THE ENCYCLOPEDIA OF UNUSUAL SEX PRACTICES

THE ENCYCLOPEDIA OF
UNUSUAL SEX PRACTICES

BRENDA LOVE

INTRODUCTION BY
MICHAEL PERRY, PH.D., A.C.S.

BARRICADE BOOKS, INC.
FORT LEE, NEW JERSEY

WARNING
The author and publisher do not advocate
practicing any of the activities listed herein.
Many are dangerous and some lethal.
People who choose to engage in these activities
do so at their own risk.

Published by Barricade Books Inc.
1530 Palisade Avenue, Fort Lee, NJ 07024
Distributed by Publishers Group West
4065 Hollis, Emeryville, CA 94608

Library of Congress Cataloging-in-Publication Data

Love, Brenda.
The encyclopedia of unusual sex practices / Brenda Love.
p.   cm.
ISBN 0-942637-64-X: $29.95
1. Sex customs—Encyclopedias. 2. Sex—Encyclopedias.
I. Title.
HQ12.L68   1992
306.77'03—dc20   92-16420
CIP

Printed in the United States of America.

CONTENTS

DEDICATION

This book is dedicated to Mark, Matilda, Martin, Linda,
Peter, Alex, Aaron, Joseph, Adrian, and Nelson, the special friends
who helped me survive both the earthquake and the death
of my mother while trying to complete this book.

ACKNOWLEDGEMENT

A special thanks goes to the people who helped me compile
information for this book. In addition to my editors they are Diego,
Michael, Tanith, Joe, Grant, Vinci, Bruce, Ron, Enrique, Janet,
Russ, Cheryl, MD, Jamie, Doug, Stephen, Angela, Erich, Crimson,
Robert, Wayne, Jay, Pete, Mark, Jim, Barry, David, Ted, Robert,
Jonathan, Dan, Katheryn, Phil, Allen, Steve, Tim, Steve, Mark,
Karen, Bernie, Michael, John, Ann, Bruce, Brad, Dwight, Susan,
Paul, Lorna, David, Israel, Joseph, Hal, John, Nawana, Rick, Walter,
Pat, Jack, Dwight, Carol, Tim, Chaz, Joanna, The Society of Janus,
The Institute for the Advanced Study of Human Sexuality, Skin II,
Mad Dog Tattoo, Platinum Films, Fetish Times, Back Drop Club,
Club Mud, British Museum Library, Mother Goose Productions,
QSM, Katharsis, San Francisco Sex Information Switchboard,
Stanford Lane Medical Library, The Gauntlet, Mr. S,
Romantasy Boutique, Desmodus, Inc.

SPECIAL ACKNOWLEDGEMENT

Many of the terms in this encyclopedia were coined by
Dr. John Money and this special acknowledgement is
given to him in gratitude for the many accomplishments
he has made in the science of sexology. A list of
his terms can be found under "Sexology."

EDITORIAL BOARD OF ADVISORS

investigation lasted ten months and gave Rodrigues in-depth background in this area. Detective Rodrigues' experiences have given him unique insight into this sub-culture from which he has given the author guidance in this topic.

K.C. ROURKE has always been interested in people. She has explored herself and her fellow humans physically, emotionally and sensually through several "adult-oriented" occupations; she reads extensively about how people think, feel and act; she has learned much from thousands of assorted personal encounters. In the late 1960s she joined BackDrop Club and explored the role of power dynamics in sex and in life. She has since found great satisfaction in becoming the slave of a skilled and understanding Master. She has also found a compatible husband, and spends her time creating a comfortable discreet space where people with fetish/fantasy interests can play.

ED SARGENT, M.D. is a family physician in Oregon who has in the course of his practice provided medical care to some in the S/M community.

GREG SAWIN is a medical editor at ALZA Corporation (Palo Alto, CA) and has a B.A. in psychology from San Francisco State University (1979). He is also a director of the International Society for General Semantics (Concord, CA) and writes the "Dynamics of Thought and Behavior" feature in the ISGS quarterly journal *Et cetera*. One of his other interests is anthropology.

KRISTINA STONE, M.F.C.C. received her Masters in Counseling from the University of San Francisco and has studied in the field of Human Sexuality. She is presently in private practice as a licensed Marriage, Family and Child Counselor in Los Gatos, California. She and her husband, Steve Stone, reside in Saratoga, California.

STEVEN STONE has a background in engineering and law and is presently practicing law in California, specializing in patent, trademark and copyright matters, primarily in the medical, pharmaceutical

and biotechnology fields. By virtue of their different backgrounds, Steve and Kristina were able to provide the author with some unique insights during the evolution of this work.

In addition to the above mentioned consultants there were many people who made contributions to the book, only some of whom are listed in my acknowledgements.

ILLUSTRATORS

PHOEBE GLOECKNER, M.A., Biomedical Communications, is an illustrator of medical texts, as well as a painter and cartoonist. Some of her other work may be found in *The Atrocity Exhibition* by J.G. Ballard (Re/Search Publications), and *Twisted Sisters, A Collection of Bad Girl Art* (Penguin). Born in Philadelphia, she was moved at the age of twelve to San Francisco, where she continues to reside (as do all the artists who contributed to this book). Her chosen profession leaves absolutely no time for hobbies or amusing pastimes of any sort. Fortunately, she is able to glean satisfaction from her work. She has inadvertently become known as an artist who provides pictures for texts of salacious content. This book may represent a departure from past work, since its intent is, of course, *to educate*, rather than to *inspire prurient feelings.*

JAKUB KALOUSEK, originally of Prague, Czechoslovakia, is a painter as well as a rap musician and film producer. His most recent recording is titled *Slickety-Lick*. He is known in some circles for his films, remarkable for their atmosphere of concrete ambiguity.

PAUL MAVRIDES is an artist of unbounded enterprise who is fluent in a variety of media. His work may be found in various cultural tidepools.

JULIE NEWDOLL, currently engaged in the demanding discipline of computer-generated medical art, cools her heels at the easel whenever time permits and inspiration insists.

INTRODUCTION

BY MICHAEL PERRY, PH.D.

It can be said of very few books that they are unique. But this one certainly is. Its original title, BEYOND FANTASY: 500 UNUSUAL SEX PRACTICES has been eclipsed. This encyclopedic work has gone beyond the original 500 listings, beyond the unusual to the truly bizarre and beyond fantasy to the outskirts of reality itself. It carves a path through sexual history and cultures and practices, both local and foreign. It will take you down byways whose very existence will amuse and possibly delight you. It will carry you into dark backwaters that will repulse and may even sicken you.

The nature of the book is truly encyclopedic and so is its format. Each entry is self-contained so you can start anywhere or you could start with Acrotomophilia (being sexually aroused or attracted to an amputee) and end up somewhere around Zelophilia (being aroused by jealousy). It is a readable commentary on all things sexual. Well, nearly all; look for the sequel. It will enable you to distinguish Pediophilia (sexual attraction for dolls) from Pedophilia (sexual attraction of an adult toward a child). There are listings for sex conferences both scientific and hedonistic; clothing-optional hotels and obviously more games, devices and concepts than even the most sexually adventurous could ever try in many lifetimes. Perhaps this is the ultimate "how-to" marriage manual to put spice back into a wilting relationship.

Brenda Love birthed this encyclopedia after four years of gestation. The seeds of this book are international with research accumulated from S/M lectures in San Francisco, West coast sex conferences, counselor training for the San Francisco Sex Information Switchboard, 19th century literature at the British Museum Library, street interviews in Amsterdam, and discussions with consultants from around the world. Many types of sexual behavior have recently been defined by Dr. John Money and these have been included, among others, in this book. Dr. Money brought prominence to the term paraphilia (a love for or an attraction to something outside the usual). He also named and defined many of the -philias contained here. (See Sexology /John Money)

Brenda Love and I met as volunteer counselors on the San Francisco Sex Information Switchboard, S.F.S.I. to those of us who know it well. S.F.S.I.'s non-judgmental spirit together with the compassion we both felt for distraught callers helped to further develop an interest in understanding the multi-faceted expressions of human sexuality.

THE ENCYCLOPEDIA OF UNUSUAL SEX PRACTICES is more than an encyclopedia with over 700 entries. Ms. Love's root theory, her philosophy and psychology of sexuality is best elucidated in two entries: "Paraphilias" and "Love." A careful read here reveals that "deviance" merely means "not usual," "away from the norm," a non-judgmental "paraphilic" classification. By dissecting neurological cycles, imprinting, primal needs and compensation, Brenda explores how different people form their own "lovemaps" (term coined by John Money) and how certain stimuli may engender a flight or fight reaction in one person and love or attraction in another. This may also explain why actual pain inflicted by an attractive person can generate arousal. Ask a dental technician! This theory delineates how elevation of energy, or stress necessarily leads to fight, flight, or love/sex in order to properly arrive at conflict resolution and homeostasis. The reactions are enmeshed. Resolution is necessary otherwise disease lingers and deepens.

THE ENCYCLOPEDIA OF UNUSUAL SEX PRACTICES will be a reference for the serious sexologist, a curiosity and source of amazement for those interested in sex and all its variations and damning proof for the puritanical that we are truly going to Hell in a handbasket—bound and flogged.

PREFACE

"The World is full of apparent contradictions, and every highest truth is the union of opposites."—HAVELOCK ELLIS

The fantasies people create in their imaginations know no bounds. Those things that two or more consenting adults do are no longer limited by arbitrary and often cruel rules based on religious beliefs. Nevertheless, there remain two immensely important constraints on human sexual behavior. First, one human being should not coerce another into sexual activities. In particular, older individuals must never use their physical or emotional power over children and adolescents, either to obtain sexual services, or to initiate habits which, although pleasurable, may diminish a young person's personal freedom of choice later in life. Second, people must not be led by their sexual drives to dangerous or mutilating practices that they subsequently regret. THE ENCYCLOPEDIA OF UNUSUAL SEX PRACTICES documents a wide range of sexual activities. Many are behaviors which are enjoyed by the vast majority of individuals while others have been associated with injury or death. It is the aim of the encyclopedia to provide objective information about how human beings behave; where you draw the line must be your own informed choice.

I have attempted to write without bias. Believing that individuals and groups engaging in certain activities are entitled to explain their own conduct, I have consulted or quoted from the practitioners themselves wherever possible. I next sought to corroborate the information I received from the practitioners with input by respected sexologists, psychologists, physicians, biochemists, anthropologists, attorneys, and law enforcement personnel.

Given the diverse backgrounds of my sources and editorial board, there were several obstacles to gaining a consensus of opinion. The medical community views unusual sex practices from a health standpoint, psychologists view paraphilias as compulsives, and many in the S/M community don't feel they fall into either category since they only engage in activities for experimentation. You the reader will need to keep in mind that almost any activity in this book can be engaged in for reasons that vary from coercion from a partner, religious ritual, experimentation, supplementing penis/vagina sex, building self-esteem, reducing stress, revenge, or it may be an exclusive act which the person feels unable to control.

The information contained within THE ENCYCLOPEDIA OF UNUSUAL SEX PRACTICES is only as accurate as its sources. These include other authors and practitioners, individuals whose lectures I have attended, sometimes with demonstrations by people whom I have interviewed. I have not knowingly included any false information.

A major dilemma has been how much detailed instruction to include in the text. Knowing people's tendency towards experimentation, I have felt that it is my obligation to provide enough safety precautions to forestall unnecessary injury. At the same time, it is not my intent to write a user's manual, or to endorse experimentation or specific sex groups. My purpose is to educate readers, and to do so without censorship.

I have used the acronyms B.C.E. (before common era) and C.E. (common era) instead of B.C. (before Christ) and A.D. (Anno Domini—in the year of the Lord of the Christian era) purposefully. My book has been written for a world audience of all religions and I prefer not to offend my non-Christian readers with Christian dates. I have also used poems on a few occasions because poems express the intensity of experiences and emotions in a way that I cannot in my writing.

I would like to extend an invitation to anyone interested in giving me their comments or sharing their experiences for a possible revised edition and videotaped slide show to do so by writing me care of my publisher, Barricade Books, Inc., 61 Fourth Avenue, New York, NY 10003.

A

ABDUCTION Bondage, struggle, and intimidation are often involved in abduction play just as in ancient times when men abducted future brides from other tribes, afterward keeping them in bondage to prevent escape. Bride capture existed in various forms until the 19th century in parts of Europe. (The ritual of a husband carrying his bride over the threshold stems from this tradition.)

Today some people use abduction as part of a negotiated sex scene that involves a mock capture of a hostage, prisoner, slave, or rape victim. The scene is acted out in the privacy of the home using a bedroom, closet, or garage as a jail cell. Others are more daring and stage their abduction scenes in a public place. The amount of physical resistance in this case is limited because potential observers may not know that the abduction is consensual. Costumes and uniforms are used in scenes, particularly for military or police arrests. Couples also make use of handcuffs, thumbcuffs, rope, tape, blindfolds, and other types of bondage paraphernalia. CAUTION: Physical resistance during abduction sometimes leads to accidental injuries.

(See also BONDAGE, FANTASY PLAY, INTERROGATION and SLAVES)

ABRASIONS (Carpet burns—on carpet) People create abrasions by using metal emery files, brushes, or other items that are rough to the skin but that do not leave residual particles of any type. Abrasions are generally less severe than rug burns. Nipples are sensitized by sanding lightly with a file and the glans penis or labia is brushed with a fingernail or an artist's oil brush to accomplish the same effect. This type of torture builds in intensity as time passes and most stop short of creating pain. The desired effect is simply to make the area much more sensitive to normal touch. CAUTION: Locations on the body are selected that will not be rubbed by clothing nor have pressure on them. Non-sterilized instruments can cause infections.

(See also BITING, BLOOD SPORTS, CUPPING, DEPILATION, PYROPHILIA, PHLEBOTOMY, SCRATCHING, SENSORY ENHANCEMENT, TICKLING, TOUCH and URTICATION)

ACOUSTICOPHILIA (Melolagnia—music) An acousticophile (acoustico: sound; phile: person with attachment) becomes aroused by sounds. Sounds preferred may be in the form of music, song, love poems, verbal abuse, sexual commands, comments in a foreign language, screaming, panting, moaning, groaning, sighing, heavy breathing, as well as any other natural sounds people make during sex.

People who do not normally vocalize feelings of arousal—but who would like to develop this skill—do it during masturbation by concentrating on sounds that express ecstasy. Sounds don't need to be loud and are preferred when natural and spontaneous. These sounds not only stimulate the person making them but also serve as a very effective method of communicating pleasure with a particular caress, position, or act. This helps the partner learn the techniques needed to keep them aroused.

Group sex can be very exciting for people because of the variety of sounds in close proximity. Some duplicate similar sounds by making a recording (or video) of their love-making and orgasms to play during the next interlude. Others are aroused by hearing or speaking curse words.

Certain music has become associated with sex. One concert pianist said he was capable of eliciting various emotions in his audience by different notes, using "middle c" for sexual arousal. "The Spanish Flea" is used for stripping, and "Bolero" is popular as an accompaniment to sex. Other classical pieces are Wagner's "Tristan and Isolde," Beethoven's "Kreutzer Sonata," Stravinsky's "Rite of Spring," and Berlioz's "Symphonie Fantastique." People who enjoy lying in front of fireplaces on rainy nights purchase recordings of rain storms or the sound of ocean waves. In a similar way, music such as dirges or funeral hymns are used to help the mood for some necrophiles. Hard rock music triggers a sexual response as well, however in an altogether different manner. Michael Koss, who is the president of Koss Stereo Headphone Corporation, is cited by Jillyn Smith in her book, *Senses and Sensibilities*, where she says, ". . . the excitement that people, especially teenagers, get from high-decibel music results from activation of the peripheral nervous system by low frequency sound waves beating against the body." Koss contends that "people can get 'high' from this feeling, because it switches on the body's fight or flight mechanism, bringing a rush of adrenalin (a reason for battle music?)" (p. 39).

(See also AGREXOPHILIA, CONFESSIONS, COPROLALIA, ECOUTEURISM, EROTOGRAPHOMANIA, FANTASY PLAY, HOMILOPHILIA, HYPNOSIS, JACTITATION, LOVE POTIONS, NARRATOPHILIA, OBSCENE PHONE CALLS, PHONE SEX, SERENADES and TEASING)

ACROPHILIA   Acrophilia (Acro: highest point; philia: attachment to) refers to a person who is sexually aroused by heights. Sky diving and bungy cord jumping are high altitude activities that elevate one's adrenalin. This excitement can then be transferred to passion and sex. Both of these activities include a form of bondage, vertigo, and suspension.

S/M partners who suffer from acrophobia are sometimes blindfolded and made to climb ladders. If this is done often the phobia seems to dissipate and along with it the sexual charge it first produced. ("Terror," QSM lecture by J. C. Collins, November 28, 1990)

Another popular form of acrophilia is having sex at a high altitude. This is humorously referred to as becoming a member of the "Mile High Club" and is done in airplanes or other aircraft. (Conversely one wonders if there is a "Mile Low Club" for submarines.) There was a group of pilots in New York that had their own version of a Mile High Club. The requirements were that the pilot and passenger went up in an

open cockpit bi-plane, and when they reached an altitude of 6,500 feet, the passenger would disrobe, climb out on the wing and into the back seat, returning to the front seat after having sex with the pilot. All without falling off the wing! (Personal communication, 1980)

Aerobatics can be sexually arousing for a few people. Stunts in a small plane offer 4-5 negative G-forces and 3-4 positive Gs. These affect the body by pushing the blood into either the head or the lower body, and result in feelings of lightheadedness, floating, or sinking, depending on the maneuver. There is a tremendous adrenalin 'rush' and a simultaneous sense of power over the airplane and submission to it. The feeling of being bound is greater in stunt flying than with other sports because the belts have to hold both body weight and chute through every maneuver. There are very few sensations that compare with hanging upside down while one's weight pulls them toward the glass bubble that separates the pilot from the rapidly approaching ground. This feat provides enough sexual stimulation to cause at least one female pilot to experience spontaneous orgasm. (Personal communication.)

Finally, there are people who claim to have been captured by creatures from outer space and impregnated while aboard flying saucers. Their stories have provided many with a sexual fantasy, one that is acted out with the aid of readily available space costumes.

(See also AGORAPHILIA, CLAUSTROPHILIA, FANTASY PLAY, PHOBOPHILIA and SUSPENSION)

ACROTOMOPHILIA   (Amelotasis— attraction to the absence of a limb) An acrotomophile (Acro: extremity; -tomy: to cut; philia: attachment to) is a person who is aroused by the thought of having sex with an amputee or by fantasizing about it.

Acrotomophiles sometimes convince a consenting partner to wrap a hand or foot in bandages. Dr. Eustace Chesser tells of a man who used a form of pseudoacrotomy by having his wife limp across the bedroom

with crutches before engaging in sex. He became impotent if she didn't comply (*Strange Loves*, p. 40).

People may become attracted to amputees for many reasons. These include fetishes, vicarious sadism, low self-esteem, a legitimate excuse for poor performance, respect for an amputee's adjustment to a handicap, need to rescue and care for an amputee, and fear that this loss could happen to them.

People in any of these categories have apparently developed an amputee attraction through a previous childhood experience. They may have escaped possible injury themselves or saw someone else injured. They were introduced to the concept of amputation at an early age. The fear or compassion which they felt at that time could have made such a strong impression that they may experience an erotic reaction when they next see an amputee. Those persons can be male or female, straight or gay. That initial erotic arousal then becomes the key to their adult sexuality.

Others may react by taking solace in the knowledge that someone else has worse problems than themselves. For some men the preference of an unusual sex object or practice is due to sexual repression and guilt imposed by parents. They select safe objects onto which to direct their lust. They may select a prostitute because she cannot be violated, or a handicapped person because the request for sex is compensated for by nurturing of the individual.

Conversely, a person with a low self-esteem may feel that someone with a handicap would provide a secure relationship as no one else would compete for them. They may also feel that the amputee could not afford to be too critical or demanding. This false sense of security and arrogance may lead a few into abusive behavior in their relationships with amputees. Men who have been constantly criticized by parents sometimes feel that if they had been amputees they would have been nurtured more and criticized less, therefore the amputee possesses a quality that this person feels he or she needs. They gain that quality by vicarious association. Their sexual inhibitions are lowered.

Clubs exist that provide introductions or referrals for amputees, and literature exists that provides written materials and photos. *Fascination* magazine features only photos and stories about female amputees. There is a book, *Amputees & Devotees* by Grant C. Riddle, which provides a detailed study of this phenomenon.

(See also APOTEMNOPHILIA, AUTOMASOCHISM, BINDING/FEET, COUVADE SYNDROME, DYSMORPHOPHILIA, HARMATOPHILIA, MASOCHISM, PSYCHROCISM, SADISM and VICARIOUS AROUSAL)

ACUPRESSURE Acupressure is the art of stimulating the self-healing or pleasure centers of the body by direct pressure on specific areas. It is widely used in India for holistic care. Not only are the person's muscles manipulated, but so is their energy flow. Yoga masters are said to have the ability to use acupressure to give or take away knowledge, spiritual enlightenment, and energy. Sex is only a small part of this complex form of healing and spirituality.

The two areas most responsive to acupressure are the hands and feet. Twenty minutes of acupressure applied to them can result in increased sexual energy. Every square inch of the feet and hands is given individual attention by using firm pressure and a rotating mo-tion. This should not create pain when done correctly.

Sensual acupressure points also include the ears and big toes, which are particularly sensitive to being sucked or fellated.

Other pressure points are on a person's torso. These areas are on the nipples, inner collar bone, center of 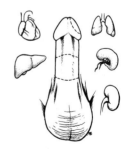 chest between nipples (of small breasts) just under the navel, at the top line of pubic hair, at the base of the spine, and around the anus. The exact spots will vary slightly from person to person, and some spots may not provide stimulus at all.

Acupressure is also used to delay ejaculation in men. These pressure points are listed by Ramsdale and Dorman as follows in their book titled *Sexual Energy Ecstasy, A Guide to the Ultimate, Intimate Sexual Experience*:

PROSTATE POINT—midway between scrotum and anus, pushed frequently and firmly before ejaculation is imminent. Some men are able to tighten the anal/Pubococcygeal muscle enough to pump the prostate.

SOLAR PLEXUS—pit of stomach right below breastbone, pressed with fingertips of both hands.

SACRUM—inverted triangle of bone at base of spine, fingertip or thumb pressure used.

PUBIC BONE JUST ABOVE PENIS—pressed with third finger.

TESTES—pulled to keep them from rising up toward body.

In keeping with acupressure therapy, Ramsdale and Dorman also include a list of genital pressure points and their corresponding list of organs that receive rejuvenation (i.e. lungs, heart, spleen, liver, and kidneys). The inside wall of the vagina has similar pressure points with the heart being the organ stimulated by the deepest penetration. The lungs are at the second deepest point. This acupressure theory suggests that there is a definite health advantage related to regular intercourse or masturbation.

(See also AXILLISM, BINDING, BITING, CLAMPS, CORSETS, CUPPING, GENU-PHALLATION, LIGHTING, MASSAGE, PINCHING, SCRATCHING, SENSORY ENHANCEMENT and TICKLING)

ADOLESCENTILISM—PARAPHILIC
(Ephebophilia—attraction to adolescents) Paraphilic adolescentilism refers to people who find sexual pleasure in dressing like a teenager or acting out this role.

(See ANACLITISM, GERONTOPHILIA, INFANTILISM, NYMPHOPHILIA, PEDIOPHILIA and TRANSVESTITES)

ADULTERY
(Apistia, Affair, Open marriage—consensual, Nonmonogamy—lifestyle that does not restrict number of partners) Adultery is the sexual union between people when at least one of them is married to someone else. It is rarely used to describe a man who frequents prostitutes or for a wandering partner in a homosexual marriage. Most often the reason for engaging in adultery is an unbridled desire for ecstasy or passion; second is the opportunity to fulfill basic needs that are not met elsewhere; and third is the inability to say "no."

Adultery, or nonmonogamous sex, was probably common among clans of primeval man and resembled the social system in some American Indian tribes. Adultery for women may have offered a few of the same advantages we find in some animals. Bachelor bands, such as the langur monkeys, are one example. These clans are ruled by a dominant male and are often raided by the younger outcast males. During raids these males rape straggling females and kill their young. The female is sometimes able to avert this fate by slipping away from the clan and having sex with several of the male outcasts. Her reward is that neither she nor her young are attacked during the raids. They are in fact protected by her adulterous partners, all of which consider themselves the father of her young. Females in other primate clans use adulterous liaisons to guarantee babysitters for their young. The mother signals one of her lovers to watch her young while she enjoys a few hours of leisure and again each male assumes this to be his responsibility as 'the father'. Thomas Gregor, in his book *Anxious Pleasures, The Sexual Lives of an Amazonian People*, seems to attribute the continued survival of small Amazonian tribes to the cohesion created by the numbers of members who engage in adultery. Lovers, especially men, tend to give presents of food. This type of support, or exchange, balances their economic system.

The love bonds and the presence of children by various women deter a young man or widower from leaving to marry someone from another tribe.

In modern societies, adultery became a threat to the family unit. It was still tolerated, but most often in the form of prostitution. The Bible provided one of the first restrictions against adultery for women, but even then women were rarely punished. Numbers V tells of a ritual used to expose adulterous women. Most people, unfamiliar with Jewish history, interpret this adultery test as unfair, chauvinistic, and cruel. In reality, no guilty woman's stomach ever swelled and caused death as the law warned. The test consisted of simply dissolving the ink inscription of god's name off a parchment with water. The intention of the rabbi or priest was to restore the husband's faith in his wife and therefore discourage divorce or retribution. This was done without regard to her guilt or innocence. The test eventually lost its credibility because all the women proved innocent by the application of this test.

Adultery continued to be tolerated by societies that practiced pre-arranged marriages or that enforced laws against divorce. Catholicism did not campaign to stop adultery but had its influence by primarily condemning the sex act; for them adultery did not carry much more stigma than carnal lust in marriage. The first real campaign against adultery came from the Protestant reformation. The Protestant leaders thought it wiser to discourage arranged marriages and to sanction sex within a marriage. Their hope was that families would be bonded more closely if couples married for love. In turn, the Protestant ecclesiastical courts demanded chastity until engagement, and fidelity forever after. This law was for the economic protection of a society that did not have a welfare system or a job market for women.

The English Puritans, upon relocating to the Colonies, abolished the ecclesiastical courts and made sex offenses capital crimes in civil courts. There are still many states that have statutes and penalties against adultery. Enforcement, however, has become impossible due to increased anonymity in metropolitan areas and a lack of motivation by neighbors or relatives to report offenders, among other factors.

The Puritans must have been appalled when they were first exposed to the open sexuality of the adjacent Indian culture. John D'Emilio and Estelle Freedman, in their book *Intimate Matters, A History of Sexuality in America*, discuss the sex habits of Puritans and American Indians during this time. The Indians unabashedly practiced homosexuality, adultery, polygamy, transvestism, and zoophilia. Likewise, being human, not all of the Puritans remained pious and many of those who settled in Plymouth openly adopted these Indian customs, even reviving some of the pre-Christian religious fertility ceremonies. The leader, Thomas Morton, was eventually deported to England for a while, and only returned shortly before his death. In time, the majority of Puritans prevailed and forced all settlers in the new colonies to follow the Puritan code of morality.

This intolerance, however, was not restricted to their fellow colonists; it was imposed on the surrounding Indian tribes as well. In *Women and Colonization: Anthropological Perspectives* (quoted in *Intimate Matters*), a Jesuit, confronting a Montagnais Indian, said, "It is not honorable for a woman to love anyone else except her husband," for this sexual promiscuity meant that a man "was not sure that his son...was his son." The Indian, pointing out the cultural differences of the intruder, replied, "You French people love only your own children, but we love all the children of our tribe." This attitude made unwanted pregnancies and split families less of a psychological burden. Women and children were also recognized as valuable and their contributions to the success of the tribe were viewed as equitable and necessary. The Indians, unlike the Europeans, did not use wages, sexual fidelity, and closed educational institutions to suppress women.

Colonists later used the promiscuity and cultural differences of the Indians as proof of the latter's racial inferiority. This helped the colonists to justify their extermination program.

Adultery was also tolerated by societies when the ratio of men to women was disproportionately high, or when the offense was by a man against a lower status slave, servant, or prostitute.

Today, there seem to be differences between male and female affairs. Men usually are not looking for a replacement for their wives. They use adultery to relieve stress, alleviate boredom, get revenge, remedy a lack of affection from a spouse, temporarily escape responsibility, boost their ego, increase their sexual knowledge and proficiency, or to ease the transition period between being a promiscuous bachelor and being married. Many men also marry for practical reasons and not because the one chosen was the most sexually appealing. Women have affairs for many of the same reasons, but tend to fall in love with their new partner much more often. This can be a problem, because, unlike men who may also fall in love, women are less likely to separate sex from responsibility and often do not give up their lovers simply to keep peace in the family.

Affairs are often painful for the single partner. While they may feel a high level of self-esteem initially, it is depleted when the adulterer goes home every night to someone else. Often in the end the person who was the center of the adulterer's world becomes an embarrassment, a mistake, or a scapegoat, so that breaking up becomes the only remedy.

Spouses desiring an open marriage may be able to negotiate for what they feel is necessary for their emotional survival. However, much depends on the value their partner places on fidelity. Statistics show that most people don't file for divorce on a first offense, but one can expect spouses who feel helpless and betrayed to go through a stage of wanting to control or know about all their partner's activities. This is temporary and necessary for some to reestablish trust in a partner's fidelity.

Others may seek revenge by having an affair with a close friend or relative of their spouse.

Married partners who accept an open marriage will generally negotiate for things such as secrecy, discretion, restriction on gifts, time allocated, locations for sex, type of person selected, type of sex, safe sex, etc. Some couples use group sex with strangers as an equitable compromise because both parties are present and there are very few emotional liaisons established in this environment. Nonmonogamous marriages, whether consensual or undiscovered, are thought to take longer to break up because the adulterous partner is usually happy and rarely takes out their frustrations on their spouse. There are exceptions, for while some adulterers will feel guilty and treat their partners with more respect, others turn guilt into hostility and false accusations against their spouses.

Adultery involving homosexuality can be traumatic to the spouse who has a limited interpretation of human sexuality, thereby adding more guilt and shame to the event. Counseling is beneficial for most people who find themselves in this predicament. The book by Jean Schaar Gochros, Ph.D., entitled *When Husbands Come Out of the Closet*, may be of benefit for those facing this particular problem. CAUTION: An assumption of implied consent regarding open marriages or use of deceit may have severe consequences. Diseases and unwanted pregnancies can also create problems.

(See also CANDAULISM, CUCKOLDRY, GROUP SEX, FESTIVALS, HAREMS, HETAERAE, ILLEGAL SEX, LOVE POTIONS, MARRIAGE, MENAGE À TROIS, PROSTITUTION and WIFE SWAPPING)

AGALMATOPHILIA (Galateism, Pygmalionism, Statuophilia) Pygmalion was a mythical Greek sculptor who fell in love with Galatea (one of his female statues). At his request, the goddess Aphrodite brought her to life. Today this term refers to people with a statue or mannequin fetish.

Several historical cases of agalmatophilia have been documented. Clisyphus evidently "violated the statue of a goddess in the Temple of Samos, after having placed a piece of meat on a certain part. In 1877 "a gardener fell in love with a statue of the Venus of Milo and was discovered attempting coitus with it" (*Psychopathia Sexualis*, by Richard Von Krafft-Ebing, p. 351).

The practice of having sex with a statue was common among worshippers of the god Priapus where virgins were to first be pene-trated by him. This practice was later relegated to a priest or magistrate. However, even in our own century, young Indian virgins have been known to use sacred phalluses to break their hymens before marriage.

A few ancient statues had removable penises to facilitate their use as dildos. Several statues of Catholic fertility saints, including among others St. Foutin, St. Guerlichon, St. Gilles, and St. Rene were equipped with a large phallus. The Protestants demolished a church at Orange in 1562 to find a large wooden phallus that had been covered with leather and 23 years later at Embrun found people still worshipping the statue of St. Foutin by pouring wine onto his penis (*Sex in History*, by G. Rattray Taylor, pp. 269-270).

Today some men still prefer the multi-dimensional aspect of these forms to two-dimensional printed erotica. One case was reported of a man who as a 12 year old boy became enamored of a life-size statue at a museum when his mother called it obscene. Later, he spotted two small statues in a store window and purchased them. He began using them while masturbating and at the age of 34 had not broken the habit even though he was married. Another case was that of a window dresser who felt compelled to masturbate whenever he saw a nude manikin. His first sexual experience was at the age of 14 when he was forced to perform fellatio on his supervisor as they sat on manikins. He developed the desire to not only rub against a manikin to masturbate

but to have another man watch (*The Sexual Fetish*, by Robert Tralins, pp. 27, 46).

A few people in today's S/M community use a psychological form of restraint where the person, like a statue, is not to move or respond to the fondling actions of their partner. And people everywhere seem fascinated with the royal guards at Buckingham Palace for their statue-like imperviousness.

(See also AMAUROPHILIA, ANDROIDISM, EROTOMANIA, FETISHES, FORNICATORY DOLLS, FROTTAGE, HEIROPHILIA, PEDIO-PHILIA, PHALLOPHILIA and PORNOG-RAPHY)

AGONOPHILIA (Pseudo-rape) Agono-philia (agon: struggle; philia: attachment to) refers to those who enjoy engaging in a pretended struggle before overpowering their sex partner.

(See also FANTASY PLAY, HARPAX-OPHILIA, RAPE and WRESTLING)

AGORAPHILIA (Bushie mall—sex in open park) Agoraphilia (agora: public place or assembly; philia: attraction to) refers to arousal from being in public places. People who desire to have sex in their back yard, a park, or other exposed area more than likely experience an unusual level of excitement from being outdoors. Agoraphiles experience sexual excitement from being outdoors just as agoraphobics experience fear.

One of the parks in San Francisco is a popular meeting place for gays who enjoy semi-public sex. The city tried to discourage their activity by having many of the shrubs cleared away. This simply resulted in the gays having sex without the protective covering of shrubs.

(See also ACROPHILIA, CLAUSTROPHILIA, EXHIBITIONISM, HODOPHILIA and PHOBO-PHILIA)

AGREXOPHILIA Agrexophilia refers to those who become aroused by the knowledge that others may become aware of or hear their lovemaking. This can occur in hotels, group sex scenes, outdoors, or during visits with friends or relatives.

(See also DOGGING, ECOUTEURISM, EX-HIBITIONISM, GROUP SEX and JACTITA-TION)

ALGOPHILIA (Doleros) Algophilia (algo: pain; philia: attachment to) refers to sexual arousal gained by pain sensations. An algophile may be involved in S/M, however it seems the majority are not. Kinsey, in 1953, reported that about 50% of the people he surveyed admitted feeling sexual arousal from being bitten.

Primitive tribes, with their painful rituals for entering adulthood, valued their ability to endure pain as a prerequisite for marriage. The hostile and formidable environment hunters and gatherers lived in made this an essential qualification. Paul Bohannan, an anthropologist who wrote a paper on his field work in Nigeria between 1949 and 1953, reports a conversation he once had with a group of the Tiv tribe:

The aesthetic of beauty, insofar as it is represented by scarification and chipping of teeth, is involved with pain. I once asked a group of Tiv with whom I was discussing scarification whether it was not exceedingly painful. They turned on me as if I had missed the entire point—as, indeed, I had. 'Of course,' one of them said, 'of course it is painful. What girl would look at a man if his scars had not cost him pain?' The effort to 'glow' must be obvious; the effort to be dressed up must involve expense and trouble; scarification, one of the finest decorations, is paid for in pain. The pain is the proof positive that decoration is an unselfish act, and that it is done to give pleasure to others as well as oneself (*Marks of Civilization, Beauty and Scarification Amongst the Tiv,* edited by Arnold Rubin, p. 82).

Tribes also used the pain of these scarifications to induce passion, and thus fertility, in much the same way as people today use biting.

The registration of pain is caused by the release of chemicals such as bradykinin, substance P, and prostaglandins and can be divided into two types, somatic and visceral. Somatic pain occurs most often in the muscles or skin. This pain is relatively mild compared to visceral pain which radiates from internal organs, causing nausea and weakness. The testes are part of the visceral system and injury to the testicles is traumatic.

We detect somatic pain by stimulation of the free nerve endings that lie near the surface of the skin. Once activated they transmit a signal to the brain, however, this is not a guarantee that the sensation will be perceived as painful. The message may be thwarted in several ways. First, certain nerves, the ones that transmit sensations of deep pressure, vibration, heat and cold, can override pain signals. This is why cold compresses, heating pads, and chemicals seem to help reduce discomfort. Second, a person's mood affects this process and if he is anxious the pain will be sharper, whereas if he is sexually aroused, feels safe, in control, and submits to the partner, the sensation may even seem pleasant. In a study conducted by Drs. Miczek, Thompson, and Shuster it was discovered that in mice it was not the amount or length of painful stimulus that triggered the analgesic response but rather the mouse's resignation to defeat ("Analgesia Following Defeat in an Aggressive Encounter: Development of Tolerance and Changes in Opioid Receptors," *Annals of the NY Academy of Sciences, Stress-Induced Analgesia,* Vol. 467, p. 16). Extroverts are thought to require stronger tactile and mental stimulation than introverts and will not register pain as quickly. Once pain has been registered the body will try to adapt in various ways. Steady pain requires rapid firing by our nervous system and the body's tendency is to adapt to constant stimulus by slowing this process, meaning that the intensity of pain dissipates accordingly. Once pain has been registered for 20-40 minutes the body will begin to produce opiate-like chemicals to reduce pain sensations.

People playing with pain normally desire to create enough to trigger the release of these chemicals with their anesthetic, euphoric, and trance-like qualities. The pain game is precarious because the pain/pleasure threshold is not constant and can be unintentionally crossed over, bringing an end to one's hard earned sexual euphoria. Gene Bylinsky, in his book *Mood Control,* explains: On the surface, the effects of stress, fear, and arousal on pain perception look paradoxical. Moderate anxiety increases the response to pain, whereas high levels of anxiety, including terror or fear, *decrease* the response to pain. But in terms of survival such a response makes a great deal of sense. Perception of pain depends on environmental situations and on the state of arousal at a particular moment. As one scientist explains it, "Thus, being hit in the mouth by a mugger, in a perhaps life-or-death situation, may cause little or no immediate pain, while the slightest touch by a dentist of a patient's tooth may readily elicit wincing" (*Mood Control*, by Gene Bylinsky, p. 35).

An additional aspect of pain is that it can trigger a reaction from the autonomic nervous system causing an increased rate of breathing, heart rate, and blood pressure; all of which can enhance sexual sensitivity or experience.

Modern society views pain as an affliction and does everything possible to inhibit its effects. We may someday have a better understanding of its biochemical properties and pain may prove to have more therapeutic value for our ability to recuperate from emotional trauma than we realize. Most of the twelve-step programs, and many psychologists, advise people to recognize psychological pain, feel it, and cope with it rather than suppressing it with chemicals before a natural resolution has been reached.

Some people consciously hold onto emotional pain after the dissolution of a relationship, sometimes for years. The pain appears to be the only thing remaining of their love affair and they are unwilling to completely let go of it, turning instead into romantic masochists. CAUTION: Pain produced from activities that harm the body can cause serious health problems. If blood is involved it would also be considered unsafe sex.

(Refer also to AUTOMASOCHISM, CICATRIZATION, FLAGELLATION, MASOCHISM, ORGASMS, PARAPHILIAS, SADISM, TORTURE and TOUCH)

ALLORGASMIA　Allorgasmia refers to those people unable to orgasm without fan-tasizing about a more desirable partner than the one with whom they are having sex. The condition in heterosexual females or gay men is called alloandrism and in heterosexual men or lesbians is known as allogynia.

(See also ADULTERY, FANTASY, FANTASY PLAY and SEX MAGICK)

AMAUROPHILIA　(Lygerastia—arousal only in darkness) Amaurophilia (Amaurosis: blindness; philia: attachment to) refers to those who are aroused by a sex partner who is unable to see them and does not apply to two blind partners. Amaurophilia usually manifests itself by an inhibition of sight with either one or both sex partners using a blindfold or having sex in total darkness. This may be caused by reasons such as religious guilt about nudity and sex, low self-esteem, or feelings of inadequacy.

Other amaurophiles may have become conditioned to respond sexually only when a partner is asleep or has his or her eyes closed. They may have had childhood experiences of sex with siblings who were either sleeping or feigning sleep. Necrophiles also may be aroused by their partners keeping their eyes closed, but would further require a lack of movement.

There is also a natural physical condition that causes people discomfort when attempting sex under bright lights. This discomfort can be great enough to interfere with some people's sexual performance.

An advantage of darkness is that tactile stimulation can reach the greatest sensitivity when all other senses are inhibited, particularly sight.

(See also BLINDFOLDING, FETISHES, PARAPHILIAS, SENSORY COMPENSATION and SOMNOPHILIA)

AMPUTEES　See ACROTOMOPHILIA and APOTEMNOPHILIA

ANACLITISM　Anaclitism is the act of achieving adult sexual arousal by activities or objects one was exposed to as an infant. These may include breast sucking, enemas, toilet training (urophilia and coprophilia), soiled clothing (mysophilia), bondage (womb confinement), spankings, humiliation, biting, nudity or exhibitionism, circumcision, submission, being bathed, nurtured, throwing temper tantrums, wearing infant apparel, having the penis slapped for masturbation, or playing with dolls.

Similar activities were ritualized by the ancient Greeks, who believed that is was necessary for any man who had fallen fatally ill to undergo a rebirth upon recovering. He was passed through a woman's lap, washed as a newborn, dressed in in-fant's clothing, and nursed.

Fetish objects can be very arousing when introduced into sex play. Most often these items include rubber pants, rubber aprons, shoes, fur, and stuffed animals. Partners usually know which items they find erotic. The fetish value of some objects originates during the period before a baby sees well. These are tactile and the person may only respond to them by touch. An example of this was the woman who noticed a sense of

nurturing when a dental hygienist or nurse leaned over her, brushing her uniform against her skin. The mere sight of uniforms had no effect; the stimulus had to be

tactile. A history of the woman revealed that she had been born two months premature and had spent the first months of her life being cared for by nurses in uniform. (Personal communication.)

Some people interested in this type of sex play have formed adult baby clubs that provide contacts, photos, and paraphernalia for others who want to experiment with this form of erotic play. CAUTION: Anaclitism in which a partner is exposed to body secretions is not considered safe sex.

(See also BONDAGE, EXHIBITIONISM, FETISHES, HUMILIATION, INFANTILISM, KLISMAPHILIA, LACTAPHILIA and UROPHILIA)

ANAL SEX (Sodomy, Buggery, Coitus analis, Arsometry, Anocratism, Anomeatia —female partner, Androsodomy and Catamite—male partner) The male

prostate, similar to the female G-spot, can have an orgasmic response to pressure or manipulation. The prostate is about two inches up the front wall of the rectum and is shaped like a small firm disc.

Anal sex has been practiced throughout history for pleasure, birth control, and to avoid breaking a virgin's hymen. While common in some cultures, others put restrictions on this type of intercourse just as they did with abortion or birth control. Rules concerning birth control either ensured an adequate supply of soldiers or servants for the country or prevented overpopulation, which was a strain on economies that didn't have welfare programs or a stable agricultural base.

The anus, in addition to its response to tactile stimulation, is a sensory area that produces a pleasure response in the brain when stimulated. Primal man evolved so that a pleasure sensation would occur in the brain whenever he engaged in a life sustaining body function. This encouraged men to eat until full, drink, sleep, urinate, defecate, and so forth. An example of this reaction is the kiss. Men have discovered that stimulation of the mouth during sex produces a euphoric chemical reaction for what our body thinks is eating. The nipples and ears are also utilized in this manner without much guilt or shame; however, using the anus in sexual activity is taboo in some cultures, ours included. Clinically there is no difference between stimulation of the mouth, ears, nipples, feet, or anus in the production of pleasure sensations to the brain. None of these activities have a direct role in reproduction so it seems inconsistent for people to accept some and not all points of arousal in sexual activity.

In 1990 there were still seventeen states with statutes that made consensual anal sex or sodomy illegal. *Playboy* reported the case history of one Indiana husband who was imprisoned for having anal sex with his wife. The husband's letter to *Playboy* in part read:

I want to express my appreciation to the Playboy Foundation for helping me fight for my liberty. I have been in prison since August

1965 for having had anal intercourse with my wife. Your readers may find it difficult to believe that a person can be imprisoned for a form of sexual expression performed within the privacy of the marriage bed, but I ruefully can testify that it is true.

These are the facts: My wife and I were married in 1953 . . . Whatever quarrels we had were always made up amicably after we'd had a chance to cool off. Even though we were having a particularly difficult time of it during the spring of 1965, I was nonetheless shocked to learn one day that my wife had signed an affidavit accusing me of committing "the abominable and detestable crime against nature" with her. To this day, I do not know for certain why she did this—although during subsequent conversations, I have gathered that at the time she was particularly angry with me, following an argument, and that a meddlesome friend had goaded her into trying to "put me away" for a while. I do know that whatever my wife and I did in bed was as much her wish as it was mine.

Even though his wife changed her mind and wanted to drop the charges she was informed that she no longer had the legal right to withdraw her allegation; the state of Indiana became the plaintiff.

The trial took place and to his amazement the judge sentenced him to "not less than two nor more than fourteen years." Fortunately, an attorney from the Playboy Foundation became interested in his case and assisted him in filing an appeal attacking the constitutionality of the Indiana sodomy statute. Mr. Cotner spent almost three years in prison before receiving a retrial (*From Playboy: Sex American Style*, Edited by Frank Robinson and Nat Lehrman, pp. 247-250).

There are many types of sex that involve the anus. The following subsections are variations of anal play.

ANOLINCTUS (Anophilemia—kissing anus, Hedralingus—licking anus, Proctotit-illia—tickling anus) Anolinctus is the act of licking the anus. Some people prefer their partner to clean the area first, and others prefer the natural state. The tongue is run along the inner buttocks and the anus is licked or tickled with the tongue. In another form of anolinctus, a person uses the tongue like a penis, thrusting it between the buttocks, and ramming it against the anus. (See also COPROPHILIA and FLATULANCE)

ANOLINGUS Anolingus, or rimming, is similar to analinctus but refers to actually inserting the tongue into a partner's anus. This activity can transmit diseases such as AIDS, hepatitis, and giardia unless a dental dam or plastic barrier is used. Another reason precautions should be taken is that there are also indigenous parasites living in the lower intestine that can cause disease when ingested and relocated to the upper intestine of the one who does the licking.

AUTOPEDERASTY Autopederasty refers to a man inserting his penis into his own anus. This is not physically possible for all men, but can be pleasurable for those who achieve it. The anus is lubricated, the testicles are pushed to one side and the semi-erect  glans penis is pushed into the anus. Orgasm is not considered possible due to the position and detumescence of the penis.

FELLCHING Fellching is a term used to describe the act of sucking semen out of a partner's vagina or anus. Fellching gives pleasure to some sex slaves as an act of submission even when the semen belongs to previous lovers. The woman sometimes squats over the face of her slave and lets the semen drain into his mouth, others assume the usual positions for cunnilingus. The term fellching may also be used to describe the use of a live animal in anal or vaginal sex. (See ZOOPHILIA)

FISTING Fisting involves inserting the hand, fist, or forearm into the rectum or vagina. See the section on FISTING for additional information.

PEDERASTY (Proctophallism, Sota-dism, Corephallism—with young girl) Pederasty refers to the act of penetrating a partner in anal intercourse. It is also used interchangeably with pedophilia. Pleasure is sometimes increased for the pederast by pressing together their partner's buttocks to squeeze the shaft of the penis. CAUTION: Anal play carries with it the potential of disease and bacterial infections because the rectal epithelium is thinner and more easily damaged than the vaginal wall. New or nonmonogamous partners often use a latex or rubber barrier to prevent direct contact between the anus and the penis or instrument and they avoid switching from anal intercourse to vaginal intercourse without properly cleaning the penis or instrument. Men who do not use condoms often wash after anal penetration to prevent breaking out with a possible bacterial rash the next morning (this is often mistaken for herpes—which takes at least two days for initial infection to appear). Some people use presex enemas to reduce the amount of bacteria in the lower rectum. The cell wall in the rectum is very thin and can be easily torn. Foreign objects, toys, fingers, and fingernails are checked to make sure they are free of any rough edges. Nylon hosiery run across an object can test its smoothness. Condoms and latex gloves are also used. The four basic rules observed before engaging in anal sex include the following:

Communicating with partners, not surprising them.

Lubricating well with a water- based lubricant and using a condom.

Relaxing and pushing out with the anus muscles—some find that lying on their side is the easiest position for entry.

Objects are not poked into the partner, but rather held in place as partner slowly pushes back onto them.

People experimenting with anal play begin by using one of their fingers or a small dildo or butt plug. Anything inserted into the anus has a flange or is securely anchored to prevent the internal sphincters from sucking it out of the fingers and up into the intes-

tine. People have actually used light bulbs and other glass or plastic instruments that have broken once inside, causing tissue damage that required surgery. (Refer to section on GENITAL/ANAL INSERTS for additional information.) The following symptoms of injury are watched for and reported to a physician:

Sudden change in number of times defecation occurs

Abdominal pain

Pain with bowel movement

Black or bloody feces (internal bleeding)

Discharge of mucous from rectum (other than semen)

(See also BIRTH CONTROL, COCKTAILS, COPROPHILIA, FLATULENCE, GENITAL /ANAL INSERTS, KLISMAPHILIA, PARAPHILIAS, SAFE SEX and SHOWERS)

ANASTEEMAPHILIA (Nanophilia—short partner) Anasteemaphilia (anasteema: height; philia: attraction to) refers to people who are attracted to a person because of their difference in height. This preference is most likely to be noticed when the man is shorter than his female companion. Our society accepts the preference women have for taller men but not the reciprocal desire some men have for taller women.

Some men are attracted to small women because they say it makes them feel more significant as a protector, and that the small women are more feminine because of this difference. The opposite is true for the women.

Men who are enamored of tall women often tend to be short themselves. One such man stated that the attraction for his six foot companion was because when they walked into a room together everyone noticed her beauty and this boosted his self-esteem. The flaw to his reasoning was that his girlfriend was not beautiful by the standards of other people, but she was over a foot taller than he and undoubtedly did attract attention when they walked into a room together.

Short men may feel that the height of a partner in some way compensates for their stature.

(See also ACROTOMOPHILIA, CHUBBY CHASERS, DYSMORPHOPHILIA, FETISHES and GERONTOPHILIA)

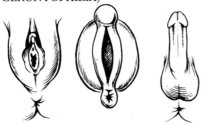

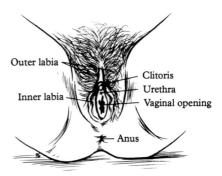

ANATOMY Male and female embryos have the same sex organs. It is only after testosterone, the male hormone, is released that the clitoris grows, becomes elongated, and forms a penis. The testicles and ovaries are formed in the abdomen and once the infant's sex is determined by hormone production a male's will descend into the scrotum. The scrotum is formed from the labia on either side that join to encase the area that later holds the testicles. What would have been a female's vagina and uterus shrinks and ends up near the male's prostate gland.

The glans penis and the clitoris have the same number of nerve endings and similar sensations, as do the other genital areas:

MALE	FEMALE
Glans penis	Clitoris
Muller's ducts/	Tubes, uterus
prostate gland	and vagina
Shaft	Inner labia
Scrotum	Outer labia

Both the length of an average erect penis and the average depth of the vagina is 6". Penises, however, can vary considerably. The circumference of the penis, vagina, and urethra also vary, with individuals commonly being smaller or larger than what is considered average (*Fundamentals of Human Sexuality*, by H. A. Katchadourian and D.T. Lunde, p. 28).

The G-spot, named after the gynecologist Ernst Graefenberg, is not shown but it is approximately 1" inside the front wall of the vagina. It is the size of a dime and feels like a disc of fatty tissue. Women have vari-

ations in the size and shape of the inner labia as well as the distance between the clitoris, urethra and vagina. The vagina changes in size according to the stage of arousal; it begins in a constricted state and then lubricates and relaxes allowing for deeper penetration and deposit of the sperm near the cervix. The vagina, after orgasm, returns to its original shape, forming a type of spoon-shaped pocket at the base of the cervix. This function holds the sperm against the canal to facilitate their travel into the uterus.

People often get their impression of a "normal-size" penis from erotic movies; this is misleading and can damage many male egos. The porn industry intentionally hires men with penises and stamina that others

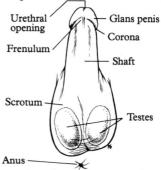

will envy; therefore, these movies are not the place to take a random sampling of normal-sized penises.

Many books are available that elaborate further on the subject of anatomy. These brief explanations and diagrams are included in this encyclopedia only to provide the reader with basic information and to act as a reference for the vocabulary used herein.

(See also DYSFUNCTIONS)

ANDROIDISM

Androids (andro: male or human, eidos: a form) is used to describe robots or programmable machines that resemble humans. Movies such as *Barbarella, Flesh Gordon, Alien, Westworld, Futureworld,* and *The Stepford Wives* have depicted or implied sexual activity between humans and androids.

Pseudo android-ism is practiced in sex play. An example is the woman behind the "Back Drop" booth (a fantasy and fetish club) during the 1990 San Francisco Exotic Erotic Halloween Costume Ball. She wore a g-string, silver wig, glasses with small flashing lights, and a coating of silver on her body, patterning her mannerisms to resemble the movement of a robot.

Fantasy magazines that feature seductive poses of half naked female androids are popular. However, this fascination is not restricted to men. The character 'Data' on the television series *Star Trek: The Next Generation* is reported to receive more fan mail from women than any other male cast member.

(See also ANTHROPOMORPHIC CARTOONS and AGALMATOPHILIA)

ANDROMIMETOPHILIA

Andromimetophilia, coined by John Money, refers to those who are sexually aroused by females who imitate males.

(See also ANDROGYNY, GYNEMIMELO-PHILIA, TRANSVESTITES and TRANSSEX-UALS)

ANISONOGAMIST

An anisonogamist is a person attracted to a partner who is either much older or younger than themself.

(See also CATAMITES, GERONTOPHILIA, MARRIAGE, NYMPHOPHILIA and PEDO-PHILIA)

ANTHROPOMORPHIC CARTOONS

Anthropomorphism (anthropos: human, morphosis: change of form) means attributing human characteristics to other entities, particularly animals. The sexual aspect of anthropomorphism involves cartoon characters that are part animal, object, etc., and part human. These are portrayed in print as engaging in sexual activity with each other. One reason for the popularity of these cartoons in the United States and Europe is that, although it is illegal to depict humans in photographs of zoophilia, sadism, homosexuality or other activities, it is legal for cartoon characters to be shown engaging in these activities.

Another advantage of using cartoons is that one is able to draw scenes that would be physically impossible for humans to perform.

Two magazines featuring such cartoons are titled *FurNography* and *FurVersion*.

ANTHROPOPHAGY

(Anthropophag-olagnia—includes rape) Anthropophagy (anthropo: man, and phagy: the practice of eating) is the act of cannibalism. Cannibalism has been practiced by many cultures throughout history, the first record being that of the Peking Man who lived 500,000 years ago and whose fossils where discovered in 1927 in Choukoutien China. The remains indicated that one group had killed and eaten another group.

Many lust murderers, including Jack the Ripper, were suspected of anthropophagy, often carrying away part of the female organs to eat later. In a different part of the world, Montezuma was said to have eaten the same type of young boys with whom he preferred to have sex (*The Homosexual Matrix*, by C. A. Tripp, Ph.D.). The Aztecs are reported to have sacrificed and eaten no less than 15,000 victims a year. According to one theory, the reason for such an exaggerated number of victims was that it controlled the population, as did many infant sacrifices in ancient Europe and the Middle East.

Cannibalism was used by cultures to terrorize intruders, or to acquire desirable traits of a victim. Males among many tribes would not consume females for fear of emasculation. Tribes in New Guinea suffered from Kuru, a slow virus, carried in the brains of deceased relatives that were consumed as a ritualistic practice. This caused shivering and led to eventual death.

Cannibalism was also used in magical and ritualistic ceremonies. These ancient rituals required that a person consume a small amount of blood or flesh from the sacrificed victim. The Greeks sacrificed a priest who symbolized god and by eating his flesh these congregates were to become one with their god. This custom very closely resembles the rationale of the sacrament of the Eucharist.

People who have consumed human blood and flesh reportedly claim to experience an intoxicating euphoric effect. This reaction is similar to that experienced by anyone who satisfies a strong sexual craving that is not considered normal (exhibition, necrophilia, rape, etc.). However, in this case, it must have reinforced the beliefs of worshippers that indeed their god was present in the victim. Reports indicate that cannibalism is still practiced as part of ancient religious and magical rituals.

Cannibalism was also practiced by the medical profession. The famous first-century Greek physician, Galen, compiled a reference of all known medical remedies; these included potions consisting of human brains, livers, flesh, and burned bones.

We find sexual cannibalism in spiders, scorpions, crickets, praying mantises, empis flies, and some grasshoppers. However, it is doubtful that this act ever existed in humans as any sort of natural reaction. In a society that doesn't practice cannibalism, those who kill their own victims are assumed to suffer from sociopathy.

Three other varieties of anthropophagy are autophagy, necrophagy, and parthenophagy.

AUTOPHAGY Autophagy refers to ingesting one's own flesh. Krafft-Ebing recorded the case history of a man who at 13 became infatuated with a young white-skinned girl. However, instead of desiring intercourse, he was overwhelmed by the urge to bite off a piece of her flesh and eat it. He began stalking women, and for years he carried a pair of scissors with him. He was never successful in accosting a woman, but when he came close he would cut off and eat a piece of his own skin instead. This act produced an immediate orgasm for him.

NECROPHAGY Necrophagy (necro: corpse, death, and phagy: the practice of eating) is the act of cannibalizing a corpse, usually one whose death the molester did not cause. Many cases of reported necrophilia include cannibalism or other forms of sadism and it is believed that many others fantasize about doing it. One of the more bizarre cases was in the southern United States. A woman repeatedly invaded the caskets of her family vault and ate the genitals of her deceased husband, son, and brother (*Perverse Crimes in History*, by Masters/Lea, p. 118).

PARTHENOPHAGY Parthenophagy (parth-enos: a virgin, and phagy: the practice of eating) is the act of eating young girls or virgins. Several lust murderers were known to consume the flesh of their victims. Fritz Haarmann (England, died 1924) and his male companion ate away the throats of 24-50 victims. Albert Fish (Washington, D.C., died 1935) confessed to having cannibalized 8-15 children by cutting them up and using the meat in stews. Fish claimed to be the Christ who had come to take vengeance on a depraved society and prided himself on never having penovaginal sex with his victims; he would masturbate instead. Another cannibal, Menesclou (1880), was convicted of murdering a four-year-old girl and removing part of her body to be eaten later.

CAUTION: Anthropophagy is illegal and, because it involves body fluids, is dangerous. Certain diseases carried by 'slow viruses', such as kuru and Creutzfeldt-Jakob disease, can be transmitted by cannibalism.

(See also COPROPHAGY, LUST MURDER, MUTILATION, NECROPHILIA, ORGIES, RITUAL SEX, SITOPHILIA, VAMPIRISM and ZOOPHILIA/BESTIALSADISM)

APHRODISIACS An aphrodisiac is a chemical that increases or enhances sexual desire and stamina. The term comes from Aphrodite, the Greek goddess of love and beauty.

Authorities generally agree that the best aphrodisiac is found in good health, supplemental vitamins, meditation, exercise, and rest—not in recreational drugs. Orgasms use a lot of stored energy. If a person's energy level is low, they may not be able to achieve the orgasmic intensity they would like. A person who is ill, physically exhausted, on certain prescription medication, caffeine, nicotine, or who is under stress may not have the energy required for a dynamic orgasm and should not expect it.

Narcotics and alcohol are not recommended for sex play, with the possible exception of the small quantities some people need to feel relaxed and loosen inhibitions. When a person uses a depressant to make them feel relaxed they may compromise the intensity of their sensations during the sexual experience. Drugs and alcohol are never recommended for sex and a particular warning applies for any type of sex play that requires mental, verbal, or physical skills.

A natural aphrodisiac is that of prolonging the courtship phase of a relationship. Time is needed to build anticipation, affection, and respect for a partner. People who have casual or spontaneous sex with a fairly new acquaintance may compromise the intensity of the act and may feel they need artificial methods to elevate arousal. The first episode may have the excitement of something novel and daring, but that fades in successive episodes. Strangers or casual acquaintances tend to be much more critical of sexual performance than a long-term friend; therefore, with strangers there is more emphasis on performance, perfect bodies, and the overall rating of how a partner compares to a fantasy lover. This situation makes the use of an aphrodisiac seem more necessary than it would be ordinarily.

Many people use aphrodisiacs to compensate for feelings of inadequacy, to build the intensity of passion in a partner to match that of a fantasy model, to overcome exhaustion, or to create desire for a person who otherwise wouldn't be of interest. There are two variations of aphrodisiacs: dietary and drugs. Each will now be discussed separately.

DIETARY

BLOOD: Many cultures have believed in the power of blood to increase vitality but some attributed sexual potency to blood. Historians wrote of Romans rushing into the arenas to drink the blood of slain gladiators with the hope of restoring their sexual libido.

TESTES: Throughout history people have eaten all types of animal testes for virility. These contain testosterone, the male hormone, and may have had some positive effect for that reason.

KOREAN GINSENG: This is taken as a supplement and acts as a stimulant. People take this daily for no more than two consecutive months.

DAMIANA TEA CONCENTRATE: People add a drop to their drink 15-30 minutes before they have sex.

VIGOREX FORTE: This product is extracted from oats and, in studies conducted by the Institute for the Advanced Study of Human Sexuality, it seemed to enhance sexual performance for the majority of men. Blood samples showed an increase in the level of testosterone for those who had low or normal levels prior to taking the extract. The recommended dose is 300mg per day.

VITAMIN B-6 (NIACIN): A dose of 50-100mg is taken at least 1/2 hour before sex.

VITAMIN C: People begin with a 1,000mg dose every day and build to a dose they can tolerate. Vitamin C is also thought to improve the immune system and to restore collagen to aging skin, but this is not proven.

VITAMIN E: The highest levels of this vitamin are found in the testes, adrenal glands, and the pituitary. Some people claim that it restores not only sexual vitality but fertility in men. The recommended daily dosage is about 25mg, but a person can take as much as 1,000mg a day without serious complications. Vitamin E is found naturally in asparagus, wheat germ, sunflower seeds, almonds, peanuts, and olive oil.

DRUGS   In general, drugs, even when taken in moderation, will lower inhibitions and have a slight analgesic effect, making it possible for some premature ejaculators to last longer; however, many make orgasm impossible. Drugs do not initiate sexual arousal, but enhance the feeling if it is already present.

ALCOHOL: Champagne, beer, and wine are used in small to moderate amounts. However, too much is a depressant and can have negative results. Heavy use can lead to impotence later in life.

AMPHETAMINES: These create a sudden burst of energy that the body will have to replace later. The drugs speed up a person's cardiovascular system—an effect similar to that of adrenalin. Some people are able to have sex in this condition and some aren't. A danger is that amphetamines are psychologically habit forming.

AMYL NITRITE: (Also called poppers.) This drug is used by heart patients to dilate arteries, thus decreasing blood pressure and giving a sense of slow motion and lightheadedness. This makes the orgasm seem to last longer for some people.

BARBITURATES: These are depressants (or "downers") and are sometimes used to induce sleep or to counteract the effect of amphetamines. They are likewise addictive and an overdose can kill.

COCAINE: For some, this drug increases sex drive and loosens inhibitions. There is an immediate increase in heart rate and blood pressure; people report feelings of contentment, exhilaration, relief from fatigue and depression. It also has a local numbing effect. It can be eaten in its natural leaf state, used intranasally, smoked, injected, or used topically. The long-term negative effects are fatigue, restlessness, and irritability. It can damage the nasal passages if snorted, and can do irreparable damage to the penis if injected directly into that region. It is extremely psychologically habit forming and its use can be fatal.

ICE: Ice is methyl amphetamine, and when smoked it has effects similar to cocaine but with an action that lasts for 12-24 hours instead of the regular 20 minutes for crack cocaine. Ice is new in the United States. It also is extremely addictive.

KETAMINE: This is either injected or snorted, with the effects lasting 10-20 minutes. The person loses sense of everything around them until the drug starts wearing off. This produces an effect of slowly becoming aware of oneself as having a body, followed by an emerging recollection of one's memory or identity, also known as a 'rebirth' experience.

LSD: This is a hallucinogen that may intensify any mood of the user. Its effect is like the altered state of consciousness that mystics achieve by fasting, deprivation, or flagellation. There may be a transposition of sight and sound, that is, people report seeing music and hearing objects move. Another possible effect is depersonalization; the person loses the sense of having a separate body and seems to dissolve into part of a liquid or flowing universe. (See ORGASMS /ALTERED STATES) LSD is an unpredictable drug.

MARIJUANA: This drug is smoked or eaten in food to create an increased awareness of body sensations, analgesia, and euphoria. A person may have the sense of being able to think clearly and have faster reflexes, although research has proven that the opposite is true. It is a hallucinogen and may also compromise the immune system. Regular use may destroy a person's ability to cope with stress and weaken their ambitions for the future.

MDA: This is an amphetamine that has a mild psychedelic effect. It speeds up the cardiovascular system but slows reflexes. It also has a euphoric effect that can last up to eight hours.

MDMA: Known as "ecstasy" or the "hug drug," it is an amphetamine and empathogen similar to MDA and is reported to induce the desire to give and receive affection or to caress a partner. The first-time user often reports retaining a long-term attraction for the person or object they interacted with on this drug.

MESCALINE: This is a derivative of the peyote cactus. Its effects are similar to a higher dose of marijuana, but supposedly without loss of mental acuity. Mescaline is not thought to be addictive; however, what is sold on the streets is usually a substitute or mixture of other drugs.

NITROUS OXIDE: Also known as "laughing gas," it produces light-headedness and acts as an analgesic. Prolonged use or overdose can cause brain and liver damage.

QUAALUDES: These are depressants that induce a state of euphoria and confidence. They can become addictive and fatal with even a small overdose.

SPANISH FLY: This drug is made from the wings of the Cantharis vesicatoria beetle. It causes dilation of blood vessels that can produce prolonged erections. It also causes the genitals to itch intensely when the drug passes through the urethra. People are driven to sex as a method to relieve the itching this drug causes. A dose of more than .06 grams can be fatal and, therefore, until recently was used only in breeding animals. Anal electrical probes now replace this drug in large farm animals.

TRAZONDONE: This drug is prescribed for depression and is known to cause priapisms (erections that may last several hours) and has recently been documented as causing an increased libido in three women. In one case the patient began masturbating and initiated sexual relationships with three men. After ending the therapy, her sex drive, to her disappointment, slacked off to what it had been before treatment. Two other cases were similar. (Nanette Gartrell, M.D., "Increased Libido in Women Receiving Trazodone," *American Journal Psychiatry* 143:6, June 1986, p.781)

YOHIMBINE: This chemical originally came from the bark of a tree that was considered part of the pepper family. It is a CNS agent that raises blood pressure and, like Spanish fly, creates itching or irritation of the urethra. Its use for impotence is controversial, but it does cause castrated rats to mount female rats. It has sometimes had serious side effects when mixed with some medications.

CAUTION: There are many issues involved in a decision to use alcohol or drugs to improve sexual arousal. Some drugs are extraordinarily destructive. A self analysis would involve questions about one's emotional security, fear of impotence, sexual boredom with current partner, fear of intimacy with casual partners, risk of chemical addiction, and performance anxiety. A person who insists on using drugs to enhance the sex act may also risk damaging the partner's self-esteem by making him or her feel sexually inferior or inadequate.
   (See also CHARMS, FERTILITY RITES, LOVE POTIONS and RELICS)

APOTEMNOPHILIA (Amelotation— loss of limb) Apotemnophilia (apo: away from; temp: to pull; philia: attachment to) describes people who are aroused by the idea of themselves losing a limb or having a body part surgically removed. Such people will occasionally injure themselves to an extent that requires amputation by a surgeon. However, most are content to fantasize about the loss as they masturbate. A few men crossdress as females and fake some sort of disability.
   There are many theories for this behavior. One explanation is similar to that for why men cross-dress. As children, these men felt that females and amputees received special compensations. As adults, they prefer an unusual sex object or practice due to early-life sexual repression and guilt imposed by parents. They select safe objects for their lust. These may be prostitutes or a handicapped person. CAUTION: Actual removal of body parts causes personal disability and if it is done under unsterile conditions serious infections may result.
   (See also ACROTOMOPHILIA, AUTO-MASOCHISM, CICATRIZATION, DYSMOR-

PHOPHILIA, MASOCHISM, MUTILATION, NECROPHILIA and TRANSVESTITES)

ARACHNEPHILIA Arachnephilia (arachne: spider; philia: attachment to) refers to those who are aroused by sex play involving spiders. Spider scenes utilize a person's fear of spiders to increase adrenalin. The bottom may be tied down and the spider either brought close to them or placed on their body to crawl around. CAUTION: Poisonous spiders are dangerous because there is a chance that the bottom will be bitten.

(See also FORMICOPHILIA)

AUCTIONS Slave auctions were common until a hundred years ago in the United States. The New Orleans bordellos were among those who bid for fair-skinned young female slaves. Interbreeding was so common at this point that some slaves had blue eyes and blond hair. Other slaves were white children who were either abducted from northern farms by the slave brokers or were bastard children purchased from slave women in whose care the unwed mother had left them. The slave  brokers often kept the fairest for their own sleeping companion business, in which a man was able to lease a fair skinned slave for one night, a month, a year, or whatever he wished. Two of President Thomas Jefferson's educated auburn-haired daughters (born to him by Sally Hemings or "Black Sal," an octoroon) were sold upon his death in 1826 and taken to New Orleans for this fate. The youngest escaped and committed suicide. They weren't the only slave daughters of an American President; twenty years later President Tyler's mulatto daughter tried to elope with her white fiance to another country, and upon being caught, her father commanded that she likewise be sent to New Orleans and sold on the slave block (*Sex and Race* by J. A. Rogers, p. 197).

A few European men sold their wives in lieu of divorce (a total of 387 cases reported in England between the 16th and 19th centuries). Some of these were sold to the wife's lover in order to gain some recompense (*Untying the Knot* by Rodrich Phillips, Cambridge Press, p. 85).

Although auctions of women for prostitution no longer exist, there are still those who illegally barter with the future of those under their control. Now they use a facade such as an international employment agency for models or entertainers. Once in a foreign country without government assistance, money or friends, many will end up working in the sex industry for their abductors.

The pseudo-slave auctions found in America today are legal and consensual. Often a popular charity will sponsor an auction to raise money. Men are used and the item bid on is the date rather than sex with the man, although women often let fantasies cloud their expectations. Local businesses donate dinners for two, theatre passes, and so forth. The money bid by the winning women goes to the charity.

The other type of auction is sponsored by S/M clubs; at these events consenting dominants and submissives are auctioned off for S/M play. The Society of Janus has an annual event with an auctioneer and a crowd of 200 bidders. The Back Drop Club in Richmond, California has a slave auction every Friday night where people introduce and auction themselves for the type of activity in which they want to participate. Typical of most S/M participants, these people use the drama and intrigue surrounding the original auctions to set the stage for sex play. These auctions are legal because only play money is used and there are house rules against genital penetration. The following is an account of a female who was auctioned at one of these parties:

What does one wear to a slave auction; would I have the nerve to buy a man and what would I do with him? These questions occupied my thoughts for a week. The evening approached and I had rationally decided to take a slave collar and dog leash with me in case I rallied the nerve to bid. I entered the older San Francisco home and paid my $20 cover charge to the club that gave most of their proceeds to an AIDS organization. I was given $10,000 of privately printed S/M buckaroos to use as play money during the bidding. I immediately entered the auction hall to check out the participants and get instructions on bidding. The auctioneer was handing out forms to the participants. Many people were getting into costume and others had begun to barter for buckaroos. It seems that an hour is spent before the auction, engaging in every sort of negotiation. This is apparently necessary if a woman is to be purchased. Everyone begins with the same amount of money, $10,000, and bidding for a female starts out above that amount. A man on the corner of the stage was collecting $2,000 a minute for letting others suck on his lover's nipples. At this point, I was overcome with the desire to get into costume myself. I stripped off the remnants of my chaste persona leaving only black garters, hose and panties. I studied myself in a wall mirror and decided that the outfit looked out of balance, so I placed the black leather collar around my neck. The time for the bidding came closer, and with the encouragement of others, I decided that in order to get the fullest benefit from the event I should allow myself to be auctioned. Without deliberating further I asked the auctioneer for a form. I gave my name, experience (none), sexual preference, and S/M role preference (top, bottom or switch) and then waited in terror. I looked around the room, selecting those I most wanted to have bid on me and then those I worried about winning and how they might want me to perform. These fears quickly subsided as the first slave walked on stage and the bidding began. The room was now packed with what must have been over 200 people. Soon there was a good-looking male slave in his late 30s and without caring about his particulars I jumped into the bidding and won. He came over and collected the amount and we agreed to get together after the auction to negotiate on the type of play in which we wanted to engage. Then another good-looking guy was up for bid, a brunette from Los Angeles, I bid, but soon lost to a female friend. However, not one to accept defeat, I bartered with her for access to her new slave for 20 minutes in exchange for the bal-

ance of my buckaroos. She graciously accepted. The bidding continued as 10 or 15 more slaves were sold. The best of the show was a couple of bi-sexual females who were auctioned as a pair, just before me. They waited until they were on stage to simultaneously expose their breasts, immediately driving up the bidding. Now it was my turn, I didn't expect to still be apprehensive or have stage fright, but I did. The auctioneer began the bidding for what I think he called a virgin; the bidding continued for 20 minutes or more as the room divided into competing factions. All were willing to donate money at this point because there was no reason left to save it. Soon people were obviously bidding more money than it was possible to have and the auctioneer stopped the bidding. One gentleman in the back of the room suggested that everyone put their money together and buy me. The auctioneer then sold me to the whole room. I doubt that many people have had to make decisions while in a state of shock. My concern was to be fair to all those who seemed intent on winning, therefore I suggested that they get into a line and I would spend four minutes with each. One man volunteered to be the time-keeper and we began. Most men wanted to be massaged, to have their nipples squeezed, or to be kissed. One gorgeous man asked me to simply run my finger down the front of his latex vest for the full four minutes. A transvestite, who told me that as a male he was a bottom and as a female he didn't know what he wanted to be yet, asked to run his long, red, manicured fingernails down my body while we stood in front of the mirrored walls. One older male had me switch in a spanking scene and when the time-keeper's turn came, he pinched my shoulder and tried to make me submit to his dominant commands. Unfortunately, I became overwhelmed and exhausted before everyone had their turn and after apologizing, got dressed and drove home with memories of what will probably be the most unique experience of my life.—K.H.

(See also PEDOPHILIA, PROSTITUTION and SLAVES)

AUTAGONISTOPHILIA (Exhibitionism) Autagonistophilia (*autos*: self, *agonistes*, dramatic actor, philia: attachment to) refers to those who are aroused by being on stage or performing for a cameraman.

(See also EXHIBITIONISM and HOMILO-PHILIA)

AUTOASSASSINOPHILIA   John Money coined the phrase autoassassinophilia which refers to "stage-managing the possibility of one's own masochistic death by murder." Money cited an example in *Lovemaps*:

The masochistic drama of erotic death and atonement may be enacted not as an autoerotic monologue, but as a dialogue with a coopted partner in collusion. The partner is not necessarily a paraphilic sadist, but rather a daredevil hustler or mercenary given to trying almost anything for kicks, or for profit. This was the type of hustler whom a young man with a paraphilia of homosexual masochism would pick up, one or more at a time, on the waterfront. With his beguiling brand of macho, he would cue the hustlers into their roles in his masochistic drama. First he would supply them with squeeze bottles of mustard or catchup and a spray can of shaving cream to squirt on him as he lay naked, masturbating. Then he would direct them to bind him with rope, urinate on him, degrade and abuse him verbally, hit him, and kick him with their heavy boots, harder and harder, until he would ejaculate, not knowing whether a blow on the head would wound or kill him (p. 43).

People engaging in this activity do not appear interested in dying but rather find the mortal fear itself arousing.

(See AUTOEROTIC ASPHYXIA, HARPAXOPHILIA, HYBRISTOPHILIA and MASOCHISM)

AUTOEROTIC ASPHYXIA   (Asphyxiaphilia, Hypoxyphilia, Autoerotic Strangulation—strangulation for arousal, Scarfing—use of scarf for autoerotic strangulation) Autoerotic asphyxia refers to self-induced strangling or suffocation during masturbation. This is estimated by some to take the lives of 250 to 1,000 men every year.

This practice appears to be ancient. Professor Leopold Beitenecker, Director of the Institute of Forensic Medicine at the University of Vienna "claimed that the technique had been practiced by Eskimos and by Asians before it was introduced to Europe by French Foreign Legionnaires returning from war in Indo-China, where the technique was performed by prostitutes to increase the client's sensation of ejaculation" (Michaldimitrakis, M., "Accidental Death During Intercourse by Males." *Am J Forensic Med Pathol* 1986; 7:74. Cited in "The Pathology and Medicolegal Aspects of Sexual Activity," by William G, Eckert, M.D., Steve Katchis, and William Donovan. *The American Journal of Forensic Medicine and Pathology* 12(1):3-15, 1991, p. 12). Sexual asphyxia was also portrayed in the Japanese movie *In the Realm of the Senses* which was based on the true story of a couple during the 1930s.

Very little is known about people who practice asphyxia because most do not seek therapy and do not otherwise come to the attention of the medical profession unless they die. Two leading authorities on this subject, Ray Blanchard and Stephen J. Hucker, both of Toronto's Clark Institute of Psychiatry, have collected a vast data bank of coroner's reports and other materials to try to understand this phenomena. They have found a correlation between this practice and other paraphilias in their study of 117 males who died of autoerotic asphyxia. "This study investigated the relationships between: asphyxiator's ages; two paraphilias commonly accompanying autoerotic asphyxia, bondage and transvestism; and various other types of simultaneous sexual behavior...Data concerning sexual paraphernalia at the scene of death or among the deceased's effects were extracted from coroner's files using standardized protocols. Anal self-stimulation with dildos, etc., and self-observation with mirrors or cameras were correlated with transvestism. Older asphyxiators were more likely to have been simultaneously engaged in bondage or transvestism, suggesting elaboration of the masturbatory ritual over time. The greatest degree of transvestism was associated with intermediate rather than high levels of bondage, suggesting that response competition from bondage may limit asphyxiators' involvement in a third paraphilia like transvestism" ("Age, Transvestism,

Bondage, and Concurrent Paraphilic Activities in 117 Fatal Cases of Autoerotic Asphyxia"; *The British Journal of Psychiatry*, September 1991, Vol 159, pp. 371-77).

People have different reasons for engaging in this activity. However, these can only be guessed at because most cases are only learned of after the victim's death. We do know that asphyxiation itself creates excitement and eventual euphoria because of the adrenalin produced when the body perceives a life-threatening condition. Suffocation also causes light-headedness. Scarves or ropes can be part of an auto-bondage game which develops a simultaneous fear of death, control, and submission. A person builds a feeling of power or control by bringing themselves to the edge and then releasing the device. Fear is one of the strongest effects and it is usually enhanced either by using bondage with asphyxia or by having another person control the scene. This is similar to bondage, as in the case of one woman who took strangers home to tie her up. She was not interested in submitting to people she knew because that lacked the risk or fear element. John Money has written an entire book, *Breathless Orgasm*, based on one asphyxiaphile's case history. It appears that this man became fixated on the idea of asphyxiation as a child in the same manner others have become acrotomophiles (attracted to partners without a limb). This man specifically writes, "And then the girl who I thought was my sweetheart hopeful drowned while swimming at the beach; and then my fascination of the word asphixia [sic] came into play. I used to sit and try to imagine her nude body drowning underwater, and I wondered what it was like to drown; and I started having dreams while sleeping about swimming underwater and drowning, and then swimming like a fish where I didn't need any kind of air tank. But I could swim and watch other people drown, mostly girls. Then I started to masturbate..." (*Lovemaps, Clinical Concepts of Sexual/Erotic Health and Pathology, Paraphilia, and Gender Transposition in Childhood, Adolescence, and Maturity* by John Money, p. 246, pub. Prometheus

Books). This man eventually used strangulation techniques on himself. CAUTION: Autoerotic asphyxiation is of particular concern because of the frequency of deaths associated with it. ("Breath Control and Carotid Artery Play" by Michael Decker, QSM lecture, January 11, 1992)

(See also BONDAGE, OXYGEN REGULATION and PHOBOPHILIA)

AUTOMASOCHISM (Deliberate self-harm syndrome, Borderline self-mutilator, Sergeism—infliction of injury to suppress arousal, Munchausen's syndrome—reopening a wound, Traumaphilia—arousal from trauma) Automasochism is the conscious act of inflicting pain or injury on oneself as a means of stimulating orgasm, an altered state, or an emotional release that would act as a substitute for orgasm.

Examples of automasochism are lying on a bed of nails, flagellation, cutting, piercing, burning, sun dancing, bell dancing, binding, corsetting, and tattooing. Many cultures have used forms of mutilation as part of their tribal or religious rituals. A physical mark was used as verification of an adult's ability to conquer pain.

People who engage in any of these acts to relieve stress or for subliminal sexual gratification are referred to as self-mutilators. The fundamental reasons for automasochism and self-mutilation may be similar. Many mutilators have low self-esteem, feelings of guilt and self-denigration, depression, difficulty in expressing or verbalizing emotions, are from broken homes, or have emotionally distant or physically abusive parents. The more serious mutilators (e.g. removal of penis) are considered psychotic or schizophrenic.

Motives for self-mutilation vary. It can be done to gain attention and love, control aggression, reduce tension, or end a state of depersonalization or emotional numbness. Events that often lead to an episode are arguments with family or the threat of losing a lover.

Some people sabotage their health with the goal being surgery and afterward they may reopen the wound. This is referred to as Munchausen's syndrome.

People who compulsively injure themselves seem to follow a consistent five stage pattern: "(1) the precipitating event (such as loss of a significant relationship), (2) escalation of the dysphoria, (3) attempts to forestall the self-injury, (4) self-mutilation, and (5) the aftermath (for example, relief from tension)" ("The Inner Experience of the Borderline Self-mutilator," by E. Leibenluft, DL Gardner, RW Cowdry, *Journal Personality Disorders*, 1987; 1317-1324).

Automasochism has the same neurological effects as discussed in the Masochism section. These range from sexual arousal, euphoria, depersonalization, and altered states. People who perform self-mutilation to end the depersonalization phase of the stress cycle may be subconsciously effecting a speedier recovery. People who suffer physical injuries after a disaster "often fare better ultimately than those who escape unhurt" ("And Now, Emotional Aftershocks," by Anastasia Toufexis, reported by Andrea Dorman/New York and Joseph J. Kane/Atlanta, *Time* magazine, October 30, 1989, p. 46). Speculation based on historic remedies involving acupuncture, bloodletting, cupping, electric shock, slapping someone who becomes hysterical, etc. suggests that post-traumatic infliction of pain or injury triggers the neurological recovery cycle or immune system of a patient.

Self-mutilation is common in hospitals, prisons, and asylums. This is logical because of the extra stress felt by patients or prisoners who are separated from their family, and who have a new strict routine imposed that severely limits their personal freedom. People naturally go through a normal stress cycle when experiencing trauma: fear, avoidance behavior, anger, compulsiveness, depression, depersonalization, and numbness. Scientists have observed that "practically all known reports of self-injury in macaques [a primate] have been recorded when the animal is physically restricted and usually when isolated" ("Self-

injury: toward a biological basis," by I. Jones, *Perspect Biol Med*, 1982; 26:p37-150).

People who engage in automasochism may find professional therapy, self-help groups, or guidance in communicating emotions and anxiety beneficial. Medication such as "dopamine antagonists, serotonin reuptake inhibitors, and opiate antagonists may be of value" in some cases ("Self-Injurious Behavior: A Review of the Behavior and Biology of Self-Mutilation," by Ronald M. Winchel, M.D., and Michael Stanley, Ph.D., *Am J Psychiatry* 148:3, March 1991, pp. 306-315). CAUTION: Cutting can damage nerves and arteries which can lead to serious health complications.

(See also ACROTOMOPHILIA, ALGOPHILIA, CICATRIZATION, HUMILIATION, MASOCHISM, MUTILATION, SADISM and SLAVES)

AXILLISM (Hircusophilism—preference for underarm hair, Maschalophilous—arousal from armpits) Axillism (axilla: armpit; ism: act) refers to the use of the armpit for sex. This is more common in Europe, where women allow their armpit hair to grow. This area is very sensitive to the flicker of a tongue or the warmth of a penis. Unshaven hair is also said to retain pheromones, the sex hormones that cause arousal when inhaled.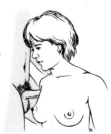

The advantages of axillism for men are that of a tight fit, friction against the penis, close proximity to the breasts, and no risk of pregnancy or disease. Axillism, when engaged in within a day of shaving, produces more sensation but later underarm stubble can cause irritation of the penile skin.

(See also COITUS A INTERFERMORIS, COITUS A MAMMILLA, GENUPHALLATION, HEAD STANDS and PYGOPHILIA)

B

BATHS Baths have been used throughout history for personal hygiene, health, religious rituals, luxury, socializing, distraction, sexual arousal, and meeting prostitutes.

The importance of a tradition can sometimes be determined by the extravagance some use in their indulgence. For example, the Japanese Funabara Hotel allows guests to bathe in a solid gold tub that is carved in the shape of a chicken. The ancient Roman Baths of Caracalla were a mile in circumference and could hold 1,600 bathers. In Bath, England the baths were part of worship. Here the Romans built a temple to the goddess Sulis Minerva over natural hot springs. Worshipers believed that hot springs were a gate to the fiery underworld and one could petition the gods' favor by bathing there or by throwing coins or valuables into the water. People still throw coins in fountains but usually without the knowledge of its religious significance.

Public baths lost their popularity during the Dark Ages when Christians, particularly those of the ascetic movement, condemned bathing with perfumes as self indulgence and nudity as immoral. They managed to convince others that a dirty body was a proper method of mortifying the flesh as a penance for sin. Public baths did not become popular again until the crusaders returned from the Arab countries enthused about the Turkish baths they had seen. Public baths became popular as social gatherings with wine and music being provided for the bathers. Brothels soon began to use these baths as a way to increase their business. This continued until the bubonic plague caused their extinction in the 15th century.

Public baths in the United States now consist of hot tubs, spas, steam baths, and jacuzzis. They may be part of an apartment complex, private club, or house party. There are establishments that specifically cater to sexual encounters, sometimes providing private rooms that can be rented. Their clientele will usually consist of either gay and bi-sexual men or heterosexual couples. Group sex houses often have hot tubs on the premises. Some individuals have formed private pseudo-swing social groups. They have weekly potluck dinners where guests may undress and relocate to the hot tub or bedroom after eating.

Most of the gay baths have been closed as a result of the campaign against AIDS. There is serious doubt that AIDS is spread through chlorinated water but the sexual activity engaged in before gays became aware of AIDS and safe sex practices did put many at risk.

(See also COITUS A UNDA and SHOWERS)

BED OF NAILS Lying on a bed of nails is a passive form of masochism. A bed of nails is an apparatus which consists of a rectangular piece of wood the length and width of the body, that has 4-5" long, 2 gauge or larger nails driven through at 1/2-1" intervals.

This bed has been used in Eastern religions to create intense sensations, possibly sending the person into an altered state of consciousness. Today it is done in India, primarily as a tourist attraction. Some American S/M communities have adopted it and use it as it was originally intended.

The pain felt while lying on the bed directs attention to the body and its sensations. This helps one to ignore the emotional pressures from the rest of the day. It becomes a 'stress purgative.' The sensation is painful for the first few minutes but becomes dull and decentralized after about 20 minutes. Physical pain that one has control over stimulates a person's immune system and people who engage in this type of activity may regenerate the immunity that long term stress compromises. The experience leaves the user feeling invigorated in much the same manner as jogging or tennis. (For more discussion on the effects of pain please see the sections on ALGOPHILIA and MASOCHISM).

Placing the nails close to each other reduces the risk of pain or accidental piercing. The tips are also uniform with a level top surface. People who construct these beds modify them to their own body. CAUTION: The greatest risk of being injured is when the person gets on or off the bed. Men will wear a pair of leather briefs or jock straps and most use a firm pillow to support their head. The person next straddles the bed, squats into a push-up position, and lowers himself or herself onto the bed so that the torso of the body receives even and level support. They next bring their legs into position and place the pillow under their face. The body remains still because moving around or twisting can cause nails to puncture the skin. However cautious a person is who uses a bed of nails, there is always a risk of being accidentally pierced and people rarely lie on the bed while alone. Additionally, if blood contaminates the nails it can be a transmitter of blood borne diseases such as AIDS or hepatitis.

(See also ALGOPHILIA, AUTOMASOCHISM, BELL DANCING and FAKIR MUSAFAR)

BEE STINGS (Melissophilia; Entomocism—use of insects, Entomophilia—arousal from insects, Formicophilia—arousal from ants)

Bee stings are used to extend the duration of orgasm, enhance sensations of the penis, and increase its circumference.

Bee stings were once used as a folk remedy by arthritis sufferers. The insects were captured and held on the affected joint until they stung. The poison and swelling it caused alleviated much of the pain in their joints.

One male, having observed his grandparents use bees for this purpose and later having a female friend throw a bee on his genitals as a joke, discovered that the sting on his penis extended the duration and intensity of his orgasm. Realizing that the bee sting was almost painless, he developed his own procedure. This procedure consisted of catching two bees in a jar and shaking it to make the bees dizzy to prevent them flying away. They were then grabbed by both wings so that they were unable to twist around and sting. Each bee was placed just below each side of the glans penis and

pushed on to encourage it to sting. (Stings to the glans do not produce desired swelling and the venom sack tends to penetrate the skin too deeply, causing difficulty in removing them.) Bees leave their stinger in the penis and are not able to sting other parts of the body. Stingers have a small venom sac that pumps the remaining poison into the flesh before

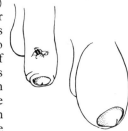

removal. Stings on the penis, unlike other areas, resemble the bite of a mosquito. The primary discomfort is produced by subsequent itching, although the penis will also become tender and swell. A thick twine or leather strip tied around the base of the penis, allowing enough space to insert two fingers between the penis and string, restricts the swelling in the penis from dissipating into the body but will not cut off circulation. In this case the circumference of the man's penis increased from 6 1/2 inches to 9 1/2 inches. Swelling is greatest on the second day. There are two unexpected effects, however. The swollen outer skin may restrict blood flow into the penis and the swelling can become lopsided or uneven if pressure is applied on only one side. CAUTION: Poisonous venom can have serious effects on about 5% of the populace. Any of the following symptoms of anaphylactic shock following a bee sting require emergency medical care:

difficulty breathing

chest pain

dizziness

nausea or vomiting

edema or general swelling

blue coloration of lips

weak pulse

(See also FORMICOPHILIA and ZOOPHILIA)

BELL DANCING (Ball dancing—balls or fruit hanging from skin hooks) Bell dancing is a form of ritualistic self flagellation where the dancer pierces the body to hang ornaments by strings into his or her flesh. Flagellation was one of the various  methods shamen used to achieve an altered state. Other forms were fasting, drugs, and dances. Bell dancing combines the festive dance ritual with self flagellation. This combination seems to speed up the neurological process of obtaining an altered state of consciousness.

Bell dancing is performed by religious sects using bells, balls, lemons, or other fruit. These are usually attached to sutures at one end and sewn into the skin on the other. Enough ornaments are sewn on so that they eventually form a necklace or belt around the person. The person then dances to percussion instruments or possibly a flute. The dance or swirling causes the dangling objects to beat against the person's body and to pull against the pierced skin where each strand is attached. The dancer's primary desire is to experience an altered state.

Bell dancing is a mixture of spiritual and sensual sensations and, like other types of masochism, it can give the dancer a sensation similar to but much more intense than a normal orgasm. CAUTION: This is considered a blood sport and unprotected contact with a partner is not considered a safe sex practice.

("Rituals," by Fakir Musafar, Society of Janus lecture, November 30, 1989)

(See also ALGOPHILIA, BED OF NAILS, CHOREOPHILIA, CORSETS, FLAGELLATION, MASOCHISM and SAFE SEX)

BELLY DANCING (Danse du ventre—fertility dance) Belly dancing is a modern version of an ancient religious dance signifying sex and childbirth. It can be traced throughout history in countries such as Phoenicia, Turkey, Egypt, Africa, and Greece. It was introduced into the United States by Sol Bloom as an exhibit in the 1893 Chicago World's Fair.

One of the earlier forms of the belly dance was called the "awalem" and was used as sex education for newlyweds in Egypt. The dancer(s) would stand in one spot and imitate the different sexual movements required for coitus. The belly dance still consists of various body contortions performed in a restricted space. The dancer changes positions only to give the audience a different perspective of the movements.

A second ancient dance, the "ghaziyeh", had only dancers with a scarf or piece of cloth that they would swirl around and pull back and forth against their genitals until orgasm. The dancers were females who had clitoridectomies performed while young and therefore had to stimulate their genitals by intense and prolonged rubbing. Unlike the silent belly dancers, these women would scream and moan like wild beasts until orgasm was reached; it was not until then that the dance ended and the orgy began (*Cradle of Erotica* by Allen Edwardes and R.E.L. Masters).

Jacobus X wrote of another dance, one performed by African Senegals. "In the anamalis fubil, the dancer in his movements, imitates the copulation of the great Indian duck. This drake has a member of a corkscrew shape, and a peculiar movement. The woman, for her part, tucks up her clothes, and convulsively agitates the lower part of her body by the motion of her haunches; she alternatively shows her partner her vulva, and hides it from him, by a regular movement, backwards and forwards, of the body" (*Untrodden Fields of Anthropology* by Jacobus X, 1898). Victor Robinson, a turn of the century medical doctor, documented the verbal instructions given by a village priest for an African Dance of the Bride-Elect:

1. Prepare your skin (vibration). Go to your place.

2. Walk (with hip swings) as though to Huge Sacred Phallus.

3. Vibrate your body. Ardently wish the phallus was entering you.

4. Behold! It is standing to greet your wish, royally erect like the rising sun.

5. Vibrate your body. The power of your ancestors is concealed within you.

6. Wonder of wonders! My depths are entered by the Royal Phallus.

7. Ah! What glorious sexual union has come to me.

8. Let us clamp our bodies together—tighter and tighter—closer and closer.

9. Lean to the left side.

10. Lean to the right side.

11. Ah!!! What glorious sexual union has come to me. Ah...(ejaculation).

12. We tremble at the knees.

13. He becomes like sawdust: I am breathless: we collapse.

14. Soon he boasts to me—he will rise again soon.

15. We close together in another glorious sexual union.

16. Still closer and closer—he will fill me with great progeny.

17. Ah, ah, behold! Great and Royal generations will arise (from this union).

18. Again we tremble at the knees.

19. We salute our posterity (swing to the left).

20. (Swing to the right). Soon we will clamp our bodies together again.

21. Hurrah! he has risen again: he goes down my path: I dance with joy.

22. He moves closer and closer, deeper and deeper into me.

23. Still closer—still deeper.

24. Hurrah—he goes down my path—I dance with joy.

25. I groan as he presses closer and closer, deeper and deeper.

26. He cleaves me royally—I am amazed how gloriously he cleaves me.

27. Behold he (his life) gushes forth again.

28. I let go the juices of my loins.

29. I give up every drop.

30. I will soon return to him—restored and refreshed.

31. Now my eyes are full and my throat swollen.

32. I am forced to my knees—I collapse.

33. My navel and chest sink inwards.

34. I open and shut my mouth with hugh breaths.

35. I long for the Sacred Phallus again—strong, erect, glorious. Ah! I faint with longing—I sleep (*Encyclopaedia Sexualis*, by Victor Robinson, M.D., pp. 166-7).

Belly dance motions are no longer overtly sexual. Instead they have become an art form that allures, teases, and promises an exotic experience that is more fantasy than reality. The dancer must also express strong emotions such as happiness, sorrow, love, and anger. These humanize the dancer and if done well can create a bond that is emotionally and sexually stimulating.

The belly dance follows a basic routine. It begins with the dancer entering, moving with the grace of a serpent hypnotized by the sound of a flute. The music then gains in tempo to become a folk dance. The dancer shakes and rolls her shoulders, head, stomach, and hips to the new rhythm. The music becomes deeper and as emotions intensify the dancer moves around the floor. She selects a spot on which to go down to her knees and lean back into the floor routine. The dance ends as it began and she shimmies her way back into the harem or Turkish street whence she came.

There are books and classes where men and women can learn this erotic art form. Belly dancing, while gaining in popularity in the rest of the world, has seriously declined as an occupation among women in Egypt. In November, 1989 there were only 50 licensed dancers remaining in that country. CAUTION: Belly dancing can cause back problems for some people.

(See also CHOREOPHILIA, SEX SHOWS and STRIPPING)

BESTIALITY See ZOOPHILIA

BI-SEXUALISM (Ambisexual, Amphisexual, Androgynophilia, Sexoschizia) Bi-sexuals are attracted to either sex as partners. This predisposition is thought to be based on biological (genetic, hormonal, and neurological) factors. Harry F. Harlow, who led the research into primate psychology, stated in his book *Learning to Love* that "Bisexual potential is a fact in humans and monkeys, and judgment of any sex-role behavior as normal or abnormal is only in relation to some manmade standard, real or fictitious" (p. 93). In tests, more than 50% of females in a group sex scene responded to same sex intimacy compared to only 1% of the males. However, when anonymity is guaranteed the ratio of male bi-sexuals increases to an almost equal level.

Bi-sexuals may have dating relationships with men and women at the same time or may be serially monogamous with either. Some married bi-sexuals have affairs with others of the same sex, but never with the opposite sex. This is because they separate love from lust and do not consider passionate sex with same sex partners a threat to the love and commitment they feel for a spouse.

There are various reasons for bi-sexual attraction. Some feel that all people are the same (i.e., a body is a body). Others find a distinct energy that uniquely characterizes each sex. Bi-sexuals may be nurturing or passionate with either sex. However, they usually separate the two, being only nurturing with one sex and passionate with the other. Famous bi-sexuals in history include Julius Caesar, who was said to be every woman's husband and every man's wife, and the Emperor Hadrian.

Bi-sexuality can offer a person who only responds to their partner with passion or nurturing an opportunity to enhance and complete their sexual and emotional needs.

At the same time such a person may benefit from therapy to help them discover the reason for this emotional dichotomy and to enable them to get both nurturing and passion in a single relationship.

(See also GAYS, HETEROSEXUAL and HOMOPHOBIA)

BIASTOPHILIA (Raptophilia) Biastophilia (biasto: rape or forced violation; philia: attachment to) refers to those who are only aroused when sexually assaulting an unwilling victim. The rapist loses interest if their victim submits. They need to see fear or tension in the partner.

(See also DACRYPHILIA, LUST MURDER, RAPE and SADISM)

BINDINGS Binding restricts movement and may include an area such as the genitals, feet, face, breasts, or all of the body, as in the form of mummification. Mummification requires that a person totally submit to their partner, however with binding one only relinquishes control of a certain area, usually the genitals or breasts, but not always. Binding is pleasurable to some due to the sensation of compression. It may also be included with other types of bondage.

Any area of the body can be bound but the following will only describe breasts, face, feet, penis, and mummification.

BREASTS Breasts are bound with soft rope, scarves, Saran Wrap, Ace bandages, soft leather strips, etc. They can be partially bound, so that the base is squeezed and the front area is left exposed for nipple play, or they may be completely bound for sensation from pressure. This type of breast binding is used by transvestites for crossdressing purposes.

FACE Occasionally people enjoy having their face or head restricted. A person's head is bound with scarves, soft thin rope, leather straps, or latex hoods. These can be lethal if they slip out of place. Most tops don't leave the room while their partner is bound. Latex also causes perspiration and the partner's discomfort determines how long the hood remains in place. CAUTION:

Closing off the mouth and nose together or using the throat area as an anchor can be dangerous and even fatal.

FEET Foot binding was originally practiced in 950 A.D. among dancing girls of the Chinese T'ang dynasty. It spread throughout the different levels of society and continued until the emancipation of women in the 1911-12 revolution. There are several theories related to its popularity. The binding of a wife's feet made her more subservient and more dependent. The binding of feet and the resulting effort required to walk was thought by some to aid in the tautness or development of muscles in the vagina. This theory is controversial and the bindings may have become popular simply because men are aroused by frailty, pain, or discomfort suffered by the opposite sex, especially when it is done for sexual reasons. This handicap was also a status symbol in the same way as the aristocratic Chinese male's incredibly long fingernails, both being symbols of wealth and leisure.

Today many women wear high heels that are uncomfortable or cause a similar slow delicate gait. Women seem to wear this type of shoes as much for themselves and their own sense of what makes them feel sexy as to please men. (See also ACROTOMOPHILIA, APOTEMN-OPHILIA, DYSMORPHOPHILIA, MASOCHISM, PODOPHILIA and SADISM)

MUMMIFICATION Mummification involves wrapping the whole body. The ancient Egyptians preserved their dead in this manner. Today it is used in the S/M community as a form of bondage. If the bound partner prefers to play during the time they are encased, the genitals, nipples, or anus are left exposed. Negotiation is very important and a safeword is always agreed upon between partners before they play. (See NEGOTIATION)

The materials used for mummification are bandages, scissors, a ceiling hook that can support the weight of their partner, a chain, panic snap, a head harness, padding for between the person's knees and ankles, material for wrapping, duct tape, a large towel, and their partner's favorite sex toys. Wrapping materials consist of Saran Wrap, Ace bandages, or latex strips. Once the person is wrapped they are ready to be entertained.

Head harnesses are used to give maximum support under a person's chin and the back of their head. The top of the harness has a ring with which to attach the panic snap and chain. These are not designed to support the weight of the person, only to assist their balance while standing.

The typical mummification scene proceeds by a person undressing, having the head harness fitted and then hooked to the chain that attaches to the ceiling. This is done to make sure the person is comfortable and has the proper support before the wrapping begins. Next the padding is placed between the ankles and knees and the wrapping then begins at the ankles and moves upward. The person wrapping watches to make sure that he has not left any exposed skin between the wrapping to which the duct tape might stick. Many prefer not to wrap the person with their legs or arms touching other skin because of the discomfort. The wrapping is continued, leaving the genitals or breasts exposed, and finished by loosely wrapping the neck. Duct tape is applied to secure the wrapping material, and a blindfold is occasionally used. When the game is over, bandage scissors are used to cut the mummy out of the wrapping. The material may be cut loose while the person is still suspended or afterward. Head harnesses are not unsnapped unless the partner is strong enough to support their body weight because many people are unable to stand on their own after mummification. Cutting is begun at the bottom between the back of the ankles and continued to the neck. The mummy is usually perspiring and has to be wrapped in a large towel or blanket. A simpler type of mummification is done with restraint type body or sleeping bags.

Another form of mummification is the wrapping of one's partner in toilet paper as they stand. They are next sprayed (using a water pistol or bottle spray) with a favorite liquid. The partner or partners then proceed to lick the wet paper off their body. This game is called "squirt and lick." CAUTION: It is psychologically important to the mummy to be touched and talked to by their partner. The mummy is much more likely to panic without constant reassurance. Many people have died attempting mummification while alone or with a partner who wasn't aware of proper precautions.

PENIS Many methods are used to bind the penis. There are prefabricated leather harnesses with rings, snaps, and even attach-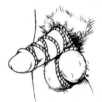able vibrators. Some have a ring that can accommodate a leash which is used to lead naked men around at S/M parties.

The penis is also bound or wrapped with 6 feet of rope, thin leather boot laces, strips of 1/2" garment leather, or Ace bandages. Bandage scissors are kept in an accessible location in case of an emergency. A sample wrapping beginning with the center portion of the strand being anchored gently under the scrotum, both ends brought up, crossed at the top front of the scrotum, brought up and across the top of the penis, and from there continues until the desired effect is achieved. CAUTION: It is dangerous to wrap the binding too tightly. Penis binding is restricted to no longer than 10 minutes and shorter if a tingling sensation develops. Safewords are used to signal the need for immediate release. If the bottom is gagged, an obvious gesture is agreed on in the event of any discomfort, nausea, or pain. Serious damage can occur if not done safely.

(See also BONDAGE and CONSTRICTIONS)

BIRTH CONTROL Documented efforts to prevent pregnancy are ancient. The Jews first recorded coitus interruptus as a form of birth control in Genesis. Efforts at birth control are also found in Egyptian papyri as early as 1900 B.C. The Egyptians used many different methods. One was a barrier of lint that was covered in acacia powder, another was a mixture which included crocodile dung, both being used by females. More recently the 18th century Casanova used half lemons which must have acted as an acidic spermicide and cervical cap. Abortion and sterilization are also types of birth control that are ancient.

Historically, governments have had the most control over sex, abortion, birth control, adoption, or the number of males and females allowed per family. These restrictions were usually based on a country's need for additional soldiers and workers. Most cultures had little or no provision for welfare, therefore, their only solution in preventing hunger was to control the birth rate or population of their citizens. A woman who accidentally became pregnant had the option of aborting before delivery, abandoning, selling, or killing the child after its birth.

Religions eventually became involved with restriction on birth control and, in some cases sex in general. Europeans and Americans alike found that after the censorship of sexual information during and following the 19th century period of Victorianism birth control information was not available to the general public. A few notable people fought to bring women this information. People such as Francis Place, Richard Carlile, Annie Besant, John Stuart Mill, Charles Knowlton, Dr. Aletta Jacobs, and Dr. Marie Stopes fought for people's right to choose birth control. Even the management of Syntex Labs had a struggle in bringing the first birth control pill to the market.

One of the last great social reformers was Margaret Sanger, who in 1914 spearheaded a movement to educate women on this subject. She was a nurse who had not only seen first hand the agony unplanned children had on poor families but had tended a patient who died of an illegal abortion. It was she who first coined the term 'birth control' and began writing literature on the subject. She soon found herself indicted under the directive of Anthony Comstock, the special agent of the Post Office and lobbyist for the Comstock Act, which made obscenity a felony. Comstock especially felt that birth control was a major evil. Mrs. Sanger left the country to avoid prosecution and this angered Mr. Comstock. To get revenge he set up her husband just as he had unsuspecting physicians in the past to provide information about birth control to a supposed couple who were desperately in need of it. Mr. Sanger mailed the information, was convicted, and imprisoned. Mrs. Sanger founded the American Birth Control League in 1921 which consolidated with another agency in 1942 and became the Planned Parenthood Federation of America. Even with her intense lobbying to undo the harm accomplished by Comstock there were statutes against birth control information being distributed through the mail or devices being sold until 1970. Many voters do not realize that some evangelical lobbyists today not only want anti-abortion laws but are just as adamant about wanting to rescind people's right to use birth control. (See also ANTHONY COMSTOCK)

The governments of many countries now recognize the need to control their own birth rates, some even giving incentives to restrict the number of children in a family. When family planning is made available, the birth rate has fallen in many third world countries two to four times as quickly as it did in the West at a similar stage of development.

ABORTION   Ancient methods used to induce miscarriage were often concoctions of herbs. The Hottentot women drank hot badger urine, which when ingested for several days, often caused the fetus to abort. Australian women had the abdomen beaten with large stones or a stick; or might also lean against a tree and have two men roll the stick down across her stomach. The pushing was not only hard enough to cause the death of the fetus but sometimes that of the mother as well. In the Middle East slaves who were well endowed were sometimes used to abort pregnancies in their master's harem. This was accomplished with violent thrusts of the slave's penis.

Abortion had been practiced throughout history without much restricting legislation because it was not considered murder at that stage of prenatal development. That is,

not until Tertullian interpreted Exodus 21:22, which refers to legal action being taken against a man who injures a pregnant woman, as encompassing a mother, doctor or midwife who performs an abortion. This Church doctrine later became incorporated into secular legislation. Women in the United States receive 1.5 million abortions a year. World-wide the number is estimated at 50 million with 200,000 related deaths. The number of abortions always rise with the inability to obtain other forms of birth control.

Abortion clinics are currently operative in most of the United States although often under protest and harassment by "right-to-life" groups. A woman checks into these clinics, is interviewed, and has several expandable sticks of seaweed (laminaria) inserted into the opening of her cervix, causing it to stretch open overnight. The patient goes home and returns the next day for a vacuum aspiration (a tube is inserted into the womb and the suction removes fetal tissue). This procedure is effective for up to fourteen weeks into pregnancy. Small underground groups of women have formed to learn of alternative methods if abortion becomes illegal.

ANAL SEX   Anal sex is today considered a high risk activity for contracting AIDS, although in the past it was used in some cultures both in preventing pregnancy and loss of virginity before marriage.

CERVICAL CAP   A cervical cap fits over the tip of the cervix and is made of rubber, metal, or plastic. They cannot be used by all women because of the difference in individual shape of cervixes. The cap is similar in appearance 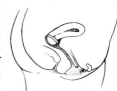 to the diaphragm but smaller and more difficult to get into the proper position. They are manufactured in England and more popular in Europe than in the U.S. The estimated success rate is 75-95%.

COITUS INTERRUPTUS   This refers to withdrawing the penis from the vagina before ejaculation and is one of the oldest methods of birth control. It is used by approximately 35 million people in the world today. Its success rate is 70-95%.

CONDOM   Condoms have also been used throughout history. Goat bladders, lemon halves, sheep intestines, fish intestines, seed pods, linen, silk, and leather have all been used to create a barrier between the penis and vagina. Condoms are available in different shapes, textures, and sizes. The diameters begin at 1 1/4" but can be larger (Mentor's Magnum, and Fourex). However, most condoms are between 1 1/4" to 1 1/2" in diameter, and are 7 1/2" long. The body of the condom stretches but the ring at the base can cause discomfort if it is too tight. There is also a new condom on the market that only covers the glans penis.

Proper placement of a condom requires several steps. First, the tip of the penis is lubricated with a water based lubricant (an oil based lubricant will cause the latex to deteriorate). Next, the reservoir tip is held closed as the condom is rolled onto the glans penis. Men who are not circumcised pull the foreskin back to expose this area. The condom is then rolled over the rest of the penis taking care not to catch the hair at the pubic region. Some men find that by using a lamb skin condom first and then putting a latex condom over it they create more sensation for both them and their partner. Additional water based lubrication can be added to the outside of the condom if the man feels it is necessary. Caution is taken before withdrawing the penis after ejaculation by holding the bottom base of the condom tightly to avoid it slipping off as it is pulled out. One condom manufacturer, Mentor, has adhesive added at the base to help prevent this from happening. A condom is 80-95% effective against pregnancy.

In addition to birth control, condoms protect people from many sexually transmitted diseases. A way to increase the safety factor is to use a spermicide with nonoxynol-9 in conjunction with the condom, although latest tests reveal that this is not a guarantee for avoiding infection from the AIDS virus. Some condoms already contain a small amount of this ingredient in the lubricant. CAUTION: Condoms do sometimes break. The ratio is 1 in 165 for vaginal sex and 1 in 105 for anal sex. The risk can be minimized by only using fresh condoms and additional water based lubricants.

A new female condom, WPC 333, has been developed by the Wisconsin Pharmacal Company. It is now scheduled for clinical trials with no expected marketing date. The device has two rings, one that is inserted internally, in a similar manner as a diaphragm, and the other end lies against the outside of the vagina. Its efficacy has 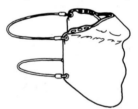 been rated as superior to the male condom and can be used without the necessity of a sustained male erection to hold it in place. It also has the potential to reduce the possibility of herpes transmission (The Helper, by the American Social Health Association, p. 9). The female condom appears to be adaptable to sex play as a receptacle for stuffing food or drinks into the vagina. (See STUFFING) Names selected for this device are Reality and Femidom.

There is a patent held by Ricardo J. Esqueda for a facial prophylactic that protects the wearer from transmission of diseases while engaging in oral sex. The mask covers the person's face from the top of the nose to under the chin. The person breathes through a shaft that passes from the nostrils to the top of the mask.

CONTRACEPTIVE IMPLANT   This product was introduced into 17 countries in 1991 and has approximately 500,000 users. Small silicone rubber capsules are inserted under the skin of a woman's arm to provide protection against pregnancy for about five years. These may be removed at any point in time. The implant is almost 100% effective and lasts about five years

DIAPHRAGM The diaphragm was invented in 1882. It is a half-ball-shaped thin rubber device with a metal rim. A spermicide is placed into the cavity and the top rim is pinched together in the center for insertion into the vagina before sex. The diaphragm, when in place, covers the cervix and prevents sperm from entering through the opening. The spermicide is only effective for 12 hours and needs at least 6 hours to kill sperm after intercourse.

The diaphragm can slip during intercourse and for this reason it is rated as only 80-95% effective.

DOUCHE A douche is the flooding of the vagina by a liquid, usually water, but it may have another additive such as vinegar. Disposable plastic bottles with nozzles (douche bags) are available at drug stores. Sperm can enter the cervix in as little as one minute after release of pre-ejaculate and for this reason douching is rated as being the least effective form of birth control, falling behind the rhythm method.

HOME OVULATION DETECTOR A home ovulation detector is under development by a California firm. This unit provides a convenient method for women to monitor the progesterone level in their urine. A rise in progesterone signals the end of ovulation for a particular monthly cycle. This product may be available by 1993. If used properly, this method should be 100% effective. The disadvantage is that sex without risk of pregnancy can only be guaranteed for 10 to 14 days a month.

IMMUNOCONTRACEPTION Immuno-contraception is currently under research. This method works by using a vaccine to build antibodies to bind proteins onto the surface of the woman's egg, thus making it impossible for the sperm to penetrate its surface. Another method vaccinates the woman against sperm. The immune period lasts for up to five years, afterward dropping to a level that permits fertilization. ("Have it your way," by Margo Schneidman, *Stanford Medicine*, Spring 1992, p. 23)

IUD Intrauterine Devices have been used intermittently since the nineteenth century.

The idea was conceived from the observance of female camels having their fertility period delayed by the insertion of a stone into the uterus before long trips across the desert. In 1930 E. Grafenberg began using a coiled silver wire with success, however, due to controversy among gynecologists the device did not gain popularity. In 1959 two more physicians, W. Oppenheimer and T. Ota documented a success rate of over 97.5% with no significant complications and the device became a popular birth control method. Two million Indian women were wearing these IUDs within 4 years after introduction. IUDs have lost popularity in the United States due to complications involving infections among women exposed to sexually transmitted diseases. However, they are still popular in China and safe for most any female in a monogamous relationship.

IUDs seem to work by interfering with the ability of the fertilized egg to implant itself in the uterine wall. An inflammation can occur for the first few days after insertion, but will usually disappear. Women may have later complications resulting in infertility. Therefore, they are only recommended for women with established families.

Two IUDs are currently marketed in the United States. One is GynoPharma's Paragard and the other is the Progestasert. Both look similar. The Progestasert was invented by Dr. Alejandro Zaffaroni in 1976 and marketed by ALZA Corporation. This IUD differs from others in that it releases progesterone to the uterus over a period of one year. This low dosage of hormone does not produce the same side effects found in contraceptive pills and seems to have fewer complications than other types of IUDs.

The Progestasert is about 97.5% effective against pregnancy.

MENSTRUAL EXTRACTION Menstrual extraction, or suction of uterine contents, is done soon after a woman discovers her menstrual cycle is late. This particular technique has been endorsed by a few women's groups for almost 20 years but has only recently gained attention due to new laws threatening a woman's choice to obtain a legal abortion. Menstrual extraction is used by some every few months as a precaution against possible pregnancy. This home health technique is performed on women by other women through support groups. The technique itself requires a special skill and most practitioners are trained by other women. The actual suction device consists of a syringe with a by-pass valve, a cannula, tubing, a mason jar, and other attachments. CAUTION: Infections and serious injury are possible, especially when the procedure is performed by women not trained in menstrual extraction.

PILL—CONTRACEPTIVE Scientists discovered in 1934 that ovulation could be inhibited through administration of estrogen or progesterone but the doses needed were too large to be practical in humans. Then in 1951 Dr. Carl Djerassi succeeded in synthesizing steroids that were more potent and thereby practical for administration in pill form. Further testing was done by Gregory Pincus and the first contraceptive pill was marketed by Syntex in the early 1960s.

There are an estimated 65 million users of the contraceptive pill. These are taken for 20 to 21 consecutive days beginning with the fifth day after the menstrual cycle begins. There can be side effects for some, however, the rate of effectiveness when the pill is taken properly can be 100%. Some women are able to take 100 mcg of estrogen within 24 hours after sex and repeat that 12 hours later to prevent pregnancy. The continual use of the pill for several years greatly reduces a woman's risk of ovarian or endometrial cancer.

A male pill is being researched. One method suppresses the gonadotropin-releasing hormone which in turn inhibits the production of testosterone and sperm production. To prevent a loss of sex drive, men are given a bi-weekly injection of synthetic testosterone. The other method requires a weekly injection of testosterone which blocks the pituitary secretion of hormones and the production of sperm. The level of testosterone in the bloodstream remains normal. There are many more psychological factors involved with a male's decision to use the pill than exist for a woman. If a male pill is introduced it may not be until around the turn of the century.

PILL—CONTRAGESTIVE RU 486 is the only contragestive pill on the market and as of 1992 was available in France, China and England. This pill can be taken after conception and up to nine weeks during the gestation period. It is called a "death pill" by antiabortionists. The dosage of three 200mg pills, followed by a small amount of prostaglandin 48 hours later, is administered by a physician. The success rate of embryo expulsion is 96% within the first day of receiving the prostaglandin. Some physicians fear that this drug might be sold on the black market where, without medical supervision, a woman might take the pills after the nine week limit, potentially causing her death as a complication of hemorrhaging.

RU 486 was developed by Etienne-Emile Baulieu in the late 1970s while consulting for Roussel-Uclaf. Boycotts were threatened by both opposition and supporters of the new pill. It was not brought to the market by Roussel until French health minister Claude Evin said that the pill was the moral property of all women and threatened to transfer the patent to another pharmaceutical company. FDA approval for RU 486 has not yet been filed in the United States ("News and comment," by J. Palca, *SCIENCE* (Vol. 245), Sept. 22, 1989, pp. 1319-1324).

RHYTHM METHOD (Natural Family Planning) Women have different fertility cycles and the purpose of this method is to restrict sex to the cycle during which the woman is not able to conceive. The number of days from ovulation to menstruation is fairly consistent at 13-15 days, however, the number of days from the first sign of menstruation to ovulation varies greatly. Problems also arise with differences in cycles between women and irregularity in the same woman brought on by stress or illness. Sperm can also live up to 5 days inside the vagina and some women can ovulate twice. The rate of effectiveness is 65-85%. This is the only type of birth control approved by the Roman Catholic Church, who adopted St. Augustine's belief that sex other than to produce children was a sin. Judaism differs from Christianity in that the scripture that tells one to reproduce and fill the earth is interpreted as only applying to men. Women therefore are given authority over their own bodies and can practice birth control if they choose. The form of birth control, however, cannot be something that depends on the male (condoms or vasectomy).

SPERMICIDE   Spermicides kill sperm on contact and come in the form of gels, creams, foams, suppositories, and sponges which act as repositories for the chemical. These have to be inserted before intercourse and are all available without prescription in drug stores. Spermacides have a rating of 70-90% effectiveness.

STEROID INJECTIONS   Injections of steroids are popular in Asia and Latin America. A 150 mg dose of medroxyprogesterone acetate is injected to prevent pregnancy. The body absorbs this steroid for up to 90 days and the woman during this time remains infertile. Side effects are reported by as many as 36% but the effectiveness rate is greater than 99%.

TUBAL LIGATION   Women sometimes choose sterilization by having their fallopian tubes severed. This is a surgical procedure and is done in a hospital and is completely effective against future pregnancies.

Surgical reversal has become possible, but the success rate is very low. If a woman chooses to reverse this procedure, locating a micro surgeon with a high success rate is recommended. In 1988 the expense of physician and hospital for a reversal was approximately $5,000.

VAGINAL RING   A vaginal ring is under development that emits steroids in the vagina to prevent ovulation. Like the birth control pill, it is used for three weeks and then discontinued for one week to permit menstruation. The ring is shaped like a small thin donut and has only minor side effects. The advantage over other methods is that the woman has only the date of insertion and removal with which to be concerned. This device may be on the market by 1997.

VASECTOMY   This surgical procedure for sterilization has been done on about 45 million males. The physician is able to perform the procedure in his office. First anesthetizing the scrotum, he makes a small incision, locates and ties both vas deferens in two spots, cuts out the section between, and the procedure is over. Birth control needs to be practiced for an additional 12 weeks or 20 ejaculations to guarantee that all remaining sperm are no longer potent. Hormone secretion continues as usual. The only detectable difference is in the milder flavor of his ejaculate. Reversal of vasectomies is also sometimes possible.

(See also ILLEGAL SEX and SACRIFICES)

BITING   (Odaxelagnia—arousal from biting) Biting and nibbling is used by some to sexually excite their partner. It is done on the neck, ears, lips, nipples, back, buttocks, genitals, inner thighs, etc. The pressure one uses depends on their partner's pain tolerance. Biting can be very light or can leave marks and be painful. Novices usually begin with light nibbling, having their partner signal when it becomes intense. They start with ears and work their way down the back to the thighs and back up, alternating bites, nibbles and licking. A few men respond to firm biting of the shaft of the penis just below the glans.

Biting is one of the easiest and most accepted methods of light S/M play. The increased sensation brings some individuals who are emotionally stressed out of their physical numbness, back into touch with their bodies.

Biting was recommended for lovers in the Kama-Sutra. Vatsyayana first listed the types of bites as follows:

The hidden bite leaves on the skin only a passing redness. The swollen bite occurs when the skin has been seized and pulled, as though with pincers. The line of jewels is formed by a bite involving all the teeth. The broken cloud is a broken line of points undulating around a curve, due to the space between the teeth. The bite of the boar is imprinted on the breasts and the shoulders and consists of two lines of teeth marks, one above the other, with a red gap.

One can convey one's desire to a woman by making nail or teeth marks on the following objects which she wears or owns; any ornament of the forehead or ears, a bunch of flowers, and a betel or tamala leaf.

When a lover bites his mistress hard, she must, with feigned anger, bite him back twice as hard...If she is very excited, and because of his passionate condition starts a kind of fight with her lover, she will take him by the hair, pull his head towards her and bite his lower lip; then, in her delirium, she will bite him all over his body, with her eyes closed.

Kinsey reported that about 50% of people surveyed showed sexual arousal from being bitten during sex. A more sadistic type of biting was portrayed in two scenes in the 1960's movie Barbarella. The first was when she was tied to a column and dolls with metal teeth were unleashed on her. The second was when she was thrown into a glass cage and parakeets swarmed over her body, supposedly biting off bits of flesh before she was rescued. Marilyn Monroe was known to draw blood by biting the lips of her partners.

Animals such as cats, horses, and turtles use biting to arouse their partners to the high levels of passion necessary for ovulation or ejaculation. CAUTION: Bites that draw blood are considered unsafe sex.

(See also CLAMPS, CUPPING, PINCHING, SAFE SEX, SCRATCHING, SENSORY ENHANCEMENT and TICKLING)

BLINDFOLDING   Blindfolding, or manually impairing the vision of a partner accomplishes several results. A person who temporarily loses their sight develops an increased awareness of their other senses, such as touch. The person blindfolded can also experience a sense that their mind is detached from their body. Blindfolding releases some from their inhibitions and can have a depersonalizing effect on both partners. Blindfolding is used to reduce the power of the bottom and give it to the top. An example is that of a dominant husband

who wants to temporarily submit to his normally timid wife.

Blindfolding makes it possible for a top to act out the role of anonymous serial lovers in a scene without the inconvenience of changing costumes. It is used in group sex for the reverse effect.

The blindfold used most often because of its comfort and restricted vision is the adjustable leather blindfold that is lined with padding or fur. CAUTION: Contact lenses can cause injury if worn with blindfolds of any type. A slight mental disorientation can occur after any extended period of blindness and caution is taken when removing the blindfold. If the person is under any other type of restraint, the blindfold is removed first.

(See also AMAUROPHILIA, BONDAGE and LIGHTING)

BLOOD SPORTS   Blood sports are those sex activities in which skin is broken. This would include activities such as cutting, phlebotomy, cicatrization, piercing, carpet burns, abrasions, shaving, scratching, vampirism, flagellation, caning, branding, burning, etc.

Cutting the skin or drawing blood creates an adrenalin rush, trust for partner, and a sense of personal conquest for the participant. It may also help relieve stress in some people.

People involved in blood sports only use shallow cuts on certain padded areas of the body, like thighs, upper arms, and shoulders. This type of scene is performed only by those in the medical profession or those who have a vast amount of cutting or piercing experience.CAUTION: Activity involving unprotected contact with the blood of a partner is considered unsafe sex and cutting areas that have a concentration of nerves, arteries, veins, tendons, ligaments, or bone can be dangerous.

(See also ABRASIONS, BITING, CUPPING, DEPILATION, FLAGELLATION, PHLEBOTOMY, SAFE SEX and SCRATCHING)

BODY PAINTING   Body painting probably had its beginning with prehistoric hunting tribes and is still a ritual art form in

Africa where natives decorate themselves to resemble wild animals or sacred spirits. American Indians used face painting when

they went to battle so their gods wouldn't recognize them and hold them responsible for the injury or death of other humans. This philosophy is successfully used by those who feel guilty about experimenting with sex. It is also simply a sensuous way to savor the contours and crevices of one's partner. Many begin preparation by giving the partner a full body massage using oil which acts to seal dry porous skin. The music and location is then selected to match the desired mood. The paint is then applied along the contour lines of the person's body with particular attention being paid to sensitive areas such as hands, feet, face, ears, nipples, and genitals. Body paints come in an assortment of colors and some even glitter. Motif transfers of birds, snakes, and roses are added to enhance basic designs. Some people prefer to simply use a dry brush or warm massage oil instead of paint which needs to be washed off later.

Body painting is not limited to two people; it is sometimes modified (adding a g-string) to become entertainment at a party. Here some people substitute various edible love oils and let guests experiment by brushing one of these onto the model and then licking it off. CAUTION: Body painting may block the sweat glands, resulting in a potentially dangerous compromise of the body's ability to regulate its own temperature. For this reason, covering the entire body with paint should be avoided. Also, some people may have an allergic reaction to toxins in the paint.

(See also CICATRIZATION and TATTOOING)

BONDAGE (Vincilagnia—arousal from bondage) Bondage refers to the act of restricting the movement of a person.

Bondage can be physical or symbolic and may involve many different methods. Primitive cultures used bondage on stolen brides to prevent their escape. This form of restraint eventually evolved into symbolic bindings around the waist, legs, wrist, and, according to some, the finger. The tradition of carrying the bride across the threshold also comes from this custom. There was a strange twist to sex and bondage during the 19th century when parents were encouraged to bind the hands of their sons behind their backs to prevent them from masturbating. Adult men were not exempt and were often expected to have the same thing done to them.

Today television programs are full of abduction and bondage scenes. Children play cowboys and Indians using rope bondage. And in 1989 over 40% of the patients in American nursing homes were put into restraints. Regardless of the popularity of bondage, it is not always socially acceptable for adults to utilize it for sex play.

The benefits individuals receive from bondage vary. Simple solitary bondage is like meditation for many practitioners. The brain seems to release more alpha waves, causing a floating or hypnotic state similar to when one drives on a highway late at night.

Other people prefer to pull against the restraints, building a rush of adrenalin and euphoria. Men who are much stronger than their partner, but still want a passionate reciprocal exchange of physical power, benefit from partial bondage. This handicaps the man so that the woman appears to have equivalent or superior physical strength. Some build up immense confidence and self esteem by being able to work their way loose from the restraints. Many find that bondage relieves them of always having to sexually perform. This allows them to relax and not feel guilty about enjoying the sensations their partner is creating.

Bondage often serves as simple support. Secure and comfortable bondage allows the bottom to relax completely, without worrying about balance or other practical distractions. Imaginative sexual positions may move from ridiculously awkward to fun with such support.

A major effect of bondage, when used during sex, is the release of normal inhibitions. A prisoner or victim does not feel as personally responsible when obeying commands, especially ones they have fantasized about but didn't have the courage to try. The person performing the bondage experiences a similar release of inhibition due to the tremendous increase in feelings of personal power. However, sexual etiquette requires that the top not use the situation to exclusively fulfill their own fantasies, particularly ones that the bottom doesn't find arousing.

Bondage scenes are negotiated ahead of time which enables both people to determine what type of scene they want to act out and what paraphernalia might be needed. A safeword guarantees that the sexual limits of the bottom will be expanded but not violated. The safeword is also a command to end the game, whether it is because the bottom feels discomfort, boredom, or their limit has been reached. Regardless of why the safeword was used, it is the responsibility of the top to get them out of bondage within a few seconds.

Bondage also creates trust and appreciation for the top. Those bound are for the first time not able to reciprocate acts of affection and stimulation received from a partner. They become fully aware of the role their partner plays in expressing affection and controlling sexual arousal. Many bottoms become extremely grateful and submissive upon finally being released.

Bondage, like other sex games, will generally not produce an erotic effect unless one is sexually attracted to their partner or has an overpowering lust for bondage, in which case the partner is of lesser importance. In addition, most safety conscious people do not play with people they don't know.

Bondage, unlike other types of sex, may require a long period of time, up to 48 hours. This necessitates the partner being diverse and having the physical and mental stamina required to keep the game intense,

focused, and progressive. The top is often more exhausted than the bottom at the end of the bondage scene. CAUTION: Bondage, like mountain climbing, skydiving, body building, and car racing can be dangerous if not done properly. People who practice bondage read about the safety of new equipment or positions they can use on their partners. Positions are selected according to the length of time in which the partners have to play. Many positions seen in magazines are extremely uncomfortable and would not work for more than a few minutes. Pulling a person's arms upward while they are bound behind their back (strapado torture position) can easily dislocate their shoulders. A person is never left unattended while bound. Furthermore, the person who is bound is constantly monitored for breathing, circulation, skin tone, and temperature of the fingers and toes. Nothing is put near the neck except properly fitted collars. Ropes, blindfolds, hoods, or other restraints can slip out of their original position and cause suffocation. The restrictive cuffs or ropes match on each side of the body in order to produce the proper sensations. Those learning bondage add additional paraphernalia slowly, avoiding gags, latex hoods, impaling, lacing, and crucifixion.

The following are specific examples of common bondage play.

BARS Spreader bars are used in conjunction with leather cuffs, and sometimes chains. They are designed to alleviate the need of anchoring a person to a chair or bed. A leg or knee spreader also keeps the bottom from closing their legs to protect or hide their genitals. This type of vulnerability is particularly exciting for women who enjoy being exhibited. 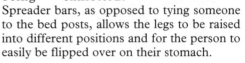 Spreader bars, as opposed to tying someone to the bed posts, allows the legs to be raised into different positions and for the person to easily be flipped over on their stomach.

CAGES Cages are used to imprison partners without the need of additional restraints. Cages are made to resemble wire chicken coops, coffins, or wooden boxes. The type of cage one selects is determined by the feelings one wants to produce. If the fantasy involves an interrogation of a prisoner, bars are often used. If the slave is impersonating a pet, the chicken wire pen or kennel sets the proper mood. Necrophiles and vampires prefer coffins. Wooden boxes with holes for ventilation are versatile in most cases and claustrophiles (people who are aroused by being trapped in small areas) enjoy being placed in them.

Cages may or may not be large enough to permit the slave to stand or lay fully stretched out. The size of the cage determines how long a person is left inside. Cages are used as beds, for punishment, or during a recess in S/M play. Some tops have anchored male prisoners wearing Prince Albert penis rings (metal ring that pierces the urethra and exits near the frenulum) to the cage bars by wrapping his penis around a bar and fastening the Prince Albert to a cockring at the base end of his penis.

People practicing long term bondage who need to leave the house for a couple of hours often leave their partner in a cage. This is considered safe, on the assumption that the chances of the house catching fire or the top getting into a car accident are extremely slim.

CHAINS Chains are used for suspension or attaching one restraint to another. They are also used for ornamentation or to connect various ring piercings on the body. Chains, because they rattle and feel cool, add tactile and auditory sensations to the bondage scene.

Chains are preferred by some for suspension because they are heavy duty and various items can be hung from the links. A 3" or 4" panic snap is added to provide for immediate release. The disadvantage to using chains is their weight and bulk if people take sex toys with them on a trip.

COLLARS Collars are worn by slaves and bottoms. They act as a visible and physical reminder of their submissive state. The collar is often black leather with a buckle and some include chrome studs as decoration. It is either worn alone or with a leash attached to a "D" ring. Others use an ordinary necklace with some type of charm or emblem to signify their commitment. Pet slaves sometimes have personalized dog tags attached to their collar.

Wrist restraints are occasionally attached by a chain to the "D" ring with the arms in front of the body or to the sides. This is dangerous if done from the back because it can cause self-strangulation.

CRUCIFIXION Crucifixion consists of suspending a person by the wrists and ankles from a stake. It was originally done by Phoenicians, Assyrians, Egyptians, Persians, and Romans as a method of execution. Nailing the wrists and feet usually meant a fast death from blood loss while using ropes meant that the person would live several hours before suffocating. Death could take several days if their weight was supported by something. The Carthaginians used crucifixion as a form of ritual sacrifice. Malcus, in order to ensure himself victory in battle, dressed his son, had a crown placed on his head, and then crucified him as a sacrifice to the god Baal. Once dead, the victim was usually burned with the cross. The Romans developed four more types of crucifixes: the Y, X, T, and H. The latter involved hanging a person horizontally by one leg and one arm.

Leather cuffs are preferred for most, but people also wrap their ankles and wrists with ropes using Ace bandages to give some protection underneath the binding. The rope binding is to be secure but not too tight.

A few people find crucifixion games arousing and powerful because of its religious association with pain and sacrifice. CAUTION: There is a danger that setting the restraints too loosely may cause permanent crushed nerve damage. Constant monitoring of the extremities for circulation is done by all who play with restraints.

Some choose to have an orgasm during suspension. However, the body tolerates more pain before orgasm than afterward and they risk experiencing increased pain.

Positions that require one's arms to be separate and support their weight will put stress on the lungs and can cause suffocation. The least painful position is one where both hands are hung together above the head and the ankles are spread but still have support. This can be tolerated by some for as long as 10-15 minutes, depending on the person, their weight, and the type of bondage (*Dungeon Master*, No. 11, July 1981, "When in Rome," by Fledermaus, pp. 41-43).

CUFFS   Leather cuffs are 2-3" wide leather strips that fit around the wrists or ankles. They have buckles, latches, or padlocks and may be lined with fur for comfort. Cuffs are simpler to use, more restrictive than rope, and can be removed faster. Chains, leather straps, or spreader bars are sometimes used to attach cuffs to each other.

ENCASEMENT   Encasement is a type of bondage that also involves sensory deprivation. The Sadhus of India used this method as one way of preventing orgasms while trying to achieve an altered state of consciousness. It is also used as a type of chastity device ("Fakir Musafar" by V. Vale and A. Juno, *Modern Primitives*, p. 20).

Encasements of heads were used in the form of hideous helmets or metal masks during the Middle Ages as a form of humiliation. This type of torture was portrayed in the movie "Man in the Iron Mask" with Richard Chamberlain, and if this had a similar effect on the head as it does the penis, we can only imagine the psychological torment it could cause.

A man usually encases his penis in a

metal ball or other material that will not come into constant contact with the penis. Both of these have a small hole for urine to pass. Encasements make it impossible for the person to achieve an orgasm and there is no sensation in the penis while encased. However, after several days have

passed and the ball is removed the penis becomes extremely sensitive to the touch.

(See also BONDAGE/HOODS, ORGASMS /ALTERED STATES, and PENIS MODIFICATION/NEGATION)

GAGS   Gags are used to render people speechless, which has a great psychological impact. Some bottoms prefer gags because they muffle their screams of ecstasy. Those using gags establish an alternative signal to replace the safeword. Some have their partner hold a marble and drop it if they want the game to end.

There are many types of gags. They include bridles, ball gags, mouth covers, muzzles, adhesive tape, stuffers, dildos, and bar gags.

Most movies depict adhesive tape placed across the mouth. This, like any gag that does not restrict movement of the jaw, is technically ineffective. Removal can also be painful.

Ball gags are effective and safe as long as they are anchored or strung onto a strap that is wide enough to be comfortable.

Penis or dildo gags are available with the penis mounted on the inside of the mouth, the outside, or both. Penis gags are used for humiliation, sex, punishment, and teasing. People strap on the gag with the dildo that protrudes outward and then mount it. They also have the option of sitting on the partner's gag and sucking on their genitals. Head harnesses are available in Japan with a high-heel shoe attached to the front so that the toe penetrates the mouth.

Muzzles or head harnesses are used by many because they are comfortable, generally anchor the jaw, permit breathing, and do not chafe the lips. The person is not rendered completely speechless but the sound is muffled. CAUTION: There is a risk of the person not being able to breathe adequately through their nose, gagging on saliva, damaging their teeth on hard objects put in their mouth, swallowing or choking on vomit or stuffings that can be bitten off or come loose from the mouthpiece, or the mouth becoming uncomfortably dry. Many only use gags for two minutes at a time.

HANDCUFFS Handcuffs are adjustable and when applied correctly it is impossible for the victim to escape. They are easy to apply and are a convenient form of restraint for those wanting to move their partner to another location.

Generally mitts, socks, or boots are used to protect against the discomfort caused by the metal pressing against the skin. Good quality handcuffs with built-in safety locks that keep them from tightening after being locked are used in the S/M community. Those who have more than one set usually have them all keyed the same and keep extra keys readily available during bondage play as a safety precaution. Handcuffs are applied so that the key hole faces away from the body, making them more accessible and easier to remove. CAUTION: For safety, handcuffs are carried closed. This guarantees that the key is available before play begins and padding (gloves or Ace bandage) is used on the wrists to protect them from abrasion.

HANGING Pseudo-hanging in S/M games is done to keep the partner restricted to one location. This is accomplished with a knotted rope noose or a chain that is attached to an 'o' ring on a leather hood and connected to a supporting hook on the ceiling. Others use a string that breaks if the bottom slips and falls. CAUTION: Hanging with a rope is very dangerous because the person who is bound can not catch themselves if they lose their balance. Those who use hanging must be physically strong enough to support the bottom's weight until the noose is removed. Do not leave the bound partner unattended.

(See also AUTOEROTIC ASPHYXIA and OXYGEN REGULATION)

HARNESSES Body harnesses are used for decorative attire, suspension, and to anchor onto other restraints. Decorative harnesses are made of rope in bondage scenes and of leather for costumes.

Harnesses used most for suspension are parachute harnesses which are available for purchase in many Army Navy surplus stores. (See also BONDAGE/ROPE)

HOODS Hoods are used to depersonalize a partner. This anonymity gives the top more power, both parties fewer inhibitions, and focuses the bottom's sensations entirely on their body.

Hoods are made of soft or hard leather, latex, silk scarves, or wooden boxes. The sensations, smell, and sound effects obviously differ. Some opt for pin holes that allow restricted vision. Others are specifically designed for oral sex and the only opening is over the nose and mouth.

The wearing of hoods is not limited to use by bottoms. Frightening effects are also created by only the top wearing a hood or mask. These have eye and mouth openings. CAUTION: Latex hoods having only a few holes under the nostrils have been known to accidentally slide around and cut off the person's oxygen supply.

IMPALING Criminals were often executed by being sat on the sharp point of a stake. Their weight drove the stake up into their torso, causing a slow death. Ancient Assyrians developed this into a form of torture where the victim could live a day or more before expir-ing. Impalement has since evolved to include any penetration of the body that restricts a person's ability to move.

Impalement for sex play purposes is accomplished by any of several methods. It may be done by hammering a stainless steel needle through the webbing between the fingers in a crucifixion, a nail through the soft area of the glans penis and into a piece of wood, or  through a woman's breast into a wooden chair back. Impaling is done more for psychological effects rather than pain. A person bound in this manner does not pull against the restraints as they would with other devices; submission is immediate and complete.

The other type of impalement used to immobilize people is to nail a dildo to the floor or other object and bind the victim so that the dildo penetrates the vagina or anus. CAUTION: People follow the same sterilization techniques as for any type of piercing. In addition, the tip of the nail or needle going through the wood is cleaned with alcohol before pulling it back through the skin. This is a blood sport and therefore considered an unsafe sex practice.

LACING   Lacing, when used in bondage, is similar to impalement. It involves piercing the skin with a needle, tying a string around 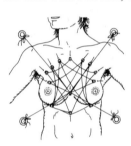 the needle, and then attaching it to an immobile object. Macrame designs are sometimes woven between needles. It is less dramatic than using a hammer to pierce the skin, but safer and more versatile. CAUTION: Lacing is a blood sport and is considered unsafe sex by those who practice it. Sterilization techniques are followed. (Refer also to SUTURING)

MITTENS   Mittens are put on a bottom to prevent them from using their fingers to untie rope, loosen buckles and so forth. Mittens also provide skin protection from metal, rope, or unlined leather restraints. They are available in lengths extending to the shoulder with zippers to facilitate easy removal. Others are masonite cardboard or made of leather and shaped like ping pong paddles to prevent the grasping or curling of fingers. Bottoms lose a lot of their perceived power when they are unable to use fingers and hands for fighting or protection. Mittens are also being used more by Nursing Homes in the United States in place of the more restrictive forms of bondage to keep patients from pulling out IVs.

PADLOCKS   Padlocks are used on chains, metal extensions, and the O-rings on leather restraints. Some have been used around the top of the scrotum, and small decorative ones are sometimes used through permanent piercings in place of jewelry. People who use more than one padlock usually have the locks all keyed the same. This is not only for convenience but an important safety feature. Searching for a key when a partner wants to be released is awkward and potentially dangerous. There is also the hazard of mistaking the wrong key for the padlock and not being able to find the correct one. Because of this a man in Texas had to drive a long distance to a hospital emergency room to have a padlock around his genitals removed with a hacksaw. (Personal communication.)

RAPE RACKS   (Romantic chairs—special Chinese rape chair) A Rape Rack is designed to position and immobilize a person so that their genitals are accessible. These are often used by scientists to aid male animals in breeding with noncooperative females.

The 18th and 19th century Chinese had 'romantic chairs' that were used by outlaws and certain landlords. The chair was designed with clasps that would automatically snap in place around an unsuspecting woman. The chair then unfolded into a bed.

Today a bed, table, or saw horse is used for this purpose, the most popular rape rack being the saw horse. It is modified by padding the top for comfort and mounting eye screw bolts that act to anchor the wrists and ankles to the bottom of the legs. This position can be humiliating to the bottom as well as making them very vulnerable. CAUTION: There is a danger of the partner being injured by loose splinters.

ROPES   Ropes are often used for bondage. They offer a technical challenge to the top and are versatile in their application and effect. Rope is inexpensive and can be purchased in hardware stores. People often use silk curtain sashes, soft nylon rope, or the magician's rope found in magic shops. Rough ropes are used for those into punishment or cowboy scenes.

Erotic rope play is done by pulling a long rope very slowly across the genitals and breasts, or wrapping it between the fingers and toes. The rope essentially takes the place of caressing hands. Once the person has used all the rope, the bottom is then slowly released in the same manner. The whole process may take an hour or longer.

Thorough planning of a scene is done ahead of time. If the bottom wants to be spanked or have their partner play with their genitals they make sure that hands and rope don't obstruct the area. Arms are bound separate from the body to facilitate occasional movement or relocation which prevents much discomfort as time passes.

Rope is washed after use if a person has more than one partner. It is usually put in a pillow case or laundry sack to prevent tangling and dried at the highest temperature to kill bacteria. CAUTION: Knots are not placed on areas where veins or arteries come close to the surface: near the joints, the inside wrists, upper arms, elbows, upper thighs (femoral artery), behind the knees, above the ankles, and the front sides of the neck. Pressure on the lower rib cage is also dangerous. The ankles and knees may need additional padding and are not bound together unless the person is lying down, sitting, or supported by a harness while standing.

There are many other safety precautions used with rope. The bottom is placed in a comfortable position, unless the game dictates otherwise. The diameter of rope is usually 1/4-1/2". It is always applied doubled or in twos, which decreases the risk of cutting off circulation because it broadens the area of pressure. The correct pressure for rope is discernable by a slight indentation in the skin. A person's body swells during the application of rope and takes about five minutes to return to normal. The rope can slip out of position after this time and can be dangerous if it ends up around a partner's neck or another area that could cut off circulation. The top constantly monitors the rope for tautness and their partner's extremities for circulation (warmth) comparing the color of the fingers with what they looked like before the bondage scene began. The top also requests that the partner move their hands and toes to check for numbness because many people don't notice it until they move. A pair of bandage scissors is always kept near to cut a person loose if their circulation is cut off or if they use the safeword. The partner does not leave the room while the bottom is in bondage.

("Bondage with Ropes," Society of Janus lecture, October 12, 1989, and "Rope Harness and Other Simple Bondage Techniques," QSM lecture by Hal, October 13, 1990)

SHACKLES   Shackles are restraints made of metal strips that cuff the ankles, neck, or wrists. They have a loop that allows the attachment of chain or a locking mechanism. Shackles are popular in authentic medieval dungeon scenes but are uncomfortable and can cause injury if not padded for a fantasy scene. The strong psychological impact of shackles overrides the concern for comfort for many who use them.

SPECULUM   The speculum, otherwise fondly referred to as the "cold spoon," is the dilating device commonly used by physicians when doing pelvic exams. These are also used for med-  ical bondage play where the partner does such things as look at the cervix, insert fingers, food, or urinate into the vagina. Couples who are concerned about STDs are able to examine the female for genital warts with this device. This is done by bathing the vagina in diluted white vinegar and then conducting a thorough exam of the accordion-like skin. The vinegar turns the tiny grass-shaped warts white in color, making them easier to detect. Physicians do not always have the time required for this tedious task, but once a person is diagnosed with genital warts the physician can find and alleviate them.

Physicians sometimes use disposable speculums and will often let the patient keep one if asked. CAUTION: Mucous tissue is sensitive and it may cause yeast infections if these items burn or contain sugars or oils.

 **STOCKS** Stocks were often used in colonial America and Europe to restrain people as part of public humiliation, discipline, flagellation, and confinement.

Stocks or similar apparatus were also used by the Spanish conquistadors in South America to punish slaves. The victim was put in stocks for several days, being vulnerable in many instances to rape during the night. European townspeople often tortured the female victims of stocks to death by beatings, mutilations, burnings, and forcing feces into their mouths and wounds.

There were several types of stocks, including those in which the person stood while their head and hands were bound, and those where the person sat with their legs bound. Others were disk shaped, binding the person's head and wrists in the center, but allowing them to walk. There are modified vise-like stocks that restrain the male genitals and there are those placed across the chest to pinch the breasts together.

STRAIGHTJACKETS Straightjackets are used in bondage play and have been patterned after those used in prisons and mental hospitals. They are constructed of sail-cloth or coarse fabric and have strips of leather or metal. This allows a patient or prisoner to fight and work off energy without harming anyone else. At the same time it makes them aware of the futility in resisting authority.

Houdini thrilled crowds with his ability to escape from this symbol of power. Many suits designed for S/M have modifications that make escape even less likely. They are available in all leather but for some this can become uncomfortable due to the additional weight and body heat. The chance of having a partner escape from one of these is lessened by adding straps. One also secures the bottom of the jacket by passing the strap under the crotch area. A strap is placed on each wrist over the jacket sleeves and one is used to cinch the elbows and lower arm to

the body to prevent forward or side movement. ("Bondage Equipment—Non Rope," by Mark, Society of Janus lecture, November 9, 1989)

SYMBOLIC BONDAGE It is easier to play bondage and discipline games with a visible symbol of restraint. Symbolic bondage can be achieved by either loose-fitting restraints or restraints that fit on wrists and ankles but which are not anchored. An example would be silk scarves, ties, and hosiery. These are not used in serious bondage scenes because the knots tend to tighten and may cut off circulation. This often requires having to cut an expensive silk scarf. The Flash knot is the only one recommended for fabric of any sort. This begins as a cow's head knot; the rope is folded, the two sides held together six inches below the fold, the top loop dropped down, and the two rope lengths pulled through to form a noose. One of the sides of the noose is then given an extra twist. A hand or foot is then put through both loops and the two ends are pulled taut. The advantage is that the knot will rarely slip tight enough to cut off a person's circulation.

A dog collar and leash is used to symbolize bondage and submission. Another method includes having the bottom sit without moving or having the bottom hold his or her hands together above their head with a coin between their fingers. They are then told that the game is over if they drop any of the coins.

THREE LEGGED BLOOMERS These are found in Europe and are used to restrict or focus a person's attention on their partner's genitals. They may be permitted to perform oral sex and will probably at least  have their hands placed in restraints. The fabric is either made of thin material or latex with holes punched on the sides to make it safe for breathing. These garments resemble regular pants or panties which have been modified by a slit in the crotch. Around this slit a hood is attached with a corresponding opening over the face. The opening is placed slightly forward in the male's crotchless latex pants.

(See also BINDING, GROPING APPARATUS, KNIVES, SAFE SEX, STAPLING, SUTURING, TAPHEPHILIA and TOURNIQUETS)

BORDELLO (Brothel, Ficaro, House of Prostitution, Red light district, Whorehouse; Floating hog ranches and Flower boats—bordellos operated from boats, Green bower—establishment used for sex but which does not supply partners) A bordello is a structure where prostitutes conduct their business. Bordellos have been sponsored and managed by religions, government, business investors, and by prostitutes themselves.

Bordellos gained popularity once temple priestesses were no longer available and when polygamous societies permitted wealthy men to have private harems. Poor men had a similar although temporary arrangement at the bordellos. The cost per visit was very reasonable in comparison to the overhead of a private harem.

The Greeks and Romans had many bordellos. They viewed them as necessary to keep men who were not sexually satisfied in their marriages from breaking up those of others. Roman bordellos provided entertainment for clients as well as a wide variety of sexual pleasures such as geese for avisodomy, glass floors for coprophilia, males for homosexual acts, virgins, and infants for fellatio and coitus interfermoris.

The Chinese were infamous for their Hoa-Things, or flower boats. These varied in size, with the largest being up to eighty feet long and fifteen feet wide. The large boats were often lavishly decorated with expensive carpets and crystal which hung from the ceiling. One could listen to professional musicians or indulge in drugs, drink, delectable meals, and beautiful young girls. The females were purchased from parents or a merchant while the young were trained in much the same way as the Japanese geisha or Yoshiwara. These girls were dressed in expensive silks and trained to enhance their appearance with cosmetics. Like the geisha, they entertained their guests with socially polite conversation before retiring to one of the small boats anchored to the main flower boat.

The American West had a less illustrious version of the flower boats. These were called Floating Hog Ranches. Madams, as they travelled west with their entourage, would purchase boats and conduct business from the river while enroute.

At one time assignation houses were used by lovers for clandestine meetings. They differed from bordellos in that women were not on staff. Men brought lovers with them. The decor and exterior were plain so as to avoid suspicion.

Bordellos became popular in the 19th century United States, both in the West where the male to female ratio was high and in the South among slave brokers who provided out call or sleeping companion services.

The red lights used to symbolize houses of prostitution appear to have originated with the Chinese who used red silk bamboo lamps outside their "wine houses" (bars where illegal prostitution often occurred). Chinese emigres appear to have brought the tradition of red lights with them to California (*Sex in History*, by Reay Tannahill, p. 191).

Bordellos today are usually managed and owned by a madam. Often she is an experienced prostitute who brings her own clients with her, although a list of clients may be purchased from other prostitutes or madams. A retiring California madam in 1980 sold her list, which included a personal introduction to the buyer, for $50,000.

A madam recruits her working prostitutes from former girlfriends, street prostitutes, bored housewives, bars, and group sex parties. Lesbians are said to do well financially because of their lack of romantic involvement with male customers. The madam instructs her new employees in the type of sex she plans to offer her clients and in the standard of conduct and hygiene she expects from them.

The basic protocol followed in a bordello begins with the customer selecting a partner, sometimes after a conversation with several prostitutes. The couple then adjourns to a private room. The client may be asked if he is a police officer, although in California entrapment is now legal and an officer may respond with a 'no' and arrest a woman who he propositions; a simple smile can be construed as an affirmation on her part. (In some cases, an officer has gone to group sex houses and engaged in sex with a woman on several occasions. Then one night he offers her money and arrests her if she accepts or is not explicit with her refusal.) Bordello clients negotiate to determine which fantasy the prostitute is willing to perform and for what price. Next the money is exchanged and a visual inspection of the male genitals is conducted. If a yellow discharge, herpes, venereal warts, syphilitic lesions, scabies, or crabs are discovered the customer will be asked to return after he is cured. (Sex workers themselves are often required to be inspected weekly by physicians.) The customers who pass inspection either shower or are washed by the prostitute before getting onto her bed. Kissing is not usually engaged in by prostitutes due to the feeling of intimacy it elicits, and because it spreads diseases that can decrease the number of hours she earns money. Once the sex act is over it is possible to either negotiate for more time, leave, or take a break and choose another partner later. Respect must be mutual. If the client is courteous the workers are much more likely to reciprocate.

Bordellos sometimes have a menu from which a client can select. A sample menu from the Salt Wells Villa Ranch in Fallon, Nevada offers the following:

1. Binaca blast
2. Peppermint French
3. Emotion lotion
4. Alka-seltzer
5. Movie & party
7. Doubles
8. Trip

9. Around the world
10. Bubble bath
11. Champagne party
12. Salt & pepper
13. Having fun now
14. Frenzy explorations
15. Sweet preserves
16. French sensations
17. Socrates pleasures
18. The apparatus drive
19. S&M (B&D)
20. Uninhibited free for all
21. The wind the rain the lava
(*The Official Guide to the Best Cat Houses in Nevada*, by J.R. Schwartz, p. 46)

The selection of bordellos is limited in comparison to what could be found in the past or in other countries. Some do specialize in things such as offering gay males, minors (illegal), the obese, podophilia, S/M, infantilism, coprophilia, and urophilia. One bordello was recently publicized because they had their workers dressed to impersonate famous movie stars. A bordello that cannot fill a client's request is usually able to refer them to one that does.

(See also AUCTIONS, DUNGEONS, ESSAY-EURS, GEISHAS, GROUP SEX, HAREMS, HETAERAE, ILLEGAL SEX, PIMPS, PROFESSIONAL DOMINATRIXES, PROSTITUTES and SLAVES)

BOTTOMS (Masochist, Sex servant, Sex slave, Submissive) People who play the passive role in sex play are referred to as bottoms. Those who orchestrate the sex games are referred to as tops. Bottoms are not always masochists because many sex games do not involve pain or degradation. The S/M community prefers the term bottoms because it is indicative of the broader and more diverse roles that are used for sexual pleasure.

(See also SWITCHES and TOPS)

BRADYCUBIA Bradycubia (bradyr: slow; cubare: to lie down) refers to a sex technique where the male slowly thrusts in and out of his partner's vagina or anus. This is usually done at the beginning of the sexual encounter.

(See also KABAZZA, SEX POSITIONS and TANTRA)

BRANDING Branding is done by burning a symbol onto a person's skin and was used by governments, religions, and among various tribes. The Egyptians, Greeks, Romans, French, English, and Americans used it to mark their slaves. Government penal systems also used branding as a judicially prescribed way of identifying which crimes were committed by an individual, thus marking him for life.

Others brand themselves for social or religious reasons. A Christian sect in Russia called the "White Doves" used a branding iron to mutilate their genitals as a ritual in a convert's baptism by fire. Political branding is now illegal in most areas, but is still practiced on prisoners in some countries. One African tribe brands themselves by taking a small section of dried plant, tying it against their skin, lighting it, and letting it burn out. This leaves a design in the desired location.

People who use consensual branding today are either involved in "modern primitive" movements or S/M. Branding is permanent and one chooses this for similar reasons as others choose to be tattooed. People with dark skin have traditionally used scarification and branding for marking or decorative purposes because tattooing does not provide the needed color contrast.

The design of the brand is made of simple lines or curves. The brand can not  have closed circles, triangles or squares because this will cause the skin in the middle to react and perhaps fall off. The width of the brand lines expand to four times that of the original burn, therefore, thin lines are always used. A pattern of small brands are often repeated for any desired distance. A popular brand is that of arrow heads: <<<>>>.

People select flat locations such as the chest, back, thighs, calves, stomach, buttocks, or shoulders.

Chosen designs often have life-long meaning to the person. People who have been branded with their partner's initials and later split up found that the brand was at the very least an embarrassment. The brand is more prone to resentment by a new partner than a tattoo because the brand is often done by the former lover and can symbolize ownership.

The burn takes 2-6 weeks to heal, depending on the size, depth, and natural ability of the person's body to heal. The skin may also shrink as it heals and this is allowed for in the design and placement of the brand. If a person's scars normally tend to darken, they wear a sun block on the area for six months.

There is one professional piercing studio in San Francisco which recently began offering branding to its clientele. CAUTION: This activity causes unnecessary scarring and possible infection if the correct procedures are not followed. ("Branding and Burning", QSM lecture by Fakir Musafar, November 18, 1989)

(See also BODY PAINTING, CICATRIZATION, FAKIR MUSAFAR, PENIS MODIFICATION, PYROPHILIA, RINGING, SAFE SEX, SLAVES and TATTOOING)

BREAST SHAPING Women have sought to alter the shape of their breasts for several thousand years. The women of Africa's Nandi tribe wore two wire plate-shaped disks around their neck, hanging just low enough to press against the top of their breasts. Over time these would flatten their breasts so that they hung like pancakes against their body. Flat breasts were symbols of motherhood and were much more respected among the tribe than full round breasts. Most other cultures preferred augmentation.

AUGMENTATION Breast augmentation, artificially enlarging the size of breasts, has been done throughout history. The priestesses of Aphrodite wore breast shields made of wood and inlaid with jewels to enhance their form. Women continued utilizing different types of padded bras until recently when surgeons have made it possible to increase the size and improve the shape of their breasts with silicone implants. Implants are only recommended for women who need breast reconstruction after a mastectomy.

One study has emphasized the importance of immediate reconstructive breast surgery in these cases. "Patients who had reconstructive breast surgery at the time of mastectomy (immediate) or within 1 year (early) had significantly less recalled distress about their mastectomy than those who had it more than 1 year later (delayed)...The wish to wear a wider range of clothes and the wish to be rid of the external prosthesis were common motivations for reconstructive surgery. The desire to improve sexual relations or one's marital state was less common and should be viewed with caution when presented as the primary motivation for this procedure" ("The Sooner the Better: A Study of Psychological Factors in Women Undergoing Immediate Versus Delayed Breast Reconstruction," Wendy S. Schain, Ed.D., David K. Wellisch, Ph.D., Robert O. Pasnau, M.D., and John Landsverk, Ph.D., *American Journal of Psychiatry* 142:1, January 1985, pp. 40-46).

Those whose self esteem has seriously been impaired by having small breasts and topless dancers who use augmentation for professional reasons risked accidental severing of nerve endings during surgery. These nerves make it possible to detect light pressure, deep pressure, pain, cold, and heat and a person can lose any or all of these sensations with nerve damage. Partners of women with augmentations should be aware that she may only be able to feel one or two of the normal sensations and may want to adjust their tactile stimulation accordingly.

Silicone implants are a recent medical development and there remains concern as to whether possible leakage from the silicone bag could damage healthy tissue. Many women have needed secondary surgery due to a build up of scar tissue or silicone leakage years later. More important, there is also concern that one type of implant may increase the risk of cancer.

A woman having augmentation surgery has it performed under a local or general anesthesia by a plastic surgeon. The woman is allowed to select the size of the silicone implants she desires within the constraints determined by the current size and elasticity of her breasts. A woman who begins with a natural bust size of 32A cannot become a 40D. Rather she will end up with about a 32B or 32C bust.

The normal surgical procedure is done by cutting a two to three inch incision underneath the bottom outside edge of each breast or under each armpit (some will cut around the areola). The surgeon then separates the frontal breast tissue from the ribs and pushes the silicone sack inside and then stitches closed the incision.

There is a period after surgery when the woman will not be permitted to raise her arms or lift any heavy objects. This is followed by a period of time where the breasts have to be massaged to prevent scar tissue from forming and distorting the natural shape of the breasts.

Silicone implants are used by some transsexuals who are not happy with the size of their breasts after hormone therapy and some transvestites elect to only have the breast augmentation performed without taking hormone therapy. CAUTION: The United States FDA, concerned with possible carcinogenic effects, have recently restricted breast implants to only those females in need of reconstructive surgery following a mastectomy.

REDUCTION Woman of all ages have breast reduction surgery. Large breasts create aesthetic problems, tissue damage where the bra straps rub, back pain, bad posture, and inability to participate in many sports. Reduction can also be used to correct natural sagging as the woman grows older.

Breast reduction is more complicated than augmentation and always requires general anesthesia and a short hospital stay. In 1989 the cost ranged from $10,000 to $15,000. The surgeon reshapes the entire breast by making several incisions, usually six for each breast, and enough tissue is removed to reduce the size of the breast. Many woman need to have the areola relocated and made smaller so that it remains in proportion to the rest of the breast. To accomplish this some surgeons use a device resembling a cookie cutter on the areola.

This ensures correct roundness. So far no woman is known to have requested any alternative shape for the areola.

(See also PENIS MODIFICATION)

BREASTS See BINDING, BREAST SHAPING, COITUS A MAMMILLA and LACTIPHILIA

BULL FIGHTING The bull fight is a surviving remnant of ancient fertility rituals and of Roman games.

The conquest and slaughter of a wild beast by a human is prehistoric and documented by early cave drawings. Religions celebrated the mating of animals, germination of crops, slaughter of an animal, and anything else that meant production of food; thereby ensuring the survival of their tribe. Many tribal rituals have required that a boy kill an animal as part of entry into manhood. The American Indians had to kill a buffalo, bear, or other feared animal. The Roman and Cretan fertility rituals or orgies of Dionysus may have had similar roots. People also practiced phallomancy, fortune telling by reading a bull's penis.

The Moors brought bull fighting to Spain during the 8th century. The muleta (red cloth supported by a stick) was not introduced until the 17th century; before that men used an animal skin on their backs as camouflage and protection. As time progressed the bull was killed by a nobleman on horseback. The bull was often baited by dogs, pikes, knives, and the cape.

The people of Rome used the fights and death of animal or man as an emotional stimulus. For many, this meant sexual arousal and orgasm in the stadium during the performance. Today bull fights offer the only legal arena in which to watch the violent death and mutilation of man, bull, and horse. (*Death in the Afternoon* by Ernest Hemingway)

(Refer also to EXECUTIONS, PHOBOPHILIA, and VICARIOUS AROUSAL)

BUNDLING (Shunammitism, Lectamia —caressing in bed without coitus) Bundling refers to the practice of a dating couple sleeping together fully clothed, sometimes separated by a board. This was an ancient Nordic practice that competed with the Christian tradition of bridal virginity. It provided for the need teenagers had to experience recreational sex before they committed to establishing a family. The general custom was for the couple not to become married until the woman became pregnant. This custom stems from farming and fishing cultures that were more egalitarian. Women were viewed as important to the survival of the social system and family unit just as were the men. Both were expected to enjoy sexual freedom before marriage. The male ownership philosophy did not exist, therefore no judgments were made of women who chose their own sex partners. A Christian compromise of this original tradition was the practice whereby two or more people slept together, nude or clothed, for the purpose of exchanging sexual energy. As a general rule it did not include penetration of any sort and, to ensure this, some mothers tied their daughter's legs together. Certain cultures were allowed to engage in penetration if orgasm did not occur.

Bundling was also used by some for health purposes. This is the reason King David and other older men hired virgins to sleep beside them when they were tired or ill. Catholic monks engaged in this practice from about 400 to 1500 C.E.

Ramsdale and Dorman, in *Sexual Energy Ecstasy*, describe bundling during the 18th century:

Young knights offered "courtly love" to women who were not only married but wedded to a nobleman or other male power figure. This was known as a donnoi relationship. Again history is vague as to the details, but in addition to sleeping together in the nude, nude caresses, nude embraces and ravishing the naked noblewoman's body for hours with eyes, the young knights may have also practiced coitus reservatus on occasion or even frequently... According to their own reports, these relationships fired their imaginations and lifted their psyches to planes of feeling much higher than ordinary sexual relations usually did. In fact, the knight's "courtly love" relationship is probably the predecessor of our contemporary romantic love ideal.

This romance also seems to be reached in affairs when the two parties refrain from consummating the union.

Bundling fills a basic physical and psychological need to be held or touched. Studies have shown that orphaned infants who were held did much better than those left alone in nurseries, the latter suffering from autism and in some cases death. All humans function better with a proper amount of intimacy, nurturing, and touch from others. Even a sincere smile or acknowledgement from another person can make people feel better.

(See also MARRIAGE, TOUCH and TROUBADOURS)

BURNING　See BRANDING and PYROPHILIA

BUTT PLUGS　See GENITAL/ANAL INSERTS

C

CANDAULISM　Candaulism refers to a group of three people where only two of them engage in sex and the other watches, sometimes from a closet. In early 20th century France, men would take their wives to brothels to watch special stage shows where a cast of prostitutes acted out a performance. Females playing the roles of men wore "artificial phalli." Afterward men would persuade their wives to have sex with another male customer while they watched. Those who didn't have obliging mates would often resort to befriending a gentleman and offering to pay for a prostitute of his choosing, in exchange for being permitted to watch.

At the beginning of the century people considered the viewing of explicit films to be similar to that of engaging in orgies. Men who watched films of couples engaging in sex were dubbed perverts; while curiously the young women who ventured into these theaters were merely said to have been out for a 'thrill.'

Swing clubs often have several men who enjoy watching their wives with other men. One man was extreme in that he was actually incapable of having sex with any woman unless he had first seen her be penetrated. A swing house in southern California once had benches around the group room until some of the women complained to the owner that they didn't like the men watching them perform. The owner kindly removed the benches and soon found that he lost most of his guests. It seems that many of the men were only interested in coming to a group sex house if they could watch their wives. The benches were reinstalled. These same men were said to get extremely excited if they saw their wife being propositioned by a regular guest, who happened to be black and very well endowed; this seemed to be the ultimate experience for the husbands. (Personal communication, 1990.)

(See also GANG BANGS, GROUP SEX, MENAGE À TROIS, ORGIES and TROILISM)

CANNIBALISM　See ANTHROPOPHAGY

CASTRATION　(Ablation, Emasculate, Evirate, Geld; Atestus—testes, Ederacinism—tear out sex organs by the roots, Penectomy—penis only, Shave—penis and testicles)

Castration is defined as the removal of the testicles, scrotum, penis, clitoris, or ovaries. Castration, both consensual and nonconsensual, has been used throughout history for political, religious, economic, medical, and sexual reasons.

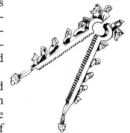

The most feared form of castration among men is the complete removal of both the penis and testicles. Charles Panati, in his book *Panati's Extra-ordinary Endings of Practically Everything and Everybody*, describes the ancient surgical procedure for this type of castration. It began by placing the victim on a table, immobilizing him, tying a cord around his penis and scrotum that cut off the circulation, slicing the genitals off with a razor, and cauterizing the open wound with a hot poker. The victim was not allowed to eat or drink for several days and then was given water so that the urine flow would open the urethral passage. Only about 20% survived this surgery. Other methods were similar, except the slave was given alcohol and a hot bath to decrease the pain. After the penis and testicles were tied off and severed, alum and antiseptics were applied. A feather quill was then inserted into the urethra to prevent its healing shut. Those undergoing this procedure had a 40% survival rate. Castration may also be a tragic result of battle. The Romans in about the third century used a bronze castration clamp. "The penis was drawn through the oval ring to keep it out of harm's way, while the scrotum and testes were pulled through between the arms of the clamp, so that when everything was locked in position the serrated edges gripped the folds of the skin joining the scrotum to the body. It took only a single stroke of the knife to cut away scrotum and testes, and the cut edges were then either sewn up or cauterized" (*Sex in History* by Reay Tannahill, p. 251—cited from *Transactions of the Royal Society of Medicine* (January 1926) by Alfred G. Francis).

Soldiers in World War I sometimes suffered gun shot wounds in the genital region. The slang term for this injury was D.S.O. (dick shot off). One California policeman discovered during riots that militant men dropped their weapons much faster if he pointed his gun at their genitals rather than their head. (Personal communication, 1985.)

The effect of testicle castration on a prepubescent male is weight gain, increase in height and length of limbs, reduction of body hair, and retention of prepubescent voice and demeanor. The testicles produce the largest amount of testosterone, the male hormone, with the adrenal gland producing the second highest level. Historically short men were assumed to have increased sex drives because additional height was associated with the castrated eunuchs.

Castration due to disease or trauma to the testicles after pubescence may produce a decrease in mental acuity, physical vitality, aggressiveness, desire for social interaction, appetite, and sex drive. The effects can take several years to develop or may not at all if the adrenal gland functions properly. If side effects do occur a hormone replacement therapy is required to keep the prostate gland functioning. Many men who have only had their testicles removed lead an active sex life. The orgasms may feel different and be more difficult to achieve, but they are not impossible. This applies to men who have undergone penectomies as well. As long as the prostrate remains intact for tactile stimulation an orgasm is theoretically possible.

PROFESSIONAL EUNUCHS Castrati were popular in the 18th century. They were used in choirs for the church and as actors in plays that didn't yet permit females. Their voices remained prepubescent but grew in strength, creating unique and highly prized sopranos.

The eunuch castrated before puberty was preferred by some men for use as guards due to their additional height, low sex drive, and submissive behavior.

Eunuchs, castrated after pubescence, were occasionally used to sexually satisfy their shiek's wives due to their inability to father children. These men needed prolonged stimulation before they could orgasm, therefore they were able to satisfy many women. Intruders who sneaked into harems were at great personal risk. While sex with a eunuch chosen by the master was permissible, a stranger was not tolerated. Many of these uninvited guests soon found that wives and concubines would sadistically attempt to tear off their testicles during sex.

MEDICAL Romans and Greeks as early as the 5th century B.C.E. performed castration on young boys (probably those with partially descending testicles) to prevent the occurrence of hernias later in life. The French used castration to cure rheumatism, leprosy, and gout. Earlier this century castration was routinely done in the United States on the insane and epileptics. In discussing the value of this procedure one physician in Havelock Ellis' book, *Studies in the Psychology of Sex*, states:

It is often forgotten that the physical and psychic qualities associated with and largely dependent on the ability to experience the impulse of detumescence, while essential to the perfect man, involve many egoistic, aggressive and acquisitive characteristics which are of little intellectual value, and at the same time inimical to many moral virtues (Vol. II, I, p. 184, 1936).

In other words, the mental or physically handicapped should not be permitted the same pleasure the 'perfect' man derives from erection and masturbation because it embarrassed, threatened, and offended their prudish caretakers. Castration also slows the patient's mental, sexual, and physical capacities; making control easier for their wards. Other physicians recommended castration for homosexuals, alcoholics, Jews, and others, considering them to be social misfits. Castration is done today for health reasons due to disease, such as cancer of the prostate, unrepairable traumatic injury to the genitals, and as part of the surgical procedure for either hermaphrodite or transsexual conciliation.

Human and ram testicle implants were used for experimentations at San Quentin prison beginning in 1918 by Leo L. Stanley, M.D. and his associates. They performed over 600 implants and injections of testicle tissue, uncovering much of what we know today about the effects of testosterone. The prison was an excellent field for research. The doctors were in a position to use the testicles of executed and unclaimed prisoners (about 3 a year) and to procure willing volunteers from the prison inmates. This research ended when the government restricted the use of humans for unsafe medical experiments.

POLITICAL A few states in the 18th century permitted castration of black slaves for raping white women. However, most suspected of this crime were hung.

Use of castration was again advocated by some physicians in the early 20th century for rape, sodomy, zoophilia, pederasty, and even habitual masturbation. Castration was used for a short time as a punishment for sex offenders but it was soon discovered that when done nonconsensually it caused an already emotionally unbalanced person to develop even more anti-social and criminal activities (*Studies in the Psychology of Sex*, Vol. II, III, pp. 612-4).

PSEUDOCASTRATION Pseudo or mock castration is often used in S/M play due to its being one of the greatest of men's fears. Pseudocastration is done with verbal threats or different types of modified and consensual genital torture. It is used in fantasy play to reinforce cross-gender play, male rape, or humiliation scenes. It may also be done symbolically with instruments, piercing, stretching, restraints, a modified chain saw, biting, or sucking. Some men consider anal penetration to be demasculinizing and therefore a form of castration. Prior consent is obtained before attempting any type of anal penetration. Men react in various ways when faced with anal sex; they can feel indifferent, lose an erection, become emotionally traumatized, feel liberated, assume their partner is immoral, or become extremely aroused. If this is his first experience he may not know how he will react himself until it's too late.

PSYCHOLOGICAL Psychological castration occurs when one becomes convinced that they lack sexual desirability or the social criteria that determines one's feminine or masculine identity. This is often imposed on someone else, as the term "castrating bitch" implies.

RELIGIOUS Castration was at one time believed to have been performed as a religious ceremony on young boys. The extracted genitals were then sacrificed on an altar to the gods. Sacrifice may have had the added benefit of supplying the upper classes with docile non-militant servants. Religious castration among Christians is usually symbolic and is accomplished through a vow of chastity. However, an early monk named Origen had himself castrated to prove his commitment to celibacy and to provide an example of pure chastity for others.

SEXUAL AROUSAL Some women seemed to enjoy watching the castration of men as a means of sexual arousal. Emperor Justinian's wife, Theodora, was reported to enjoy masturbation while watching men being castrated. A prostitute from Kabul, Afghanistan had her lovers seized and castrated after coitus.

The Roman emperor, Nero, had a lover castrated so he could pass as a female. The two had an elaborate wedding ceremony and Nero presented Sporus, his new bride, with a dowry and a wardrobe of feminine apparel.

Castration is common during anthropophagy and mutilation murders. The genitals of the victim are eroticized in different ways. One person may want to consume genitals they consider sexually stimulating, while others only want to remove or discard the part of the anatomy they consider evil, immoral, and responsible for either their own unrighteous lust or that of the victims, particularly in the case of prostitutes. Insects also engage in castration of lovers. Hy Freedman in his book Sex Link tells of the following two examples of castration during the mating processes of insects. A new queen bee leaving the hive to start one of her own will be followed by 200 males. While in flight one will mount her, copulate, fall to the ground, and bleed to death. His severed penis now acts as a plug to hold in the sperm which will fertilize 2 million eggs over the next 5 years. The rest of the male bees return to their hive where, no longer serving any purpose, they soon starve to death. In a different type of ritual, the female bristle worm, after watching a courtship dance, will bite off her partner's genitals, and swallow the enclosed sperm. This fertilizes her eggs as the sperm passes through her digestive tract.

(See CIRCUMCISION, CLITORIDECTOMY, EUNUCHS, PENIS MODIFICATION, STAPLING, SUTURING and TESTICLES)

CAT FIGHTING Cat Fighting is a fight between two women without rules. They scratch, bite, gouge, pull hair, and rip clothing. Cat fights appeal to men who hope to catch a glimpse of forbidden flesh as fighters tear clothing.  Fighting also provides vicarious thrills similar to when one watches professional male boxers and wrestlers. However, the difference between them is that men do not want to see serious injury or nose bleeds on the women. They want the abuse to be verbal, preferably squabbling over a man or undergarments and the physical violence restricted to ripping clothes or pulling hair. A description of a cat fight was given by a female participant in an adult newspaper, *Fetish Times* (No. 191):

Some people say I'm a bossy dom but the way I see it is I just don't like to be pushed around. When my roomie took my best black bra without asking for it I blew my stack. Ripping it off her tits I gave her a hard slap across the face. She grabbed my hair and yanked and the fight was on. Tripping her with my foot I dived on top of her and got her in a tight wrestling hold. Just as I thought she was beaten the little bitch slipped free and smacked my ass. Rolling over to protect myself I let myself open for a shiner. Seeing stars I grabbed out blindly and grabbed her by the pussy hairs. She screamed and I pulled. Then I caught ...

Cat fights between saloon girls and even the leading lady seemed to be more common in western movies before the 1980s. Today mail order video tapes are available of cat fights, female boxers, and males and females engaged in hand to hand combat. Live performances are also staged for gamblers in the United States. The women and their sponsors travel to different locations setting up events that are evidently similar to that of a cock fight (both being illegal). (Personal communication.) Mud wrestling is a similar sport that became popular in the 1970s.

(See also ABDUCTION, DEFILEMENT, INTERROGATION, PHOBOPHILIA, QUEENING and WRESTLING)

CATAMITES (Bardajes, Pathicus)
Catamites were boys that were used as personal lovers for older men. An example in mythology was that of Zeus taking Ganymede as his lover and appointing him water bearer in his court. The early Greeks followed Zeus' example and boys often left home with their parents' permission to be a companion for an older man. The man took great care in seeing that he received an education, relieving the parents of this financial obligation.

The Mayas had a custom where a young man's parents would provide him with a slave boy to be used for sex. He was forbidden to select his own or to have sex with women until he was married. This strategy was designed to protect other men's wives from overly anxious young males (Sex in History by Reay Tannahill, p. 290).

(See also GAYS, HETAERAE and PEDOPHILIA)

CATHETERS (Catheterophilia—arousal from catheters) Catheterization has been practiced for at least 4,000 years. Ivory and jade catheters have been found in ancient Chinese tombs and ritualistic catheterization scenes decorate Mayan pottery.

Today catheters are used in sex play as a symbol of total control over a partner. This type of sex play is similar to the catheterization found in health care facilities. The sterilized catheter is inserted up through the urethra and into the bladder which allows the flow of the urine to be controlled by the dominant partner. The stimulation seems to trigger the brain's pleasure center that ordinarily responds to urination or ejaculation.

Catheters are available in different styles. A Foley has a blow up bulb at one end which allows it to stay inside the bladder without having to be held in place. The Robinson has a straight tip on both ends and has to be held in by hand or taped at the end to the submissive's genitals. The tip of the catheter is sometimes clamped to prevent urine from dripping out.

The instruments used for catheterization are also sterilized. If the catheter is used again by the same person it can be washed in soap and water and then boiled for 30 minutes. The partner is prepared by washing the genitals with soap and water and rubbing with Betadine. Sterile surgical latex gloves are used to insert or spread a water based lubricant, Surgilube, onto the catheter. Most people purchase small tubes or bottles of lubricant to prevent contamination. If the bottle has been used before they squeeze out and dispose of the first small portion, then they squeeze the amount needed onto a sterile surface and roll the catheter in it. Dipping fingers into the jar of lubricant contaminates the whole jar. The top next inserts the lubricated catheter into the partner's urethra. The partner feels like they want to urinate or orgasm as the catheter passes through the canal. If the catheter does not insert easily, it is not forced but is instead removed. If there are no obstructions the procedure is  continued until the tip reaches the sphincter of the bladder. The tip is never forced in, but rather held in position with slight pressure until the sphincter opens on its own. At this point urine will flow out the end of the tube. Those using the Foley will push the catheter an additional three inches and then inflate the tip by injecting about 5-10 ccs of sterile water or sterile saline solution. The amount of liquid injected is measured to guarantee release of that same amount before they withdraw the catheter. Some men are able to ejaculate while urine flows through the tube. Their semen passes between the catheter and the wall of the urethra. This practice is not considered safe because if there is not adequate space left in the urethra the violent force of the semen at ejaculation is thought to increase the risk of internal injury. The amount of urine drained from a bladder is also measured for safety. There is danger of potential complications if the bladder is forced to hold over

1,000 ccs or one quart. Likewise, a person who starts with a full bladder is not made to hold it for very long. Catheters, after deflation, are removed by simply letting them slide out. The urethra is often sore and burns for 1/2 an hour afterward. (Society of Janus lecture on "Water Sports," dated June 8, 1989 and "You are going to put a what up my what??" *Dungeon Master*, by La Farge, pp. 17-20)

There is a type of noninvasive catheter available that is called either a Texas catheter or an External Male Catheter. These resemble a thick condom with a large reservoir tip that has a nozzle to facilitate the attachment of a tube. People use these to control a partner's urine flow without having to go through the ordeal involved with sterilization procedures.

A national club exists for people who share an interest in catheterization. CAUTION: This type of play is potentially dangerous and is usually done by people who work in the medical profession. Even nurses have been known to accidently injure hospital patients. Not everyone can be catheterized, since some people have scar tissue or strictures on the sides of their urethra which can tear if a catheter is forced past them. Most people begin with the smallest sized catheter available. Symptoms of possible damage to the urethra are a change in frequency of urination, the color of urine (orange or brown), or the presence of pus. If strict sterile technique is not followed, there exists a significant chance of bladder infection, kidney infection, sepsis, kidney failure, or death.

(See also BONDAGE, COCKTAILS, GENITAL/ANAL INSERTS, KLISMAPHILIA, MEATOTOMY, PHALLOPHILIA, RINGING, SCROTAL INFUSION, SHOWERS and SOUNDING)

CELIBACY (Abstinence, Aphallatia, Chastity; Agenobiosis—couple who lives together without sex, Asceticism—religious self-denial, Lagnocolysis—inhibition of sex urge)

Celibacy refers to sexual abstinence or the state of not being married. Celibacy is encouraged by various institutions, governments, and religions for different reasons.

At one time celibacy was the only recourse for women who chose not to submit to a marriage that would place them in servitude to a man. Others, out of necessity, used celibacy to protect their reputations. Conversely, those in arranged marriages took advantage of the pious admonitions of the Church by using it as an excuse not to have sex with their spouse (agenobiosis). Many people chose to remain celibate during the absence of their lovers. Others chose it out of fear or hate from having been sexually or emotionally abused. And many were forced into celibacy due to a lack of available partners. This was true for early male Chinese immigrants in California.

Government has imposed celibacy on people throughout history as a method to control population, disease, and for economic reasons. The U.S. military in World War I, prodded by moral reformers and concerned over potential loss of manpower due to venereal disease, encouraged the celibacy of their troops by using propaganda which portrayed sexually responsive women as spies, prostitutes, and disease carriers. Military police were stationed in areas where local women and prostitutes frequented. Sexually active women came to be viewed as prostitutes with many being arrested en masse. Ironically, those who were less permissive were often viewed by the men as the spoils of war. None of these attitudes created respect for women and their sexuality in a soldier's mind.

Religious homosexuals who have wanted to remain in a favorable standing with their church have chosen celibacy.

Abstinence can be seen as character building. However, it can also be seen as sexual repression with definite negative consequences. The occupants of convents and monasteries were known for their sadistic propensity and, like the accusers during the European and Salem witch hunts, reveled in the sexual expose's of others' deviances. Religious celibacy also serves the purpose of focusing the follower's attention on a god, looking only to Him for love and approval. This may bond a person to the church but at the same time destroys any chance they have of learning to look to each other for nurturance, support, and unconditional acceptance. Not everyone accepted the Church's stance on celibacy. In 1061 a number of Lombard bishops and nobles organized a rebellion, marched on Rome, captured it, and appointed Cadalus, Bishop of Parma, as Antipope, naming him Honorius II. This revolt ended two years later due to internal politics.

Eighteenth century Shakers practiced celibacy in communal groups. This religion gained popularity during a time when there was no social welfare. Many followers joined for financial assistance, health care, or companionship needs. The Shakers imposed many social restrictions on themselves to avoid erotic stimulation. The members were not allowed to have pets because these might mate in front of them, nor were they allowed to touch, speak, or walk with someone of the opposite sex. Members were permitted only one covert sexual release, that of frantic ritual dancing which led some into an altered state orgasm.

There are many others who practiced celibacy in order to experience altered states. St. Augustine and St. Thomas Aquinas, early men who formed the doctrines of the Catholic church, were influenced by this method rather than by flagellation. St. Augustine was also a major instigator in transforming sex from something sacred to something sinful.

The Victorians and their views on sex were influenced, not by religion, but by the medical scare of the 18th and 19th centuries. The physicians of this time taught that the loss of semen caused a wasting away of all the vital energies to the point of insanity and death. Therefore, the only justifiable and necessary type of orgasm was that done to propagate the species. This meant that any type of sex other than penis/vagina was viewed as unhealthy. Claude-Francois Lallemand, in 1939, published a book that cited a report from the Massachusetts State Lunatic Hospital which showed that out of 407 patients 55 had become insane due to excessive masturbation. In the early 1900s certain writings of the medical profession claimed that fellatio and cunnilingus could

cause cancer and anal coitus would have a worse consequence. Masturbation was considered more dangerous than homosexual coitus because of the frequency in which a solitary person could indulge.

Two famous celibates and anti-orgasm advocates during this time were Sylvester Graham and John Kellogg. It was their belief that spicy foods could excite the sex centers and this led them to invent the then-tasteless crackers and cereal. Their successors later added sugar to increase sales.

Celibacy is no longer considered a medical prophylactic or cure-all. However, it is still sometimes recommended for psychological reasons. The 12-Step Program support group called Sex and Love Addicts Anonymous recommends it as a necessary process to recognize and control an 'addiction' to sex. Mystics use abstinence to reach altered states of consciousness and Witches, yoga masters, and religious leaders use celibacy to maintain a high level of concentration on a desired thought or activity.

There is no documentation on the long term physical effects of total abstinence but one might be concerned about atrophy of the pubococcygeus muscles, which serve to control the spasms during orgasm. There is some concern whether it is possible for a woman to orgasm after ten or twenty years of not using this muscle properly.

(See also CASTRATION, CHASTITY DEVICES, CHOREOPHILIA, EUNUCHS, INFIBULATION, ST. AUGUSTINE, SUPPORT GROUPS and VICTORIANISM)

CHAPERONS   Chaperons were popular in the 19th century. It was their responsibility to protect and supervise the behavior of young women, couples, or groups. Most often it was the young woman's mother, aunt, or a paid matron of respectability. In addition to guarding the maiden's virtue, the chaperon might also investigate young men as to their character, intentions, and wealth. Once satisfied with the findings she would arrange a formal introduction to the young lady. If either person found the other unsuitable during the evening it was socially acceptable to return to the chaperon and part company on friendly terms.

Most chaperons performed their duties admirably but there were those who couldn't hold their liquor at parties or who fell into lascivious conduct themselves.

The young wards soon learned evasive strategic maneuvers. Couples would go sailing hoping that the chaperon would spend more time hanging over the stern than watching them. They also rollerskated through park paths and walked briskly up hills trying to wind the older matron. Then came the invention that propelled ladies into lasting freedom; the bicycle. Corsets and petticoats which had created the frail feminine image soon became a burden and were discarded for all but formal wear.

Today we still see mothers chaperon their daughters in small towns in Central and South America. Town parks sometimes have benches around the edge facing outward toward the streets. Here the parents sit and talk as their teenagers socialize inside the park. In a small coastal town in the Mexican state of Sonora mothers take their daughters to what appears to be a modern disco. They then line up outside along a four foot high wall in the front that looks through a large window. Above this wall one can see the heads of a dozen five foot tall mothers who resemble solemn nuns in their black head scarves and dresses as they watch to make sure their daughters conduct themselves appropriately.

Women of all ages in Moslem countries are required to have chaperons. Many other European and Middle Eastern countries also expect a lady to be accompanied if she ventures out in the evening, the exception of course being for prostitutes. Female tourists can save themselves embarrassing moments by inquiring about local customs when traveling abroad.

(See also COURTSHIP)

CHARMS   (Good luck pieces, Talisman) Charms refer to chants, objects, or gestures that are believed to have magical powers. Belief in charms has been commonplace throughout man's history. The advent of science seems to have freed many people from their former reliance on superstitions, magic, and charms. Yet many people still consider certain items lucky.

Charms were used to increase fertility, improve virility, ensure the attraction or fidelity of a partner, determine the sex of a child, to ease childbirth, or to break spells. Female genitals were also believed to hold great powers. A woman could break evil spells or control weather by simply exposing them. It was at one time common for Roman women to wear amulets of genitals around their neck and for them to be found on the entrances of many temples. These later came to resemble a ring or open circle. The upside down horseshoe found above doors for good luck is a surviving remnant of this tradition. Some lesbians use this above their doors as a sign of their sexual preference.

Ancient Romans used amulets of penises or symbols of both sexes to ward off the evil eye. The current gesture of "giving someone the finger" is a remnant of that early custom. Many Roman homes had phallic replicas above their doors with an inscription underneath that read "Hic habitat felicitas—Happiness dwells here." Others used figures of a satyr or the phallus alone in their gardens to protect their crops. The middle finger was also used by Roman gays as an invitation to others as well as by men in battle as a signal of surrender. The Roman emperor Caligula was known for making this sign with his hand as he stretched it out for subjects to kiss. The Trobriander men believed that those who possessed a "charmed finger" could seduce women by inserting it into their vaginas.

It was also thought that one could increase one's virility by wearing the right testicle of a donkey on a bracelet or holding seeds that resembled testicles in one's hand during sex. Chinese eunuchs, hoping for regeneration of their lost sexual organs, would eat the warm brains of newly decapitated criminals (*The Illustrated Book of Sexual Records*, by G.L. Simons, p. 26).

(See also APHRODISIACS, FERTILITY RITES, LOVE POTIONS, PHALLOPHILIA and RELICS)

CHASTITY DEVICES (Day belts, Florentine Girdle, Girdle of Venus; Fibula—stitching of skin, Vertugadin—wire-looped skirt) Chastity belts are similar to a jock strap that is worn around the waist to prevent a person from having intercourse. The chastity belt designed for women makes it impossible for a male lover to insert

an erect penis into the vagina or anus. The male chastity belt has either a small hole or metal guards in the front to prevent the pulling of an erect penis through the device. These belts are more common in Europe than in the United States.

Homer's *Odyssey*, in which Hephaistos forged a girdle to ensure the fidelity of Venus after she had an affair with his brother, may be the source of chastity belts during the 16th century. Two nuns that were known for wearing chastity belts and other forms of self mortification were canonized as St. Rose and St. Marina. Older styles of chastity belts evolved into the 19th century "Day Belts" that were used on young girls by their mothers as insurance of the former's virtue during unchaperoned day excursions. Husbands, often with the wive's blessings, locked their wives in a chastity belt when traveling through dangerous territory or when their area was invaded by soldiers as a protection against rape. The belts were not designed for long term wear.

Women in several cultures, including Borneo, kept their husbands chaste during trips away from home by inserting a large (4" diameter) penis ring through the husband's penile piercing. This stayed welded together until he returned home (*Modern Primitives*, by V. Vale and A. Juno, p. 20). These were also used on Roman slaves. The holy men of the Mussulman sect in Africa wore these rings as a symbol of their chastity and were honored by women who would kiss the ring in worship.

Later years brought changes to the chastity device concept. The Spanish and French used wide crinoline skirts that were reinforced with whalebone. The name "vertugadin" (virtue guard) suggested that its purpose was primarily one of protecting virtue, rather than only being a current fashion.

Parents during the Victorian era devised a cage, some with spikes, that fit and locked around the penis of their sons to prevent masturbation. This was during a time that wasted semen was believed to cause poor health and possible insanity. Boys who showed intellectual promise particularly had to be dissuaded from this dangerous practice (*History of Sexual Customs*, p. 20).

Belts may be ornamental or symbolic. They are sometimes used in fantasy play and available with attachable vibrators and dildoes. Spare keys are kept for all locking belts as a safety precaution. Like all types of sexual activity, the decision to wear a chastity device is consensual and never imposed on a partner.

(See also BONDAGE, CASTRATION, CELIBACY, EUNUCHS, INFIBULATION, RINGING, STAPLING and SUTURING)

CHEMISE CAGOULE A chemise cagoule (cagoule: separate and combine) was a heavy night shirt used by Catholic men during the Middle Ages. It ensured that they would not derive any unnecessary tactile pleasure while impregnating their wife. The chemise had a hole cut in the front to allow the erect penis access to the vagina. There were also additional regulations as to the position a couple might use to avoid other

sinful stimulation (*The Mysteries of Sex*, by C.J.S. Thompson).

(See also CHASTITY DEVICES, GLORY HOLES, ENDYTOPHILIA, NORMOPHILIA, ST. AUGUSTINE, SEX POSITIONS and VICTORIANISM)

CHEVALIER D'EON

Chevalier d'Eon or d'Eon de Beaumont was one of the first controversial cross dressers in Europe and the person from whom the phrase Eonism was coined. He lived from 1728 to 1810 in France and during this time no one was positive of his true sex. His father held a prominent position in government and d'Eon was educated in law and received his post upon graduation. He became skilled in fencing and was appointed by King Louis XV to carry out special missions such as a trip to Russia in the guise of a female. Later, he was appointed as an envoy to England and after confiscating secret documents that indicated Louis XV's plan to invade England, he was pursued by both the French and the English. D'Eon once again dressed as a woman to escape detection. King Louis finally prevailed upon d'Eon to relinquish some of the secret documents in exchange for financial compensation and a political position. He once again found himself in good standing with the upper echelon of society. However, his cross dressing escapades began to cause a stir. His friends began waging bets on his true sex and although he denied being female, the gossip continued. A reputable envoy of the French government came to believe the story and told the King and his court that d'Eon was female and had disguised himself as male when in France. The King was shocked but believed his source. Upon the King's death d'Eon asked permission to return to his homeland and after some negotiation he was permitted only if he lived out his life dressed in female attire, as befitting his sex. D'Eon, having been unsuccessful at convincing people otherwise, resigned himself to this fate and returned to France. Marie Antoinette soon took an interest in him and had her designer create an extravagant dress for him. D'Eon wrote his feelings about this effort. "Mlle. Bertin undertakes to turn me into a passably modest and obedient woman. Only my extreme desire to appear irreproachable in the eyes of the King and my protectors could impart to me the strength I need to conquer myself and adopt a mildness of disposition in conformity with the new existence which has been forced upon me. It would be easier for me to play the part of a lion than that of a lamb." He found life intolerable because of the notoriety he was receiving and left for England where he gave public fencing performances dressed as Joan of Arc to support himself. He died in poverty at the age of 81. A surgeon was immediately appointed to identify his true sex and end speculation forever. Those who wagered on his being male won.

(See also TRANSVESTITES)

CHOREOPHILIA

Choreophilia (choreo: choral dance, and philia: attachment to) refers to people who are sexually aroused by dancing.

One of the first ritual dances was done as worship to fertility gods. The Hawaiian hula dance is a modern day example. Melodies and dance have often been combined for erotic excitement and were often prohibited during times of repressive religious rule. Calvin was quoted as saying, "Dauncyng, the cheefe mischeefe of all mischeefes, dauncers are mad men, dauncyng stirreth up lust." It is "vnpossible that dauncyng should bee good." It was often thought that people who danced in festivals were possessed by demons.

Many of the ancient festivals, such as Dionysia, Bacchanalia, May Day, Saturnalia, Feast of Fools, and Carnival, encouraged people to dance until they reached a state of euphoria. Catholic clergy often condemned dancing and other forbidden games in their churchyards during these festivals. (It seems that missionaries made a practice of building their churches over pagan altars, therefore during festivals people would naturally gather to these sites.)

The Arab Sufis, or whirling dervishes, Wiccans, American Indians, various African tribes, and the Sadhus of India all use dancing to induce a euphoric trance. Christian groups such as the Quakers and Shakers did this as well.

Dance halls were started in the United States by bar owners who hired females to dance with their clients, thus attracting larger numbers. Some of the women were prostitutes who seized the opportunity to offer men other services. In the early 20th century female wage earners began frequenting dance halls, amusement parks, and theaters that were away from the watchful eye of parents and neighbors. Single men quickly opted for sexually integrated establishments as opposed to all male clubs and the popularity of mixed dancing began in America.

(See also BELL DANCING, BELLY DANCING, FESTIVALS, FLAGELLATION and LAP DANCING)

CHREMATISTOPHILIA
Chrematistophilia refers to those who are aroused by being charged for sex or robbed. Payment for some men may give them a feeling of power because the partner is now obligated to do their bidding and there is no guilt in not reciprocating.

(See also AUCTIONS, AUTASSAINOPHILIA, HARPAXOPHILIA, HYBRISTOPHILIA, PHOBOPHILIA and VICARIOUS AROUSAL)

CHUBBY CHASERS
A chubby chaser is the nickname for someone who is sexually aroused by an obese partner. The term Chubby Chaser is shortened to Chaser and the term Chubby is used here to refer to the obese object of their love.

Ford and Beach, when investigating sexual preferences from many different societies, discovered that the majority preferred women who were plump. Holmberg tells of the Siriono of Eastern Bolivia:

Besides being young, a desirable sex partner—especially a woman—should also be fat. She should have big hips, good sized but firm breasts, and a deposit of fat on her sexual organs. Fat women are referred to by the men with obvious pride as ere'N ekida *(fat vulva) and are thought to be much more satisfying sexually than thin women* (Patterns of Sexual Behavior, *by Cellan S. Ford, and Frank A. Beach, Ph.D., pp. 88-89).*

There are several theories as to the reason for this preference; however, no single pattern fits everyone.

A small majority have at least one parent or close family member that is obese.

Reasons may be similar in some cases to those of acrotomophiles.

This preference is often developed at an early age and could have a complex hormonal, genetic, and environmental cause.

The chaser may feel nurtured by the size difference (i.e. parent/child) just as others seem attracted to tall partners.

The chaser prefers the physical sensations of being with a large, soft, pillow-like body. One chaser describes contact with a chubby as a "mountain of flesh enveloping one, as lying on a sack of pudding with flesh oozing between the fingers and gushing over arms and legs, and being enveloped or consumed alive as one sinks into those silky depths" (*BUF*, February 1990, p. 40).

Cleopatra was assumed to have been rather obese. But in 1988 it was discovered that the statue that was thought to be of her was of another queen. Obesity has always been a sign of affluence in Africa and young girls are still sent to special farms to be fattened into marshmallow physiques before marriage. The school also gives them instruction in maintaining a household. The Japanese seem mesmerized by their obese Sumo wrestlers but I have not seen data to suggest that their fascination is a fetish.

There are several erotic magazines that cater to this taste in lovers, both heterosexual and gay.

People interested in meeting others attracted to chubbies have a bulletin board that accepts personal ads.

(See also ACROTOMOPHILIA, AGAL-
MATOPHILIA, AMAUROPHILIA, ANAS-
TEEMAPHILIA, ANDROIDISM, DYSMORPH-
OPHILIA, GERONTOPHILIA and INFAN-
TILISM)

CICATRIZATION Cicatrization or scarring has probably been practiced much
longer than can be documented. The first
evidence was found on 4,200 year old
Egyptian mummies. These were women
from the neighboring country, Nubia, who
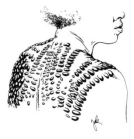
were associated as
either priestesses
or dancers for the
fertility gods.
They bore a series
of lines across
their abdomen,
these being made
by an ancient
method of tat-
tooing (dyeing freshly cut skin). The
abdomen symbolized childbirth, and therefore a woman's sexuality.

Women in certain African tribes used
scars to increase their fertility until the early
20th century. The explanation for efficacy
is that the scars create some level of mild
pain for a period of three to four years.
When this sensitive area is touched by her
husband and the brain releases neurotransmitters in response to the pain, the woman
becomes aroused by the stimulus and has
sex with her husband. The more sexually
active the woman is, the more likely she is to
conceive, thus validating the ancient claim
that scars can increase one's fertility.
Cicatrization was and is done for many
other reasons as well. Pubescent girls had to
prove their ability to endure the pain of
childbirth by rites of passage that involved
painful scarification. Young boys also had
to show courage and endure a similar rite of
passage, proving their ability to withstand
the hardships of hunting and providing for a
family. Those not choosing to be marked
were viewed by the tribe as cowards,
unwilling to suffer for a loved one, and not
worthy of marriage. The scars represented
one's inner qualities of beauty and their
physical constitution.

Strategically placed scars provided historical documentation of one's position,
accomplishments, bravery, and tragedies
during a time when they had no written language. Multiple scars on a person were
respected in much the same way as the stars
of a military general are today (*Marks of
Civilization*, by Arnold Rubin).

Cutting has always been a basis for emotional healing. Today many people in
mental institutions, hospitals, and prisons
engage in cutting as a form of self-mutilation. The reasons given for this behavior
vary, but most feel it puts them back in
touch with their bodies so they feel human
once again.

Cutting for facilitation of the healing process after a traumatic event was not only
prevalent in primitive societies but can be
seen in the fairly recent practices of cupping, phlebotomy, bleeding with leeches,
and acupuncture.

Cicatrization is also used as an art form
and reported to be less painful than tattooing. The person desiring the body art
selects a design and has a professional cica-
trist cut it into their skin. Cutting requires a
special knowledge of where and how deep
to cut the skin as well as an artistic flair.
The chosen design has a personal significance to the individual. Some people prefer
this form of cutting for self healing rather
than random mutilations, saying that it is
more empowering. An example of this are
those who were raped or were abused and
who use cutting to overcome that memory.
People are programmed or conditioned by
stimulus that has a strong emotional impact.
People can reprogram phobias much faster
by creating a strong emotional state and, at
this point, using positive affirmations to
reprogram past messages. For instance, if a
father had always referred to his child as
stupid, the child would now think or do
something that gave him an adrenalin rush
and state to himself, "I am intelligent, I am
a good, kind, respectable person worthy of
love." Cutting creates an intense moment
and display of personal power over the
person's fate. The person's cicatrix acts as a
constant affirmation of their new found

power over pain and tragedy. ("Cutting," by Raelyn Gallina, QSM lecture, January 6, 1990) CAUTION: Activities that expose one to another's blood are considered unsafe. Cutting also requires a knowledge of the cardiovascular system and neurology to prevent serious injury.

(See also AUTOMASOCHISM, BODY PAINTING, MASOCHISM, MUTILATION, PARAPHILIAS, SAFE SEX and TATTOOS)

CIGARS (Capnolagnia—arousal from watching others smoke) Cigars are used as tools of arousal. There is a club called "Hot Ash" where men interested in cigar play can contact each other. There are also films available such as "Red Dog Saloon" that feature men smoking cigars, blowing smoke at others, rubbing a victim's face in an ash  tray that contains cigar butts and ashes, removing a cigar from someone's mouth, replacing it with a penis, and using a cigar as a dildo.

There are specific cigar fetishes where men collect the discarded cigar butts of men they find appealing, and later masturbate while holding the cigar to their lips.

Cigars are used by women on stage and in nude modeling for magazines. Some performers are able to blow smoke rings after placing a cigar in their vagina. CAUTION: Using a cigar as a dildo is very dangerous if the rectal wall absorbs the nicotine or if the cigar slips out of the top's fingers into the rectum. Tobacco can also be irritating to vaginal tissue.

(See also FETISHES, HOT WAX, ICE, KNIVES, POWER TOOLS and PYROPHILIA)

CIRCUMCISION (Acucullophallia, Apellous, Peritomy, Posthetomy) Males are circumcised by cutting away the foreskin that covers the glans penis and females by cutting the hood that covers the clitoris. Women who are only sexually aroused by circumcised males are referred to as acucullophiles.

Circumcision of the hood of the clitoris was traditionally done on young girls among the Moslems. They felt that the hood would restrain the clitoris from enlarging, the removal of the hood then exposed the clitoris to more direct stimulation during vaginal penetration. This surgery is occasionally done on women in the United States who cannot orgasm because the hood occludes the clitoris.

The practice of circumcision is quite ancient as evidenced by a prehistoric stone carving of a circumcised penis. The Egyptians sacrificed the foreskin to a fertility god by burning it. Some feel that Abraham modified one of the existing religious customs that required the first fruits of sex, either the first born infant or a genital sacrifice, to appease the fertility gods. Circumcision came to be a symbolic sacrifice of one's life force and reproductive power. Americans often have circumcision done on baby boys before they leave the hospital by a technique that involves crushing the foreskin with a clamp and then cutting it off after about 10 minutes. Jews have a special ceremony (berith or briss) when the boy is eight days old. A professional *mohel* slices the foreskin off an infant in a couple of seconds while he is held by his father. The Moslem tradition is to perform circumcision when the boy reaches thirteen years old although today it is becoming acceptable to do it years earlier. Arabic Bedouin tribes would circumcise the male the day before he was to marry and during this operation the groom was to sing, thus proving his conquest over pain to the surrounding crowd. This was his initiation into manhood. Other cultures, such as the Nandi, circumcised their boys with a glowing iron that burned off the foreskin as another held it out-stretched; afterward the fat from the udder of a cow was applied to the wound. This technique was called circumbustio. The Kikoyu tribes only cut away the top half of the foreskin, leaving a flap that hung off the bottom tip of the penis.

Circumcision became popular among Christians during the early 19th and 20th centuries when doctors and religious leaders believed tight foreskins led young boys to masturbate.

Male circumcision may have some medical advantages later in life. There are diseases that afflict only the uncircumcised, such as penile carcinoma, posthitis, phimosis, and balanitis. In addition, there is ten times the risk of getting urinary tract infections. It is reported that nine out of ten uncircumcised men have difficulty or experience pain in getting the foreskin to pull backward upon erection. The smegma or secretion that is produced from the glands around the bottom of the corona or rim of the glans penis is thought to be carcinogenic for women, as there is a lower rate of cervical cancer among women who are married to circumcised men. This secretion is also known for rapidly developing an unpleasant odor. There appear to be some recent indications that infection with the AIDS virus is more prevalent among uncircumcised men in Third World countries. This does not hold true in Western countries where the standard for hygiene is often higher.

The United States has the highest number of circumcised men but that figure is dropping. This is primarily due to some insurance companies dropping their medical coverage for this procedure.

Foreskins vary in size. They range from long and loose to short and tight. The short tight foreskins are very similar in appearance of those circumcised. Some men resent having lost their foreskin and may blame their parents or even suffer from depression. If this happens it is good to talk to the person(s) one feels was responsible, replace the foreskin if possible, or seek counseling. (For more information on penis reconstruction, see section PENIS SHAPING—Foreskin Restoration)

Men sometimes incorporate their fear of circumcision into sex play as a means for arousal. They fake a circumcision by having their partner blindfold and bind them, placing a reservoir tipped condom and then slicing off the tip with a knife. Some do this as part of a hospital scene. Their partner dresses like a doctor and goes through a convincing sterilization procedure.

Sometimes men who were never circumcised use their foreskins in sex play by doing such things as putting a clothespin or electrode on it, stretching it over another man's glans penis, or putting ice inside and tying it closed with a string. Masturbation techniques can differ greatly between circumcised and uncircumcised men.

(See CASTRATION, CLITORIDECTOMY, EUNUCHS, FESTIVALS and NYMPHOTOMY)

CLAMPS   Clamps are small devices that are placed on nipples, genitals, or any other part of the body. The throat and lactating breasts are unsafe areas. The amount of tension varies according to the user's wish. Clamps can be part of highly developed sex play used to induce more severe pain, or to apply mild tactile sensation to the nipples while leaving the partner's hands free to arouse and stimulate other

parts of the body. The most widely used clamps are those with an adjusting screw where the person sets their own tension.

Clamps that are used to increase mild sensation have a weaker bite than others. While they are slightly painful when attached they are designed to provide extra sensitivity while being worn. If clamps are left on over a few minutes the area becomes painful when removed. People reduce some of this pain by using their fingers to pinch the tissue as the clamp is removed and then slowly releasing the tension to allow blood to gradually enter back into the area. This method is especially used when wooden clothespins are applied to the inner labia. Here also the moisture of the mucous membrane tends to be absorbed by the wood, causing it to stick to the skin.

People who want to reach the upper limit of the pain-pleasure barrier do things like joining two tit clamps together by a cord or chain and pulling on it slowly. They may add small weights, pierce the nipples, or drip hot wax on them. This is sometimes referred to as tit torture and can be dangerous if engaged in by novices. Other locations used for clamps are under the arms, on the penis, scrotum, labia, and on the anal sphincter. Plastic clothespins are often used on mucous membrane areas because in addition to not sticking to the skin they can be soaked in a solution of water and 10% bleach to disinfect.

Clamps are used on the testicles in several different ways. The scrotum is sometimes separated and stretched with several clamps placed at strategic points. Clamps may also be placed on the scrotum in symmetrical lines. Most scrotums can hold 40 to 50 clothespins. Excessive stretching is avoided because it can cause small vessels to break, although this is not usually serious. Pinching the upper scrotum is serious, however, because it can damage the vas deferens.

Body art includes things ranging from clamp-on nipple jewelry to temporary body markings and live puppets. Clothespins are most often used for body art. These are carefully selected to ensure against defects such as rough edges, breaks, twisted wire, or uneven edges. They are next painted or dyed to the color preferred, black being the most common. Bird representations are done with combinations of black, deep red, and white. Clothespins are placed down each arm, across the chest, abdomen, and sometimes on the back until one finally has a form representative of a bird. Skin markings are different in that the shape of the design is not evident until the clothespins are removed. A common mark is called a zipper and is made by placing clothespins side-by-side in a line. These are usually joined by a leather string run through the center of the wire spiral and at the designated moment the group of pins is pulled off with one swift stroke. Various effects are created by placing clothespins at different angles so that the lines curve and by using clamps that have distinctive bites. A few people have endured over 300 clothespins on their body. The placement of the clamps is done from the bottom of the torso and worked upward. Those who start at the top and work down for some reason find that their partner becomes lethargic.

Human puppets are made by running a string through clothespins placed on the person's legs and arms. They are then gently pulled on to make the puppet walk or move. Some people prefer threading these strings through an eye bolt in the ceiling for a similar effect. CAUTION: As with any type of play that involves tactile pain there are special precautions that are taken. Neither person uses drugs that would desensitize the pain to the extent that the bottom doesn't recognize their physical limit. Stress or distrust of a partner can increase the sensation of pain. Orgasm is often avoided before clamps are removed because this almost always intensifies the pain. Clamps themselves may leave blood blisters or cuts if not enough skin is placed between the tips or if the tension is too tight. There are subtle changes made in the flow of blood through the veins and fainting may occur. Alligator teeth clamps are not safe for use on more than one partner unless they can be sterilized. It is dangerous to clamp normal skin tissue for over six hours or muscle for longer than a few minutes. The lack of oxygen causes tissue to die. ("Clothespins: The Scene from the Corner Store," by Joseph W. Bean, QSM lecture, July 13, 1990)

(See also AUTOMASOCHISM, BINDINGS, BONDAGE, JEWELRY, PINCHING, RINGING and SENSORY ENHANCEMENT)

CLAUSTROPHILIA   Claustrophilia (claustrum: place shut in, philia: attachment to) refers to those sexually aroused by being confined in small compartments.

People who are claustrophobic experience anxiety from being confined. Some individuals take advantage of this fear to create arousal in their partner. This is done by putting partners who are claustrophobic in confining surroundings. The types of compartments or equipment used includes closets, boxes, caskets, cages, and straightjackets. A partner with a more severe case of claustrophobia may be aroused by simply taking them on a crowded elevator ride, through an amusement park's "house of horrors," or by having sex with them in a walk-in closet, a lower bunk bed, or a cave.

It is also possible that a person who starts playing with this phobia can become desensitized after a while and along with losing their fear of enclosures they will also lose the sexual arousal associated with it. Conversely, the partner is never pushed very far beyond what they think they can handle.

(See also PHOBOPHILIA)

CLITORIDECTOMY (Exmuliebrate, Spay, Thelectize) A clitoridectomy is the name of the surgical procedure used in removing the clitoris. Clitoridectomies were performed on American women as late as the early 20th century to prevent habitual masturbation.

The clitoridectomies used by other cultures were not designed so much to inhibit female orgasm as in the States, but rather to enhance vaginal orgasm by male penetration and thus discourage the lesbianism practiced in harems. The surgery was usually done by a woman who held the protruding clitoris between her thumb and forefinger until it stiffened and at this point she sliced it off with a razor. The girls of the Nandi tribes had their clitoris inflamed with nettles and then burned out with a glowing coal held on it with a wooden "spoon" until it became charred. Clitoridectomies were taken seriously because it was believed that children of a girl not undergoing this surgery would die. Because of this infants born to these mothers were strangled by pushing cow dung down their throats. The girls in the Nandi tribe were confined for four months in a hut and at the end of that time a strange ritual was performed. Several matrons would go into the woods to find a lion. One of the matrons dressed in a fur garment then began stroking and binding it, and then brought it to the hut of the girls. There it was tied to a stake outside their hut.

"The girls, who can hardly distinguish the contours of the beast of prey in the dark, are so frightened that they urinate. Now they must eat all the insects off the lion, then the lion urinates, and its urine is sipped up by all the newly-circumcised girls. . . The girls must eat

still other such repulsive delicacies. Women bring them fleas and lice in the leather of their clothing; they also lick clean a ring dipped in the mucous of the vagina" (Voodoo Eros, by Felix Bryk, p. 141).

(See also CIRCUMCISION, INFIBULATION and NYMPHOTOMY)

COCK RINGS A cock ring is one of the oldest mechanical sex aids used for sustaining an erection for a longer than ordinary period.

One of the oldest cock rings was called a hairy ring (also happy ring or goat's eyelid). This dates back to the Orient in the 13th century and was made from the eyelashes of slain goats. These were chemically treated and inlaid in rings that fit over the glans penis. Today's version has soft bristles or blunt points—all designed to provide extra stimulation of the vagina during coitus. Powders and rings can have bad effects for some and most people use them with caution until they are certain the item is safe.

Another device similar to the hairy ring is the rubber beaded erection ring that doubles as a cock ring and vaginal or anal massager when worn at the base of the glans penis. The Japanese have a sulfur ring that fits around the neck of the glans penis, desensitizing the penis while at the same time acting as an astringent to tighten the vaginal walls.

Metal or plastic cock rings are placed in position by first inserting one testicle through the ring, followed by the second testicle, and finally the flaccid penis is pulled through. The penis must be flaccid when putting on a metal ring. Rubber rings are occasionally used under the glans for penile stimulation but are removed for intercourse.

Rings are available in sizes of approximately 1 1/2–2" in diameter and are designed to fit at the base of the penis below the testicles. A simple method used in measuring for the size is that of tying a string around the appropriate area while erect and using that measurement to determine the circumference.

Leather snap-on cock rings are placed around the base of the penis below the testicles and are adjustable in size because of the selection of strategically placed snaps. This type of cock ring is fairly safe because it's easy to remove. Metal rings have special uses in sex games; they hold their shape when cords or ropes are passed through for bondage purposes, and they conduct electricity for cock torture games. Gates of hell are used in S/M play. These are cock rings that have several leather straps or metal rings that fit at intervals along the shaft of the penis. They may also have spikes on the inside to discourage erection. This type of device is safest when it can be unsnapped. CAUTION: A cock ring is removed if the penis begins to tingle or burn. If the cockring is metal this may create a complication because an erect penis must become flaccid before it can be removed. This is normally accomplished by either wrapping an Ace bandage around the penis or placing cold compresses on it. If neither of these methods work a physician is consulted as soon as possible. Prolonged venal constriction can cause thrombosis of the veins.

(See also BINDING, BONDAGE, GENITAL/ANAL INSERTS, PENILE MODIFICATIONS, RINGING, TESTICLES and TORTURE)

COCKTAILS (Coprophilia—arousal from feces, Mysophilia—arousal from soiled objects, Urophilia—arousal from urine)

The word cocktails is a term used in sex play to describe the drinking of body fluids such as blood, semen, urine, and enema contents from a glass or chalice. CAUTION: These body fluids may carry bacteria and viruses and therefore cocktails are not considered safe sex.

BLOOD AND SEMEN COCKTAIL The mixture of blood and semen was used to symbolize human life and was common among ancient goddess rituals. Today salt water or mixtures of herbed teas or wine are used in witchcraft ritual. Some also dip the athame (knife) into the contents of the chalice to symbolize sexual union.

Blood and semen, or other body secretions, are used in symbolic goddess worship sex games. In these the worshipper drinks secretions from the sex goddess to prove his devotion.

ENEMA COCKTAIL An enema cocktail is made with the liquid expelled from the rectum after a water or wine enema. This fluid is collected or poured into a cocktail glass for one of the partners to drink.

GOLDEN COCKTAIL The golden cocktail is comprised of urine. This drink may be used as part of a goddess sex ritual where the submissive drinks, or as part of a formal group dinner where everyone imbibes prior to an orgy.

(See also COPROPHAGY, CUM ETIQUETTE, FLATULENCE, HYGROPHILIA, KLISMAPHILIA, LACTAPHILIA, MUCOPHAGY, MYSOPHILIA, OCULOLINCTUS, SALIROPHILIA, SITOPHILIA and TOILET TRAINING)

COITUS À CHEVAL Coitus à cheval, or sex on a horse, has been practiced in many cultures throughout history. The Turkish soldiers, while invading villages, would capture women and children, place the victim in the rider's lap, and rape them while riding away on horseback. The loping horse provided a rhythm that was used during penetration.

Lovers also utilized the rocking rhythm during journeys on a horse, camel, or elephant. Lord George Herbert wrote of such a love story in *A Night in a Moorish Harem*:

We were borne along at an unflagging gallop. Hasan held me in front of him like a baby in his arms, often kissing me, his kisses constantly growing more ardent; and then I felt his stiff shaft pressing against my person. He suggested that I ride astride for a while and rest myself by a change of position. I obeyed his suggestion, turning with my face towards his and putting my arms around his neck, while my thighs were spread wide open over his own. He let the bridle drop over the horse's neck, whose headlong pace subsided into a gentle canter which was like the rocking of a cradle.

Hasan put his arms around my loins and lifted me a little, and then I felt the crest of his naked shaft knocking for entrance between my naked thighs. I was willing to yield to Hasan anything he wished; but no sooner had the lips of my sheath been penetrated than I involuntarily clung more tightly around his neck and, sustaining myself in that way, prevented him from entering further. Hasan's organ seemed adapted to the place and excited a sensation of pleasure. I offered my mouth to Hasan and returned his passionate kisses with an ardor equally warm. A desire to secure more of the delightful intruder overcame my dread of the intrusion...

There are several types of sex drama using coitus à cheval. One consists of a slave who prefers to be worked like a horse on a farm. He is made to plow the field naked, stabled at night in the barn, and whipped if he enjoys flagellation as punishment.

Less intense forms of sex play include having the bottom wear a special bridle (wrapped in leather for comfort), a harness, and possibly blinders, a saddle, or ornamental head feathers. The top then mounts the stallion and saddlebreaks it by sometimes slapping its flanks or using a riding crop on the more spirited animal. The horse isn't supposed to speak, therefore, a specific

sound is selected during negotiation to signal the end of the game or to indicate a desire for the partner to dismount. After the ride, the horse is sometimes watered, fed, given sugar cubes, or groomed. Grooming involves body worship. A stallion is flattered on their strength, beauty (their mane is fondled), long muscular legs, and told how sexually aroused the rider got with the rocking motion against their thighs, and the enormous size of their genitals. Those who remain in role to have sex with their stallion do not use the missionary position, but rather the horse remains on their knees or all fours. CAUTION: A human's back is not designed to withstand constant weight.

(See also ANDROIDISM, CAT FIGHTING, COSTUMES, DOMINANCE/SUBMISSION, FANTASY PLAY, SEX POSITIONS, SWINGS, SYBIAN and ZOOPHILIA)

COITUS À MAMMILLA (Mammagymnophilia—arousal from female breasts, Mazophallate—penetrating between breasts) Coitus à mammilla is the act of ejaculating between breasts. This is particularly exciting for men who have a breast fetish. The woman generally leans backward as the man places his penis on the sternum between her breasts and thrusts. The woman controls the pressure by

pushing her breasts together. The slang term for this is "a pearl necklace." Two women engaging in sex may masturbate against the breasts and nipples.

(See also AXILLISM, COITUS INTERFERMORIS, FROTTAGE and GENUPHALLATION)

COITUS À UNDA (Albutophilia, Undinism; Coitobalnism—in bath tub) Coitus à unda refers to sex in water as opposed to water sports which generally involve urine or enemas. People are often fond of masturbating or having sex in the shower, rain, ocean, swimming pool, and jacuzzi. Fellatio, during which the partner holds hot water in their mouth, is another form of water sex that is sometimes mentioned.

Tiberius Caesar was inventive with aquatic sex sports. He had young boys trained to swim after him and come up from below to suck and nibble on his genitals. He called these boys his "minnows" (*Perverse Crimes in History*). Some women used the water flow from their bidet (a basin that sprays water upward for a woman to clean her vagina) for masturbation. This is called bidetonism.

Bars sponsor entertainment such as naked women swimming in a large aquarium and wet t-shirt or jock strap contests. In bath tubs soap is often used as a lubricant to insert fingers, toes, and toys into openings. Gloves, brushes, or chemical scrubs are used for body massage and some people bind their partner's wrists with rope or blindfold them. Those involved in infantilism may run a bubble bath for their partner and add their favorite rubber duck or toy boat for the baby's entertainment. CAUTION: Electric or battery operated devices are dangerous near water as is sex in a swimming pool or outdoor body of water during a storm. Nudity in ocean water has led to some men having had their uncovered genitals stung by jellyfish.

(See also BATHS, INUNCTION and SHOWERS)

COITUS INTERFERMORIS Coitus

Interfermoris consists of penetration between the thighs of a person, sometimes a child or infant of either sex. This does not include vaginal or anal sex; therefore, it was used by many as a form of birth control before marriage.

This practice is quite ancient. The Jewish Talmud mentions neighboring tribes "who rub their rods between the legs of children; i.e. those who practice masturbation by way of limbs." The distinguishing evidence of a child having been assaulted in this manner is of inflamed inner thighs or perineum (*Perverse Crimes in History*, p. 193).

Penetration of the thighs is done one of four ways. Ancient Greek pedophiles used the younger males' thighs for penetration while they stood or reclined. Middle Eastern tribes would place the person on the lap of the male with their back toward him, the penis was then thrust between the legs and against the perineum. Another method was that of laying the person on a bed or chair on their back, raising their legs in the air, and crossing them to form a small cavity between the upper thighs and perineum into which the penis was thrust. The fourth was to hold a young child upside down by the ankles or knees and penetrate between the legs in this position.

This type of sex is used more as a form of masturbation because it creates more intense sensations of abrasion and pressure than vaginal entry. It is much less common in the United States than in some Eastern countries.

(See also AXILLISM and COITUS A MAMMILLA)

COMPUTER SEX (Teledildonics)

Computer sex refers to computer user networks or bulletin boards where people exchange information about sexual subjects, jokes, personal ads, fantasies, and sexual graphics between two on-line operators. Sex toys and other paraphernalia can be ordered through on-line catalogs. Computer networks are also used as introduction services for singles, swingers, gays, and sadomasochists. A few are set up to enable couples to engage in private communication that lead some to masturbate. These messages are referred to as "one-handed postings." The process is awkward because one has to type in order to keep communication open. A few have not only mastered this but are able to do it at their desk during work hours.

Most user groups either have a questionnaire or ask for a short biographical description. Networks that are explicitly sexual may ask personal information such as sexual preference, body measurements, amount of body hair, length of penis, and best physical attributes.

Similar to most other user networks there is a monthly fee and long distance charge when applicable. The computer has to be equipped with a modem, communication software, and a phone line.

Future technology includes the ability to create tactile sensations from three dimensional video projections called virtual reality. Some think this will lead to X-rated programs of female film stars performing fellatio on the computer user, etc. This has led to the term 'teledildonics'.

There are computer software games such as Leisure Suit Larry Sexxcapades, and a version called MacPlaymate that is designed to allow the player to make special requests of a model who performs these on screen. Other services provide a catalog of color photos that can be viewed on individual monitors. ("Computer Erotica," by Adele Aldridge, Ph.D., and Eve Gregory, Mensa Sexyg Gathering Conference in San Francisco, February 17-18, 1990)

(See also ANDROIDISM, DATING SER-VICES and PORNOGRAPHY)

ANTHONY COMSTOCK   Mr.

Comstock (1844-1915) was appointed by President Grant as Special Agent of the Post Office Department. His responsibility was to prevent 'obscene' material from passing through the U.S. mail. Comstock had very little education and came from a family of 14 children. His mother died young. But instead of coming to appreciate the horrors women endured because of the lack of birth control, he saw his mother as a martyr in his fight against it. Comstock worked as a porter, shipping clerk, and salesman until he became involved in a Y.M.C.A. campaign to suppress pornography where he was successful in obtaining the arrest of a publisher. He continued his affiliation with the Y.M.C.A. and soon helped to form the N.Y. Society for the Suppression of Vice. He came to the attention of President Grant when he successfully lobbied for passage of postal legislation preventing pornography from being sent through the mail. His campaign included raids on the Knoedler's New York Art Gallery that was displaying reproductions of Paris Salon Prize Winners and the American Art Student's League to confiscate their male nude artworks. He also had nude manikins removed from New York clothing stores, filed charges against George Bernard Shaw's *Mrs. Warren's Profession* (1894), "protested against photographs of athletes exercising in trunks," and had many physicians arrested for sending information about birth control to their patients. (See section on BIRTH CONTROL.) Comstock was proud to have accomplished the destruction of 175 tons of 'obscenity', nearly 4,000 arrests, and over $237,134 collected in fines. The most disturbing figure, however, was the number of suicides among those he had arrested. This totalled 15 after only five years and the next 37 years of his career brought many more. Yet, despite many protests, he remained in his capacity as Special Agent of the Post Office Department until his death in 1915

(*Encyclopaedia Sexualis* by Victor Robinson, M.D., pp. 144-147).

(See also BIRTH CONTROL, ILLEGAL SEX, PORNOGRAPHY and ST. AUGUSTINE)

CONDOMS   See BIRTH CONTROL /CONDOM

CONFESSIONS   Confessions, in the

Catholic Church, enable people to be absolved of their 'sins.' But they also produce sexual torture for many priests.

Peter de Rosa, a former Jesuit priest, explains in his book *Vicars of Christ* that new priests were susceptible to temptation after being trained in a seminary for years away from all women. Between 1215 and 1614 these priests suddenly found themselves alone in the same room with attractive women at their feet confessing in detail to every type of sex they experienced, desired, or even fantasized about. Many priests succumbed to temptation under this strange form of sexual seduction.

The sexual temptations of priests were not restricted to young maidens but included married women, nuns, men, and boys. A few priests would demand that a female disrobe and be whipped as penitence, some having the woman flog them in reciprocation.

The Church invented the confessional box and made its use compulsory in 1614, hoping to alleviate the former temptation. A urologist in 1841 reported that the priests had a dramatic increase in the number of seminal losses after hearing confessions. Therefore the confessional box evidently helped, but did not provide a solution for the young priest trying to remain chaste under this type of sexually stimulating environment. The confessional box also came to be used by laymen who were able to pose as the priest and get women to confess details of their sex lives. The Church only considered this to be a serious offense if the laymen gave absolution to the women.

The penitents were at times asked to divulge explicit information about their sex lives because the Church suspected certain groups of perversions. The following set of questions was used in 1697 for the Tarascan tribe in Western Mexico:

> Are you a married woman, or a widow, or a virgin, or have you lost your virginity?
>
> How many times?
>
> Did you want anybody?
>
> Are you relatives?
>
> In what degree are you relatives?
>
> Have you sinned with a woman?
>
> Were they your relatives?
>
> Did you commit sin with some woman using both parts?
>
> Have you kissed any woman?
>
> Was she your mother, the one who gave you birth?
>
> Have you committed sodomy?
>
> Have you touched the lower parts of a man with pleasure, wishing to commit a sin?
>
> Have you committed sin with any beast?
>
> Have you committed sin with a woman while she was lying down like an animal on four feet, or have you put her like that, wanting to sin with her?
>
> And how many have sinned with you?
>
> And was one your father, the one who begat you?
>
> And was one your elder brother?
>
> And was one your younger brother?
>
> And have you sinned with another woman as if you were man and woman?

Manual de administrar los Santos Sacramentos a los espanoles y naturales de esta provincia de Michoacan (1697) fols. 150-54. by Angel Serra—cited in *Sex in History* by Reay Tannahill, pp. 299-300).

Confessions and a commitment of trust have strong aphrodisiac qualities for both parties. The person confessing can give details of their sexual exploits, cry about being abandoned and used by a lover, and about their current relationship status (usually available), with intense emotions of guilt, sadness, or anger. All of this can be very emotionally stimulating for the person whose shoulder they are crying on, bringing out in them a need to nurture the victim. Both men and women replace old lovers with this covert seduction routine.

(See also AGREXOPHILIA, COPROLALIA, HIEROPHILIA and NARRATOPHILIA)

CONSTRICTIONS (String bondage) Constrictions are used to induce a trance-like state or simply to create different body sensations than one normally experiences with sex. Constrictions are done by wrapping string around the body. Each strand is made into a slip knot, wrapped three times around an area, and tied. CAUTION: Wrapping the neck area can be dangerous. String constrictions can be left on for several hours. However, if an area begins to tingle or turn blue the string is removed immediately.

COPROGRAPHY (Graffiti) Coprography (copro: feces, graphy: written) literally means to write with feces but is used here to describe someone who writes vulgarities on the walls of public toilets.

> *Here I sit,*
> *Waiting to ....*

This irresistible urge has been felt by people for as long as there were public latrines. The Romans resorted to having symbols of their gods painted on latrine walls to prevent frustrated poets from ruining them. The Romans shared a common wiping stick, the "bum swab," which might have been used to write on the walls as people wiped the stick to clean it off; thus the literal translation "written feces." Aristocrats wiped with disposable feathers.

Public toilets entice people into writing vulgarisms on their walls more so than any other location. This may be due to the anonymity it offers, the ability to outwit the last guy, the urge to educate others, brag about sexual exploits, or because one's mind is focused on the genitals. Dr. Georges Valensin, in *A Complete Guide to the World of Sex, Sex From A to Z*, refers to the author of graffiti as being "momentarily liberated from tension by his scriptural ejaculation." These semi-public bulletin boards have also served a political purpose in cultures were the people were repressed and could not express their discontent by any other method.

Another form of coprography is used by many sex criminals. They write descriptive letters to the police or parents of their victims describing in gross detail the form of torture they used for their last murder. This is not only a popular form of excitement for the murderer himself, but also for many others who write to the police claiming credit for the same crime. Sex offenders very often document their crimes with photos, film, or in the case of Gerald Thompson, a convicted sex murderer, a diary. This diary and several hundred photos were later used as evidence against him in court.

Vulgar letters may be sent to public figures as well. A popular television talk show host, Geraldo Rivera, mentioned having received threatening letters from viewers containing feces (July 30, 1991 Geraldo program).

(See also ANTHROPOMORPHIC CARTOONS, EROTOGRAPHOMANIA, JACTITATION, NARRATOPHILIA, STATIONERY and TATTOOING)

COPROLALIA   (Cunnilalia—talk about vaginas) Coprolalia is the act of using words that are considered obscene, usually during sex, to arouse the person speaking and/or their partner.

Words, especially those involving humiliations, are negotiated with the partner before the sex act. While some men or women may become extremely aroused by the sound of rarely used obscenities, it can make others lose their interest in sex. Negotiation is specific; a partner may say they enjoy hearing or using dirty words during sex but fail to mention that the word "tramp" does nothing while "slut" brings them to orgasm.

Some people enjoy having their partner speak obscenities, but would never use obscenities themselves. Likewise, one can have a partner that loves to use dirty words during sex, but if one responds in a like manner, they pass judgment.

Fantasies offer a much broader selection of sexual exploits than is humanly possible; the use of dialogue increases one's potential for safe sexual diversity and experimentation.

(See also ACOUSTICOPHILIA, CONFESSIONS, JACTITATION, OBSCENE PHONE CALLS, PHONE SEX and NARRATOPHILIA)

COPROPHAGY   Coprophagy (copro: feces; and phagy: to eat) is the act of eating feces for sexual arousal.

Coprophagy has a long history, losing its popularity only within the last three centuries. The use of feces had many applications. John Money, in *Love and Love Sickness*, tells of Eskimo mothers who at one time licked their soiled infants clean, which is also a natural maternal action among many animals. An ancient aphrodisiac consisted of a formula of semen mixed with the feces of hawks. Human feces was also a common medical remedy used to cure a wide variety of diseases. As late as 1905 the February 19th issue of *Journal de Medecine* of Paris carried an article by Dr. Schurig wherein he listed coprophagy along with various other medical lore of the past 200 years. Specific types of feces were also used in medicine for different ailments. The following list from John Bourke's book, *Scatologic Rites of All Nations*, lists the type of feces recommended for each ailment:

TYPE OF FECES	INDICATION
human	burns
	breast cancer
	inflammations
cow	gout
	rheumatism
dog	dysentery

dog	epilepsy
	colic
dove	headache
	vertigo
goat	jaundice
	spleen trouble
	hawk sore eyes
pig (dried and inhaled)	nasal hemorrhages
peacock	convulsions
cat	gout of feet
donkey	insomnia
	nose bleeds
horse	pleurisy
	colic
crocodile	facial blemishes
	freckles
lion	anti-epileptic
mouse	child constipation

People have not only used feces to cure ailments under the direction of the medical profession, but it has been found in common rituals and religious services throughout history. The prophet Ezekiel was told to bake his bread with human dung:

And thou shalt eat it as barley cakes and thou shalt bake it with dung that cometh out of man, in their sight.—Ezekiel 4:12

God's admonition to Ezekiel is surprising because of the fastidiousness of the Jews in matters governing excrement. The *Code of Jewish Law* (by K.S. Arulch) explicitly lists many of these regulations, including not thinking of holy things while in a latrine, making sure that there is not even a small particle of excrement on the anus before entering the house of prayer, and not praying in the vicinity of a soiled infant or child.

Some cultures included feces in their festivals. "In Thuringia a sausage is stuck in the last sheaf at threshing and thrown with the sheaf on the threshing floor. It is called the "barrenwurst" and is eaten by all the threshers" (*Scatologic Rites of All Nations*, by John Bourke, p. 466).

The ancient followers of the deities Baal-Phegor were all trained to eat feces. The Christian church only dropped their coprophagy requirement in the last couple of hundred years. The Church used it as a means by which an ascetic was to prove symbolic self-mortification. In March, 1904 Brenier de Montmorand wrote an article titled "Ascetisme et Mysticisme" in *Revue Philosophique* where he quoted Madame Guyon and Marguerite-Marie's description of their experience and the repugnance they were forced to overcome. He also said that "the Christian ascetics are almost all eaters of excrement." Havelock Ellis, in quoting Mr. de Montmorand, assumed his last statement to be an exaggeration. G. Rattray Taylor, in his book *Sex in History*, cites more ecstatics who engaged in similar activities. "The Alacoque, for instance, dwelt on these ideas with an irresistible compulsion. In her diaries she describes how once, when she wished to clean up the vomit of a sick patient, she 'could not resist' doing so with her tongue, an action which caused her so much pleasure that she wished she could do the same every day" (p. 48).

Reasons given today by people engaging in coprophagy vary. First is that of latent defiance toward their mothers who commanded them not to play with it while young. Second, this strange substance comes from their own body and complete examination has never been permitted. Third, eating feces can represent one's total and unconditional approval of and submission to a partner; showing love for anything that comes from their body. And fourth, it can be a form of masochism or self abasement when one experiences a low point in their life.

Coprophagy may be the primary intent of the individual or may be a secondary result of analingus, or fellatio after anal penetration. The threat of coprophagy is also used by a top to intimidate or frighten a bottom. Some mistresses, after using a butt plug on a slave will, without his knowledge, put a new condom on it and place it in his mouth demanding that he lick what he thinks is his own feces.

People sometimes substitute food for feces. Dominatrixes train slaves by using beef hash and insert it into the anus before defecating it onto a plate. A rapist nick-named the "Peanut Butter Kid" would smear peanut butter on the genitals of his victims and lick it off. (For those interested, feces supposedly has a charred or sour flavor but otherwise tastes similar to whatever was consumed.)

Movie videos and magazines are available from Europe that feature coprophagy (usually with a squatting woman defecating directly into the mouth of a male), enema cocktails, or smearing feces on the face of a partner. CAUTION: Eating anyone else's feces is considered a risk because of AIDS, hepatitis, giardia, amebiosis, and many other diseases. Even one's own feces must be kept away from cuts due to the risk of infections from dangerous organisms and bacteria. For these reasons some people use cellophane as a protective barrier.

(See also ANAL SEX, ANTHROPOPHAGY, COCKTAILS, COPROPHILIA, CUM ETIQUETTE, FLATULENCE, HYGROPHILIA, KLISMAPHILIA, MUCOPHAGY, MYSOPHILIA, OCULOLINCTUS, SAFE SEX, SALIROPHILIA, SITOPHILIA, TOILET TRAINING and WORSHIP/GODDESS)

COPROPHILIA (Coprolagnia, Scat; Chezolagnia—masturbating while defecating, Coproscopist—person watching, Defecolagnia—arousal from defecating) Coprophilia (copro: feces; philia: attachment to) refers to one who is sexually aroused by feces. This person may or may not be a coprophagist or mysophile. The reasons for playing with feces, however, may be similar.

One type of coprophile will tend to want to play with feces in a similar manner as a child who has not been taught that it is disgusting and filthy. Some people consider it psychologically healthy to analyze one's childhood and act out all the things that one wanted to do as a child but was prohibited from by overprotecting parents. This was one rationale behind a private club in San Francisco (before AIDS) that comprised of men who would save their excrement in baggies and bring it to the meeting where they removed it and used it as finger paint or modeling clay. John Money gives an example of a coprophilic "plumber" who collected feces from public toilets after turning off the water supply. He later used the feces to eat or smear on his body (*Lovemaps*, p. 48). Another woman liked to rub feces on a dildo and then use it on herself. A San Francisco man who couldn't find women willing to engage in coprophilia was able to get several to smear panties containing chocolate frosting on his face. Others have sent soiled panties to pen pals in the mail.

One form of behavioral conditioning was described by Havelock Ellis in the case history of a man from the 19th century who as a young boy was allowed to stay in the same room with the maids while they defecated in a portable toilet. He gradually began to eroticize the female buttocks and the act of defecation. As an adult, he was caught masturbating over a similar portable toilet containing the feces of a woman to whom he was attracted. In this case, his own feces had no appeal, nor did feces of those to whom he was not sexually attracted. This holds true in the case of many fetishes.

Some people become aroused by having a bowel movement. This can be explained because the anus is one of the areas abundant with nerve endings. Therefore, like the nipple, mouth, and genitals it is one of the primal body functions that releases opiates in the pleasure center of our brain.

There are those who love the feel and texture of feces and some couples will rub it between their bodies during sex for the slippery effect it produces. Some enjoy watching their partner defecate, although they have no desire to touch the feces itself. These people have devised gimmicks such as lying under a glass coffee table while their partner defecates from above, or using a glass plate in lieu of the table. Romans too seemed to have no compunction against using feces. Bordellos sometimes had a glass floor that was designed for this purpose. Practical use was also made of feces. Roman charioteers rubbed the dung of boars onto their bodies hoping that the odor would keep the horses from trampling them if they were thrown from their chariots (*Those About to Die*, by Daniel Mannix). Until as late as the early 20th century African Semi-hamite tribes used cow dung instead of soap for washing hands and polishing metals.

A small bi-annual newsletter, titled *Religion of the Month Club*, is published in California for those interested in the topic of feces. It comes complete with illustrations, a centerfold, famous quotes, and a Scratch 'n' Sniff strip.

(See also ANAL SEX, ANTHROPOPHAGY, COCKTAILS, COPROPHAGY, CUM ETIQUETTE, DEFILEMENT, FLATULENCE, HYGROPHIILIA, KLISMAPHILIA, MUCOPHAGY, MYSOPHILIA, OCULOLINCTUS, SAFE SEX, SALIROPHILIA, SHOWERS, TOILET TRAINING, UROPHILIA and WORSHIP/GODDESS)

CORSETS (Girdles—usually restricts lower abdomen or designed only to hold up hosiery) Corsetting refers to a restriction placed around the waist, the effect of which creates difficulty in breathing deeply and decreases the size of the waist. It is thought to have originally been a form of bondage used on women who were captured to prevent them being able to run away, but still allowing them to perform assigned tasks. Women in Crete wore large rings around their waists to make their waists smaller.

Westerners began wearing corsets as a result of Christianity's use of abrasive clothing as a form of penance. Men and women began by wearing abrasive shirts, next they used tight bands of cloth on their arms, and eventually wore corsets on their waists. Corsets may also have gained popularity among women because a small waist signals males that she is not pregnant and therefore worth his investing time in trying to mate with her.

Many materials were used as corsets evolved, including iron, cloth with wooden supports, whale bone, metal strips, and finally plastics. Mid-18th century women wore daggers in the front of their corsets which were often tied with a ribbon. They would give these as relics to their favorite beaus who then sewed the string of lace on his hat; thus evolved the modern hat band. When garment styles dictated the wearing of full skirts, corsets were essential in lending basic support needed to carry the weight. Clothing became so layered that at times a woman's complete apparel could weigh up to 35 pounds. In the late 19th century a few women actually had surgery to remove their lower ribs so that they could corset their waists more tightly. Corsets began losing their popularity during World War I, but are again resurfacing. There is now a national corset club headquartered in San Francisco.

Old fashioned corsets not only restrict breathing but push the internal organs up and in, all of which is necessary to decrease one's waistline. This technique can reduce a normal waistline down to 19" within six months. A few women have been able to shrink their waists to 13", however this can create internal problems and the shape created becomes almost too exaggerated to be considered flattering. ("Corsets," by B.R. Creations, Outcast lecture, San Francisco, August 18, 1989)

The reasons people use corsets in sex play vary. Theoretically, the restriction of the waist would force a woman to breathe with her chest and would make some women become aroused and reach orgasm easier; it might also cause them to experience euphoria and light-headedness during sex play. One woman enjoyed them because after exercise, such as dancing, she would automatically experience an orgasm upon its removal. Male transvestites use corsets to shape and contour their torso. Submissive homophobic men and lesbians are made to wear corsets during sex play as a form of humiliation. Many simply find the binding sensation or the full rounded breasts protruding over the bra to be erotic.

(See also BINDING, BONDAGE, COSTUMES and OXYGEN REGULATION)

COSTUMES Costumes can play an important role in sex scenes. They create an illusion of sexual variety, a different sense of oneself, and provide the proper visual effects for a theatrical sex scene.

People who use costumes to maximize or minimize their power during a theatrical scene choose costumes to aid in acting out their role. These are characters that tend not to be too commonplace or offensive, nor so obscure as to simply confuse one's partner. Examples of commonplace costumes are business suits, regular military uniforms, school teacher outfits, or construction worker gear. Religious costumes can offend some people. Costumes that are most popular in sex play are those of Indians, cowboys, police, nurses, doctors, maids, harem girls, slaves, fetish attire, belly dancers, cross-dressers, infantilism, nuns, priests, the renaissance era, witch trials, animals, or aliens.

People who have studied a certain period of history or particular event have an advantage in being able to set the stage and be convincing in their portrayal of a character from that time. Knowledge of a foreign language can be beneficial as well.

Finding or making an authentic costume can take a lot of time, research, and skill. The real authority on costumes will be able to tell if a military uniform has the wrong buttons or insignia.

If one's preference is for military or American western costumes, traveling gun shows are excellent resources for information and material. They also advertise rendezvous campouts that sponsor target shooting and other contests of skill and courage. Proper attire, weapons, and gear for that period is required. ("Clothing and Costumes," by Karen W., Society of Janus lecture, September 28, 1989)

Role playing does not have to be restricted to the home. It may be done for social events that encourage costumes, such as parades, gun shows, some sexually oriented conventions, S/M lectures, group sex houses, transvestite clubs, leather bars, or midnight showings of *The Rocky Horror Picture Show*.

(See also COITUS A CHEVAL, DRAG QUEENS, FANTASY PLAY, FEMALE IMPERSONATORS, INFANTILISM and PETTICOAT DISCIPLINE)

COURTSHIP Courtship is the act of showering attention on someone in order to receive love and/or marriage in return. This attention often comes in the form of writing letters, staring, caressing, kissing, handholding, dancing, baby talk, giving gifts, using pet names and cute phrases, and stroking the hair or face.

Courtship is the period that allows each person time to discern the sincerity of the other as well as their ability and willingness later to commit to possible child rearing efforts. Adherence to a schedule of spending time to get to know each other and to bond often alleviates one night stands that leave the abandoned partner feeling hurt and confused.

In the West, the romantic interest in women developed in the 12th century during the Crusades. Husbands left their wives in charge of large estates and these women reaped the respect and admiration formerly only known to powerful men. Women became the benefactresses of travelers, among whom were the singing minstrels or troubadours. Many of these troubadours rewrote their ballads to express affection for matrons. The sentiment spread rapidly and rooted itself in many European cultures.

A view of how courtship is used in nature might heighten our understanding of human behavior. One function courtship serves is to excite both partners, providing the stimulus necessary to release the hormones that prepare the reproductive organs for coitus and impregnation. Another function is discussed by Edward O. Wilson, in his book *Sociobiology*.

Pure epigamic [attracting the opposite sex during the breeding season] display can be envisioned as a contest between salesmanship and sales resistance. The sex that courts, ordinarily the male, plans to invest less reproductive effort in the offspring. What it offers to the female is chiefly evidence that it is fully normal and physiologically fit . . . . The courted sex, usually the female, will therefore find it strongly advantageous to distinguish the really fit from the pretended fit. Consequently, there will be a strong tendency for the courted sex to develop coyness . . . . Males invest relatively little with each mating effort, and it is to their advantage to tie up as many of the female investments as they can. This circumstance is reversed only in the exceptional cases where males devote more effort to rearing offspring after birth. Then the females compete for males . . . . At each point in time there will be a temptation for the partner with the least accumulated investment to desert the other. This is particularly true of the male immediately following insemination (pp. 159, 162, 163).

Humans, with their intelligence, have devised legal procedures to ensure a commitment from both parties and for financial support if the contract is broken. A dissolution is often a result of one or both partners misrepresenting themselves, their intentions, interests, or needs.

Today, courtship can serve to build intimacy and bonding between a couple before there is a risk of pregnancy. It creates a foundation of love that can be built on as a relationship progresses. A woman who has even once been charmed by a romantic display of quaint courtship knows its virtues (*A History of Courting*, by E.S. Turner).

(See also BUNDLING, CHAPERONS, FANS, LOVE, LOVE ADDICTION, LOVE POTENTS, PERSONAL ADS, ST. VALENTINE, SERENADES and TROUBADOURS)

COUVADE Couvade is the custom of the male joining his wife in experiencing symbolic labor and delivery during the birth of a child. In some cases, the father would even be required to stay in bed or be isolated for a period of time after the delivery.

This custom is widespread and of ancient origin. Early man was not always aware of the role he played in fertilization. This ritual seems to have served in bonding him to the infant. It is also assumed to be a ritual that symbolically transferred the wife's pain and susceptibility toward evil spirits onto the husband. Couples exchanged clothing for the same purpose (J. G. Frazer, 1910, *Totemism and Exogamy*, Vol 4, London, Macmillan).

COUVADE SYNDROME (Chipil) Men rarely practice couvade rituals today. However, many do have sympathetic psychosomatic symptoms during the period of their wife's pregnancy and childbirth. Many men have taken it upon themselves to assist their wives during labor and to be present during their child's birth. Lennart Y. Bogren, M.D. reported that in recent studies as many as 20% of husbands suffer some type of sympathetic pain during a wife's pregnancy. These men tend to be those who identified more closely with their mother ("The Couvade Syndrome," by Lennart Y. Bogren, M.D., *International Journal of Family Psychiatry*, Vol 7, 1986, No. 2, pp. 123-135). Another study done in 1985 by the University of Wisconsin-Milwaukee School of Nursing estimated that 90% of men had symptoms such as cravings for food, weight gain, nausea, or swelling stomachs during their wives' pregnancies.

(See also COUVADE)

CROSS DRESSING See ADOLESCENTILISM, ANDROIDISM, CORSETS, COSTUMES, DRAG QUEENS, FANTASY PLAY, FEMALE IMPERSONATORS, GYNEMIMETOPHILIA, INFANTILISM, TRANSSEXUALS, TRANSVESTITES and VICTORIAN LACE

CUCKOLDRY This Renaissance term derives its name from cuckoo birds who select males other than their mates to father their young. As in eugenics this practice allows them to benefit from the highest quality genes available. Women occasionally prefer a male other than their husband to parent a child. This may inadvertently improve the gene pool but is more often the result of a simple desire to be with or have a child by a particular lover. The "cuckold" is the hapless husband.

(See also ADULTERY and EUGENICS)

CUM ETIQUETTE Ejaculate or vaginal secretion's (ungation) consistency, flavor, and quantity varies from person to person.

The quantity seems to be genetic and age related. The consistency of male ejaculate changes almost immediately after release by becoming thicker. This evidently functions as a plug to keep the sperm from dripping out of the vagina before insemination.

The flavor of ejaculate varies and is determined primarily by the factors listed below:

BITTER: Smoker (cigarettes or marijuana), alcohol

SHARP: Red meats, sperm, asparagus, broccoli, spinach, and some vitamins

MODERATE: Having only one or two of the Sharp ingredients and none of the Bitter ones

MILD: Vegetarian, lots of celery, no sperm

SWEET: Borderline diabetic or diabetic

A man who has ejaculated several times within a couple of days will have increasingly milder ejaculate. Partners that have difficulty swallowing ejaculate sometimes separate it into smaller portions and swallow it a little at a time. Some people have satisfied their curiosity about its taste by dipping their finger in their emissions and inserting it in their mouths. This is also done while french kissing with consenting partners.

The odor of the genitals can play an important factor in flavor. The male and female both have glands around the base of the glans penis or clitoris that produce a cheesy substance called smegma. If the foreskin and clitoral hood are not pulled back periodically and cleaned the smegma can produce a very potent smell.

A small percentage of woman have an  ejaculate from the Skene glands that surface on each side of the urethral opening. The ejaculate is similar to the consistency of urine but has been proven through chemical analysis to be different. The female who ejaculated in this manner was until recently considered incontinent. The amount of her ejaculate varies from a few drops to a couple of teaspoons which shoots from the openings in the same pulsating manner that semen shoots from the penis.

Genital secretions are used in sex games for brushing or rubbing cum onto the breasts, face, buttocks, and stomach. People playing a dominance game occasionally ejaculate into a glass and have their partner drink it, either alone or mixed with another liquid or food. Men are often forced to ejaculate in their own mouth for the amusement of their dominant partner. CAUTION: Allergies to semen can cause a rash in a few people. Consumption of a partner's secretions is not considered a safe sex practice.

(See also CUNNILINGUS, FELLATIO and SHOWERS)

CUNNILINGUS (Clitorilingus, Gamahucheur; Oral sex—fellatio or cunnilingus) Cunnilingus (cunnus: vulva, and lingus: tongue) is the act of licking the female genital area and is very common throughout cultures in history.

"Empress Wu Hu, who ruled during the great T'ang Dynasty (700-900 C.E.), created a peculiar sexual custom designed symbolically to elevate the female and humble the male...Consequently, all governmental officials and visiting dignitaries were obliged by royal decree to pay homage to her Imperial Highness by performing cunnilingus upon her. Old paintings depict the beautiful empress standing and holding her ornate robe open, while a high official or kuan is shown kneeling humbly before her and lavishly applying his lips and tongue to her protruding clitoris" (*The Cradle of Erotica*, pp. 319-320).

Cunnilingus is often used as a tool for men to control premature ejaculation due to the length of genital contact it takes before their partner can orgasm, which may be twenty minutes or more.

Some prefer to clean the clitoris before engaging in cunnilingus. This is done by pulling the hood of skin back by using the fingers to press in an outward direction or on both sides of the head until the clitoris protrudes. The area is then wiped clean with a wash cloth or cotton swab. Caution is taken not to pull the hood back too far because like the foreskin, it can become caught behind the corona of the clitoris. If this happens one side of the upper labia is stretched and a finger used to gently press down on the top of the protruding clitoris.

Communication with the woman is important to learn the appropriate amount of pressure to be used against the clitoris. Some women prefer not to have direct or firm stimulation on the clitoris until they are near the peak arousal stage. Some find it easier to have the women demonstrate exactly how she masturbates.

Insertion of an object into the vagina or anus is not usually necessary but can enhance the sensations for some. Not all women can have orgasms by cunnilingus, just as all men are not able to orgasm with fellatio.

The G-spot is a secondary point of stimulus. It is just inside the front wall of the vagina and feels like a round raised area of fatty tissue about the size of a dime. About 15% of the women who have G-spot orgasms ejaculate liquid from the Skene glands which lay on each side of the urethra. The following is a description of cunnilingus by a heterosexual male.

MALE TO FEMALE It is important to first convince some women that you love cunnilingus, the aroma and flavor of their genitals. This can be done by telling her you love it, moaning during cunnilingus, showing her by being comfortable, with performing cunnilingus on her while watching TV, or at other times when there is no expectation of reciprocation. Partners may both feel less inhibited if they bathe before oral sex. If this is not done and you have a concern about the secretions of smegma under the hood of the clitoris, the odor can be taken care of by five seconds of licking. You may hold your breath for the five seconds, as smegma has an odor but no obvious taste. Some women have a stronger flavor or larger amount of lubricant. Relax and enjoy getting her juices all over your face. Wiping it off, being timid, or lack of movement will send her a negative signal.

Another suggestion for etiquette involves inconspicuously getting a strand of pubic hair out of your mouth. This can be accomplished by licking her thighs and leaving the hair there.

If your goal is to bring the woman to orgasm plan on spending five minutes to two hours. Prepare for the marathon scenario by learning to conserve the muscles in your tongue, and using a variation of pressure and types of licking. Licking with the relaxed flat position of your tongue is also pleasurable to your partner. You aren't in a race. Keep your neck supported by resting your head on the inside of her thigh as you are both on your sides. You may also switch positions and have her squat or sit above you. You don't have to isolate your activity to the genitals in the same way as you would for a man. Women enjoy nongenital stimulus as well, so move around, lick the inside of her thighs, perineum, buttocks, anus, abdomen, etc.

Begin cunnilingus with foreplay, and gradually work your way down to the genitals. Unlike many men, women enjoy being teased by lingering on her waist, around the top of the mons pubis, and down the inside of the thighs; don't feel you have to immediately proceed to the clitoris. When she is ready for direct clitoral stimulus she will either tell you or signal by pressing her clitoris toward you.

You will now be able to locate the clitoris by finding the small protrusion to the front of the genital area. Many females will direct you by their body movement; however, ask her to put her finger on it if you can't locate it yourself. Next, move your tongue slowly around the vagina and into it, lick softly around the clitoris, slowing bringing the tongue closer to the protruding clitoris, increasing pressure as your tongue comes into direct contact with it. Move your tongue in a circle around the clitoris then rapidly go up and down or across it. If she backs away you will need to slow down. Women vary in the amount of pressure or direct stimulus they can tolerate. For those who are extra sensitive you will need to only apply pressure to the sides of the clitoris. Alternate licking with sucking or use a combination of the tongue and lips by following the tongue with the lower lip and vis-a-vis. Some women enjoy being nibbled on in the genital area; however, avoid the clitoris. You may want to delay orgasm as long as possible. Women respond to being built up by peaks of arousal in the same manner as a man. A woman will move as long as she is stimulated. If she becomes bored or over-stimulated she will either say something or you will notice her once protruding clitoris disappear. Many women prefer to have vaginal penetration before they orgasm rather than continued cunnilingus. The woman will usually let you know at this point, by telling you she wants you inside or by pulling you into position. Otherwise, you will find that her clitoris swells more at orgasm and this is the time to suck, being careful not to use the tip of your tongue as the clitoris will be extremely sensitive at this point, and for some this is true after orgasm also.—Contributed by Pete Pappas

(See also CUM ETIQUETTE and FELLATIO)

CUPPING Cupping refers to placing a suction device on the skin, the purpose of  which is to draw blood closer to the surface. This was a form of bloodletting (similar to leeches) that was used in Europe, Turkey, and China as late as the 18th century as a leading form of medicine in the treatment of a wide variety of diseases. Glass inspirator cups were placed against a person's oiled skin and then the inside air was heated with a small torch, creating a vacuum effect, drawing blood to the surface in about 30 minutes. Some people in the S/M community use a mild form of cupping with the purpose of increasing the sensitivity of the skin. Sometimes this produces such sensitivity that running a feather across the area will produce orgasm.

The most popular cupping devices are the rubber suction cups from small Cutter snake bite kits. A larger cupping device is sometimes made from a transmission fluid funnel. The edges of this funnel flare outward and therefore do not cut or dig into the skin. It is adapted for sex play by putting a 3" long soft rubber tubing over the nozzle. The skin area is licked to ensure a good seal. The funnel is placed on the area, usually a breast, and the air is sucked out through the rubber hose. Once this is accomplished the hose is pinched shut and a flat binder clip is placed on the tip to keep in the suction. Some hook a chain or rope onto the clamp and lead the person around the room, but the primary benefit is nipple sensitivity. There are special cupping devices sold through S/M catalogs. These have a nozzle that is equipped with a one-way shut off valve that leads to two plexiglass cups. Extreme pressure such as that caused by hooking up artificial vacuum devices, like a fish tank pump, to a cup is dangerous. CAUTION: This is a blood sport and therefore not considered a safe sex practice. Welts are common. ("Branding and Cupping," by Fakir Musafar, Society of Janus lecture, August 8, 1991)

(See also BITING, MASOCHISM, PHLE-BOTOMY, PIERCING, PYROPHILIA and SAFE SEX)

CUTTING See CICATRIZATION and MUTILATION

D

DACRYPHILIA (Dacrylagnia) Dacry-philia refers to people who become aroused by seeing tears in the eyes of their partner. One man described his pleasure in seeing a young Asian prostitute cry as he thrust his penis into her small vagina. He had met her at a bar earlier and she had seduced him even though he had had sex only a short time before.

(See also SADISM)

DATING SERVICES Marriage brokers have been used for centuries by parents seeking suitable alliances for their children and now have become popular in countries where the young make their own marriage decisions. The age of computers has made collation and matching of thousands of questionnaires simple. Some will send a club member photos of several matches a month and a few services have video-taped interviews of members that can be viewed before making a selection. There is usually at least one televised dating show such as the "Love Connection" where one person interviews and selects a partner.

Special interest groups have their own services. There are interracial dating services, younger male and older female, The Big Board in Danville California for the obese, herpes groups such as New Friends in Santa Cruz, California, bi-sexual groups, and specific Christian or pagan dating services. There are quick and inexpensive telephone services where a person dials a 900 number, is asked personal questions by a computer, presses the keys on the phone pad to answer, and then is immediately matched and given several people's phone numbers.

The clubs that offer private parties or socials can have an advantage over others since they allow people to actually meet. This presents a distinct advantage over services which rely on matching compatible questionnaires; sexual chemistry will only become evident in a personal meeting.

Japanese men tend to be more formal and normally family friends provide introductions, however this is not always successful. A man named Satoshi Noguchi started a modern marriage school that teaches businessmen how to look sexy and what to say to impress the women they meet. Armed with this knowledge and self-confidence they are sent to compete with other men at dances and singles bars.

The common guidelines for women using dating services is that their home address is not given prior to the first date. The first meeting is arranged in a public place and both partners should keep the appointment. Many do not.

(See also COURTSHIP and PERSONAL ADS)

MARQUIS DE SADE Donatien-Alphonse-Francois Comte de Sade (1740-1814) was a French nobleman and author of pornographic novels such as *La Nouvelle Justine, ou les Malheurs de la Vertu, Juliette, ou la suite de Justine, La Philosophie dans le Boudoir, Les Crimes de l'Amour, ou le Delire des Passions, Les 120 Journées de Sodome, ou l'École du Libertinage,* and others.

His novels of Justine and Juliette chronicle the lives of two sisters who were separated and had to leave a convent because of their father's death. Justine was an innocent and naive 14 year old girl who was thrown into the clutches of evil, being raped or violated by all those from whom she sought refuge and safety. Conversely Juliette, her older sister, revels in vice. When they finally meet years later Juliette has led a noble and gratifying life while Justine has lived in poverty, been tortured, and barely escaped death on numerous occasions. The moral is then divulged by a cavalier who says: "There you see the Misfortunes of Virtue! And, my friends, the Fortunes of Vice!" as he pointed to Justine and Juliette respectively.

De Sade was an avid reader and managed to exhaust an innumerable volume of literary works. It was through historical records, 18th century literature, and personal contacts that he was able to compile a complete record of sexual deviances and characters with which to fill his novels. He dramatized the sex acts by portraying them as part of a nonconsensual torture scene ending in murder, and casting many victims as close relatives or children. One example of sexual deviance was his story of Justine who one day while sitting on the bank of a pond:

saw a child thrown into the water. She saved it but was surprised by the angry murderer who threw the child back into the pond and led Justine to his castle, where this monster lived alone. He had the peculiar mania of abusing each woman only once for the sole purpose of child-rearing. The children were raised until 18 months and were then thrown by him into the pond. At the moment he had thirty girls in his castle. He was a vegetarian and anti-alcoholist and also gave the girls plain fare so that they would be better fit to bear children. He also bound them to a machine before coition and had them afterwards lie in a bed for 9 days with their heads bent and feet high. That was his method of aiding conception. He conducted his own operations and took especial pleasure in the Caesarean. Just as the choice fell upon her she was freed by Coeur de Fer whom she had let into the castle and who gave her her freedom" (Marquis de Sade, His Life and Works, by Dr. Iwan Bloch, p. 181).

The Marquis de Sade himself was schooled in one of the finest French colleges, and was devoted to fine arts, music, dance, and literature. He then joined the king's regiment in a war against Germany and rose to the rank of captain of a cavalry regiment. It was undoubtedly during this time that he was exposed to pederasty, sexual torture, and masochism. Flagellation was learned from his early school years and persisted as one of his sexual preferences. Once out of the military he was forced into an arranged marriage by his father. The eldest daughter of a prominent military leader was chosen, despite the fact that he and her younger sister had fallen in love and pleaded with both families to allow their marriage. His mother-in-law exiled the love-struck younger daughter to a convent for the next nine years. His attempt to locate her was not successful and he apparently turned to extreme forms of sexual diversions which resulted in a prison sentence at 23 years of age. Of his remaining 51 years he spent 27 incarcerated, during which time he became a prolific writer. When de Sade finally did become reunited with his original love he choreographed a death sentence and threat of suicide to gain her sympathy and convince her to escape with him. They fled to Italy where as misfortune would have it she died of an illness only a few months later. He was again imprisoned but later was sent to an insane asylum at Charenton at the request of his wife and mother-in-law. The conditions here were superior to prison, and according to letters written by the resident physician, de Sade managed to engage in unbridled perversions, became a favored poet and dinner guest of the asylum director, and was allowed to establish and direct theatrical comedies, concerts, and balls until near his death. He was described during this time and the periods when he was free as being charming, polite, solemn, well groomed, handsome, and sympathetic to attractive women. While incarcerated he, like many other prisoners, became hostile, violent, and misogynistic. It was the need to vent anger and revenge that found expression in his novels.

De Sade's alleged crimes consisted of sodomy, accidental poisoning of prostitutes with bonbons laced with spanish flies (cantharis beetle), flagellation, and the cutting of a woman named Rosa Keller. His greatest offense was of a political nature and it is thought by some historians that this was the true reason for his constant imprisonment. His insolent political pamphlets undoubtedly provoked Napoleon who was notorious for sending even the slightest offenders to prison without a trial.

DEFILEMENT   (Anophelorastia—arousal from defilement, Mysophilia—arousal from soiled clothing) Sexual defilement involves polluting, destroying, violating a fetish object, sex partner, or oneself (known as automysophilia). The stimulus is similar to a mother who sees her child track mud on her new carpet; however, in this case the anxiety is transferred into a sexual response.

Hirschfeld and Ellis cite cases of men who were sexually aroused to the extent of orgasm by cutting, burning holes with a cigar, throwing ink, acid, or other defiling liquids onto women's white skirts as they passed on the street. It also brings some men pleasure for a partner's hand to be dirty while manipulating their penis.

Urination onto a victim is a more common form of defilement. Boys become fascinated at a young age and begin by urinating on pets, flies, or anything else within range. Adult men sometimes continue this practice and have been known to secretly urinate on their partner while showering. Others have been caught urinating onto strangers on the street in much the same manner as an exhibitionist.

A consensual form of erotic defilement is mud. Mud wrestling gained popularity because of the anxiety of seeing someone getting dirty mixed with two virtually naked women groping each other. There are actually three major taboos violated in this case (getting dirty, fighting, and pseudo-lesbianism).

Club Mud was formed in California for people who get aroused by seeing their fetishes being defiled. Boots, jeans, and leathers are featured in the films with defilement by mud, water, crankcase oil, or urine. There is also a 900 number for those wanting to listen to descriptions. Specific material is available for separate groups, i.e., sexual, nonsexual, and gay. Similar clubs exist in other areas. Flint Michigan has one called Wet & Muddy Clothing Club and San Diego's is called Mud Buddies. More serious enthusiasts are depicted in X-rated videos where the dominant male urinates on his partner in a barn and makes him roll in the mud and squeal like a pig.

Other types of defilement involve food. Small groups sometimes advertise for new members who are sexually aroused by having pies thrown in their faces and for those not aroused by pies or mud, video tapes are available of women wrestling in jello. CAUTION: Exposure to body secretions of a partner is not considered a safe sex practice.

(See also COCKTAILS, COPROGRAPHY, COPROPHILIA, MYSOPHILIA, PIE THROWING, SHOWERS, TOILET TRAINING, UROPHILIA and WRESTLING)

DENDROPHILIA Dendrophilia refers to those aroused by trees. Trees were ancient symbols of fertility and men on certain holy days would go into the fields and ejaculate onto the trees. Thomas Gregor, an anthropologist, spent time with the Mehinaku tribe of South America during the 1960s and told of one folk tale involving a man with a tree:

I have been able to find only two other stories of masturbation, and in both, men are the principal actors. In one tale, we learn of a man who discovered a remarkably gratifying hole in a tree, which he began to use to the exclusion of his wife and girlfriends. In the second story, a man made an artificial vagina of leaves to which he became similarly attached. In both myths, the culprits were seen by other villagers who hacked away the hole with an ax and tore the leaf vagina to shreds. In both stories, the masturbators behaved as if their leafy companions had been real women. They wailed for the deceased plants, cut their hair short, and took off their belts as a symbol of mourning (Anxious Pleasures, The Sexual Lives of an Amazonian People, by Thomas Gregor, p. 67).

(See also FESTIVALS/MAY DAY, FETISHES and MARRIAGE/MOCK)

DEPILATION (Electrolysis, Shaving, Waxing; Acomoclitic—arousal from hairless genitals, Medocure—clipping or perfuming of penis)

Depilation is the removal of hair by cutting, shaving, electrolysis, pulling, or using wax and creams. People in other cultures have used shaving as a way to control lice. However, many types of depilation have had erotic undertones.

Shaving or removal of pubic hair was practiced in Rome, the Middle East, Japan, China, India, and North Africa. Sex in many of these countries began during prepubescence before either partner had developed pubic hair. The male and female often became conditioned to respond sexually to bald genitals. Some later in life even became impotent at the sight of pubic hair on a partner. A few women have been  known to become frigid if their partner has a hairy chest. This problem was sometimes solved by having the man wearing a t-shirt during sex.

The act of pulling out clusters of pubic hair was used to produce an orgasm in some men. This was a service offered in Moorish baths by women who were skilled at this art. Physicians in France during the late 16th century revived this practice and used it as a cure for hysteria in women. Hysteria was thought to stem from sexual dysfunctions and this type of depilation must have had what appeared to be a sobering effect.

Sex was associated with the cutting of hair in the Biblical case of Samson and Delilah. According to Jewish history Samson was abducted by the Philistines after losing the power associated with his long hair. Delilah, a Philistine lover, cut it off during his sleep. Samson was then used as a stud to breed strength and courage into the progeny of the Philistines. The reason given for the Philistines having blinded Samson was to enhance his sexual response and to keep him from discriminating between attractive and ugly women. God supposedly allowed him to commit suicide to prevent the further parenting of a new and stronger breed of Philistine soldiers.

Depilation was used as a deterrent to sexual arousal as well. Ancient tribes often shaved the heads of wives to discourage other men from capturing married women. The Phoenicians required any woman with an unshaven head to act as a temple prostitute during certain seasonal rituals. Jewish women practiced head shaving upon marriage and would wear a scarf or a wig. The Catholic Church continued to require this type of depilation for nuns as a symbol of their marriage to Jesus.

There are case histories of men who have cut off hair of strangers in public and either had an orgasm then, or used the hair to masturbate with later. A man in Chicago was arrested during the late 19th century for having clipped off the tresses of over fifty women. Some paid; a woman in Paris earned money by letting men caress her long hair but had to constantly watch the men to guard against it being clipped.

Today depilation or shaving is used in sex play as part of body worship and bondage. It may also be necessary for aesthetics in infantilism, body painting, or transvestism. Shaving plays a practical role in wearing chastity belts or strap-on dildos, in branding, and in piercing. A top will sometimes shave their slave to put them into a psychological role of submission, exposure, humiliation, and shame. It may also be done to elicit fear as in the case of areola or breast shaving. The application of lotion and baby powder prevents itching for some people. Others alleviate discomfort by using Hibiclens, Neosporin, or apricot scrub, or shaving in the same direction as the hair grows. Cotton underwear is preferred by some women because it reduces the sticking problem. The contrast of sensations before and after shaving is substantial and many people consider the added sexual pleasure to be worth the effort of shaving.

The three methods used to accomplish permanent hair removal are electrolysis, thermolysis, and blend modalities which over the period of one to two years will destroy all the hair follicles. Each method involves some type of pain and for this reason sessions are limited to 15 to 60 minutes. The current can also be lowered to cause less pain, but then needs to be left on each follicle longer. The old method of electrolysis took up to five minutes of current on each follicle. The blend methods can accomplish the same effect in three seconds to a minute. Thermolysis uses alternating current and the heat produced cauterizes the tissue, whereas electrolysis uses direct current that produces a sodium hydroxide that decomposes the tissue. The blend modality uses a combination of the two other methods. Treatments have to be repeated for up to two years because many hair follicles are dormant and take that long before the hair emerges. The expense for these treatments is usually just under $60.00 an hour.

Movies and magazines are available for those interested in seeing men or women shave part or all of their bodies. There is also an international club that is open for membership to people with this interest. CAUTION: Shaving is considered a blood sport and therefore an unsafe sex practice. Safety razors and sterile techniques are used. Straight razors are generally only entrusted to professional barbers.

DEVIANCE   See PARAPHILIAS

DILDOS   See GENITAL/ANAL INSERTS

DIPPOLDISM   (Sadomasochism by proxy—arousal from watching others disciplined) Dippoldism refers to those who become sexually aroused by beating or flagellating children. The term came into use during the early 1900s when a notorious German tutor by the name of Andreas Dippold caused the death of one of his students. Dippold had been entrusted with two young boys aged 10 and 14. He was reported by Magnus Hirschfeld as having tied the boys in their beds and beaten them with rods until they broke, accusing the boys of masturbating. At other times he would grab their genitals and squeeze until they bled; They were made to write confessions of sexual conduct and to appear naked for different functions. One of the boys fell ill and Dippold made him rise early, take a cold shower, and do strenuous exercises until he became unconscious and later died.

Corporal punishment has since been phased out of most schools but during the times when caning was practiced there were numerous cases of sexual misconduct by both men and women. Children were made to strip naked, were tied down, hands of the adult wandered down against or near the child's genitals, and young men were sometimes allowed to put their hands or faces against the breast of a female assistant as they were flagellated. In one instance a headmistress allowed a banker to watch as her female students were lined up, skirts raised, and disciplined for various infractions. She was paid weekly for this favor (*Sexual Anomalies and Perversions* by Magnus Hirschfeld, pp. 349-375).

Today parents are the primary disciplinarians. While few deliberately cane their children to become sexually aroused, there are those who sometimes unconsciously become aroused. While most people would not recognize this impetus, John Money became aware of its existence in several case studies and in a 1982 *Money and Werlwas* paper coined the phrase, *sadomasochism by proxy*. Couples who confessed to having extremely passionate sex after whipping their children considered their sex lives normal and would never have considered engaging in consensual S/M games.

(See also FLAGELLATION, INCEST, PARAPHILIAS, PEDOPHILIA and SADISM)

DISCIPLINE   Discipline is a term used in S/M to describe rules for obedience training, and may also refer to the forms of punishment used to enforce them. A person can not technically be a slave without some form of restriction. They must be given regulations. These may or may not be obeyed, but the rules must be there along with an authority figure to enforce them.

The type of punishment is determined based on the severity of the disobedience and the type of sex play that the bottom enjoys or wants to experience. This is a game designed to create anxiety or fear and transfer it into sexual arousal and passion. The types of punishment are also selected with this in mind. (Many S/M players, however, try to avoid games that cause fear or anger in a partner.)

The top or master may imitate anger while disciplining their partner but will not feel it. S/M play is NOT used to work out the top's aggression on a victim. The top is, in reality, the servant that does everything in their power to provide the conditions and tactile stimulation needed for the sexual pleasure of the bottom. The severity of any verbal or physical punishment is, or should be, negotiated ahead of time. The bottom also has a safeword they can use to immediately stop the game. (See NEGOTIATION)

Many bottoms use sex play in order to feel secure; they revert back to the relationship role of parent and child. The bottom makes none of their own decisions, regardless of whether they are playing butler, slave, pet dog, or maid.

Other bottoms use these games to build their self esteem. This is done by flawless implementation of strict regulations and complex instructions. They receive gratification from this accomplishment as well as by an immediate reward for their endeavor. This type of bottom is rarely punished or likely to have an orgasm from this encounter.

Light physical punishment, if the bottom wants any type of tactile stimulation, is used with an unlimited amount of threats. Verbal threats are the top's best tools if they are ones that can be enacted. An example would be that of telling a partner they have until the count of five to orgasm and if they don't succeed the sex act is discontinued. Threats to throw a person off a cliff are not realistic and would not be perceived as a danger by the bottom.

There are discipline organizations that train servants. Ireland has a club for women that offers Victorian domestic discipline to maids and school girls. CAUTION: People who use humiliation spend a cooling down period at the end. For instance, if one called their partner a slut they compliment them on their fidelity, if they said their partner was repulsive they give an honest and flattering appraisal of the partner's value as a person, and so forth. The wise top doesn't use an insult that comes too close to the truth. ("Discipline," by Peter Fiske, QSM lecture, November 15, 1990)

(See also ALGOPHILIA, BLINDFOLDING, BONDAGE, CHASTITY DEVICES, DEFILEMENT, DOMINANCE/SUBMISSION, HUMILIATION, INTERROGATION, PETTICOAT DISCIPLINE, PROFESSIONAL DOMINATRIX, TORTURE and VICTORIAN LACE)

DISEASES A French doctor named Jacques de Bethencourt named syphilis "morbus venereus" or the sickness of Venus, goddess of love. With time the term venereal diseases (VD), came to include all sexually transmitted diseases. Today the term VD has been changed to Sexually Transmitted Diseases (STD) to reflect a broader scope of transmission. There are currently 32 organisms and 26 syndromes that are thought to be transmitted sexually.

The following information is brief because it is not intended to be used for self diagnosis. Many other diseases have similar symptoms and only a physician is qualified to make a diagnosis.

Diseases are transmitted primarily through an exchange of blood, genital secretions, and skin to skin contact with an infected area. Pathogens such as viruses and bacteria do not normally penetrate through outer skin, but we are more susceptible to sexually transmitted diseases because mucous membranes are involved. Due to the normal enthusiasm experienced during sex, genital tissue can easily be abraded or torn. This is what makes it easier for the pathogens to enter our bodies during sexual contact.

There are many STDs and individuals vary in the types or severity of symptoms they will suffer. Any change in the amount, odor, or color of discharge, and inflammation or texture of the skin may indicate an infection. Physicians recommend that people examine themselves thoroughly to determine a standard or baseline appearance in tissue and discharge. There is a surprising number of small bumps and color variations on the genitals that seem okay now but which can cause sleepless nights if a sex partner confides that they have been seeing someone else and they don't have this baseline reference.

The paramount problem in the transmission of many STDs is that they are asymptomatic (the person will have no symptoms). This is why asking one's partner if they are "clean" or "safe" is not a guarantee of safety. This is also why its important to notify sex partners that may have been exposed to the disease. Most of these diseases are not fatal to an adult and it is easy to justify avoiding the embarrassment of calling old lovers; however, they can cause sterility and other serious complications. It is impossible to foresee how many people an ex-lover can expose to the disease.

It is everyone's individual responsibility to practice safe sex if one is sexually active outside of a primary relationship. In working for a national switchboard dealing with sexually transmitted diseases, I discovered that the majority of people contracted these diseases from 'monogamous' partners. This is because most people let down their guard in what they believe are monogamous relationships and therefore are at more risk when their partner strays than people who practice safe sex in open relationships.

DISEASES	INCUBATION	SYMPTOMS	COMPLICATIONS
AIDS	2 Weeks to 10 years	Diagnosis is based on positive antibody test and one more of the opportunistic diseases as defined by the Centers for Disease Control (CDC)	Destruction of body's immune system and death
CHLAMYDIA	Difficult to Determine	Possibly none Discharge Painful urination F/only) bleeding after intercourse and pelvic pain	Sterility Infection of sex organs Tubal pregnancy Death
GONORRHEA	1-10 Days	Possibly none Discharge Painful urination	Sterility Infection of sex organs Arthritis Endocarditis
HERPES	2-20 Days *May take years	Painful blisters Will dry up and disappear in 5-21 days	Blisters may reoccur May be passed to infant at birth
TRICHOMONAS	Difficult to Determine	Itching, discharge foul odor	Epididymitis Prostate problem Recurrent infections
VAGINITIS	Difficult to Determine	Change in Discharge Itching or burning Painful urination	May occur spontaneously
VENEREAL WARTS	1-6 Months	Cauliflower-like painless bumps near genital Slight itching or burning	May lead to cervical cancer in female May spread to anus Difficult to remove
SYPHILIS	10-90 Days 6-8 Weeks 2-40 Years	PRIMARY: Chancre at site of contact, heals in 7-21 days, swollen lymph glands SECONDARY: Lowgrade fever, headache,weight loss, lymph nodes, hair loss in spots,swollen growth resembling genital warts. Possible recurance of secondary symptoms for several years. TERTIARY STAGE: Large ulcers on skin or bone, cardiovascular and CNS disorders	Eventual paralysis, blindness, insanity, death, transmittable to fetus if not treated within 12 weeks

Safe sex includes things like massage, body rubbing, dry kissing, self masturbation, consensual voyeurism, exhibitionism, or anything else where body fluids are not exchanged. Possible safe sex practices include the use of condoms, french kissing, external water sports, and masturbating one's partner (one can check for undetected cuts by first rubbing peroxide on the skin). The proper use of condoms (refer to section on Birth Control—Condoms) cuts down risks, but only if the condom covers the infected area and does not break. Spermicidal foam, cream, or jelly that has Nonoxynol 9 listed as an ingredient can provide additional protection, although it poses a risk for some women as it can destroy bacteria and cause vaginal yeast infections and it does not completely protect against the AIDS virus. Minimal precautions such as washing with warm soapy water and urinating after sex will reduce the risk of other bacterial infections. Some wash a partner's genitals with a warm wash cloth after sex as a special way of showing affection. Douches are not recommended for a prevention for STDs because the water can push the pathogens farther back into the vagina.

Herpes is often spread during oral sex if a partner has a history of cold sores or during unprotected genital contact with a person who has had outbreaks. The majority of diseases are spread by people who are either not aware that they have the disease or by ones who think they are only contagious when they have an outbreak.

The National STD Hotline provides operators who are available to answer questions and refer people to clinics or physicians. That toll-free number is: 1-800-227-8922. People who have specific questions about AIDS may contact operators at: 1-800-342-2437.

(See also DYSFUNCTIONS, HANDICAPS and SAFE SEX)

DOCKING Docking is a form of masturbation that involves two people, usually men. The foreskin of one partner is pulled back and the other's foreskin is stretched over the tip of his penis. The two penises, after being locked into place, are then stroked so that the skin is moved back and forth over the two glans. It may not be considered docking, but a few women have substituted a dildo for the second penis.

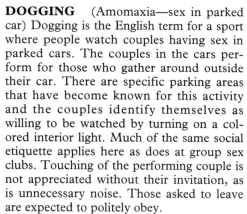

(See also BEE STINGS, BINDINGS, CASTRATION, CHASTITY DEVICES, CIRCUMCISION, COCKRINGS, PENILE LIGATION, PENIS MODIFICATION, PHALLOPHILIA, SACOFRICOSIS, TESTICLES and WEIGHT TRAINING)

DOGGING (Amomaxia—sex in parked car) Dogging is the English term for a sport where people watch couples having sex in parked cars. The couples in the cars perform for those who gather around outside their car. There are specific parking areas that have become known for this activity and the couples identify themselves as willing to be watched by turning on a colored interior light. Much of the same social etiquette applies here as does at group sex clubs. Touching of the performing couple is not appreciated without their invitation, as is unnecessary noise. Those asked to leave are expected to politely obey.

Other couples engage in oral sex or nudity on the highway for the purpose of attracting attention from truck drivers.

(See also CANDAULISM, EXHIBITIONISM and GROUP SEX)

DOMINANCE/SUBMISSION (Cataphilist and Pageism—male submitting to female, Passivism—submission, Top/Bottom—Dominance/Submission) A role of dominance or submission is used in sex play to increase the intensity of emotions and bonding of partners. Dominance in any arena usually involves control which is reinforced by threat of emotional or physical pain.

Dominance and submission both seem to fall into a human's need for security. Clans of primates or groups of animals usually have a dominant figure who regulates the behavior of others. Nature seems to have designed the brain of most species to produce a pleasure response to either type of behavior if engaged in by parties who trust and care for each other. Submission may be induced primarily by accompanying forms of stimulus such as a loss, restriction, or humiliation. Laboratory tests on mice revealed that in a fight endorphins (pleasure response) are released in the injured mouse only at the point of submission. Thus submission, rather than pain, was the critical factor in creating a euphoric response. (See ALGOPHILIA)

Dominance can produce euphoria because it is associated with attainment of a goal, or an object of security. A person who loses control over one facet of their life often tries to compensate for it by overcontrolling in a different area. This behavior may manifest itself in abused children with something as simple as consistent and compulsive placement of shoes in a closet. However, in an adult relationship this compulsive behavior is often acted out through demands and manipulation of another person. Here dominance serves to re-establish a feeling of security or self esteem for the person under stress.

Sexual dominance and submission are used to enhance the role of the characters in fantasy play. Costumes are often used to reinforce each role and makes physical or verbal abuse less necessary. Costumes that project power include policemen, military, doctors, and black leather. Accoutrements used to enforce submission are diapers, feminine lingerie, whips, slave or dog collars, and bondage equipment. A dominant who is only experienced in corporal punishment would not be a match for a submissive who follows orders perfectly and is not into pain. Alternately, a submissive who enjoys punishment for misbehaving or verbal warfare is not a match for a dominant who can't handle competition for control.

The submissive controls the intensity and direction of the game. People often select roles because it provides a change from the ordinary. People who have inhibitions or guilt associated with sexual experimentation find that this seems to relieve them of personal responsibility for their actions. Total sexual submission is used by some as a way to express love. A person who lets a partner

put a dog collar on them feels they are expressing love in a way that words never will. This is perhaps why submissives can sometimes appear to go to extremes.

Dominant sex play is also often engaged in as an entertaining way to refine the management skills needed in all types of professions.

(See also ALGOPHILIA, BLINDFOLDING, BONDAGE, CHASTITY DEVICES, COITUS A CHEVAL, DEFILEMENT, DOMINANCE/SUBMISSION, HUMILIATION, INTERROGATION, PETTICOAT DISCIPLINE, PROFESSIONAL DOMINATRIX, TORTURE and VICTORIAN LACE)

DOMINATRIX, PROFESSIONAL

A professional dominatrix, or mistress, is a woman who is paid to act out an S/M scene with a client. It is much less common to find women who will play the submissive role as this entails much more risk to her health. Those who do submit or bottom rarely work alone. Professional dominatrixes are not considered prostitutes and remain legal so long as they do not engage in sex. The fee for a session ranges between $100-150 an hour depending on the location, type of equipment, whether photos are taken, and the dominatrix' reputation. The woman learns her profession by either having been involved in S/M previously, having an S/M friend teach her, or by  beginning work in an established "dungeon" or organized S/M house that hires and trains dominatrixes. The house gets approximately half of the fee and the professional dominatrix the balance, including tips. One can make a substantial income with a full schedule, although most see only one or two clients a day and spend a lot of time waiting on no-shows. A good dominatrix is intelligent, quick witted, and creative. She has to be good at improvisation to keep clients aroused, submissive, and entertained for an hour. This is much more demanding and difficult than sex.

Europe has many attractive, skilled, and well known dominant professionals. The United States seems to have fewer women enter the profession and fewer still that remain. One reason is that many are unwilling to participate in the variety of practices for which Europeans are known to engage. There are only a few American dominatrixes that have gained a national reputation.

Mistresses find clients by referrals and advertising in fetish magazines or newspapers. Mistresses as well as clients come from all social and professional groups. The only prerequisite for the client is that they pay, obey the no sex, drugs, or alcohol rules, and inform the mistress of acts or humiliation they do not find erotic. The dominatrix should have some knowledge of S/M, bondage and discipline, and safety. In addition, a safeword is assigned that will immediately end the game. The dominatrix has to appear or sound authoritative and in control of the submissive client. A professional can develop such an expertise at dominance and aloofness that often clients complain that she doesn't seem to enjoy the session. Costumes are important to set the proper tone. Black leather, latex, or a whip symbolizes authority and restraints placed on a client ensure submission. It appears that the largest percentage of clients engage in bondage, corporeal punishment, anal play, and cross dressing during the sessions.

Men who are not able to visit professional dominatrixes are provided with optional methods to experience this type of arousal including audio tapes and personal letters. Regular phone sex businesses may have women experienced in domination and some may specialize exclusively in these types of fantasies. (Personal communication with Lady Tanith, California, June 8, 1991.)

Gini Graham Scott, Ph.D., a sociologist-anthropologist, documented her study of dominant women and submissive men in her book titled *Erotic Power, An Exploration of Dominance & Submission*. In this book she interviews professional dominatrixes and their clients as well as non-professionals who find this lifestyle fascinating.

(See also DISCIPLINE, DOMINANCE/SUBMISSION and WORSHIP)

DORAPHILIA (Hyphephilia—arousal from touching skin, hair, leather, fur or fabric) Doraphilia (dora: skin, philia: attachment to) is the love of fur or skin. This attraction is usually for animal skin or leather, which has been used as clothing throughout human existence. It is considered a fetish when it has to be present during sex. Human skin holds a fascination for some people. The 1950s sex criminal, Edward Gein, who derived pleasure from skinning female corpses he exhumed from local graves and then wearing them like a garment, is reported to have become fascinated with the idea of changing himself from male to female. There have been cases where people have used human skin to make purses, lamp shades, belts, and upholstery. This was apart from similar things done to men with tattoos during the Holocaust. Captain John Bourke wrote of human flesh being used as girdles or mummies that were worn by pregnant women to assist them in labor.

The feel and smell of leather gives many people a feeling of power. Some explain this as subconsciously taking on the character of the animal with whose skin they cloak themselves. This was a common belief of holy men during their ancient religious ceremonies. The Roman emperor Nero dressed in an animal skin and then emulated the beast's ferocious behavior as he sexually assaulted the people he had tied to stakes.

An explanation for the continued appeal of leather or fur is that some people feel secure and nurtured by being wrapped in skin, a sort of surrogate mother effect. Clinical studies showed that rhesus monkeys who had their mothers replaced by inanimate objects responded better or clung to the ones that were wrapped in some type of fur.

Many people who use leather for erotic feelings or as a symbol of their sexual power prefer the color black. The motives behind this preference are not clear. Historical facts regarding the color reveal that the ancient Egyptians revered the color as a sign of fertility because black was the color of the rich soil along the Nile. This may also be the origin of the black gowns used in witchcraft or other ancient religions. The Japanese, some Egyptians, American Indians, Christians, and Hindus saw it as a sign of destruction or death. Europeans dressed in black garments to attend funerals so that they would not be recognized as human and harmed by ghosts. Conversely, black Africans dressed in white clothing at funerals for the same reason. Today black is perceived as a symbol of evil, elegance, authority, and religion (*Stories Behind Everyday Things*, by J. Polley, ed., Reader's Digest).

Erotic leather apparel can be purchased at some lingerie and leather shops or ordered from Europe. Leather jock straps (some with chrome studs), bikini panties with zippered crotches, body suits, bras, corsets, dresses, skirts, pants exposing the rear, costumes, and accessories are all available.

(See BINDINGS, BULL FIGHTS, FETISHES and ZOOPHILIA)

DOUCHES   A douche is a jet of liquid that penetrates into the vagina or rectum. Douches are used for hygiene, birth control, and sex games.

ANAL   Anal enemas are often referred to as douches by gay men. These are done for hygienic purposes prior to anal intercourse. This differs from klismaphilia (enemas) which is part of the sex play and is administered by a partner.

GOLDEN DOUCHE   This is another type of douching used in sex play. It is the act of urinating directly into the vagina or anus after ejaculation. The partner has the sensation of being filled with semen for a second time. This is mechanically difficult and something very few men accomplish. CAUTION: Golden douches are not considered safe sex.

VAGINAL   There are sex games where people insert the top rim of a champagne bottle into a partner's vagina and drain the contents. The champagne is then sucked out of the vagina. Vaginal douching is most often used as a method of birth control. This is often not effective because it takes as

little as two minutes for sperm to enter the cervical canal. CAUTION: Frequent douching is not recommended by physicians as the vagina cleans itself by a natural flow of lubricants. The vagina also has a regulated amount of bacteria and chemicals that can be thrown out of balance by spermicides, alkaline, and deodorant douches. Women wearing an IUD are particularly discouraged from this practice. Commercial deodorants and douches have been known to prevent conception in otherwise fertile women. A more serious risk is that of having the liquid, under high pressure, enter into the uterus, Fallopian tubes, and eventually the peritoneum, where it can cause serious damage and possibly require surgery.

(See also BIRTH CONTROL, KLISMAPHILIA and STUFFING)

DRAG QUEENS   (Cross-dressing—wearing clothing of the opposite sex or age group, Gynemimesis—female impersonation in male who is unable to become sexually aroused by females) Drag queens vary in style and purpose. There are gays who dress as women, male prostitutes who are trying to pass as female, and others who find the character change cathartic, challenging, amusing, or entertaining.

Drag queens who enjoy entertaining frequent bars, parades, fairs, or other events where they can perform. One San Francisco area drag queen had developed several characters and used them according to which event and statement he wanted to make. He attended the gays' protest demonstration against a group of fundamentalists as an omnisexual that was half feminine and half masculine (i.e. corset and jock strap). This was a character that could flirt with any sex and did. He attended the Folsom Street Fair as Mrs. Trauma Flintstone, who being recently divorced from an abusive husband, didn't care at all about sex but loved to sing and perform for the crowd.

Male prostitutes who are attracted to heterosexual men are sometimes successful in hiding their male genitals when they restrict their activity to fellatio and keep the partner's hands out of their panties. Drag queens have become the rage in Italy, where heterosexuals prefer their outrageous costumes and the fact that they can have sex with a man without feeling particularly gay themselves. Often men who live in countries where females are expected to be virgin upon marriage are more tolerant of prostitutes and drag queens. A man in these cultures is not considered gay unless he takes the receptive role.

Gays are divided on whether they want a partner to dress in female attire. A gay male in Utah enjoyed preparing candlelit dinners for his date and meeting him at the door in women's lingerie. His dates had reactions that ranged from pleasure and amusement to indifference or disgust.

(See also TRANSVESTITES)

DUNGEONS A dungeon is a room that is specially furnished for sexual activity.

The room is designed to offer complete privacy and some have additional soundproofing. Equipment and toys may or may not be displayed. People decorate their dungeons to look like medieval torture chambers, stages, barns, child's rooms, guest bedrooms, special fantasy scenes, or they just take a room and hang a collage of their favorite equipment on the walls.

Dungeons may be used exclusively by the owners and their guests, rented to friends, the public, or clubs for play parties and lectures. The basic rental dungeon will

include hooks and chains in the ceiling for suspension, a 6"x6" beam for standing bondage (probably wrapped with rope for comfort), a mattress, wall mirrors, a chair, and bathroom. Extra items may include a hanging chair swing, rape rack, body harness, cage, box, stocks, gynecological exam table, hospital gurney, dental or barber chair, and stereo. People usually supply their own costumes, flagellation equipment, or toys.

The two sketches of dungeons show the diverse range of possibilities. One dungeon

displays an array of S/M equipment, such as a mask, cane, riding crop, ostrich feather, candle, lubricant, puppet, mirror, scarf tie, 4 bed posts, razor and basin, brush, hooks for suspension, bridle, slave collar, leash, bull whip, penis whip, and horse. The

other dungeon has a wall mirror, hanging chair sling, 6"x6" beam with chains, and wrist straps.

(See also BONDAGE, FANTASY PLAY, FLAGELLATION, GENITAL/ANAL INSERTS, KNIVES, MEDICAL SCENES, PROFESSIONAL DOMINATRIX and SWINGS)

DYSFUNCTIONS Sexual dysfunctions are either physical or psychological. A few are listed as follows:

AZOOSPERMIA Azoospermia is the partial or total absence of spermatozoa in ejaculate. It is caused by a blockage between the testicles and urinary tract or can be caused by testicles that do not produce spermatozoa. Azoospermia sometimes responds to treatment or surgery.

CRYPTORCHIDISM Cryptorchidism is the failure of one or both testicles to descend after a male is born. If the testicle fails to drop into the scrotum before puberty, it will be sterile and will eventually atrophy. Surgery is usually successful when done early. Later, plastic testicles can be surgically implanted into the scrotum for aesthetic purposes. Hitler was thought to have had only one descended testicle, although his close friends denied this as propaganda.

EPISPADIAS Epispadias occurs if the urethra opens up on the upper surface of the penis instead of extending through the center to the tip of the glans penis. This condition is called hypospadias when the urethra opens on the underside of the penis. Both conditions can be corrected by surgery.

FILARIASIS This is commonly referred to as elephantiasis and is an enlarging of an arm, leg, or scrotum caused by a prolonged obstruction of circulation in the lymphatic vessels by filarial worms. It is common in tropical countries and is carried by

mosquitoes. The scrotum of some men become so large that they have to be carried in wheel barrows.

GYNECOMASTIA is the condition where a male will have enlarged breasts. It is caused by fatty deposits and can occur in eunuchs or men being treated with female hormones to arrest prostate cancer. This condition is also common in boys during puberty but will usually disappear itself within a few months. Male hormone treatments are available for those who become concerned with their condition.

RETROGRADE EJACULATION This is an ejaculation where the sperm is pushed into the bladder instead of out of the urethra. It occurs when the internal bladder sphincter opens and the external urethral sphincter closes, causing the semen to enter the bladder. This condition may be caused by injury, diabetes, use of some tranquilizers, or prostate surgery. For couples wishing to have children it is possible for a physician to immediately remove semen from the bladder with a tube and insert it into the female partner's vagina.

PENIS DEVIATIONS This deviation refers specifically to bent penises. One may be born with this or it can be caused later due to an injury. It can be sustained during sex by the penis being bent into a crooked position, occur as a result of natural hardening of the corpora cavernosa when a man grows older, or due to an illness such as Peyronie's disease. Most deviating penises curve toward the body when erect but a small percent curve forward, sometimes making entry and thrusting painful for a partner. The direction a penis curves in this case may simply be due to the position the man kept his penis in as a child. For example, a forward curving penis can sometimes be caused by a boy tucking his penis back

between his legs. A urologist can be consulted if the bend seems abnormal.

PRIAPISM Priapism is the condition where the penis stays erect. This is often painful and can be caused by acute cases of gonorrhea, leukemia, prostate problems, spinal injuries, or an overdose of drugs that treat impotence. At one time leeches were used to suck out the blood. Today common treatments include wrapping with elastic bandages, cold baths, and sometimes surgery.

SIAMESE DEFORMITIES Daniel P. Mannix, in his book, *FREAKS: We Who are Not as Others*, mentions a man named Frank Lentini who had two complete sets of genitals. Lentini was born in 1889 as a partial siamese triplet. The only portions of the parasitic brothers that attached themselves to Lentini were a set of genitals, a leg, and two feet. Lentini joined the circus at a young age and earned a fortune with his performances. There is no information as to whether both penises were functional, however, he did marry and father four children.

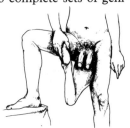

SPERM DEFECTS Sperm itself can be defective and not capable of fertilization. They can become two-headed, tailless, small or large headed. None of these conditions facilitate the rapid movement necessary to enter and reach a waiting egg. The mucosal plug that blocks the entrance of the cervix likewise acts as a screening mechanism, allowing only healthy and well formed sperm to enter. (*How to Get Pregnant* by Sherman J. Silber, M.D.)

(See also DISEASES and HANDICAPS)

DYSMORPHOPHILIA (Morphophilia—arousal from person with a different physique) Dysmorphophilia (dys: abnormal, morphe: form, philia: attachment to) refers to those who are sexually aroused by deformities in their partners. These may include things such as club feet, scars, dwarfs, mastectomies, hunchbacks, etc.

There are bordellos that cater to these tastes and recently a London fashion magazine featured photos of models with long fake noses or ears.

The attraction to people who possess these features is similar to the attraction of those who find amputees appealing. For some the strong sense of compassion or fear may condition them to overreact later and possibly confuse this excitement with sexual arousal. Others feel emotionally secure or in control when their partner does not have the perceived ability to leave them for someone else. Others need to nurture or rescue a sex partner to feel love or bonding and some are simply attracted by novelty.

(See also ACROTOMOPHILIA, APOTEM-NOPHILIA, CASTRATION, CHUBBY CHAS-ER, HERMAPHRODITE, PARAPHILIAS, PODOPHILIA and TRANSSEXUALS)

E

ECOUTEURISM   Ecouteurism is similar to acousticophilia in that sounds arouse the person. However, ecouterism is nonconsensual and the stimulus comes more from this fact rather than from what is heard. This is similar to the kleptophile who is aroused by the danger and courage involved in stealing rather than by the object they steal. This is also true of a peeping Tom, exhibitionist, or obscene phone caller. Similarly, an ecouteurist will use the stimulus from eavesdropping as an aid for masturbation.

Sexual ecouteurism involves intentionally listening to someone else's personal conversations or sexual exploits through doors, walls, telephone lines, and with special electronic listening devices. Some of these devices look somewhat like a megaphone and are capable of picking up low level noise from 100 feet away. An ecouteurist may be a voyeur as well, but the two do not always occur simultaneously.

Many people are aroused unintentionally by overhearing a couple engaging in sex from an adjoining bedroom or when attending a group sex function. This is a normal reaction for most people.

(See also CANDAULISM, COPROLALIA, JACTITATION and VOYEURISM)

ELECTRIC SHOCK   (Electrophilia—arousal from electricity)Electric shock is used as a form of titillation or light torture depending on the amount of voltage chosen by the recipient. This type of sex play always elicits some type of excitement; however, technical knowledge of the apparatus and a partner's physical safety is essential. Many scientists have accidently been executed while experimenting with electricity. Benjamin Franklin was probably the first to deliberately use it to take life as he experimented with animals. A century later, in 1886, a scientist employed at Edison's laboratory patented the electric chair. After demonstrating the  chair to a government commission by electrocuting a cow and a horse, he took this act on the road to entertain crowds throughout the United States.

This contraption was endorsed by the government and prisoners began being executed in this manner, soon rendering hangings obsolete. Humans electrocuted in these chairs were given 1,700 volts of alternating current for 30 seconds. Unconsciousness was almost immediate and death came in 2-3 seconds. The approach was merciful when the system functioned correctly; of course, there were prisoners that had to be electrocuted twice.

Shock as a form of sex play is a modified and safe version of the types of electrical shock government officials used in different countries to interrogate political prisoners and by American prison guards to control their prisoners.

Most devices used in sex play are inconsequential by comparison. They are small battery operated gadgets that resemble a flashlight. Other devices, such as the titolator, two-celled cattle prods, used medical machines, and telephone magnetos (which are used to make shock units that feature a hand crank and wire contact) can be purchased or modified. The lubricant or solution used on the electrodes that touch the body have a salt content; some simply add salt to KY-gel or aloe vera.

It is dangerous to place the electrical contacts above the waist. The reason for this is that electric current travels from one contact point directly to the other. Therefore, to avoid the risk of the current passing near or through the heart the contacts are never placed on the chest, arms, or nipples. Both people take time before the shock treatment to make a final safety check for liquids or metal objects that could be touching their bodies.

House current with isolation or GFI (ground fault interrupters) and transformers are mandatory. DC batteries are safer but many complain that they create skin burns and the person usually only feels the power come on and go off. Human tissue varies in the amount of resistance (measured in ohms) it gives to electrical current; therefore, what is safe for one person may cause injury to others. Some tops prefer to give the control of the rheostat to the bottom. This makes the person responsible for their own decisions ("The shocking art of electrical torment" by Fledermaus, *Dungeon Master No. 8*, January 1981, p. 18).

The Japanese use a special battery operated device to induce orgasm in men. This box has two wires with electrodes, one is attached to the end of the penis and the other is inserted into the rectum. The man then regulates the current with a rheostat until orgasm. This device is used by physicians to eject sperm from impotent men to use for artificial insemination and similarly by veterinarians for breeding livestock. American inventors sold an electrical device in the early 20th century making boasts, backed by a guarantee, that it not only cured impotency and nocturnal emissions, but could increase the size of men's organs as well. (*EROS*, by R. Ginzburg, Spring,

1962) CAUTION: People have died from miscalculating voltage and time restrictions while masturbating alone. ("Electrical Applications," by J. Bruce, QSM lecture, December 2, 1990)

(See also ALGOPHILIA, GENITAL/ANAL INSERTS, INTERROGATION, POWER TOOLS, SAFE SEX, SENSORY ENHANCEMENT and TORTURE)

EMETOPHILIA   (Roman shower) Emetophilia (emein: to vomit; philia: attachment to) refers to those who are aroused by vomit or vomiting. These people usually ingest wine or urine and then vomit it out; sometimes onto their partner. A few men have deliberately encouraged their date to overeat and drink. Afterward, using this condition to stimulate vomiting by using their penis during fellatio to start a gag reflex in their partner.

(See also SHOWERS)

ENDYTOPHILIA   (Endytolagnia) Endytophilia refers to people who prefer their sex partners to be dressed rather than naked. (See CHEMISE CAGOULE, FETISHES and TRANSVESTITES)

ENEMAS See KLISMAPHILIA

EROTIC BALLS   There are several world renowned erotic balls. The San Francisco Exotic Erotic Ball is held every year for Halloween and New Year's Eve. Thousands of people with exotic costumes crowd into large warehouses near the wharf. Constance Enterprises hosts an annual Fall fetish costume ball and fashion show in New York. The author of *The Safer Sex Maniac's Bible*, Miss Tuppy Owens, sponsors an annual Sex Maniac's Ball in London as a fund-raiser for people with disabilities. Guests wear costumes from their favorite fantasies. The Eccentric Fashion Show attracts people to Switzerland every year and Melbourne Australia hosts an annual Hookers and Deviants Ball.

Many of the sex oriented symposiums such as Lifestyles and the National Sexuality Symposium have a Saturday evening erotic ball for attendees.

The San Francisco Exotic Erotic Ball has been compared to an indoor Rio Carnival; however, the Latins wear more revealing costumes. Attendance at this Halloween ball begins with waiting in line outside the building for up to an hour. At least, unlike theatre lines, this one is quite entertaining— or enough so that crowds of spectators gather around all evening to catch glimpses of what people are wearing under their trench coats. People finally enter the gigantic rooms already filled with thousands of excited voices and music from live bands. Most people either take photos or model. Photographers often convince women to pose in an erotic fashion for them or with them. People wear costumes of vegetables, vampires, witches, monsters, cave men, half naked brides, human dildos, robots, doctors, and priests. The S/M and leather people attend in their regular playwear. One year a dominatrix gave a whipping and fisting demonstration with her slave, but this is a rare event. Ordinarily the most one sees is an occasional couple discreetly engaging in fellatio or lap dancing. The crowd begins to thin at midnight and those remaining are often inebriated.

(See also SEX CLUBS, SEX CONFERENCES, SEX HOTELS and SEX SHOWS)

EROTICA Erotica is a term that currently refers to literature or photography that depicts sex in a more subtle or socially redeeming manner than does pornography.

(See also PORNOGRAPHY)

EROTOGRAPHOMANIA Erotographomania refers to a strong desire to write love letters or poems. This was more common before the invention of the telephone.

(See also COPROGRAPHY, COURTSHIP, JACTITATION, OBSCENE PHONE CALLS and PHONE SEX)

EROTOMANIA (De Clerambault's syndrome, Groupies, Old Maid's Insanity, Psychose passionelle)

Erotomania (abnormally strong sexual desire) is a term that has come to refer to someone who develops an "overwhelming conviction, amounting to a delusional

belief," that someone with whom he or she has little or no actual contact is deeply in love with him or her ("De Clerambault's Syndrome," by Joyce L. Dunlop, MA, MB, BCh. BAO, MRCPsych, DObst. RCOG, British Journal of Sexual Medicine, August 1989, pp. 306-7). This person's love objects are often prominent figures who are not even conscious of their existence other than the fan's repeated letters and appearance at stage doors waiting for autographs or souvenirs. Some may throw underwear at their love object as they perform on stage. Gloria Estefan is said to have at least twelve pairs of men's underwear thrown at her feet per performance. (Of course, not everyone throwing underwear at a performer has the delusion that the performer returns their admiration.) P. Ellis and G. Mellsop listed eight criteria for this syndrome:

delusions of amorous communication which have not been initiated by the patient

higher rank of love object as perceived by the patient

perceived approach by the other person

sudden onset

single unchanged object

explanations of paradoxical behavior given by the patient

chronic course

absence of hallucinations

("De Clerambault's Syndrome—A Nosological Entity?"; by Ellis P., Mellsop G., *Br J Psych*, 1985; 146: 90-93).

People who suffer from erotomania have a similar background to those who are attached to fetishes. They generally experience some type of isolation or emotional distancing from parents while young. A normal relationship is difficult and each has replaced their need for love with a fantasy object.

Problems not only arise from the fan's efforts to spend time with the celebrity but also when the fan's love turns to revenge because of perceived rejection. Several movie stars have been assaulted and some murdered due to this psychosis. The erotomaniac does not always return the affection they think the other person gives them. Jonathan H. Segal, M.D. included an example of one of these cases in the October 1989 issue of *American Journal of Psychiatry* 146:10:

Ms. B, a 65-year-old retired clerk, was admitted for psychiatric treatment following her attack on an elderly bank manager who lived in her apartment building. She claimed that although he had never spoken to her out loud, he had been contacting her telepathically for months with romantic messages; she 'hinted' that these messages contained sexual overtones. She said that she could tell he was interested in her by the way he looked at her. After she accosted him several times to protest, he denied any interest in her and obtained a restraining order barring any contact between them. Unable to restrain her indignation, she followed him to his office, leaped at him across his desk, and allegedly tried to strangle him. Later, however, she admitted only to having touched his tie... (Erotomania Revisited: From Kraepelin to DSM-III-R, p. 1264).

(See also FETISHES, LOVE, LOVE ADDITION and PARAPHILIAS)

ESSAYEURS   Essayeurs were men whose services were retained by Parisian brothels. It was their responsibility to fondle the prostitutes and engage in overt sexual behavior in front of timid male clients. This relaxed the clients enough for them to participate themselves. This is the same psychology used by some casinos when they employ shills to encourage others to gamble.

(See also BORDELLOS, CANDAULISM, PIMPS and PROSTITUTION)

EUGENICS   Eugenics refers to the philosophy that offspring should be controlled for genetic purity. This has been attempted throughout history by several methods. Nature usually destroys its weak or diseased by spontaneous abortion or miscarriage. Deformed infants who escaped nature's selection process were often disposed of after birth.

There are several men who have gained notoriety for their belief in eugenics. A respected lawyer in ancient Greece, Lycurgus, favored preconception selection and encouraged weak or old men to let younger men impregnate their wives in order to improve the race. Much later, John Noyes, founder of the late 19th century Oneida Community, implemented the practice of propagation by scientific selection. A limited number of healthy men in this community were allowed to impregnate women, although all were allowed to perform a type of coitus reservatus with consenting women. Conjugation could last an hour with the purpose of letting the woman have as many orgasms as possible during this period of time. However, the man himself was not allowed to ejaculate even after withdrawal and masturbation was forbidden.

The Nobel Sperm Bank was founded in 1980 by Robert Graham in Escondido California. Graham believed that for a Nobel winner or other notable achiever to die with only a few heirs, or perhaps none, was a sad waste of genes.

There is controversy about whether intelligence and achievement is genetic and concern over the pressure some parents put on children who are conceived for this purpose.

(See also BIRTH CONTROL, CUCKOLDRY, LESBIANS and SPERM BANKS)

EUNUCHS   A eunuch is a man who does not have functioning testicles, or whose testicles and/or penis have been removed.

The worshipers of Aphrodite, the Goddess of Love, had an annual ceremony where a young priest was sacrificed and in the ensuing frenzy other men would cut off their penises and splatter the blood on her statue as their personal sacrificial offering. Those surviving then joined her service as eunuch priests.

The eunuch priests of Cybele conducted similar rites, offering their severed penises on her altar and afterward adopting women's clothing, and dedicating themselves to temple service which often included prostitution. The Catholic Church has a law that no pope may rule who has been castrated or whose genitals are otherwise deformed. Cardinals at one time acted as inspectors and would walk past the pope, who sat in a special chair exposing his genitals, confirming their approval by chanting "testiculos habet et bene pendentes."

It became common for slave traders to castrate male slaves. These were then sold throughout the Middle East as guards, servants, and managers. The orient commonly used castrated men as servants, cooks, musicians, guards, executioners, and torturers. The use of slaves in harems began in the 7th century and still exists in parts of Africa and Saudi Arabia.

Middle Eastern eunuchs were able to gain political power within the confines of the harem and many acquired great wealth and status. A black Turkish eunuch, Kislar Agha, came to exercise supreme power and when he died, left a sum of 30,000,000 piasters along with many other riches. He had been purchased for 30 piasters. Other eunuchs led revolutions, deposed sultans, or were given respectable titles and very high ranks. As late as 1877 a head eunuch, Hafiz Beheram, was said to have more power than the Grand Vizier or Prime Minister. The hiring of eunuchs in the Church was finally forbidden by Leo XIII in 1878; primarily to end the misuse of castrati.

(Refer also to CASTRATION, CELIBACY and HAREMS)

EXECUTIONS   Some people experience vicarious stimulation through watching others face death by execution. Once a person becomes anxious it is possible to transpose any of the basic emotions caused by the fight, flight, sex response. The spectators at a public execution who might have been angered by the crime of the victim may also feel avenged by the death; sympathy is absent.

Casanova and Hirschfeld were only two who wrote about women who masturbated while viewing or waiting for the finale of an execution and the orgies that followed. Englishmen knew that to break down a woman's resistance or scruples he simply had to get her to attend a public execution.

This was said to work much more efficiently than wine.

The Romans mixed violence and lust at their Theatre on a much grander scale. The games involved rape of children by men and beasts, followed by mutilation and murder. Even the Empresses Messalina and Theodora masturbated and had sex in the stands while watching the events. Daniel Mannix, in his book *Those About to Die,* told of young boys who learned to position themselves next to unescorted women and when they became overly ecstatic at the sight in the arena the boy seized the opportunity to grab and fondle them. Prostitutes worked below the stands and lined the roads leading out of the arena to service the numerous men who as yet had not relieved themselves. The Romans were not all mere spectators; there were those who enjoyed molesting and taunting prisoners as they were marched into the arena to face death. Mannix, in addition to describing the Roman lust for executions, cited an example during the 20th century of the wife of an officer at Buchenwald, who would in a similar fashion fondle prisoners on their way to the gas chamber.

Castrations, tortures, and hangings were public spectacles in the States until quite recently. In 1936 20,000 people gathered to watch the hanging of a 22 year old who had murdered an elderly woman in Kentucky. Once "pronounced dead, souvenir hunters fought over the hood that covered his head, ripped off pieces of his clothing and even tried to cut chunks of flesh from his hanging body" (*The Encyclopedia of American Crime,* p. 241). R.E.L. Masters and Allen Edwardes, in their book *Perverse Crimes in History,* wrote of the Arab-Israeli conflict when scores of stripped and castrated Haganah men were photographed by Muslims. These photos of dead and mutilated Jews were reproduced and sold. The public purchased them "like hotcakes."

Military leaders were usually aware of the death/sex phenomenon among soldiers in action and provided prostitutes, permitted rape, slavery, and marriage of the conquered. At other times military leaders, influenced by religious zealots or Victorian physicians, imposed severe penalties for those who engaged in any form of immorality or sex.

(See also BULL FIGHTS, LUST MURDER, MORTALITY, NECROPHILIA and PARA-PHILIAS)

EXHIBITIONISM (Peodeiktophilia—arousal from shocking others with exposure of genitals) An exhibitionist or scopophile is one who derives erotic pleasure from the display of genitals or other body parts that are normally considered taboo. Exhibitionism is common among primates and humans as foreplay. The exhibitionists, however, usually expose themselves without the consent of their audience or the intent of consummating the act.

Historically exhibitionism has been an essential part of certain fertility rites or worship service to gods who themselves were represented with exposed organs. Fertility gods are still worshiped in parts of the world. East Indian priests during the early 20th century would walk through the streets naked ringing bells to call out female devotees from their homes. The women would then pay reverence to the priest's reproductive organ by embracing it. Women, in a few societies, use the exposure of their genitals to catch the eye of a favored male. Ford and Beach wrote of the West African Dahomean women using this method. Those belonging to a serpent cult wore a short shirt and would drop it to expose their genitals to any man catching their eye. Blackwood describes a method used by females of the Kurtatchi [Solomon Islands]:

A woman desiring sexual intercourse with a man who does not make advances to her will, when opportunity arises, lie down in his presence with her legs apart, a position otherwise regarded as indecent. . . . If a woman exposes her genitals, even unwittingly, as in sleep, the situation is liable to be taken advantage of by any man whose passions may thereby be aroused (*Both Sides of Buka Passage*, by B. Blackwood, p. 125).

There are many degrees of exhibitionism and reasons or benefits obtained therefrom. The act may be consensual or nonconsensual; however, it must provide enough per-ceived ego boost, novelty, embarrassment, defilement, or other discomfort to produce the high level of stimuli needed to create the physical sensations necessary for orgasm. If the display or act does not produce the amount of adrenalin and hormones needed for a psychic or genital orgasm, the individual will supplement with masturbation, sex with a partner, or end the experience with whatever level of arousal was produced.

A certain amount of preliminary anxiety or arousal is present with exhibition, as with many other forms of anticipated sex. An exhibitionist will become stimulated as they plan what to wear, where to flash, and to whom or what type of person they want to flash. Coordinating the right sequence of events and location can add to the tension. The exhibitionist will get some level of excitement from the experience whether they are successful in exposing themselves or not. Some men walk around with their penis protruding from their zipper but hidden beneath an overcoat.

Most exhibitionists feel at some level that the stimulation is mutual. It is an adult game of "I'll show you mine, if you show me yours." The fact that they generally select the young indicates that they may be fixated on a childhood experience. This type of voyeur/exhibitionist is generally found on jogging trails, around swimming pools, or ladies restrooms. The exhibitionist sometimes feels their exposure is reciprocal due to either the revealing swimsuit of the victim or to the previous type of genital activity in which the women engaged while in the toilet.

Other exhibitionists derive pleasure from assumed defilement of the religious or innocent. This type would not be stimulated or risk exposing themself to anyone who might give any response other than horror. This exhibitionist chooses to expose themselves at churches, in school yards, and to children from inside their cars.

Comedian exhibitionists love the shock effect. This is probably the only type who doesn't mind laughter. This group usually "moon," or expose naked buttocks to victims of their own age group and because the excitement comes from shock rather than sexual fantasy. Their victims can be of either sex. An example of this type of exhibitionism taken from another culture is that of the Egyptians in Portside City. Ships, after the end of World War II (1948), would travel along the Suez Canal and as they passed a desolate area as many as 20 naked native men would line up along the shore. Each man had a drum that he would thump with their erect penises in rhythm to a song that sounded much like: "Hubba Hubba - thump thump - Hubba Hubba - thump thump." (Personal communication.)

The exhibitionist does not always have to be present to experience the thrill; some men mail nude photos to women they assume will be shocked. This practice is common among people responding to personal ads. Swinger magazines that allow photos to accompany personal ads seem to afford exhibitionists the opportunity of consensually exposing themselves to hundreds of readers. Some of these people, including couples, eventually mail each other photos on a regular basis. The common stereotype is that of a stalking male in an overcoat; however, many couples participate in this form of excitement by having sex in public where there is a risk of discovery. This is done at nudist camps, in cars, parks, elevators, backs of theaters, hot tubs, swimming pools, or in a guest bedroom during a party. Some hosts are aware of this proclivity and provide a bedroom for this purpose by placing a sign on the door that identifies its inevitable function, such as: "For Participants Only," "Voyeurs Permitted," or "By Invitation Only."

Some people get excited by exposing their intentions to others, as in the case of those who purchase magazines or books with explicit sexual photos or titles when there is a person at the register to whom they are sexually attracted, hoping that person will initiate a conversation with them.

Exhibitionists also consist of those who don't expose themselves but rather get a vicarious thrill from having their partner do it. Women are encouraged to go without underwear and to expose their genitals to other men during excursions. They may also be requested to undress in a place where there is a risk of discovery.

Women rarely get accused of exhibitionism even when they wear short skirts and no underwear. A man, on the other hand, is judged much more harshly and no place is found in a formal social gathering for revealing and seductive attire. One of the reasons for this is that of implied consent and power. Men are much more willing to give consent to a display of nudity by a woman (other than their wife or daughter) than to one by a man. A woman almost always feels threatened by the difference in physical strength and potential aggression between the sexes. A woman does not consider herself capable of stopping a man who might decide to extend this type of teasing foreplay into a nonconsensual sex act. Women are socialized to be prudish and are offended more by the nudity; however, when the threat of aggression and social mores are lifted women have the capacity of becoming overtly aggressive. Women who attend professional male strip shows often unleash their passion because they feel they are in a safe environment.

Women engage in partial exhibitionism in the form of revealing clothing. This began in America when arranged marriages became obsolete and women were thrown into competition with each other for suitable mates. Personal appearance in both sexes gained significance. The ads  that previously displayed women as matronly and dowdy now exhibited young, pretty, and fashionably dressed women. Women began selecting their own mates; it was no longer an arrangement made between the father and future husband. The courtship period gave many women power over men for the first time, power being in the hands of the possessor of something someone else wants. Therefore, a woman who was attractive and/or exposed herself just enough to titillate a man without sacrificing her reputation created an advantage in marriage negotiations for herself. Conversely, men during this time lost the power they previously enjoyed. They could no longer barter for a wife, they had to win her heart by showing compassion, respect, charm, bravery, social status, and so forth. Letters written between betrothed couples changed in content from a discussion of friends, relatives, and marriage arrangements to love, affection, grief due to separation, and sex. Many men felt frustrated, inept, and sometimes resentful over this new role reversal. For the first time in American history, they began to use whistling, cat calls, or verbal propositions to humiliate attractive women on the street. For some this was a way of venting anger for the power women now had over their egos. Other men, similar to the exhibitionist, used these verbal insults and compliments as a way of saying: "Look at me, aren't I desirable, aren't I worth your attention" (*Intimate Matters, A History of Sexuality in America*, by John D'Emilio and Estelle B. Freedman).

Nudist colonies, group sex houses, and S/M play parties allow people to indulge in legal nudity or exhibitionism. Many people find exhibitionism to be arousing, whether the excitement comes from strutting one's physique, defying taboos, being placed in bondage and put on display, teasing or seducing a potential partner, or having sex with a partner while others watch.

A person who uses nonconsensual and illegal exhibition as their primary sexual outlet would benefit from professional assistance and support. CAUTION: Police and psychologists consider exhibitionists to be relatively harmless. In any case, it is potentially dangerous for a woman to go near a man in an isolated area, whether he is exposing himself or not.

(See also AGORAPHILIA, AGREXOPHILIA, BODY PAINTING, BONDAGE, CANDAULISM, DOGGING, DRAG QUEENS, ENDYTOPHILIA, EROTIC BALLS, EROTOGRAPHOMANIA, ESSAYEURS, GROUP SEX, HANDKERCHIEF CODES, HOMILOPHILIA, JACTITATION, NUDITY, PHOTOGRAPHY, SACOFRICOSIS, SEX SHOWS and STRIPPING)

F

FAINTING   Hyperventilation is a common cause of dizziness and fainting during sex. People, as they become overly excited, breathe quickly, lowering the carbon dioxide in the blood and changing its acidity. Breathing into a paper bag can stop hyperventilation. If a person faints they will return to consciousness without any assistance; this is not usually considered a medical emergency.

There are also other reasons people pass out. People who get involved in sex play learn their partner's medical history in order to determine whether they fainted out of ecstasy, a pacemaker quit, insulin shock, a seizure, new medication, or haven't slept for three days. If a person has a medical condition that may cause them to pass out, the exact procedure and who needs to be called is written out for their partner ahead of time.

Fainting can be caused by an injury that occasionally results from suspension, or blood sports; this requires immediate attention. The person's pulse and breathing is monitored for a couple of minutes and they are not moved unless they aren't breathing in which case it is necessary to open an airway or to give CPR. A person gaining consciousness may be dizzy and in need of assistance. A person may experience headaches for up to a week after a head injury. An ambulance is called for major bleeding wounds, after having a clean compress held against them. The exception to this is a wound caused by sharp foreign objects (broken glass) that may still be in the skin. This will require pressure on vessels around the wound if the amount of blood loss demands it. Embarrassing sex equipment is not moved from the room because the emergency crew needs to get a visual impression of how far the person fell, what they may have fallen onto, whether the marks on their body were due to the fall or flagellation. A person who gets injured often goes into shock and therefore many automatically treat them for shock. Symptoms of shock appear as a feeling of weakness, nausea, thirst, dizziness, coolness, trembling, weak and rapid pulse, shallow breath, pale moist cool skin, sweating, or dilated pupils. A person is made to lie down, with feet slightly elevated (exception is when there is severe bleeding above the hips). Their clothes are loosened to make it easy for them to breathe. They are covered with a blanket if they feel cool but not if it is hot. The person is also calmed and made to feel safe. If a person can walk, and is not actively bleeding, weak, dizzy, or short of breath, it is often appropriate to simply drive the person to an emergency room.

(See also ORGASMS and SAFE SEX)

FAKIR MUSAFAR   Fakir Musafar is the pseudonym of a genteel and quite amiable San Francisco advertising executive who ventured on a path of ritu-
alistically probing and
expanding the confines of
the physical body with
techniques   used   by
shamans and other early
twentieth century primitive
tribes while still a child.
Fakir labeled himself a
modern primitive but kept
his experimentations secret until his early fifties. He has gone public with his amazing feats of endurance in order to bring the long forgotten mystical entity back into the lives of a stoic and undisciplined culture. Fakir quickly gained the awe and respect of even the most accomplished sadomasochists. It is doubtful that any human in history has personally experienced all the cross-cultural rituals of passage and shamanistic ordeals. There are probably very few if any Christian mystics who have had as many out-of-body spiritual experiences.

Fakir has engaged in primitive piercings, stretchings, bindings, bandings, American Indian Sun Dancing (hanging from a tree by a string connected to two sticks pierced through the pectoral muscles), genital encasements, tattooing, encumberments, pinching ordeals, wearing weights hung on hooks, corsetting, gilding, hanging his whole body from flesh hooks, lying on a bed of nails, lying on the edges of a group of six razor sharp knife blades, as well as enduring numerous Eastern Indian Kavandi bearing ceremonies where a cage is formed from sharp spears sticking into the chest and the shaman dances as they dig deeper into his body.

Fakir lectures, conducts international workshops, and private sessions to educate others on the value and beauty of a dying spiritual tradition. He has recently developed a line of quality pierced body jewelry and a School of Branding and Piercing for professionals and has published magazines with photos of his rituals.

(See also AUTOMASOCHISM, BRANDING and PIERCING)

FANS   Fans were used by many 17th and 18th century ladies of Europe. This instrument proved invaluable in the art of flirting. It was used as a shield to avoid recognition or to end a conversation, it covered blushing cheeks or the lack thereof, it served as a weapon against roving hands, it could cover a low neckline or be lowered to expose enough breast to tease a suitor, and of course fanning circulated the air.

Fan dances were popular for centuries among oriental dancers who used them to shield their nude bodies while on stage. They were introduced into America during the 1930's.

(See also MASKS)

FANTASY   (Sexautism; Gendoloma—fantasizing during sex to hasten orgasm, Hemerotism—fantasizing about sex or nudity, Oneiropornism—fantasizing about sex or prostitutes)

Fantasies are desires people have for specific new experiences. Sexual fantasies may receive their potency due to the guilt or fear felt by the perpetrator. Many fantasies begin in childhood and remain as primary sources of pleasure for some throughout their life, others change fantasies with regularity. There may be some connection between whether a person finds pleasure in engaging in sexual experimentation and their ability to utilize new fantasies.

Men and women commonly fantasize about being overpowered by a sex partner. This entails female seduction of men in their fantasies, and the use of physical force in female fantasies.

Certain fantasies tend toward visualizing situations they would not want to experience in real life. These are specifically designed to increase adrenalin or excitement level to the point of being able to have sex without a partner. Some of these fantasies can be quite sadistic or violent, as in the case of some fantasy magazines. Sadistic fantasies may serve the purpose of relieving stress and aggression more than sexual tension.

People who feel guilty because they consider their fantasies to be extremely violent will probably find that they are docile compared to the following sample scenario from a fantasy magazine.

"The end came however, as the funnel was filled and the cow piss spilled over the sides and ran down into his mouth and nose. He coughed and choked as his lungs, already caked with blood, filled with the piss. Jerry shook violently, trying to gain air and only was getting piss. Saddcheda stomped the round mound of Jerry's belly. His weight caused it to explode, spewing guts, body fluid, blood, and cow piss all over...Rocco's face was nearly gone as the rats were feasting. His mouth was gone and his teeth shown bloody...One rat was now gnawing up into the right eye socket. The mice had done in the giant cock quickly, and now they were chewing into the lower belly through the hole they had started in the pubic hair. The snake was wriggling out of Rocco's ass-hole which was clenching, trying to expel it..." (*Ganienkeh*, by C. Williamson, *The Magazine*, Issue Thirty-Eight by Katharsis, pp. 106-107).

Katharsis, a distributor for a huge variety of fantasy magazines, offers a selection of fantasies ranging from sex with aliens, gladiators, and slaves to castration, beheading,

sacrifices, executions, bondage, women luring men to their deaths, selling and trading them, using them for furniture, food for their pets, etc. Many of their contributing writers are priests, ministers, movie screen writers, and one is a former military interrogator.

There is a Transformation Salon in New York where people can pay someone else to dress them in a favorite fantasy costume and to assist with appropriate makeup. Photos are provided upon request. CAUTION: People who fear that they are beginning to act out fantasies that would harm others are encouraged to seek professional counselling.

(See also ALLORGASMIA, FANTASY PLAY and PARAPHILIAS)

FANTASY PLAY   Fantasy play involves people symbolically acting out their sexual fantasies. Acting out a scene broadens or enhances the sexual experience by including intellect and emotions that may not be stimulated in ordinary sex. It is the equivalent of adding a plot to an X-rated movie.

Of course, fantasies such as hanging from the chandelier, cross gender experiences, and sex crimes cannot be physically acted out. However, many of these types of fantasies can be done symbolically. An example would be the cross gender fantasy where a male lover decides he wants to act out a lesbian scene. It is not only necessary for him to dress in female attire for the role, but to psychologically prepare himself. He may be put through a mock castration scene with his partner verbally reiterating that he is no longer male and describing his new female organs to him. He would be pampered, complimented, degraded, or in general treated in the manner he feels a sexy female would be under the same circumstance. Mirrors help reinforce his new role but only if he is in costume. Of course, a name change is often used. This same scenario could as easily turn another man off; therefore, the fantasy scene is discussed or negotiated prior to enactment.

Contrary to what most believe, it is not advisable to act out a person's favorite masturbation fantasy. This is because reality with its physical limitations can never match the diverse activity and timing possible in the mind. A person can easily come to have unrealistic expectations in regard to their favorite fantasy and will often be disappointed, or perhaps even blame their partner for a sloppy performance. People find it more advantageous to create new fantasies that lend themselves to physical reenactment. Some of the most popular are abduction, burglary, sex slave, rape, military games, prison, pirates, college fraternity initiations, police arrest, Indian capture, and space ships.

Pseudo-group sex scenes might include Bo-peep searching for her missing sheep. The sheep are symbolic and with the exception of the partner are made of a sheep drawn on a sealed paper bag, each of which has a different sex toy inside. The sex partner hides all of the bags and himself. Bo-peep then begins her search. The same type of scene is acted out with an Easter egg (sex toy) hunt. The player inevitably finds a woman in a bunny costume. Game rules vary, but usually the hunter has to find a minimum of two toys and if they don't choose to use one of them they have to replace it with two others, making a total of three. One does not have to use toys, some prefer using written sexual suggestions instead. A similar fantasy includes a seduction of Santa Claus. In this fantasy sexy lingerie or toys are put into gift wrapped packages.

A sample pseudo-group sex scene, and one that is more difficult to act out, is of male who is captured by a wicked queen and taken to her dungeon to be tortured by her servants while she watches. The prisoner is blindfolded and bound (unless one changes costumes several times) to a table or bed. The queen then instructs a woman called the French tickler to slowly titillate every inch of the captive's body. He finally screams for release and promises to perform any type of sex the wicked queen wants. She rewards him by commanding one of the women from her harem to give him a sensual warm oil massage. As the wicked queen watches, she tells him exactly what she wants. Horrified, he refuses. She expected this and now commands her guardian of ice

to take a piece in her mouth and slowly glide it over the most sensitive areas of his body. After 10 minutes he has failed to surrender. The tyrant queen next orders her favorite slave, Marquita de Sade, to punish him until he promises to submit himself totally to her passions. Marquita is ruthless, but he still refuses to surrender. At this, the queen becomes furious and condemns him to the ultimate torture. She turns and offers the first woman who can fill a cup with his love juices their immediate freedom.

A simple but entertaining game played at parties requires everyone to anonymously write out their favorite fantasy or sexual experience on a piece of paper, drop it in a box, and once everyone's fantasy is in the box, they are read aloud to the group.

There are several books that list fantasies to give couples ideas. One is titled *Fantascenes: Games Lovers Can Play* from Lady Tanith, P.O. Box 7925, Berkeley, CA 94707-0925.

(See also ABDUCTION, COITUS A CHEVAL, DRAG QUEENS, PHONE SEX, SLAVES and TRANSVESTITES)

FECES   See COCKTAILS, COPROPHILIA, COPROPHAGY and SHOWERS

FELLATIO   (Blow, Corvus, Irrumation, Penosugia; Oral sex—fellatio or cunnilingus) Fellatio (fellare: to suck) refers to the ancient practice of mouth to penis sexual contact. This form of stimulus is quite common in the animal kingdom. The book *Sex Link* tells of the dragon fly that demands a form of fellatio before coitus. He joins his partner during flight and bangs her head against his primary sex organ until he decides to finally turn around and mate.

The ancient Phoenician and Egyptian prostitutes were the first to wear lipstick which was used to advertise their specialized talents of fellatio and cunnilingus. Cleopatra, while not a prostitute, was known for her love of fellatio. Her enemies spread rumors of the queen fellating huge numbers from among her army in one night.

The following sections describe techniques involving autofellatio, female to male, and male to male fellatio. (See also CUM ETIQUETTE and CUNNILINGUS)

AUTOFELLATIO   Autofellatio is performed by a male on himself. G. L. Simons  writes of hermaphrodite gods who had penises as long as their torso because some primitives thought these gods reproduced by inserting their penis into their own mouths. Others believed in their god's ability to insert its penis into its own vagina (*Sex and Superstition*, p. 21, reproduced with permission of Blackie & Son Ltd.).

Kinsey reported that 2-3 males in a thousand practiced autofellatio. In order to perform autofellatio the man has to be limber and have a rather long penis. The position that offers the deepest penetration is upside down on a couch with the head and shoulders resting on the bottom cushion, the backbone against the back of the couch, and the knees resting on either side of the shoulders. The penis is then in front of the mouth at this point and if the man's proportions are right he can reach up with his mouth and take hold of the tip. Some men enjoy ejaculating into their mouths, and others like the feel of it on their skin, or the sound of it as it shoots past their ear. One man who engaged in autofellatio as a teenager claimed that most of the sensation occurred in the mouth rather than the penis. This is logical because there is a higher concentration of nerves in the tongue and lips than in an erect penis. Therefore, the primary sensation is more like that of giving fellatio to someone else and the secondary sensation like that of receiving it.

The following are contributions describing fellatio made by individuals who enjoy this type of sex.

FEMALE TO MALE   *"Men's sexual response occurs in cycles. The more times they are brought close to an orgasm the more intense it is when they release. Therefore, when performing fellatio remember to watch for signs of his nearing climax or better yet ask him to signal. The areas that are the most sensitive, in*

order, are the frenulum, corona, glans penis, urethra opening, shaft, and scrotum. If one uses anal play with fellatio the prostate can provide extreme sensitivity.

"Now, to set the mood, think of yourself as a toothless carnivore, and forget expressions like giving head, sucking, licking, eating and caressing. Think of teasing, devouring and consuming. In addition to the techniques mentioned here a person wants to constantly think of new sensations and techniques to try on their partner.

"Tell him what you are going to do to his penis and ravage his ear with your tongue. Slowly work your way down his neck, armpits, nipples, torso, buttocks, and to the groin area using varying degrees of pressure and movement with your tongue. Men vary in the amount of pre-genital contact they desire for fellatio; be aware of whether his emotional intensity is increasing.

"Make sure you are in a position to be able to move freely so that eventually you end up in a position where you are facing toward his feet. This allows the natural curve of his penis to match the curve in your mouth for easier penetration.

"Use very light fingertip strokes around the whole groin area and say your last words. Next begin at the base of his penis or testicles and very gently flick your tongue up and down the shaft several times, getting it wet. Then blow up and down on the wet area to make it cold and next alternate with exhaling warm air. Lift the penis gently. As you tease and tickle with your mouth wide open, hold his penis in position with your lip and tongue just below the glans penis. You don't want to touch the tip yet. Use your fingertips to gently tap or tickle the shaft. Your lips and tongue can be used to lightly massage his shaft as you move the penis deeper into the throat, still trying not to put pressure on the glans penis.

"Moan as if you can't stand the teasing yourself and firmly grip his penis at the base with your hands and pull it toward you. Hold the penis and then with your tongue very gently tickle the urethra entrance and release the tension of your grip on the shaft. Now retighten your grip and push your tongue firmly into the tip of the urethra. This time work your mouth, tongue and lips down his

penis massaging it with more pressure. The light touch should coincide with his approaching orgasm to forestall it and the harder pressure is used to rebuild intensity. Some penises have obvious indications of strong arousal: they throb, spasm, increase in temperature, have lots of pre-ejaculate emissions, and the testicles rise toward the body; however, others show very little indication of inevitable orgasm.

"If the partner's penis is flaccid and not fully erect you will be able to place your mouth firmly around the base of the glans penis and by working with the loose skin you can keep it in place against your lips but have the penis slip back and forth beneath the extra skin. You then suck the tip of the penis swiftly back and forth in and out of your mouth. Take your hands and roll the shaft of the penis between them as though you were rolling a small ball of cookie dough. Next devour his testicles and perineum. You may want to hum while they are in your mouth to create a slight vibration. Once the penis is erect, move back up to the glans penis and cover it with your mouth (no teeth). Use your tongue to gently tickle the underside of the corona. With your mouth over his penis insert an index finger into your mouth so that the fingertip can rub back and forth on the frenulum as you lower your mouth and tickling tongue as far down on his shaft as possible. Get your hands back into the flat rolling position and this time when you roll the penis between your hands, hold your lips over the glans penis and make the tip bounce off the insides of your mouth.

"In order to deep throat a penis, get into the position facing toward his feet and slowly glide the penis as far back as you can without gagging. Then take a deep breath and swallow. This will allow you to hold the penis in your throat longer and for many stops the gag response. Many women also find that the closer they are to orgasm the less of a gag reflex they experience. The man should also know before ejaculation that he needs to pull his penis back slightly so that the woman can breathe and swallow, preventing a gag reflex from occurring if the ejaculate squirts directly into the throat. You may place your hand around the base of the penis and pull toward you during the man's orgasm, but because the penis becomes extremely sensitive immediately after ejaculation, all pressure on the penis should end at this point. You may tell him you are going to suck out every drop, but don't. If you want to maintain intimacy either place your head and hand on the abdomen near the penis or stretch out beside him and cuddle. At orgasm, the sensation of hot squirting semen from an undulating penis can be so powerfully intimate that it is possible to orgasm yourself. Semen varies in taste, quantity, and speed at which it is expelled, all of which can effect the palatability. Semen, like all strong flavored foods, is an acquired taste. If you have not yet acquired the taste it is better to either dilute it with water before swallowing or discreetly rinse the mouth and discard it back into the glass. (Keep two glasses in case he wants a drink.) Men can feel rejected or hurt if a woman immediately spits the ejaculate out or refuses to take it into her mouth.

"Anal play can be introduced at any point. Make sure that if you plan on using your fingers your fingernails are short and smooth. If you have a plug make sure that it has a flange on one end to prevent the sphincter muscle from sucking it into the rectum.

"You may experiment with creating extra sensations by using a variety of substances in your mouth. For example: warm water, ice chips, mint flavored toothpaste, cool soothing action cough drops, champagne, Pop Rocks (candy that fizzles), or lotions made specifically for oral sex. Do not use anything too hot, like deep heat rub, some menthol cough drops, or hot liquids."—Anonymous Contributor

CAUTION: The exchange of body fluids is not considered a safe sex practice.

MALE TO MALE   "Fellatio is begun, after preliminary washing, by selecting a kneeling position near the edge of the bed to allow extended performance without physical discomfort. The exception would be if you are playing with bondage or acting out an interrogation scene.

"It can be very intriguing for your partner if you hide the condom in your mouth without their knowledge. It can be kept between the teeth and cheek without notice. Place the glans penis in your mouth and with your tongue locate the condom and position it over the tip of the penis. Begin rolling it down with your lips and tongue (4-5 strokes). This creates a grabbing or squeezing sensation he doesn't expect. Avoid getting hair caught in the condom or your mouth by stroking the hair downward with one hand as you take the penis deeper into your mouth. Learn to enjoy the flavor of latex so that it won't distract you.

"Take your tongue and tickle inside the crease at the top of the thighs and under the scrotum. Next lick up to the top of the penis. Circle the head with the tongue, quickly taking one gulp. The man will gasp and at this point have him take hold of your hair and guide your head as you begin the rapid bobbing motion. Men with longer penises can be easily handled by keeping one hand wrapped around the base of the penis as an extension of the mouth. It is important to keep the penis and hand lubricated well with saliva to make this work. The hand will also need to stay against the lips and to follow the motion of the mouth. You may stroke the penis with the right hand, but try to use the left to hold the condom in place. This hand position also protects you from having the person shove his penis too far down your throat; it puts you in control of how much you take into your mouth. You can also create more pressure with your hand than your mouth (lips should be kept over teeth at all times, never bite). Flick the frenulum with your tongue repeatedly. Another technique is to hold the penis in your mouth and create an airtight seal with your lips, suck all the air out of your mouth, and hold your tongue tightly against the penis. Next roll the tongue muscle from the tip to the back so that it feels to your partner like you are milking or swallowing his penis.

"Delay his orgasm by holding your fingers together like a cup and slowly pulling the testicles back down into the scrotum. Some men enjoy having their testicles squeezed, but not all. If your partner is safe and is not wearing a condom you can take the penis out of your mouth and coolly blow up and down the shaft, then follow it by warming it with your breath. If you want to intensify these sensations you can alternate small ice cubes and hot chocolate or coffee. Carbonated liquids create a strange sensation for the partner.

"If your partner has difficulty reaching orgasm, lubricate your finger and insert it into his anus to massage his prostate. Hold his ejaculate in your mouth until you get next to his ear and swallow with a big gulp. Pull back and show him how much you loved the experience by a satisfied and lustful smile.

"If your jaw ends up feeling sore, massage it behind the ear where the jaw ends before you go to bed. This will help ensure it not being as sore in the morning."—Contributed by Mike Bergen, San Francisco

CAUTION: The exchange of body fluids is not considered a safe sex practice.

(See also CUM ETIQUETTE, CUNNILINGUS, DOCKING and PHALLOPHILIA)

FELLCHING Fellching (fellare: to suck, fell: animal hide) refers either to stuffing animals into the vagina or anus, or to a partner sucking semen out of one of these orifices.

(See ANAL SEX, OPHIDICISM, SAFE SEX, STUFFING and ZOOPHILIA)

FEMALE IMPERSONATORS (Crossdressing) Female impersonators refers to those men who perform or entertain in front of an audience while dressed in women's clothing. Females were not permitted in many European and Asian stage plays until the last couple of centuries; their roles were filled by young male actors dressed in appropriate garb. Rewards for impersonators are financial rather than sexual. Many do not crossdress for any other occasion; in this way they differ from transvestites. Drag Queens, however, perform on stage for personal gratification and for money and will crossdress on other occasions as well.

Most large cities have a restaurant or theatre featuring this type of performance. Las Vegas probably has the most elaborate performances and most expensive wardrobes. Portland, Oregon has a comedy show with many of their performers pantomiming famous vocalists. Here there is a combination of all ages and sizes among the performers. The owner of the club is often invited to prestigious civic functions with the only condition being that he attends in costume.

(See also DRAG QUEENS, INFANTILISM, PETTICOAT DISCIPLINE, TRANSSEXUALS, TRANSVESTITES and VICTORIAN LACE)

FERTILITY RITES Fertility, or the bearing of children, has always been important. The early religions were based on people's needs for fertile crops, animals, and progeny. The first two were essential for immediate survival and the third for survival of the species. Thus, man celebrated when the crops germinated and the animals mated.

Sex became sacred and at one time was part of Temple worship in most cultures. The Egyptians at Mendes considered goats as sacred and able to increase virility and fertility. The goats lived in the temple and during their fertility rites the priest let the goats out of their stalls to run among the worshipers who quickly tried to touch and kiss them. Many of them were successful in coitus. Other worshipers, not fortunate enough to catch a goat, settled for cohabiting with another human. In some temples the priest began temple orgies by deflowering a virgin or offering some other sacrifice. Today's counterpart of this priest, at least in name, is "reverend." This title has its roots in the ancient worship of the sex goddess Venus (venery, venereal, venerate, revere). Sex, love, and worship were once all part of religion, as the definitions of these words indicate.

The penis came to be worshipped as a symbol of fertility in many religions. Virgins believed that if they broke their hymen on the phallus of the stone god that they would be guaranteed fertility. The practice of defloration by stone statues or priests still survives in parts of India. The Indians also had a ritual in honor of fertility gods whereby a horse was slaughtered and a woman laid with him under an opaque sheet where, according to Tawney (1924) "She performed a very obscene act with the horse symbolizing the transmission to her of its great powers of fertility" (*Sex and Superstition*, by G.L. Simons, p. 60, reproduced with permission of Blackie & Son Ltd.). The Romans wore amulets of penises as jewelry and until recently the Holy Prepuce, foreskin of Jesus, was not only revered but in the French diocese of Chartres worshippers believed it to have the power to restore fertility in women. (Several churches in Europe claim to be proprietors of the same foreskin.)

Fertility rites were used for animals and crops by many ancient cultures. People in parts of medieval Europe sought to ensure the fertility in their herds of cattle by having naked men build two fires between which they drove the herd. Monks performed this rite for people; however, instead of cattle, they held up a phallus.

People in farming communities during the 20th century in both North and South America are reported to have sex in their newly plowed and seeded fields to ensure germination. This practice is thousands of years old.

(Refer also to APHRODISIACS, CHARMS, FESTIVALS, LOVE POTIONS, ORGIES, RITUAL SEX, SEX MAGICK, and PHALLOPHILIA.)

FESTIVALS Most of our present day holidays are remnants of ancient festivals. These festivals served as a temporary relief from the burdens of a repressive, laborious, or tedious life. People were permitted to switch partners, cross dress, or go against any sexual taboo that controlled their behavior the rest of the year. Ancient moralists condoned this temporary outlet of energy as necessary. It was believed that if a person didn't let their negative energy out in this manner it would surface in a more heinous or violent form.

The following are synopses of several of the more notorious historical festivals, most of which are described in detail in B. Z. Goldberg's book, *The Sacred Fire*.

APHRODITE—DAY OF BLOOD Aphrodite was the hermaphrodite goddess of life and sex. She was a virgin mother who bore a son, Attis, by holding a pomegranate between her breasts. Attis was later compelled to castrate himself, which he did while leaning against a palm tree (symbolic of virility). This proved fatal for Attis and, just like nature, he began a cycle of death in the winter and rebirth in the spring.

Each winter the worshippers of Aphrodite mourned for Attis by fasting and abstaining from sex. The Spring "Day of Blood" began with the cutting of a palm tree. It was decorated with flowers and wrapped with cloth to resemble a corpse. A young priest was tied to the tree and sometime during the night was mysteriously stabbed to death. The next morning other priests gathered around and symbolically shared this death by cutting themselves and spattering their blood on the altar of Aphrodite. Music and dancing ensued, building the crowd into a frenzy which resulted in some male worshippers castrating themselves and beating their severed penises against her statue. These eunuchs then became temple priests. The festival continued throughout the day until the tree was again erected. A tomb was opened to symbolize Attis' rising from the dead and a new priest resembling the sacrificed one now worshiped at the altar. As morning broke people dressed in disguises and were able to do whatever they pleased. The festival ended with the palm tree being taken to the brook and washed, decorated with roses, and returned to the temple in a procession.

BAAL   Baal was one of the early gods. He died during the winter and resurrected himself in the spring. People mourned his death in the winter by fasting, women baring their breasts, abstaining from sex, and shaving their heads. Women who did not cut their hair in the winter had to offer themselves sexually during the spring festival. As the first day of spring arrived worshippers would travel to the Sacred Hill, bringing with them the first fruits of their crops and first born of their animals. These were offered to Baal by the priests and then were used to provide a feast for the worshippers. Finally the last sacrifice, a lamb, was brought to the altar. Music would sound to summon a priestess who would walk to the altar with her eyes closed. The priest would dip his finger into the blood of the lamb and place it in her mouth. She now opened her eyes, plunged her hand into the open cavity, tore out the heart, and placed it on a platter. Dancing priestesses entered and as the passions rose the worshipper chose a priestess by touching her navel and giving her a coin.

She followed him to a tent and together they consummated a prayer of love to their god.

CARNIVAL   This international festival is one of the surviving versions of the Dionysus and Saturn festivals. The word carnival is taken from the Latin word carnelevarium (caro: flesh, and levar: to put aside), thus the abstinence from meat during Lent. People wear masks, have parades, indulge in drink, music, dancing, and sex.

DIONYSIA   This was a festival in honor of Dionysus, the god of wine, women, and song. The festival began at sunset with a procession led by a chariot, torch bearers, then followed by worshipers carrying wine and fruit, with the musicians and phallus bearers at the rear. All wore masks and scanty costumes of nymphs, satyrs, or other creatures. They wore phallus symbols or carvings either on their heads or dangling from their waists. Their songs and dialogue were deliberately sexual. When they reached the woods a pig was sacrificially roasted and a feast began. The statue of Dionysus was brought out of its chest and soon all were disrobed and the orgy of men, women, and children began. This Greek festival was later introduced into Rome but became so violent that the Senate banned it in 186 B.C.

MAY DAY   The Maypole is a form of tree worship that survived into the 20th century. In some cultures the men would wander through plantations naked to fertilize the trees with their semen. The Maypole symbolizes the penis and is decorated with flowers just as the palm tree in the worship of Aphrodite. Worshipers of May Day entered the woods the night the pole was to be cut and are rumored to have passed the night in a revelry of unbridled sex. The next morning the worshipers brought the decorated Maypole into town, paving its path with flowers and branches. Once the Maypole was in place they ended the festival with ceremonial dancing.

(See also DENDROPHILIA)

MOLOCH   Moloch was the Phoenician's masculine god of bounty. He had the head of a bull and the body of a man. The pedestal of his statue served as a furnace where all sacrifices offered to him were burned. This fire was prepared at sunset and male worshipers would bring sacrifices to throw into the flames. At this time women were not allowed to attend the dancing or the male orgies that occurred during the night. Here eunuch priests and trained temple dogs could be purchased for the worshiper's sexual pleasure.

The high priest eventually decided to permit women but required them to remain separate from the male worshipers. The women installed their own prostitute priestesses and offered sacrifices to Moloch for his blessing. The level of passion was concomitant to the value of the sacrifice and some of these women began throwing their infants into the fire as a sacrifice. This produced enough stimulus to allow them to experience the maximum level of sexual passion.

SATURNALIA   This is the ancient Roman festival in honor of Saturn, the god of agriculture. It began on December 17th and lasted for 7 days. People unwrapped the woolen swathing that was kept on the statue of Saturn for the rest of the year and began the festival. They exchanged places with their slaves, or at least invited them to share in a feast as social equals, gifts were exchanged, and moral restrictions were relaxed. A ritual king was chosen each year at the beginning of the festival and an idol of him was symbolically burned at the end to signify Saturn's death.

(See also FERTILITY RITES, ORGIES and RITUAL SEX)

FETISHES   (Crurofact—leg, Genofact—genitals, Mastofact—breast, Morphophilia—arousal from person with a different physique, Organofact—part of body) A fetish is an object that replaces another human as the primary love object. The fetish may be partial (such as breasts, feet, hair, buttocks, obesity, or navel) or inanimate (such as shoes, fur, latex, leather, hats, gloves, panties, lace, jock straps, or used condoms). The fetish can be sense specific. The person may be aroused when they see the object, feel it, smell it, hear it, taste it, or any combination thereof. Fetishes tend to involve objects which give a feeling of nurturance. For example, it would be unusual to find a spider or scorpion fetish.

The selection of the fetish involves conditioning or learned behavior and requires a strong stimulus for it to register. Conditioning of a fetish occurs from infancy to preschool and again during puberty when the child's sex drive emerges a second time. (Judd Marmor, in *Modern Views of Human Sexual Behavior*, states that this sexual latency in children seems only to occur in societies that enforce sexual repression by threats of punishment, loss of affection, and indoctrination that sex is a sin.)

A fetish can require progressively increased intensity in order to achieve orgasm. A hair fetishist may first experience orgasm by fantasizing about hair; soon he will want to see it, watch the woman comb it, touch it, masturbate into it, and possess it by cutting it off (or stealing it from) a non-consenting stranger. The fetishist is also often polygamous: a shoe fetishist is not satisfied with only one shoe throughout his life but rather continuously seeks new shoes and often keeps a 'harem' of such.

There are occasionally disadvantages involved with partial fetishes. For example, if a man marries a woman primarily because of a fetish, and then she cuts her hair, loses weight, or has to have a mastectomy, the sexual attraction can disappear overnight, sometimes even causing total impotence within the marriage. The worst scenario for a married fetishist is to have their fetish rejected by their spouse; this only alienates them more and creates more dependence on the fetish object.

Men appear more apt to rely on fetish objects than females.

There are fetish newsletters or magazines available that have personal ads of people selling photos of feet, hair, shoes, or sports scenes. Those not interested in photos can custom order specific worn or used underwear.

It is impossible to list all of the fetish objects people use but some of the common ones are as follows:

BOOTS OR SHOES (Altocalciphilia—high heels, Retifism—shoes) This fetish is most likely selected and conditioned during early childhood. A shoe is the first thing a  crawling child sees before its mother picks them up to nurture them. It becomes their cue for being cared for and loved. The shoe may need to be a certain style and color or can remain nonspecific. They may prefer to have a person to which they are attracted wear them but not always. The appeal of the shoe has a long history and is not limited to humans alone. There was a case of a male chimpanzee who was raised in captivity. He developed a boot fetish and would masturbate by rubbing on the boot of the caretaker.

Hirschfeld counseled a priest whose fetish was for a set of man's and woman's shoes together. He often stopped outside doors where people had left their shoes and would kiss, smell, and caress them. He even paid hotel employees to let him clean guest's shoes.

High heels are the most appealing type of shoe and are said to have their beginning with Catherine de Medicis, a 16th century Italian who married Henry II of France (their son married Mary Queen of Scots). Catherine was very petite and brought with her shoes that were custom designed to give her height. This started a fashion rage among the aristocratic ladies. The first heels must have been extremely difficult to maneuver in because male escorts often had to carry these dainty ladies up and down stairs. The majority of Americans were not exposed to high heels until a French prostitute brought several pairs with her to an elite New Orleans brothel during the mid-nineteenth century. The madam, Kathy, noticed that men were willing to pay more for this girl and quickly ordered French heels for all the women in her brothel. Other brothels did the same and men soon ordered them for their wives, creating enough

demand that in 1880 a Massachusetts shoe factory opened to supply their needs (*The Sex Life of the Foot & Shoe*, pp. 141-143).

The shoe fetish is not always limited to the sight or touch of the shoe. One case history taken from Moraglia, *Archivio di Psichiatria*, vol. xiii, p. 568, refers to a man who would reach orgasm by following women whose shoes creaked. This phenomenon was the result of being conditioned at age 17 by hearing the sound of his partner's shoes creaking as they had sex on a staircase.

Men in the S/M community often have a different reason for being in awe of a shoe. Several have commented that the extremely high and spiked heel is arousing because of the potential danger if a woman decides to use it as a weapon against them. It is true that many S/M magazines feature photos of a woman's spiked heel resting against the genitals of a submissive male. The greatest height for a heel is about 9", this being almost impractical for walking and is used exclusively for fetish play.

Most men, however, are attracted to the foot or shoe due to the change in posture and the frail gait that characterizes a woman who wears high heels. The wearer's posture is altered with a more dramatic curve of the spine which causes the buttocks and calves to appear to be more rounded, the bust to protrude, and the hips to have an exaggerated sway. The frail gait widens the division of power between the man and woman and appeals to his desire to protect and possibly to his feeling of self-esteem. People are also often aroused when they see pain in a person of the opposite sex. This could be part of a predatorial instinct to be alert to the lame or weak. For example, sharks often attack ailing or injured fish that are near the top of the water, and lions stalk animals that lag behind a herd. In humans, this tendency to actually prey on the weak is usually thwarted by morals, but the initial attention remains. (Refer also to BINDING/FOOT and PODOPHILIA)

FURS Fur fetishes seem to come from the sensations or tickling produced by family pets, stuffed animals, fur coats, rugs, feathers, or velvet chairs. The fetish is usually tactile rather than visual. Rabbit fur and ostrich feathers are often used in sex scenes to enhance the senses, particularly if the partner is bound. (See also DORAPHILIA and TICKLING)

GODS   The definition of fetish as found in *Webster's New World Dictionary* (1972, p. 517) states: "Fetish - any object believed by superstitious people to have magical power . . . any thing or activity to which one is irrationally devoted . . . any non-sexual object, such as a foot or a glove, that abnormally  excites erotic feelings." The god usually demands something in turn from his devotee and while this makes the relationship slightly more difficult, the sacrifice serves to bond the individual even more. A doctrine of religious celibacy contributes to emotional isolation from the intimacy of other humans and binds the devotee even more. The vow nuns took during the Middle Ages stated "I love Christ into whose bed I have entered . . . There in glowing love embrace your beloved (savior) who is come down from heaven into your breast's bower, and hold him fast until He shall have granted whatsoever you wish for" (*Sex in History*, by G. Rattray Taylor, p. 42).

This form of fetish was easier to recognize among ancient fertility religions when people used the idols of their gods to masturbate against or have sex with a surrogate priest or priestess. Christianity began a movement to repress the sexual relationship with God, leaving only the Platonic love. The early Corinthian Christians celebrated Agape feasts in imitation of the Last Supper, but included a Eucharistic rite that was very similar to those of fertility gods. [Author's note: People now fantasize an emotional intimacy with God rather than a sexual union. However, the result can be the same. Like any other fetish it can interfere or replace the primary intimacy normally shared with other humans. The Inquisition was only one example of what happens when people use their devotion to god to justify prejudice or religious intolerance of others.]

LATEX AND RUBBER   Many of today's adults were exposed to rubber as infants in the form of rubber pants or sheets. Tactile stimulation is important with this fetish. Many fetishists buy or have underwear or costumes made of rubber or latex. These include nun's habits, sheets, underwear, vests, skirts, whips, and hoods. Latex pants can include an anal plug or reservoir for the penis. Latex clothing causes a person to perspire after a short time. Tight fitting latex can also be difficult to get into and some people have solved this problem by using talcum powder on the inside.

LEATHER   (Please refer to section titled DORAPHILIA.)

UNDERWEAR   Underwear is a popular fetish. It can offer tactile, visual, and olfactory stimuli. Men collect women's underwear for several reasons. Transvestites have a collection to wear regularly, others steal or collect panties from sexual conquests, and some men take a pair of their lover's underwear with them when they travel. If these men use the panties to masturbate it is usually done by associating the panties with a specific person. This is true in gay relationships also. The true fetishist, however, will use the odor or texture of the underwear as a primary stimulus by which they masturbate. They may fantasize about a lover but have little desire to be with them. The person with a partial or weak fetish would only be aroused if the underwear was being worn by their lover. (See also ENDYTOPHILIA)

FIRE   See BRANDING, ELECTRIC SHOCK and PYROPHILIA

FISTING   (Hand balling; Brachioprotic eroticism—arm in anus) Fisting involves the insertion of the hand into the vagina or anus. Double fisting can refer to simultaneously fisting the vagina and anus, or having two hands inserted into the anus at the same time. The depth of penetration can be as great as 11-15 inches. This activity is practiced by heterosexual and gay alike. Fisting is rarely mentioned in historic literature; however, there was a scene in the movie *Caligula* of the Roman emperor fisting a groom after his wedding.

There are variations in the type of sensation people enjoy during anal and vaginal fisting, usually involving differences in depth, width, and "punching." Depth is accomplished by carefully following the vaginal cavity to the end or the anal chamber through the rectum and descending colon to the transverse colon (which feels as though it's lined with fur). It is from this position that the fistor can access the spleen and descending aorta, which is what most fistors assume is the heart because of its contractions. "Punching" refers to the slow rhythmic stroking or repeated thrusting penetration of the fist into a cavity. Width is accomplished by rotating a fist, spreading the fingers once inside, insertion of a second hand, penis, testicles, or dildo. CAUTION: Fisting can lead to serious physical injury and is not considered a safe sex practice.

ANAL   Fisting requires special preparation by both partners. The fistee prepares by cleaning out the lower intestine with an enema. The fistor removes any rings and examines the hands for cuts or hangnails. Nylon hosiery is sometimes carefully run over the hand to locate any roughness. Latex gloves are often used as a protection for both parties.

The hand and arm are generously lubricated with vegetable shortening and additional lubricant is applied to the fistee's anus. The fistor next inserts one, then two fingers, and when the partner's anal muscles seem relaxed, the hand is pushed in fingers first with the tips together in a closed ring fashion. Next the hand is slowly worked up inside. There are several sphincters or valves that block progression and these are opened by massaging or stretching the entrance area then pushing one or two fingers through and pulling some of the intestinal wall back through. Pain can be an

indication of improper or dangerous manipulation.

The fist is slowly removed from the anus to prevent the hand from creating a vacuum effect and pulling a section of the intestine out with it; this is called a rosebud and is not deadly. (Ancient yogis voluntarily expelled their intestines into a bowl of water by manipulating their muscles.)

Fisting creates an unusual sensation of pressure and fullness and may activate the brain's pleasure center associated with defecation and digestion. For others this intimate activity creates a tremendous level of trust and bonding between partners. Others compare the pain and pleasure as similar to a woman giving birth. People combine fisting with other sexual activity such as nipple play, fellatio, and cunnilingus (*TRUST/THE HAND BOOK: A guide to the sensual and spiritual art of handballing*, by Bert Herrman) ("Fisting," QSM lecture, April 24, 1991, by Bert Herrman). CAUTION: The anal wall is very thin and if torn can necessitate surgery and the need to wear a colostomy bag. The rectal perforation rate for fisting has been estimated at 1 per 2,000 penetrations (*DungeonMaster Yearbook II*). Symptoms of injury include a gradual building of internal pain that may not be noticed for one to two days, followed by illness. There may not be a noticeable discharge of blood. The fisting is ended if the fistor encounters red blood or feces that was not flushed out with the initial enema. Those who engage in this activity a lot often eat yogurt or drink acidophilus milk to keep their natural intestinal flora in balance.

AUTO-FISTING   Auto-fisting is rare and those who practice it find that the angle of the hand and wrist is awkward and the depth is naturally restricted.

VAGINAL   Vaginal fisting does not require a prior douche. It differs from anal fisting in that vegetable shortening is not used (it sticks to the inner walls and collects bacteria). Water-based lubricants are preferred instead. The hands and fingernails are prepared so that there are no rough edges or cuts. The vagina is then opened with two or three fingers by stretching the opening until it can accommodate all of them. These are then pushed gently into the inner cavity until the hand is inside. There is a point at which the fingers are curved inward into a fist or cupped around the mouth of the cervix. Vaginal chambers differ in length and this determines the depth one is able to reach with the hand. Females are capable of being fisted anally and vaginally at the same time. However, a fist in the vagina reduces the area available in the rectum and vice-versa. The procedure used may require inserting the fist into the anus beyond the rectum and then pushing the hand into the vagina. For some, but not all, punching or cunnilingus during fisting can be arousing.

(See also ANAL SEX, COPROPHILIA, GENITAL/ANAL INSERTS, KLISMAPHILIA and SAFE SEX)

FLAGELLATION (Ecorchement, Mastigothymia and Rhabdophilia—arousal from flagellation) Flagellation, the use of whipping to arouse passion in a sexual partner, is an ancient practice. People in other cultures seem to have understood early on the aphrodisiac effect of pain and used it to their benefit. Vatsyayana wrote explicit instructions for striking a partner during sex in the *Kama-Sutra*:

Blows are a form of love play...The parts of the body which may be struck out of passion are: the shoulders, the head, the chest between the breasts, the back, the jagdana, the hips and the sides. Such blows may be administered with the back of the hand, with the fingers together like a pad, with the palm of the hand and with the fist...During intercourse it is customary to tap between the two breasts with the back of the hand, faster and faster as the level of excitement rises, until the end of the sexual act; at that point one should repeat the sound 'hin', or some other preferred sound. When the man strikes the woman's head with the end of his fingers held tightly together, he utters the sound 'phat', while the woman replies with the cooing sound.

Flagellation has also held an important position in medicine and religion. Those thought to be mentally ill were flagellated from the 17th through 19th centuries on the advice of prominent physicians. Forms of flagellation were also used by holy men or shamans in the earliest religions to induce a trance-like state (mystical out of body experience) in which they believed they could commune with god. Flagellation continued to be used as part of religion and was adopted by the worshippers of the fertility or sex gods. The goddess Diana's religious ceremonies included contests to find the boy who could endure the most pain. Religious floggings were also used in the fertility rites of the Roman god Lupercus, and women during the Thessaly (Greek) festival of Aphrodite used flagellation to build their passions in preparation for sexual orgies. Barren Greek women were stripped naked and beaten in the temple of Juno to cure their infertility.

From fertility religions, flagellation eventually found its way to Christianity. Christian monks adopted flagellation as part of their self-mortification rites. Flagellation was appealing for celibates because it substituted for the imposed restrictions on physical sensations or nurturing their bodies naturally needed. The strokes are capable of awakening the senses to the point of orgasm, or can lead to the even more desirable mystical out-of-body experience.

Not all monks, priests, and bishops were satisfied with self-mortification, some were caught implementing this type of penance on naked nuns and parishioners. The term "Cornelian Discipline" was named after a priest, Cornelius Adriansen, who became notorious for demanding that his penitents be totally nude. Some monasteries not only humiliated their monks by having them flogged naked, but carried out the punishment in a town square with an audience of villagers.

In 1210 a Christian sect of flagellants appeared in Italy. The monk, St. Justin of Padua, gave an account of their ritual in *Chronicon Ursitius Basiliensis* (quoted from *A History of the Rod*, pp. 102-3):

To such a degree were they affected with the fear of God, that noble as well as ignoble persons, young and old, even children five years of age, would go naked about the street without any sense of shame, walking in public, two and two, in the manner of a solemn procession. Every one of them held in his hand a scourge, made of leather thongs, and with tears and groans they lashed themselves on their back till the blood ran: all the while weeping and giving tokens of the same bitter affliction, as if they had really been spectators of the passion of our Saviour.

By the year 1261 this sect had expanded into Germany and Poland and by the year 1349 had spread throughout Europe.

Proselytizing monks, Jesuits, and missionaries would many times convince female tribal natives of the value of Christian doctrine by beating them until they agreed to convert. In addition, Saint Junipero Sera is said to have held the children of potential converts hostage. *Chronique Scandaleuse* (quoted from *A History of the Rod*, p. 99) documents an incident in 1634 in Africa when a Jesuit missionary discovered the Queen of Matamba and her attendants carrying an idol.

...he enforced his arguments against idolatry by the application of a whip to the body of her sable majesty! It is astonishing, he says, how the process of flagellation gradually opened her understanding, till she at length confessed herself wholly unable to resist such sensible proofs of the excellence of his doctrine.

Conversion and obedience induced by whipping was used in Paraguay, Mexico, Africa, and probably other countries as well.

Flagellation has of course been used by most forms of government and military. France, until 1756, sometimes punished a prostitute by tying her on a donkey with her buttocks toward the front of the animal, a straw hat placed on her head, and an inscription on her back. The prostitute was then whipped by the crowds as she was paraded through the towns on her way to prison. This may be the remnant of a more ancient punishment for adulterous wives in which the donkey not only carried her through town but she was forced into sexual union with it (*Encyclopaedia Sexualis*, by Victor Robinson, p. 37).

Flagellation has been common in bordellos for centuries as a method to reduce impotency in men. The English bordello fee in the late 1960's for caning was 1 pound per lash. One client wrote a letter to a Madam before his visit detailing the treatment he desired as well as the price he would pay, this being regulated by the amount of blood the woman was able to draw.

Caning became most popular in English schools and as a result sexual flagellation is more common in that country than any other. At one time whipping clubs were common even among young people. These included games of forfeit, similar to strip poker, where articles of clothing were lost until eventually the person ended up naked. The clothes could only be redeemed by submitting to a set number of strokes with the rod. Today there are English diners where sexy waitresses apply the rod to willing patrons who do not eat all the food served on their plates.

In 1671 England, a phantom spanker named "Whipping Tom" was arrested for abducting women and carrying them into a dark side street. There he would pull up their dresses and spank them until they screamed for help, at which point he would make his escape.

People today use flagellation in sex play because the pain awakens or focuses the mind of a stressed person onto their senses and away from the pressures of a job. The cessation of whipping also causes the bottom to feel extremely grateful and even more willing to please their partner.

Flagellation or pain can also sensitize a numb body. People who sustain an injury or suffer emotional pain seem to release neurotransmitters that have an analgesic effect on the body; therefore, in order for this person to feel anything, the pain or stimulus has to be greater than it would under ordinary circumstances.

Erotic whipping is rarely abrupt. A warmup period is common whereby the top runs their hand over the area, massages it, pinches it, and when the whip is used, the intensity is built up slowly. Time is allowed for the person's brain to produce the neurotransmitters causing analgesic and euphoric states. The bottom's ability to tolerate pain is in direct proportion to the release of these chemicals. This is why most

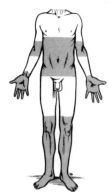

people are able to endure more pain as they approach orgasm. Many prefer to end the flagellation after orgasm because these chemicals wear off almost immediately. People differ in their preferences and therefore flagellation must be negotiated.

There are areas of the body that generate more erotic responses than others. The most erotic spot is the lower or inner part of the buttocks. The closer the stimulation is to the center, the more erotic sensation they create. A kneeling female may have her knees apart but for safety a male should have his knees together to protect his sex organs. CAUTION: The physical environment for erotic flagellation is important as people respond better if the climate is warm and the light dim. People who practice erotic flagellation adhere to the following safety guidelines found in *Sandmutopia Guardian 5, Fundamentals of Flagellation*, by The Quartermaster (April 1989, pp. 28-33): The wrists and ankles, if

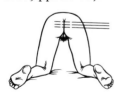

bound, are constantly monitored. Improperly placed strokes or repeated strokes on the same area can become distracting to the bottom and ruin the scene. Accidental pain is NOT erotic. It is dangerous to strike a person on the front or back of the head, neck, elbows, waist, hands, knees, feet, abdomen, shins, chest, and spine.

It is also risky to let the end of a whip or cane wrap around the person's body. Lashes are aimed so that the end of the instrument lands in the center of the far buttock or shoulder. Padding is sometimes used to protect the abdomen, the most common types being leather belts designed for body builders, pillows, or rolled up towels.

As a general rule, the thinner the whip or cane, the sharper the pain. These may also cause cuts in the skin. A paddle, whip, or riding crop that is soft and wide at the end will create less pain and have more of a sensual feeling. If the instrument is wide and heavy the impact with be felt deeper in the muscle tissue, like a thud. People vary in the types of sensations they prefer.

People use bondage for the safety of the bottom as it prevents them from accidentally moving during a blow. Bondage also draws a person's focus toward the sensations of their body rather than trying to move or escape.

Many bottoms now provide their own flagellation equipment due to AIDS and the possibility of contamination from anything that draws blood.

BASTINADO Bastinado is a form of foot torture that originally was used on criminals, many of whom never walked again. Feet are sensitive and delicate, and they also have to carry the weight of the individual, which makes any injury dangerous and, in the very least, inconvenient. Only short whips with soft leather are used in sex play and these are applied with light strokes.

BIRCHING Birch rods or bunches of birch twigs have long been a common instrument for flagellation. Birching was not only popular in saunas, where people whipped each other to stimulate their skin, but was also popular for sex play.

Birching had several advantages over caning or flogging. Birches can be used safely over most of the body (excluding face and neck) and they cause only superficial effects. It takes fairly severe use of a birch to break the skin and cause bleeding, but the wounds are very minor and, once the blood is washed away, only a few scratches are visible. CAUTION: Birch twigs get thin toward the tips and may break off. Trimming them periodically during flagellation helps prevent the tips from causing problems by wrapping around on the sides of a person. Those birching a partner on the shoulders have them wear goggles, blindfolds, hoods, or masks to protect their eyes from tips that can break loose. Once a batch of birch is used on one partner it cannot be used safely on others because of possible contamination from the scratches.

CANING   Canes are made from rattan or bamboo. The domestic cane is straight and has a grip at one end, while the school cane has a crooked handle, and the Malacca cane has a knob at one end.

Novices begin with the shorter and less flexible canes because they are easier to aim and control. Each type of cane has a different effect and feel in addition to the sensations caused by the power, rhythm, and location of the stroke. Successful disciplinarians are aware of all their options and are able to apply their lashes in a manner that brings the most pleasure to the bottom. Training and knowledge of the proper location to strike and the power of each stroke is essential for caning because without it one can cause serious injury.

A student begins training by getting the feel of swinging the rod. They stand in a room, away from any objects, and swish the cane through the air with varying degrees of speed, up and down, sideways, and in an arc. Once the student has the feel of the swing they work on accuracy of aim by using a pillow. Different positions are used for the pillow, laying it on a bed or binding it in a vertical position to a piece of furniture. They replicate any position they may use for their partner, as each height and angle requires different strokes. The novice practices until the cane hits the center of the pillow and only three-quarters across to the other side. The next progressive step is to be able to apply strokes such that they lay parallel to each other and are properly spaced. Once these skills are mastered, the student applies the strokes to their own buttocks to adjust the power of the stroke accordingly.

The student next practices on a live volunteer. Safety precautions are still used and the person places a heavy towel or pillow over them to protect against stray strokes that might land on their lower thighs, or upper or far side of the buttocks. The strokes are kept light in order to get the most strokes out of the practice session. A powerful stinging type of swing is usually done for punishment and is limited to two or three strokes. Regardless of the position selected, the strokes will either be parallel or perpendicular to the floor. Strokes are applied at intervals of about 10 seconds. (*The Fine Art of Caning*, by Nan)

FLOGGING   Flogging is usually done on the upper back while in a standing position. The person, if bound, is positioned in a manner that does not cause their shoulder blades or spine to protrude. Whips with wider strips of leather can have the same effect as a good massage, and many enjoy being flogged  because of this. The position is also more macho, depicting the pirate, prisoner, or military style of punishment.

GENITAL WHIPPING   Genital whipping is usually attempted only by the very adventurous. A much gentler stroke is used as well as a special type of penis whip (6") or riding crop. These whips only require a slight wrist action, not the full swing common with some other types of flagellation. Intensity is built up by increasing the number of strokes in a given period, not by hitting harder. The genitals themselves have small areas that are much more sensitive than other parts, and these are either protected with a hand or avoided. The three most sensitive areas are the clitoris, testicles, and glans penis. Genital whipping is enjoyed more when erotic stroking is alternated with lashes of the whip. The flagellator sometimes holds the palm of their hand 7" opposite to where the whip lands so that on the return swing it stings their palm, thus ensuring awareness of the intensity of the stroke given to the partner's genitals.

PADDLING   Paddling is a semi-intimate form of punishment carried out on the buttocks of an individual who is either bending over, leaning against a wall, or lying across the lap of their partner. American schools seemed to prefer the use of paddles over the English cane.

There are a variety of paddles used in this form of flagellation. Leather paddles, some with decorative chrome studs on one side, make a heavy thud when they hit and like the genital whips are manipulated by wrist action alone. Slappers are similar but are designed to make a noise. These are formed by placing two pieces of leather together and leaving them unsewn on the paddle portion. Tawses are designed the same as the slapper except they are cut to form fingers. The fourth type is the wooden paddle. Light weight paddles are safer but, as with any instrument, caution is still exercised. Some people use wooden kitchen spatulas and spoons for a paddling scene. CAUTION: Heavy wood paddles can cause physical damage. Fraternity paddles are, as a rule, too heavy for S/M play.

SLAPPING   Slapping a partner is done more for arousal by humiliation than for pain. CAUTION: Slapping a person's face can be very dangerous. The technique used for slapping requires one to put their hand on the opposite side of the partner's face, giving support to their head and preventing damage to the vertebrae in the neck. The slap is aimed to land just below the cheek bone, NOT on the jaw area or near the eyes. Of course, only wrist action is used, never an arm swing.

SPANKING   Spanking can be one of the most intimate forms of flagellation and is done by having the victim lie over the lap of the disciplinarian, who then repeatedly slaps the person's buttocks. Different psychological effects are achieved by the type of verbal communication used, and whether the truant removes any of their clothes before submitting. The type of clothes or

fetish objects worn also plays an important role. Some disciplinarians wear latex skirts or pants that create a slippery sensation against the penis. Cross-dressing of the truant adds a different dimension to this game. Men experience what it would have been like to have had their dress lifted and panties pulled down for a spanking. Rubbing, dildos, or the insertion of fingers are sometimes used to induce orgasm.

Other forms of spanking are done during intercourse, in either the missionary (the person on bottom spanks the one on top), or doggy style (the mounting person spanks the one on bottom). Less dialogue is used for this type of spanking and the slap is sometimes followed by grabbing the buttock and gently squeezing or

massaging. Again, sporadic or sharp pain is not erotic.

STRAPPING   Strapping is done with a belt or strip of leather. This was the typical woodshed style of father/son discipline. The same risks apply with regard to safe aim. Shorter straps are used because they give the best control. The victim is made to stand, bend over (knees together), lean against an object, or lie down. Replicating the strap or belt used on the victim as a child makes more of an emotional impact (this could be either a positive or negative experience).

WHIPPING   Whips are designed to give increased or decreased power to the hand. Whips made of feathers, velvet, or rubber soften the blows. Long whips made of leather with weights at the end of each strip produce the most pain and are usually reserved for punishment. Today's S/M punishment whips are more innocuous versions of the lethal historic cat o' nine tails, the Roman flagellum, and the Russian knout. However, even the modified version, if not used properly, can injure the partner. One method of swinging the whip is in a circular motion perpendicular to the person's buttocks. If done correctly, the tips of the whip graze the lower buttocks in the upward sweep of the circle. The lighter the strokes given, the longer the game can last. Many novices forget that the whipping is for arousal; not punishment. When purchasing whips consideration is given to how the handle fits one's hand and that the grip is properly balanced with the rest of the whip. That is, the handle is the same approximate weight as the tail. Riding shops offer a good selection of whips, the best quality usually coming from England. There are individual craftsmen that cater to the S/M community and create beautiful whips of excellent quality ("Slave Training," by Lady Tanith, Backdrop Club lecture, January 26, 1991).

(See also ABRASIONS, ALGOPHILIA, BED OF NAILS, BEE STINGS, BITING, CLAMPS, DISCIPLINE, DOMINANCE/SUBMISSION, PARAPHILIAS, PINCHING, RHABDOPHILIA, SENSORY ENHANCEMENT, TICKLING and URTICATION)

FLATULENCE (Flatuphilia, Eprocto-lagniac and Eproctophilia—arousal from flatulence) Flatulence refers to the passing of intestinal gas. The French once had a stage act where a performer attracted large paying crowds merely to watch him pass gas. Serious flatuphiles request that their partner release the intestinal gas directly into their awaiting face or mouth. The following is an excerpt from a letter submitted to me by an anonymous flatuphile describing one of his sessions:

My audio cassette player was running during this time—it didn't record too clearly, but you can hear her say that she had to fart and then ask if I was ready.

I answered yes and she blew a huge fart right into my face! The fart itself is very clear on the tape.

I could smell nothing because her ass pressed against my nose and closed it. We tried a couple of times to have her fart while on her hands and knees so I could then pull my face back and smell her farts but that never seemed to work out.

About 15 minutes after her first fart, she announced she had another one and asked again if I was ready, she then ripped another big one right in my face!

She has a friend who lives much closer to her who she has gotten into some things she enjoys—golden showers [see Urophilia]—which I don't really do. Therefore, I suspect I will not be as interesting to her. But, I wrote to her last week and suggested she meet with me on a more professional basis and I would pay her for each "full blown" fart she lets in my face while the recorder is very close by...

People place personal ads to assist them in finding consenting partners. Here is one:

My mouth is your toilet,
Fart up my nose,
Sit on my face and let
me deep sniff your love box,
Rim slave, wants master to
fart in my mouth...

CAUTION: Holding a lighter to the buttocks as they release gas is very dangerous because the gas is combustible and can create an explosive effect if the flame enters the anus, thus seriously damaging the rectum.

(See also COCKTAILS, COPROPHILIA, DEFILEMENT, DOMINANCE/SUBMISSION, HUMILIATION and SHOWERS)

FOOD/EATING See ANTHROPOPHAGY, COCKTAILS, LACTAPHILIA, MUCOPHAGY, PIE THROWING, STUFFING, UROPHILIA and VAMPIRISM

FOOT BINDING See BINDING/FEET and PODOPHILIA

FORMICOPHILIA See ZOOPHILIA/FORMICOPHILIA

FORNICATORY DOLLS (Dame de voyage, Inflatable dolls, Pediophilia—arousal from dolls) Fornicatory dolls are those that are produced with the specific intent of being used to accommodate genital penetration. There are several types of sex dolls available in today's market. Fornicatory dolls are made in Asian countries, Africa, Europe, and the United States. They are about half the size

of a human, with pliant breasts or a realistic penis. The most common type are the inflatable dolls that come equipped with vibrating penises, breasts that can be filled with warm water, and several orifices. The more expensive types were once popular among European sailors and had pubic hair and even a clitoris. There is also the inflatable sheep (Luv Ewe) or pig that is equipped with an opening under the tail.

Fornicatory dolls are used as a third person for group sex, the cold partner for a necrophile, same sex partner, and consensual partner for spanking, coprophilia, or S/M where a submissive is commanded to have sex with the doll. However, they are most often used as jokes. The June 21, 1991 San Francisco Chronicle carried the story of inflatable dolls being passed around among Red Sox fans at a Fenway Park baseball game. Some of the crowd became offended by the blatant fondling of the dolls and security guards confiscated them. People occasionally use other dolls for sexual purposes as in the June 1991 case of the stolen Ronald McDonald who, several days after his abduction, was found in an apartment closet dressed in female underwear.

It is possible for the inflatable dolls to come loose at the seams and deflate. The plastic can also be ruined by oil based lubricants.

(See also AGALMATOPHILIA, GENITAL/ANAL INSERTS, PEDIOPHILIA, PENETRATION TOYS and SYBIAN)

FROTTAGE (Toucheurism, Haptosis—non-consensual touching) Frottage is the act of rubbing one's body against another person or object for sexual arousal. Today it is highly recommended as a safe sex practice in lieu of intercourse. There are two common manifestations of non-consensual frottage, one is when someone rubs against a person in a crowd and when confronted apologizes as though it were an accident. The usual cue is the obvious pressure of an erect or semi-erect penis against the victim's buttocks. The other type of frottaphile is the "goose and run" offender.

Robert Tralins, in *The Sexual Fetish*, gives the case history of several frottaphiles.

One would follow women who were endowed with particularly large buttocks up escalators and push his penis against the rails to induce orgasm. Another followed obese women into revolving doors and was aroused by rubbing against them. Of course, not all frottaphiles are aroused by the person they are rubbing. Men with silk or fabric (hyphephilia) fetishes will only rub women in silk dresses, and so forth. Some podophiles, as well as other varieties of fetishists, engage in frottage almost exclusively. They not only fondle the foot or shoe but some are actually aroused by feigning accidentally stepping on a woman's foot in a crowd. These usually apologize immediately.

Men are not the only offenders. For example, there are women who enjoy such things as squeezing through men packed into gay bars and watching them jump as they suddenly realize that a pair of breasts have just brushed against their backs.

(See also AGALMATOPHILIA, OCHLOPHILIA and TOUCH)

FURTLING Furtling (furtivus: stolen or hidden) refers to the once popular entertainment of manipulating one's hand underneath a photo that had a small area cut out where the legs, breasts, or genitals were located. Placing one's hand behind this space gave the illusion of seeing real life genitals or buttocks. Burton Silver and Jeremy Bennett have written a book that contains examples of this erotic art form with a history of its appeal and its demise  under Victorian influence. In their book they cited the following portion of a 19th century physician's address to the West London Scientific Association in defense of furtling:

AS A DOCTOR I cannot speak too highly of this book of original engravings, which, by the simple contrivance of holes auspiciously placed, affords an entertainment most enjoyable and vitalizing. However, let me at once warrant that the purpose of this work is not merely to amuse and entertain, but, in so doing, to assuage the sorrow of the heart, lift the load of melancholy from the desponding mind, and restore to the wounded spirit its wonted elasticity. Indeed it has been my pleasure to demonstrate the workings of this fine book to more than a few patients, and I can assure you that even when a severe prudery was evident, I have never experienced a failure. The appropriate fervours have always been quickly aroused and harmlessly released in a manner most therapeutic and becoming (The Naughty Victorian Hand Book, Furtling: The

Rediscovered Art of Erotic Hand Manipulation, by Burton Silver & Jeremy Bennett, in forward).

The reason the word furtling is used is because the sketches are all of normal people who are unknowingly or unintentionally exposing themselves to others; such as a woman watching a nude male swimmer towel dry through a telescope, or a woman who just had the front of her skirt bitten out by a horse, exposing her genitals. There are hands drawn on each previous page giving instructions on exactly how to hold the fingers behind the hole.

(See also KOKIGAMI, SEX GAMES and VOYEURISM)

G

GANG BANGS   A gang bang consists of serial sex with more than two partners. A few claim that this may possibly be the type of sex for which our bodies are physiologically designed. This assumption is based on the difference in average time for orgasm between men and women. Some men orgasm in two to three minutes and some women take twenty minutes. A clan of primal humans could gain many advantages from having more than one man inseminate each woman. Sex and suspected paternity of many of the offspring bonds members of the clan together and ensures sharing of food and protection when necessary. It is also the type of behavior engaged in by some of our closest relatives, the primates.

Gang bangs differ from a Menage à trois (a married couple with an outside lover), troilism (three lovers), candaulism (one person watching a couple) and a "Mongolian Cluster" (simultaneous sex with multiple partners). The term is frequently used in rape situations where there is more than one rapist. However, it can also be organized and consensual. There is a group in the San Francisco area that allows women to select sex partners from a photo album. The coordinator then calls the men selected and invites them to a private party. Those attending are then able to meet the

woman and decide whether to participate or to leave. Those who stay take turns until the woman is satisfied. Waiting in line has many merits according to participants. Men sometimes find that watching others having sex is informative as well as stimulating. The tension and anticipation is probably much higher than in ordinary group sex where everyone's attention is either scattered or focused on their current partner(s). (A few group sex houses cater to the wishes of women who announce that they would like men to line up for a gang bang.)

People similarly engage in impromptu gang bangs at private parties where one person slips away and has sex with numerous people during the evening.

A slightly different form of gang bang is the "two-minute parking lot test." This is staged at singles bars and is designed to ensure selection of the most competent or sexually compatible candidate for the night. One woman described her technique as follows:

First a potential partner is screened by dancing. A close dance with a man gives me a quick answer to whether our bodies fit together, there is sexual chemistry, compatible body rhythms, whether he caresses or gropes, and how easy or difficult it would be to get him aroused. The dance can also reveal how long he can maintain an erection once aroused, and a possible estimate of his critical dimensions. Once he passes the screening and intimates his desire for sex, he is given the opportunity to take the "two-minute parking lot test." If in that time he performs well and proves to be sexually compatible he qualifies as a sex candidate for the rest of the evening. The advantages to this method of selection are that I don't end up spending the night with someone who doesn't meet my needs. A commitment doesn't have to be made before sampling more of the merchandise, and my reputation stays intact because no one suspects that two people leaving and returning to the bar within three to four minutes have had any form of sex. The rejected men are usually content because they received a consolation prize of two minutes of phenomenal sex and left with a great story. The victor gets an ego boost, and I leave with the best possible sex partner.

Prearranged gang bangs may have a special theme such as Santa Clauses at Christmas, men in diapers or long beards on New Year's Eve, valentine costumes on February 14th, or "bring a sex toy to share" party. Games such as "Little Bo-Peep" or "Hide and Seek" add to the intrigue. (See FANTASY PLAY) CAUTION: Safe sex practices are the responsibility of each individual. If a condom happens to break during penetration, the session ends or is restricted to a different orifice.

(See also ADULTERY, CANDAULISM, FESTIVALS, GROUP SEX, MENAGE À TROIS, ORGIES and POLYITEROPHILIA)

GAYS (Commasculation, Gay, Homophilia, Homoeroticism, Iterandria, Invert, Lung-yang, Sexual inversion, Sarombavy, Uranism, Zwischenstufe)

A RITUAL OF JOINING
Two pairs of eyes that burn with feeling, meet
And measure bodies toned from fight and flight
That tense, aroused, and lift to reach a height
Which threatens each and each allows to greet
Antlers thrusting, meeting antlers, hooves beat
Air. And bone caresses bone with crushing might.
Heaving sides glisten bright, the source of light
Bursting, twitching, shimmering. And the heat

Of two bodies together fends off night.
When one is seen walking it seems that two
Are there. Or perhaps it's the two seem one.
Two may be seen to rear as if to fight
A battle, an old struggle to renew.
It's the passion, the ritual begun.

–Nelson Graff, 1991

A predisposition toward homosexuality, bisexuality, and heterosexuality is based on biological (genetic, hormonal, and neurological) factors. Gays usually notice an attraction for the same gender at a very young age, even before they are aware of the physical aspects of sex. The exact causes of human or animal sexual preferences are still unknown, therefore this text will not endeavor to explain them. One recent development by a scientist at the Salk Institute, Dr. Simon LeVay, is worth mention. Dr. LeVay found evidence of a structural difference in the brain's hypothalamus region between heterosexual and gay men, the latter's being more similar in size to heterosexual females. The study is still preliminary and no theories have been substantiated.

Homosexuality is found among other species as well. Pigeons, ravens, and dolphins are known for general acceptance of same sex mates, some taking a mate of each sex. Most primates that become isolated from the opposite sex mate in captivity will mate with same sex partners. G.L. Simons states an interesting observation in his book, called *Sex and Superstition*. "The biblical word for sodomite, a translation of qadesh, properly denotes a man dedicated to a deity, and so the early Jewishhostility to 'sodomites' may have been nothing more than opposition to a rival cult. The Sodomites, it appears, were consecrated to the mother of gods, the famous Dea Syria, whose priests or devotees they were considered to be. Sodomitic acts were committed with male and female temple prostitutes" (p. 121).

Throughout history about 10% of the total population is believed to have been gay. A few notable gays or bi-sexuals have included Nero, Tiberius, Julius Caesar, Socrates, Michelangelo, Leonardo da Vinci,

Alexander the Great, Hitler, and very probably, J. Edgar Hoover.

Many people assume that gays are all effeminate because this type is easiest to recognize. However, there are many gays who are homomasculine ("bears"). These cultivate the biker, body builder, lumberjack, or construction worker images.

Often women will become lesbian for a short time after a traumatic experience, particularly rape. Young men who have been violently raped by another male often become gay as well. The reason given is that it is a way to abandon identity with the male race that he considers abusive and he becomes the passive "female" during sex encounters, sometimes dressing the part. Not all male victims react this way.

A common explanation men give for their change to same sex partners is that of discovering sex with other men is much more physical and passionate than with past female partners. Likewise, women will prefer the gentle nurturing and extended foreplay other women offer. People who are confined in areas for an extended period of time with only a few people may temporarily make a switch to whatever sex is available. Others simply prefer the common interests shared by someone of the same sex. Many travelers practice homosexual behavior in other countries, with whatever the indigenous race, but would not engage in it at home. J. A. Rogers, in *Sex and Race*, spoke of living in the West Indies, where pharmacists had to put out an extra supply of lubricants when English sailors ported.

A current philosophy or political strategy is that of gays becoming open about their sexual identity. This is designed to force people into recognizing the prevalence of gays and by this mass exposure cause them to respect the rights of gays to live without persecution or disparagement. Some gays are currently forcing others into exposure by a ploy called "outing." This is accomplished by leaking a prominent gay's name to the media.

Gay lifestyles are very similar to those of heterosexuals. Those who form live-in relationships divide chores according to talents and preferences rather than social roles. A gay couple has potential to be financially more secure than a heterosexual couple because they have a double male income and no dependents (the opposite is usually the case for lesbian couples; however, they in turn, have an economic advantage over a single female parent). Gay couples rarely have a problem understanding the puzzling psychological differences of the opposite sex. Not all gay men engage in sex, but those who do anatomically have more options and no menstrual cycles with which to deal. The male-male relationships can last through the decline of passion due to a close bonding and compatibility, but they seem to face more internal pressure for challenge, sexual passion, and adventure. However, most of the problems gays face in a partnership arise from the prejudice of smaller communities, families, or employers. There are support groups available for gays and their families in larger cities and a national organization called "Gay and Lesbian Alliance Against Defamation" that unites gays in defending themselves against bashing and prejudice. Gays are often objects of persecution. Even today, Iran's government executes gays by beheading, burning, or stoning. A 1990 Soviet survey conducted by the Moscow Institute of Sociology reported that 30% of those questioned favored isolation of gays and 33% favored extermination. The majority opinion in America most likely differs. However, gay bashing still occurs.

People who participate in sex with a same sex partner will often deny their gay status by claiming that it is only the receptive partner who is gay, that this is only a temporary way of getting sex until the right or perfect heterosexual mate comes along, that they were seduced while intoxicated and therefore innocent, or that the person they are involved with is a very special friend and they wouldn't consider having sex with any other same sex partner. Others say sex doesn't count if they are not emotionally involved. Everyone has the prerogative to select a label to express their own sexual identity. A person's label won't always be consistent with Webster's definition, but social etiquette dictates that the term they select be respected. This is also true for transsexuals, transvestites, and bisexuals. Three examples of men who claimed identities that seemed in conflict with their actions were 1) a man who said he was heterosexual but went on to say that he does have five or six male friends with whom he really enjoys having sex, 2) a male prostitute who says he is heterosexual but has only had sex with a woman once while on drugs. All of his other sexual encounters were with men while he played the role of female, often in female attire (other transvestites accept this as heterosexual behavior), and 3) a 40 year old virgin male who claims to be gay.

Gays rarely change their sexual preference through therapy and many therapists believe it is more valuable to simply help them adjust to their lifestyle rather than change it. The Masters and Johnson Institute does, however, offer a "short term intensive intervention" program for those with a strong desire to change their preference. Some feel that only bi-sexuals are able to make these changes and the program is certainly not guaranteed to effect a change. (Masters and Johnson Institute, St. Louis, MO)

(See also BI-SEXUALS, CATAMITES, DRAG QUEENS, HOMOPHOBIA, LESBIANS and PEDOPHILIA)

GEISHAS   A Japanese geisha is a female who is taught to entertain men with contrived charm. She was at one time purchased while young from her parents, just as were the Yoshiwara (prostitutes), except this girl became educated and later chose her own sex partners. She began her education at the age of twelve and for the next six years she was taught social etiquette, ancient dances, songs, rituals, and the precise hand and body movement enacted during the tea and flower arranging ceremonies. Hendrik de Leeuw quite eloquently describes the experience of being entertained by these professionals in the early 1900's.

A charming hostess greeted us at the door. She was attired in a charming Japanese costume, and she moved unimpeded by the rich cloth of her kimono. She led us into the reception room. There I saw many geisha girls in gay kimonos, their hair dressed formally and elaborately. They crouched in little groups, chattering as usual. . . . As if to talk gaily of nothing at all was one of the lessons they had learned well at school.

The tea ceremony began. It was beautiful, indeed; and a solemn thing, in a way, conforming in all its many details of movement to a ritual conceived ages ago and by the weight of those far times still taught as an important part of education.

The movements of the leader were captivating. She was seated on a lacquered stool. Before her was a table, richly decorated. On it was a bronze stove and this was topped by a water vessel of brass, from which a vapor rose as the fire heated it. As she sat solemnly at her post, two of her assistants, leaving her side with identical inclinations of the head and graceful liftings of the hands, burned incense. Another arranged the flowers in a beautiful vase of porcelain. Each touch of her fingers was a motion produced by long practice. It was poetry of the hands. I watched eagerly as the flowers slowly assumed the precise position required by custom, one yearning toward the ceiling of the room as if toward the sky and the sun, another turning gently downward, gazing into a pool that was not there. All this motion—of the burning incense, of the flower arranging, and the solemnity of the presiding officer, flowed into a harmony of action, sound, and color. It unfolded itself like a flower under the morning sun.

The geisha at the table rinsed the dainty tea cups with boiling water, dried them with a piece of red silk, mixed green leaves in the cup and slowly poured the hot water over them. She paused, then took a solitary quill and brushed, although my eye could not discern them, specks of ashes and tea dust from the shiny table. Then there was another moment of rest. Once more she poured the precious decoction from one cup into another until, at last, one cup of true tea was prepared. This was offered to me, because I was the guest of honor, and I tasted it. I must confess that I was not able to tell exactly what subtle delicacy had been added to the drink by the ceremony, but I was quite willing to sip for a long time if sipping would cause a continuation of the pretty tableau.

Also I was somehow glad when I looked about into the freshly painted faces of the geishas that there was no need for them to fashion their coiffures for the rude embraces of townsmen and foreigners (Cities of Sin, pp. 37-8).

The Japanese culture during this period placed little emphasis on romantic love. A wife was a servant and mother, not someone with whom to converse or to shower with socially unaccepted displays of affection. Therefore, the Yoshiwara (prostitutes) served men's need for passion and the geishas provided feminine conversation and companionship. Men, while able to enter into a sexual relationship with a geisha, often resisted temptation due to the financial and social responsibilities involved. It was the equivalent of committing to a mistress. Male children born to mistresses/geishas were generally adopted by the father and his legal wife; daughters were raised by the geisha. Today geishas choose the profession for themselves, often coming from working or middle class families. However, the majority are daughters of geishas or tea house owners. Western influence has lowered the status of geishas and prostitutes in Japan. Mr. de Leeuw illustrated the polarity of moral values between the two cultures when he said, "If the Japanese can be accused of being unmoral and cynically realistic in their official attitude toward sex, the West may be said to be outwardly sentimental and hypocritical. Certainly to the Occidental mind, and especially to the Christian, the Yoshiwara is sinful. The Japanese think otherwise since morality and chastity are, to them, something more than the abandonment of all sexual activity. They are aware that a 'chaste' woman, as she is described in the Western countries, may be the epitome of all the established virtues and yet be a highly immoral being."

(See also BORDELLOS, HETAERAE and PROSTITUTION)

GENITAL/ANAL INSERTS (Bouginonia, Butt plugs, Dildos, Godemiche, Olisbos, Paraphallus) Dildos are artificial penises or plugs that are designed to fit into the mouth, vagina, or anus and act as aids to masturbation. They have been made of leather, stone, clay, wax, ivory, rubber, fruit, vegetables, plastic, and polyurethane. These devices are quite ancient and even the Bible makes reference to artificial penises:

Thou hast also taken thy fair jewels of my gold and of my silver, which I have given thee, and maddest to thyself images of men, and didst commit whoredom with them.—Ezekiel 16:17

ANAL INSERTS   Anal plugs are specially designed for anal insertion. They are shaped like fingers or inverted cones and can be used alone or in conjunction with penile-vaginal sex. Males find the plug adds stimulus to his prostate and on the female it fills in the rectal area which presses against the inner vaginal cavity, making it smaller and thereby giving one a fuller sensation. Anal plugs range in length from 4" to 8", and those longer than 4" need to be very pliable beyond the 4" point to facilitate the curve in the rectum. An anal insert is available for the heterosexual couple that is very small in diameter and which has a ring at the base allowing it to slide over the penis for intercourse. CAUTION: Butt plugs are designed with a flange on the bottom to prevent the rectal sphincter, which acts like a vacuum, from sucking the lubricated object up into the body. If this does happen and the person is unable to defecate or pass the object out within a day a physician can either administer drugs to relax the intestine and facilitate the object's expulsion, or use other treatments.

The ancient Orient is known for having invented many types of artificial inserts. One of these is the Chinese Love Bead, String of Pearls, or Siamese Strings. These consist of a string that has small rubber balls or pearls attached at 1/2"—1" intervals. They are inserted into the anus and pulled out as the person ejaculates. These are only intended for use by one person. Another device is the Ben Wa Ball which is made of steel and plated with chrome or gold. Two of these are inserted into the vagina to produce titillation while the woman goes through the day. Most women find that Ben

Wa Balls don't produce any type of special sensation and, worse yet, can fall out when they walk. Women who leave them inside  the vagina during intercourse say they derive pleasure this way. The original or more authentic Ben Wa Balls were constructed differently, with one having a hollow center containing mercury that resonated with movement. Others acted as bells to add music to the sex act. It is usually difficult for women to have an orgasm without any form of clitoral stimulus, therefore it is doubtful the balls are adequate in themselves.

Hawk Metals has invented a similar set of toys for men known as Ass Weights or Ass Eggs. They weigh slightly over a pound each and are shaped like eggs. Some have a small longitudinal hole through the center that allows one to pass a string through and attach it to another egg or to use it as a handle for removal. The weight of the eggs makes them easy to remove with mere gravity. These eggs are worn during any type of ride that bounces the wearer around. Motorcycles are highly recommended in advertisements.

DILDOS   Other early records of dildos go back to Egypt and Greece. French troops gave them to their wives before marching off to war as masturbatory aids. Tipu Sahib, a sultan of India, allowed the 600 women in his harem to use dildos to keep themselves sexually satisfied, thus discouraging lesbianism and adultery. Women also used a mulierre (special 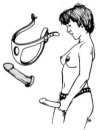 strip of fabric pulled up against their genitals and fastened to a belt by straps) to create stimulation by rubbing when they walked.

Today people purchase their own dildos which come in a variety of shapes, sizes, colors, and textures. One 10" dildo is sold that was made from a mold of the porn film star Jeff Stryker. Some dildos include vibrators.

Dildos specially made for the purpose may be worn attached to chastity belts, latex underwear, harnesses, gags and chin straps. Anal plugs can be added to chastity belts, and double ended dildos can be worn on harnesses. The Japanese have face masks that are worn over the groin, the nose being very long and shaped like a penis. Dominatrixes sometimes will have their "pets" fetch a dildo and present it to them in their mouth as part of a humiliation scene.

Some dildos have flexible shafts that rotate to stimulate the G-spot along with an external clitoral stimulant, such as the "Pet Turtle." Some are equipped with suction cups on the base, which are used to  anchor the device, attach to a flat headed vibrator or, as in the case of strippers in a sex show booth, to a glass window.

The Japanese have designed a type of dildo that slips over the penis and releases fluid at the appointed time. We have dildos that expel fluid but they are not as elaborate. Other dildos are simple rubber sheaths that fit over a semi-flaccid or erect penis to give the effect of a larger penis when the partner is penetrated. CAUTION: Condoms are put onto dildos before use. If the condom breaks, the dildo is cleaned in warm soapy water or soaked in a solution of water and nonoxynol 9 to destroy viruses. Only water-based lubricants are safe on the condom as oil dissolves the rubber. Safety also requires that dildos and plugs have a chain in the center, rather than a dangerous nonpliable metal shaft, to prevent pieces from breaking off inside the body.

VIBRATORS   Vibrators are mechanical devices that produce vibrations (small rapid jerks) and which are placed against the skin for a massage effect. Their power comes from either batteries or house current.

Some people use vibrators against the genitals for sexual arousal and orgasm.

Dildos have been designed to house the battery operated mechanisms so that they may be safely inserted into the vagina or rectum. Some electrical vibrators have add-on attachments for penetration or clitoral stimulation. A few vibrators have a cup attachment for the glans penis.

Vibrators can end years of inability to orgasm but others may find that it desensitizes the area. People respond differently to different types of vibrators and should not assume that because a battery operated hard plastic vibrator does not bring them to orgasm that other types won't either.

Small vibrators are also used on nipple and clitoral clamps. (*Good Vibrations, The Complete Guide to Vibrators* by Joani Blank)

(See also ANAL SEX, CHEMISE CAGOULE, CATHETERS, ELECTRIC SHOCK, GLORY HOLES, PENETRATION TOYS, POWER TOOLS, RINGING, SAFE SEX, SCROTAL INFUSION and SYBIAN)

GENUPHALLATION Genuphallation is the act of rubbing the penis between a partner's knees.

(See also AXILLISM, COITUS A MAMMILLA, COITUS INTERFERMORIS and HEAD STANDS)

GERONTOPHILIA (Alphamegamia— older man, Anililagnia—older women, Chronophilia—age difference, Graophilia— older female, Matronolagnia—older female) Some people have a sexual attraction for people who are significantly older than themselves. There are even rapists who only attack elderly women (anoraptus). Gay gerontophiles are common as indicated by the number of personal ads requesting father figures. Personal ads of gays are usually more direct than those of heterosexuals. The following are typical::

30 yr. into shaving, ripe crotches looking for Daddy

Boy seeks leather daddy to serve

WM wants Daddy Bear for manly sessions of safe sex

Bearded Daddy wanted to teach me the ropes and serve his needs

Gerontophiles are thought to have been conditioned to respond to older parents or relatives because they were kind to them. It may also be an attempt to reconcile a lack of affection from a parent. Many others simply prefer the compassion, intelligence, experience, and charm of people who have achieved their life goals and now live to enjoy and share life with others.

Special dating clubs such as Anachron in New York cater to the needs of gerontophiles as do some bordellos. Magazines such as *Over 40* or *Over 50* feature photos of older women and stories of their sexual escapades with younger men (see Appendix). There is even a video called "Grandma Does Dallas."

(See also ANISONOGAMIST, DYSMORPHOPHILIA, INFANTILISM and MATURATION)

GLORY HOLES See GROPING APPARATUS

GOLDEN SHOWERS See SHOWERS

GROOMING Grooming of a sex partner is most commonly found among primates but humans too, in addition to the normal grooming one does before a date, use grooming as foreplay.

Ford and Beach found this to be true among the Siriono, Dusun, Plains Cree, and Trobrianders. Holmberg wrote of the Siriono's of Eastern Bolivia:

Lovers also spend hours in grooming one another—extracting lice from their hair or wood ticks from their bodies, and eating them; removing worms and spines from their skin; gluing feathers into their hair; and covering their faces with uruku . . . paint. This behavior often leads up to a sexual bout, especially when conditions for intercourse are favorable (The Siriono, by A.R. Holmberg, p. 182).

Sex slaves often prefer performing tasks that involve the grooming of their masters. These rituals include bathing, manicuring their partner's nails, and shampooing or styling their hair.

(See also COURTSHIP, and SLAVES)

GROPING APPARATUS These are devices that create a barrier between people but at the same time enables them to have sexual contact by inserting their hand into  strategically placed holes. There are grope suits made of latex or leather where only the genitals or breasts are exposed and boxes that one person stands in and other people can reach in with their hands. An alternate form is the glory hole (a wall or box that has a hole only large enough for the insertion of a penis) which allows both partners to protect their anonymity. These are popular in X-rated video rental stores. The Suaheli of Africa were said to use a hole in the fence around their yard for rendezvous with lovers.

"In the yard, near the fence, there is a gate-like board in which there is a hole about a yard from the ground. Early in the morning the negress takes her stand there with her back to the board and facing her husband, who, though still lying in the hut, can watch her well from his bed. Her lover comes to the gate as pre-arranged, she bends down forward, acts as if she were washing the cooking utensils, and calls out some chance phrase to her husband, who suspects nothing, while her lover has her through the hole in the board" (*Voodoo-Eros* by Felix Bryk pp. 216-7).

Latex suits are available with small rubber fingers or fibers over nipples and genitals. These create a tickling sensation as the person moves or perspires.

There are similar groping games where one person walks between two rows of people in the dark or while blindfolded.

Humans are not the only species to use groping apparatuses. The female thread-worm pokes her vagina through the skin of her host vegetable when she is ready for sex. The males crawl around the surface until they find one of these female occupied holes (*Sex Link*, by Hy Freedman).

(See also CHEMISE CAGOULE and GLORY HOLES)

GROUP SEX (Orgy, Swinging, Wife swapping; Bigynist—one male/two females, Bivirist—one female/two males, Marty-machlia—arousal from having others watch during sex, Ochlophilia—arousal from being in crowds)

Group sex involves sex between more than two people. Humans, like other species, can experience a high level of sexual energy from an environment where they hear, see, touch, and smell others engaged in copulation. The opportunity to engage in sex without the usual commitment or intimacy likewise relieves pressure for many. Many ancient religions used orgies in the worship of fertility gods. These rituals gave widows, homely virgins, and spouses of infertile mates the chance to conceive; the offspring of such unions were considered sacred.

Today the North American Swing Club estimates the number of active swingers in the United States to be five million. There is a diversity of establishments, individuals, or groups that support this activity. They range from sex houses, special group sex cruise ship excursions, hot tub parties, S/M clubs, fetish clubs, gay baths, nudist colonies, gang bangs, religious rituals, and intimacy workshops. The most common establishment is one run by a couple who open their home as a group sex house one or more nights a week. The couple usually provides clean sheets, towels, lockers, snacks, drinks, condoms, and lubricants. In return each person donates a small amount of money to help them cover the expenses. This contribution does not pay for sex, and just like a singles bar one can leave without having sex. The house will have several rooms. One is used as a room for people to socialize, usually clothed early in the evening and semi-clothed later. There is a kitchen where people snack and socialize as well. Hot tubs are common and usually one's first invitation is to undress and soak in the tub. The next progression of events takes one to either a group sex room or a semi-private room. The difference between these are in the distribution of mattresses; group rooms have them joined together to cover the entire floor, whereas semi-private rooms have them arranged farther apart. In addition, the house rule restricts anyone else from joining a couple in this room without their invitation. The rule for a group sex area is that people can only join a couple or group with their permission. There is an important difference between invitation and permission. The first requires the couple to ask another to join and the latter allows the couple to be interrupted with requests of others. Often, being touched or caressed by others is used as a subtle substitute for the verbal request. Once this inquiry has been made it is each individual's responsibility to say no or gently push them away. People who refuse to take "no" for an answer or who are too aggressive will be asked to leave and not asked back. There are house rules governing the type of sex allowed on the premises. Often overt sadomasochism is prohibited, and generally men are not allowed to engage in genital contact with each other, although it is often encouraged between women. Once compliance is made to these rules the type of sex and number of participants vary.

A visitor to a group sex scene will see a few who masturbate alone, couples engaging in oral/genital sex, and groups of three or more together using an array of positions. There are groups of three people satisfying each other with a variety of oral, genital, anal, and overall body tactile stimuli. Mongolian Clusters consist of more than three people. These usually have more men than women and each woman will have several men penetrating her or groping from the outside of the cluster. Some women use the anonymity of this environment to experiment with different forms of same sex intimacy. These may either engage in mutual titillation with each other or work together as a team to provide sexual variety (one female may not enjoy some sex acts—cunnilingus, fellatio, anal or vaginal penetration—and the other will cover for her.) In addition to the Mongolian Cluster, other positions include the Rainbow, which is a cluster of people who have different skin colors, and a Row Boat is where a female

sits on a reclined male's penis and fellates two men, one standing on each side. Daisy Chains are the circles formed by a group of people, each performing oral sex on the person in front of them. No one is forced to swap partners and many couples simply go to watch others have sex or to have sex themselves while others watch.

Sophisticated group sex establishments may offer videos, mirrored ceilings and walls, grope boxes, see through glass dance floor, fashion shows, strip tease classes, pubic hair trimming, and massage lessons. A house in Florida requires that both partners attend a sensitivity class prior to being allowed into the club.

Group sex houses offer women many benefits. They are able to engage in casual sex in an environment where there is little need to be concerned about rape or physical abuse. Participants are not restricted to depending on one partner to satiate their appetite. Casual sex can help relieve the tension or frustration experienced by those who don't have a regular sex partner. It is a way of accepting responsibility for one's own physical needs rather than letting an unsympathetic socioreligious system dictate deprivation. Establishing control of one's own life creates a feeling of empowerment and keeps a person from directing frustration toward others, or of internalizing these feelings and suffering from depression and low self esteem.

In addition to these types of group sex houses, there are those that cater to special interest groups such as S/M, scat, golden showers, cross dressing, and fetishes. CAUTION: Many couples assume swinging will save a marriage. However, it more often destroys a weak relationship. Likewise it is an activity that has to have the enthusiasm of both partners to be successful. Sexually transmittable diseases are a major concern for many. However, it is often easier to insist that a casual partner use condoms than it is to ask a steady lover. ("Swingers," Mensa Sexyg Gathering Conference, San Francisco, February 17-18, 1990; "Are You a Swinging Virgin," by Shirley Sez, Lifestyle Conference, August 17-18, 1990; "ABC's of

Swinging," by John and Honey-bear, Lifestyle Conference, August 17-18, 1990)

(See also ADULTERY, CANDAULISM, FESTIVALS, GANG BANGS, MENAGE À TROIS, ORGIES, POLYITEROPHILIA, SEX CONFERENCES and WIFE SWAPPING)

GROUPIES See EROTOMANIA

GYNEMIMETOPHILIA Gynemimetophilia (gyne: female; mimos: mime), coined by John Money, refers to those who are aroused by a male who is impersonating a female or a male-to-female transsexual.

(See DRAG QUEENS, PETTICOAT DISCIPLINE, TRANSVESTITES and VICTORIAN LACE)

H

HANDICAPS Handicaps include physical disabilities and, in this text, includes incurable sexually transmitted diseases. People suffer from many different handicaps but only a couple were selected for discussion here. These should give the reader a general concept of the problem and possible recommendations to facilitate adjustment.

Paraplegics cannot feel anything from the waist down, but orgasms similar to wet dreams do occur. It is possible for the paraplegic's partner to rub the penis, creating an erection that will enable the two to have penetrative sex. Paraplegics become aroused from tactile stimulation done above the waist. A sex surrogate is sometimes used to train the person or couple in adjusting to this condition and there are organizations that offer resources and support to disabled people.

Men whose genitals have been removed are still able to have pleasurable sensations by stimulating the nerves in the prostate region. Ancient eunuch priests used this method of pederasty to continue their sex lives. Men who have lost testicles after puberty can often have an active sex life; however, orgasm is usually more difficult to achieve. Anal stimulation of the prostate can be of benefit for them also. A doctor is able to monitor these men to make sure their adrenal gland is producing enough testosterone to replace what was once produced by the testicles. If this hormone is not present the prostate can atrophy.

Multiple sclerosis and Lou Gehrig's disease are diseases that attack the central nervous system. Sensation in the genitals may diminish and make sustained erection and orgasm more difficult. The use of a cock ring may benefit a partner and a urologist can be consulted if orgasms do become a problem. Support groups exist in some areas that assist in working out many other concerns.

Support groups and clubs are available for many categories of special handicaps. People who are under five feet tall have a club called "Little People of America" that sometimes serves as a resource for meeting others. Not everyone considers it necessary to restrict their selection of a spouse to those with similar handicaps.

Personal ads are excellent for people who live with STD's such as AIDS and herpes, or for people who are deaf, blind, have colostomy bags, are amputees, etc. The person placing the ad remains anonymous and does not risk personal rejection. One should never think one is alone in his or her suffering. For instance, 9 1/2 million people in the U.S. are restricted to wheelchairs, an estimated 40 million have genital herpes (some reports have indicated that from sample screenings as many as 50% of Americans carry the virus) and as of December 1991 there was a cumulative of 206,392 reported cases of AIDS.

(See also ACROTOMOPHILIA, DISEASES, DYSFUNCTIONS and DYSMORPHOPHILIA)

HANDKERCHIEF CODES Handkerchief codes are used by some S/M and gay groups. Colors denote preference for specific sexual activities and placing the handkerchief on the left side of the body tells potential partners the wearer is a top (one who does this to another). Colors on the right side of the body signal that the person is a bottom (one who has the act done to them). Therefore, people look for matching colored handkerchiefs on the opposite side of the prospective partner's body. The following chart shows the significance of specific colors:

COLOR	SIGNIFICANCE
Black	Heavy SM
Blue, dark	Anal Sex
Blue, light	Oral Sex
Blue, robin's egg	Light SM
Brown	Coprophilia
Gray	Bondage
Green	Prostitution
Lavender	Group sex
Lemon	Catheters
Maroon	Vampirism/Menstruating
Mustard	Food games
Olive Drab	Costumes/Military
Orange	Anything
Pink	Breasts/Lactaphilia
Purple	Piercing
Red	Fisting
White	Novice
White lace	Corsets, etc.
Yellow	Urophilia

Codes are not perfectly standardized, and embarrassing mistakes have occurred. At one time right and left sites had opposite meanings for those living on the East and West Coasts.

(See also EXHIBITIONISM and PERSONAL ADS)

HAREMS (Gynecaeum, Seraglio) Harems rose from the practice of polygamy. Keeping women sheltered was a way of guarding wives and concubines from the sexual escapades of men in the community and possible reciprocation from the women. The term harem is used for Moslem seraglios, where the women were kept under lock and key, but its meaning, "that which is sacred, set apart, or forbidden," alludes to the former religious custom of maintaining priestesses for sexual purposes in the temples. The isolation of married women in harems was consistent with an oriental practice of purdah (hiding women behind veils and gowns) that predates Mohammed, and

of the Greek's gynecaeum, where women stayed at home, having servants shop and do errands. A Greek woman of social status was rarely ever seen on the streets—this was a place for female servants, peasants, slaves, and prostitutes. This isolation doomed the women to social illiteracy, many being condemned as superstitious and intellectually unfit to rear male children. Harems were outlawed in the early 1900's but some still exist. The King of Morocco is reported to have over 200 women in his harem.

Ancient Chinese kings and emperors had as many as 121 women in their seraglios. Special "sex secretaries" were employed to keep tally of whose turn it was to have sex with the king and whether she became pregnant as a result. Finally in "the early eighth century, girls who slept with the emperor were rubber-stamped afterward" (*Sex in History*, by Reay Tannihill, p. 238).

The Moslem injunction is religious and even without the locked doors of a harem the Arab women prior to the 20th century would not choose to walk about the streets exposing themselves to strange men. Most harems consisted of only one wife and a few concubines. The Koran limited men to four wives; however, they were permitted additional concubines. Only the wealthy could afford this luxury because in addition to the wives the man had to support the necessary servants or slaves needed to care for the women and children. The lives of the women were leisurely. They had private gardens, talked, bathed and gossiped. Some engaged in alternative or illicit sexual adventures and others escaped boredom through the use of opium.

(See also GEISHAS, GROUP SEX, HETAERAE, MARRIAGE and ORGIES)

HARMATOPHILIA Harmatophilia (harmostes: to govern or bring harmony, tomy: to cut, philia: attachment) refers to one who is aroused by mistakes or rules being broken. Harmatophobia refers to those who are frightened of making a mistake. A great majority of men are aroused by their partner having less sexual knowledge or competence than themselves. This bolsters their self esteem and makes them feel more secure in the relationship. Of course, this preference for sexually inept females can cause some women to either feign incompetence or prevent them from wanting to experiment or learn more about sex.

(See also MASOCHISM, PECATTIPHILIA, SADISM and ZELOPHILIA)

HARPAXOPHILIA (Chrematisto-philia—arousal from being robbed)

Harpaxophilia (harpax: robber, philia, attachment) indicates sexual arousal from robbery.

Certainly there is an adrenalin rush experienced while being robbed.

Consensual sex scenes or fantasy play that utilize the stimulus produced when being robbed often consists of having the

victim retire and sometime later being awakened by a scantily-clad cat burglar crawling through the bedroom window. The victim pretends to be asleep while the burglar searches for valuables. At some point there will be a struggle with one person ending up bound. This person will be interrogated as to where the jewels have been hidden and then can expect to be sexually molested.

Fantasy scenes of cat burglars seem to work because we react emotionally when we lose something regardless of whether or not it was voluntary.

(See also ABDUCTION, FANTASY PLAY, HYBRISTOPHILIA, KLEPTOPHILIA, PARA-PHILIA, PECATTIPHILIA, PHOBOPHILIA, SACRIFICE and SYMPHOROPHILIA)

HEAD STANDS Couples may enjoy

having sex with the female in a head stand position (head and hands forming a tripod-like pose on the floor).

In one couple, the female preferred having orgasms in this position because the blood that settled in her upper extremities created a lightheaded sensation that produced intense orgasms for her.

The exact position required that she position herself in a head stand on something soft and spread her legs. Her partner then straddled her between the legs so that one of his feet was on each side. Bending forward he was able to insert his penis and thrust until orgasm.

Other similar activity includes only engaging in oral sex with the partner doing the headstand or lying on a bed with the upper body hanging over the edge.

(See also OXYGEN REGULATION and SEX POSITIONS)

HEBEPHILIA Hebephilia refers to the

attraction of a person to teenagers.

(See also CATAMITES, ILLEGAL SEX, INCEST, NEPIOPHILIA, NYMPHOPHILIA, PEDOPHILIA, PORNOGRAPHY, SEX RINGS, SNUFF FILMS and VIRGINS)

HEDONISM Hedonism (hedone: plea-

sure) refers to the lifestyle of those who plan their lives primarily for the experiencing of pleasure.

(See also HODOPHILIA, PECATTIPHILIA, PHOBOPHILIA and ZELOPHILIA)

HERMAPHRODITES (Ambisexuality,

Gynandromorphous) This is a disorder where an individual has both male and female genital characteristics due to the body producing irregular amounts of male and female hormones during prenatal development. They may have a modi-

fied vagina, ovaries that hang in the outer labia (labial ectopy) an enlarged clitoris, a small penis with testicles, a developed penis with an empty scrotal sack (crytorchidism), or any number of combinations or internal alterations of the normal. A hermaphrodite with functioning testicles or ovaries and uterus can parent children with a partner of the appropriate sex. These variations often account for the cases reported of veteran soldiers giving birth to children. Many ancient gods were portrayed as herm-aphrodites and were thought to be able to parent children without a partner.

Hermaphrodites in America were often hired by circuses and exhibited naked as freaks until the mid 20th century. Chinese in the third century were warned that this was the result of bi-sexual parents. Europeans in the Middle Ages thought that the condition could be cured by having the hermaphrodite engage in sex with a recently deceased virgin. Today parents in India have infants with this dysfunction castrated and raised to be dancers and prostitutes. Surgery and hormone treatments can often correct this condition if done while the child is young.

There are a few magazines and movies featuring hermaphrodites engaged in sex. They differ from pre-operative transsexuals in that the latter still have a similar physique as to when they were male and they still have scrotal sacks and testes with no vagina. One movie featured a couple of hermaphrodites who were feminine except for well developed penises. They performed in various positions including simultane-ously penetrating each others' vaginas with their penises and then each withdrawing to ejaculate. Such movies are often just farces in which females wear glued-on dildos.

(See also ANATOMY, DYSFUNCTIONS and TRANSSEXUALS)

HETAERAE   (Courtesans) The Greek hetaerae were female companions and entertainers during the 4th and 5th cen-turies BCE (before common era or BC). They were the highest of the three classes of Greek prostitutes. The second class were called auletrides. These played musical instruments at feasts and used prostitution as a secondary source of income. The lowest class was the dicteriades, whose pri-mary talents were sexual. Most hetaeraes were originally slaves; Greek women rarely were allowed to pursue intellectual interests. Hetaerae were comparable to the highest class of European courtesans. These women chose to remain single and pursue an educa-tion. Although often financially supported by their lovers they were still allowed much

more freedom than other women who, after marriage, were confined to their gynecaeum or homes.

It was extremely difficult for women to gain any type of positive recognition in Greece but several of the hetaerae are men-tioned by historians. Aspasia became the intellectual and beautiful mistress of Athenian statesman, Pericles, who ruled Athens for many years. The infamous Thais, mistress of Alexander the Great, is credited with persuading him to burn the city of Persepolis in Persia. Evidence exists that some of the hetaerae led campaigns to educate other women and to improve their status.

(See also ADULTERY, CATAMITES, GEISHAS, HAREMS, MARRIAGE and PROSTI-TUTION)

HETEROSEXUALS   (Androphilia, Heterophilia, Heterosexualism) Heterosex-uality is the preference of a person for a partner of the opposite sex. It is determined by biological factors that include genetic, hormonal, and neurological components. Our sex preference does not seem to be determined by casual sex experiences. A large number of boys experience homo-sexual contact before they settle into a het-erosexual lifestyle. Furthermore, many ancient or primitive tribes practice active homosexuality on young boys before mar-riage. This is socially accepted and after their marriage seems not to effect their het-erosexual role.

Society does not seem to be able to manipulate people's sexual preferences, but can influence how people perceive them-selves in their selected role. Successful implementation of husband/wife roles usu-ally necessitates a proper role model by par-ents. Children reared in single parent homes often have difficulty in determining appro-priate roles or behavior and families por-trayed on television can often create unrealistic expectations for a partner or one-self. While having poor role models rarely leads to homosexuality, it can cause broken marriages or decisions to remain single.

(See also BI-SEXUALS, GAYS, HOMO-PHOBIA and LESBIANS)

HIEROPHILIA Hierophilia (hieros: sacred or holy; philia: attachment to) refers to those who are aroused by sacred objects.  This may include such things as masturbating with crosses or while sitting in the church pews. Some have even broken into churches at night and had sex on the altar. (Personal communication, Austin Texas, 1969.)

Many of the early goddess religions revered sex and included it as part of their worship. Statues, animals, priests, and priestesses were all provided for congregants' sexual gratification at one time or another.

(See also CHARMS, FERTILITY WORSHIP, FESTIVALS, PHALLOPHILIA, SEX MAGICK and YONI WORSHIP)

HODOPHILIA (Nomavalent, Ecdemolagnia) Hodophilia (hodos: path, philia: attachment) describes the sexual arousal people feel while traveling to new or strange places. Travel often entails anxiety, pleasure, autonomy, and additional hours for entertainment. People feel more tempted to break out of their normal routine and experience their new environment to the fullest, especially if the country has a legal red light district.

(See also COITUS A CHEVAL, SIDERODROMOPHILIA and XENOPHILIA)

HOMILOPHILIA (Autagonistophilia— arousal by being on stage or on camera) Homilophilia (homilo: sermons, philia: attachment) refers to feeling sexual arousal while listening to or giving sermons and speeches. Public speakers are often dynamic and this combined with adrenalin can produce sexual arousal for both the speaker and their audience.

Religious services were once designed to arouse devotees sexually in preparation for the ensuing orgies. Today, tent revivals still appeal to the emotions of those gathered by promising that God will forgive their sins and love them. Occasionally people will fall

on the ground in mild convulsions that are indistinguishable from some tantra practitioners whose bodies go limp during exercises due to sudden orgasmic vibrations that last ten to twenty minutes. Spiritual arousal at revivals, however, was not always limited to God and the individual worshiper. In 1873 D. J. Davis recorded his experience of old time American camp-meetings.

Those who think that a camp-meeting is no place for love-making are very much mistaken. When passions were aroused and moral restraints gave way for miles around the camp hundreds of couples could be seen prowling around in search of some cozy spot (History of the City of Memphis, p. 173, as quoted in Sex and Race, by J.A. Rogers). Rogers continued with this explanation: "Since the camp-meeting was a primitive affair, those human beings who were nearest to original Nature, were the leaders, thus the chief stirrers of the sexio-religious emotions of the whites were Negroes, most of whom could neither read nor write. Surcharged with primordial feeling, these totally illiterate blacks would whip their white audiences to the heights of frenzy" (331).

In small towns, lacking more sophisticated meeting places, the back rows of tent revivals were popular 'cruising' spots for both gay men and heterosexual prostitutes during the 1950's and 1960's.

Another group of speakers that seem to project sexual chemistry are trial attorneys. These people have to deliver intense emotional pleas in defense of clients. This responsibility and strong emotional display sometimes induces erection in male attorneys. They are often warned by their professors not to fixate on a female juror because she can pick up on the sexual energy and feel uncomfortable.

The ability to emotionally or sexually arouse an audience appears to be necessary; without it an audience will not respond to the desires of the speaker, whether this is to purchase an object, convert, volunteer, or change their position on an issue.

Speeches that are about sex do not have to condone it. Often the guilt associated with a minister's admonitions against this 'vile' act can create greater arousal than a lecture discussing its merits.

(See also ACOUSTICOPHILIA, AGREX-OPHILIA, COPROLALIA and NARRATO-PHILIA)

HOMOPHOBIA Homophobia is defined as the fear of homosexuality and its perceived emasculating consequences. A more appropriate word might be "femmephobia" because this feeling is generally applicable only to the fear of becoming the passive partner. To most heterosexual men being gay means being weak, effeminate, and powerless. It means that if a man takes the aggressive role and approaches them they lose their powerful masculine status; they are being pursued and have to say "no" to sex, something with which most men have little experience. A feeling of helplessness then is easily transformed into anger and aggression.

After World War II, gays became more open. But Puritan morals argued that any form of sex other than penovaginal is deviant and that those who practice it are not capable of any type of ethical behavior. A Senate committee released a report in December 1950 that warned that even one...

sex pervert in a Government agency tends to have a corrosive influence upon his fellow employees. These perverts will frequently attempt to entice normal individuals to engage in perverted practices. This is particularly true in the case of young and impressionable people who might come under the influence of a pervert...One homosexual can pollute a Government office.

"Gays, because of this new social stigma, were considered a security risk being easy targets for blackmail by Communist spies. The FBI was given the responsibility of investigating, exposing and dismissing anyone proven to be homosexual" (*Intimate Matters* by John D'Emilio and Estelle B. Freedman, pp. 288-293).

Homophobia can have a negative effect on a man's ability to maintain close friendships with others. Men have as much need for close same sex friendships as do women but only a few support groups exist to provide a forum for discussion of personal problems, fears, and goals. A person who cannot communicate their frustrations often releases their tension in inappropriate or unhealthy ways, therefore it benefits everyone in a family to let others have time and permission to cultivate same sex friends.

A few men have begun gathering in the form of support groups where they are making an effort to share their emotions and fears with other men. A goal is to overcome the homophobia that keeps many from developing the type of close supportive relationships that women seem to cultivate.

(See also GAYS, HETEROSEXUALS, LESBIANS and PHOBIAS)

HOMOSEXUALITY See GAYS

HOT WAX Hot wax in sex play is used to increase adrenalin and thus arousal. The most famous enthusiast was St. Pazzi, a 16th century nun who would have others drop hot wax on her body while she was tied to a bed post and humiliated (*Very Peculiar People*, by E.J. Dingwall).

People engaging in hot wax play hold the candle over a partner and drip wax, sometimes until a large mound is formed. Occasionally people will drip wax on their partner's genitals or insert a long candle into the anus and let the wax run down the sides of the candle until the anal area  is obscured. CAUTION: Both partners experiment with the wax on themselves before using it in a game. A plain wax candle, with no scents, beeswax, or metal coloring, is used. The temperature is also regulated by the distance the candle is held above the person, becoming cooler in proportion to its height. Ice is kept on hand for accidents or simply to alternate the sensations. Areas with dense body hair are avoided unless depilation is desired.

(See also ALGOPHILIA, BODY PAINTING, CIGARS, ELECTRIC SHOCK, ICE, MASOCHISM, PYROPHILIA, SAFE SEX, SCRATCHING and SENSORY ENHANCEMENT)

HUMILIATION (Asthenolagnia— aroused by weakness or humility) Verbal humiliation in sex play produces passion for some.

Humiliation has long been a popular form of discipline for governments and religions. It was used as a form of abuse by the Visitantines, a Catholic order of nuns formed by Francoise Fremoit de Chantal to replace chastisement with birches. The Rev. William M. Cooper, B.A., in *A History of the Rod* (p. 81), states:

Novices were obliged to wear a fool's cap, immense spectacles, or to tie heavy pieces of wood on themselves, or be laden with stones and blocks like an ass. If a novice lay too long in bed, she had, as a punishment to carry a pillow into the refectory; and if a similar fault was committed a second time, she was obliged to extend herself on the ground, and say to the nuns, 'Dear sisters, have pity on me, that I am so lazy.' On a third offence, the delinquent was treated like a little child, wrapped in swaddling clothes, and fed with pap, and only as a last resource would the Mother Superior give a good birching. Some of the nuns thought the rules too mild, and left the community for a more rigid order.

Humiliation was also used by the Scottish Puritans who sometimes placed the sinner in an iron collar and fastened them to the wall in front of the congregation to be harangued for half an hour every Sunday, sometimes for up to a year.

Today humiliation is used in almost any form of sex play, but is consensual and something a partner can transfer to a sexual response. There are people who do not become sexually aroused this way, and others who enjoy insults when they are feeling well psychologically, but not when they are depressed. Therefore, a safeword is used with humiliation just as one uses it with flagellation or bondage.

Humiliation is more effective for some when they are bound or being forced to do something menial or embarrassing. It may also take a physical form that involves the use of urine, feces, or shaving. CAUTION: People have personal limits they don't want violated. A sample contract may state, "You can call me anything you want, but don't say anything about my mother, the size of my penis, or my tattoo." There may be subjects from one's childhood that are too painful to address, while others use humiliation to reprogram negative experiences into a satisfying erotic one. A general guideline used in humiliation is that of not using insults that one will later have trouble denying. For instance, a person would never call an obese partner a "pathetic fat-assed pig."

Humiliation is like bondage play in that after the game the partner has to be released. In humiliation this is accomplished by spending time nurturing and reassuring the partner of their value and attributes. This part of the game is essential, and not taken lightly.

(Refer also to COPROPHILIA, DEFILEMENT, DEPILATION, DOMINANCE/SUBMISSION, INTERROGATION, SLAVES, TOILET TRAINING, UROPHILIA and WORSHIP/GODDESS)

HYBRISTOPHILIA Hybristophilia is defined by John Money as "a paraphilia of the marauding/predatory type in which sexuoerotic arousal and facilitation and attainment of orgasm are responsive to, and dependent upon, being with a partner known to have committed an outrage or crime, such as rape, murder, or armed robbery [from Greek, hybridzein, to commit an outrage against someone + -philia]. The partner may have served a prison sentence as a convicted criminal, or may be instigated by the hybristophile to commit a crime and so be convicted and sent to prison" (*LOVEMAPS*, pp. 263-4). Dr. Money used Bonnie and Clyde and Charles Manson's "Family" as examples of this phenomenon. Men living in prison often have

ongoing relationships with three or four women. These men offer excitement, mystery, and intrigue to women who usually have low self esteem, or a fear of physical intimacy. Masters and Lea wrote of a notorious mass murderer named Vacher whose trial was attended by a large number of women, some of high social standing, who were obviously aroused by the murderer.

Some male criminals are attractive, but that does not explain the phenomenon. Certainly, Vacher was not a man at whom women would look twice—unless in revulsion—were he not glamorized or somehow charged with eroticism by his crimes. Philip Lindsay (The Mainspring of Murder) describes him as having a pallid countenance, splotched with yellow. Hair straggled down his cheeks, black and matted. He had a harelip, adding also a speech defect to his debilities. And still additionally, as a result of a gunshot wound sustained in a suicide attempt, his right eye was damaged and suppurating; while the right side of his face was semi-paralyzed, the consequence of the severing of a nerve (Perverse Crimes in History, pp. 165-6).

Women would often pass suggestive notes to the defendant, flirt, and at times create such a disturbance that they were asked to leave the courtroom.

Prisoners benefit from these liaisons by conning the women into smuggling drugs, cash, and cigarettes into the prison. Visiting hours are usually spent fondling each woman. It is possible for relationships to evolve into marriage but most of them end if the prisoner is released (*Prisoners of Love*, by Richard Cone; *Pacific Northwest*, May 1989, pp. 53, 102).

(See also ACROTOMOPHILIA, HARPAXOPHILIA, PHOBOPHILIA, SADISM, SYMPHOROPHILIA and VICARIOUS AROUSAL)

HYGROPHILIA Hygrophilia (hygro: wet or moisture, and philia: attachment) refers to sexual arousal attained from contact with any type of body secretion. This includes nasolingus (nasal mucous), tears, saliva, salirophilia (perspiration), vampirism (blood), urophilia (urine), coprophilia (feces), semen, and vaginal secretions.

People may derive their pleasure from direct contact with the secretions, prefer to find it in articles of clothing, or to simply smell the odors or pheromones these produce.

Hygrophilia is not limited to the secretions of their partners; some have engaged animals or deceased humans for this purpose.

(See also COCKTAILS, CUM ETIQUETTE, KLISMAPHILIA, LACTIPHILIA, SAFE SEX and TOILET TRAINING)

HYPHEPHILIA Hyphephilia (hyphe: web, and philia: attachment to) refers to those who are aroused by touching fabrics or other garments.

(Refer to DORAPHILIA, FETISH, FROTTAGE, OCHLOPHILIA and TOUCH)

HYPNOSIS Hypnosis is a trance-like state that resembles sleep wherein the person is susceptible to suggestion by the hypnotist. There are several degrees of hypnotic states: the lethargic state that resembles a coma, the major state wherein one is oblivious of all outside stimuli except the hypnotist's suggestions, and last the minor state wherein the person obeys suggestions to a lesser degree.

There are historical records of cases where hypnotists were able to use hypnotic suggestions to facilitate intercourse. Hirschfeld was consulted during a trial where an impotent husband filed sexual assault charges against his wife's physician. The doctor confessed that he ordered her to "raise her skirt, lie down, spread her legs, take out his penis, introduce it into her vagina, then, during the act, perform parallel movements until mutual orgasm occurred." Suspicion was aroused when she became pregnant and a detective was then hired by the husband, who confirmed his fears (*Sexual Anomalies and Perversions*, by Magnus Hirschfeld, p. 378).

Hypnotic suggestion is also used by therapists to create an aversion to particular types of sex. A case cited by C.A. Douglas Ringrose was of a young male who developed a sexual attraction for his mother-in-law. He sought counseling and Quad 'P' therapy was used. This is a "combination of self hypnosis, behavior modification, biofeedback, personal acupressure, and autogenic programming." The patient was put in a trance to explore his past. Then his "memories were modified to associate sexual thoughts of the mother-in-law with an unpleasant taste (castor oil) and an unpleasant aroma (ammonia)...Post-hypnotic suggestions were given to associate any new sexual thoughts of the mother-in-law with the aversive stimuli...During a subsequent series of three sessions, a penile self-slap was added." The patient finally achieved relief from his problems ("Case Report Quad 'P' therapy for rapid relief from Sexual Aberration," by C.A. Douglas Ringrose, *British Journal of Sexual Medicine*, May 1989, p. 194).

People who experience sexual phobias (impotence or frigidity) have sometimes been successfully hypnotised to overcome this fear and thus can experience orgasms. Others have used autohypnotic suggestion to induce orgasms for themselves. Cases are mentioned in the annals of hypnosis that describe hypnotist-induced hallucinations that are visual, auditory, and tactile. These hallucinations are said to be of seductive women who sing, dance, and provide the tactile stimulation needed for orgasm (*Perverse Crimes in History*, p. 181).

A Florida hypnotherapist, Michael Stivers, uses hypnosis to enlarge women's breasts and offers a money back guarantee if the patient fails to see results after several treatments. (KNTV, Chan. 11 News, December 30, 1991)

(See also SEX MAGICK, SUBLIMINAL TAPES and SUBPERSONALITY)

I

ICE Ice is used to enhance tactile stimulation, confuse or surprise the partner, delay orgasm, as a catheter, a light form of torture, or as first aid for mild burns.

A sample S/M ice scene is as follows:

Male: Has waiter of restaurant seat him and his date in a secluded corner. As he whispers his desires into her ear he takes the opportunity to slowly guide his hand discreetly up her dress and along her thigh.

Female: Responds by taking a piece of ice from her water glass and hands it to him, saying, "If you want to play I make the rules. Take the ice and run it in circles up my inner leg, pull my panties aside, and insert it. If you don't do it right I'll order the most expensive item on the menu."

Ice can be run along the body at any time, but it is especially effective during bondage or massage. A few heavy S/M participants will blindfold their partner telling them they are going to brand or burn them and instead use ice. The initial sensations are very similar. They also alternate heat and cold for added intensity.

Other uses of ice include placing a few chips in the mouth as one fellates a partner. This will usually delay orgasm by causing the penis to become flaccid. A small amount of ice is occasionally inserted into the vagina or rectum during sex or is placed inside the foreskin and the end is then taped or held shut. Fellatio is used to speed the melting process. CAUTION: It is unsafe to put more ice into an orifice than will dissolve within a couple of minutes. Ice catheterization requires a special clean procedure and can be dangerous if the ice rod has rough edges or breaks before it melts.

(See also CATHETERS, CIGARS, ELECTRIC SHOCK, MASOCHISM, PSYCHROCISM and SENSORY ENHANCEMENT)

ILLEGAL SEX The government once regulated which days married couples could have sex, positions (missionary) they could use, type of sex (penovaginal, kissing, and caressing), and denied them the use of birth control. Europeans broke the ties between religious sanctions and civil law long ago. However, in the United States legislators stalled, fearing that support of changes in the sex statutes would label them as immoral. Therefore, a country which is progressive in every other way has kept its archaic civil regulations on sex between consenting adults until quite recently. The manufacture and sale of condoms was illegal in the United States until December, 1930. This is an item that has been available in one form or another for 3,000 years. Condoms purchased before 1930 were obtained on the black market and thus were not subject to quality control. The American Law Institute, in 1955, wrote a new code recommending that all laws imposing fines and imprisonment for sexual activities performed between consenting adults in private be abolished. Despite the fact that in 1948 Kinsey released data showing that the majority of Americans engaged in illegal sexual activity, these puritan laws continued to be enforced. (Kinsey reported that 59% of Americans engaged in oral-genital sex, 70% used prostitutes, 37% had participated in homosexual behavior, and 17% of those raised on farms had engaged in zoophilia.) The new *Model Penal Code* was not accepted by any state until Illinois reformed its laws in 1962. In 1965 a landmark decision was rendered by the U.S. Supreme Court in the case of *Griswold v. Connecticut* which gave married couples the right to use birth control devices without having their privacy invaded by the imposition of criminal sanctions, but still arrests continued. In 1967 parents had their college student daughter and boyfriend arrested in Illinois for alleged fornication. The father stated "I'd rather see her in jail than debauched." In 1963 a prominent entertainer was arrested on charges of sodomy (fellatio with two consenting females) and spent two years of a ten year sentence in prison before attorneys were able to get him released. These were only a few of the many cases where people were convicted for having deviant sex with a consenting adult. At the end of 1990 Idaho, Utah, Arizona, Oklahoma, Minnesota, Louisiana, Mississippi, Alabama, Georgia, Florida, South Carolina, North Carolina, Virginia, Maryland, Massachusetts, Rhode Island, and the District of Columbia still had statutes against heterosexual fellatio, cunnilingus, anal sex, and the use of dildos. Adultery is illegal in some states. Recently a couple of women were arrested and convicted on the mere accusation of adultery by

their husbands. One woman had already asked for a divorce. Today most other states permit consensual sex between adults. Sex acts most commonly prosecuted as criminal are rape, prostitution, child molestation, exhibitionism, voyeurism, homosexual behavior, and pornography. California's legal age of consent (adult) is 18 years. Touching a child 13 years and under is considered molestation and is a felony. If the child is 14-18 the charge is changed to "child annoying" and is a misdemeanor. Zoophilia is a misdemeanor. Homosexual behavior is legal unless it occurs in a state prison. Incest is illegal regardless of the age of the participants. There is also a law against child pandering which, in addition to pimps, includes a father who talks a prostitute or friend into showing his son the ropes if the son is younger than sixteen.

California law has made provisions for anyone who technically breaks a law but one that was obviously not intended for their case. This law permits an attorney to inform jurists that they can nullify an unfair law if they feel it is too harsh in a particular case. This is called Jury Nullification and the jurists use it by simply voting "innocent" regardless of the defendant's plea.

Americans are at risk of even greater intervention and regulation of sex between consenting couples by the government. Within the last few years, the FBI has used the RICO law, originally designed to confiscate all of a drug lord's property, against video store owners and x-rated movie producers. The complainants are usually from the religious right or originate from traps set by FBI investigators. If the investigators can get three convictions in a small religious community, they can use the RICO act to confiscate property from people in other states; even when laws in the other state permit them to produce the material. In addition to this type of government censorship, Senate Bill 1521 has been introduced "which would allow victims of sexual assault to file a civil suit against producers and distributors of 'obscene' material." (*Californians ACT*, Vol. VI, No. 4, by Bobby Lilly, Nov. 14, 1991, p. 2). This bill was introduced despite evidence by the

President's Commission on Obscenity and Pornography (1970) that pornography, a 20th century innovation, does not "cause" sexual violence against women and children. This bill is serious because it could provide rapists and child molesters possible legal defense for their criminal acts and make prosecution even more difficult. Another tragic effect of this bill would be to potentially increase the number of sex crimes. The majority of sex offenders don't take personal responsibility for their violence; this is why they repeat their acts. A bill that would shift responsibility enables them to continue in their violence without remorse once they are acquitted or paroled.

America is not the only country that is becoming more repressive with their laws against sex. The Canadian Supreme Court recently (1992) ruled that pornography could cause violence against women. This assumption was based upon lobbyists' arguments that within the last few years, along with the rise in pornography, there has been a rise in sexual harassment and rape. This assumption is not necessarily valid. It is worth noting that historically societies enduring economic distress experienced an increase in spouse abuse, hate crimes, rape, theft, and so forth. People who undergo stress due to loss a of livelihood either release their anger on the weaker or compensate for their loss with overeating, sex, alcohol, or drugs. It is quite possible that instead of pornography being the cause of an increase in sex crimes, that an increase in pornography was only one of many symptoms of a suffering economy. Another country, England, recently (1992) used a prior ruling on fights (originally used to prohibit consensual but deadly duels) to apply to consensual sex acts. If allowed to stand, this law makes illegal in England any consensual act that would break or bruise the skin. Technically this includes love bites, spanking, and many other S/M activities. ("Controversy over court ruling on sadomasochism" by Nick Cohen, *London Independent*, February 20, 1992, pp. 1, 3).

("Sexual Lifestyles and the Criminal," by Norma Jean Almodovar, Lifestyle Conference, August 17-18, 1990; "Sex and Censorship," by Bobby Lilly, National Sexuality Symposium lecture, February 16-18, 1991)

(See also ADULTERY, ANAL SEX, BORDELLOS, PEDOPHILIA, PORNOGRAPHY and PROSTITUTION)

IMPOTENCE (Astyphia, Asynodia, Invirility, Pareunasthenia) Impotence is the inability to sustain an erection long enough for penetration of a partner, but orgasm usually remains possible with the right amount of stimulation. This condition affects almost 10  million people in the United States including as many as 40% of men over 65 years old who are not in good health.

Normal erection depends on many factors. It may begin with an increased level of dopamine and adrenalin in the brain or with stimulus to the parasympathetic (involuntary) nerves of the penis. These cause the smooth internal muscles of the penis to relax, allowing blood to enter through two main dilating arteries in the penis, filling tiny sinusoid veins with blood. As these expand they create pressure on the veins that control blood flow back into the body. The penis at this point becomes erect. After one eventually achieves orgasm, the two arteries return to normal, the muscle contracts, the pressure on the veins is diminished, and the blood drains back into the body leaving the penis flaccid. A disease, injury, or temporary debility of any of these components can cause impotence ("Impotence" by P. Church, *Harvard Medical School Health Letter*, September 1989, pp. 4-6, and October 1989, pp. 3-4).

Anxiety and stress can cause temporary impotence but doesn't seem to interfere with erotic desire. On the other hand, depression and anger cause a decrease in sexual arousal without creating actual impotence.

If a person suspects impotence with a psychological cause, an old fashioned but simple method of testing for this is that of sticking a row of postage stamps around the shaft of the penis before retiring. If the perforations are torn in the morning the person has experienced normal involuntary nocturnal erections (normally 3-5 a night) and psychological impotence can be suspected, although not proven. A urologist should be consulted if physical impotence is suspected. This specialist will be able to test arterial blood flow, condition of sinusoids, and possible leakage of veins. The urologist can make an initial diagnosis with an injection of papaverine. If the male gets a full erection and maintains it his problem is probably psychological. If he only becomes semi-erect or it comes on slowly he usually has a problem with arteries that flow into the penis. If he has an erection but it doesn't last very long his problem may be due to the veins leading out of the penis not closing. All these problems are now treatable with surgery and have a 50-70% success rate. The physician may be able to diagnose certain diseases or ailments that often cause impotence, such as diabetes, nervous system disorders or injury, atherosclerosis, or a deficiency of testosterone (male hormone). Impotence also often occurs after surgical removal of the prostate, bladder, or part of the rectum due to cancer.

In addition to inherent physical or emotional problems a person can suffer impotence due to drug abuse, or as a side effect from certain prescription medications (beta-blockers, tranquilizers, and antidepressants among others). Tobacco has recently become suspect as contributing to impotence. Studies conducted on dogs that were made to inhale the equivalent of one to two cigarettes resulted in temporary impotence. Alcohol is another cause of impotence. Autopsies on the penises of alcoholics have revealed that many of these men had very few if any of their penile nerves remaining ("Impotence," lecture by Tom Lue, M.D., Palo Alto, May 30, 1990).

Some men are impotent at night but are capable of having sex at other times. Dr. Martin Blinder, in his book *Choosing Lovers* (p. 211), states: "Incidentally, as men age, there is a change in the time of day when their sexual biorhythm and consequent peak potency occurs—typically to earlier in the day. One patient who reported he could 'barely get an erection once the sun went down,' proved insatiable at noon."

Treatments for impotence vary according to its cause. Drugs like papaverine (dilates the vessels) and prostaglandin E1 (PGE1) can be injected to produce erections that will last about 30 minutes. The needle is very small in diameter and only causes  slight pain for most men. There is a risk that the drug's effects will last too long (4+ hours) and cause further damage. A physician needs to be contacted if this happens, in order to inject a counteracting drug. A priapism (long term erection) that is not relieved within 6 hours causes pain, and if allowed to continue untreated for 24 hours can cause gangrene and require surgery. A man wanting to relieve erection before the normal time has elapsed can take 30mg of Sudafed (decongestant), assuming he did not overdose on the amount of his injection. Impotence treatment incurs an annual expense of $1,000-5,000. The newest approach has been with a mixture of three drugs: papaverine, prostaglandin, and phentolamine. A larger majority of men responded favorably in a test; there were no prolonged erections, no pain, no fibrosis, and the cost was only $2.50 each (*Men's Health*, "Injections That Cause Erections," by Mike McGrath, Vol. 6, #8, August 1990, pp. 4-13). An alternative injection device has been invented and is awaiting FDA approval in the United States. It is a small plastic tube that is held just inside of the urethra and squeezed so that the medication drains down into its center. This method is an improvement over needle injections because the needle sometimes causes scar tissue to develop over time.

Vacuum devices are much less expensive but can be cumbersome. The vacuum

device has a cylinder that is placed over the penis; the air is pumped out, thus pulling blood up into most of the penis. Once the penis becomes fairly engorged (3-5 minutes), the vacuum device is removed and a ring is placed around the base of the penis to prevent the blood from flowing back into the body until after orgasm. Tissue damage can occur if the ring is left on for more than 15 minutes. A similar semi-rigid device produced in England and called Correctaid is left on during intercourse (*British Journal of Sexual Medicine*, June 1990, p. 175).

Implant devices vary slightly. The simplest, the malleable, consists of two cylinders that can be inserted into the shaft of the penis under local anesthesia. The penis will be semirigid and can be bent forward for sex and back toward the body the remainder of time. The penis will not

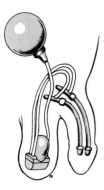

increase in size or swell, but the rigidity will allow penetration and orgasm. A more complicated implant consists of two inflatable cylinders, a pump, and reservoir. The pump and reservoir are placed in the scrotum. The pump can be pressed to push the fluid held in the reservoir into the inflatable tubes, producing a more natural erection. The pump is pressed again after orgasm to release the fluid from the tubes back into the reservoir. These implants can range in cost from $10,000 to $20,000 (*Mayo Clinic Health Letter*, December 1989, pp. 4-5).

Sexologists or other professional health care workers are recommended for any couple attempting adjustment to the husband's impotence or restoration of sexual activity. Renewed sexual activity causes many women to feel jealous of other women for the first time and they may need counseling and support in adjusting to this change.

Men suffering from impotence in other cultures have used alternative methods of achieving orgasm. Most of these involve flagellation or some other form of sensory stimulation that leads to an altered state/orgasm. These techniques are effective in inducing orgasm without genital contact; therefore erection is irrelevant. Prostitutes were often experts in employing flagellation, and many bordellos specialized in this type of remedy. The man had an additional advantage with these women as he did not have to feel guilty or embarrassed at not having an erection to facilitate penetration and hence her pleasure, since she derived this from payment. Thomas Gregor documented cures used today by primitive tribes in the Amazon. These include simply rubbing phallic shaped fish, turtles, or plants against the penis while chanting or having another male blowing onto the penis as if trying to revive fading embers. The most unpopular technique was to have the penis scarred, afterward rubbing medicine into the wounds (*Anxious Pleasures, The Sexual Lives of an Amazonian People*, p. 140). The Chinese acupuncture method was used in 1989 on a group of one hundred men who failed to respond to other forms of treatment. Of these 63 were able to have sex twice a week and ten could do so once a week (*Journal of Traditional Chinese Medicine* as quoted in Se*x Over Forty*, Sept. 1990 issue, p. 5).

There is a self help group called I-Anon that is headquartered in Maryville, Tennessee for those needing emotional support.

(See also CELIBACY, DYSFUNCTIONS, FLAGELLATION and HANDICAPS)

INCEST

SLEEPING BEAUTY

Laid out
Under the gauzy veil
Of sleep,
I feel the hall light strike
Me in the chest,
And I curl around it,
Roll away
Into dreams,
Away

From the creased frown
And darting, hungry eyes,
Hoping that this time
The burning incandescence will fade
To cool, empty blackness.
But when the light dies,
It leaves a stirring in the dark
That cleaves to my dreams,
Breathes into them a rising spinning life,
That smooths the wrinkles,
The eyes unchanged,
And I wish for a needle,
Immune to kisses,
To drain me for the last time
Of cursed wakefulness
And heat.

—*Nelson Graff, 1992*

(Fratrilagnia—brother, Matrincest—mother, Oedipus complex—repressed desire to have sex with parent of opposite sex, Patrolagnia—father, Thygatria—father/daughter, Sororilagnia—sister)

The taboo against incest originated for several reasons. Genetic defects in offspring has been cited most often. However, many tribes only restricted marriage between relatives; not sex. The taboo was used to promote kinship with other tribes, and to avoid sexual disruption or confusion of roles in the family unit. Sibling incest was once thought to produce only female offspring. This belief might have been one reason patriarchal societies prohibited these marriages.

Incan royalty is thought to have used incestuous marriage to keep power and wealth in the family. The Egyptian royalty used matrilineal descent in choosing successors because they couldn't prove paternity. Royal sons could only rule if they married their sisters. Sometimes they were married at birth. Cleopatra was one of the most notable females who engaged in incestuous marriage. At 14 she was married to her 10 year old brother. They vied for power until, at about age of 19, her brother mysteriously drowned in the Nile. Caesar had Cleopatra married a few years later to another young brother as a cover, while he lobbied for a law permitting polygamy. But then Caesar was murdered before he could wed

Cleopatra. Before her return to Egypt, the second brother/husband disappeared even more mysteriously than the first (*The Nile, The Life-Story of a River*, by Emil Ludwig, pp. 464-9).

Father/daughter incest is the type of incest that is prosecuted most often in court. Often, the men are religious, passive, poorly educated, and married to wives who are usually unavailable emotionally due to illness, alcohol, or drug addiction. The daughter often has to take over the mother's housekeeping responsibilities. These, or other problems, can create an environment where both the child and father crave nurturance. The father's moral values prevent him from even considering having an affair outside the marriage, a sin of adultery. Therefore, over a period of several years the father and daughter may sit together on a couch and watch television, gradually becoming more physically intimate, each time with the father reprimanding himself and swearing not to let it happen again. Of course, both have weak resistance and eventually engage in petting, oral sex, intercourse, and so forth. A key factor involved in father/daughter incest is often the father who lacks parent/child bonding due to the father not having participated in diapering, feeding, and caring for the child as an infant.

Mother/son incest, the third type of incest, may begin after a divorce when a toddler is allowed to sleep with the mother and a few nights runs into several years; however, actual penetration is rare in this situation. Typically, the dangers are greater when the toddler or other male child is past puberty and the mother is divorced, widowed, or not receiving an adequate amount of affection from a husband. The young men react in different ways, including having deep feelings of guilt. A teenager who feels guilt for seducing his mother needs to be reminded that, unless he raped her, seduction is impossible without the mother's consent. Teenagers are often traumatized by sexual advances made by their mother/guardian. It is important for these mothers to know that the psychological damage could make it difficult or impossible for their sons to trust or maintain normal relationships with women as they grow into adults.

Same sex parent/child incest can be the most traumatic for a child because it involves breaking two of society's taboos.

All individuals need to take responsibility for their own sexuality. The adolescent should say "no" without guilt, find a consenting person their own age, or seek professional help before incest occurs. Seeking counsel before an incident is very important because it may prevent incest, and because counselors are required to report cases of incest, thus making it almost impossible to seek assistance after incest has occurred without the risk of someone being arrested. Too many parents view incest as limited to the physical act. Incest can have traumatic emotional ramifications for the rest of the child's life. Adults who were either sexually abused or engaged in incest as young children often suffer from low self-esteem, guilt, shame, impotence, poor interpersonal relationships, obesity, and suicidal tendencies.

Incest is illegal but not unnatural. If it were unnatural we wouldn't need such stringent laws. The strength of the taboo counteracts the strength of the desire. There's nothing wrong with having fantasies; however, as mentioned previously, merely touching someone under thirteen in California is a felony and incest has no statute on age. Before engaging in incest both the parent and teenager might consider the consequences involved with having a parent (father or mother) imprisoned, and the ensuing isolation and guilt imposed on the child. The law does not acknowledge mutual consent between immediate relatives; therefore, this defense cannot be used in court.

Family rape is very traumatic and a child in this predicament may speak to a school nurse or counselor. There are many agencies whose purpose it is to protect children from incest and rape.

(See also ILLEGAL SEX, NYMPHOPHILIA, PEDOPHILIA and RAPE)

INFANTILISM (Autonepiophilia—arousal from playing role of infant, Infant-ophilia—arousal from playing role of infant) Infantilism refers to people who prefer to remain children and who often have an aversion to their adult bodies, facial or genital hair, or wearing adult clothing. There are cases of sexual and non-sexual infantiles. Infantilism differs from anaclitism in that the former consists of people who want to regress or act out the role of a child and the latter is a fetish relating to objects or acts from childhood.

There are cases of adults who act out their desires alone and without a partner. They may dress as a young boy and sit at home all day looking at themselves in the mirror or they may take a break and go to a park and play innocuous games with children. Others keep their body hair shaved, dress in children's clothing, and photograph themselves. One man took extreme pleasure in checking into a hotel and urinating in bed during the night. Infantilism was popular enough among the general populace for Germans to participate in adult baby balls after Lent.

Other adults find willing partners and create a multitude of scenarios. An infantile scene can last for many hours and the length is negotiated ahead of time because of this. The responsibility placed on the parent of a demanding infant can be very exhausting. The adult is not always a parent. He or she may be a young male child being baby-sat by a teenager who tucks them in, reads a bed time story, and tries to seduce the bashful but aroused young person. Scenes are also acted out where each partner dresses and plays the role of a child. Games of doctor and show me yours are also used.

Infantilism is on the increase because people are able, for a time, to have burdensome adult responsibilities taken away, and thus find it possible to "let go" emotionally (and perhaps sexually) in ways that would not be permitted the "adult." They are also allowed to demand nurturing and attention from their surrogate parent. They are now in total control and can have every whim fulfilled without feeling guilt. The act of getting by with things that they were punished for as a child creates a sense of empowerment and excitement. In addition to the emotional rejuvenation the child actor feels, a bond of trust and love is built between partners.

Infantilism can be therapeutic for people who are only able to accept unconditional nurturing by reverting to infancy or childhood. Others use this method to make up for the nurturing they didn't receive from their parents.

Infantilism does not always involve nurturing. It may be used in any S/M scene. Those trying to induce fear in a partner usually find it easier when the male is made to cross dress and to play the role of an innocent young girl.

Professional dominatrixes are often hired to act out adult roles for infantiles and there are magazines and clubs that provide information and paraphernalia. ("Alternate Personas," by Sybil Holiday and William Henkin, Ph.D., Society of Janus lecture, August 24, 1989)

(See also ANACLITISM, FANTASY PLAY, FETISHES, LACTAPHILIA, PARAPHILIAS, PEDOPHILIA, PETTICOAT DISCIPLINE, and TRANSVESTITES)

INFIBULATION (Episioclisia, Labiorrhaphy and Hymenorrhaphy—surgical closure of labia) Infibulation (in: inside, and fibulate: that which fastens) is the term used for either the sewing or fastening of the foreskin over the penis, sewing the labia 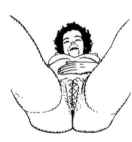 minora or labia majora together, or sewing the scrotum around the penis. The type of penis infibulation determines whether it prevents full erection or only penetration.

The *Oetang* ring was used as a chastity device, whereas stitching was done to prevent both coitus and masturbation. Penis infibulation was used by European parents on their sons to prevent night emissions or masturbation during the 19th century when this was thought to be harmful to their health. The Russian government, during a time when they restricted many soldiers from marriage, had a wire pushed through the foreskin of the soldiers and a seal soldered onto the ends to prevent unauthorized removal.

Infibulation, following the cutting of the labia minora, was used on young girls in parts of Africa to ensure their virginity at marriage. The husband was responsible for first opening the scar tissue protecting her hymen. Cultures varied in their rituals. Some only did this once, others closed it after the woman became pregnant, opened it in time for her to give birth, and sewed the vagina closed again after she became pregnant.

Today a few people practice a temporary form of infibulation or lacing in their sex play. It is a psychological game of having one's partner impose chastity on them. The stitches are placed through either the labia or foreskin and can remain there up to several days. Infibulation is only performed by people experienced with sterile techniques. They may first shave before cleaning the genital area with Betadine or Hibiclens. The skin is pinched up and away from the body, then a sterile suture (or needle and thread) is used to pierce the skin and sew the edges together. CAUTION: This is a blood sport and infection can occur if the person fails to use sterile procedures.

(See also BLOOD SPORTS, BONDAGE/LACING, RINGING, SAFE SEX, STAPLING and SUTURING)

INSECTS See BEE STINGS, FORMICOPHILIA and ZOOPHILIA

INSUFFLATION Insufflation, or blowing air into a person, has been done to almost every human orifice. The medical profession uses it to revive an asphyxiated person with mouth to mouth resuscitation and pharmacists in 19th century France used a form of rectal insufflation with tobacco smoke to revive or invigorate languorous patients and drowning victims. People have used insufflation during sex play but it is never recommended. CAUTION: Air inadvertently pushed into the rectum during enemas usually causes cramps and if a large amount of air is forced into the rectum or vagina, it may rupture a blood vessel. It can also carry a bubble of air (embolism) to the brain or heart, causing instant death. (See also KLISMAPHILIA and STUFFING)

INTERROGATION Forms of interrogation have been adapted by many for sex games of dominance and submission. The "prisoner," "rapist," "transvestite," "burglary victim," or "shoplifter" is bound, humiliated, intimidated, "tortured," and at some point "forced" to perform sex on the interrogator.

Some of these scenes have lasted up to two days without the bottom confessing or giving information. The length of the game is usually predetermined in negotiation and can be canceled at any time.

People speed the process by setting up the interrogation room with bright lights, a cold temperature, and an uncomfortable position for the prisoner. A dripping faucet or some sort of distracting noise can be used, but not music. Some men crossdress;

which makes it easier for them to surrender or cooperate without losing their dignity.

(See also ABDUCTION, DISCIPLINE and FANTASY PLAY)

INUNCTION (Aliphineur—person using lotion to arouse partner) Inunction (inunction: act of rubbing ointment, or lather) refers to those who have their body lathered up or rubbed with an oil and then use a partner or object  to slide against. Americans during the 60's would have Mazola parties where all participants would undress, rub their bodies with oil, and wrestle or play on a plastic sheet. There are bath houses in Bangkok, Thailand that offer a similar service. A client has the choice of lying on a lathered air mattress with a lady wriggling on top of him or of being lathered and lying between two writhing women. The ointment alleviates friction and produces a sensation that is drastically different from normal skin-to-skin contact.

Rubber mitts are sometimes used that have soft pliable nubs to add more sensation to the application of oil or soap.

(See also COITUS A UNDA, LUBRICANTS and MASSAGE)

J

JACTITATION Jactitation refers to those who become aroused or derive pleasure from bragging about their own sexual exploits.

(See also AGREXOPHILIA, CONFESSIONS, COPROGRAPHY, COPROLALIA, EROTOGRAPHOMANIA, NARRATOPHILIA and OBSCENE PHONE CALLS)

JEALOUSY (Othello's syndrome) Jealousy is a feeling of envy or anger directed toward someone deemed as a rival for a loved one. The fear of a loss actually creates a stronger reaction because the person has to act to prevent the loss, where a permanent loss will create eventual depression. There are also people who use

jealousy as an arousal technique for group sex.

Jealousy increases in direct proportion to our dependency on our partner and our fear of losing them. Often people who were in some way abandoned during their childhood or kept overly dependent on a parent will suffer more from jealousy. They unconsciously feel they will die or not be able to function without this surrogate parent. Many people effectively deal with this fear by building up their independence and self esteem, thus taking the burden of creating happiness or security off their partner.

This formula for self esteem sounds simple, however a person has to be strong to overcome the critical little voice inside that says "you can't," "you're ugly," "you're stupid," "I will deal with it later," and so forth. One must learn to yell back using honest arguments such as "I can," "my nose is a little larger than I would like," "I'm poor at math but I can speak three languages," "I will work on this project two hours every night for a week."

It is not easy to win this battle, because most people have relied on this voice to protect them from failure or embarrassment. One is turning a former ally into their worst enemy, but with courage and persistence victory is possible. Salesmen, who have to deal with constant rejection, have a simple but effective slogan: "Ask for what you want, you can't lose something you don't already have." Two people who have mastered control over low self-esteem and jealousy can live together without either party feeling burdened by the other's overwhelming demands for something neither has the capability of filling.

Jealousy can be healthy if it focuses a straying partner's attention back on their spouse. The couple can use this opportunity for honest discussion of their fears and negotiate any areas of concern.

(See also HEDONISM, LOVE, PECATTIPHILIA, SADISM and ZELOPHILIA)

JEWELRY Jewelry has been specially designed for people's breasts and genitals. (The jewelry for permanent piercings is discussed in the section on RINGING.) Nipple rings are used by women who like the look of pierced jewelry but who don't want to make a permanent commit-

ment. One type, called Sweater Bumpers, fits around the nipple in the same manner that a ring slides over a finger. These come in many designs and can be purchased in San Francisco sex boutiquesor piercing salons or can be ordered direct from the manufacturer. A different type was made from elastic material and joined by a

decorative chain. These are called Tit-Ilizers. Both types of nipple ornaments cause the nipple to stand erect and feel more sensitive.

A Clit Clip was designed by Judy Kirk which slips over the labia and clitoris like a paper clip. It holds the clitoris out and cuts off enough circulation to keep it engorged in a similar manner as a cock ring does to the penis. The clip is decorated with crystals or bells that hang from small chains.

Cock rings are available for men that are decorative and fit around the bottom of the glans. Other men wear leather cock rings with metallic studs.

(See also COCK RINGS, RINGING and TATTOOS)

JUVENILISM, PARAPHILIC See ADOLESCENTILISM and INFANTILISM

K

KABAZZAH (Pompoir, Kegal exercises, Snapping pussy) Kabazzah is translated as "holder" and refers to the Eastern technique where the male partner is passive and the female uses only abdominal and vaginal muscle contractions to 'milk' the penis. Both partners simply relax and enjoy the sensations of the union while she moves her muscles. Women train for years before

becoming proficient. It is a form of tantra designed to increase and enhance time spent with a loved one. There are still some Eastern prostitutes who have this expertise.

KAREZZA (Male continence, Coitus reservatus) Karezza, to caress, was coined by Dr. Alice Bunker Stockham in her book, *Tokology* (1883). Stockham not only recommended staying in sexual union for an hour but also saying prayers during this time (*Sexual Energy Ecstasy, A Guide to the Ultimate, Intimate Sexual Experience* by David Alan Ramsdale and Ellen Jo Dorfman, Peak Skill Publishing, pp. 228-234).

John H. Noyes, the founder of the Oneida Community, believed in karezza for a different reason. He founded a group marriage commune in the late 19th century based on eugenics. Here only the most fit men were allowed to impregnate the women. Other men in the group could penetrate the women and bring their partner multiple orgasms but could not ejaculate themselves. The act required relaxation for the male because tension could bring on the desire to ejaculate. Noyes discovered that practicing kabazza, in addition to accomplishing birth control, improved the intimacy and love between he and his wife.

(See also BIRTH CONTROL, EUGENICS, SEX POSITIONS, SEX SHOWS and SEXERCISE)

KISSING (Basoexia, Osculocentric and Philemamania—craving for kissing) Kissing is accomplished by a person placing their lips against an object or another person. Kissing is a social act between persons of all ages. It is also used during sex as additional stimulus in many, but not all, cultures.

Cultures that restricted social contact in the form of kissing or shaking hands usually did it under the auspices of eliminating sexual temptation or desire. This restriction may also have served to prevent transmission of disease causing bacteria during epidemics.

Cultures in which kissing is sexual often assume that it is a natural display of affection and method of sexual arousal; however, in the biological sense this is not accurate. Our bodies are designed to produce anxiety or pain if we ignore vital duties such as eating, sleeping, urinating, defecating, and so forth. Once we engage in an action at our body's prompting it produces biochemicals that create a pleasure sensation. Stimulation of any of these centers can produce pleasure because our body is fooled into thinking that we are carrying out a necessary function. For instance, when we kiss our body thinks we are eating, when our nipples are massaged our body thinks we are nursing, when our urethra is touched our body thinks we are urinating, and it rewards us with a pleasure sensation each time.

The physical act of kissing takes several forms. Some pucker their lips and make a cursory smacking noise as they touch them to the other person's lips, cheek, forehead, or hand, each site often having a different social implication. The more the kiss lingers, becomes repetitive, or intimate the more it is interpreted as having sexual implications. The most arousing is the French kiss where the kisser probes their partner with their tongue. For this reason, a French kiss can make some people feel uncomfortable when initiated in public, without foreplay, or with a person who has not expressed reciprocal sexual interest.

Kissing is used to build intensity during foreplay and to convey unspoken desires. Females often have a specific limit on what type of foreplay or sex in which they are willing to engage. For instance, she may allow kissing and touching on the outside of her clothes but not underneath. She may allow cunnilingus but not vaginal penetration of any sort, etc. The rules are not always logical to the partner but should still be obeyed. Males seem to be different than females in this respect. They will rarely continue dating a person with whom they would not be willing to engage in sex. Compromises can often be negotiated with partners who are not willing to be penetrated, but who want to be sexual. They may be willing to experiment with coitus a mammilla, fellatio, or mutual masturbation instead. The following is a scenario that uses kissing for seduction.

Seduction begins by touching the partner's hand followed by stroking their hair or face with the back of the hand. The chin is then held while gently kissing their face and lips (no Frenching at this point). If the partner is responsive one hand is used to cradle the back of their head and when the partner responds by caressing or pulling closer, the fingers of the hand can be slowly lowered down the outside of the clothes to lightly feel the breasts. The hand is then gradually brought to cup the full breasts with more pressure. Kissing may now progress to using the tongue to lick the other's lips or to gently suck on them. The partner may now give permission to slide a hand underneath her blouse and bra. Kissing and sucking are next directed to the neck and ears. If the partner doesn't remove their clothes, sucking on the outside over the nipples may provide encouragement. Watch for a positive response (faster heart rate or breathing) before proceeding. When the nipples are uncovered these may be kissed and then covered with the mouth in a sucking action alternating with the hardened tongue probing circles around the nipple or gently flicking back and forth across it. At this point one hand may be slowly run down the waist or up the leg toward the genitals, allowing time for the partner to adjust to the suggestion. If the partner is not ready slow down and repeat the above procedure. Once they are receptive to genital stimulation accelerate the intensity of kissing, position their head so that it is underneath and yours on top. At this point harden the tongue into the shape of a penis and gently push it into the partner's mouth while simultaneously adding pressure to their genitals. Voice your desires and continue thrusting your tongue deep in the partner's mouth (without the lips parting) . It is best to get a verbal agreement at this point even if they pull you closer. Asking her if she wants you or if you can take a second to put on a condom makes your intent clear. Foreplay is then started with French kissing and pressing the bodies together before penetration is attempted. The whole seduction process may take anywhere from 15 minutes to an hour depending on the people. Proper communication is strongly recommended to avoid false expectations or accusations of rape later. A person who is not held gently or caressed for a few minutes after sex and asked for another date may assume the partner just used them for sex, thus turning a wonderful experience into one of feeling violated. There are two individual people, separate morals, and emotions involved in each sexual venture.

(See also CUNNILINGUS, FELLATIO and SEX POSITIONS)

KLEPTOPHILIA (Kleptolagnia; Kleptomania—compulsion to steal) Kleptophilia (klep: to steal or hide, and philia: attachment to) is the act of becoming sexually aroused by stealing objects. This differs somewhat from the kleptomaniac who usually has an uncontrollable urge to steal items they don't need. The word kleptomania was coined in 1838 for several kings who had the habit of stealing worthless goods. Kleptomania was not only practiced by kings but also by St. Augustine, one of the founding fathers of the Catholic church. In *Confessions* he states: "Yet I lusted to thieve and did it compelled by no hunger, nor poverty."

Men and women both have participated in kleptophilia. William Stekel, in *Sexual Aberrations*, refers to the case of a woman who had a doll fetish. Her husband discovered her playing with them one afternoon and destroyed her collection. She went into a depression and later resorted to stealing replacement dolls. A man in the late 1800's was arrested and sentenced several times for stealing ladies' used handkerchiefs and spent a total of 7 1/2 years in prison for these crimes. He tried to cover the theft by buying handkerchiefs and attempting to exchange them without the woman's detection. He also devised a scheme whereby he threw a handkerchief down on the street in front of a pedestrian, hoping she would step on it as she passed. This producing immediate orgasm for him.

The kleptophile prefers stealing fetish items and will have an orgasm either while stealing them or later by fondling the objects. For instance, a person with a panty fetish will steal ladies' underwear; one with a hair fetish may come up behind a woman, cut her hair and flee. This also applies to fur or other articles of clothes where a piece can be cut off in a crowd without immediate detection. Men with shoe fetishes have sometimes accosted women and fled with their shoes. One woman only stole pencils, afterward using them to masturbate while she fantasized about "an infantile penis" (*Encyclopaedia Sexualis*, by Victor Robinson, M.D., pp. 139). A kleptophile does not always have a particular fetish.

They will instead steal intimate items such as tampons, menstrual pads, bras, and hygiene sprays. Some are satisfied stealing from stores and others only want items that have already been worn by a person. Another kleptophile category is one where men steal a casual sex partner's underwear as a personal souvenir.

People suffering from kleptomania may not have a direct sexual motive but in case studies that include sexual histories there seems to be a correlation between sexual dysfunctions and stealing. Marcus J. Goldman, M.D. stated this in a research paper: "No information was given concerning sexual preoccupations, behaviors, or dysfunction for 17 of the 26 patients in table 1. In the nine studies reporting such information, the patients reported experiences such as vaginismus, nonarousal, promiscuity alternating with abstinence, and a preoccupation with sterility. Some reported orgasm or sexual excitement during thefts." Goldman continues with a description of these people. "It would appear that the average person suffering from kleptomania is a 35-year-old married woman who has been apprehended for the theft of objects she could easily afford and does not need. Her stealing began at age 20 and she has been caught several times. A search of her house reveals piles of unopened packages of stockings and cans of jam. Her acts of theft bring her great relief from tension, and she may attempt to force herself to remain indoors for fear that she will steal...She seems to suffer from a powerfully necessary, pervasive, repetitive, and ultimately self-destructive act. A personal history reveals that she is unhappily married, may have sexual difficulties, and has been dysphoric and moody for many years. She very likely has had a tumultuous and stressful childhood. Furthermore, she may have a personality disorder" (Kleptomania: Making Sense of the Nonsensical, by Marcus J. Goldman, M.D., *American Journal of Psychiatry* 148:8, August 1991, pp. 986-996).

Regardless, the act of stealing, with its inherent risk of detection, naturally triggers an adrenalin rush that gives one the same physical responses they have during sex. The theft of a fetish object seems to act as an aid in turning the experience into that of sexual arousal. Also fetishists who become desensitized to their love object may use the extra excitement that stealing produces in order to orgasm. Kleptomania may be connected with our primeval drive to gather and collect. These activities once ensured our survival during winter months. The kleptophile may also be trying to compensate for a lack of parental love during childhood, similar to the fetishist. CAUTION: Stealing is illegal and an inconvenience and hardship to those being robbed.

(See also FETISHES, PARAPHILIAS, PYROPHILIA and RELICS)

KLISMAPHILIA (Enemas) Klismaphilia (klisma: enemas; philia: attachment to) dates back to the ancient Egyptians and was also popular with the French, Greeks, Romans, and Americans.

The Egyptians used enemas for relief of constipation. They believed that all sicknesses were caused by a buildup of toxic wastes in the body. Healers used laxatives, vomiting, and enemas to alleviate this disorder. The Egyptian's sacred bird, the ibis, when constipated used its  long beak to remove feces and many of their enema tips were modeled after this bird.

The 19th century French revived this belief and used purging as often as four times a day. Enemas were thought to improve the complexion, add vigor to one's constitution, and cure impotence. Charles Panati, in his book, *Panati's Extraordinary Endings of Practically Everything and Everybody*, enlightens us as to the once popular customs. "Limonadiers des posterieurs," or pharmacists trained for giving enemas, would arrive with an assortment of herbs and syringes. Herbs were mixed and one could chose from exotic clyster tips such as tortoiseshell, mother-of-pearl, or gold. Tobacco enemas were popular, giving the person a rush to which they soon became addicted. These enemas led to another form of rectal medication, the smoke clyster. The "Limonadier" used a special pipe which he inserted in his patient's rectum and blew tobacco smoke. This became a popular procedure in reviving fainting women. It is dangerous to blow too much air into the rectum because this could cause a fatal embolism.

Americans have used enemas for constipation, dieting, before a date as insurance against flatulence, as preparatory cleaning for anal sex, and for sex itself. Wine enemas and coffee enemas are popular, due to the effects of the alcohol or the caffeine content. The slow warm stream of water into the rectum, or by the prostate, seems to enhance sex play for some. There are clubs that cater to this interest in the United States. CAUTION: Enemas can cause damage if not done safely. Precautions used for enemas:

Lots of lubricant is used on both the anus and nozzle. Warm water, soap, drugs, or alcohol can damage tissue if they are not diluted with one quart of water for every 1/2 jigger of additive.

The enema bag is held no higher than the waist. This allows the water to flow gently. The sensual stimulus is caused by the stream of water, so the flow of water is prolonged as long as possible.

Letting water pass through nozzle before it is inserted avoids getting air into the rectum, causing cramping and possible embolisms.

Preliminary enemas are used by people who are embarrassed about expulsion of feces.

Proctitis can develop when one engages in this activity too often.

The rubber Whoopee Cushion is used in enema play for those who like enemas but find the purgatory effects to be unpleasant. The nozzle of an enema bag is inserted. A rubber band is used to secure the nozzle in place and the hose is attached after the bag has been filled with warm water. The cushion is rubbed with a water based lubricant and pushed into the anus. The enema bag is next slowly raised until the cushion is filled.

Enemas have been used by rapists as well. There was one case during the 1960's of a man who would raid a female college dorm and tie up all the students, strip them, administer enemas to all, and then selecting the one to whom he was the most attracted would give her a second enema before leaving.

GOLDEN ENEMAS   Golden enemas use urine instead of water. This is accomplished by a man inserting his penis into a partner's anus or vagina and then urinating. This is physically difficult and only a few men are able to urinate while semi-erect. Some people simply fill the enema bag with urine and administer it instead of water. CAUTION: Urine may contain particles of blood, viruses, or bacteria and because of this golden showers are not considered safe sex.

(See also CATHETERS, COCKTAILS, LACTAPHILIA, SAFE SEX, SCROTAL INFUSION, SHOWERS, TOILET TRAINING, UROPHILIA and VAMPIRISM)

KNIVES   Consensual knife play is used in sex games to create a feeling of fear, anxiety, and ultimate trust. These passion games usually consist of cutting underwear off a partner. Additional threats are not necessary for the majority of people. There are a few heavy S/M players who use knives in interrogation or pseudo-torture games, but even they rarely cut their partner. Some will rub tomato catsup on the back edge of the blade and pull it across the victim's flesh leaving a red line that resembles a cut.

The technique used to cut away clothes depends on the item itself. Clothing over the breasts may be cut by pinching the fabric lying against the nipple, pulling it away from the body, twisting it, holding it across the edge of the knife, making sure that no skin is near, and then cutting the fabric. A fairly round hole is left, exposing the breast. Underwear is cut away by pulling the fabric away from the body, placing the knife under the fabric with the sharp edge always facing away from the skin and slicing the fabric. Knife play may be performed with or without a blindfold and bondage, but is negotiated ahead of time with a partner, so as not to cut away an expensive article of clothing.

Some men find it extremely stimulating to dress in ladies' apparel and then to have their panties cut away in a pseudo-rape scene. CAUTION: Knife play is a blood sport and can be dangerous. Care is taken not to let the blade point or sharp edge make contact with a partner's skin.

(See also ABRASIONS, CICATRIZATION, CIGARS, ELECTRIC SHOCK, PHOBOPHILIA, PYROPHILIA, SAFE SEX and SEX TOYS)

KOKIGAMI   Kokigami (koki: a cloth worn around the waist by Japanese actors and used as a prop, gami: paper) is the art of wrapping the penis in a paper costume. The 8th century Japanese aristocrats practiced the art of *Tsutsumi*, or packaging. They wrapped their organs with silk and ribbons in complex and intricate designs and upon entering the bed chamber offered them as gifts to their lovers. He then enjoyed the physical sensations as she carefully unwrapped her prize. Today the authors Busch and Silver have invented a similar form of art. However, instead of rib-

bons, paper is used as a disguise or costume. The lovers then act out their roles based on the type of figure selected. There are geese, fish, squid, and dragons. Busch and Silver, in their book of Kokigami cutouts, suggest the following dialogue and play for the latter: "The crafty Dragon likes to breathe his fire into the dark jeweled cave. Ravaging, vengeful, sly... Where are my precious jewels? My treasures? My trophies? Are they hidden there in your dark cave? The Reply: Come on hot stuff! Careful the iron gates don't  snap shut and sever your burning tongue!... With arms outstretched and fingers curled like claws, move forward warily with the knees bent. The hips may be flicked about spasmodically accompanied by the low seductive roar of a raging furnace" (*Kokigami, The Intimate Art of the Little Paper Costume*, by Heather Busch and Burton Silver, p. 18).

The Japanese also used samurai face masks over the groin region with a dildo protruding as the nose. Those not interested in artificial phalli cut out the nose and put their own penis through it.

(See also FANTASY PLAY, MASKS and SEX GAMES)

L

LACTAPHILIA   (Eretithia; Erotamastia —masturbation playing with own breasts, Mastofact—breast fetish, Tithiolagnia— orgasm while nursing, Tithioscopia— arousal from watching infant nurse) Lactaphilia (lactate: secretion of milk, and philia: attachment to) is a term used for sexual arousal caused by lactating breasts. At one time milk from a nursing mother was thought to have healing powers. The milk from both a mother and daughter was used as a prophylactic against eye diseases.

A few nursing mothers will experience orgasm during infant feeding, and any orgasm will cause milk to spurt from a lac-

tating nipple. Orgasm during nursing (tithiolagnia) is not exclusively a female trait. Hirschfeld wrote of a man who experienced only three orgasms during his life and these all occurred while attempting to nurse an infant. People used to wonder why males are born with nipples since "most" are not capable of nursing. The natives of ancient Gallas (near Ceylon) remedied this discrepancy by amputating the nipples of male infants. They feared that this female symbol would create cowards in battle (*Sex and Superstition*, by G. L. Simons, p. 43, reproduced with permission of Blackie & Son Ltd.).

People can be aroused by lactation for many reasons. It may be a conditioned response from having been breast fed as an infant or be viewed as a form of female ejac-ulate. Others find the scene of a woman sucking her own breast to be very erotic. There are magazines that cater to this interest with photos of women squeezing milk out of one or both breasts. Some have the drops of milk lying on their breasts and others fill glasses for the camera.

As mentioned in the section on SIT-OPHILIA, a woman can simulate lactation by pouring cream over her breast. Some men prefer wine instead and this is referred to as oenosugia.

(See also ANACLITISM, COITUS A MAM-ILLA, FETISHES and SHOWERS)

LAP DANCING Lap dancing seems to be the modern creation of the Mitchell brothers. It began at their O'Farrell Theatre in San Francisco. While a stripper performs on stage others work the audience for tips. The city ordinance forbids genital contact with a man or exposure of his genitals, therefore lap dancing has strict regulations. A stripper dressed in sexy apparel will approach a man in the audience, negotiate a price, and then facing him will put a knee on each side of his legs and, lean forward enough so that his nose is between her cleavage. He is not allowed to caress her as she goes through her pelvic thrusts.

(See also BELLY DANCING, CHORE-OPHILIA, SEX POSITIONS, SEX SHOWS and STRIPPING)

LESBIANS (Cymbalism, Gynecozygous, Harem effect, Tribadism; Homophilia and Homosexualism—male or female gays) The name lesbian is taken from a tragic Greek account of a woman named Sappho who lived around 600 B.C. She supervised a school for girls on the island of Lesbos. Sappho fell in love with one of her students but this girl, Phaon, was unresponsive to Sappho's advances. Finally in despair, Sappho drowned herself at sea. She left behind a rich collection of love poems, almost all of which the Catholic Church later burned. The Greeks too were intolerant of lesbianism but ironically certain types of male-male relationships were respected.

Lesbians have varying tastes in the type of partner they select. They may prefer women of a different race, those who appear masculine ("flat shoe dykes"), those who are feminine ("lipstick dykes"), or those who are androgynous in appearance. The type of partner selected may or may not match their own appearance.

Many lesbians would say that sex does not play a major role in their lives. The type of sex they do engage in varies. Some have a phobia against any type of penetration, while others prefer mutual penetration with fingers or dildos. Cunnilingus is engaged in by some lesbians, but not others. A lesbian couple's sex life, if one exists, can lose intensity after a few years because physical and emotional similarity destroys passion for many. Lesbians today have one advantage over gay males and that is the ability to have and rear children in a homosexual marriage. This is accomplished by either partner choosing to have children by artificial insemination (often with a turkey baster at home), or sex with a male friend.

Lesbians have support groups and organizations that offer assistance. Larger cities have bars that cater to lesbian clientele with special attractions such as all female strip shows, leather contests, and costume parties. Events such as the annual SF Lesbian and Gay Freedom Day Parade and Celebration support lesbians and is usually led by a group called "Dykes on Bikes" who seem tough enough to make even the macho "Hell's Angels" yield right-of-way.

(See also BI-SEXUALISM, GAYS and HET-EROSEXUALS)

LIGHTING Both women's fertility and men's virility are influenced by circadian rhythms (the body's natural metabolic, glandular and sleep rhythm cycles).

Research has proven that an absence of light throws this system off its regular cycles. Eskimo women do not menstruate or ovulate during the Alaskan winters and men have a decreased amount of spermatozoa during this time. Bright light is an essential part of our sex lives, but at the same time can be uncomfortable to the eyes. For this reason some prefer to have sex in the dark; others use blindfolds during the types of sex play that require bright lights.

The type of light selected for romantic foreplay can be important. Ordinary light bulbs tend to tinge flesh with tones that are not flattering, and also seem to expend a person's energy at a faster rate. Romantic interludes require forethought if one wants their partner to feel comfortable and eventually undress. The following chart compares an environment that is not conducive to one that is:

Hard chair	Soft spacious sofa
Caffeine drink	Wine cooler or light liquor
A bright light that enhances possible flaws	Dim light or candles that hide flaws
Natural background noises or television	Soft background music to mask distracting sounds
Cool room	Warm temperature

The color light one chooses can also enhance one's mood and create specific illusions. Green can slow down a man's erection time and red can speed it up, but may also trigger arguments. The combination of blue and green can create the illusion of larger breasts and penises. Everyone's favorite; candlelight and fireplaces, seem to enhance the shape and color tone of the body and in general add to an erotic mood (*Sexual Energy Ecstacy*, by David Alan Ramsdale and Ellen Jo Dorfman).

People experiment with light by using a combination of candlelight with colored glass candle holders. Dimmer switches allow people to modify the light intensity during the evening, and timer devices are sometimes strategically set for bedtime.

(See also COURTSHIP)

LOVE Love and sexual attraction are emotional reactions stimulated by the brain. Infantile love begins as a survival instinct at a time when the child is dependent on parents for all its care. Although a child later develops a desire to explore and play with peers, the need for love and nurturing at this stage is evoked more by a sense of danger, at which time the child seeks out its mother. It is natural for both humans and animals to gradually teach their young survival skills and if necessary to "push them out of the nest." If parental love or protection is withdrawn too early a child may transfer their love attachment to an inanimate object and have difficulty later in trusting a partner in a relationship. If the detachment is done late a child may remain too dependent on their parents or others. A high self-esteem results in being able to care for one's own needs whereas love is perceived as a dependence on someone else to care for those needs. The two are on a continuum, meaning that a person who doesn't feel they can provide themselves with all their needs will rely more on a love object for survival. A person who is independent will not be as dependent on a love object. Nature seems to endow normal teenagers with an inflated self esteem. This probably gives them the extra courage needed to leave nurturing parents and face the world on their own.

Adult love seems to follow a similar pattern to that of childhood, with anxiety creating a perceived need for a love object.

Several experiments have been conducted to gain insight into love. Julius Fast and Meredith Bernstein, in their book, *Sexual Chemistry, What It Is—How To Use It*, cite an experiment done by Drs. G.L. White, S. Fishbein, and I. Rutstein where they divided men into four groups. The groups then were exposed to one of the following stimuli: a boring lecture on the anatomy of frogs, a comic routine, the story of a murdered and mutilated missionary, or just told to run in place. The men "were next all shown a videotape of an attractive young woman talking. When asked if they'd like to date this woman and kiss her, the three groups who had been stressed by exercising, a comic routine, or a horror story all responded more positively than the men who had sat through the dull lecture on the frog."

A similar study was done by a group of psychologists who conducted an experiment on men who had just walked across a swaying bridge. A woman was stationed at the end of the bridge and stopped people to ask questions for a survey. She gave her phone number under the pretext of making available the survey results. A large percentage of men called to request dates. The men in this study had confused or transferred the fear and anxiety response they felt from crossing the bridge into a feeling of attraction for the woman.

What elements then need to be present in order to trigger the love response instead of anger or fear It seems that the primary factor is the sexual attractiveness and receptiveness of someone in the immediate vicinity. The male is generally more susceptible to love at this point, whereas females tend to screen the man for an emotional or a financial security potential. Next, to bond the relationship, the two partners must have complementary needs, or think they do. This is similar to the concept of power, and in a love relationship it can place the more needy partner in a submissive role. Mutual physical nurturing is a major need for both individuals. Other needs may be for excitement, power, security, personality characteristics, beauty, and companionship. Someone who is constantly under stress, good or bad, is likewise often susceptible to falling in love. Recognition of specific needs that are being gratified by a partner is important before a commitment is made. Ask whether the needs are temporary and rational. Also, are there other methods that could be used to satisfy them?

Bonding after a marriage is facilitated by a continued matching of needs and gratifications, compatible interests, open communication, and compassion on the part of each towards the other. This bonding may also be influenced by other factors such as insecurity, financial gain/loss, social pressure, and so forth.

An excellent resource for those interested in reading more about relationships and why people enter them is Dr. Martin Blinder's book, entitled *Choosing Lovers*.

(See also JEALOUSY and LOVE ADDICTION)

LOVE ADDICTION   A love addiction, or more appropriately, a love compulsion is an irresistible impulse to fantasize about a love object, expecting it to provide a solution to problems. Daydreaming itself seems to trigger opiates to numb pain. The compulsive lover is simply a person who becomes fixated on romance or sex and tries to avoid loneliness, fear, stress, or other basic unfulfilled needs in this manner. The negative aspect of fantasizing is that it numbs the pain everyone must experience in dealing with life and by doing this a person destroys the incentive to work on real issues; the anxiety is transferred instead to possessing a love object. The person makes themselves more dependent on others and becomes less capable of functioning on their own. Ironically, they become enslaved to this self destructive cycle which will inevitably include pain.

There are many ways to battle a compulsion whether it is for love, sex, drugs, food, fetishes, working, gambling, etc. The most common advice is to build up one's self esteem. This means taking control of life, becoming more egotistical and self nurturing, improving one's appearance (if it keeps them from socializing), and avoiding harsh judgments and restrictions on oneself. Pain is faced and resolved rather than masked or avoided. When something traumatic occurs the person tries to first handle it alone, and not use this as an excuse to find a romantic fix. Personal goals are set as well as maintaining a good balance of activities. A method used specifically for relationships involves analyzing the qualities that are usually present in the people with which one normally falls in love. Once this is done a person selects one or two of these attributes and works on making them part of themselves. This defuses some of the attraction they feel for lovers and individuals improve their own self-esteem. They become the special person others want to date.

There are support groups that people can attend such as the twelve step program called "Sex and Love Addicts Anonymous." Here members, if single, are encouraged to give up sex until they gain a proper perspective on love and relationships. It is not until sex and fantasies are given up that one realizes that the urge to do these things is triggered by something painful in our everyday lives—things such as having a friend move away or not getting a promotion. The first urge is often for sex. Once a person says "no" the next urge is to have a drink, eat, or anything that will distract one from feeling the pain. The more appropriate solution for a person is to learn to deal with pain, grieve, and address the real issue so that it can be resolved.

Not everyone agrees that people can have too much sex. The National Organization for Sex Enthusiasts (N.O.S.E.) was founded by Roger Libby, Ph.D. and advocates sex as healthy and a natural body function.

(See also JEALOUSY and LOVE)

LOVE POTIONS Love potions are different from aphrodisiacs in that a special magic ritual is performed over the concoction. These were popular in societies where spouses were not monogamous. "Juvenal, a first-century satirist, reproved Roman women for dosing their husbands with love potions from Thessaly which only caused premature senility, dizziness and loss of memory" (*Sex and Superstition*, by G.L. Simons, p. 67, reproduced with permission of Blackie & Son Ltd.). The Siwans of North Africa believed that if a man could slip his semen into the food of a favored woman, this woman would fall in love with him (*Patterns of Sexual Behavior*, by C. Ford and F. Beach, p. 101).

The book *The Satanic Witch*, by Anton LaVey, tells how the gingerbread man was once used as a popular love potion. The gingerbread man was made as a replica of the person on which the spell was to be cast. A love-sick female usually approached a witch seeking assistance in casting a spell on the man she wanted to be her lover. The ritual began with the girl undressing and lying on a bench. The witch would then place a wooden board across the top of the girl's genitals, mix the cookie dough using ginger, a once popular aphrodisiac, mold it into the shape of a man, and place it onto a small stove that was now placed on top of the wooden board. The cookie baked  while the witch chanted and in explicit language told the girl what type of sex she could expect from the man. The girl was to intensify her passion until she achieved an orgasm, sometimes having to be assisted by the witch or a local male. Once the orgasm occurred, the cookie was removed and wrapped. The girl was then instructed to deliver it to the object of her love and wait for the spell to take effect.

The ancient witch also used liquid love potions that contained alcohol. Some of these recipes are available commercially such as Advokaat, Chartreuse, Creme de Noyaux, Drambuie, Goldwasser, Mezcal, Parfait Amour, Sloe Gin, and Vermouth.

Spells that used visualization and goal setting were also popular. An example of one of these is when one would hang a loving bell in an open window facing toward the west. A chant was then spoken:

Little bell of love, I hang you to whisper my need for love on the breezes and winds.

Little bell of love, speak of my need for love to your brothers and sisters.

Little bell of love, I ask you to speak softly and draw to me someone who listens.

—*Earth Power* by Scott Cunningham

Another method mentioned by Cunningham was a love binding where one takes a small piece of clothing from one's lover, ties it together with a piece of one's own clothing, and hides it in a safe place.

(See also APHRODISIACS, CHARMS, FERTILITY RITES and RELICS)

LUBRICANTS Men and women both secrete a natural lubricant to facilitate intercourse. Male lubricant is in the form of pre-ejaculate and the female's is released from the walls of the vagina during arousal.

Saliva is used most often as a supplement for genital lubricants and serves to titillate the breasts, ears, mouth, and body as well. The longest lasting but least common body lubricant is nasal mucous. This is generally used during masturbation rather than with a partner.

Other lubricants may be purchased at sex video stores, S/M leather outlets, pharmacies, and through catalogues. The important criteria for lubricants is that only water based lubricants are used with rubber products such as condoms or dildos. This is because oil will deteriorate rubber and can cause a condom to break during coitus.

The most recommended water based lubricant is a polyethylene oxide called Slippery Stuff which was originally invented for scuba divers to get into their wet suits. When used without condoms this lubricant is so slippery that it reduces vaginal friction to the point that many men are able to stay erect for an extended period of time. Another popular water-based lubricant is Astroglide. It is clear, odorless, and tasteless. Probe is a lubricant that was formulated to resemble our natural sexual lubricants.

Flavored gels such as Joy Jelly are also popular; it comes in blueberry, strawberry, orange, and lemon-lime. Other gels are available that are designed to numb the sensations of the penis so that a man can stay erect longer. However, for some men the numbing effect causes them to lose their erection.

Some gels and lotions contain glycerin which warms up when exposed to the carbon dioxide in a partner's breath. Sodium hydroxide is a lye which leaves a bad taste; it is added to adjust the pH balance of the lotion. Propylene glycol also adjusts the pH but without the bitter flavor.

Oil based lubricants are preferred for masturbation, anal sex (without condoms), and latex gloves (the latex on gloves is thicker and can withstand the deterioration caused by oil better than condoms) because it doesn't dry out as fast as the water based type. Petroleum gels and mineral oil are not carcinogenic but they trap yeast and bacteria in the vagina. Glycerine is a safe lubricant.

There are moisturizers specially formulated for older women or those who no longer produce a satisfying amount of natural vaginal lubricant. One recommended in medical journals is REPLENS which lubricates for up to three days with only one application. CAUTION: Some people use special chemical lubricants such as Tiger Balm or Vicks in serious sex play to create intense sensations. These can cause tingling, burning, or numbness. People use a small portion on a small area of mucosal tissue before proceeding to rub over the genital area. Many of these chemicals can feel pleasurable on one person and yet cause extreme burning or itching on another. People who find the sensation is too intense often dilute it by mixing the chemical with a plain lubricant until the desired sensation is obtained. A condom can also confine these effects to the person who enjoys them (Communication with Wayne Cooper, Ph.D.). Soap is sometimes used for lubrication but often abrades the delicate genital tissue.

(See also INUNCTION, MASSAGE and SAFE SEX)

LUST MURDER (Dacnolagnomania, Erotophonophilia, Sexual sadist killer; Lagnonector—person who kills in order to have sex with corpse) The primary cause of most murders is anger and where some would direct it toward the person responsible, others transfer their aggressive behavior or sadism to a stranger.

There are two famous cases of lust murder. One was of Gilles de Rais, born in 1404. He was the Marshal of France under King Charles VII and the Lieutenant and protector of Joan of Arc. After an unsuccessful attempt to rescue Joan from torture and burning, he became bitter and vengeful against the God who allowed her death. Gilles soon squandered his fortune and elicited aid from alchemists and magicians in his attempt to convert base metals to gold. After many failures, he became involved with black magic, convinced that committing gross deeds would enable him to enter into a pact with the Devil to restore his wealth. Gilles began a reign of terror wherein he strangled and slit the throats of nearly 800 boys, performing coitus interfermoris, mutilation, vampirism, and necrosadism. He was finally brought to trial in 1440 and sentenced to death by strangulation. Two hundred years later the Countess Elisabeth Bathory of Hungary murdered approximately 600 girls. She kept them shackled in a dungeon, bled them, and then bathed in their blood in the belief that it would restore her youth. Upon finishing these baths she preferred to have her slaves lick the blood from her body instead of using a rough towel (*Perverse Crimes in History*, by R.E.L. Masters and Eduard Lea, pp. 23-30).

Lust murderers sometimes have a particular fetish or ritual they perform. Recently, a fetish lust murderer was apprehended in Oregon. This man would pick up young prostitutes, kill them, chop off their feet, and carry one foot with him. This ritual brought about his conviction when police discovered a metal shoe buckle in his wood stove matching the one belonging to a recent victim.

Many lust murderers begin torturing animals as children. Eventually these acts lose their original intensity and the person begins attacking people. Some murderers pride themselves on humanely strangling their victim before proceeding with torture or mutilation. Others photograph or tape the torture and screaming to use for their own excitement later. A lust murderer also derives sexual release from killing and for this reason the victims are generally people the murderer finds sexually attractive. Gays kill males, pedophiles kill children, and heterosexuals kill those of the opposite sex. Richard Rappaport, the chief psychiatrist in

the John Wayne Gacy case, reveals the following information about a lust murderer's victims. "The killer's victims were usually of the same sex, in the same age group and shared many similar physical characteristics. Theodore Bundy murdered young college women with dark hair parted in the middle; Gacy's victims were young men or adolescents; the Atlanta murders all involved young black children; the 'Night Stalker' in Los Angeles focused on occupants of homes painted white or yellow and located near a freeway. The existence of this kind of similarity among victims seems to indicate that the killer's victim has been invested with a personal, intimate—and delusional—meaning for the murderer. The victim, far from being a random encounter for the murderer, seems far closer to being an object of his compulsive desires" ("The serial and mass murderer: patterns, differentiation, pathology" by Richard G. Rappaport, M.D., *American Journal of Forensic Psychiatry*: Vol IX, No 1, 1988, pp. 39-48).

Orgasms achieved by these murderers may occur due to masturbation, frottage, or can be spontaneous. Many of these men either carry a part of the clothing or body with them or later return to the site of the murder and masturbate.

Rappaport (cited above) explains the reason behind this compulsion. "Murder then represents a compulsive attempt to solve an internal conflict, the repetition evidencing that there is no lasting benefit from killing as a method of resolving the internal conflict. Some researchers maintain that the motivating force involved in these repetitive violent acts is pleasure. The author's [Rappaport's] view is that the quest for relief of pain (the inner, unresolvable turmoil) is the essential dynamic which impels the murderer to reenact his bizarre and furious crimes."

There are those who take it upon themselves to pass judgement on gays or prostitutes and consider it their religious obligation to rid the planet of them. Some feel that murdering their sex partner expiates their sin. In addition, passing judgement on a victim serves to abate normal guilt. CAUTION: People can reduce the risk of becoming a victim by avoiding close contact with strangers. Some murderers use clever tactics in abducting victims. Ted Bundy used disguises such as wearing a cast on his leg and asking women to help him pick up books he had dropped and carry them to his car. Others have run women off the highway at night or dressed in police uniforms.

(See also ANTHROPOPHAGY, MASOCHISM, MUTILATION, NECROPHILIA, PARAPHILIAS and SADISM)

M

MAIEUSIOPHILIA (Cyesolgnia; Alvinolagnia—stomach fetish) Maieusiophilia (maieutikos: to bring forth children, as in midwives, philia: attachment to) refers to those who are aroused by women who are going to give birth.

Our early ancestors carved innumerable statues of pregnant women and goddesses. 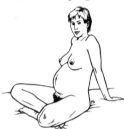 One of the more famous was the Earth Mother of Willendorf that is dated at about 25,000 B.C.E. These carvings were worn as amulets and buried with people when they died. Pregnant goddesses brought forth the world, seasons, other gods, and humans. Pregnant women evidently must have at one time held a highly esteemed position in society.

Today many women feel sexually unattractive during the last few months of their pregnancy. However, there are a number of men who consider them extremely titillating—enough to buy magazines titled *Milkin' & Poppin' 1*, and *Milky Mamas*.

(See also FERTILITY RITES, FETISHES and LACTAPHILIA)

MARRIAGE Marriage is a verbal or written contract that implies some sort of emotional or financial commitment between two or more people. Contrary to popular belief, humans have not lived in monogamous marriages ordained by God since the time of Adam and Eve. A study by C. S. Ford and F. A. Beach revealed that "monogamy as a compulsory pattern of mateship...occurs in only a minority of human societies—only 16% of 185 societies studied...(Even in that 16%, less than one-third wholly disapproved of both premarital and extramarital liaisons)" (*Modern Views of Human Sexual Behavior*, p. 241). Polygamous marriages were not banned by the Church until the 6th century C.E. Consensual monogamy, where individuals select their own marriage partner, has only existed for the last couple of hundred years in Europe and the United States. Primal man lived in clans and even when marriage became popular adultery was common. Monogamy was regulated when couples began to live alone away from the community. A description of the following types of marriage should not only give a historical perspective of the evolution marriage has gone through in some cultures but help in understanding the small contingent of people today who still practice many of these marriage forms.

ARRANGED Marriages for most of the last three thousand years were arranged by fathers. Children were betrothed and married before they finished puberty, certainly before they were old enough to demand a freedom of choice. Marriages were entered into for the financial and political advancement of the family as a whole and children's preferences were not acknowledged. Most Europeans and Americans have only been able to freely select their own marriage mates since the late eighteenth century.

Arranged marriages still exist in America among some small ethnic or religious groups.

CAPTURE This is an ancient form of marriage and in some cultures has existed until the early 20th century.

Primal men, who captured their brides from other tribes, were given a higher status due to the courage and strength required in the feat. Customs varied and where some immediately raped the woman, others kept her in a separate house hoping she would consent. If she didn't, a tribunal would hear testimony and make a decision as to whether she would be returned to her parents or forced to marry the captor. Other marriages were temporary, as in the case of some forest tribes in the Congo where the man would capture a bride, take her into the forest while he hunted, and return her to the village after she had given birth to a child and weaned it. The husband would then give the wife half of the game in exchange for the child.

Bride capture was practiced in England until the end of the 15th century, in Ireland as late as the 18th century, in Crete at the end of the 19th century, and until recently in parts of South America. In medieval France a woman was not safe even when escorted by a knight because other knights had the right to attack her protector; if victorious they could do as they pleased with the female. Cultures in north east and central India practiced a pretended capture of the bridegroom. It is speculated that this tradition stems from a time when fathers captured young men from other tribes to provide husbands for a surplus supply of unwed females (*Sexual Life of Primitive People*, by H. Fehlinger, p. 34).

There are several wedding rituals that have survived from capturing brides: the carrying of a bride over the threshold, the use of groomsmen, and the honeymoon. The captured bride not only had to be carried but was often bound in some manner to prevent her escape. Symbols of this type of bondage could still be seen in 19th century African tribes with their use of wide metal bands that fit tightly around the waist, leg bands, and wrist restraints. These no longer serve a practical purpose, but they have remained as part of their wedding rituals. Groomsmen were originally fellow tribesmen who assisted in the capture of the bride because discovery meant having to fight. The honeymoon was the period of time needed for the bride's family (in some cases husbands) to give up their search. Brides were not only captured to become a sex partner and mother, but were often destined to become only one of several secondary wives who were primarily used to work the fields.

The Koryak, a tribe to the south of eastern Siberia, have a marriage ceremony with a capture symbolism. A groom, after obtaining permission of the bride's parents, will wait for an opportunity to capture her. The bride must not only resist but, having been warned, has her friends sew her into a chastity garment. The groom attacks at the appropriate time and in a struggle takes a knife and cuts enough of the garment loose to reach inside and touch her genitals as a symbol of consummation. The struggle ends and they return to her tent as a married couple (*Strange Customs of Courtship and Marriage*, by William J. Fielding).

CHILD BETROTHAL Child betrothal has been practiced by many cultures but child marriages have been used by only a few. A female child may be betrothed to a male child or, as is more common, to an adult male. This custom survives for many reasons but is usually economic. In parts of Africa the older husband is financially responsible for the infant bride and will pay the child's mother for her care. In other areas dowries for younger girls are less expensive, and for some financially destitute parents a daughter is their only collateral. Other factors include a possible shortage of females in a tribe, the risk of an older unbetrothed girl eloping with an undesirable match, the cultural emphasis placed on virginity, the existence of multiple family dwellings (a young girl is more submissive to the older female in-laws and therefore preferred), and of course social or religious pressure.

COERCION People sometimes, perhaps often, use forms of coercion to hasten a partner's commitment. Pregnancy at one time had this effect because of societal mores. Impregnation could be premeditated by either partner. Couples also used this as a method to gain their parent's consent.

A few people today have been reported to use untreatable sexually transmitted diseases to trap a partner in a relationship. These people assume that their desired partner will be too traumatized or embarrassed to pursue new partners. (Of course, most episodes of transmission are due to a lack of education about the disease and its contagiousness, or because of simple carelessness.)

CONCUBINAGE Concubinage began as a union between soldiers and women captured during battle who became servants to the soldier and his wife. The soldier often had sexual relations with these women. Young males used for the same purpose by a dominant male owner were called catamites. As part of the master's property concubines could be distributed to heirs upon his death. The Romans, in their effort to keep the blood line pure between themselves as conquerors and the defeated, ruled that marriages were only official between free Romans. They allowed for a type of monogamous concubinage in instances where a Roman male desired to marry a woman of lower status.

A distinction is still made between wives and concubines in Moslem countries. The Koran permits each man to have four wives but allows as many concubines as he can support.

DOWRY Dowries are the gifts given by the bride's family to the groom. The Greeks were expected to give the equivalent of 1/10 of their property as a dowry. The Romans and Arabs also gave dowries. However, these were protected by law and would revert to the daughter's ownership if she became widowed or divorced. Dowries were often a form of inheritance during a period when all property was left to the firstborn son.

Brides sometimes earned dowries themselves. Belly dancing was an acceptable method in some cultures and prostitution was normal in others, including among the Natchez of Louisiana.

ELOPEMENT Couples who marry without parental consent are said to elope. This was often done when a lover did not meet with the bride's parents' approval, was unable to meet the amount required for a dowry, or had been betrothed as a child to another person. Elopements also occurred between married women and their suitors.

GROUP Group marriages were once common among members of certain tribes. Men and women were both permitted to have multiple spouses and concubines. Couples often lived in separate quarters either alone, with parents, or in same sex communals.

Today a group marriage consists of at least three people where each has a sex partner. The sexual preference of each spouse is predetermined to suit the needs of the others. A heterosexual male may require that all other partners be heterosexual. If under this arrangement anyone later discovers they also enjoy bi-sexuality, they may be asked to leave, the converse is also true of marriages established on bi-sexuality.

Sleeping arrangements vary according to house rules. People may be left to select their own partners for the night or may have them assigned. Others, in addition to private bedrooms, have a group bed in which anyone so inclined may retire. There are several support groups in California for people involved in group marriages. (Expanded Family Network meeting, February 1989.)

LEVIRATE This was the Jewish custom requiring a widow to marry her husband's brother if the former had not provided her with a son. The first born son of this union would then be named after the dead brother and considered to be his son. Surviving brothers who, for different reasons, did not want to follow this tradition were required to remove their shoe and have it spit on in public. Today Orthodox Jews sometimes go through a similar symbolic shoe ritual.

MAIL ORDER Mail order brides were the predecessors of today's personal ads for partners. The commitments, however, were much more serious due to the expense involved and perils of travel. Men often used this method for finding a bride because they lived in an area that did not have eligible women from which to select; if there were women at all. New settlers or immigrants are generally male. If they brought women with them they often died within a few years. The men who desired companionship then had only a few options; they could marry a local female who was not of their race or religion, become homosexual, or send for a bride from home. His parents or family often acted on his behalf in this case.

Today mail order brides are primarily used to find a bride who is from a different culture. This is generally a match between an American male who desires more submission and loyalty from a wife and a foreign bride who prefers a less dominant and more financially secure husband. There are magazines to which men can subscribe at a cost of over $300 a year that display ads and photos of women from Brazil, England, Scandinavia, the Philippines, and the Orient. Some offer a translation service for correspondence. CAUTION: Marriages between Americans and foreigners that are entered for monetary compensation in exchange for American citizenship are illegal and carry a heavy penalty. Immigration authorities expect the two people to have proof that they knew and spent time together within the previous two years. Ads are not always legitimate. Women of any country responding to foreign ads for brides or models face a risk of ending up as slaves to a prostitution ring. Likewise, men can often be defrauded by "confidence games" in which they are asked to forward money for a bride that does not exist.

MATRIARCHAL SOCIETIES   Matriarchy refers to domination of a family lineage by females. This type of rule preceded our current patriarchal system. In matriarchal primal clans, women did most of the labor, male infants were sacrificed, girls were educated, and males moved into the home of the bride's family, sometimes taking their name. Often a woman or her family could annul the marriage if they became dissatisfied with the husband. A wife could openly flaunt affairs, but a husband could be severely punished by a legal council for the same offense. In some cultures women ruled, worked, and fought, while men stayed at home weaving and caring for the children (*When God Was a Woman*, p. 36). Matriarchal cultures such as some American Indian, African, Asiatic and Polynesian tribes have survived until today. These societies were agricultural and are attributed with ecological conservation. They are also believed to have been defensive rather than responsible for propagating wars.

MOCK   Mock marriages were common in India among Brahman men. They were not allowed to marry until after their older brothers took a bride. While this law seems logical all sorts of complications arose in trying to implement it. A solution was soon devised that permitted the older brother to marry a tree, thereby freeing his younger brother to marry. A similar form of mock marriage was practiced by the Punjab, also of India. Here a superstitious ritual was performed to protect the third bride of a widower. The bride sat nearby while a marriage ceremony took place between the groom and a tree or sheep that had been disguised in women's clothing. It was believed that if the groom possessed an evil spirit that was killing his wives it would destroy the surrogate bride instead of the human one (*The Sacred Fire*, by B. Z. Goldberg).

PATRIARCHAL SOCIETIES   Patriarchal societies developed as people began breeding animals instead of farming, fishing or hunting game. The care of herds took men away from in-law domination for long periods of time, breaking down the social conditioning that required their submission to women or family. Men eventually proved they could not only provide food, but could also capture slaves to work the fields. Men now owned possessions of their own and instead of living with the wife's family, men began paying their in-laws to take the brides to live with them and serve their families.

War-like patriarchal clans soon formed, eventually conquering most of the farming matriarchal groups throughout Europe.

The true paternity of children became important under patriarchy. Now instead of the clan providing care for children with them inheriting the mother's possessions children were fed and educated by the father, later inheriting all his property.

POLYANDRY Several cultures permitted women to have multiple husbands. Polyandry was common in Sparta among the poor. Here a farm could only be left to the eldest son and there was no means of support available for his brothers. Therefore, the eldest son would sometimes let his brothers remain on the farm and share his wife. Polyandry was also necessary for the survival of wives and children in areas were there were frequent invasions by other tribes and the husbands had to be away for extended periods of time. The Mongols permitted one woman to marry four brothers, one always remaining behind to provide protection. Polyandry produced fewer children but more adult providers. It is still practiced in parts of Nepal and Tibet where land is difficult to cultivate. The excess females either remain single or leave their tribe for the low lands.

POLYGYNY Polygyny, or polygamy, is a marriage between one male and several females. Women benefitted from this arrangement when the ratio of men to women was low. It provided women who were widowed or would otherwise have to remain unmarried a chance to have a family. Her domestic burdens were also lightened because these were shared not only by other women but by additional children. The polygynous unit seemed beneficial to communities where women worked or had a skill while the converse was true of those who did not permit the wives to leave the house or to educate themselves. Problems developed among the men in cultures where the ratio of females to males was not balanced and only a few men were able to possess the majority of available females.

Polygyny among Indians was condemned by the American colonists, yet ironically these men justified raping the same women they were supposedly trying to save from the abuse of polygyny. "Seventeenth-century Pueblo Indians had petitioned the Spanish government because soldiers so often forced Indian women to have sex. Some Indians also complained against the Catholic clergy, and at least one priest was accused of raping Indian servants...the church opposed polygamy, and friars physically punished Pueblos who continued this custom...When white Americans became the conquerors in western territories, they too claimed sexual access to native women and tried to obliterate Indian and Mexican sexual customs." Polygamist Mormons during the 19th century suffered from people's wrath, despite the fact that their sexual morals were rigid and fellow Mormons found engaging in adultery, zoophilia, or incest were executed (*Intimate Matters, A History of Sexuality in America*, pp. 91, 118).

There are some families in Utah that practice a form of polygamy and from some reports the men and women both agree that it is a preferred life-style. The internal criticism seems to stem more from "arranged marriages" rather than the number of wives. Pro-polygamist Mormon women before the Woodruff Manifesto argued that polygamy gave them freedom and equality. Utah universities have been open to women since 1850 and almost all the first female doctors were Mormon. The feminist movement joined forces with anti-polygamist Mormons and, using condemnations of immorality, worked up the sentiments of religious Americans to support them in stopping this practice. While Susan B. Anthony and Elizabeth Stanton were concerned with equality rather than morals which had only been a convenient tool, other factions of the feminist movement were never able to separate the two issues and continued on a moral campaign directed at men and their female victims of vice.

PURCHASE The custom of giving a bride away at a wedding is a ritual that has survived for several thousand years. A form of purchase of brides evolved with the capture marriage. A gift to the parents of a bride often kept peace between two tribes and reduced the risk of the bride being avenged or escaping on her own after capture. It was also used during the change from matriarchal to patriarchal societies. The groom, instead of living with his bride's family and serving them, gave her parents some type of compensation in exchange for their daughter.

There are tribes that, instead of giving money or animals, would exchange brides. If the father had both a son and a daughter he would often exchange his daughter for his son's bride. The daughter would then become a bride for one of the groom's relatives or a secondary wife of the father-in-law (*Strange Customs of Courtship and Marriage*, by William J. Fielding).

RAPE   Rape was used by some Australian aborigines to symbolize marriage. Grooms stalked neighboring tribes and, finding a woman, hit her over the head with a club and dragged her away. Once she recovered the man forced her to follow him to his tribe where he raped her in front of witnesses as testimony of their new bond. This union was often short lived because attractive women were soon captured by men of other tribes and the same rape ritual repeated (*Strange Customs of Courtship and Marriage*, by William J. Fielding).

ROMANTIC   It was not until the late eighteenth century that marriages were entered into based on romance. Until this time marriage had been a result of capture, purchase, or barter between parents. Romance was restricted to extramarital affairs. A woman's appeal quickly changed from being based on meekness and spirituality to being attractive, endowed with large breasts, and a small waist. Letters between engaged couples no longer discussed or negotiated a division of property and wedding arrangements but rather expressed affection. Parents who did not readily sanction a child's marriage could often be coerced with the announcement of pregnancy.

SORORATE   This was the right given to a husband to take as wives all or any of his wife's sisters. Sororal marriage was common among many primitive tribes and has existed until recently among American, Fiji Island, Australian, and African tribes. These tribes also often required that the eldest daughter be married first. The man marrying the eldest then had first right of refusal on all others as they came of age. The animosity found among multiple wives in other cultures was almost nonexistent in these families. Likewise, children fared better because an aunt made a more considerate stepmother than did a stranger. Marriage of sisters was not always necessary for the husbands to enjoy sexual liaisons with his sisters-in-law because many tribes granted these liberties anyway. The requirement of marriage seemed to evolve at a later period.

The Todas of India had a reciprocal group marriage arrangement between wives and husbands. The paternity of children was determined by order of birth, the first born of each wife belonging to the eldest brother, the second born of each wife belonging to the second eldest brother, etc. (*Strange Customs of Courtship and Marriage*, by William J. Fielding).

TRIAL   Pre-marriage trial periods are accepted in cultures such as those of Eskimos, American Indians, Africans, Arabs, and Tibetans. The period of time differed; some societies expected a trial period of a year before couples could legally marry and German communities practiced a trial night whereby the girl and her suitor could determine their sexual compatibility before continuing a romance. An Anglo-Saxon ordinance in the 10th century permitted a seven year trial marriage, and the Scottish permitted trial marriages until the 16th century.

Peruvians encouraged trial marriages, taking a dim view of chastity. Sexually inexperienced women whose marriages ended were blamed for not having learned enough about sex before marriage to please their husbands.

Indian braves leaving on a long hunting trip would enter a short term marriage contract with a woman to accompany them. She helped to cook and was their sex companion. The game was shared at the end of the trip and the contract was terminated (*Strange Customs of Courtship and Marriage*, by William J. Fielding).

(See also HAREMS, LOVE, LOVE ADDICTION, WEDDINGS and WIFE SWAPPING)

MASKS Masks were popular during the 18th century in Europe. Prostitutes originally used them to hide their identity but later they became pop-

ular among women of higher social status. These masks provided anonymity between lovers, or from gossips and spies. Women wore masks to the theatre so that others would not see them blush and in the gardens so that they could flirt in public. Masquerade balls were organized and the tedious requirement of proper social introductions not only became unnecessary but at many parties it was mandatory that people not reveal their identity at all. Flirtations and roving hands at these events provided extremely intriguing entertainment for an otherwise sexually repressed society. It took more than a hundred years for these masquerade balls to be suppressed by disapproving religious leaders.

(See also BONDAGE/HOODS)

MASOCHISM

[A fourteenth century monk] shut himself up in his cell and stripped himself naked . . . took his scourge with the sharp spikes, and beat himself on the body and on the arms and on the legs, till blood poured off him as from a man who has been cupped. One of the spikes on the scourge was bent crooked, like a hook, and whatever flesh it caught it tore off. He beat himself so hard that the scourge broke into three bits and the points flew against the wall. He stood there bleeding and gazed at himself. It was such a wretched sight that he was reminded in many ways of the appearance of the beloved Christ.
　　—*The Pursuit of the Millennium*
　　　by Norman Cohn

This is an example of extreme religious masochism which would rarely, if at all, exist among sexual masochists today. In fact, the term sadomasochism now refers primarily to the consensual exchange of power between two people whether the method used to achieve this is psychological or physical. Rape, lust murder, and spouse abuse for our purposes are not considered forms of sadomasochism. They are nonconsensual and therefore will remain in categories of their own. The term masochism was first used in the late 19th century by Krafft-Ebing, the psychologist, who wrote *Psychopathia Sexualis*. Krafft-Ebing used the novels of Leopold von Sacher-Masoch to learn about men who gained sexual pleasure from having a woman inflict pain. While the prominent writer was still alive, Krafft-Ebing labeled his acts as a sickness. One has to wonder what influence male chauvinism had on this label because during this same period a child, wife, and servant were all expected to endure a lashing without complaint. The similarity between these cases can be seen in the assumption that if a wife didn't submit to corporal punishment she was being disrespectful and rebellious. She would also be suspected of not loving her husband. A wife who showed total submission to a tyrant was respected but a man who wanted to submit to a woman was considered sick. However, a few thousand years earlier the opposite was true. Men living in a matriarchal society would have found the desire to please or submit to mothers natural.

SM is a consensual and negotiated game between two or more people which may be stopped at any time by any partner. The purpose of the game is to push the masochist to the same level of emotional and physical exhaustion found in an extremely passionate love affair. Would the monk mentioned in the beginning of this section have felt as devoted to Jesus if he had not suffered so much because of his love for humanity? Submission and suffering can both be components of a strong love bond.

Men and women differ in the way they view the importance of sex in a relationship in some cultures, and it is this role that they choose to sacrifice in masochistic games. Men value sex and tend to judge the quality of a marriage by whether their sex life is satisfying while a woman will put sex into context with the rest of the relationship and if that seems healthy they will not be concerned. Male masochists willingly give up all their power, masculinity, and demands for sex to prove, by sometimes extreme methods, the intensity of their love. Conversely, female masochists tend to abandon sexual inhibitions displaying or offering their bodies willingly; thus, sex becomes the sacrifice that proves love for a partner. The reason people feel a need to convey love in this manner often lies in their past environmental conditioning. Many were neglected or had emotionally distant parents. Some of these people use masochism to win the love of their partner because, to them, love and nurturing were never given freely. In addition, these people probably only received nurturing from their parents when they were injured or ill, therefore, they may feel that the only time they are permitted to receive nurturing is when they are weak or injured. Similar conditioning is now considered a contributing factor for people who become sexually aroused by piercing and cutting. These fantasies were discovered in children who underwent surgery as infants by Dr. John Money.

Another dimension of masochism is that of physical pain. Pain is on a continuum that runs from very mild sensations, such as tickling, to extreme levels that are produced in mutilation. People who use pain during sex often set limits to how much and in what manner the pain is to be administered. A simple experiment that often clarifies the use of pain to increase sensation is that of holding one's hands up, taking notice of how they feel, and then clapping them together for five seconds. There should be a tingling sensation that most would define as pleasurable, especially if spread throughout their body during sex. Most people would not normally define this tingling sensation as pain, or think that clapping their hands was a form of self-flagellation. Yet, for most

practitioners, this is what masochism is all about. The level of pain is chosen according to the desired effect: for example, relaxation, sexual arousal, to clear free floating anxiety, or to awaken feelings in a numbed body. Masochists involved in heavy pain use it to either produce opiates in the brain for an euphoric effect or to reach altered states of consciousness.

Masochism plays a role in creating a feeling of self empowerment or self esteem. The masochist faces fear, pain, or humiliation and not only survives but has an orgasm or receives love as a reward. Scientists discovered that laboratory rats took much longer to drown when thrown into a vat of water than did their captured cousins (5 minutes vs. up to 24 hours). The reason given for the laboratory rat's survival was that until then he had always survived, no matter what injury he might have sustained. This gave him stamina that his country cousin lacked. People are able to gain this type of courage themselves by overcoming fear-producing obstacles. A person who learns to endure pain and conquer fear will rarely panic or think that all fear and pain end in failure or death.

The automasochism or self mutilation that is so often seen in prisons, psychiatric wards, hospitals, cult groups, convents, and monasteries is a manifestation of primal aggression or fear triggered by anxiety that has been turned inward rather than acting it out toward another person. Our bodies were designed to produce relief from trauma whether we were the aggressor or the victim in a conflict.

There are many private S/M clubs and these all vary in character. S/M clubs may be heterosexual, gay, all female (some will allow transvestites in female attire), pansexual, male dominant, or female dominant. Most clubs sponsor occasional play parties, some give educational lectures, many restrict activities to bondage, a few have a religious undertone, and others are political in nature. Acts that look safe and simple, such as bondage, can be very risky and even cause a partner's death in a very short time. Therefore, the primary purpose of clubs is to provide education for novices and a safe environment in which to practice and acquire the skills needed for play. S/M clubs are not group sex houses and many have regulations against even a married couple engaging in genital penetration during a play party. Individuals who sponsor private parties set their own rules. CAUTION: Masochistic play may not be safe for some types of people. Those who may need to exercise caution include veterans who were in active combat, people who were abused as children, and women who were violently raped. Any of these people can "flip out" if triggered by a familiar word, piece of clothing, a certain touch, and so forth.

There have occasionally been cases of masochists who regressed into what appeared to be past lives involving torture during play and experienced emotional stress because of this. Like others who have survived trauma, they may need professional assistance in coping with the memories. In addition, if these people continue to play the masochist role, it is their responsibility to inform future partners of things that set them off, enabling the partner to avoid repeating the same mistake.

(See also ALGOPHILIA, AUTOMASOCHISM, BONDAGE, DOMINANCE/SUBMISSION, FLAGELLATION, HUMILIATION, PARAPHILIAS and SADISM)

MASSAGE (Tripsolagnophilia and
Tripsophilia—arousal from being massaged, Tripsolagnia—arousal from having hair manipulated or shampooed) There are several types of massage that will be discussed in this section. There are basic massages that are used to create intimacy with a partner without expectations of sex. Others are used in bondage or torture play. A massage does not have to cover the entire body or be done while reclining. Partial body massages of areas such as the head, face, hands, feet, legs, shoulders, neck, chest, buttocks, or genitals can feel wonderful and they lend themselves more to spontaneity and reciprocity. Time spent on massages can vary greatly.

FACE The face is often one part of the body that gets ignored. The procedure for a basic face massage is for one person to position themself behind the partner and,

having them close their eyes, place the middle fingers softly in the center of their forehead. The pressure is slowly increased and massaged with thumbs toward the temples followed by the use of circular motions on them. Next the thumbs are placed one on each center corner of eyebrows and pushed toward outside edges. The thumbs are then  rubbed down the sides of the nose toward the nostrils, then placed on the sides of the nose and pushed outward across the cheek bones. This is followed by massaging the areas above and below the lips. The chin is then massaged by running the fingers and thumbs from the center along the jaw bone. Last, the outside edges of the ears are gently held between the thumbs and forefingers, covering as much area as possible with the grip.

SENSUAL FULL BODY Those indulging in full body massages first take precautions to avoid being interrupted. A warm dark room is necessary for people to be able to relax and enjoy the experience. Background music is often appropriate but sometimes takes away from the personal intimacy between partners who may prefer to hear soft sighs, moans, or deep breathing.

A person does not have to be a trained in massage if the pressure used is light or moderate. Most people plan ahead so that everything they need is nearby. Movements are never hurried, and one hand stays on the partner at all times, even when reaching for something. Those using vibrators make sure that the batteries are fresh and that rubber parts do not come in contact with massage oil.

Many people use heated vegetable based oil for massage. Olive oil, light mineral oil, almond, or sesame seed oil are best for the skin. Other common oils are baby oil and commercial massage oils. The important information needed when selecting the latter is to know that they are often scented or have chemical additives. Scented oils often arouse a partner, therefore they are not be used if sex is not the ultimate goal. An oil that produces chemical heat may be appropriate for a partner with sore muscles.

Several groups sponsor massage parties where couples bring a food dish to share, bathing suits for the hot tub, and supplies for giving a massage.

BONDAGE AND TORTURE People who prefer playing or being tortured during bondage submit to various sensory enhancing techniques such as being tickled with an ostrich feather or fur mittens, or being rubbed with leather gloves.

Blindfolding is used in sensory play because a lighter touch can be used to give the same effects as higher intensity play. People wanting stronger sensations have their partner nibble, scratch, run ice chips over the body, or use light biting.

FOOT Feet are either massaged with the fingers or can be caressed by the mouth to stimulate a partner in sex play. This is done by sucking or running the tongue in and out through all the toes; some do this to each other simultaneously.

A dominant partner often demands that their servant soak their feet and give them a pedicure. A dominant partner may also massage a slave's back or genital area while wearing spiked heel shoes.

GENITAL Genital massages are used to become familiar with a partner's genitals during a time when sex is not the primary goal. Oils reduce the friction of the skin and provide visible evidence of areas not yet explored.

(See also ACUPRESSURE, BINDING, BITING, CLAMPS, CORSETS, CUPPING, LIGHTING, OLFACTION, PINCHING, SCRATCHING, SENSORY ENHANCEMENT, TICKLING and TOUCH)

MASSAGE PARLORS Massage parlors offer people various types of massage. In addition, some for an additional fee will massage the genitals or masturbate a client. There is usually a basic fee for the massage and time is limited to a specified number of minutes. The foremost concern of workers in these parlors is whether new customers are involved with law enforcement. Regular customers and those who convince the masseuse that they are trustworthy can often have the massage finished off with manual stimulation of the genitals. A new customer uncertain of the appropriate gestures or information to divulge usually ask the woman what he could do to prove he is not affiliated with the police. If the masseuse provides any type of sexual service she will then give the client an idea of what is available and for how much. Sex does not automatically come with the basic price and masseuses do not perform a wide variety of sex acts. Etiquette for men in a massage parlor includes not grabbing or gouging the masseuse and not joking about being a policeman. Gentlemen ask permission or attempt contact by gently stroking the masseuse with the back of a hand. These men are much more apt to receive a favorable response. Unless additional money is received a man is not automatically entitled to feel her body; he has only paid for a massage.

The women who work in massage parlors may be young, inexperienced, lesbian, married, or professional. Some are masseuses because they really enjoy the work, others for the excitement, and some because it's a quick way to make money. Many build up a regular clientele with whom they develop a good rapport, and some have even married clients.

(See also BORDELLOS, MASSAGE and PROSTITUTION)

MASTURBATION (Ipsism, Onanism; Amatripsis—rubbing labia together, Manuxorate—male using hand, Maritate—female alone, Siphnianize—anal, Syntribate—rubbing thighs together, Triborgasmia—wife who masturbates husband) Masturbation generally refers to bringing oneself to orgasm using manual stimulation. If this is accomplished with the assistance of a partner it is then referred to as mutual masturbation, petting, or foreplay. Masturbation is considered a normal process in a person's sexual development and can begin at a young age. Boys generally first ejaculate between the ages of 10 and 13 years. James Weinrich states that "experiments in primates show that if this sexual rehearsal play is interfered with, the result can be an adult who cannot or does not function sexually as well as other individuals who were permitted such play" (*Sexual Landscapes*, p. 244).

The early 18th century marked the beginning of a two hundred year period where masturbation came to be viewed in Western societies as a form of unhealthy self-abuse by the morally degenerate or mentally ill. The Puritans condemned the practice because sex was for procreation. However, the Victorians were concerned more because of its perceived health risks. These fears arose from books that were written warning that almost every sort of ailment could be caused by men wasting their vital life energy. Physicians erroneously assumed that losing semen created the same effects as seen in castrated men. John Todd wrote several books, wherein he quoted the superintendents of an insane asylum as saying that masturbation is not only "the cause of bringing many of their patients there, but an almost insuperable obstacle in the way of their recovery" (*The Horrors of the Half-Known Life, Male Attitudes Toward Women and Sexuality in Nineteenth-Century America*, by G. J. Barker-Benfield, p. 166). This was the start of a public phobia that led many parents to use painful penis harnesses to prevent erections in their sons. The case of a young girl was reported in an 1894-5 edition of *International Medical Magazine* where a doctor in Ohio decided to eliminate the girl's desire to masturbate by cauterizing the clitoris. When this failed to produce the desired results he infibulated the area with silver wire. These she tore loose and in a final effort he cut out the clitoris. Adults were castrated. As late as 1897 a man was documented to have had his penis amputated as a cure for masturbation.

Masturbation is not usually thought of as a tool for torture, but even this pleasurable experience has dreadful consequences when overdone. Messalina, the wife of the Roman emperor Claudius, is said to have ordered men to be masturbated until they either became permanently impotent or died. At one time several nomadic Northern African tribes used a similar form of torture on their captives. Even today repeated masturbation is used on male rape victims or in bondage scenes, but not to the same degree.

Normal masturbation is educational, prepares people for sex with partners, and allows them a safe environment in which to experiment with methods and sensations that are stimulating. The role of masturbation in one's life can have even more dramatic psychological benefits. A new form of sex therapy has enabled people to replace harmful substance addictions by forcing themselves to masturbate daily. This act transfers the pleasure stimulus to an activity that is healthy and one that can lead to an intimate relationship with others (*ESO, Extended Sexual Orgasm*, by Alan Brauer, M.D. and Donna Brauer, p. 48).

Masturbation is tolerated by most cultures except when it totally replaces a person's desire for the opposite sex. It is easy for people to become conditioned or reliant on one method of stimulation. If that method can be easily modified to allow orgasm through genital penetration there is no problem. However, if the stimulus needed is one that cannot be adapted in this manner both people will suffer. The following chart identifies a few masturbation techniques and categorizes them according to a criteria for penile-vagina sex.

PARTNER COMPATIBLE:
Thrusting against pillow
Rubbing with fingers, towel, heel of foot
Use of lubricants, condom, fruit, liver in milk
    carton, or rubber genitals
Anal stimulation
Ben-wa balls
Nipple stimulation

PARTNER INCOMPATIBLE:
Vibrators
Boudoir water spray
Rubbing against photos
Use of fetish object
Rushing through act
Watching own genitals in a mirror
Douches
Urethral stimulation
Rough handling of genitals

Some would say regular masturbation helps one's ability to orgasm by keeping the pubococcygeus (PC) muscle in tone. This is the muscle that covers the genital region from the mons pubis to the anus. A physician named Arnold Kegel developed an exercise that improves people's muscle tone thereby intensifying or adding control to orgasms. These are named Kegel exercises. A person can exercise this muscle by simply stopping and restarting the flow of their urine. The next step is to continue exercising this muscle from time to time throughout the day. People gradually work up to two or three sessions of 100 contractions a day, trying to hold each one for several seconds. The improved strength of the muscle can be tested if one is a man by hanging a towel over an erect penis and trying to raise it higher. A woman can place a pencil or finger in the vagina and squeeze or push with her PC muscle. An improvement of muscle tone should be noticeable within a few weeks.

There is an organized group in San Francisco that sponsors Jack and Jill Off parties. They meet almost monthly to engage in mutual masturbation. Safe sex kits are supplied and many people add to the festivity by wearing costumes. Unescorted men and women are permitted to attend and bi-sexuality is encouraged due to the higher ratio of men to women. CAUTION: There is no universally accepted restriction as to how often one should masturbate. Some men regularly masturbate as often as six times a day with no apparent harm. However, men who masturbate excessively may risk getting their penis accustomed to the stimulus of the hand, which can be much stronger than the stimulus in intercourse. Abstaining from masturbation for a period of time can restore sensitivity. Excessive masturbation can only be determined individually, based on the number of skin abrasions, bruises, or the time spent on this activity and whether it keeps one from engaging in other necessary activities. In part, our desire to masturbate involves needs that may extend beyond sex or morality. Masturbation can be seen as a thermostat for our emotional wellbeing, and can be used according to a person's needs.

(See also AGALMATOPHILIA, CHASTITY DEVICES, CUNNILINGUS, FELLATIO, GENITAL/ANAL INSERTS, ORGASMS and SEX TOYS)

MATURATION   Maturation, or aging, has several effects on a person's sexuality. These are all as normal as any other aging process and are experienced by everyone to some degree. Many partners find that they even benefit from the lingering effects of arousal and orgasm. Disease, boredom, or an unreceptive partner creates many more sexual problems than does aging.

An issue of *Sex Over Forty* listed most of the changes that men encounter as they age. These include a longer time before obtaining erection, the need for more tactile stimulation of the penis, some loss of firmness in the erection, a prolonged period of erection before orgasm, and faster detumescence afterward. The force of the ejaculate may not be as strong and period of time between erections and the desire to orgasm often increases. Men also begin focusing more on total body intimacy with a desire to please their partner rather than on genital sensation only. Regular sexual activity is recommended to prevent muscles from losing their tone and to keep tissue healthy ("Sexual changes in men over forty," by S.H. Rosenthal, June 1982).

(See also DYSFUNCTION, GERONTOPHILIA, IMPOTENCY and MORTALITY)

MEATOTOMY   See PENIS MODIFICATION/MEATOTOMY

MEDICAL SCENES   (Iatronudia—arousal from exposing oneself to physician) Medical scenes are arousing for many. Iatronudia refers to those who are aroused by pretending to have an ailment so that they can undress in front of a doctor.

Others set up their own version of an adult sex game of "playing doctor." This may involve any type of role play involving a character from the medical profession and a patient. Less often it might include a dominant and submissive playing the role of veterinarian and dog. The types of activity vary and include simply wearing costumes,  taking vital signs, giving physicals, enemas, catheterization, sounding, pap smears, cupping, prostate exams (very popular at professional S/M houses), bindings, bondage, genital modifications, mock castration, cicatrization (scarring), coprophilia, shaving, electric shock, phlebotomy, piercing, lacing, scrotal infusion, toilet training, defloration, suturing, or stapling.

Some dungeons come equipped with gurneys or gynecological tables to assist in making these popular games more realistic.

Medical games are popular because they are connected with the anxiety that many people feel when visiting a physician which leads to a natural increase in energy in a sexual experience. CAUTION: Sterile procedures are used any time the skin is broken, along with other precautions.

(See also BONDAGE, CASTRATION, COPROPHILIA, DEPILATION, GENITAL MODIFICATIONS, LACING, PIERCING, PHLEBOTOMY, SAFE SEX, SCROTAL INFUSION, STAPLING, SUTURING and TOILET TRAINING)

MÉNAGE À TROIS A ménage à trois is a group sex scene involving three people, two of which are married. These may technically be of any sex or sexual preference. If a heterosexual couple lives in an area where prostitution is legal they may simply hire a third person. Singles often advertise in local swinger newspapers for couples interested in a ménage a trois and couples advertise for singles. Some prefer a regular partner who is bi-sexual or willing to engage in sex with a third person. (A woman who feels like she is being used as a pawn or pimp for her partner's pleasure may resent the relationship.) Unless the couple is gay, generally it is easier for the female to approach the third party. The ménage à trois relationship that has potential for lasting longest consists of same sex partners, followed by two bisexual women and a male or two men and a

woman, and last by one male and two heterosexual females.

One's focus is often divided between two people and if a male orgasms before the female(s), the sex play may be over, if the women are not bi-sexual. There is also the risk that if one is enjoying a particular sensation, someone stroking or probing another part of the body becomes distracting. This often happens with two people who are excited about experimenting with bi-sexuality for the first time. If something goes wrong it is better for someone having a poor experience to stop immediately; no one is obligated to stay in the group until the others are satisfied. Husbands and wives often have strong opinions about which types of sex their partner can use with the outside lover. These rules are best discussed prior to approaching the third person, and then discussed again with the third person so that their wishes may be taken into consideration by the couple as well.

Sexual positions used during a ménage à trois vary according to the type of sex the people enjoy. People can be stimulated with the tongue, mouth and hands—some even use their feet to gain contact with the third person. Jessica Stewart, in *The Complete Manual of Sexual Positions*, includes a chapter with photos of group sex. CAUTION: Safe sex should be used in all group sex scenes to prevent the transmission of disease.

(See also ADULTERY, CANDAULISM, FESTIVALS, GANG BANGS, GROUP SEX, ORGIES, POLYITEROPHILIA and TROILISM)

MISCEGENATION (Allotriorasty) The word miscegenation was first used in the 1860's and refers to sex or marriage between two people of different races.

According to a survey conducted by Louis Harris in 1971 an average of one in five Americans have dated someone of a different race. Most interracial relationships were not entered into based on this difference but rather by similar criteria as would apply to anyone of the same race. The couples who deliberately select a partner of another race do so for reasons such as sexual novelty or the appeal of submissive women from other cultures. In America it is common for some young caucasian girls to seek out black boyfriends as part of a larger pattern of breaking away from their parents'  values. This is especially true if parents are both overcontrolling and racially prejudiced. The men they choose, who are usually poor and uneducated, are flattered by this and consider it a mark of status. These relationships, when based on defiance of parents and social strictures, can involve a lot of negative behavior (drugs, truancy, prostitution, etc.) to flaunt the rebellion, and the relationships seldom work.

Societal bias may influence minority or immigrant sexual ideals with the advertising media. In the United States models, movie stars, and dolls are often blond or fair skinned. Even ethnic magazines use women with light skin and facial features that could pass as Anglo. These groups often develop anglo criteria for beauty and an aversion to women who fail to meet that standard.

Personal prejudice against one's own race is also a motivator when marriage occurs outside a cultural group; sometimes being an attempt to deny one's identity as a minority or to increase social status via a spouse.

Americans have disapproved of most types of miscegenation since the beginning. Marriage or sex with Indians, Irish, Jews, Catholics, and Chinese was discouraged. However, sex with blacks seemed to incite the greatest indignation. Blacks, unlike slaves during other times, were discriminated against because of color. This phenomenon was due in part to Christianity's interpretation of Ham's curse of his descendants being turned black and made to serve as slaves. This misinterpretation coincidentally began in America as new labor was desperately needed in the production of molasses (the product that was the first mainstay of the new American economy). When the theory of evolution became popular in the 19th century it also condemned blacks to a lower status. Despite created prejudices against blacks, white slave

owners were sexually attracted to their black slaves. The legal system unfortunately supported sexual harassment and subjugation of black women, not only during slavery, but also after their emancipation. One of these laws was passed during the 17th and 18th centuries by the English colonists which pronounced mulatto offspring between slave and freeman to be slaves. In contrast, the Spanish colonies granted children of mixed unions their freedom. Winthrop Jordon, in his book *White Over Black*, stated "If he [white man] could not restrain his sexual nature, he could at least reject its fruits and thus solace himself that he had done no harm...By classifying the mulatto as a Negro he was in effect denying that intermixture had occurred at all" (p. 178).

The legal reforms won after the 1863 Emancipation Proclamation by blacks were short lived. The right of a black woman to sue for financial support of her half white illegitimate children was repealed. Laws that would make concubinage illegal and force whites to marry black women with whom they lived never passed.

The 19th century saw a continuation of black lynchings. However, now instead of accusing black men of conspiracies, insurrections, and plotting the murder of slave owners they were charged with rape. This indictment was made against males engaged in consensual unions because "it was impossible for a white woman to freely succumb to a black man." The accusation of rape served the white men well because it was an act that even the most liberal supporter of equal rights would not condone.

There are disagreements as to whether intermarriage to the point of homogeny would alleviate prejudice among humans. If we use examples of amoebas, bacteria, viruses, or female worker bees which are genetically identical, the answer is yes. Frank Baird, Jr., a professor of science and curator in entomology, explains that "Sex is an antisocial force in evolution. Bonds are formed between individuals in spite of sex and not because of it. Perfect societies, if we can be so bold as to define them as societies that lack conflict and possess the highest degree of altruism and coordination, are most likely to evolve where all of the members are genetically identical. When sexual reproduction is introduced, members of the group become genetically dissimilar. Parents and offspring are separated by at least a one-half reduction of the genes shared through common descent and mates by even more. The inevitable result is a conflict of interest." Professor Baird goes on to state that "To diversify is to adapt; sexually reproducing populations are more likely than asexual ones to create new genetic combinations better adjusted to changed conditions in the environment. Asexual forms are permanently committed to their particular combinations and are more likely to become extinct when the environment fluctuates" (*Sociobiology, The Abridged Edition*, pp. 155-6).

The nature of humanity, so long as we sexually reproduce, seems to embrace aggression. People who live in predominantly homogenous societies, where skin color and facial features are similar, direct their aggression or prejudice against members of other religions, caste systems, schools, or companies. The solution, if there is one, lies in individuals learning to control their own aggression, to appreciate racial and cultural variety, and to cultivate compassion for those who are different or weak.

People who choose to add racial variety to their sexual repertoire have dating services such as the Ebony Ivory Society that cater to their needs. One will also find erotic magazines like *Cocoa 'n Creme, Your National Guide to Interracial Swinging* that lists personal ads such as the following:

Hot, white couple, seeking well-hung, black men to take care of sexy wife's needs. See picture of her first gang bang while on vacation...

Do I look like a church secretary to you? Thank God. I live in a small town...Just dressing like a slut makes me wild with desire....

Black Goddess accepts TVs, TSs, females, males, and couples for her slaves....

(See also ANTHROPOMORPHIC CARTOONS, CANDAULISM, EUNUCHS, HODOPHILIA and SLAVES)

MISOGYNIST   This term is applied to men who hate women. This hate is often based on low self-esteem and a fear of suffocation or abandonment by the woman-hating partner. To prevent abandonment, or soothe the feeling of inferiority, he degrades her, accuses her of cheating or not loving him, and otherwise tries to reduce her level of self-esteem to something lower than his. We gain self-esteem by learning to handle our own problems and becoming independent from our parents. When this separation is thwarted or a child is abandoned early, a son's confidence in himself suffers. He will feel dependent on others, fear abandonment, and may be unable to handle frustrations. A misogynist resents his partner, rather than his mother, for these feelings.

Dr. Susan Forward explains the dynamics behind misogyny. "Mother is the nurturer and the boy's primary source of comfort, while Father helps him to pull away from Mother so that he does not become overly dependent on her. However, in the family backgrounds of misogynists, just the opposite occurs.... so that the boy has no other option than to make Mother the center of his universe." Dr. Forward's book, *Men Who Hate Women & The Women Who Love Them*, offers additional insights on this relationship.

The adult male grows up attributing the same power or needs of his mother to all women. Men will also hate women because of mothers who emasculated them by overprotection or humiliation. Weak mothers can make sons feel helpless by asking them to take on impossible responsibilities of care, protection and nurturing. A major part of healing comes from learning to communicate fears or anger without blaming a partner. Society condones anger and violence as tools for masculine power. However, anger stems from fear of being helpless and most would not consider this manly. (Some people can relieve anger by immediately breathing deeply and asking themselves why they are feeling helpless.) Each person is responsible for their own problems. A partner can lend support but should not be blamed or expected to mend things. A marriage is between two adults, not a parent and small child. For people who do not have a clear understanding of their role and what should be expected of them Dr. Susan Forward lists a "Personal Bill of Rights" for couples:

1. You have the right to be treated with respect.

2. You have the right not to take responsibility for anyone else's problems or bad behavior.

3. You have the right to get angry.

4. You have the right to say no.

5. You have the right to make mistakes.

6. You have the right to have your own feelings, opinions, and convictions.

7. You have the right to change your mind or to decide on a different course of action.

8. You have the right to ask for emotional support or help.

10. You have the right to protest unfair treatment or criticism.

These rules are for the benefit of both people. If one person doesn't feel they can ask them of their partner they may not think it is fair for the other person to make the demands. The relationship works better if kept balanced. If one person asks for a favor the other should request something in exchange (i.e., if a husband wants to spend Thanksgiving with his family then the wife might ask for another holiday with her family—not a mink coat and a new Jaguar.) This may seem strange or unromantic in the beginning but it will stave off a lot of resentment and feelings of betrayal in the future. Equality prevents either person from feeling totally used.

(See also BIASTOPHILIA, LUST MURDER, PHOBIAS, ST. AUGUSTINE and SEXUAL HARASSMENT)

MORTALITY   There is probably no greater anxiety than to see or face death.

Seeing mutilated or dead bodies stimulates some people. Many people driving along a highway will slow down to get a better look at accidents. Some men have reported sexual arousal and even orgasm to their psychologist because they are confused by this reaction to mutilated bodies.

Some couples, surviving a near miss with death themselves, find their passions aroused. Others experience an increased sex drive after losing a close friend and in two cases women who had lost a child became nymphomaniacs. The latter propensity would certainly contribute to the survival of a species who has historically had a high infant mortality rate.

(See also BULL FIGHTS, EXECUTIONS, LUST MURDER, NECROPHILIA and SADISM)

MUMMIFICATION   See BINDING/ Mummification

MUCOPHAGY   Mucophagy, consuming nasal mucosa, is done as a matter of course in nasolingus. Others may engage in mucophagy because of the implied self degradation, or simply the novelty of it. Like consumption of other body secretions, mucophagy can be used to demonstrate total acceptance and love of a partner.

(See also COCKTAILS, COPROPHAGY, UROPHILIA and VAMPIRISM)

MUTILATION   (Colobosis—castration, Mazoperosis—of breasts, Perogynia—of females) Mutilation refers to inflicting physical injury on someone; usually by stabbing, tearing, or cutting.

Deliberate mutilation was used by leaders and rebels in battles to evoke terror in enemies and reinforce their own feeling of power. However, the flaw in this strategy is that often those who had been terrorized generally retaliated. Mutilation in battle seems inhumane but is tolerated by many societies as necessary. Mutilation for the purpose of sexual arousal concerns people much more. Jacobus X, a physician in the French army during the late 1800's, related two examples in his book, *Crossways of Sex.* One was Joseph, a young cook in the Navy, who would have erections when he slaughtered fowls or rabbits. He would "then cut off its testicles and go outside to eat them and masturbate." He was previously dismissed as a goat herder after he nearly killed a he-goat for disturbing him while he was engaging in intercourse with one of the nannies. This man's sexual fantasies included performing pederasty on a prisoner or Chinaman and toward the end cutting off the victim's penis. Jacobus X refers only to Joseph's childhood molestation by an older brother as an explanation for his interest in mutilating male organs. The next case study was of a doctor who became aroused when performing autopsies which included dissecting penises. He transferred to a hospital that served sailors and convicts because he detested working on females. This doctor and his bi-sexual lover found it amusing to take these dismembered organs and slip them into the beds of unsuspecting prostitutes who quite often suffered violent consequences when their horrified clients discovered these under the sheets. Jacobus X did not offer an explanation as to what might have led to this man's strange arousal.

While rarely performing mutilation themselves, there are several examples of women who were aroused by viewing it. During the 1919 Sparticist uprising in Berlin, Hirschfeld wrote that he "accompanied a woman to the mortuary where, among hundreds of bodies, some of which were shockingly mutilated or had their throats slit, we discovered her son...In the identification hall an endless stream of people, mainly women, were filing past the unidentified bodies and an attendant who knew me called my attention to some girls who had for several days continually rejoined the queue, evidently because they could not tear themselves away from the sight of the male bodies which lay, entirely stripped, before them...The expression on their faces was similar to that with which I had seen the women of Madrid and Seville watch the bull-fighters in the ring." Then Hirschfeld compared this to an execution he had attended a few years earlier. "Next to me stood the State Attorney's wife, who followed the horrible scene—the condemned

man screamed and fought the executioners who were dragging him to the scaffold—with a heaving chest and ecstatic groans that sounded almost lustful. As the axe fell the woman behaved as though she were passing through the moment of orgasm" (*Sexual Anomalies and Perversions*, by Magnus Hirschfeld, p. 313).

Mutilators often begin with animals. This was particularly true in the past when many people killed their own game or fowl. Case studies often do not include reference to prior zoophilia in these instances but this may be due to the automatic death penalty most societies imposed and thus the victim's understandable hesitance in admitting to it. Another factor is that masturbation generally took place only after mutilation and without penetration of the animal, therefore courts did not view this as falling into their normal definition of zoophilia.

Men who are homosexual will most often mutilate those of the same sex, heterosexuals mutilate those of the opposite sex, and pedophiles mutilate children. Hirschfeld even mentioned men damaging statues but did not specify as to whether they had a history of engaging in agalmatophilia.

Severe stress, such as the threat of losing a lover or arguments with the family, sometimes leads to the person entering a state of mind where reason and compassion are overshadowed by a blind desire to mutilate. In normal confrontations one animal or human will halt their attack when they see submission, pain, or injury in the same species. This may come in the form of tears, an expression of sadness, or remorse. However, for those who either feel justified in severely punishing the victim or who are not capable of the sensitivity required to empathize with emotional expressions of pain or surrender, a physical manifestation of injury is necessary. These people are often physically abused as children to a degree that leaves them emotionally numb. Expressions of emotional pain in others do not register with them because they cannot relate to something they have no memory feeling; these people only recognize pain caused by physical injury. Dr. Loren Roth described several characteristics that violent prisoners had in common. "The violent prisoners . . . had missing, alcoholic, criminal, or abusive fathers . . . were age 12 or under at first arrest . . . [and] had attempted suicide or self-mutilation" (*Clinical Treatment of the Violent Person*, edited by Loren H. Roth, p. 219). A person who does not learn to feel emotional pain cannot feel remorse or guilt for their actions.

(See also AUTOMASOCHISM, CASTRATION, EXECUTIONS, LUST MURDER, MASOCHISM, PARAPHILIAS and SADISM)

MYSOPHILIA Mysophilia refers to becoming aroused by smelling, chewing, or rubbing against a foul smelling soiled jock strap, pair of panties, menstrual pad, bra, or other object. The most common secretions  used are genital discharges, menstrual blood, feces, and milk. Locker rooms provide abundant odors for the mysophile, who often pilfers used jock straps. Necrophiles who prefer decaying flesh, as opposed to a fresh corpse, fall into this category also. One case involved a male who had been almost blind since birth. He was compensated for his loss of sight with enhanced smell and touch. He confessed to wanting to mutilate, wallow in, and eat a person. He was only able to find animals. Attempts to convince his grandmother to leave him her body were unsuccessful. His most common behavior consisted of searching for garbage and eating feces (*Perverse Crimes in History*, p. 130).

It is possible that some mysophiles have increased sensitivity to pheromones that are produced in body excrements.

Underwear is occasionally taken off a partner in bondage and used in place of a gag. Fake excretions are safe when made from things such as peanut butter, mayonnaise, or ketchup. These are smeared onto the underwear or body.

Fetish magazines carry ads that offer photos, videos, and, recently, worn and unwashed panties. CAUTION: Ingestion or exposure to body secretions of other persons is not considered a safe sex practice.

(See also COCKTAILS, COPROPHAGY, PHEROMONES, SALIROPHILIA, SHOWERS and UROPHILIA)

N

NARCISSISM (Autophilia, Ipserotic) Narcissists derive sexual gratification from their own bodies or intellect. The term is a derivative from the mythological Greek character named Narcissus who was known for his beauty. Echo, a nymph, fell in love with Narcissus but because he was so consumed in admiring his own reflection he was unaware of her need for him to speak. She was only able to use the echo of his voice to express her love for him. When she died of grief, Nemesis, the goddess of equity and retribution, avenged her death by making Narcissus unable to leave the river. He finally drowned by falling into the water while trying to kiss himself. At the point of death the goddess turned him into a flower by the same name. Philosophers and writers have since interpreted the myth at various times as not only symbolizing self-love, but abstinence, morality, masochism, sadism, fetishism, and the use of dildos.

Narcissism is considered normal in the early development stages of youth, but not upon maturity. The types of activities in which a narcissist may engage include one or more of the following: kissing oneself, prolonged use of a mirror, excessive grooming, masturbation, collecting trophies and photos (often of own genitals), exhibi-tionism, homosexuality, and attraction to partners because of similarity to oneself. A few Narcissists have gone to even more extreme measures, such as being aroused by listening to their own stomach noises, passing gas, performing autofellatio, and drinking their own urine or semen. CAUTION: Narcissism can cause a breakdown in bonds between family and friends. These bonds give meaning to life, a sense of worth, security, and love.

(See also LOVE and LOVE ADDICTION)

NARRATOPHILIA (Selgolalia, Lagnolalia; Cunnilalia—talk about female genitals, Gymnocryptosis—females talking about sex life of husbands, Medolalia—about penis, Moriaphilia—jokes, Phallolalia—talk about penis) Narratophilia (narrare: narrate; philia: attachment to) refers to those who are aroused by telling sexual stories or jokes or reading love poems or novels that include material with a sexual content to a sex partner.

(See also AGREXOPHILIA, CONFESSIONS, COPROLALIA, HUMILIATION, JACTITATION, OBSCENE PHONE CALLS and PHONE SEX)

NASOPHILIA Nasophilia (naso: nose, philia: attachment to) refers to arousal from the sight, touch, act of licking, or sucking a partner's nose. The reasons people are enamored with this activity varies. Eskimos rub noses when greeting others and Sioux Indians traditionally rub noses to express affection; they do this just as other cultures kiss on the lips.

Magnus Hirschfeld related the case of a young writer who made wax noses and put them over his own, admired himself in the mirror, and with a "slight manual manipulation he brought about an ejaculation." Another would hire a gay prostitute, take him home, and having placed a wooden clip on his nose had the prostitute pull on an attached string while saying "I hope this nose is going to be so big that everybody will be surprised at it." This was necessary to induce orgasm. Another man became fixated on the size of female nostrils, thinking that if large enough they could be penetrated. He drew and kept sketches of his large nosed feminine ideal. One day, while

on the bus, he spotted a young woman who had large nostrils. Infatuated, he followed her home and proposed marriage on the spot. She refused and when he continued to come to her home she had him arrested (*Sexual Anomalies and Perversions* by Magnus Hirschfeld, pp. 411, 551-2).

People sometimes use nasolingus (licking or sucking nose) as a substitute penis during intercourse, occasionally asking their partner to blow their nose in simulation of an ejaculation. CAUTION: This is considered an activity that exposes a partner to the body secretions of another and is therefore not considered a safe sex practice.

(See also ANAL SEX, AXILLISM, LACTAPHILIA, OCULOPHILIA, ODONTOPHILIA, PHALLOPHILIA, TESTICLES and YONI WORSHIP)

NECROPHILIA (Necrocoitus—penetration of corpse, Necrochlesis—sex with corpse) Necrophilia (necro: corpse; philia: attachment) is defined as an erotic attraction to corpses and is considered a rare paraphilia.

The necrophile often views the corpse as having a personality which is pure and incapable of heartless acts (e.g. rejection). Necrophiles often chose a profession that allows them free access to their love objects. A Greek historian, Herodotus, in writing about ancient Egypt said: "As far as concerns the noble ladies, their bodies are not immediately given to the embalmers, especially those who were of great beauty and who attracted great attention during their lifetime, but were given them three or four days after death. These precautions are taken because it is feared the embalmers will violate the corpse." At one time a fiance in India was required to deflower his future bride if she died before the wedding. The girl could not be cremated until this ritual was carried out in front of the village priest (*Perverse Crimes in History* by R.E.L. Masters, p. 174).

During war, conquering soldiers performed pederasty on their dead or dying victims in order to experience the victim's anal spasms which occur at death. Soldiers during the Moroccan campaigns of 1919-26 and the Russo-Turkish war were violated in this way on the battlefield (*Perverse Crimes in History*, pp. 113, 204).

A current case study of a necrophile was submitted at the Eighth World Congress for Sexology in Heidelberg, West Germany (June 14-20, 1987) by H. Martin Malin, Ph.D., FACCS. The patient was brought to his attention and that of his colleague, Dr. Jackie Davison, after having been arrested for photographing partially nude children posing dead in a coffin. Other photos were found with models or corpses "on embalming tables, in caskets, and in shrine-like natural settings." Other than children's books of *Snow White* and *Sleeping Beauty* he was unable to find suitable pornography and had to create his own. He also visited funeral parlors and when alone would fondle the breasts or genitals of a corpse. The patient seemed to have a sexual interest in corpses since the age of four. He used "playing dead" as a sexual game with another boy and in masturbation fantasies when alone. The patient explained his fascination with death and corpses thus:

"I had to find sexual expression I could live with since according to my mother real life sex was so dirty. My four-year old mind had to find some way to do it...I had to find an escape...She practically destroyed me...I was afraid of females altogether...so that by envisioning them as dead, they were totally passive and there was no condemnation."

Dr. Malin wrote, "To my mind, this case vignette bears eloquent testimony to the mechanism of the pathogenesis of at least this paraphilia. With a native 'love map' severely vandalized by the forceful repression of masturbation — an early form of juvenile sexual rehearsal play — our patient was forced to devise a strategy to reclaim his right to be erotic." Drs. Malin and Davison began to treat this patient with a combination of insight oriented psychotherapy and the antiandrogenic hormone medroxyprogesterone acetate, also known by its trade name of Depo-Provera. Dr. Malin explained, "While we believe we are the first to use this approach with a patient suffering from necrophilia, this regimen has been used with considerable success in treating other paraphilias, especially pedophilia, at the Sexual Disorders Clinic at The Johns Hopkins Medical Institutions as well as other clinics. The patient was started on weekly 500mg intramuscular injections of Depo-Provera and continued to receive intensive individual psychotherapy. Within three weeks, he reported that for the first time in his entire life he felt that he had some chance of getting his sexuality under control, rather than being at its mercy. Our treatment plan for him was based upon continuing his Depo-Provera as an adjunct to long-term psychotherapy aimed at helping him make an adjustment towards a more socially acceptable form of sexual expression. Unfortunately, our patient is being denied the therapeutic benefits of Depo-Provera which he has found to be so helpful. He is incarcerated in a State which, despite substantial clinical evidence, considers the use of Depo-Provera in the treatment of paraphilias to be experimental..."

There are many more people who engage only in necrophilic fantasy. Necrophilia may be triggered by performance anxiety. B.R. Burg, a sexologist, observed that "[n]ecrophilia involving sex acts with corpses, despite Freud's assertions to the contrary, seems usually to be accompanied by other relatively severe psychological disorders. Rejection, alcohol abuse, and object loss also seem more than coincidentally common among both those committing necrophilial acts and those experiencing necrophilial fantasies" ("The Sick and the Dead: The Development of Psychological Theory on Necrophilia from Krafft-Ebing to the Present," by B. R. Burg, *Journal of the History of the Behavioral Sciences*, Volume 18, July 1982, p. 242-254).

Types of sex practiced on corpses include kissing, fondling, cunnilingus, fellatio, pederasty, and penile/vaginal intercourse. Others are described in the following text:

FETISHES Necrophiles, similar to the general population, often have special fetishes having to do with hair, breasts, or eating toe nails. Some necrophiles masturbate during funeral sermons or dirges as they sit in a crowd of mourners. The patient in the case reported by Dr. Malin included the removal of a few pubic hair, panties, and once a tampon as trophies from corpses.

MYSOPHILIA A few necrophiles ingest body fluids of corpses, particularly urine. A mysophile may want to roll their body in the open wounds or secreta of a corpse.

NECROSADISM Necrosadism involves sadistic acts on a corpse such as biting, dismembering, cutting, or stabbing for sexual arousal. Those who mutilate corpses often cut away the genitals or breasts, as in the case of Jack the Ripper. Others, such as Victor Ardisson and Jeffrey Dahmer, have been known to severe the head and keep it with them until decay makes disposal necessary.

NOSOPHILIA (Nosolagnia) Nosophilia refers to those who are aroused from the knowledge that a partner is terminally ill. Hirschfeld wrote of men who fell in love and married women who were thought to be terminally ill. The sexual relevance became evident when upon the women's miraculous recovery their husbands became impotent. CAUTION: True necrophilia is not legal and if relatives of the deceased discovered this type of sexual violation it would make their grief even more unbearable.

PSEUDONECROPHILIA Pseudonecrophilia (pseudo: pretended, necro: corpse, philia: attachment to) refers to sex play where one partner pretends to be dead. The scene is occasionally enhanced by having the acting partner lay on a covered block of ice or dusting their body with baby powder. There was a case in Oregon of a man who would call ahead to a bordello and request that a woman lie still waiting for his arrival and remain motionless through intercourse until he departed. The client was a local mortician.

A case in Texas involved a patient at a nursing home who raped comatose or paralyzed victims. The man's justification was that he had often seen it done by the night orderlies (Personal communication). Geoff Mains spoke of a man in California who

enjoyed being mummified and temporarily buried by his friends (Urban Aboriginals, p. 90).

(See also AMAUROPHILIA, ANTHROPOPHAGY, EXECUTIONS, SACRIFICES and SOMNOPHILIA)

NEGOTIATION Negotiation, or discussion and agreement, on activities to be engaged in during sex can alleviate the misunderstandings that otherwise often occur between partners. Successful negotiation requires that people be free to discuss their expectations and limitations without being judged. The first difficulty many encounter is one of embarrassment or inhibition. An effective technique in overcoming this shyness is that of using a written questionnaire. The form is better if it is specially designed by the couple for themselves. The couple then may enter into the second stage of negotiation.

This second stage involves looking at costumes and experimenting with toys. The negotiation becomes increasingly complex in direct relation to the complexity of the sex acts and paraphernalia incorporated into play.

The initial questions may sound rudimentary for "vanilla" practitioners (people who only engage in penile/vaginal sex), however they are necessary for sadomasochist games. Vanilla sex often lasts 10-30 minutes, whereas bondage may last from two hours to two days. A misunderstanding about the amount of time can create a problem if the personwho is put into a gag and restraints for 12 hours only expected to be there for two hours and has planned to attend a black tie dinner that evening.

Experienced players have the option of using a safeword or signal. These are used rather than a "no" because "no" is used in fantasy scenes; therefore, a different word is selected such as "red," "uncle," or "pansy." The criteria is that it must be easy to remember and pronounce. Two more words may be selected to let the person in control know whether to intensify the game or to slow it down. The control words, red, green, and yellow, are popular when using his formula. Some limit the number of

NEGOTIATION QUESTIONNAIRE

DATE_____TIME_____

LOCATION_____

PREFERRED ROLE

TOP/DOMINANT ( ) BOTTOM/SUBMISSIVE ( ) SWITCH: TOP/BOTTOM ( ) NONE ( )

SAFE WORDS STOP:_____CAUTION:_____INTENSIFY:_____

SAFETY PHYSICAL LIMITATIONS, HEALTH, MEDICATION, SAFE SEX, BIRTH CONTROL, RECENT PIERCINGS:

_____

_____

GOALS

NURTURING AND INTIMACY

ACUPRESSURE( )	INFANTILISM( )	BATHS( )	BODY PAINTING( )
TANTRA( )	MASSAGE( )	PEDICURE( )	PHOTOGRAPHY( )

FANTASY OR CHARACTER PLAY

COSTUMES( )	ACROPHILIA( )	ANAL SEX( )	ACOUSTICOPHILIA( )
AXILLISM( )	BITING( )	STUFFING( )	SEX GAMES( )
CUNNILINGUS( )	CUPPING( )	DEFILEMENT( )	EXHIBITION( )
FELLATIO( )	FETISHES( )	FLAGELLATE( )	SEX POSITIONS( )
HARPAXOPHILIA( )	HUMILIATION( )	ICE( )	MUD PLAY( )
CROSS DRESSING( )	SITOPHILIA( )	SHAVING( )	SPITTING( )
TEASING( )	TICKLING( )	WEIGHTS( )	HIEROPHILIA( )

BONDAGE

BINDINGS( )	BLINDFOLDING( )	CORSETS( )	CHASTITY BELT( )
GAGS( )	GROPING SUITS( )	HOOD/MASK( )	THREELEGGED
RAPE RACKS( )	SLINGS( )	SLAVECOLLAR( )	BLOOMERS( )
			SPREADER BARS( )

times a bottom can use a safeword because excessive use means that either the chemistry between the two people is not working or the fantasy chosen is not appropriate. At this point the two may either switch to vanilla sex or end the scene.

Physical limitations and health are important for everyone to reveal and discuss. In addition to the normal questions about birth control and safe sex, people need to know if their partner has any medical conditions of which they need to be made aware. If so, they should also know the medication needed for the condition or the name of their doctor in case of an emergency.

The next decision made involves the type of emotion or passion the individuals desire to achieve and type of play that will fulfill their goal. The sample questionnaire is divided into categories that facilitate that choice.

The last stage of negotiation entails the selection of costumes, perfumes, lighting, music, the use of paraphernalia such as flagellation tools, sensory devices, dildoes, vibrators, and bondage equipment. Any item that has potential to cause discomfort is tried on both partners to determine the degree of pressure or pain that they will use.

People select their style of sex in a similar manner to which they choose food. In the same way that one would not expect a person to eat anything that happened to be on a menu, the questionnaire is not to be used to persuade a partner into experimenting with forms of sex that they don't find arousing. A partner's selection of sexual activity must never be taken as a personal rejection.

(See also BIRTH CONTROL, HANDKERCHIEF CODES and SAFE SEX)

NEPIOPHILIA (Nepiolagnia, Nepiphtherosis) Nepiophilia (Greek, nepios: infant; philia: attachment to) refers to an adult's sexual attraction to an infant of the opposite sex. This was more common in the past when the care of infants was often left to servants.

Edwardes and Masters wrote that there "was a rather extensive literature of English and European complaints about masturba-tion of infants by domestic servants. The act is most often performed ostensibly for the purpose of stopping the baby's crying, or restlessness, although it seems obvious that the servant often derives erotic titillation from her behavior. Later, these same servants, or their successors, frequently initiate the male children into other mysteries— copulation, fellatio, and cunnilingus; and, sometimes, perversions" (*Cradle of Erotica*, p. 251).

The ancient Romans openly engaged in nepiophilia. They may have been originally influenced by the practice brothels had of allowing their prostitutes to keep nursing infants on the premises. These brothels often kept chickens and other animals for the pleasure of their clients. The use of infants for sexual purposes or to pass time while waiting for the infant's mother may have been a natural progression. This type of conduct was not restricted to brothels but found its way to the top of the social hierarchy. Tiberius (emperor of Rome) placed infants in his lap and had them suck on his penis.

Asian child pornography during the 1960's included photos such as an old man sucking on the genitals of an infant. CAUTION: Nepiophilia is illegal. It can be considered a form of child abuse that may be ruinous to the future development of any children involved, since they are being introduced to adult sexuality long before they are ready.

(See also COITUS INTERFERMORIS, INCEST and PEDOPHILIA)

NIDDAH (Menstrual taboo, Natural family planning) Niddah is a Jewish religious observance that requires married couples to maintain physical separation for approximately 10-14 days a month. The admonitions in Arulch's *Code of Jewish Law* can sound extremely harsh. However, Orthodox Jews today who practice niddah do nothing but praise the tradition. Couples who have been married for twenty years describe each sexual encounter as being as exciting as their honeymoon. Passion and desire is rekindled during the period of time they do not touch.

This law supposedly came into existence when Aaron, the compassionate brother of Moses, was approached by women of the tribe with complaints of husbands who seemed to take them for granted, demanding sex and servitude from them without showing sensitivity or appreciation in return. Aaron was sympathetic to their needs and as a solution implemented niddah. Periodically doing without something we love often helps us appreciate it more. This was not a unique strategy; Judaism has many laws pertaining to food and behavior that restrict indulgence during designated times. Hence, the sex act became holy and mandatory during specific times and a defilement or unclean at others. Niddah was codified by defining this period of unclean time as from the first moment a spot of menstrual blood is seen to seven days after it ceases. A ritual immersion in water was to follow as a symbol of purity and sexual availability to her husband. The punishment imposed on any who had intercourse during the forbidden period was exclusion from the tribe and those who were found caressing during niddah were flogged. The *Code of Jewish Law* continues with detailed instructions for conduct.

The husband in that period should not touch her even with his little finger. He is not allowed to hand anything to her, be it even a long object, nor to receive anything from her. Throwing anything from his hand into her hand, or vice versa, is forbidden .... He is not allowed to eat with her at the same table, unless something separates between his dish and hers . ... They are not allowed to sleep in the same bed .... they may not sleep facing one another [in parallel beds], unless there is a big distance between them .... She is forbidden to pour water for him to wash his face and hands, and bathe his feet, even if the water is cold .... He is not permitted to scent her perfume, and to hear her sing (Chapter 153, pp. 21-23).

Irrespective of religious beliefs, psychologically a husband who is not permitted to touch his wife or have her serve his needs is soon reminded of her value. Wives are thus given a reprieve once a month from being a sex object and servant. Couples learn to express their affection through other methods. Catholics who practice natural family planning experience a similar feeling although Catholic couples are permitted to touch.

The discipline that niddah requires is difficult to follow without the ritual and moral inducement that religion bestows.

Niddah is thought by some to have been an adaptation of primitive views of a female's menses. This taboo was quite common among ancient tribes who feared that some type of supernatural being was mutilating the inside of the vagina and if they had sex during this time they too would be injured. William Stephens, in a cross-cultural study of menstrual taboos, found "that all but fourteen of a sample of seventy-one tribal cultures have significant menstrual taboos. . . . Nearly twenty-five percent of the societies in Stephen's sample went so far as to seclude women in special dwellings for the duration of their menstrual period" (*Anxious Pleasures, The Sexual Lives of an Amazonian People*, by Thomas Gregor, p. 141).

This rule applies to members of the Nandi tribe but only for ordinary husbands and men. It seems the medicine men are not only exempt but satisfy the sexual lusts of many of the tribal women during their menses. The one striking feature that distinguishes niddah from other menstrual taboos is that an extra seven days was added to this period of separation for Jewish couples. Therefore, it would seem to have a purpose other than to just allay fears of castration in men.

(See also ORGASM, PRISHA, PURDAH and TOUCH)

NORMOPHILIA Normophilia, coined by John Money, is a condition of being in sexual conformity with the standard as dictated by customary, religious, or legal authority.

(See also HIEROPHILIA, PHOBOPHILIA and SEX POSITIONS)

NUDITY (Actirasty—exposure to sun's rays, Alloerasty—using nudity of another person to arouse partner, Gymnophilia, Nudomania and Omolagnia—arousal from nudity)

Nudity is taken from the Latin word nudus, meaning naked or unclothed. The historical acceptance of nudity can be measured to some degree by the liberties a culture gave to its artists. Mass portrayal of nudes engaged in explicit sexual acts implied a lax attitude at least among the upper classes. Ancient Greeks were probably the last European culture that was most comfortable with nudity, even revering it as sacred. Greeks who participated in athletic games, beauty contests, and dances often performed while in the nude. Depiction of nudes in European art was common until about the 2nd century C.E. The Christian influence then drove it underground and it remained there until about the 15th century.

Christianity demanded that the body be covered and draped in drab clothing for almost 1,000 years. During the reign of Napoleon III, when not even statues could be naked, sculptors rebelled against this law by depicting animals, where it was still permissible to show every anatomical detail. Parks became filled with statues of tigers, lions, horses, and wild boars *History of Sexual Customs*, by Richard Lewinshohn, MD, p. 301). Medicine likewise suffered during the Middle Ages because physicians weren't permitted total freedom in closely examining human anatomy; the Church forbade dissection of cadavers.

Even recently, examples of repression around nudity are rampant. *National Geographic*, with its graphic depiction of naked tribes, was one of the first sources; mail order catalogues advertising underwear was another. Kinsey's 1953 report showed that one-third of the women born before 1900 wore clothes while engaging in sex.

Today there is a growing interest and participation in recreational nudity. This includes excursions to nude beaches, spas, ocean cruises, clubs, resorts, hot tub parties, and participation in intimacy workshops.

Advantages for indulging in group nudity are best explained by nudists themselves who claim that it is very relaxing, that without clothes they relate to others in a more egalitarian way; and everyone feels vulnerability which develops into a mutual trust. Nudity also reveals everyone else's flaws and many feel relief in not having to compare themselves to professional nude models or movie stars. Nude resorts rarely, if ever, permit public sex or overt cruising, the fear of which would make many couples apprehensive of attending nude social functions.

Professional nudist clubs offer more than a place to hang clothes. They often provide tennis courts, hottubs, massage, dances, dining, movies, and comedy acts. For example, the Ponderosa Ranch outside Dallas, Texas, has special events such as lingerie dances, potluck dinners, mud-wrestling, and an annual Mr./Ms. Nude Texas Pageant. The contestants are judged on evenness of suntans, public speaking ability, and their attractiveness. They first appear on stage naked, next in swim wear, and finally in formal wear as an audience of several hundred nudists applaud and scream for their favorite contenders. The National Ms Nude America is hosted every October in San Jose, California.

(See also EXHIBITIONISM, GROUP SEX, SEX SHOWS and STRIPPING)

NYMPHOMANIA (Andromania, Arrhenothigmophilous, Clitoromania, Coitolimia, Furor uterinus, Hyperphilia, Idiosyncrat, Lagnoperissia, Pareunomania, Sex addiction)

Nymphomania (nympho: female; mania: abnormal craving for an act or object) is the term used for women who have an insatiable appetite for sex.

Hirschfeld cited the case of a young man who had his marriage annulled after six weeks due to his wife's insistence that he perform to her satisfaction. "In fact during the six weeks of the marriage the husband had not more than an hour's sleep per night, as the woman always prevented him from falling asleep by various sexual manipulations...she compelled him to engage in the sexual act for hours and when this became impossible owing to repeated discharges she demanded that he should manipulate with his fingers for hours, until, as he says, his arms ached" (*Sexual Anomalies and Perversions*, by Magnus Hirschfeld, p. 105).

Jews tried to guarantee wives sexual satisfaction while still taking the husband's physical limitations into consideration. The *Code of Jewish Law* did this by regulating sexual performance according to a husband's profession. "Men of a strong constitution who enjoy the pleasures of life, having profitable pursuits at home and are tax exempt, should perform their marital duty nightly. Laborers who work in the town where they reside, should perform their marital duty twice weekly; but if they are employed in another town, only once a week. Men who convey freight on camels from distant places, should attend to their marital duty once in thirty days" (Chapter 150, p. 15).

Common male fantasies have always included that of finding a nymphomaniac. These were often portrayed in art as water nymphs who floated in waves near the

 shore, sirens who sat on rocks and enticed sailors with their beautiful voices, and mermaids who swam near boats; all were believed to lure men to their death. Threats of death no longer loom in the minds of impassioned men, but seduction by a nymphomaniac is still thought to have negative consequences. Dr. Charles Wahl reports the emotional reality of men who have found their real-life nymphomaniac: "Curiously enough, encounters with the real thing; that is, a true nymphomania, do not live up to either literary or personal fantasies. On the several occasions when patients have described experiences with so-called nymphomaniacs and on other occasions when I have been told of such experiences by friends or acquaintances, they have turned out to be both unpleasant and anxiety-producing for the men involved. The inability to gratify such women and the demands for further experience have mobilized whatever fears and anxieties these men have had, no matter how latent, regarding their sexual adequacy—and, in the case of patients, severe castration anxiety, not to mention an unpleasant state of physical exhaustion" (*SEXUAL PROBLEMS Diagnosis and Treatment in Medical Practice*, pp. 164-5).

This warning seems disheartening for men, but fortunately the religious vindictiveness against the female as perpetrator has somewhat diminished in the last hundred years. At that time men were warned:

Chronic conditions of nymphomania are apt to weaken public morality and lead to offenses against decency. Woe unto the man who falls into the meshes of such an insatiable nymphomaniac, whose sexual appetite is never appeased. Heavy neurasthenia and impotence are the inevitable consequences. These unfortunate women disseminate the spirit of lewdness, demoralize their surroundings, become a danger to boys, and are liable to corrupt girls also, for there are homosexual nymphomaniacs as well (Psychopathia Sexualis, by Krafft-Ebing, pp. 322-3, printed with the permission of Scarborough House.

Nymphomania was considered even more dangerous for the woman herself, being on occasion potentially lethal. The most extreme cases, involving "acute deadly nymphomania" were likewise cited by Richard von Krafft-Ebing, a neurologist and psychiatrist who lived during the late 19th century.

Moreau (op. cit.). . . *A young girl became suddenly a nymphomaniac when forsaken by her betrothed; she revelled in cynical songs and expressions, and lascivious attitudes and gestures. She refused to put on her garments, had to be held down in bed by muscular men (!) and furiously demanded coitus. Insomnia, congestion of the facial nerves, a dry tongue, and rapid pulse. Within a few days lethal collapse.*

Louyer-Villermay (op. cit.). . .*Miss X., aged thirty; modest and decent, was suddenly seized with an attack of nymphomania, unlimited desire for sexual gratification, obscene delirium. Death from exhaustion within a few days. Cf. three other cases with deadly result by Maresch, Psychiatr. Centralblatt, 1871.*

These cases are viewed with much skepticism and Krafft-Ebing has been criticized for citing cases that offered no proof of validity as to the women's cause of death being nymphomania.

More commonly the word is used by men to describe a woman who has multiple partners or a greater sexual appetite than they themselves can handle. Most people only suffer from this condition periodically, and it is rarely considered serious in itself. However, complications arising from adultery or an inability to form lasting bonds with a lover create emotional problems that lead some to seek therapy. Wide variances exist in the number of times people engage in sex. Therefore, no quantitative definition can be given to nymphomania. For example, most American adults have sex ranging from once to four times a week, but when we compare this to other cultures we find our sex appetite is low by comparison. Dr. Eustace Chesser revealed that primitive societies such as the "Aranda of Australia have intercourse three to five times each night. The polygamous Chagga of Tanganyika do not regard it unusual to have intercourse ten times in a night; and the Thonga of Mozambique copulate with three or four wives in a single night" *(STRANGE LOVES, The Human Aspects of Sexual Deviation*, pp. 182-3).

(See also ORGASMS and SATYRIASIS)

NYMPHOPHILIA (Blastolagnia) Nymphophilia (nymph; young female, philia; attachment) is the love of a female adolescent by an adult. The idea seems remarkable today, but until the last century the age of consent for common law marriages was between ten and thirteen years of age in many countries, including the United States. Historically, early marriages could provide children with better living conditions, and simultaneously relieve their families of economic burdens.

Early marriage is not permitted today. Therefore, all sexual relationships between young pubescents and older people are considered incest, molestation, or statutory rape.

Criminal labels given this sex act have caused us to scrutinize this propensity in an individual to a greater degree than previously. Psychologists have learned that this preference for an age group is set during pubescent development. However, the nymphophile often does not continue to mature in his sexual response as he ages. This phenomenon is often caused by the abuser having been abused physically, emotionally, or sexually while young. As he ages he may feel inferior or helpless around women. A child offers him emotional security and a sense of being in control. These offenders have the same profiles as discussed in the section on incest. James Leslie McCary paraphrases them as: ". . . . inappropriate, self-defeating attempts to combat feelings of inadequacy; opportunism, carelessness, or drunkenness; a general criminality and a callous disregard for the rights of others; mental dullness or deficiency, and various degrees of mental illness and personality disorders" (*Sexual Myths and Fallacies* as quoted in *Modern Views of Human Sexual Behavior*, p. 307).

The offender sometimes responds to therapy that educates and readjusts inappropriate attitudes about sex or the law. For instance, they are taught to accept responsibility for their actions and learn not to transfer the blame onto the other party. They are made aware of the harmful effects the abuse has on a victim, including themselves if they were molested as children. Group therapy with other sex offenders often provides support and insight into their behavior. Individual counselling for sexual dysfunctions or establishing social relationships with adults is also used. For some, additional therapy such as behavioral conditioning and medication is needed to prevent future digression.

Nymphophiles often accuse the child of seduction. While children are not legally capable of seduction, they do have a primal need to be held and nurtured. "Experts term this type of sensuality 'psychobiologic' (independent of any awareness or judgment). For example, breast-feeding prompts physiological changes of sexual arousal in infants" (*Mayo Clinic Health Letter*, "Sexual Abuse of Children," August 1989, p. 7). A boy who is weaned at a year old may several years later still manifest extreme anger at being refused permission to fondle his mother's breasts. Whatever a child's perceived sexual advances are they never justify an adult's acquiescence to temptation.

Molestation creates special concerns for the young victim as well. It is recommended that a child first be reassured that the incident was the full responsibility of the other person. The child can then be encouraged, but not forced, to discuss any details or questions in order to bring a closure to the incident. Professional therapy is particularly beneficial when the molestation involved force or when the adult is nowhere near the age of the child.

The following symptoms may exhibit themselves in the case of a sexually abused child:

Sexually promiscuous behavior

Emotional withdrawal or distancing

Abnormal aggressive behavior

The National Center for Missing and Exploited Children can offer additional information and may be reached at 1-800-843-5678.

(See also INCEST, NEPIOPHILIA and PEDOPHILIA)

NYMPHOTOMY   Nymphotomies are surgical procedures that cut away the inner labia. The shrinking scar tissue served to restrict the size of the vaginal opening, making sex more pleasurable for some men. This procedure was done on some African girls from four weeks to four years old.

(See also CIRCUMCISION, CLITORIDEC-TOMY and INFIBULATION)

OBSCENE PHONE CALLERS   (Telephone scatologia and Telephon-icophilia—arousal from talking about sex on the phone) An obscene phone call is one that is made to a nonconsenting victim for the purpose of sexual arousal. Female callers differ in that they more often use these calls for revenge or excitement rather than as an aid to masturbation.

Obscene callers may deploy techniques such as immediately hanging up, breathing into the phone until the other party hangs up, conducting a survey that often leads to provocative questions, pretending they know the victim, saying they mis-dialed, or simply beginning with sexually explicit comments or threats. Callers often adapt to suit the situation. For instance, if the caller places calls to public service hotlines that answer questions about sexually transmitted diseases he will start by pretending to be naive. Typical questions are: "Can you get a disease by masturbating?" "No, well then what do you have to do?" The questions continue until the operator becomes wise to the delayed response time and labored dialogue.

Some callers use scenarios such as lying back on their bed with something to drink, their favorite selection of music, erotic magazines, videos, and a telephone list. The caller may take several hours and during this time will place periodic calls as a method of arousal maintenance. They don't have to keep the victim on the phone to be able to orgasm, the very act of calling someone and hearing their voice is enough of an emotional charge for some. However, most prefer to orgasm while the other person is on the line.

Obscene callers are normally perceived as having motives of aggression, dominance, seduction of the victim, or ridding themselves of a feeling of inadequacy. It is true that aggression, fear, and a need for power or dominance sometimes colors the motive of a caller. However, this is just as true for many "normal" sexual encounters. In addition, the caller has both a need for closeness and a fear of intimacy; making anonymous calls while masturbating resolves this dilemma.

The type of therapy that is recommended for those needing to end the obsession is behavioral and psychodynamic (raising self-esteem). In addition, the twelve-step program called "Sex and Love Addicts Anonymous" provides an inexpensive group therapy environment and may be the first step in reinforcing social interaction.

Females who receive these calls often feel victimized or sexually violated. The most recommended course of action when receiving a call is to simply hang up without saying anything that might reinforce the caller. If the caller persists in redialing the number and the victim has a "call forwarding" feature on their phone they can temporarily forward their calls to a male friend.

(See also ACOUSTICOPHILIA, AGREX-OPHILIA, COPROLALIA, JACTITATION, NARRATOPHILIA, PHONE SEX and SEX HOTLINES)

OCHLOPHILIA   (Gregomulcia—to be fondled in a crowd) Ochlophilia (ochlos: a mob, populace, philia: attachment to) refers to those who are sexually aroused by the presence of a crowd. This may include orgies where people are surrounded by others having sex, or large gatherings where performers and revellers are semi-nude and pressed against one another. Some feel compelled to seize the opportunity that anonymity offers in a crowd and grope those near them. Hirschfeld wrote of the problem a few priests endured when London first opened the underground train system (tube) causing them to uncontrollably ejaculate because they were unaccustomed to warm bodies pressing against them from all sides.

(See also GROUP SEX, HOMILOPHILIA and POLYITEROPHILIA)

OCULOLINCTUS   Oculolinctus (oculo: eye, and linctus: lick) refers to the act of licking a partner's eyeball for sexual arousal.

This seems to be rare but there are several cases including one reported of a female who in order to orgasm would have to lick the eyeball of her obliging male lover. CAUTION: Oral herpes (cold sores) can be transferred to the eye.

(See also ANAL SEX/ANALINCTUS, CUNNILINGUS, FELLATIO, LACTAPHILIA, NASOPHILIA and OCULOPHILIA)

OCULOPHILIA   (Strabismus) Oculophilia (oculo: eye, philia: attachment to) refers to people who are sexually aroused by the eyes of a partner. For instance, Descartes was primarily attracted to women who squinted.

Many people realize that a person's pupils will enlarge when they see something or someone to whom they are attracted. To capitalize on this European women until not long ago put chemicals (originally belladonna, which means "pretty woman") in their eyes to cause them to dilate so that they would appear aroused by their suitors. Today's advertisers use this to their advantage when photographing models.

There is one instance of a more physical sexual display and this seems to involve novelty rather than a fetish or true attraction to the eye. A prostitute in the Philippines gained notoriety for soliciting men to penetrate her eye socket after removing her glass eye.

(See also LACTAPHILIA, NASOPHILIA, OCULOLINCTUS, ODONTOPHILIA, PHALLOPHILIA and TESTICLES)

ODONTOPHILIA   (Gomphipothic) Odontophilia (Odonto, tooth; philia, attachment to) refers to sexual arousal involving teeth.

Marquis de Sade claimed that his works were based on the sex life of others, many of which were documented. One of the sex acts he wrote of was tooth extraction. The passage reads,

[t]he passion of Boniface is also singular. He loves pulling out the teeth of his victims, while fucking them and being simultaneously sodomized. One who becomes the victim of these gentlemen is Fosine, fourteen years old, with a beautiful form and a rich family. She promises the ideal combination of lust and profit. Both Boniface and Chrysostome wish to indulge themselves with her, and after pulling out her thirty-two beautiful teeth, she is subjected to the Superior, who immolates her in his own fashion.

It is very doubtful that anyone today practices odontophilia in this form; however, it is possible that an occasional tooth extraction scene occurred in 1797 when de Sade wrote his book. Nitrous oxide and ether were not used to extract teeth until 1840 and Novocain was not produced until the beginning of this century; therefore, people during de Sade's lifetime were accustomed to having their teeth removed without effective pain killers.

The pulling of teeth may be arousing even with the advent of anesthesia as noted in Erich von Stroheim's film *Greed*. Here the beautiful patient is kissed by her dentist as the blood still flows from her mouth (*Sex and Superstition*, by G.L. Simons, pp. 87-88, reproduced with permission of Blackie & Son Ltd.).

(See also LACTAPHILIA, NASOPHILIA, OCULOLINCTUS, PHALLOPHILIA, TESTICLES and YONI WORSHIP)

OLFACTION (Antholagnia—arousal from smelling flowers, Barosmia, Olfactophilia, Osmolagnia, Osphresiolagnia and Ozolagnia—arousal from strong smells, Renifluer—arousal from smell of urine)

Olfaction (olfacto: to smell) refers to people's ability to smell odors. Certain molecules dissolve onto hairlike cilia receptors that extend down from the olfactory bulb of the brain and into the nasal cavity (*Senses and Sensibilities*, by Jillyn Smith, p. 96). It would be difficult to imagine life without smell. Astronauts have found it so disturbing that they carry scented chemicals with them to counteract the negative effects.

Differences in odor have sometimes been attributed a person's race [although more 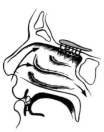 likely it is their diet]. J.A. Rogers, in his book, *Sex and Race*, quoted Iwan Block, noted sexologist, "who made a study of the sexual attraction and repulsion of the odors of the various races," and who said, "It is this strongly unpleasant odor of the black race which is one of the chief reasons for the antipathy between Negroes and whites. . . . On the other hand, the same antipathy seems to be entertained by Negroes and mixed races against white folks. Thus it has been reported that to the Masai (an African tribe) every stranger is hateful from the start; and this hatred goes so far that upon smelling the approaching stranger such repugnance is aroused that aromatic herbs must be held to the nose." He then goes on to quote a white French physician who married a Negro woman from Haiti, "who, according to his own expression, intoxicated him by her perfume. "I cannot understand," he says, "love with a white woman. She is insipid and odorless" (pp. 404-405).

The effect of odor can be enhanced by several methods. Fast and Bernstein claim that "the combination of scent and massage is a heady experience. Stimulating the olfactory center under the erotic stimulus of touch can evoke an emotional response, free a person to some degree and allow a natural chemistry to occur . . . Masseurs are usually aware of this hedonic effect, and to avoid it they will use only unscented oils during massage. 'Scented oils arouse my patients, men and women,' a professional masseur told us. 'I just can't handle that. I use a very light mineral oil, warmed up, and I don't allow scents anywhere in my studio!'" (*Sexual Chemistry*, by Julius Fast and Meredith Bernstein, p. 67).

People engaging in bondage often find the use of worn underwear stuffed into the mouth as a gag to be more arousing than the usual plastic or leather apparatus. Sensory deprivation such as blindfolding, silence, or a lack of touch also intensify the person's reaction. A person with a fetish often prefers the smell of one part of the body over the others. If they have a foot fetish, they prefer the odor of feet or shoes, and men with a breast fetish prefer the odor given from the areola glands. Other fetish odors include feces, urine, leather, hair, etc. The odor of their love object appears to be learned along with the image of the object. It is also possible that much of what people attribute to odor is actually the result of our being able to detect pheromones through the vomeronasal organ in our nose.

(See also PHEROMONES)

OPHIDICISM Ophidicism (ophidi: snake) refers to people who use reptiles. The snake in the form of a circle biting its own tail has been a representation of sex since early Egyptian civilization. The snake represented the male organ and the ring that it formed symbolized the vagina.

Today one finds magazines and movies available of women who insert snakes or eels tail first into their vaginas and masturbate as the creature wriggles to get free. Slow moving snakes that don't bite are used for this form of sex. Ancient Roman women differed only in that they inserted the snakes head first. CAUTION: People can contract salmonella from amphibians and reptiles.

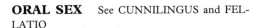

(See also BEE STINGS, FORMICOPHILIA and ZOOPHILIA)

ORAL SEX See CUNNILINGUS and FELLATIO

ORGASMS (Acmegenesis) There is no generally accepted operative definition of orgasm. *Webster's Third New International Dictionary* defines orgasm as: ". . . intense or paroxysmal emotional excitement; the climax of sexual excitement typically occurring toward the end of coitus; usually accompanied in the male by ejaculation." According to this definition, ejaculation, which many view as the orgasm itself, is rather an accompanying act of orgasm. A variety of consensus on orgasm now exists among sexologists.

Lila V. Powers, Ph.D. and Michael E. Perry, Ph.D. have studied orgasm physiology in a laboratory and conducted surveys for several years. Their studies lead them to believe that there are at least four types of orgasms: plateau, tonic, clonic, fusion. The plateau has whole body intensity but does not include ejaculation and detumescence. Tonic orgasms are felt in the pelvic muscles and do not include ejaculation or detumescence. The sensations for clonic orgasm are felt primarily in the genital region, and the fusion orgasm includes plateau, tonic, and clonic and does end in ejaculation and detumescence.

Normal (or "fusion") orgasms adhere to the following physiological responses for each sex.

MALE	FEMALE
Tensed muscles, increase in heart rate and blood pressure, nipple erection	Same
Penis becomes erect, scrotum elevates, and become enlarged	Clitoris becomes erect, labia majora testes pulls away from vagina, labia minora enlarges, lubrication begins, vagina expands and lengthens, uterus doubles in size, breasts enlarge
Muscle tension becomes more evident, heart rate, blood pressure and breathing increases, sex flush	Same
Corona increases in size, erection becomes more stable, testicles enlarge to three times original size and elevate to body, secretions may become evident	Clitoris shortens, color of labia deepens, lubrication slows, areola (area around nipple) swells
Involuntary muscle spasms, including anal sphincter	Same
Seminal fluid is collected into urethral bulb then expelled with more muscle spasms	Muscle contractions with orgasm including vagina and uterus
Muscles relax, breathing, heart rate and blood pressure return to normal, nipples slowly decrease in size, color and size of genitals return to normal	Same

(Handout of the San Francisco Sex Information Switchboard training program)

Orgasm is attainable throughout most of our lives. It has been achieved as early as six months old and by the age of five Kinsey reported that 50% of all boys could reach orgasm. Of course, this is without ejaculate because males do not produce sperm until they are between the ages of eleven and seventeen.

Orgasmic sensations vary according to the degree of emotional, biochemical, or psychological intensity; most are within our power to regulate. Dr. Alexander Lowen described an orgasmic experience "as the opening of a dam, with the release downward of a flood of feeling while the body convulses as a unit in response to each involuntary forward swing of the pelvis. Feelings of melting and streaming downward now pervade the whole body. If the acme is intense enough, the sensation of heat increases and is perceived as a glow in the pelvis and as an overall body sensation of lumination" (*Love and Orgasm*, by Alexander Lowen, M.D., pp. 197-198).

The following sections list various categories of orgasms people claim to experience along with descriptions of the associated sensations.

ALTERED STATE ORGASMS An altered state orgasm is believed to occur when the brain's level of serotonin is excessively high. The effects of an altered state of consciousness or "near-death experience" have been divided into components and a person may experience all or a combination of these. A study of 89 near-death experiences was conducted by Bruce Greyson that computed the percentages of each of these components. "A cognitive component [15%], including time distortion, thought acceleration, life review, and sudden understanding; an affective component [41%], comprising feelings of peace, joy, and cosmic unity and an experience of a brilliant light; a paranormal component [?], including enhanced vision or hearing, apparent extrasensory perception, precognitive vision, and an out-of-body experience; and a transcendental component [47%], comprising encounters with an apparently unearthly realm, a mystical being, and visible spirits and a barrier or point of no return that, had the subjects crossed it, would have precluded their return to life." Greyson further discovered that "near-death events in which death might have been anticipated (e.g., suicide attempts, exacerbations of chronic illness, or complications of surgery) were associated rarely with cognitive experiences but frequently with transcendental and affective ones." People who were victims of accidents or sudden illness are more often the ones whose life flashes before them ("A Typology of Near-Death Experiences," by Bruce Greyson, M.D., *American Journal of Psychiatry* 142:8, August 1985, pp. 967-969).

People can enter an altered state by many different methods. Timothy Leary in a *Playboy* interview claimed that "In a carefully prepared, loving LSD session, a woman can have several hundred orgasms." In order to create this same trance-like state there are often (but not always) two stages of preparation required. The first phase generally prepares the mind by using such deprivations as water, food, sleep, sex, or complete inhibition of senses (sight, sound, touch, smell, and taste). Deprivation alone can trigger hallucinations or an altered state. People who use shorter term deprivation often induce it through physical injury or flagellation. A similar method is used by various military officials in their torture of captives. Deprivation and pain causes an increase of serotonin and once this chemical reaches an abnormally high level, the prisoner goes into an altered state of consciousness.

People often have an orgasm as they approach the altered state, reducing their energy and serotonin level causing the experience to end. For this reason some have learned to negate the orgasm by physically altering their penis with stretching or other methods to guarantee an orgasm never occurs. Shamans gave up their sex lives so that the physical orgasm wouldn't interfere with their ability to obtain an altered state.

The Catholic mystics used a different discipline to reach an altered state. Paul Kurtz, a scholar in this field, claimed that religious mystics had to have two striking ingredients present. "First, there is repression and frustration, a sense that pleasures of the flesh, especially sexual enjoyments, are evil and sinful. Second, there is an apparent form of sublimation and some sexual gratification in the mystical encounter . . . Very few, if any, of the prominent mystics led a normal married or sexual life: the mystical life in a sense grew out of perturbation and perversion. It expressed a pathological response to the need for sexual fulfillment, by means of a deflected discharge of the libido" (*The Transcendental Temptation*, pp. 99-100, used with permission of Prometheus Books).

The sexual nature of this state is further evident by their use of the Song of Songs (or Song of Solomon) as the text for mystical ascent and union with God. Peter de Rosa, a Jesuit, explained that this allowed "Christian mysticism to draw upon and sublimate erotic energies . . . The celibate male can turn his affection to the person of the Virgin Mary as his 'lady', in order to repress real sexuality with women. Spiritual eroticism is to be directed to the higher, spiritual feminine that elevated and transformed the soul, rather than to the debasing, carnal female" (*Vicars of Christ* p. 147).

What does one feel or see during a mystical altered state? Individuals experience different hallucinations, several of which are cited as follows. St Francis of Sales (died 1622) described his mystical experiences by saying they were, "as melted balm that no longer has firmness or solidity, the soul lets herself pass or flow into What she loves: she does not spring out of herself as by a sudden leap, nor does she cling as by a joining or union, but gently glides, as a fluid and liquid thing, into the Divinity Whom she loves. She goes out by that sacred outflowing and holy liquefaction, and quits herself, not only to be united to the well-Beloved, but to be entirely mingled with and steeped in Him. The outflowing of a soul into her God is a true ecstasy, by which the soul quite transcends the limits of her natural way of existence, being wholly mingled with, absorbed and engulfed in, her God" (*The Transcendental Temptation*, by Paul Kurtz, p. 96, used with permission of Prometheus Books).

Another example of a Christian mystical experience is that of St. Theresa. She describes it as seeing "an angel close by me, on my left side, in bodily form . . . in his hand a long spear of gold, and at the iron's point there seemed to be a little fire. He appeared to me to be thrusting it at times into my heart, and to pierce my very entrails; when he drew it out, he seemed to draw them out also and to leave me all on fire with a great love of God. The pain was so great that it made me moan; and yet so surpassing was the sweetness of this excessive pain that I could not wish to be rid of it. The soul is satisfied now with nothing less than God" *(Mysticism*/New York: World/ Meridian, 1972).

St. Theresa's sadomasochist bent was evidently a common feature of medieval monastic literature. Rosamond Gilder, in discussing Hrotsvitha, a nun and playwright from 950 C.E., says "in two plays, Hrotsvitha gives expression to a vein of sadism, which is also associated with certain aspects of repression. She positively revels in the lurid and suggestive details of her torture scenes . . . nuns were suckled on tales of torture and martyrdom, and the more boiling oil, fiery furnaces, severed limbs, and bleeding wounds a tale provided, the greater the thrill . . . Undoubtedly also, Hrotsvitha obtained a certain release for her own emotional suppressions by elaborating these pictures of carnal dangers and the pitfalls of the flesh" (*Enter the Actress*, pp. 34-5).

Autosadism and self-flagellation were used by religious mystics, as well as by those simply seeking an altered state of consciousness for sexual pleasure. There were many monks who flagellated themselves with canes or whips. A Dominican monk, Heinrich Suzo (1300-1366), wrote about his experiences in an autobiography. He began practicing extreme asceticism and torture as a tool in overcoming temptations. He found that "he was able to achieve frequent, even daily ecstasies. However, a time finally arrived when the bleeding saint realized he could not continue in his path and still live. 'He was so wasted that the only choice was between dying and giving up these practices.' At this point, he tells us, he threw all of his instruments of torture into a stream" (*The Transcendental Temptation*, 1986. pp. 99-100, used with permission of Prometheus Books).

Today, many people who practice the more 'painful' form of S/M do it to induce this altered state and view it as a spiritual connection rather than explicitly sexual.

ASTRAL ORGASMS An astral orgasm refers to a person's consciousness leaving their physical body and traveling in their astral body. Astral projection is practiced by several occult groups. According to these people it is possible to teach steps one can use to project oneself into an astral plane at will. However, we are referring here to the unintentional experience of traveling through the universe or to distant areas of the earth. This experience is caused by extraordinarily intense emotions felt during sex. The reported cases of astral projection occurring during orgasm have involved either a psychic or an unsuspecting sex partner of a psychic. [Author's note: This phenomenon is not the type that can be verified by science and for that reason we can do nothing more than mention that this type of orgasm has been reported by several people.]

EXTENDED SEXUAL ORGASMS (ESO) Many people have become interested in extending the length of their orgasms since the 1983 publication of the Brauers' book, titled *Extended Sexual Orgasm*.

In their book the Brauers detail the rewards they claim awaits those practicing this discipline. "At the highest level of female ESO, which we call Phase II, continuous slow waves of push-out contractions of the deep pelvic muscles replace the mixed contractions of Phase I. Each contraction lasts up to thirty seconds and there are not rest periods between. Women experience this phase subjectively as a continuous orgasmic increase. . . . At the highest level of male ESO, Phase II, a man finds himself in a continuous state of orgasmic emission for thirty minutes or more. Clear fluid issues almost continuously, drop by drop, from his penis. His anal sphincter is relaxed and open. The ejaculation phase may involve twenty or more intense contractions and last twenty seconds or more (*ESO—Extended Sexual Orgasm*, by Alan P. Brauer, M.D., and Donna J. Brauer, pp. 3-4).

ESO emphasizes controlled masturbation techniques and sex exercises, particularly development of the pubococcygeus (PC) muscle that cradles the lower torso from the pubic bone to the tail bone. A person eventually learns to control muscle contractions to attain the results listed above.

One of the exercises mentioned in this book involves partial retention of semen during orgasm, this giving a man the ability to orgasm two to six times during intercourse. The Brauers call this type of male multiple orgasm "seminal fluid retention" and describe explicit instructions for accomplishing this feat. Part of the exercise involves holding one's breath and squeezing the PC muscles until ejaculation is stopped (*ESO — Extended Sexual Orgasm*, by Alan P. Brauer, M.D., and Donna J. Brauer, pp. 56-7).

FUSION ORGASMS The "fusion" orgasm is reached by stimulating two or more erogenous zones which each create a different sensation, thereby intensifying the orgasmic experience.

People learn this technique by manually stimulating different parts of the body in various ways. Once a responsive location is detected a person works it into their masturbation routine until orgasm can be reached by that stimulation alone. After several locations have been orgasmically developed they are stimulated simultaneously. Care is taken not to let one site become overstimulated into orgasm before the other. The goal of a fusion orgasm is to induce orgasm from all areas so that they peak at the same time. For example, if one is stimulating both the nipple and penis and feels orgasm approaching due to stimulation on the penis, he will lessen the intensity on the penis and concentrate on the nipples until they are again equal in intensity ("Living Up To Your Orgasmic Potential," by Dr. Herbert Otto, *Sex Over Forty, IX, 2*, pp. 1-3, July 1990).

Areas of the body that respond well to stimulation are the prostate, anus, G-spot, scrotum, ears, armpits, toes, and nipples. These areas are sensitized even more by the use of lotions, heat, and slight abrasion. The prostate can be manipulated a couple of ways. It may be stimulated from outside the body by pressing rhythmically upward on the space between the anus and the back of the scrotum. Others insert a finger or specially designed dildo two to four inches into the anus and massage the prostate that lies to the forward side of the body.

PSYCHIC ORGASMS (Psychic masturbation, Psycholagny) Psychic orgasms are those induced by methods other than genital stimulation.

The prevalence of psychically induced orgasms can be influenced by certain cultures or religious mores. Masters and Lea spoke of Turks and Arabs as being "especially prone to psychically induced spontaneous emissions . . . . Arab ethicists, for example, considering the significance of spontaneous emissions, have decided that they belong in the same category ethically with nocturnal pollutions . . . . The Arabs explained spontaneous daylight ejaculations, which occurred not uncommonly at the sight of an attractive woman, as a sacrifice made by the system in honor of beauty. However that may be, the point is, ethically, that both nocturnal and daylight emissions of this order were held to be beyond the individual's control and therefore no moral blame could be assessed" (*Perverse Crimes in History*, pp. 180-181).

People who are able to attain orgasm or sexual arousal by excitement and nongenital stimulation are discussed by several authorities. Cauthery and Stanway inform us that "women can experience orgasms over the phone, by fantasy . . . when combing their hair, when passing water . . . . rope-climbing; movement on buses, trains or 'rides' in fair-grounds; hearing a man's voice; sitting next to a man on a bus; being shouted at; being late; listening to music or poetry; dancing," etc. (*The Complete Guide to Sexual Fulfillment*, by Dr. Philip Cauthery & Dr. Andrew Stanway with Faye Cooper, pp. 44 and 122). According to Kinsey some three or four men out of more than 5000 could ejaculate by deliberately concentrating on sexual fantasies. However, most males, while not orgasming to non-tactile stimulus, do have erections to seemingly odd stimuli. Activities responsible for erections in younger boys are things such as "punishment, electric shock, fast elevator rides, fast

car driving, skiing, airplane rides, sitting in church, urinating, boxing, wrestling, high dives, being scared, near accidents, reciting before a class, tests at school, seeing a policeman, big fires, anger, marching soldiers, looking over edge of building, finding money, watching exciting games," etc. (*Sexual Behavior in the Human Male*, by Kinsey, Pomeroy and Martin, 1948, pp. 164-165).

Practitioners of Hatha Yoga can achieve orgasm without manual manipulation. Hypnotists use auto-suggestion to first induce excitement and erection and then orgasm. Some use fantasy alone to produce orgasm, many use tactile stimulation from nongenital areas of the body, and others orgasm when emotionally excited. The orgasm itself may be less intense than one experienced with a partner and men have reported them without accompanying emissions; consequently, these are often multiple, ending with exhaustion or final emission. Occasionally, a psychic orgasm can be so intense that it creates prolonged orgasmic muscle spasms or renders the person momentarily unconscious as in the case of Tantra.

SM ORGASMS There are two basic types of S/M orgasms and these can be differentiated between what the bottom (masochist) and top (sadist) experiences.

The person engaging in a pain inducing activity or sensory deprivation may experience an altered state orgasm. They may also experience intense exaggerated emotions or, if in bondage, a trance like state from which they gain ecstasy. It is described as more cathartic than the one experienced when topping.

The top (dominant) experiences more of a psychic or energy charged orgasm from watching and controlling the erotic response of the bottom. Some tops demand genital stimulation during play. However, orgasm is at times reached with a simple touch on the surrounding area. Tops choosing not to include physical orgasm in a scene still experience a euphoric high. This sensation has been described by people as a warmth in the stomach that radiates outward through the extremities, comparable to a tantric orgasm, and similar to the feeling in your stomach after a fast elevator ride.

TANTRIC ORGASMS Tantra is an Eastern form of sexual yoga. People learn to build energy by breathing techniques and then direct this energy by body positions and mental control. Physical effects vary according to the type of breathing engaged in by a person. The goal is to enter an altered state where one merges not only with their partner but also the cosmos. The path to this ultimate state abounds with diverse orgasmic experiences. These have been described as having been invaded and filled with white light, or as energy working its way up and down the spine and then extending from the body through the head and hovering over it like a cobra.

Many books have been written endorsing and describing numerous benefits of Tantra. The Kales wrote that "the prolonged sex of Tantra gives you and your partner orgasms that are indescribable in their intensity. It also brings you and your partner so close to each other that both of you will find yourselves wanting to embrace total strangers, becoming sensually receptive to an unbelievable degree, and developing an empathy that makes you one with the whole of burgeoning, fecunding, striving creation around you" (*TANTRA, The Secret Power of Sex*, by Arvind and Shanta Kale, p. 143). A further recommendation is given by Ramsdale and Dorfman in their book. ". . . [M]en and women report that while making love their bodies seem to contract expand liquefy shake burn glow melt merge they say they feel like they are flying they feel two people become one they see brilliant colors they feel like king and queen, noble and royal they feel really 'high'—naturally some even say they disappear for awhile; another words, they experience that making love expands their consciousness these people were not on drugs they were on sex . . ." (*Sexual Energy Ecstasy*, by David Alan Ramsdale and Ellen Jo Dorfman).

(See also MASTURBATION)

ORGIES An orgy is an antiquated term for group sex. It often referred to sex indulged in during religious festivals which were preceded by an abundance of food and drink. Examples of these religious orgies were the Dionysian, Baal, Carnival, and May Day festivals.

Paul Wirz documented the celebration of a religious orgy of the Ezam Secret Society of New Guinea in the early 1900's. Here the men and women were segregated during  which time the men played music on drums and bullroarers. There were intervals between the chants where initiates could enter into the woods with any woman and have sex. Upon the initiate's return he brought with him a broken branch to symbolize his success. This ritual of free sex continued for several days and nights culminating with a young woman being led into a hut to have sex with several men. One of these men was selected without his prior knowledge to be a sacrifice. The other men would pull down the timbers of the hut upon the man and woman while they were joined in intercourse. They were then immediately removed, cut into pieces, and roasted to provide a feast for the tribe (*Historical Atlas of World Mythology, Vol II: The Way of the Seeded Earth, Part 1: The Sacrifice*, by Joseph Campbell, p. 71).

Today, group sex houses in parts of Europe still begin orgies by serving a dinner during which time people become acquainted. These often end in food fights before selecting a sex partner. Group sex houses in the United States typically provide hors d'oeuvres and punch for people to casually partake of during the evening.

(See also FERTILITY RITUALS, FESTIVALS, GANG BANGS, GROUP SEX and WIFE SWAPPING)

OXYGEN REGULATION Oxygen regulation is used to intensify or delay sexual arousal. We normally breathe about twelve times a minute. If we drastically alter our oxygen intake in any way the body panics, increasing adrenalin and other biochemical responses. A milder effect can be triggered by quick shallow breathing into the upper lungs. This produces energy or excitement. Slowing down the rate of breathing and breathing deeper has a calming effect. Most often the regulation of breath is instinctive or controlled by our parasympathetic nervous system; however, people have learned to utilize techniques involving strangulation, corsetting, tantric locks, plastic bags, silicone bathing caps, gags, and gas masks to produce sexual excitement.

Some of the techniques have potential to be lethal because a person loses consciousness within three to five minutes if the supply of oxygen is cut off and dies immediately afterward. It is dangerous not to monitor a partner at all times. Oxygen play attempted on anyone over sixty or who suffers from arrythmia, asthma, strokes, arteriosclerosis, or hypertension is extremely dangerous.

People who hyperventilate (exhale too much carbon dioxide) have symptoms such as lightheadedness, drowsiness, and tingling in the extremities. They may lose coordination, become disoriented, or even have muscle spasms. The most common remedy for hyperventilation is to have the person breathe into a paper bag until they feel calmed. This brings the balance of oxygen and carbon dioxide back to normal.

The other effect created by oxygen regulation is hypoxia, or insufficient oxygen in the lungs. The symptoms of hypoxia include: drowsiness, dizziness, euphoria, a decrease in judgment, memory, alertness, and coordination, a greying of vision; fingernails and lips may turn blue. Hypoxia can be caused by a person forgetting to breathe during sex. This is particularly true during S/M play because the same neurotransmitters that produce euphoria seem to depress respiration. It helps for a person just coming out of a breathless state to make a conscious effort to breathe deeply. People can sometimes be assisted into breathing deeply with a slap on the face or a pinch on their nipples. However, slapping someone who has gone into shock may be dangerous.

Understanding the effect oxygen regulation has on our arousal cycle requires an examination of the physiology of our lungs. Oxygen is vital to our bodies; we use it to burn fuel. Our lungs are designed to take in oxygen for this combustion process which in turn generates heat and energy for the functioning of the body.

The rate and rhythm at which we inhale creates different effects in the amount of energy we generate, thus we can affect the level of passion and energy we produce during sex. Slow deep breaths gradually build and sustain energy, rapid shallow panting generates the immediate burst of energy needed just prior to orgasm, and holding our breath depletes excess energy.

Psychological stimulus is needed by some in addition to the decrease in oxygen. These people enjoy adding some dimension of panic or terror. Oxygen regulation alone lacks the same intensity. This may be why many use some form of bondage as an adjunct to asphyxia when alone; knowing this is dangerous. Others like to play with control, either giving it to a partner or by pushing their own limits. Some people enjoy both panic and control.

Breathing techniques may also be used to delay ejaculation for men. The bottom position in missionary sex is assumed and, before thrusting toward the partner, one breathes deeply (distending the abdomen) and holds his breath while tightening the pubococcygeus muscle and pushing out with the anal muscles. The breath is then released as he relaxes and pulls his body away from his partner, preparing to repeat the same cycle. This technique has the opposite effect on women and more often stimulates them to orgasm. CAUTION: Many things can go wrong during breath control play; the result can be permanent disability or death. People who insist on engaging in this activity plan ahead for most eventualities, how to prevent accidents, and how to get help if needed. If the activity involves more than one person, the one topping must also be willing to face criminal charges and/or prison if an accident occurs.

Descriptions of the various techniques used in sex play follow. (QSM lecture,

January 11, 1992, "Breath Control and Carotid Artery Play" by Michael Decker)

CORSETTING   Corsetting refers to a restriction placed around the waist, the effect of which creates difficulty in breathing deeply. Corsets are used by tops in breath control games by pushing in on the bottom's diaphragm and holding it in.

(See CORSETS)

GAGS   Gags are occasionally used to induce asphyxiation by blocking the mouth while the partner holds the bottom's nose closed. Gags and tape across both the mouth and nose carry a higher risk factor than a partner using their hand. Even latex hoods with small holes at the nose can get twisted slightly and cut off the bottom's air supply.

GAS MASKS   Gas masks are used over the face to restrict oxygen intake. The filter system is altered so that a 3/4" hollow tube can be inserted into the region of the mouth. The mask is tightened and when the top desires, they  place a finger over the tip to temporarily block the air supply. These masks are purchased at army and navy supply stores.

STRANGULATION   (Autoerotic asphyxia—arousal from asphyxia) Strangling differs from oxygen regulation in that it involves restricting the flow of blood through the carotid artery to the brain. This can be done with Velcro blood pressure cuffs that have been folded over and modified with a D-ring attached on the front edge with a rope going through it that is hung from the ceiling; if the person fails to deflate the cuff before they become unconscious, the rope pulls the collar loose as they fall. Thick leather collars are also used by attaching a lightweight string to the ceiling, or with the assistance of a partner. Some enjoy strangulation because

it produces a euphoric and light-headed sensation. CAUTION: There have reports of vegal nerve inhibition due to fear or lack of oxygen. A few people are susceptible to this lethal reaction and it is impossible to predict just who they are until too late.

SUFFOCATION   Suffocation refers to any form of cutting off the body's supply of oxygen. This is done in sex games by putting a plastic bag over the person's head and making them breathe their own carbon dioxide. The top may hold their hand over the person's mouth and nose but this is more difficult and requires more physical strength if the bottom resists. One man rigged up a basket with a plastic bag inside that hung from the ceiling. He then stood underneath and held the bag around his head. If he passed out the bag stayed suspended while he fell to the ground, and nothing would be left to restrict his breathing. Another method that slows a person's breathing is holding a pillow over his or her head. Since visual contact is lost this raises the risk level. Latex hoods or swimming caps are used by some couples. Some prefer "queening" (sitting on a person's face in a way that cuts off airflow) and one woman has her partner put his mouth over her vagina and then locks her legs around the back of his head to prevent his pulling away or being able to breathe. CAUTION: Games using gags, masks, strangulation, or suffocation can cause strokes, heart failure, blindness, brain damage, and death. Safety precautions for any of these activities require that the people know CPR, be healthy, not have eaten recently, or combine the activity with drugs and alcohol. Never do these activities alone or without making sure that every conceivable contingency is prepared for and made safe. People unwisely engaging in this activity alone often pad the area on the floor around them. This prevents head injuries if the person becomes unconscious and falls.

(See also AUTOEROTIC ASPHYXIA, CORSETS, PHOBOPHILIA, SAFE SEX and TAPHEPHILIA)

P

PANDERING A panderer is a person who procures a prostitute for a third person or who convinces a person to engage in prostitution by providing a client.

(See BORDELLOS, ILLEGAL SEX and PIMPS)

PARAPHILIA (Deviance, Divertissement, Perversion, Sexual Aberration, Sexual Anomalies) Paraphilia (Para: going beside or beyond, amiss; philia: attachment to) is defined by John Money as "a condition occurring in men and women of being compulsively responsive to and obligatively dependent upon an unusual and personally or socially unacceptable [sexual] stimulus . . . In legal terminology, a paraphilia is a perversion or deviancy; and in the vernacular it is kinky or bizarre sex." (*Gay Straight and In-Between*, by John Money, Oxford University Press, 1988.) Paraphilic disorders have several common characteristics. These are listed in DSM-III-R as: recurrent, fixed, compulsive, sexually motivated, personally or socially maladaptive, interferes with capacity for reciprocal affection. Sexual acts are only considered paraphilias if the person's internal experience matches these criteria. Only the person performing paraphilic acts can be the judge of their motivation and whether their compulsion hampers normal relations. An important method of determining which behavior is considered genetically coded and which is influenced by social pressure or religion is that of studying animal behavior as well as cross-cultural behavior. If a certain behavior is found in both these instances, it is considered "natural" or genetically coded (i.e. gays and grooming). This reasoning is not new. The 13th century church leader, St. Thomas Aquinas, said that the sex activities of animals were natural and should be a model of how God intended people to conduct themselves. Animals, not having been corrupted by the original sin, could only exhibit natural urges and therefore could not be judged as evil or sinful. However intelligent and perceptive St. Aquinas was

he could not have been acquainted with the sex habits of animals when using this argument to support the Church's view on "normal" heterosexual sex. Animals are not considered paraphiles, as in the case of humans, but do engage in similar behaviors such as giving gifts, extended courtships, grooming, missionary style sex, rape, incest, bondage, necrophilia, group sex, homosexuality, bisexuality, urophilia, lust murder, anthropophagy, and sadomasochism (*Sex Link* by Hy Freedman). Proof of St Aquinas' naivete was his support of Aristotle's account of a stallion that threw himself off a cliff upon discovering, to his horror, that he had just committed incest by mating with his own mother.

Social rules impose restrictions on sexual behavior but despite this people still engage in different or unusual forms of sexual behavior. There are many reasons for this variance in behavior.

The first objective is to understand how people become aroused by a seemingly non-sexual stimulus, whether or not the person falls into the category of paraphilic. Passion can be created by emotions such as anger, guilt, jealousy, shock, challenge, loss, humiliation, shame, surrender, fear, love, and pain. These all have one thing in common, they stimulate the body to produce  adrenalin (epinephrine) which in addition leads to the production of other neurotransmitters. Our judgment of the circumstances or sex appeal of the other person determines how the stimulus is perceived and acted upon. This change in bodychemistry cause things such as avoidance behavior, an increased heart rate, oxygen intake, and blood pressure; all of the physical responses needed to fight, run, or have sex. Phrased another way; in addition to love, anything that has the power to create fear or anger can be utilized by some people to induce passion and sexual arousal. Thus, what might have been reacted to with anger or panic is formed into passion. If a heterosexual male was cornered by each of the people in the illustration, all of which were seductively saying "Hello, big boy," he would most likely respond with anger to the weaker male, fear to the stronger male, and with arousal to the female. These reactions would differ with a cornered gay or female heterosexual, but the three emotions would remain fairly standard. People who play sex games use this knowledge to their advantage by creating strong stimuli and letting their bodies react. Once a fight, flight, or sex decision is presented the players opt for sex.

Aggression may have a different appeal as well for some because females of most species are attracted to males they perceive as strong enough to father healthy offspring and to protect his family. An immediate and aggressive response was needed under primitive conditions to ward off predators and to protect food supplies. Unfortunately, the same aggressive reaction is biologically triggered in today's society. Sometimes this primal aggressive reaction is warranted but most often it is not.

S/M players may use an existing emotional bond or feeling of love to generate passion, just as other people often do, only they express it differently. The following description is from Sybil Holiday, a skilled top, as interviewed by Michael A. Rosen:

The experience that I get from him isn't pain; he takes me somewhere else, and I ride with it. I keep opening up and letting go. He's very good at what he does—whipping. He seduces you into it. He's not vicious or cruel. He doesn't descend on people. He builds up intensity. He starts out where the touch of the whip is like a caress, a leather caress, and then it builds on my body. Usually, I've been on my back or my stomach in some sort of bondage, and I feel very secure; I can move, but I can't go anyplace. And the warmth, the heat, just starts building. It gets hotter and hotter and then it dawns on me that it's like I'm on a roller coaster and I'm starting to go up and there's no turning back and it starts getting more intense and it's very dramatic, and more intense and more intense. It's like I'm on a roller coaster and then it starts getting really fast. If I tighten up, resist, I lose it; it becomes no fun. There's nothing there for me if I'm resisting. If I surrender I find myself flying. It's release, intensity, a high; it's like a rain of fire and I'm flying inside" (Sexual Magic, The S/M Photographs by Michael A. Rosen, p. 58).

A second aspect of paraphilia pertains to the object to which one is attracted once stimulated. Ordinarily the advantages of conditioning or learned behavior is that we would be sexually attracted to our own species, bond to people, or recognize and react to repeated danger. When we bond to an inappropriate sexual object it is referred to as a fetish and the item will usually be something that was around the person when young, such as rubber pants, plastic sheets, fur, leather, shoes, silk, urine, and feces. For instance, John Money, Professor of Medical Psychology, and Associate Professor of Pediatrics at Johns Hopkins University, discovered that some of his patients who had undergone early surgery for birth defects were having fantasies about being pierced and cut now that they were adults.

For some men the preference of an unusual sex object or practice is due to sexual repression and guilt imposed on them when they were young by parents. They select safe objects onto which to direct their lust. This may be in the form of a prostitute because she cannot be violated, or a handicapped person because she appears less likely to abandon the man. Even those who engage in risky activities may be using the higher level of fear caused by a risky "sex scene" to override the fear and guilt they feel for indulging in normal sex. They may also need to generate more excitement in order to reach a similar level of intense emotions as experienced by earlier fears imposed by parents or religion for sinful masturbation.

A third aspect of paraphilias involves compulsion and it is this aspect that makes self-control of undesirable behavior difficult. The neurotransmitter that stimulates compulsive behavior is glucocorticoid which is triggered once a person becomes excited. The purpose of this neurotransmitter is to force a person to focus on the stimulus until they conquer it, resolve it, or are out of danger. A person who studies for a test at the last minute feels the effect of this chemical. In this case, once the deadline is met, the ability to focus diminishes. The same phenomenon occurs with love or paraphilias. As long as some type of excitement or arousal surrounds the love object or sexual activity the release of glucocorticoid increases compulsive behavior and makes a return to normal routine very difficult.

The fourth aspect of paraphilias is related to loss compensation. The brain is programmed to create pain and anxiety to ensure that we provide our bodies with certain items needed for survival. In return the brain produces opiates that trigger a pleasure response. Primal needs are such things as eating, defecating, sleeping, loving, having sex, security, energy or stimulus, communication, gathering, hunting, and using our senses. A problem arises when we cannot provide ourselves with a balance of these things as in the case of patients and prisoners. Our body or mind compensates for this loss by doubling up on another need, thereby using it as a source for pleasure. In essence what happens when this person feels pain from not being loved, they eat (or satisfy one of the other needs). This is thought to cause the brain to release opiates and the person temporarily feels gratified. Eventually the person will only feel the need to gratify their original need for love with food. Ideally people strive for a balance in meeting all their needs.

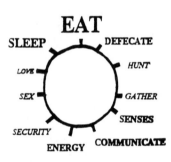

Dr. Money divides paraphilias into six stratagems. These classifications are crucial in understanding the types that commonly exist. "The *sacrificial/expiatory stratagem*

requires preparation or atonement for the sin of lust by way of penance and sacrifice [lust murder, acrotomophilia]...The *marauding/predatory stratagem* requires that, insofar as saintly lovers do not consent to the sin of lust, a partner in lust must be stolen, abducted, or assaultive and violent paraphilic rape... The *mercantile/venal stratagem* requires that sinful lust be traded, bartered, or purchased and paid for, insofar as saintly lovers do not engage consensually in its free exchange [prostitution, chrematistophilia]... The *fetishistic/talismanic stratagem* spares the saintly lover from the sin of lust by substituting a token, fetish, or talisman instead. Fetishes are predominantly either smelly (olfactophilic) or touchy-feely (hyphephilic), and both are derived from the smell and feel of parts of the human body... The *stigmatic/eligibilic stratagem* requires that the partner in lust be, metaphorically, a pagan infidel, disparate in religion, race, color, nationality, social class, or age, from the saintly lovers of one's own social group [gerontophilia, miscegenation]... [and the] *solicitational/allurative stratagems* protect the saint by displacing lust from the act of copulation in the acceptive phase, to an invitational gesture or overture of the proceptive phase [exhibitionism and voyeurism]" (*Gay, Straight, and In-Between; The Sexology of Erotic Orientation,* by Dr. John Money, pp. 136-138).

In addition to all of the above reasons for deviating from regular sex habits, people use sex to meet many other needs, such as to:

build self-esteem

learn trust for others

improve physical control

improve emotional control

sharpen intellect

get immediate gratification

reduce stress

obtain relief from guilt by acting punishments

relieve physical pain

nurture others or be nurtured

enhance or awaken senses

obtain revenge on parents or society

gain insight into one's sexuality by a gender reversal

reenact traumatic experiences to allow victim to gain control

convey love and trust for a partner by surrender or submission

express and understand their alternate personas

(See also ALGOPHILIA, FETISHES, MASOCHISM, PHOBOPHILIA and SADISM)

PECATTIPHILIA Pecattiphilia (peccatum: a sin; and philia: attachment) is the sexual arousal one gets from sinning. This may also display itself as a feeling of guilt.

Religious teenagers sometimes suffer from a dilemma when they masturbate because they are taught that God will punish or perhaps kill them for this 'perversion'. A few have grown up with a fascination for sex play that involves life and death risks in order to recapture the same emotional intensity that this fear created.

Another type of 'sinner' may intensify their feelings of guilt by seducing a virgin, a member of the clergy, wearing religious costumes, listening to hymns during sex, or breaking into a church and using the altar to engage in a form of ritual sex. They may also have their partner say things to make them feel shame or guilt.

Those suffering from extreme pecattiphilia may feel an overabundance of guilt and try to reduce these feelings by having their partner chastise or punish them before they orgasm. This seems to relieve their guilt feelings. Some develop a fear of sexually transmitted diseases afterward or salve their conscience by judging their sex partner. In extreme cases, a psychotic person will murder their victim (usually a prostitute) to expiate both their sins.

Guilt can have a positive force in our lives if it calls attention to conduct that requires more responsible action. Additional understanding of our behavior, values, and needs help us prioritize our goals and make relevant changes. Guilt can help us become more empathetic toward the weaknesses of others making it easier to develop and maintain relationships. Conversely, guilt can have negative effects when people use it to judge and inflict emotional or physical pain on themselves or others. Some psychologists believe that guilt is higher among people who have a more limited awareness of life and who are stuck in a restrictive or repressive lifestyle. A person who imposes guilt on others is practicing a form of sadism because they expect the person to self-inflict emotional pain.

(See also HIEROPHILIA, ILLEGAL SEX, PHOBOPHILIA and ZELOPHILIA)

PEDERASTY See ANAL SEX/PEDERASTY

PEDIOPHILIA Pediophilia refers to the sexual attraction some have for dolls. William Stekel relayed the case of a woman who at a young age had been molested by several people, all treating her like a doll. She evidently suppressed these memories by transferring their identity to those of dolls and toys. This came to present problems when she married and her husband caught her playing with them. He at once destroyed her toys whereupon she grew ill and remained depressed. She later became frigid and developed kleptomania, stealing dolls to replace those he had destroyed (*Sexual Aberrations*, by William Stekel, Vision Press, 1963). However, generally men have fetishes for small statues or manikins.

One California man had a doll fetish. He shaved the hair from Barbie doll heads and then swallowed the heads to produce sexual arousal. X-rays showed six doll heads in his intestines. Once these passed through the digestive tract he would boil them and repeat the process. [Personal communication.]

(See also AGALMATOPHILIA, ANACLITISM, FORNICATORY DOLLS and INFANTILISM)

PEDOPHILIA (Eopareunia—sex while young, Nepirasty—arousal from handling infant felt by childless females, Pathicant—

pederast) Pedophilia (pedo: child; philia: lust) refers to an adult being sexually aroused by a child. The adult may engage in this type of sex exclusively, restrict it to their own children, only seek out children when they are under stress or have been frustrated by an adult relationship, while intoxicated, or a few may be mentally retarded.

Child prostitution is still found in parts of Thailand and India. Societies have always differed in their acceptance of pedophilia but for most of the world it has only come to be prohibited within the last hundred years. Before this time a few cultures would use children to keep dinner guests entertained from underneath their tables. The Japanese used girls as young as five to perform fellatio in the Yoshiwaras and the Chinese had bordellos that specialized in young children. Many of these youths were purchased from parents after a drought when the father could not feed the family and the alternative was for the girl and family to starve. The sale of a daughter meant both survival of the girl and her family. Other girls were captured by bandits and sold at auctions to brothel-keepers. Hendrik de Leeuw described the horrors of one of these raids.

In the Mien'ch district, with which the report deals at length, more than one thousand villages were looted, burned, and the younger female population carried off. . .The majority were transported to slave markets and were there sold to procurers sent by the groups of capitalists who control, to a large extent, the brothels of the great cities.... Of course, many of these children never reach the slave markets. Even as they sit there, whimpering in fear and sorrow, the raiders stalk among them, drag out the least-favored among them, and attack them. This brutality continues throughout the night. The screams of the children, half-demented by the horror of butchery in the villages and by the embraces of their captors, ring out in the darkness.... . Morning reveals the true terror of the night and the true meaning of these childish cries. For, since the market for these raped bodies is not good and the price for a crazy child shows little profit, those who have

been chosen by the captors to satisfy their brutality are not carried on to the next camp. No, they are put to the knife. Then the crude meal of cold rice is gobbled and the whips are out among the train of captives, and the rifles taken up, there are scores of naked bodies flung by the black coals of the soldiers' fires. They are dead girls. One may be sure that they were happy to die, so harsh has been their fate. Their cold, small faces are bloody, beaten, and distorted (Cities of Sin, pp. 97-8).

Laws against pedophilia certainly helped to curb these types of atrocities. However, today some laws have become so extreme that parents have been prosecuted who, without an understanding of the new laws, had innocently turned in film of their children bathing. Parents who let their child take a glance at a nude photo of themselves have also been prosecuted.

Reports vary as to how many minors are molested, some statistics are as high as one in every four females and one in every six males. The National Center for Child Abuse and Neglect estimate in 1982 19% of females and 9% of males are sexually abused before the age of 12 years. The State of Kentucky Human Resource Cabinet received "32,643 complaints of child sexual abuse during the last fiscal year [1987]...the indictments filed against these residents include allegations by the children of acts allegedly committed by their mothers, fathers, uncles, grandfathers, and grandmothers. They range from child observation of a grandparent sodomizing younger males to a grandmother performing oral sex on a year-old grandson." This study also reveals that "[m]other-son sexual contact appears to be less common but is more prevalent than many clinicians may realize" ("Child Sexual Abuse: The Abusing Family in Rural America," by Thomas W. Miller, Ph.D., A.B.P.P., and Lane J. Veltkamp, M.S.W., *International Journal of Family Psychology*, Vol 9, 1988, No. 3, International University Press, pp. 259-275).

Men who were themselves sexually abused when young or who come from a home where this was acceptable do not always develop the normal social aversion to pedophilia. Young juveniles in detention centers have often experienced molestation or abuse before incarceration and many older sex offenders began this aggressive behavior as an adolescent. One report on 63 male juveniles revealed that 70% had been molested or raped prior to incarceration and some reports show that a significant percentage are sexually assaulted while incarcerated. Adolescent females were responsible for 58% of the molestations and Brannon, et al "suggest there is a population of adolescent females (i.e. friends of older siblings and babysitters) who actively victimize pre-pubescent males" ("The Extent and Origins of Sexual Molestations and Abuse Among Incarcerated Adolescent Males," by James M. Brannon, Billie Larson, Murray Doggett, *International Journal of Offender Therapy and Comparative Criminology*, September 1989, Vol 33, No 2, pp. 161-171).

In addition, people are sometimes coerced by their partners into having sexual contact with minors. One case involved a young man whose girlfriend talked him into taking drugs and having sex with neighborhood boys. These males ranged in age from six to thirteen. The girlfriend was able to coax the boys into engaging in fellatio and pederasty with her lover by promising to have sex with them afterward. More often, however, women are coerced by adult male companions.

Another concern regarding pedophilia involves courtroom testimony of child victims; the trauma for the child and accuracy of their testimony. While victims as young as three years old have accurately identified their assailant and described the details of the event others have fallen under the influence of parents in custody battles and have given inaccurate testimony against the other parent. There are many factors to consider in deciding to accept the testimony of a child. Alayne Yates, a psychiatrist, suggests that a "judge must consider whether the child can distinguish truth from falsehood, the child's appreciation of the need to tell the truth, and the child's cognitive capacity." In addition to specially trained professionals used to interview the children

Yates also recommends that a child first be "encouraged to give a narrative report of what occurred, to establish his or her knowledge base, subsequent answers would be more easily understood or redefined" ("Should Young Children Testify in Cases of Sexual Abuse?" by Alayne Yates, M.D., *American Journal of Psychiatry* 144:4, April 1987, pp. 476-480). Goodman noted that we are unsure whether children can differentiate between their thoughts about another person's actions and reality. Children can project their own interpretation of the event into the intent of the adult ("Children's testimony in historical perspective," by G.S. Goodman, *Journal of Social Issues*, 1984; 40:9-31). Some children are traumatized by having to testify and others are helped by sharing their horrible secret. This decision is perplexing; however, professional therapists can be valuable in making individual determinations. In addition, the American Psychiatric Association and the American Academy of Child Psychiatry have recommended procedures that serve to protect children from unnecessary trauma in the court proceedings.

Therapy for pedophiles prosecuted for this type of sex offense usually consists of clarifying the person's own responsibility and culpability, as well as understanding of the harm that is caused to the victim (since most pedophiles initially consider themselves the victim). Sexual dysfunctions are studied, social skills are developed to assist them in establishing relationships with other adults, behavioral modification is used to diminish their previous pedophilic conditioning, and sometimes pharmacological treatment is used as well.

A group named NAMBLA (North American Man/Boy Love Association) has been campaigning against harsh legislation since 1978. Their purpose is to educate the public and advocate changing laws to both protect minors from sexual abuse and to give them the same right to engage in consensual sex acts with a person of their choice as others have. The group formed while trying to defend 24 homosexuals who were arrested in 1977 in Revere, Massachusetts for engaging in consensual sex with teenage boys. There was often only one or two years difference in age between the felon and the victim, with the victim having admitted to being the instigator. Many potential supporters for this group are often lost because of NAMBLA's contention that the age of consent be lowered to prepubescent and their newsletter exhibiting photos of young boys.

Recommended reading for male victims of sexual abuse is *Victims No Longer*, by Michael Lew. CAUTION: Parents can help reduce the risk of possible molestation by educating children about pedophiles, being wary of adults befriending and giving gifts to their children, screening babysitters, and giving the child a secret code word to prevent friends or strangers from abducting the child from school by telling them the parent sent them. Children should also be taught their name, address, and how to dial 911.

(See also ANACLITISM, ANISONOGAMIST, CATAMITES, COITUS INTERFERMORIS, DIPPOLDISM, GEISHAS, HAREMS, ILLEGAL SEX, INCEST, INFANTILISM, MARRIAGE, NEPIOPHILIA, NYMPHOPHILIA, PORNOGRAPHY, PROSTITUTION, SEX RINGS, SNUFF FILMS and VIRGINS)

PENETRATION TOYS (Merkin—artificial vagina used for sex by men, also a wig for the pubic area) Penetration toys are mechanical devices that allow penetration of an object by the penis for masturbation purposes. There are cylinders that can be filled  with warm water (Super Sauna Pump), others utilize vibrators, or an air pump that creates a rubbing action along the head and shaft of the penis (Oro-Simulator). They may be battery operated or controlled by a rubber pump. Others, such as the artificial rubber Vaginal Pal, resemble a vagina with short hair around the labia. The interior is ribbed to create extra sensations. This type of toy is also available with two repositories, the ribbed vagina and an anus which has its interior wall covered with spiked rubber protrusions. Lubrication is added; however,

only water based lubricants are used because oils destroy rubber material. The Sleeve is an open ended lubricated rubber cylinder that slides over the penis. This simple device creates strong sensations when manipulated due to the roughness inside. It is adaptable for play with partners by rolling one end up to facilitate fellatio or by inserting it into a partner's vagina.

Most of these devices can be purchased in sex video stores or through mail order.

(See also FORNICATORY DOLLS, GENITAL/ANAL INSERTS and SYBIAN)

PENILE LIGATION   Penile ligation refers to binding or tying the penis. Young Athenian men used to tie a string around their foreskin to protect the glans penis during gymnastic events in which they appeared nude. Maoris were said to keep their foreskins tied shut out of modesty. Ligation is used in sex games today by gay men with foreskins. They join them with a string to create a form of bondage.

Penile ligation is not restricted to the sex play of two men. A different version is used by heterosexual couples who are involved in bondage games. This entails tying one end of the string around  the foreskin and the other and to a small weight, or a hook on the ceiling; thus restricting the movement of a man who has his hands tied behind his back. Similar bondage techniques are used for penis rings.

(See also MEATOTOMY, PENIS MODIFICATIONS and RINGING)

PENIS MODIFICATION Penis modification refers to any permanent physical alteration that is done to the penis. The practice is ancient and spans through recorded history. Circumcision, the oldest documented form of penis modification, was found on a prehistoric stone carving. A penis pin was discovered on a fourth century bronze dog, and the insertion of penis bells have been documented as early as the fourteenth century.

BIHARI A Bihari modification involves the cutting of the supporting ligament above the penis, causing the penis to drop forward, and in effect giving the illusion of one's being endowed with an extra inch or two of penile shaft. This is thought to have been an ancient Chinese practice. There are only a few surgeons that offer this service. One is Dr. Long Daouchou, a plastic surgeon in Wuhan China who in 1991 was doing an average of four a week. His procedure takes about 90 minutes with recovery expected in a month ("One Very Popular Surgeon," by Lena H. Sun, *San Francisco Chronicle*, Sunday Punch Section, January 12, 1992, p. 5). Another surgeon, Dr. Bihari from Cairo, was one of the first to successfully perform the surgical procedure and it is thus named after him. Dr. Brown, a plastic surgeon, has also performed a large number of these operations. He does business in Mexico (his medical license was revoked in the United States). Dr. Brown gained his expertise from doing sex change operations. CAUTION: This is a delicate operation due to the many nerves and blood vessels adhering to the muscle.

CIRCUMCISION Circumcision refers to the surgical removal of the foreskin that covers the glans penis. (Please refer to CIRCUMCISION section for additional information.)

FORESKIN RESTORATION Foreskin restorations are used to either stretch the foreskin or to surgically restore this flap over the glans penis. Foreskin restoration has been practiced throughout history to enable the circumcised male to avoid disparagement and discrimination. Africans, who were circumcised when sold as slaves or eunuchs to the Moslems, would secretly hang weights on their foreskin to stretch it, and thus restore their penis to its appearance prior to mutilation. They did this despite the fact that if detected this act of defiance could cost their life. Jews, during the period of the Roman Emperor Hadrian, (117-138 C.E.) had a heavy tax imposed upon any circumcised male. The Jews, fearing a genocide attempt because of his laws prohibiting practice of anything Jewish,

devised a bronze sheath that fit around the existing foreskin and which would eventually stretch it to a length that covered the glans. Evidently, circumcision at this time was not regulated and many mohels were only cutting off a small portion of the prepuce. Mark Waring, in his book *Foreskin Restoration (Uncircumcision)*, states that later "Jewish religious authorities introduced a method of circumcision to ensure that it would be much more difficult to restore the foreskin. The elders of the religion were disturbed that many Jews were abandoning their faith and recreating their foreskins. To make this more difficult they decided that a more radical technique of circumcision was required" (p. 5). This standardization unfortunately preceded the last attempted genocide of the Jews by Hitler's supporters. While some attempted surgery to hide their heritage, the small remnant of foreskin made it very difficult.

Today some men endure several years of discomfort in addition to expense to reconstruct their foreskins. The most recommended method is that of gradually stretching the skin while making sure it is not enough to produce pain. The slow method creates undetectable lacerations and the body responds by generating new skin cells to fill the open areas. Thus after a period of time, one will have more skin. The presence of pain is an indication that too much pressure is being applied. This almost always leads to a scarring of the penis tissue and is not recommended.

Mark Waring also describes the skin graft surgical method. This consists of cutting the ring of skin approximately an inch below the glans penis, pulling the top skin forward so that it covers the glans, then cutting two parallel openings into the scrotum that are perpendicular to the penis. The penis is then inserted into this open pocket so that the cut area on the penis is covered, yet the tip of the glans still extrudes  far enough for urination. The man is sent home and after almost a year returns for the second surgical procedure which consists of detaching the skin surrounding the penis from the scrotum and securing it into place. Complications with this type of surgery include scarring, disfiguring, and possible growth of scrotal hair on the new foreskin.

There is a magazine called *Foreskin Quarterly (FQ)* and an organization named Brothers United for Future Foreskins (BUFF) that provide essential information and referrals for those interested in foreskin restoration.

IMPLANTS   (Bulleetus, Burmese bells, Chagau balls, Tinkling balls) Tribes in Southeast Asia have used bells, stones, jewels, ivory, gold, pearls, balls, and shells to implant into the penis. "The bells ranged up to the size of a small chicken egg, and apparently were always made of metal, with a 'grain of sand,' 'dried adder's tongue,' or other object inside. The better ones were 'gilded and made with great cunning.' As many as a dozen might be inserted. Kings might remove one of theirs to bestow it on a person deserving great honor" (*The Penis Inserts of Southeast Asia*, by Donald E. Brown, James W. Edwards, and Ruth P. Moore, p. 2). This was done to enlarge the size of the penis, provide extra tactile sensation for the female, and duplicate the penis shape of local animals; such as the rhinoceros in Africa. Paolo Mantegazza wrote about bells he saw used in India. "Throughout the country [India] are found old prostitutes who sell little bells of gold, silver and bronze. The women hold great store with them for when they are sewn into the skin of the man's member they cause a swelling of tremendous length of the entire genital parts. Hence they claim their males have greater endurance and give them far greater pleasure than we poor Europeans. It is true that when there are a number of natives about, the woman will invariably choose the one with a titillating member. As soon as the boys reach puberty they rush to have the bells sewn into their members, and constantly change them for larger sizes as they grow up" (*Sexual Relations of Mankind*, by P. Mantegazza). The Chinese used a bell during intercourse but changed the design

and, instead of implanting it into the penis, they merely inserted it into the vagina.

The yakuza (Japanese mafia) still insert pearls into the area between the outer skin that slides freely over the inner core of the penis. A small hole is cut and the pearl is inserted and bandaged until the wound heals. The men perform this surgery as part of a tradition where they add one pearl to the penis for each year  they spend in jail. The pearls make the penis larger and gives it a different sensation. Women seem to disagree as to whether these penises are more sexually desirable (*Modern Primitives*, by V. Vale and A. Juno, p. 156). Koreans and some Filipinos also insert small balls under their penile skin. In 1984 Dr. S.S. Pareek wrote of a 48-year old Korean seaman who had four balls in his penis ("Unusual penile swelling—bulleetus," *British Journal of Sexual Medicine*, Oct 1989, pp. 395).

There are two common types of implants done on men in the United States today. Men who because of injury or cryptorchidism (failure of the testicles to drop) do not have visible testes often have artificial testicles inserted into the empty scrotum. The purpose is only cosmetic, saving the man from possible embarrassment. Another type of implant is a silicone tube designed to assist in providing stiffness to an otherwise flaccid penis. (For additional information **refer to section on IMPOTENCE.**) There is also a fattening operation designed to increase the circumference of the penis. The operation is described as being the opposite of liposuction and is performed by plastic surgeons.

INCISION   Incision of the penis is a practice of splitting the skin down the whole length of the penis. It is done on several islands in the Western Pacific Ocean. The penis appears similar to a circumcised one if done while the male is very young.

"Frequently, however, only completely mature young men are circumcised; in such cases the cut foreskin hangs down as an ugly brown flap" (*Sexual Life of Primitive People*, by H. Fehlinger, p. 106). Mr. Fehlinger continues with a description of one of these ceremonies among the Hamite tribe of East Africa.

Warriors visit the hut, and take away all the boys' clothes and ornaments. Then young girls visit the boys and give them a part of their clothing and ornaments. After the boys have put these on they inform their relations of the forthcoming circumcision.... After sunset they must listen to the sharpening of the operating knife. Warriors are present, and tease the boys. Later on all undress, and a procession is formed with a moterenic *at the head and rear of it. Four times they have to crawl through a small cage, where warriors are stationed at the entrance and exit with nettles and hornets. With the former they beat the boys in the face and on the sex organs; the hornet they set on their backs.... The operator kneels before the boy, and with a quick cut performs the first part of the operation; the foreskin is drawn forward and cut off at the tip of the glans penis.... Friends and relatives make merry together, while the second part of the operation begins. At this only sterile girls may be present, and also women who have lost several brothers and sisters at short intervals. Many boys become unconscious during this part of the operation. The wounds are only washed with cold water, and the boys are led back to their huts... . the foreskins are taken out of the ox horn, sacrificed to their god, and then buried in cowdung at the foot of a croton tree* (*Sexual Life of Primitive People*, pp. 111-112).

INSERTS   The use of penile inserts in the United States is normally referred to as ringing and comprises of piercings of rings or bars that are placed into the glans penis or scrotum at different angles. (Please refer to section on RINGING for additional information.)

Males and females in Malaysia and Singapore sometimes insert phonograph needles or metal charms into the mons pubis area. "In modern Malaysia and Singapore their commonest purpose is to make the person in whom they are inserted more attractive to the opposite sex (not because the needles physically alter appearance—they don't)" (*The Penis Inserts of Southeast Asia*, by Donald E. Brown, James W. Edwards, and Ruth P. Moore, pp. 10-11).

A convicted American murderer, Albert Fish (1870-1936), was reported to have had so many needles inserted into his genital region that they were thought to have short circuited the voltage from his electric chair. Fish was executed for having murdered and eaten fifteen children.

MEATOTOMY   Meatotomy refers to an incision or tearing done to enlarge the urethra. The practice often evolves from masturbation with an instrument that has been inserted into the urethra. People use increasingly larger implements in the urethra to tear tissue. Others cut one or two sides of the urethra and pack the area to keep the sides from mending together. A few men have such a large opening that they were able to  insert the glans penis of another man into the tip of their penis. (See SOUNDING for additional information.)

NEGATION   Negation, or rendering the penis impotent, is primarily done for religious reasons and involves methods other than castration. Young prepubescent boys in India of the Sadhu class hang weights on the tip of their penis to stretch it; within a few years some hang between their knees. They also push their penis inside their body and roll their scrotum around a rod; after some time they are no longer able to pull the penis from the body. Both techniques make it impossible for them to have sexual orgasm later in life. This allows them to engage in self flagellation or masochistic practices without accidently orgasming, bringing their biochemicals back to normal and preventing the attainment of an altered state of consciousness.(See ORGASMS/ ALTERED STATES)

SPLITTING Splitting the penis from the glans toward the base was a ritual practiced by a group of Australian aborigines who worshipped a totem lizard that had a split penis. Most men practiced a less dramatic form of subincision. One Anglo man successfully attempted this procedure and describes the results as follows. "My decision to surgically remodel my genitals was deliberate, of deep satisfaction to me, highly exciting, sexually adventurous, and erotically exhilarating... Full erections are still maintained as previously, but now in two complete, separate halves. The erotic zones of my penis are still the same, with orgasms and ejaculations functioning perfectly. Entry into the vagina requires a little extra effort for insertion, but once my penis is inside, its opened effect on the vagina's inner lining is more pronounced, giving better female orgasmic feelings" (*PFIQ #15*, by Carl Carroll). His account was accompanied by an actual photo. The splitting supposedly took several years to complete.

SUBINCISION Subincision refers to the cutting of part of the glans penis from the tip toward the base. The length of the cut varies according to the custom of the tribes who engage in this practice. Tribes in New Guinea used to make an incision in the glans that was up to about 3/4" in length. Some men in these tribes had two incisions that laid perpendicular to the shaft.

The ceremony of a full subincision is described as follows:

He is lifted and carried feet foremost to the shield, upon which he is placed. The assistant circumciser immediately grasps the foreskin, pulls it out as far as possible, and the operator cuts it off.... One of the men has lain face downward on the ground; a second on top of him. The initiate, conducted from the pole, is placed face upward on this living altar, and while the company sets up a great shout, a third man, mounting astride the boy, grasps and holds his penis ready for the knife, at which moment, a fourth, suddenly appearing, slits the length of it from below. In the women's camp, meanwhile, at the sound of the men's shout, the initiate's female relatives are being slashed across belly and shoulders by his mother. He is lifted from the altar, and while he squats over a shield into which the blood flows, one or two of the younger men, who have been subincised before, stand up and voluntarily undergo a second operation to increase the length of their incisions. Standing close to the sacred pole, hands behind their backs and legs wide apart, they shout, 'Come and slit mine to the root!' They are pinioned from behind, and the work is done (The Way of Animal Powers, by Joseph Campbell, p. 144).

There is a genital modification club in Chicago called INIGMA.

(See also BEE STINGS, BINDINGS, CASTRATION, CHASTITY DEVICES, CIRCUMCISION, COCK RINGS, PENILE LIGATION, PHALLOPHILIA, SACOFRICOSIS, TESTICLES and WEIGHT TRAINING)

PERSONAL ADS Personal ads are those placed in magazines or papers to advertise one's availability. This is done to meet people with anything in mind from dating, exchanging letters and nude photos, swapping partners, or connecting with someone who shares unusual sex preferences. The wording of these ads may be censored by the editor of the magazine in which they are advertised. Sample ads from various publications:

Fit, Active Blonde, W/W/F, caring, warm seeking friend and companion 59+ to share some of life's experiences. Enjoy walks, seaside, mountains, dining & sightseeing (*Trellis Singles*).

MALE VIRGINS, Very busy attractive heterosexual female. Would like discreet intimate fun with you (*Swinger's Digest*).

BEEFY RUMP, White Master, seeks slaves into spanking, paddling, ball work, wax and shaving. Take it on your beefy rump and tender testicles! (*DungeonMaster*).

STOCKING FEET, I am a Bi Woman of 40 who wishes to share experiences regarding emasculation of males via repeated masturbation and foot fetish. Sperm drawing of heterosexual, passive males for parenting purposes, administering female hormones or other ideas to assure female offspring... (*Sandmutopia Guardian 5*).

ALL BAREFOOT TICKLERS, S/M adorable with extremely ticklish feet seeks females, couples, and singles into prolonged foot bondage and tickling pleasures. All foot tickling fantasies are fulfilled and welcome ...(*Fetish Times #191*).

SEXY AND EROTIC WIFE, Young wife loves to make VHS videotapes with super-endowed black bodybuilders. I have many VHS tapes. I'm willing to share with others who share the same hot desires (*Cocoa 'n Creme #10*).

MORE THAN JUST A SNACK, My lover and I are interested in getting together with a small group of hot hung men for long safe cocksucking sessions. I am especially interested in experienced worshippers of uncut dicks. I enjoy feeding the hungry (*Drummer #133*).

There are many advantages to advertising. In addition to meeting more eligible people, one may lessen the chance of rejection at a later date by including things such as special interests, smoking, alcohol, inability to parent, herpes, sexual preference, financial status, profession, religion, race, age, weight, education, etc. The distribution and anonymity advertising offers can be very important if one lives in a small town.

Social etiquette can be important in writing an ad and in responding to replies on the phone or in person. One book available to assist people in writing straight ads, replying, and arranging meetings is *Personal ADventures, How to meet people through personal ads*, by Jay Wiseman, published by Gentle Persuasion Press in San Francisco. Familiarizing oneself with the standard protocol can alleviate much initial anxiety.

(See also COMPUTER SEX, DATING SERVICES, MARRIAGE/MAIL ORDER and PHOTOGRAPHY)

PERSONAL POWER Personal power often acts as a catalyst for partners when engaging in sex. Politicians, movie stars, musicians, sports figures, singers, and the upper echelon of corporations have this power bestowed by virtue of their profession. Some are able to keep a balance in their relationships while others are not.

Dominatrixes and tops learn to create a power image and control their partner with

it. Power over another person can create an inflated ego that leads the top into viewing the servant with contempt or at least without compassion. This is also called "top's disease." People who play in S/M roles of dominant and submissive are aware of this phenomena and work to avoid falling into this mode of thinking.

(See also BLINDFOLDING, BONDAGE, CHASTITY DEVICES, DEFILEMENT, DOMINANCE/SUBMISSION, FLAGELLATION, HUMILIATION, INTERROGATION, PETTICOAT DISCIPLINE, PHOBOPHILIA, PROFESSIONAL DOMINATRIX, TORTURE and VICTORIAN LACE)

PERVERSION See PARAPHILIAS

PETTICOAT DISCIPLINE (Petticoat punishment) Petticoat discipline refers to the discipline used on young males whereby they are forced to wear kilts without the sporran (purse) by their mother, sister, governess, or aunt. English and Scottish mothers both used this method for controlling an unruly boy. This ploy worked by humiliating and embarrassing the boy so much that he was careful not to engage in any type of activity that would draw attention to himself, thus making him easy to control in public.

The degree of modification in attire depended on the boy. For some only a bow tie, short pants, or velvet fabric was sufficient, for others lace, bows on the shoes, shaved legs, and girl's underwear was necessary.

Older males were sometimes subjected to this humiliation due to the power a widowed mother had over their inheritance. An extract from a letter to *The London Time*s sometime during the 19th century quoted a woman as saying she had "found an effective cure for my 20 year old son's flirting with young ladies. Since corsetting him and putting him into a short kilt he is unable to look a girl full  in the eyes, let alone ogle her. I heartily recommend this form of correction..."

Sexual literature often relates fictional stories of fourteen to twenty year old boys who are humiliated by a female, other than their mother. These females add frills to their shirt, shoes, or underpants. The kilt may be cut short so that lace underwear will show if the boy bends over. As often is the custom, underpants are not worn with kilts. Most of the story lines include embarrassment suffered from having others look up their skirt, pull their pants down for a spanking, or having females rub against their genitals.

Petticoat discipline differs from crossdressing or transvestism because the intent is to have the masculinity and identity of the male remain prominent. The male is not trying to pass as female; the change in gender identity would not humiliate him nearly as much.

(See also DOMINANCE/SUBMISSION, TRANSVESTITES and VICTORIAN LACE)

PHALLOPHILIA (Macrogenitalism; Teratophallic—large penises)

MALE: It's not the size of the ship that is important, it's the motion of the ocean.
FEMALE: But, only a fool would take a dinghy out on a stormy sea.

Phallophilia (phallus: swelling of genitals, philia: attachment to) implies a sexual attraction that one has for an erect penis of either extraordinary dimensions or endurance. The Greeks and Romans worshipped a god by the name of Priapus who was endowed with an exaggerated phallus. He was thought to be the son of Aphrodite and Dionysus with conflicting opinions that he was sired by Pan, Hermes, or Adonis. Priapus was abandoned by both parents and raised by shepherds, later becoming the deity affiliated with flocks, fields, and orchards. Other cultures also had their phallic gods.

Women's fascination with large penises is claimed to have affected our current male physiology. Helen Fisher, an anthropologist, contends this in her comments, "[b]ut sex attractants evolved not only on the female. Through female choice, the males evolved them too. Of all the primates the human male has by far the largest penis—much larger even than that of a gorilla, a primate three times a man's body bulk. The width of the normal penis provides extreme sexual pleasure to the female. . . It seems that the largeness of this male anatomical part has no practical function other than for sex, and undoubtedly it evolved in size long  ago because women like men with large penises" (*The Sex Contract*, p. 6). Today the average length of a penis in the United States is considered to be between five and six inches.

The Romans, in their worship of the phallus, wore amulets of the male genitals much as we wear religious saints, crosses or stars. The phallus was thought to be a charm to protect one against the evil eye and it was worn by men and women alike. Roman men also had their grave stones carved with the likeness of only their head and their genitals. Early Christians were slow in giving up their worship of the phallus. Some continued to carry the lingam in religious processions and others baked breads in the shape of sex organs. The Church finally compromised on the bread by ordaining that these buns could be accepted in Christian holidays by marking them with a cross; thus the hot cross buns. The people had fertility saints canonized, such as St. Foutin, St. Guerlichon, St. Gilles at Cotentin, St. Rene in Anjou, and St. Guignole of Landevenec. Their statues often had large penises and some were worshipped by pouring wine onto this member. "Men would present their afflicted members to the priest to be anointed with oil, and 1,400 flasks of oil were consumed every year for this purpose" (*Sex in History*, by G. Rattray Taylor, pp. 270-71). Christians became fascinated with the prepuce of Jesus and as many as 12 churches claimed to have it in their possession. This prepuce was substituted by the Church for the statues of Priapus, hoping that this would discourage his religious influence.

Today people still give undue concern to the size of their penis and its virility. Penis size that matches the length of a partner's vagina is of greater value. One that is longer than the vagina will pound against the cervix and posterior fornix causing pain with possible ulcerations for many women. Vaginas vary in length as much as the penis. Penises are also easier to manipulate during oral sex if they are not too large.

There is a dating service called the "Hung Jury" that is designed for size enthusiasts. Men must measure at least 8" in length (measured from bottom of shaft). Conversely, there is a special club, SMALL, that was begun to offer support for men who are not satisfied with the size of their penises; it has also grown to encompass those who are short in stature.

(See also AGALMATOPHILIA, CASTRATION, DOCKING, FERTILITY RITES, FESTIVALS and PENIS MODIFICATION)

PHEROMONES Pheromones, a series of short-chain aliphatic acids found in primates, are chemicals the body releases that can sexually excite a partner. These enter a person through the nostrils and cling to a receptor found in the nasal cavity (Jacobson's organ or vomeronasal organ). Unlike molecules that adhere to the olfactory system and excite the sense of smell, pheromones are diffused directly into the hypothalamus of the brain and have no odor of their own. Research is currently being done to determine exactly how this system functions in humans.

A refined ability to detect pheromones is more important for finding mates than vision or sound in species that do not live in groups. Marking trails with pheromones left in urine and feces serves to lure a potential mate. Without this ability the odds of the two meeting during the female's estrus would be very low. Advantages this has over sound or a visual cue is that pheromones can linger for days in an area, darkness is irrelevant, and predators usually don't have the ability to detect the pheromone trail of other species. Humans, because they evolved in clans, seem to have developed a primary dependence on vision rather than pheromones.

The aphrodisiac effect body odor has on people was fairly common knowledge in the past. Krafft-Ebing relates several famous cases from Europe. "The case of Henry III shows that contact with a person's perspiration may be the exciting cause of passionate love. At the betrothal feast of the King of Navarre and Margaret of Valois, he accidentally dried his face with a garment of Maria of Cleves, which was moist with her perspiration. Although she was the bride of the Prince of Conde, Henry conceived immediately such a passionate love for her that he could not resist it, and made her, as history shows, very unhappy. An analogous instance is related of Henry IV, whose passion for the beautiful Gabriel is said to have originated at the instant when, at a ball, he wiped his brow with her handkerchief." Krafft Ebing also cited the example of a peasant that had seduced many virtuous women by carrying a handkerchief under his armpit at dances and once his partner began to perspire using it to wipe her face (*Psychopathia Sexualis*, p. 20). Napoleon also seems to have been attuned to the aphrodisiac effect of pheromones present in perspiration and is often attributed with the command to Josephine, "Don't wash, I'm coming home."

(See also OLFACTION)

PHLEBOTOMY Phlebotomy (phlebo: vein; tomy: to cut) is the practice of bloodletting. People once used bloodletting as a substitute for the human sacrifices required for their deities. Bleeding also came to be used with magic to rid a person of evil spirits and as their knowledge increased they used bleeding on injuries and hematomas. These people undoubtedly noticed that animals gained relief from stress or facilitated healing of infections by tearing the area open and allowing it to bleed. The Greeks recorded their observations of manics who became calm and even fell asleep when seeing their own blood flow out of a cut. English dentists during the 16th century used bloodletting on their patients. Bloodletting remained a common medical practice of barber/surgeons until the 1850's. The barbershop blood and bandage striped pole with the receptacle basin served to advertise their profession.

Bloodletting was introduced into religious practices when early Catholic monks discovered Roman medical texts that warned against celibacy because it poisoned a man's blood. They then took it upon themselves to bleed each other to reduce the risk of toxins in their blood. This practice soon spread to single males in the general populace as a prophylactic for chastity. Females were not required to be bled because of their menses. However, some Puritan women used it as a form of abortion.

The connection between bloodletting and sex has persisted and today some people still find intense sexual arousal from either seeing blood on a partner or from bleeding themselves. This falls under the general category of blood sports; however, unlike other activities where bloodletting may be a by-product, here it is the central aspect. People often combine bleeding with masturbation, enjoying the simultaneous sexual relief that each offers. Techniques include making small cuts on the skin, puncturing a vein with a hypodermic needle, or piercing of a nipple and placing a suction cup from a snake bite kit over the area to draw and collect the blood.

(See also BLOOD SPORTS, CICATRIZATION, MASOCHISM and VAMPIRISM)

PHOBIAS   Sexual phobias are prevalent and include such things as:

PHOBIA	AVERSION TO
automysophobia	getting dirty
coitophobia	intercourse
erotophobia	sexual love
gamophobia	marriage
gymnophobia	nakedness
harmatophobia	inadequacy
hypengyophobia	responsibility
maieusiophobia	pregnancy
naphephobia	touch
pathophobia	diseases (STDs)
scopophobia	being looked at
spermatophobia	semen loss
vaginismus	penetration

A sex oriented phobia may be caused by societal guilt, a negative experience with intimacy, a lack of experience in coping with fear, temporary stress, or by separation, overprotection, or rejection by parents when young. People can feel anything from mild anxiety when confronted with the source of their fear to an extreme panic attack. One traumatic experience or a series of negative experiences in relationships that produce painful feelings or rejection can condition a person to automatically react with fear in the future. A well known, and still controversial scientist, claims that "even a single exposure to a brief stressful event— be it environmental or pharmacological— can induce extremely persistent, cascading sensitization to subsequent stressors or related stimuli which recall the memory of the original trauma (Antelman et al. 1980, 1987, 1988; Antelman and Chiodo 1983; Antelman 1988). We have recently proposed that such findings may be relevant to the development of syndromes such as delayed post-traumatic stress disorder, bulimia and panic (Antelman 1988)." (*Psychopharmacology*, (1989)98:97-101).

An example of a panic attack is the case of a woman with a phobia of relationships who when asked for a second date experiences classic symptoms such as heart palpitations, chest pain, feelings of suffocation, dizziness, and sweaty palms. Others may experience a shortness of breath, hot flashes, cold flashes, feelings of faintness, and trembling. The body responds so frantically that even if the person feels a strong attraction it becomes insignificant when compared to the relief felt when the relationship is ended. A number of people, about one in 40 in the United States, suffer from obsessive compulsive disorder. These are "haunted by disturbing thoughts, usually about contamination, violence and sexual issues." Scientists feel that this disorder is caused by a lower level of serotonin in the brain. Those suffering from obsessive fears involving sexual issues can now be helped by medication. ("Angst," by Claire Conway, *Stanford Medicine*, Spring 1992, pp. 26-30) CAUTION: Phobics who are in relationships often try coping with their fear by numbing it with alcohol or by avoiding the problem.

(See also PHOBOPHILIA)

PHOBOPHILIA   (Terror Play) Phobophilia (phobo: fear; philia: attachment)
refers to people who become sexually
aroused by fear provoking stimuli. This is
not surprising considering many people find
such things as carnival rides and horror
movies so entertaining. People who do not
perceive an event as involving real or immediate danger can transfer this anxiety to
sexual arousal. (Refer to PARAPHILIAS.)
Almost anything that can initiate the
fight/flight response can be transferred to
sexual arousal. Our bodies respond to each
of these by producing adrenalin that speeds
up our hearts, and increasing oxygen intake
to prepare us for a fight, flight, or sex. The
most common form of phobophilia is the
type where a couple has sex in a public
place, risking discovery (agoraphilia).

SM scenes are often designed to maximize the effects of fear. The black leather
and chain costumes are made to look evil,
the whips and paddles appear more inju-
rious than in reality, dungeons look cold and
menacing, and the dialogue makes one feel
inferior and defenseless.

Terror is used in S/M scenes to create
passion by capitalizing on a person's phobias. A person takes the information they
have about a partner's fear and uses it
during a scene. For instance, a person who
is afraid of heights may be forced to climb
ladders, if frightened by confinement they
may be locked in a closet, those who get
weak at the sight of needles might be
pierced, those that are afraid of losing their
temper will be pushed to the edge. The
games of terror not only produce passion,
bonding, and trust, but have the benefit of
desensitizing a person to their original
phobia. A person who successfully comes
through these experiences often feels
empowered and better able to face other
fears with courage. The technique for creating terror in a partner requires quick
unpredictable action, follow-through on
threats, using blindfolding with strange
sounds, and physical control by the size of a
dominant partner, use of bondage, discipline, or knowledge of pressure points and
wrestling holds. Dialogue and constant challenge is important in retaining power and

control. The bottom is not given time to
rest, analyze, or predict behavior. CAU-
TION: The top (dominant) is responsible
for the physical and emotional safety of
their partner. A person who is being forced
to cope with phobias may react with hysteria, screaming, violence, silence, or
fainting.

("Terror," by J.C.C., QSM lecture,
November 28, 1990)

(See also ABDUCTION, ACROPHILIA,
CLAUSTROPHILIA, HODOPHILIA, JEAL-
OUSY and PHYGEPHILIA)

PHONE SEX   (Telephonicophilia—
arousal from discussing sex on telephone)
Phone sex implies a dialogue between two
or more consenting adults with at least one
person engaging in masturbation. (Nonconsensual phone sex is referred to as an
obscene phone call.)

Couples who are not able to be together
use phone sex to simulate coitus. Others
find that phone sex offers more diversity
than they can obtain otherwise. Any sexual
deviation or otherwise physically impossible
feat becomes a reality in verbal sex. Some of
these fantasies prove educational with
regard to what turns a partner on and may
provide new ideas for inventive play. Since
one is absolutely safe from contracting a
sexually transmitted disease, phone sex is
currently enjoying unprecedented popularity.

Special newspapers or magazines advertise professional phone sex services for
interested parties. These may consist of
party lines for novices, bulletin board personal ads, a recording made by a professional, or a live professional that will follow
a person's cue as to the type of fantasy they
want to hear. The services are staffed by
adult heterosexuals, gays and lesbians. Ads
usually have a provocative photograph and
advertise such things as: "Bizarre Erotic
Fantasies"; "Dominant Bitch"; "Your
Personal Slave"; "Forbidden Games—Foot
Fetishes, Cross-dressing, Golden Showers,
Enemas," "Infantilism"; "Wrestling";
"Black Mistresses"; and "Ultimate
Telephone Torture." The erotic phone lines
in New York during 1983 received an

average of "500,000 calls daily" (*Time Magazine*, 1983). A new service has the capability of the caller seeing the woman on his television screen as she obeys his special requests

(See also ACOUSTICOPHILIA, COMPUTER SEX, FANTASY PLAY and OBSCENE PHONE CALLS)

PHOTOGRAPHY

(Pictophilia—arousal from pictures or photography) Many people photograph their partner or themselves during sex for arousal, often viewing the photos later. Self-developing cameras make complete confidentiality possible for couples.

Consensual photo sessions of nude males or females can be arousing even without any type of sexual activity or genital display. A few married couples consent to having their spouses pose nude for others to photograph as a hobby.

There are businesses in the sex districts of major cities where men can either take photos of professional women or be photographed with them in an erotic pose. These photos are popular with men who want to take a souvenir of their trip back to their buddies in a small town.

(See also COMPUTER SEX, PERSONAL ADS, PORNOGRAPHY and SNUFF FILMS)

PHYGEPHILIA

Phygephilia (phyge: flight; philia: lust) refers to sexual arousal felt from flight. The public flock to see movies about Bonnie and Clyde, notorious mob leaders, and gunfighters of the old West, many of whom may have been phygephiliacs.

There are many cases where men have toyed with the police, even giving them leads to keep the excitement going. One of these was an Englishman named Neil Cream, a lust murderer and drug addict who supported his habit by performing abortions. Cream preferred to poison his victims and then retreat to a safe place to visualize their agony. "[H]e is said to have derived further erotic pleasure from being pursued by the police—another aspect of criminal sex deviations little appreciated but

not too uncommon" (*Perverse Crimes in History*, by Masters and Lea, p. 165).

This attitude carries over into the criminal's confessions once apprehended and they often use gross details of their mutilations to shock the police and to arrogantly display their superior intelligence because, while the police arrested the killer from evidence on one or two cases, he had killed many more victims.

(See also HARPAXOPHILIA, HYBRISTO-PHILIA, PHOBOPHILIA, SYMPHOROPHILIA and VICARIOUS AROUSAL)

PIE THROWING

Pie throwing is one of the most amusing forms of defilement. There are several scenarios found in pie throwing. People at parties have thrown pies on each other, couples engage in the activity in private; and there is even a gay pie throwing club. One individual  nick-named "Pieface Brown" walks up to people at social functions or theaters and asks attractive women to pie him. Nine out of ten agree to smear the pie over his face and body. He professes to have been pied by over 200 women within a span of three months. Pieface Brown began having pies rubbed in his face at the age of eight and suddenly at the age of 18 it began to be sexually stimulating. He often records the event and, once alone, replays the giggling and comments made by the women as he masturbates. Women sometimes add to the sexual aspect of this practice by saying things such as "I would like to do this to your crotch."

Elements of arousal associated with pie throwing are anticipation, fear of rejection, thrill of acceptance, humiliation, desire that the partner will say or do something sexual and unexpected, sharing intimacy with an attractive person who might not otherwise notice them, and deceitfully engaging in a sexual and socially unaccepted act in public.

(See also COCKTAILS, COPROPHILIA, DEFILEMENT and SITOPHILIA)

PIERCINGS (Belonephilia—arousal from piercings) A piercing in this text refers to temporarily puncturing the skin. (Permanent piercings are referred to as ringing.)

Piercings were used by many ancient cultures in their rites of passage. The piercings used by some cultures were in fact much more horrendous than the skin piercings used today. There are Mayan artifacts depicting a man pulling a cord with protruding thorns through his tongue. Plains Indians have Sun Dance ceremonies where they pierce the muscle above each breast with a stick and, tying cords to the ends, hang from a tree until either the stick or the muscle tears loose. Hindu Indians have until recently used many ritualistic piercings. These include hanging by hooks, lying on a bed of nails, sewing fruit to the body, and Kavandi dancing in which a cage of spears is supported by the upper body and the ends slowly penetrate the skin as the person dances or moves. The Chinese have used acupuncture, the insertion of needles, in medical practice for hundreds of years. A different category of user, the drug addict, sometimes fixates on the needle and addicts have described its penetration and the drawing of their blood to be like masturbation (Howard and Borges, 1971, as quoted in *The Many Faces of Suicide*, p. 271).

Others have derived a more direct form of arousal from piercings. Hirschfeld wrote of a German who posed as a physician and visited schools and homes to examine young girls. In full sight of parents and teachers he would undress the girls and stick needles into them, pausing periodically to make notations. It was soon discovered that he was a farm laborer and he was imprisoned.

The most common form of piercing found in S/M play is that of simply pushing a small 25 to 18 gauge sterile hypodermic needle through a small portion of skin. These needles are not always available so barbless fish hooks, staples, and sewing needles are often substituted.

People are inventive with games devised to entertain the bottom when pierced. They may weave patterns with tinsel around the needles, put clothespins over the center of the needles, connect the needles with a cord, hang ornaments from fish hooks, and some remove needles by whipping them out. Fakir Musafar once gave a demonstration where two people were pierced, blindfolded, and joined by a cord tied to each needle. The people were then instructed to move around and gently tug on the taut cords. Some play darts by filling a syringe with water and, pushing hard and fast on the plunger, to sending the needle flying through the air to its destination. Other areas that are often pierced are the nipples. The nipple is tougher than other areas and a larger gauge needle is used. The needle is never inserted straight into the nipple toward the body but always parallel so that the tip of the needle is visible on each side of the nipple once pierced.

The labia is often pierced following the same guidelines as for nipples.

The glans penis is pierced but piercing the shaft can lead to serious damage of the cavernosa, nerves, and vessels. The glans tends to bleed more than other parts of the body. The scrotal sack is pierced more often. The needles are anchored to prevent movement. Some people use something similar to a but-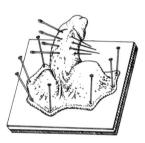terfly board. A square piece of Masonite is used and a styrofoam core of the same size is cut and placed over the board with two sheets of paper glued on top. The penis and testicles are pulled up through a round hole that has been cut in the middle and the scrotum is then stretched and pinned at the corners. Testicles are occasionally pierced but there are risks of the needle breaking, moving and tearing tissue, or introducing pathogens into the testicle.

Piercing of the fingernails is very rarely done due to the severe pain. There are a few people who are involved in serious foot torture, sometimes negotiating to have their partner insert needles under their toenails.

People fascinated with piercing explain their arousal with the description of the unique sensation of feeling something cut through their skin. It is very rarely considered a painful experience yet endorphins seem to be released almost immediately. CAUTION: Piercing the skin is a blood sport and therefore is not safe. (Refer to SAFE SEX)

("Piercing," by Raelyn Gallina, Outcasts lecture, September 15, 1989; "Play Piercing as Art and Sensation," by Celeste, QSM lecture, September 17, 1990)

(See also BLOOD SPORTS, RINGING and SAFE SEX)

PIMPS (Panderer, Procurer; Jack-gagger—if it is husband, Leno—male, Lena—female) Pimps are people who live off the proceeds gained from soliciting clients for a prostitute. The prostitutes working with a pimp do so voluntarily. However, the conditions are often deplorable for the women and would seem to fall into a similar category as that of abused wives. A procurer or panderer differs from pimps in that they deceive the victim into working for a bordello for which they are given a commission by the madam or manager of the house.

Prostitutes gravitate toward pimps for several reasons. These men, unlike most, accept their lifestyle, understand their problems, appear to remain personally unaffected by the woman's sexual power, and create an illusion of self confidence, affluence, and machismo. A prostitute usually derives her self-esteem from her ability to manipulate men and earns monetary compensation from it. A pimp profits from reinforcing this image, encouraging her to continue her work and relying on her ability to succeed. Some women receive benefits from their association with pimps, such as protection, bail money, an apartment, and even a savings account. However, others find that because a pimp has to remain in control at all times he often uses violence to win an argument. He may use addictive drugs as a means to keep women from leaving and he tears down a woman's self confidence by not encouraging her to broaden her base skills and attributes from which she achieves self-esteem.

(See also BORDELLOS, ILLEGAL SEX and PROSTITUTION)

PINCHING (Thlipsosis—arousal from pinching) Some people are aroused by pinching their partner during sex or by being pinched themselves. The most common areas are the nipples, upper thighs, and the back.

(See also BITING, CUPPING, SCRATCHING, SENSORY ENHANCEMENT and TICKLING)

PLANTS See APHRODISIACS, FLAGELLATION/BIRCHING, SITOPHILIA and URTICATION

PODOPHILIA (Foot fetish) Podophilia (podos: foot; philia: attraction to) refers to the sexual arousal certain people experience when exposed to feet. It is only considered a fetish when one either favors these in lieu of a human partner or has to focus their attention on the feet of a partner to achieve orgasm.

The Chinese have probably had the longest romance with feet, going to extreme measures in creating erotic effects. This culture practiced the binding of girl's feet, and occasionally those of catamites (boy lovers), from the 10th century until the 1930's. Other Asian countries, such as Japan, Korea, Tibet, Indonesia, and Mongolia, sometimes did this but never to the 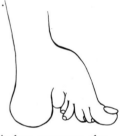 same degree. A Chinese girl's feet were first bound at the age of five to seven and continued to be bound until they quit growing at age eighteen. This resulted in a foot size of about 2" wide and 4" long. The skin on the bottom of the feet remained soft and supple because walking was restricted. The feet were perfumed and covered by embroidered satin or silk booties with padded soles. Women occasionally masturbated by rubbing their feet and lesbians would put their big toe into each other's vaginas. Males indulged in such podophilic delights as engulfing the foot in their mouth, biting, licking, sucking, thrusting their penis between the bowed arches, being masturbated by their partner's feet, washing her feet in tea and drinking it, trimming her toenails, placing almonds between her toes and eating them, and performing fellatio on her big toe (Chinese Foot Binding, by Howard S. Levy, 1972).

A few men cannot resist the impulse to have sexual contact with feet. The March 19, 1992 San Francisco Examiner carried an Associated Press article that read:

TOE SUCKER CHARGED WITH SEXUAL ABUSE
St. Louis—A man who allegedly knocked down girls and young women, took off their shoes and sucked their toes was charged with sexual abuse Wednesday. "It's kind of a humiliating thing—I think emotionally it just degraded them," said Maj. Ronald Henderson, a police commander. [E.J.], 28, was charged with assault, indecent exposure and sexual abuse in incidents from January until two weeks ago (p. A14).

There are many reasons feet are said to be arousing. Feet are often the first part of a mother or father which a toddler touches. Likewise, parents often play with toddlers by pushing them with their feet or letting them ride one of their feet. Another aspect involved in the sexual attraction of feet is that love objects always have a barrier or obstacle to attainment and feet are less available to many partners than the genitals. The feet are also less threatening for those with coital difficulty because, unlike the genitals of a partner, they do not make demands for perfect sexual performance.

The preferences for types of feet vary dramatically. Some like toe nails with a certain color polish, others focus only on the big toe and want it painted dark burgundy with the nail long and filed to a point.

Special clubs and bordellos exist for people interested in podophilia. The prostitutes engage in acts similar to those of the Chinese men, except that the roles are often reversed and men will sometimes insert their big toe into the woman's vagina. There is also a 69 position where instead of having oral sex the couples suck on each other's feet. High heels, foot tickling, erotic torture, and bondage are also available. There are foot fetish magazines that have articles, personal ads, and advertisements. One may order photos or videos of a barefoot woman pumping the accelerator of several cars, trying to start the engine, as well as many other poses of the feet. A sample ad for the Barefoot Digest Annual reads, "Full-color photo sets: TOES, FOOT-BOTTOMS, WRINKLED SOLES, DIRTY SOLES, FOOT-KISSING, FOOT-TICKLING...AND BONDAGE." There is also a "Foot Fraternity" club in Ohio that sells foot fetish material for gay males.

(See also ACROTOMOPHILIA, BINDING/ FEET, FETISHES, MASSAGE and TORTURE)

POLYITEROPHILIA   Polyiterophilia refers to those people who have to have a series of consecutive sex partners before they can orgasm. John Money refers to this phenomena in Love & Love Sickness:

This is the polyiterative subtype of hyperphilia, or polyiterophilia. It is fairly well documented in the activities of some homosexual males. Its definitive characteristic is that a man or woman builds up his or her own responsiveness towards orgasm alone or with a partner by reiterating the same activity many times with many different partners in a limited period of time...To illustrate, a homosexual male with the syndrome of polyiterophilic fellatio will be able to reach an orgasm with his own partner only after accumulating a dozen "blow jobs," that is acts of fellatio, on different men at, say, a steam bath or sauna club. (The John Hopkins University Press, Baltimore/ London, 1980, pp. 263-4. Reprinted by permission of the publisher.)

In polyiterophilia the person seems unable to orgasm with a partner without first engaging in sex with others.

(See also CANDAULISM, GANG BANGS and GROUP SEX)

PORNOGRAPHY   (Ordure; Graphelagnia, Iconolagny and Pictophilia—arousal from pornography) Pornography (porne: a prostitute; and graphos: to write) originally referred to writing about prostitutes and later came to include any text that is specifically designed to elicit sexual desire. A few feminist groups have recently modified the term to mean erotic material that leads to violence, rape, and degradation of women. Their adherence to this belief and resultant lobbying has led to an attack on pornography that indirectly threatens art, music, and even medicine.

A few fundamentalists and a majority of conformists can have a major influence on a society. As late as two hundred years ago in England private societies for the suppression of vice succeeded in banning "licentious publications" such as *The Rights of Man* and *Age of Reason* by Tom Paine. In 1820 Palmer's *Principles of Nature*, and Shelley's *Oedipus Tyrannus* were prosecuted as "seditious works." Christians were forbidden to attend the theatre or to read novels which were "instruments of abomination and ruin." People's vocabulary had to change; words like sweat, pregnant, sex, and acts of defecation had to be replaced with more delicate and evasive words. Women began describing the location of their pain to their doctors by pointing to a similar spot on a doll. Any part of their body that was between their neck and knees began to be referred to as the "liver." Even piano legs had to be covered with baggy linen so as to not arouse men because of the resemblance they had to a woman's legs. This was a resurgence of the same type of repression found in the 17th century when Galileo and Camanella were tortured and Descartes narrowly escaped the same fate because of censorship by the Church.

The United States Congress passed our first anti-pornography law in 1873 as the result of intense lobbying by Anthony Comstock, Secretary of the "New York Society for the Suppression of Vice." This man was then appointed "a special agent of the Post Office Department and granted the right to open any letter, package, book, or pamphlet passing through the mails. He personally had the power to decide what was lewd or obscene, and since he was a narrow-minded, prudish fanatic, he soon established a dictatorial reign of puritanical terror which lasted over 40 years. Many of his victims were physicians who tried to help their patients with birth control information" (*The Sex Atlas*, by Erwin J. Haeberle, pp. 377-8).

Today organizations such as the "Christian Coalition" legislate against homosexuality, abortion, and certain depictions of sex on television. Their goal is evident from a statement made by Ralph Reed, their Executive Director. "What Christians have got to do is take back this country, one precinct at a time." These people fail to show the same magnanimous attitude as our founders. George Washington made it clear in the Treaty with Tripoli (1796), that "The government of the United States of America is not in any sense founded on Christian religion."

Control of the majority by the censorship of the few is by no means restricted to the ploys of fundamentalists or feminists. The Tiananmen Square protest in China led to a year of arrests, martial law and now a crackdown on pornography. Under the new laws that became effective in November 1990, men and women arrested for selling pornography are being given tough sentences. Sexual morals have nothing to do with the rebellion or demands that the students made, but laws against sexual expression affect everyone and intimidation is the swiftest method a faltering government has of re-establishing control. On the other hand, immediately upon winning their freedom the communist block countries have begun to allow sex shops to operate more openly. Katchadourian and Lunde, Stanford professors, relate this standard political ploy. "The totalitarian states— Fascist Italy, Nazi Germany, Spain, Russia, and China—did control, or still do control, the purity of their art, for reasons which are political, rather than strictly artistic or moral. Fascist and Communist dictatorships alike have insisted that art be uncomplicated, inoffensive, and ideologically correct. Obscenity, in their view, is merely one symptom of a basic decadence. In curing the root evil, which is individual freedom, these regimes have removed their nations from participation in the mainstream of twentieth-century art and have granted their peoples and their artists the comforts of insularity—untroubled by erotic fantasies" (*Fundamentals of Human Sexuality*, p. 354).

People worry that if they are exposed to a variety of sex practices they will lose all control and indulge in dangerous or repulsive acts. The facts are that people rarely develop a desire for something they formerly considered repulsive simply because of exposure.

President Reagan approved the establishment of the "Meese Commission" to investigate pornography. Marty Klein, a prominent sexologist, elaborates further. "In 1986, Ronald Reagan created the Meese Commission with the express purpose of destroying the pornography industry. It was widely expected that the commission would issue a report linking pornography to sexual violence. . . however, things did not go exactly as planned. The Meese Commission could find no causal link between sexually explicit materials and sexually aggressive behavior. To its surprise, the commission also found that less than one percent of the imagery in the most popular porn magazines was of 'force, violence, or weapons.' And yet, despite these and other well-known findings, a surprising number of people—many of them otherwise staunch defenders of our First Amendment rights—wish to censor pornography in the interests of some greater social good" ("Censorship and the Fear of Sexuality," THE HUMANIST, July/August 1990, by Marty Klein, p. 15).

Tactics employed by opponents of pornography include emphasizing the minimal amount of "kiddy porn" and lobbying against this, as people will rarely defend this type of child abuse. The "kiddy porn" laws are then written in a way that eliminates many innocuous types of pornography or nudity.

The repression of true child pornography seems to have merit; however, the abolition of all pornography in societies has grave consequences that involve an even greater number of innocent children. Dr. James Weinrich, a prominent scientist and sexologist, holds the position that "[t]here is evidence...that *permitting* pornography can reduce child sexual abuse. In Denmark, for example, after legalization of hard-core pornography in the 1960's, child sexual abuse went down by a very substantial per-

centage, and stayed down—an effect not accounted for by liberalized societal attitudes, increased under-reporting, or less diligence on the part of the police (all of which were very carefully checked out in the study).... [A] great deal—not all—of the sexual contacts between adult heterosexual men and girls is committed by men who are not true pedophiles... Instead, much of it is contact by shy or inept heterosexual men who would prefer sex with adult women but are frustrated in their attempts: men who found, usually accidentally at first, that younger women or girls are less competent in resisting their advances... much heterosexual child molestation is *substitutional* in nature: such men apparently can resist contacts with girls if they substitute masturbation with pornography depicting their main interest, adult women" (*Sexual Landscapes*, by James D. Weinrich, Ph.D., pp. 397-8).

(See also COMPUTER SEX, ILLEGAL SEX and SNUFF FILMS)

POWER TOOLS Power tools used in sex games are drills, hedge clippers, wood lathes, weed eaters, sanders, milking machines, and modified electric chain saws. People who engage in many of these activities are in danger of mutilating themselves and causing serious injury.

Drills have been adapted for urethral play by inserting a long wooden cotton swab (i.e. those used for cleaning VCR heads) into the drill's chuck. The protruding cotton tip has a generous amount of oil based lubricant rubbed into it. The drill is then turned on and the tip of the cotton swab is inserted just inside the urethra. Some hold the flat side of a 10,000 rpm finishing sander that is attached to an air compressor on their clitoris. One man brings himself to orgasm by holding the handle of a weed-eater against his genitals while trimming grass.

Drills are also used with a modified dildo. The dildo is designed so that a projection extends through the base for attachment to the drill chuck. The dildo is lubricated and inserted in an orifice and turned on. This can be dangerous if the projection tears through the rubber cover of the dildo. Neither of these uses for a drill are considered safe. Wood lathes have been adapted for sex by lining the socket end with soft fabric and inserting the glans penis. Milking machines give a different sensation. The rubber sleeve unit is placed onto the penis and the other end of the cup is either left on the teat of the cow or closed off to produce suction. The sleeve then milks the erect penis.

Chain saws are used as part of a mock castration scene solely for the excitement of a partner. A chain saw is modified by removing the chain or blade that rotates around the groove in the protruding oblong 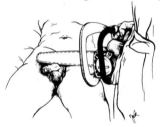 metal plate. The mock castration scene is set up by restraining the partner flat on a bed or against a wall. A blindfold is used at the beginning of the scene to prevent the partner from detecting the artificial nature of the props. The partner's genitals are then scrubbed down with alcohol and tied in a snug (but not tight) tourniquet fashion around the base of the penis. The patient is told that it is time for the castration and might be given one last request. The chain saw is started and slowly lowered so that the plate rests against the top of the genitals for a brief moment. This type of sex play is safe so long as the consenting partner has a healthy cardiovascular system. CAUTION: A chain saw without the blade removed is extremely dangerous. It may even cause injury without being turned on. Extreme care is used for all other power tools as well.

(See also GENITAL/ANAL INSERTS, SAFE SEX, SEX TOYS and SYBIAN)

PREMATURE EJACULATION (Ejaculatio praecox, Preblysis, Tachorgasmia) Premature is defined in many ways. These range from ejaculation before the couple has undressed to "when the man is unable to control ejaculation for long enough to satisfy his partner in at least 50 percent of their

coital connections" (Masters and Johnson, *Human Sexual Inadequacy*, Boston: Little, Brown). The easiest definition to remember is that of D. W. Hastings, who "suggests considering the man's subjective judgment and defines as premature any ejaculation that the man does 'not yet' want" ("Common sexual dysfunctions: I. impotence, II. ejaculatio praecox, III. lack of female response." *Psychiatr Ann I* (4): 10-31). (—both cited in *The Treatment of Sexual Disorders, Concepts and Techniques of Couple Therapy* by Gerd Arentewicz and Gunter Schmidt, p. 21). Primal man is believed to have had to catch and mate with a female either before she broke free or he was displaced by a dominant male. Kinsey reported that 75% of men surveyed ejaculated within three minutes of penetration. Other primates take about 15 seconds. This condition exists in both sexes, but society seems concerned only with the male. Premature ejaculation is common and can stem from many reasons. One is the environment where most teenage boys learn their sexuality. Here masturbation is usually rushed through to avoid detection, conditioning the person to focus on the orgasm without being able to emotionally relax and enjoy intimacy with a partner. Other causes may be a physical disorder that induces pain which acts as a stimulus, fear of intimacy, the length of time since last encounter, a new partner, or undeveloped muscle control. There are no simple cures, however. If a urologist and therapist have been consulted without positive results, one may want to experiment with some of the following suggestions:

Discuss anxiety ahead of time with the partner.

Exercise the muscles while urinating by stopping the flow several times.

Try not to focus on orgasm as the primary goal.

Masturbate before having sex with a partner.

Use condoms to reduce some of the sensations.

Have a glass of wine or beer and avoid caffeine.

Stop or withdraw the penis during intercourse if it becomes too intense.

Push upward on the perineum (1/2 way between anus and scrotum) before feeling an imminent orgasm in order to relieve pressure that is built up in the prostate gland. This may first be practiced alone during masturbation.

Pressure or slight pain on the soles of the feet may inhibit orgasm.

Tantra training or breath control is valuable for some.

Use a squeeze technique where the thumb is positioned on the frenum with the fingers on the opposite side along the rim. This is held for about 15 seconds.

Men who overcome premature ejaculation and learn to restrain themselves for long periods of time often discover that spouses remain inorgasmic. The wife's problem can often be masked by her blaming the husband. There are women, who knowing that a man ejaculates in two to three minutes, will rush to orgasm themselves, proving that timing is not always a problem. Unfortunately some women train themselves to orgasm through masturbation techniques that do not adapt well to penetration by a male. These include using fingers or vibrators in a rapid motion. A person that requires prolonged stimulus is said to have dysorgasmia.

There are many excellent resource books for people wanting to improve their sex lives. One is titled *The Complete Guide to Sexual Fulfillment, Your Questions Answered*, published by Prometheus Books.

(See also IMPOTENCE)

PRISHA   (Ischolagny—avoidance of females to prevent arousal) Prisha is the Hebrew word used to describe the separation of the sexes. Several of the ancient religions engaged in this practice and it is still found in places of worship among Hindus,

Moslems, South American tribes, and Orthodox Jews. Methods used to facilitate this separation include the use of two rooms, a curtain or partition called a machetza, or simply a distance between the two sexes. Some synagogues provide mixed seating in the middle with segregated sections to each side.

A Hindu yogi once explained this tradition to surprised Americans by saying it was as simple as separating apples and oranges; the two sexes are merely different. Rabbis explain prisha by saying people come to the synagogue to worship and God should be foremost on their mind, not romance. Therefore, temporarily removing temptation only allows for better concentration in prayer. (Females are not under Biblical command to pray together in groups as are the males.)

(See also HAREMS, NIDDAH and PURDAH)

PROFESSIONAL DOMINATRIX   See DOMINATRIX, PROFESSIONAL

PROSTITUTION   (Harlotry, Foreign woman, Scortum, Yoshiwara; Cyprieunia—sex with prostitute, Gigolos—male prostitute) Prostitute (pro: before; and statuere: to cause to stand) is the Latin word that refers to people who receive monetary compensation for sex. The Romans used the following prerequisites to determine one's status. A prostitute was one who engaged in sex *pro pecuria, palam,* and *sine delecta*—that is for money, for the public, and without pleasure. Prostitution is practiced by men, women, and children. (See Caution).

The original Hebrew word used for prostitute was *k'deshah*, which meant sacred or holy. Organized prostitution was originally engaged in by temple priestesses and the money gained used to support the house of worship. Aphrodite's priestesses usually remained in her service until their death. Temple prostitution diminished with the invasion of patriarchal tribes and later ended with the spread of Christianity.

Petrie observed that the "early prevalence of mother-right was more favorable to the sexual freedom of women than the later patriarchal system. Thus in very early

Egyptian days a woman could give her favors to any man she chose by sending him her garment, even if she were married." In time the growth of the rights of men led to this being regarded as criminal, but the priestesses of Amen, being under divine protection, retained the privilege to the last. (Flinders Petrie, *Egyptian Tales*, pp. 10, 48)

Prostitutes, regardless of social stigma, were used by kings, soldiers, crusaders, commoners, and even the notorious Pope Alexander VI who in 1501 went down in history as having the most licentious orgy at the Vatican. Burchard, a papal historian, tells how, "one evening in October 1501, the Pope ordered fifty prostitutes to be sent to his chambers. After supper, they danced with the servitors and others who were present, at first clothed but before long naked. Then lighted candles in candlesticks were placed on the floor and chestnuts were thrown among them, and the women were ordered to crawl between the candlesticks on their hands and knees and to try to pick up the chestnuts. Finally a number of prizes were produced, and it was announced that they would be given to those men who, in the opinion of the spectators, 'should have carnal knowledge of the greatest number of the said prostitutes'" (*Sex in History*, by G. Rattray Taylor p. 141).

Ancient Romans accepted prostitution to prevent men from seducing married women and thus breaking up families. They had a special holiday set aside on April 23rd as a festival of the goddess of prostitutes, originally for males and later for females. Messalina, the insatiable wife of the Roman Emperor Claudius, kept a room at a bordello where she could retire and satisfy her curiosity and lust by entertaining a multitude of clients.

Conversely, Theodora, another Roman empress and an ex-prostitute herself, decided to reform all her sister prostitutes. She created a monastery for the rehabilitation of 500 street-walkers. There they were made to conform to strict religious discipline, with the fatal consequence of many committing suicide by throwing themselves out windows while other captives went insane. However, despite her obvious failure in reforming the women, Theodora did not change her opinion as to the best strategy for their reform.

Today men who hire prostitutes may do so after a date without sex, between girlfriends, for sex that they think their partner would not perform, wanting variety, or for sex without commitment or guilt to name just a few of the possibilities. Some purchase the entire night to guarantee that the woman will not abandon them after sex, and some men reason that what they pay the prostitute is less expensive than a date.

Women choose to become prostitutes for just as many reasons. The pay is greater than other types of jobs available to women, they find it exciting, they need male attention, and for some women without job skills it may be the only job available. Almost all of the prostitutes in third world countries and many in America are mothers who are trying to support their family. Charging men makes some feel in control, others enjoy the variety of sex partners, and some do it out of revenge for a philandering husband.

Many prostitutes learn to become insensitive, since she and the client are engaged in exchanging commodities, and this can cause either to feel used emotionally. Prostitutes vary as to what type of sexual services they are willing to offer and adjust their prices accordingly. Prostitutes who work out of their own homes usually have a regular clientele with whom they meet. These address books are sold to another woman when the prostitute retires and the seller then contacts all her clients and tells them she would like to introduce them to a new person. One of these address books was sold in 1975 for $40,000. The media usually glamorizes the high priced call girl and stigmatizes the street walker. The profession as a whole is wrought with hassles from clients, pimps, the police, society, and rapists. Many people assume that this peril is brought upon the prostitute herself because of her morals. Priscilla Alexander, a feminist, disagrees. She states that the "countries with the most restrictive legal systems, including the United States and many countries in Southeast Asia, have the most problems with violence against prostitutes (and women perceived to be *like* prostitutes), thefts associated with prostitution, pimping (especially brutal pimping), and the involvement of juveniles. Conversely, the countries with the least restrictive measures, including the Netherlands, West Germany, Sweden and Denmark, have the least problems. No country, however, is totally safe for prostitutes. The stigma isolates the women, and the remaining laws still serve to perpetuate that stigma, rather than to dispel it and truly legitimize the women who work as prostitutes" (*Sex Work, Writings by Women in the Sex Industry*, "Prostitution: A Difficult Issue for Feminists" by Priscilla Alexander, Edited by Frederique Delacoste & Priscilla Alexander, p. 196). CAUTION: Prostitution is illegal in all U.S. states with the exception of some communities in Nevada. Prostitution is also legal in some states in Australia and in Holland and Germany. The client who requests a prostitute (or any woman) who is inexperienced or not trained in a specific type of sexual activity faces the risk of her not being aware of the correct safety precautions. This applies particularly to any time an object is inserted into the anus, an activity where the skin may be broken, consumption of feces or other body secretions, serious bondage, electrical shock, oxygen deprivation, and catheter play.

(See also BORDELLOS, GEISHAS, HETAERAES, ILLEGAL SEX and SLAVES)

PSYCHROCISM (Psychrotentiginosity)
Psychrocism (psychro: cold, or freezing; cism: act) refers to those who are aroused by either being cold themselves or by watching someone else who is cold.

Hirschfeld relayed the personal confession of a male patient who had a cold fetish:

The thought and sight of chilly dress or pictorial representations of it, induce in me considerable erotic pleasure. My wife naturally has no idea of my abnormal sensations in this respect, and when I make a drawing of the type with which you are familiar, say, a drawing representing a girl with bare arms and shoulders, and dressed only in the flimsiest of undies, on the ice in the skating rink, she always regards it as a joke, for she naturally does not take seriously the exaggerations in which my imagination revels. Such fantasies, accompanied by masturbation, have frequently come to me at times when sexual intercourse with my wife has been impossible for physiological reasons. These fantasies were confined to a single subject—immature girls wearing the lightest clothes in winter (*Sexual Anomalies and Perversions*, by Magnus Hirschfeld, p. 569).

Some people have masturbated by putting a towel in the freezer and then lying it on their genitals and others have used icicles. One California man has reported that on several occasions after swimming in the ocean for 30 minutes during the winter he would obtain an erection that lasted two to three hours. (Personal communication.)

Exposure to intense cold creates a sharp sensation that is similar to other types of physical stimulus that produce tension. The mind changes its focus from intellectual pursuits to physical awareness. Many S/M players use cold contact to heighten awareness of skin sensations. They often alternate cold with heat; such as ice cubes and candle wax.

(See also FETISHES, ICE, MASTURBATION and THALPOTENTIGINY)

PUBIC DRESSING (Pudendacure—female, Medocure—male) Pubic dressing refers to artistic expressions of one's sexuality through genital hair dying, shaving, waxing, body paint, glitter, or stickers.

People who dye their pubic hair prepare it by first bleaching it with the same creams found in drug stores for facial hair, adjusting the time required for bleaching to their own needs. The bleached pubic hair is then dyed with either regular hair

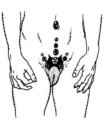

dyes or with colored pastes that come in little pots. These bright colors are applied with toothbrushes. Most other methods of coloring leave residue of the dye on the skin or any fabric that comes in contact with it.

Trimming, waxing, or shaving the genital area is done by people who prefer not to have pubic hair exposed along the legs of their bikinis or g-strings. Some women trim the hair around their labia to match the shorter length found higher on the mons pubis. Complete removal of pubic hair is sometimes done to facilitate body painting and application of stickers.

CAUTION: Shaving creates small cuts in the skin and makes it susceptible to infections, including some sexually transmitted diseases.

(See also BODY PAINTING, PUBIC HAIR SCULPTURING, RINGING, TATTOOS and TRICHOPHILIA)

PUBIC HAIR SCULPTURING Pubic hair sculpturing is done by permanently removing hair falling on the outside of the pattern a person has chosen. The most common shapes used in sculpturing are hearts and triangles. Shapes are more recognizable on people who have thick pubic hair.

Three methods used to accomplish permanent hair removal are electrolysis, thermolysis, and blend modalities which over the period of one to two years will destroy all the hair follicles. All are considered painful and can cost up to $60.00 an hour.

(See also DEPILATION and PUBIC HAIR DRESSING)

PURDAH Purdah (pardah: a veil) refers to hiding the faces of women from strangers and is practiced by some Hindus and Moslems.

Babs Rule, the mother of a woman who married a Saudi Arabian man, wrote of her first experience with purdah.

To them a woman with her hair and face exposed is tantamount to an American woman strolling topless down Main Street... My indication that I would be willing to wear the veil met with wide smiles of relief... all sought at once to show me the proper way to wear the elbays, an opaque black cape-like material which covers one from head to thigh, with a place to tuck your hands... .All this was topped with a lovely square of decorated black chiffon to cover my entire head. I could see through this, though not clearly... I was nothing more than a tall, slim, black blob... Quite a costume for the 120⁻ weather of Saudi in July... Women are not allowed to go anywhere outside the wall unless accompanied by a man. I balked at this control but was told, 'You are much too precious to have to make your way alone. We see that you are always protected and cared for. No one will dare to bother or insult you' (Everyday Life in the Harem, by Babs Rule, pp. 28-9).

Many feminists would feel that this social repression of women was abhorrent and lacked any advantage for women. The one apparent advantage was that the veil, in some instances, provided anonymity for prostitutes or adulteresses.

(See also HAREMS, NIDDAH and PRISHA)

PYGMALIONISM See AGALMATO-PHILIA

PYGOPHILIA (Pygophilemania—kissing buttocks, Pygotripsis—rubbing buttocks) Pygophilia (pyge: buttocks; philia: attachment to) refers to those who are aroused by fondling, licking, or kissing of the buttock area. Some are also aroused by rubbing their buttocks against those of their partner.

(See also ANAL SEX, COITUS INTERFERMORIS, COITUS A MAMILLA and FETISHES)

PYROPHILIA (Incendiarism mania) Pyrophilia (pyros: fire, philia: attachment to) refers to those who are sexually aroused by fire. Fire was one of man's most significant discoveries and has since been adapted for use in energy, medicine, purification rituals, branding, torture, and sexual gratification. Fire and hot liquids can cause serious injury or destruction.

Today the practice that causes greatest concern is pyrophilia or pyromania. Pyromaniacs are defined according to standards set forth in DSM-III-R psychological tests. These describe "deliberate firesetting on more than one occasion, tension or affective arousal before the act, fascination with fire, pleasure or relief when setting fires, witnessing or participating in their aftermath, not setting the fire for monetary gain, to conceal criminal activity, express vengeance or in response to a delusion." Most firesetters are male; however, a recent study involved 13 female delinquents. This study indicated that unconfirmed sexual abuse was a common factor in most of their histories. Saunders and Awad found that "there was a high rate of sexual problems: promiscuity, prostitution and questions about sexual orientation. This finding suggests that female firesetters have a history of sexual problems. However, it is not clear whether or not there is a motivational connection between the two, namely that the firesetting behavior is an expression of, or is motivated by, sexual problems" ("Adolescent Female Firesetters," by Elisabeth B. Saunders, EdD. and George A. Awad, M.D., *The Canadian Journal of Psychiatry*, Vol 36 No. 6, pp. 401-404).

Some pyromaniacs, when setting buildings on fire, seem to feel empowered and sexually aroused by having been the instrument of destruction. After setting a fire, the perpetrators often position themselves where they can watch from a distance and masturbate. Others have been found next to the building where they seem to have gone into an immediate nympholeptic orgasmic state that left them unconscious (a similar phenomenon as experienced by some necrophiles at grave sites). CAUTION: Setting fire to buildings or other property is illegal and can cause untold harm, including death, to innocent victims.

Other aspects of pyrophilia fall into the S/M arena, particularly when fire creates a sense of danger or excitement. The S/M pyrophile can feel empowered by enduring its pain or controlling its flames. Sexual games include the use of chemicals, 'frying' genitals in hot oil, hot wax, okyu, *peau flambÇ*, fire dancing, fire walking, cigarette burns, throwing matches onto pubic hair, and flagellation (tapping) with torches. Dr.

Hirschfeld wrote of a respectable gentleman in the 19th century that severely burned himself by applying acids to his body for sexual pleasure. Today chemical analgesic balms such as Vicks, Ben Gay, or Tiger Balm are used to create a burning sensation on the nipples or genitals. They may also be used on a Q-tip and inserted slightly into the tip of the urethra. Irritants are also sold that are designed specifically for sex. An Asian aphrodisiac, Chinese Red Powder, causes burning of the penis and irritation of the vagina. The ingredients are cinnamon, mustard, pepper, ginger, and various herbs. There are several varieties of these powders. CAUTION: The balm or powder is tested before general application by placing a small amount on the area where it is to be used. A balm that causes irritation is diluted with Vaseline.

Males occasionally have their genitals symbolically fried in oil. The oil is placed into a large cup and the genitals are lowered into the oil for a few seconds. The sensation is similar to the heat of the water in a hot tub and the oil is said not to burn the skin. The remaining oil is allowed to cool on the genitals to serve as a lubricant for cer-  tain sex acts. CAUTION: Vegetable shortening heated over 125 degrees Fahrenheit (using a candy thermometer) can cause burns. People with penile piercings do not engage in this activity; they are particularly susceptible to injury because the metal absorbs the heat and can burn the flesh. In addition, oil can seep into the opening of the piercing and become almost impossible to remove.

The Japanese moxibustion medical ritual consists of gluing cone shaped moxis on to a predetermined spot (usually on the back) and lighting them. The patient endures as the fire finally burns into their flesh leaving circular scars, although some have discovered that placing a thin slice of garlic or ginger root between the moxi and skin reduces this risk ("Scars of Experience: The

Art of Moxibustion in Japanese Medicine and Society," by Margaret M. Lock, *Culture, Medicine and Psychiatry* 2 (1978) pp. 151-175). Moxibustion has been modified for sex play by using Tibetan incense; cutting it into 1/4" sections and gluing it to the skin with a spray adhesive. Several of these are placed on the person's leg and lit at intervals so that the pain is continual. A milder form consists of taking a small burning incense stick and using it to touch the skin of the partner; this is more frightening than painful. One Eastern religion uses a type of burning ritual (cones are placed on the naked scalp) for emotional self-healing. This recovery technique is also emulated by some in the S/M community. This process requires the person to meditate and channel all their negative feelings and thoughts onto the spot that is burning. When the ember has burned out they visualize brushing all these thoughts away with the ashes. ("Branding and Burning," by Fakir Musafar, QSM lecture, November 18, 1989)

Peau flambé is practiced in several ways. Some people rub alcohol directly onto the skin and light it, others make special torches (wood dowel, cotton center, a Coleman mantle, and cloth cover). These are soaked in 70% alcohol, drained of excess alcohol, and lit. The torch is then either held under a person's outstretched arm, run along the skin, or used to flagellate (tap) the back or legs. ("Playing with Fire," by Celeste, QSM lecture, September 15, 1990)

There is a female artist in San Francisco whose routine begins as she carries a bowl of flames onto a dark stage placing it on the floor where she does a dance ritual around the bowl of fire then performs slow mystical gyrations in the subdued light of the fire. She then reaches in the bowl and removes blue flames that she raises in reverence toward the heavens. The dance builds to a climax as she uses torches to paint parts of her legs, torso and arms with this flame. The dance culminates in a manner reminiscent of the ending scene in the ballet "Swan Lake." ("Dancing with the Spiritual Flames," by C. Rose and E. Sweet, QSM lecture, March 21, 1991) CAUTION: Fire dancing has its own precautions. The alcohol (70% only) is left sitting in an open dish for a couple of hours to weaken its strength. The torch must be made without glue, paint, air pockets, or excess fabric that would create a hotter flame. Excess alcohol is drained to reduce the risk of cause a fire. All clothing and hair near skin areas to be used are removed prior to play. Perfume cannot be worn by either person. Areas burned are monitored for redness. A knowledge of first aid and fire safety is required.

Other types of fire play involve using a cigarette or match to burn individual body hairs without touching the skin. Matches are used by some to throw onto pubic hair. The match extinguishes itself after scorching one or two hairs. The match must be thrown accurately so as not to land on bare skin or bedding. Some use the side of a cigarette to run along a person's face, chest, or penis. This does not burn but is frightening. CAUTION: Cigarettes are not used to burn the skin because they do not create clean burns and as a result easily become infected.

Firewalking is not considered sex play but is used very effectively for stimulation. The burning sensation caused by walking across flaming embers lasts for about two hours. Therefore, some prefer to engage in sex just prior to the event. Firewalks that take place at midnight in the woods offer this opportunity. People easily slip away from the circle of people dancing and singing chants around the fire. Firewalking is being used in the United States as a form of psychological healing. People's past traumas are reprogrammed by a new frightening event, however this event is one they have conquered, helping them feel elated and empowered. (Firewalk Retreat, by Catherine Grace, April 22, 1989) CAUTION: Firewalking can cause first or second degree burns on the soles of the feet.

(See also ELECTRICAL SHOCK and SAFE SEX)

Q

QUADOUSHKA The Quadoushka sexual teachings are part of the tradition of the American Cherokee Indians. Quadoushka seems similar to Eastern sex tantra in that it emphasizes breathing techniques, energy balance, and whole body orgasms. Quadoushka utilizes Cherokee ceremonies and ritual for exploring one's sexuality. A knowledge of Eastern tantra, yoga, and chakras are recommended to enhance this training. There do not appear to be many books written specifically about Quadoshka; however, classes and seminars are taught in the San Francisco area.

(See also BRADYCUBIA, KABAZZA and TANTRA)

QUEENING The term queening refers to the European practice of a dominant female using a man's head as her throne. The woman sits in one of several positions, either on the side of the man's head or so

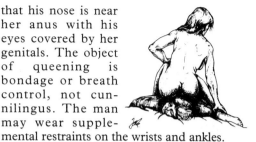

that his nose is near her anus with his eyes covered by her genitals. The object of queening is bondage or breath control, not cunnilingus. The man may wear supplemental restraints on the wrists and ankles.

A slightly comparable American sex scene is where a stripper completely disrobes and stands over a sitting male with his head tilted back so that her genitals are only a couple of inches above his face. She stays in this position moving her pelvis to the music for about five minutes. The male is not permitted to touch her in any manner during this exhibition.

(See also BONDAGE/THREE LEGGED BLOOMERS, CAT FIGHTING, OXYGEN REGULATION and WRESTLING)

R

RAPE Rape (rapere: to seize) is a term used to denote coercion of a person to engage in nonconsensual sex. Statutory rape applies to sex with minors whether it is consensual or not.

Governments have used different types of punishment to discourage rapists. The Assyrians permitted the father of a virgin to violate the wife of the rapist. The Babylonians punished both the rapist and married victims by executing them, and the English only punished the rapist if he refused to marry the female. The Persians punished men caught in harems by having their male slaves rape them before castration. To accomplish this they hammered on a tent spike to force the anal sphincter open (*Perverse Crimes in History*, pp. 202).

A clear understanding of this word is critical for many reasons. There seems to be an ambiguity between the definition and the types of rape that are prosecuted. In general, men who use weapons, seriously injure the victim, attack a stranger who resists, or rape a woman in her home seem to be prosecuted more often. The victims least able to convince a jury of rape are prostitutes, married women who charge their husbands, single women who are attacked by dates, those who are attacked by someone they meet in a bar, and those who do not sustain serious physical injury. Society's vague and inconsistent definition of rape has resulted in false convictions as well as false acquittals. Diana Scully, a sociologist who studied convicted rapists, shows the diversity in what they believe constitutes rape. One rapist remarked that "[r]ape is when a woman's life is in danger, without a doubt, or when she is beaten unconscious." At the other end of the spectrum were comments by those who had changed their interpretation after incarceration. "To dominate someone to the extent you impose your will when they say 'no', to take without consent, violently or otherwise, if the victim is scared into it" (*Understanding Sexual Violence, A Study of Convicted Rapists*, p. 87).

Rape does not appear to be found in all cultures. Peggy Sanday substantiates this in a study of tribal societies where she found that rape was nonexistent or rare in 44 out of 95 groups. She attributes rape as having evolved when the group became more dependent on men for survival than on female fertility (*The Socio-Cultural Context of Rape*, by Peggy Reeves Sanday, 1979). Scully added that other social factors seem to encourage violence against women; such as those "related to cultural attitudes, the power relationship between women and men, the social and economic status of women relative to the men of their group, and the amount of other forms of violence in the society" (*Understanding Sexual Violence, A Study of Convicted Rapists*, p. 48).

Rape may be interpreted differently by different cultures. Among certain South American tribes, women wear only ornamental strings over their genitals. However, they are extremely modest about exposing their inner labia and vagina. They define rape as when a victim is dragged off, laid on her back, legs spread for all the men to see her shame, and violently raped by all the men in her tribe. This is the punishment for some religious offenses. However, a man who catches a woman traveling down a path and forcibly leads her into the woods for sex in a sitting position is not a rapist. The tribe has as part of their social system a strong belief in compassion that includes not only the need to provide for those who are hungry but also those in need of sex (*Anxious Pleasures*, by Thomas Gregor, pp. 102-4). Therefore, here it seems that part of the definition of rape hinges on whether it was done as a punishment or out of desire and need. African Gusii tribesmen in Kenya also differ in their interpretation of rape as a crime. Their religious belief system teaches that a person who breaks taboos such as rape against relatives is a victim of mysterious spirit forces. This person or his family is either assumed to have angered their dead ancestors, or they are the victims of the evil magic of envious neighbors. Locking a

rapist away would only delay or transfer the evil acts; their answer is to find the person causing the criminal's behavior. "A diviner may ultimately determine that witchcraft is the root of the problem and, for example, direct the supplicant to purchase from a sorcerer, *omonyamasira*, retaliative magic, or *emesira*, designed to eliminate both the witch and his witchcraft. If this, the last resort, fails to alleviate the affliction, it is understood that the witch's magic, *oborogi*, is of some especially resistant sort. Accordingly, the community waits to see who will die first, the victim or the victimizer." The tribes then tolerate known rapists, as well as other criminals, living among them. Levine, who lived among this tribe, also noted that rape, "while treated as criminal behavior by the British, the Gusii people regarded as necessary for the preservation of kin-avoidance, *chinsoni*, and the prevention of *amasangia*, death following adultery" ("Crime or Affliction? Rape in an African Community," by Sarah Levine, *Culture, Medicine and Psychiatry* 4 (1980) pp. 151-165, D. Reidel Publishing Co., Dordrecht, Holland and Boston, USA).

Statistics show that up to 25% of heterosexual men admit to using force to get the sex they want. Many date rapists share common attitudes and behavior that may serve to alert women. Many disregard their wishes, or show uncontrolled anger, have unreasonable prejudices (a signal of not having compassion for others). They may also make references to other women as being weak or hysterical, and insist on meeting in isolated areas.

Diana Scully discovered that, contrary to popular opinion, the majority profile of violent rapists did not include men who had been beaten or molested as children; 71% of the acts were premeditated, the men tended to be less aggressive, less independent, most had religious affiliations, disliked their father rather than their mother, and had consensual sexual relations two to seven times a week at the time of committing rape. In addition Scully found that they had a higher ratio of physical violence against their lover than the general public but lower than felons who did not rape; were traditional in their view that "women need male protection and that they should be more virtuous than men, for example, by not telling dirty jokes;" matched traditional rather than modern masculine role for themselves; were low in general feelings of hostility toward women (the study did show that the more traditional value they placed on women the more hostile feelings they had against them); many believed that in general violence against women was a man's right; had consumed alcohol prior to attack; or used rape for revenge or punishment against a lover that angered or rejected them. If these men think at all about what the victim feels they believe that after her initial resistance she enjoys the sex.

The street rapist is often motivated by a period of stress or disagreement with a female partner or relative. He seems to transfer his anger from the person who is the source of the pain to an emotionally non-threatening target. Anger arises from a feeling of helplessness. In order for the rapist to re-establish control he needs a target who holds no emotional power over him.

A date rapist often does not have this prior trauma. He merely believes, as do most of his counterparts, that it is acceptable to use force on a woman. He justifies his act by saying women are inferior, she was teasing him, or she had an immoral character. Rape may even be more arousing to him than consensual sex because society forbids it.

Some rapists have sex once and leave, others keep the woman captive until they act out several scenarios, and a few may engage only in fetish behavior. Some become sadists who get caught up in a euphoria caused by watching fear or pain in the victim and will often continue this until she expires. Unlike people who engage in S/M they do not lose enthusiasm when they realize their partner is not aroused; nor do they have experience in how to keep this reaction from escalating. While many of these rapists do not ejaculate it is reasonable to assume that some of these do. (See ORGASM)

Often males, children, the mentally ill, deaf, and blind are targets of rape. The effect of rape on women is often deeply traumatic. They suffer from nightmares, may relocate, have difficultly in working or studying, or becoming intimate with another person. A woman who was dragged by the hair up stairs by her abductor began shaving her head to ensure that it would never occur again. Some victims become lesbian and others have had to be institutionalized. Many rapists, on the other hand, seem to suffer no emotional trauma or guilt from the act itself. Others feel extreme remorse and even beg for treatment that costs them their sex drive.

Advice about how women should react when attacked varies according to the type of rapist. There are rapists who say they would let the woman free if she screamed and physically resisted, others say it wouldn't help her, and a few say it would make things worse. Therefore, although it provides no guarantee of safety, the odds seem to favor full resistance. Many police departments, martial arts clubs, and women's groups offer basic classes in self defense.

Typically, convicted rapists are reported to be from a lower income group. A man who has control of one's income uses that as his weapon; the man who is not able to seduce and has no control over a victim's income uses physical force. A woman who has no control over the victim's income and no physical strength uses seduction. Society is tolerant of misuse of sexual power by the affluent, harshest on the poor, and ignores the female.

The initial emotional response to homosexual rape is shock, humiliation, fear, and anxiety. The victim may later become reclusive and feel guilt followed by anger and depression. Their trauma, as opposed to women, often includes confusion over their sexual identity because of their natural physiological orgasmic response to anal or oral sex. Young men may become withdrawn, feel emotionally numb, avoid contact sports, fear men, develop a quick temper, low self-esteem, and assume that they are effeminate. Parents can help reduce the risk of rape by educating their children while they are very young. Books, such as *Alice Doesn't Babysit Anymore*, are helpful.

Another recent book, titled *Broken Boys/Mending Men, Recovery from Childhood Sexual Abuse,* by Stephen Grubman-Black, was written for others who have been abused.

People sometimes unjustly accuse others of rape for personal reasons. These have been listed as "assault during or after voluntary coitus, blackmail, jealousy, fear of pregnancy or venereal disease, or revenge." They also include claims made by children because of "an unwelcomed stepfather, avoiding parental punishment for returning home beyond the curfew hour, and false accusation by a known prostitute for failure to receive payment for her services" ("False Accusations of Rape," by J. H. MacDonald, *Medical Aspects of Human Sexuality,* Vol. 7, No. 5, May 1973, pp. 170-194).

Arthur Schiff, a physician working at a Rape Treatment Center in Miami, wrote of several such cases. In one a girl was "jilted by her steady boyfriend for a new girl in the neighborhood. When the new girl moved shortly afterwards to a distant city, the boy returned to his former girlfriend. At a school dance, she seduced him and had sexual intercourse with him in the playground. She reported that she had been raped. After several hours spent untangling the various threads, it was finally learned that she had not been raped, but had given her consent. She had wanted 'to teach him a lesson' for abandoning her in favor of the new girl." Schiff also listed an 8 year old girl who reported a false rape hoping to be taken from her home and custody given to her grandparents, a 16 year old who afraid of being pregnant invented a rape story to protect her reputation, and of a 41 year old news reporter who falsely claimed to have been raped to get an inside story of how rape victims were handled inside the Rape Treatment Center ("An Unusual Case of Pseudo Rape," by A.F. Schiff, M.D., *Journal of Forensic Sciences* Vol 20, No. 4, October 1975, pp. 637-641). It is as inhumane to falsely charge another of rape as it is to rape.

(See also BIASTOPHILIA, DACRYPHILIA, ILLEGAL SEX, LUST MURDER, SADISM and SEXUAL HARASSMENT)

RELICS   (Thesauromania—arousal from collecting articles belonging to women) A relic (relike: remains) refers to an object that serves to remind one of the past. A relic can be a body part or an object associated with a saint that is kept and used in memorial services. Relics of loved ones were often used before photographs were common. Soldiers often carried such things as shoe laces, rings, a bracelet of hair, feather, or garter. Men wore these in 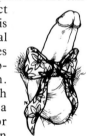 their hats, on arm bands, or over their hearts, often pausing during the day to kiss the object that once belonged to their lover. Other men, according to historical records quoted by Havelock Ellis, wore these relics around their genitals. "A captain told me that when they were rifling the dead bodies of the French gentlemen after the first invasion they found that many of them had their mistresses' favors tied about their genitories." Ellis continues with the accounts of women who had their husband's genitals cut off upon their death and kept them in small silver and gold caskets, and a man who kept the skull of his dead mistress on his desk.

Lust murderers often collect memorabilia from their victims. These are sometimes used later during masturbation.

(See also CHARMS and LOVE POTIONS)

RHABDOPHILIA   (Flagellation fetish) Rhabdophilia (rhabdos: a rod, philia: attachment to) refers to people who are aroused by being caned, or flagellated. The caning is often combined with humiliation or fear in a fantasy scenario. In order for pain or injury to produce the desired euphoric effects it must be anticipated, threatening, or part of a scene that includes a person to whom they are sexually attracted. Some people engage in self-flagellation to produce a cathartic effect without a sexual partner.

(See also ALGOPHILIA, BED OF NAILS and FLAGELLATION)

RINGING   Ringing is a term used to describe permanent piercings. These are ornamented with jewelry and can be on any part of the body where the flesh protrudes: ears, nose, nipples, penis, scrotum, labia, or navel.

Erotic piercings have been used for hundreds of years by many diverse cultures: Roman soldiers, Victorian aristocrats, natives of Southeast Asia, and even Egyptian royalty at one time wore navel rings.

People are attracted to piercings for many reasons. It may be a commitment to a leather lifestyle, purely aesthetic, practical for S/M play, to make a statement about one's sexuality, to increase sensitivity to touch, or as a way to protest the shame or stigma society has placed on the genitals by enhancing them with jewelry. Today many Europeans use genital piercings as a symbol of marriage. A gold ring on the genitals of a partner seems to convey more of a sexual commitment than a ring on the finger. Many in the San Francisco area think that only gays have pierced nipples. This misconception may be due to the fact that women do not walk down Castro Street topless. CAUTION: There are several factors involved in ringing and only an experienced person is recommended to perform this procedure. The exact location of the piercing can be critical and sterile techniques are necessary just as in temporary piercings. Anesthetics are made available by some but not all piercers. Pain has not prevented many from having areas such as the nipples and glans penis pierced. Surgical stainless steel, 14k gold, platinum, and niobium are used for jewelry. People react differently to metals; some cannot tolerate the nickel content of stainless steel, or react badly to copper in gold alloys. Substitution of other metals often clears up the problem. The needle is one size larger than the ring or bar. A piercing may take anywhere from two weeks to three months to heal depending on the area pierced. The labia heals fast while nipples take longer. A new piercing has to be washed with surgical soap or salt water for about five days while rotating the jewelry. A piercing should always have something in it to prevent it from closing. Fishing line is used because it offers partial concealment when one chooses to use discretion. If a piercing becomes infected it is recommended that the jewelry be replaced with wire filament because it keeps the wound from closing and allows pus an escape route. People are individual as to the type of metal their body accepts or rejects.

CLITORIS   Clitoral piercings are rare due to the initial pain and risk of severing essential nerves although one woman did report constant intense arousal from this type of piercing. Clitoral hood (the equivalent of the male foreskin) piercings are very attractive and if the ball of the ring hangs over the clitoral area it can provide extra stimulation.

LABIA   Labia rings do not create an erotic sensation themselves. However, some women have hung strings or chains with weights on the ends and gone dancing without underpants. The swinging weights cause the labia to rub against each other. The labia rings, if pierced symmetrically, can be used to pull the labia apart for cunnilingus or can be tied together for a mock infibulation. Women who have stretched the size of the piercing have been able to place a heart-shaped lock through both labia.

NIPPLE   Nipple rings were at one time worn by Roman centurions who used them as a symbol of their courage and some used them to anchor the corners of their capes. Victorian women wore nipple rings to increase the size of their nipples and make them more noticeable. Today men and women wear them for ornamental purposes, S/M play, or to make a serious statement about their sexuality. Diamond studded gold rings and gold shields are available at piercing salons and by mail order. ("Nipple Piercing," by Jim Ward, QSM lecture, September 23, 1989)

PENIS There are many types of rings that are worn through the penis and each offers a different benefit.

The Prince Albert was originally used by Victorian men as a way to keep their penis pulled flat so as not to protrude when wearing the tight pants that were popular at that time. The men slipped a sash through

the ring and anchored it along their inseam. This piercing is designed so that the ring enters the urethra and comes out the bottom of the frenulum. It is claimed that Prince Albert wore one to hold back the foreskin on his uncircumcised penis, making it easier to keep clean. This ring puts pressure against the frenulum and urethra during penetration and creates stronger sensations for men and their partners. For this reason it is recommended by men who use condoms.

The Ampallang was once found in ancient South East Asia, chiefly among the Dayaks. It is a bar or rod that pierces through the glans horizontally and above the urethra giving more of a feeling of firmness to the glans penis during penetration. The procedure for this ancient custom has been described as follows.

At first the glans is made bloodless by pressing it between the two arms of a bent strip of bamboo. At each of these arms there are openings at the required position opposite each other, through which a sharp pointed copper pin is pressed after the glans has become less sensitive. Formerly a pointed bamboo chip was used for this purpose. The bamboo clamp is removed, and the pin, fastened by a cord, is kept in the opening until the canal has healed up. Later on the copper pin (oetang) is replaced by another one, generally of tin, which is worn constantly. Only during hard work or at exhausting enterprises is the metal pin replaced by a wooden one. Exceptionally brave men have the privilege, together with the chief, of boring a second canal, crossing the first, into

the glans. Distinguished men may, in addition, wear a ring round the penis, which is cut from the scales of the pangolin, and studded with blunt points (Sexual Life of Primitive People, by H. Fehlinger, pp. 107-8).

These bars may be further ornamented. In the southern Philippines a ring is used that goes "completely around the penis but held in place by a pin or bar rowel-shaped ...These inserts are also

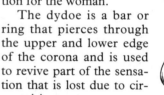

said to make intromission difficult. One report states that a person with the insert cannot deflower a woman, so servants, without the inserts, must undertake this task" (*The Penis Inserts of Southeast Asia*, by Donald E. Brown, James W. Edwards, and Ruth P. Moore, p. 3).

The apadravya is a bar placed through the glans penis vertically, being inserted just above the corona and extending down through the frenulum. The irregular movement during intercourse causes somewhat of a vibrating sensation for the woman.

The dydoe is a bar or ring that pierces through the upper and lower edge of the corona and is used to revive part of the sensation that is lost due to circumcision.

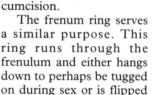

The frenum ring serves a similar purpose. This ring runs through the frenulum and either hangs down to perhaps be tugged on during sex or is flipped over the glans and used to stimulate the frenulum area and base of corona, or some use it as a cock ring to sensitize the tip of the penis.

SCROTUM Piercing the side of the scrotum is an ancient Arab tradition done at puberty to "keep the testicles from ever rising back into the body." The hafada piercing is ornamental and some add expensive jewels for enhancement. Another piercing is the guiche, which is placed slightly beneath the posterior of the scrotum along what looks like a seam running to the anus. This ring is common in the South Pacific and is said to prolong and intensify orgasms when gently pulled upon. The correct placement is crucial for the desired effect.

Many people worry that a physician may be critical or refuse health care to someone who is wearing sexual jewelry. However, most are professional and will not let their personal opinions keep them from giving any patient adequate care. Airport security alarms are rarely set to the sensitivity needed to detect a few metal rings. ("Male Piercing," by Jim Ward, QSM lecture, November 4, 1989)

(See also JEWELRY and PIERCING)

RITUAL SEX   Rituals are procedures or ceremonies that are prescribed and carried out at specified times. "The word ritual comes from *rtÅ*, Sanskrit for menses. Menses, literally month, is from the Latin, directly translated into English to denote the periods of the yearly calendar. The earliest rituals were connected to the women's monthly bleeding" (*The Once & Future Goddess*, by Elinor W. Gadon, p. 2).

Religious rituals have included some very unusual sex practices throughout history. The American Indian Hopi tribes observed a snake dance ritual where cross-dressing, zoophilia, and switching partners were common. The Roman emperor Heliogabalus performed rituals to his god that included exotic dances, dressing in the garb of a priestess, the slaughter and sacrifice of numerous animals and humans, and throwing the castrated members of young boys into a sacrificial fire. Rituals of the May Games and Feast of Fools included orgies, transvestism, and the slinging of excrement.

Satanic Black Masses were celebrated as a farce in direct opposition to religious rituals that were being forced on people. One Black Mass was described in J.A. Roger's writings. "In the genuine Black Mass, the priest officiated at a regular altar with bread, wine, and missal. He was nude save for a chasuble about the waist, which was lifted from time to time in complete exposure of himself. The altar boys were nude and so were some of the women worshippers. At a certain part of the ceremony one of the women offered herself to the priest, the rest of the congregation following his example. The sexual excitement created an atmosphere in which the worshippers felt themselves lifted on high and saw their fondest hopes being fulfilled." Black Masses have been staged in some European brothels for the benefit of curious clients (*Sex and Race in the New World*, by J.A. Rogers, p. 330).

One of the most notorious sex rituals was one practiced by a Christian sect that began in Russia during the late 18th century. The Skopzis, who referred to themselves as the "White Doves," believed that Jesus was sent to castrate men thereby making it impossible for them to sin. However, he failed and died as a martyr instead. Jesus was then replaced by their savior Szelivanov, who, like Joseph Smith, wrote his own holy scriptures called the "Book of the Dove" that takes precedence over the Bible. Szevlivanov recommended a literal interpretation of passages that spoke of amputating body parts that cause one to sin; therefore, because the original sin in their eyes was sex, it was only appropriate to castrate themselves. Szevlivanov castrated himself by baptism with a red-hot iron and convinced many others to be baptized in a similar fashion. Female converts who could no longer be sexually satisfied by their husbands were allowed to engage in prostitution; the proceeds went into the church's treasury. Some of the male converts failed in their attempt at castration by fire and were relegated to a lower position of the Lesser Seal. Soon orgies and sadomasochism became part of religious services. This was encouraged by those who had been successful in castration because they still retained sexual passion and were not only excited by watching others indulge but were able to obtain sexual release by dance and sadomasochistic activities. During these rituals a virgin was brought into the orgy to be impregnated with the savior.

She was then undressed and immersed in a tub of warm water. That her pain might be relieved, she was given an image of the Holy Ghost to hold while the old women amputated her left breast. The bleeding virgin was then placed upon an altar, and an almost inhuman orgy followed. The amputated breast was hacked into tiny pieces and grabbed by the worshippers to be eaten while still warm . . . Almost invariably the "God Mother" was impregnated in the course of this orgy . . . On the eighth day of the child's life, his left side was lanced by a finely pointed spear, and the warm blood that flowed from the wound in the infant body was drunk in the communion service. The body itself was dried and pounded into a powder . . . to be offered the worshippers on the first day of the Easter season (The Sacred Fire, by B.Z. Goldberg, pp. 259-262).

Rituals temporarily separate the participant from his normal identity, replacing his interpretation of events and response with prescribed behavior. Rituals dictate behavior, control thoughts, emotions, and when engaged in often can restrict the amount and clarity of information received. These happen to be the four components necessary for any type of mind control as reported by Dr. Steve Hassan, a former member of the Moonies (*Combatting Cult Mind Control,* p. 59).

Just as sex was often part of rituals that were associated with other aspects of our lives, rituals are used today in sex. One type of ritual is used in training sex slaves. Lady Tanith, a professional dominatrix, describes its importance. "The dominant is also expected to don a special costume and to treat the submissive in a highly ritualized manner. Enforcing certain rituals is also helpful to a submissive in internalizing his slavery. The effect of ritual behavior on the human psyche is age-old and well-documented, arousing emotions that tend to be religious in nature...When a slave is performing a series of regular, required behaviors, he is completely encapsulated in the context of the ritual. He is entirely isolated from his 'normal' environment. He literally loses himself and his sense of separate identity, submerging himself totally into his role. He does not think; he performs...the ritual begins the transition between 'normal' and 'slave-Master/Mistress' mode" (*A Tangled Web: The Art of Slavery, A Training Manual for Mistresses, Masters and Slaves, Version 1.1,* by Lady Tanith, p. 5).

(See also FERTILITY RITES, ORGIES, SACRIFICES, SATAN WORSHIP, SEX MAGICK and SLAVES)

ROBOTISM   See ANDROIDISM and COMPUTER SEX

S

LEOPOLD VON SACHER-MASOCH Sacher-Masoch (1836-1905) was an aristocratic Austrian novelist who wrote sexual tales of men being dominated, humiliated, and disciplined by beautiful women. His book *Venus in Furs* gave him the most notoriety.

Sacher-Masoch courted many women and was able to persuade several to oblige him by acting out his fantasies. The notoriety he received for his novels gained him the attention of Richard von Krafft-Ebing, a neurologist and psychologist, who decided to label his popular passion as a disease;

along with nymphomania, fetishes, homosexuality, and masturbation.

Krafft-Ebing's decision to use the term masochism was disturbing to Sacher-Masoch who was only one of many through history who wrote of this type of sexual proclivity.

(See also DOMINANCE/SUBMISSION, HUMILIATION, MASOCHISM, PARAPHILIAS and MARQUIS DE SADE)

SACOFRICOSIS   Sacofricosis refers to the practice a few men have of cutting a hole in the bottom of their front pant pocket and then sticking their hand through to masturbate. This allows men to be able to masturbate in public places with less risk of detection. The slang term is "pocket pool."

(See also DOCKING and EXHIBITIONISM)

SACRIFICES (Sphagia, Thusiai) Sacrifice (sacer: sacred and facere: to make) is the act of making an object sacred, by offering it to a god. The term is also used to refer to the voluntary forfeiture of something valuable.

People make sacrifices in relationships for similar reasons as they used to do in religious worship. It may be done as a sign of reverence, submission, a tribute, atonement for sins, a price to purchase happiness, an exchange of present pain for future bliss, or a form of masochism.

The methodology of human sacrifice varied according to culture. C.W. Jung related an example of a legend from the 5th century of a city near Rome where maidens were taken to "a certain cavern in which could be seen a frightful and terrible dragon of marvelous size, a mechanical contrivance that brandished a sword in its mouth and had shining red jewels for eyes. Every year girls were consecrated and adorned with flowers, and then given to the dragon in sacrifice. For, as they descended with their gifts, they unwittingly touched the step to which this devilish mechanism of a dragon was attached, and were instantly pierced through with the sword that sprang out, so that innocent blood was shed" (*The Collected Works of C.G. Jung*, (Bollingen Series XX) 20 vols., 5, par. 574, quoted in *Rape and Ritual*, p. 117).

Males were also sacrificed. In India female devotees of Kali the Goddess of Death "hunted men in packs. Like thugs and assassins, their aim was to spring upon the unwary traveler and sacrifice him to the Black Mother of Destruction. Torture and sexual abuse were the usual preliminaries to a death involving genital dismemberment, disembowelment, and decapitation. A common method of torment employed by the singhistriyan (tiger women) was that of slowly and persistently masturbating their victim to the point of senselessness"

(*Perverse Crimes in History*, by R.E.L. Masters and Eduard Lea, p. 203).

The Aztecs flayed the skin from a victim which a priest then wore during the ensuing ceremonial. The victim's remains were later served as the main course of their religious feast.

The female worshippers of the fire god Moloch sacrificed their infants to build passion for lesbian orgies. Goldberg describes these rites. "Thus women, too, came to serve Moloch. They had their priestesses, who prostituted themselves to the women worshippers . . . When the women came to offer their sacrifices, they cast into the devouring belly of Moloch whatever there was upon them or within their arms . . . In the heat of her ever-increasing passion, she brought the greatest sacrifice a mother could offer. It was then that Moloch first tasted the flesh and blood of the infants thrown within him by mothers gone mad with desire" (*The Sacred Fire*, by B.Z. Goldberg, pp. 150-151). It must be remembered that infanticide was a common method of population control for many cultures and the opportunity to sanctify this act was welcomed by many. This civilization eventually encountered the problem of overpopulation and modified their sacrificial offerings accordingly.

Nominal human and animal sacrifice exists today among a few Satanic cults. Most of these are individuals who attribute their lust for murder to their affiliation in a small cult. These people are responsible for an estimated 12 human deaths a year. An example of a cult sacrifice was found in a January 1986 *Penthouse* article by Dr. Joel Norris and Jerry Allen Potter. They relayed the court testimony of a woman involved in a cult sacrifice in Massachusetts. "While telling the court about the killing, Murphy explained how the group had struck Marsden in the head with rocks, cut off her fingers to remove her rings, stripped her, slit her throat, and severed her head and kicked it around. Drew then had sex with the decapitated body, and carved an X on the victim's chest while speaking 'a strange language'. He then put his thumb in the dead Marsden's blood and made an X mark on

Murphy's forehead, telling her that she was now initiated into the group."

(See also FERTILITY RITES, FESTIVALS and RITUAL SEX)

SADISM (Tyrannism; Leptosadism—mild form of sadism, Mastix—female sadist and Sapphosadism—lesbian sadism) Sadism is the name given to the sexual practices of those who derive pleasure from dominating or inflicting emotional and physical pain on others. The word sadism was formulated after the release of writings by Marquis de Sade to characterize that type of sexual cruelty. Unfortunately the term was extended to encompass consensual sex play between adults, thus causing much prejudice and misunderstanding during the next two centuries.

Consensual S/M and sadism are as different as normal sex compared to rape. True sadists are not concerned with whether the victim has a pleasurable response; people who play consensual S/M are extremely concerned.

Sadistic tendencies are inherent in humans and animals alike. Sadism is linked to our aggressive response in protecting ourselves and yet still preserving the group. Injuries are physical signals that alert us to the resolution of a conflict or the surrender of an opponent. For instance, two dogs will fight over a bone until one of them submits, as evident by a vulnerable pose or visible wound. At this point both the victor and the loser will experience euphoria due to the release of b-endorphins. In addition, the victor will experience a sense of power and enhanced self-esteem. There appears to be new evidence that the immune system is also stimulated when one is exposed to others suffering. Drs. Irwin, Livnat, and Ader address this in the following quote:

Consistent with the earlier results, only those animals exposed to the environment in which animals were being shocked (No Shock With) exhibited an increase in splenic NK [Natural Killer] activity...It may be speculated that in anticipation of such a threat, physiological changes occur which would prepare the organism to respond to the environmental challenge. Consequently, the enhancement noted in

NK activity may be the byproduct of increased sympathetic activation, or it may be an adaptive response in the face of possible physical insult. Although the nature of the cues remains to be determined, these data do indicate that the environmental context in which a stressor is applied may be an important determinant of the immunological consequences of stress exposure. Stressor Associated Cues Influence Immune Function, by J. Irwin, S. Livnat, and R. Ader, Queen's University, Kingston, Canada, K7L 3N6 and University of Rochester, Rochester, N.Y., 14642

In sadism it appears that people are capable of achieving relief of free-floating anxiety by transferring their fight-flight-sex response onto another person or object. For instance, a man who is angry at a spouse is able to humiliate, rape or mutilate another person and relieve their stress due to the signals of defeat in their victim. The fact that the sadist does not know or care for his victim makes it easier for him to carry the attack further than he normally would. A person who does attack their lover may use even greater violence because a love object creates a higher level of anxiety. People who reach these extremes of tension may lose their ability to think or behave rationally, their minds may become blank or replay other incidents, and they may beat or mutilate their partner until they regain a conscious state. Dr. Seymour Antelman et. al. have studied the results of repeated exposures to stress in animals and stated the following:

Even a single exposure to a brief stressful event—be it environmental or pharmacological—can induce extremely persistent, cascading sensitization to subsequent stressors or related stimuli which recall the memory of the original trauma (Antelman et al. 1980, 1987, 1988; Antelman and Chiodo 1983; Antelman 1988). We have recently proposed that such findings may be relevant to the development of syndromes such as delayed post-traumatic stress disorder, bulimia and panic (Antelman 1988). (Persistent sensitization of clonidine-induced hypokinesia following one exposure to a stressor: possible relevance to panic disorder and its treatment, by Seymour M. Antelman, Steven Knopf, Donna Kocan, and David J.

Edwards, Department of Psychiatry, Western Psychiatric Institute and Clinic, University of Pittsburgh School of Medicine, 3811 O'Hara Street, Pittsburgh, PA 15213, USA and Department of Physiology Pharmacology, University of Pittsburgh School of Dental Medicine, Pittsburgh, PA 15213, USA as printed in *Psychopharmacology* Springer-Verlag 1989, 98:97)

There seems to be a fear among S/M practitioners of losing control of anger in consensual sex games although there has never been any documentation of this occurring. Most injuries are accidental. War veterans may flash back to personal experiences of being tortured. It is recommended that anyone who knows they may experience this effect avoid situations that trigger it. Others who feel themselves becoming overstimulated may find it beneficial to focus on solving math, logistic, or verbal problems while they simultaneously take slow deep (into the abdomen) breaths. Another method, if practiced before the level of anxiety rises too high, is to visualize physical defeat or even an open wound on an anonymous person. This reinforces the fact that one can be responsible for their own actions by proving their ability to release anger without resorting to physical violence. Similar mechanisms work for those who when faced with anxiety feel the need to mutilate themselves; however, instead of visualizing injury on another person it may be done while looking at one's own hand.

Some sadists see themselves as compassionate because they believe in killing the victim before they begin the mutilation of their body. Those that are emotionally numb may only be able to elicit an emotional response through the sight of a wound. Their pleasure comes from this and not the fear, humiliation, or torture they inflict on the victim. Others prey on the victim's emotional reaction to their power, perhaps because their anger comes from others having psychologically abused them in a similar manner and they want to see their pain mirrored in the victim's face. This is their tool for revenge.

As intelligent humans we are able to find alternative solutions to how we achieve closure or release of anxiety. We do not need to argue or abuse our adversary or lover to the point where they display extreme remorse, pain, or suffering. Today, therapists are able to recommend treatments for controlling our own anxiety such as biofeedback, group therapy, support groups, laughter, exercise, and diet change.

(See also ACROTOMOPHILIA, ALGOPHILIA, AUTOMASOCHISM, CICATRIZATION, DACRYLAGNIA, HYBRISTOPHILIA, LUST MURDER, MASOCHISM, MISOGYNIST, MUTILATION, RAPE, SYMPHOROPHILIA and TORTURE)

SAFE SEX   Each type of sex practice requires its own special precautions. We begin by learning our partner's special needs with a discussion of their general health. A disclosure of the types of medication one takes and its purpose is essential. A predisposition to heart disease, diabetes, strokes, fainting, and hyperventilation should be discussed. Instructions need to be given for action to be taken in case of an attack and who is to be notified. A regular partner, as opposed to a stranger, is preferred when engaging in the more unusual forms of sex. Most novices will say they know how to tie a partner to the bed but their experience comes from watching movies. A lack of credible knowledge or experience on the part of a partner can potentially cost another's life in a matter of minutes.

ANAL PLAY   Anal play is considered a high risk activity for contracting the AIDS virus. Anal play includes licking the anus or penetration with the penis, dildos, fingers, fist, or enema. There are several additional dangers inherent in anal play. Feces contains many types of live bacteria and is a carrier of pathogens. The danger to the person being penetrated is that of tearing the rectal tissue. The symptoms of this injury are gradual pain in the rectal area and a worsening illness the next day resulting in possible death within several days. There is not always a discharge of blood to indicate tissue damage. Water based lubricants used in conjunction with condoms, latex gloves, finger cots, veterinarian's calving gloves, and Saran Wrap should be used as a barrier between the object of penetration and the anus of the partner. Dildos and other objects should have a flange that prevents the anal sphincter from sucking the object into the rectum.

BLOOD SPORTS Blood sports include any activity that breaks the skin, ranging from abrasions, burning, biting, shaving, cupping, and caning to cutting, stapling, suturing, lacing, impalement, and piercing. All objects touching a wound must be sterile or clean and needles that pierce the skin must be sterile and should be thrown away after only one use. Other instruments must be sterilized before being used on anyone else (see following section on sterilization techniques). Blood sports can pose a high risk for the transmission of AIDS and hepatitis.

BONDAGE The greatest dangers in bondage include suffocation, strangulation, and blocked circulation. A person can die within three to four minutes without oxygen to the brain. Therefore, it is wise to never leave the partner alone and to constantly monitor the extremities for circulation, temperature, color, and sensation. The circulatory system comes closest to the surface at the joints and pressure or knots that lay against areas such as the elbows, underarm, neck, knees, and wrists should be avoided. Ten minutes of pressure in the wrong place can easily create problems for three to six months, if not forever. The first sign of danger is a tingling or numb sensation; however, these sensations are not always perceived by the person unless they move the affected limb. For safety, rope is doubled with the knots placed on the back side of joints. Padding or leather mitts beneath cords or handcuffs are beneficial for both comfort and safety. Positions that look uncomfortable usually are and if one of these is chosen it is never recommended for more than a few minutes. These positions may also be risky if they are designed in such a way that if the person weakens or falls their arms would break, joints dislocate,

they would asphyxiate, or strain their muscles. Many of the bondage scenes in magazines are fantasy or based on real torture, they are not designed for consensual sex play.

BRANDING People use fabricated strips of galvanized sheet metal, copper, or tin as a brand. The skin is washed with soap and water (alcohol is combustible); sterilization is not necessary because of the heat. The person to be branded is put in a reclining position and the exact location for the brand is marked off with a pen. Some practice with the cold brand until they and their partner are both comfortable with the procedure. The brander then heats the metal to a cherry red and the partner is branded. The stroke is quick and even, lasting no longer than a second. Afterward, the burn is covered with an antibiotic ointment and a non-stick dressing.

BURNING Burning with fire or hot objects can easily damage the skin. If precautions to prevent burns fail and a first or second degree burn (redness, pain, or blistering) occurs, the area should be submerged in cold water until the pain becomes tolerable. A clean bandage may then be placed over the wound or blistered area. The blister itself should not be broken; it will slowly diminish over the next few days. Third degree burns will be white, gray, or charred, the skin burned away, and painless. These burns have to be attended by a physician, therefore the burned area should be covered by a clean dressing and the person immediately transported to an emergency facility. Oils or butter must never be used on burns as these tend to hold heat and pathogens on the skin, causing further complications. People with piercings do not engage in any activity that would allow hot oil into the area of the piercing.

ELECTRICITY People have died from miscalculating voltage and time restrictions while masturbating alone. A moderately high electric current flowing through the body will cause tissue damage and burns. This type of burn resembles sunburn in that there is a period of time required before one realizes the seriousness and potential pain of the injury. The person may not feel anything but warmth during the game, but the next day the injury will be obvious from the intensified pain. Therefore, electric shock cannot be regulated by the amount of pain the bottom feels. Precautions have to be taken not to use high currents at all or low ones for too extended a period of time.

An even greater safety factor involves the effect electric current has on the heart. Electricity can interfere with or stop the heart from beating.

Lower currents can be safe as long as there are no malfunctions of the equipment or human errors, and as long as the person receiving the electric current doesn't have a heart condition. (See also ELECTRICAL SHOCK)

FLAGELLATION   A bruise or hematoma may be eased by elevating the area and applying an ice pack. All leather and latex whips that break skin should be cleaned and dried before using on a different person. It is best if each person has their own supply of whips.

HYGROPHILIA   Some type of latex barrier must be used between any body secretion and the partner as protection from AIDS and other pathogens. Those desiring to smear their own feces on their bodies should avoid cuts in the skin. Ingestion is not recommended because feces can create problems if introduced into the upper digestive tract.

ILLEGAL ACTIVITIES   Exhibitionism, frottage, voyeurism, and obscene phone calls are illegal when done in public, to minors, or to a nonconsenting adult. The best precaution is to find a consenting partner with which to engage in these activities, to patronize massage parlors, join a sex club where nudity is acceptable, or find a competent sex therapist who can help people understand their motives and substitute them with ones that do not have a punitive risk.

LATEX BARRIERS   The possibility of transmitting sexual diseases can be reduced by the use of condoms, dental dams, Saran Wrap, and latex gloves. These are barriers to both pregnancy and the transmission of bacteria, and viruses. The purpose of latex is to create a physical barrier between infected skin and body secretions. It may be necessary to provide extra protection of the genital area by using underwear that has a slit in the crotch in addition to a condom to prevent contact of the testicles with the vaginal region. People who have a contagious lesion on a different part of the body may cover it with an adhesive bandage. Those who desire additional protection against viruses use a spermicide that contains the ingredient nonoxynol 9 with the condom. However, some women are allergic to this chemical. Those practicing anal sex sometimes use two condoms due to the fact that there is a higher risk of the latex tearing during this activity. The primary complaint involving latex is due to the lack of sensitivity. Some of this can be restored by using a small amount of water based lubricants (never oil because it causes rubber to deteriorate) underneath the condom near the tip of the penis. There are also condoms that have an adhesive near the base to prevent it from slipping off during sex. Men who tend to lose condoms can often make them secure and increase sensation by putting a rubber cockring over the condom at the base of the penis. Condoms may also be used over dildos or other sex toys to prevent contamination and general deterioration of the rubber when washed with soap.

PIERCING   There are many safety precautions taken when playing with piercing. Latex gloves are worn by the partner who inserts the needles, the skin is cleaned with an alcohol swab (iodine on labia), Neosporin is sometimes used on the needle to make it easier to slide through the skin, the skin to be pierced is pinched up between the finger and thumb, and the sterile needle is inserted at an angle (never straight in on any part of the body) so that the round hollow tip faces away from the skin. There may be some bleeding from a piercing and care is taken to avoid obvious blood vessels. A box of Kleenex or gauze is kept close by to dab up the excess blood. Some bleeding may be minimized by leaving the needle inside for an extended period. Muscle tissue is never pierced because a muscle can spasm, causing the needle to break. If for any reason a needle does break off in the skin the person is taken to the emergency room of a hospital immediately. If symptoms of shock develop in the partner (i.e. feeling faint or nauseous, perspiring, or coldness) they must lie down immediately with their legs raised above the level of the heart and be kept warm (not hot). If they do not improve within a few minutes one should consult a physician. Needles are disposed of in a glass jar with a lid.

PRIAPISM: A penis that is swollen due to priapism or a cock ring (preventing the blood from flowing out of the cavernosa and back into the body) can often be reduced by wrapping an Ace bandage around the penis. This starts with the glans and is worked downward toward the pubic area. Wrapping the penis with an ice bag or inducing orgasm can also lead to detumescence. If this does not work, a physician should be consulted immediately. Permanent damage can occur within only a few hours.

SHOCK Shock is caused by reduced circulation in the cardiovascular system brought on by injury or extreme emotional trauma. This physiological reaction keeps us from bleeding to death if we are wounded. However, because our body has no way of discerning the severity of the injury, it sometimes overreacts. The symptoms of shock vary according to the individual but normally include a feeling of weakness, nausea, thirst, dizziness, and coolness. These may manifest themselves as restlessness, trembling, a weak and rapid pulse, analgesia, shallow breathing, dilated pupils and pale cool or moist skin.

A person exhibiting any of these symptoms should be calmed, laid down so that their feet are elevated above their heart (if conscious, the person should be able to detect an improvement as soon as the legs are raised high enough), a blanket may be used to cover the person but only if they feel cool—do not make them uncomfortably warm. Access to fresh air is important as

well as making certain the person's clothes are loose enough to breathe comfortably. Disruptions and crowds should be minimized. A physician should be consulted if the person fails to improve within a few minutes.

SOUNDING The urethra has a sphincter at the entrance of the bladder and because of this a flange or cross bar is put on the end of a sound or object to prevent items from being pulled down the urethra and into the bladder. Another precaution people take is to make sure that anything going into the urethra is free of microscopic nicks or roughness that might abrade the delicate tissue of the canal. And last, anything put into the urethra is sterilized to prevent infection. Once a person is ready to insert the sound, sterile lubrication such as Surgilub is put onto the instrument. The handle is never released because, once inserted, dropping the heavy sound can cause internal injury and so can using force to get the sound into the desired position; the sound is merely allowed to sink.

STERILIZATION TECHNIQUES Any time the skin is broken, abraded, or burned all instruments are sterilized. Instruments that are reusable are sterilized by placing them in an autoclave. If one does not have access to this type of medical device the items may be placed in a pressure cooker for 1/2 hour or on aluminum foil in a conventional oven that is set at 300 degrees for 1/2 hour. Metal objects, pans, and scissors may be heated in a conventional oven. The metal for these devices should be unplated stainless or surgical steel.

The 'surgeon' first washes their hands twice with soap, then dries them with a freshly bleached and laundered towel. The 'patient's' skin is prepped by using prepackaged rubbing alcohol swabs or Betadine with clean cotton swabs over the area to be cut. The swab is firmly rubbed over the skin in such a manner that it does not wipe over the same area twice. The alcohol does not sterilize the surface skin, rather it simply removes dirt and oil and kills a few viruses. Betadine does sterilize the area. The packaged equipment is laid onto a fresh towel and care is taken not to let anything sterile touch fabric or other things that may be contaminated. Care is also taken not to contaminate needle tips that project through the skin because they will at some point be pulled back through an open wound.

URETHRAL PLAY   Inserting a catheter or sounding devices into the urethra require medical knowledge and use of sterile techniques. (Please refer to these sections for details.)

ZIPPER ACCIDENTS   Scrotal or penis tissue often gets stuck in between the teeth of zippers. It is advisable to keep a pair of dikes (small wire cutters) in the tool chest. These are used to clip the front guide portion that separates the teeth as they pass through the zipper. This one small section holds the top and bottom of the zipper together and when it is cut the zipper falls apart and the teeth can easily be pulled apart. ("Ask the Doctor," by F. Gordon, lecture September 19, 1990)

(Please refer to individual sections for additional discussion.)

ST. AUGUSTINE   St. Augustine (354-430 C.E.) was a North African from Tagaste (Algeria). He, along with St. Jerome and St. Gregory (the Great), formulated the doctrines of the early Catholic Church. The Church's position on birth control, papal celibacy, divorce, and their loathing of women was due to their interpretation of the original sin as having been the act of sex. They won despite a heated debate with many notable church leaders who presented arguments to the contrary.

St. Augustine had a strong passion for women but due to the influence of the popular sex-negative religions like Manicheanism, Stoicism, and Neo-Platonism he decided that his sexual lust was evil. Pleasure was to be spiritual, not physical. St. Augustine was an intellectual and lived during the time that great philosophers put a value on one's ability to control their passions. Christians and Jews were criticized due to their more natural view of sex. Therefore, when St. Augustine and others gained credibility among intellectuals of

their day because of their endorsement of celibacy, many Church leaders supported their effort. This gave Christianity a social respectability which to this point had been lacking.

St. Augustine was a prolific writer. In his autobiography, *Confessions*, he revealed his struggle with love, lust, and passion for the Roman arena. As a Manichaean he led a normal life with a mistress and fathered his beloved son Adeodatus (died at 18). However, after thirteen years his mother persuaded him to send his mistress back to Africa and to marry a girl of higher social standing. This he did at a great emotional cost. He relays in his own words "The woman with whom I was in the habit of sleeping was torn from my side on the ground of being an impediment to my marriage, and my heart, which clung to her, was wounded and broken and dripping blood...Nor was the wound healed which had been made by the cutting off of my previous mistress. It burned, it hurt intensely, and then it festered, and if the pain became duller, it became more desperate." His mistress left vowing never to give herself to another man and it is conceivable that St. Augustine's later vow of celibacy was made easy by his devotion and possible guilt over abandoning her. Christian celibacy gave him an excuse not to betray her by marrying another woman. The new marriage never took place because while he was waiting for the girl to mature he converted to a chaste Neo-platonist sect of Christianity.

He never conquered his desire for women and even forbade his sister, a nun, to speak to him without witnesses present. The more his body desired the female touch the more he condemned sex as evil.

(See also CELIBACY, EUNUCHS, ILLEGAL SEX, KLEPTOPHILIA and VICTORIANISM)

ST. VALENTINE   St. Valentine's day is celebrated on February 14th and is the feast day of two martyrs named Valentine; one of Rome and the other of Terni. Both these men died in about 269 CE (Common Era/A.D.). The date was only one day before Lupercalia, an ancient Roman fertility festival that honored Juno (goddess of women and marriage) and Pan (god of nature). One of the rituals involved in this festival included priests who walked through town striking all the women with goat skin thongs, to ensure fertility. February 14th is thought to be the first day that birds begin their mating season and therefore lovers during the Middle Ages used this occasion to send love notes. They were originally hand made by the man doing the courting and left on his lady's door step. Technology advanced and by the mid 19th century elaborate cards were being purchased and sent by mail. Suitors were then relieved of having to write poetry and decorate cards.

The Europeans not only sent cards to those they were trying to impress but it was acceptable to send vulgar and insulting ones to the handicapped and old maids. One such card read as follows:

If the devil step'd, old lady, from his regions just below,

He couldn't find a picture like the one before me now:

No doubt you know the gentleman, a sable one is he,

And he's said to be Papa of all the lies that yet might be.

Your eyes are false, your nose is false, and falser still your tongue,

Your breast is false, your heart is false, as ever poet sung;

And if disgust did not prevail, upon my present will,

I could speak of something villainous, and yet more filthy still.

(See also FESTIVALS)

SALIROPHILIA (Idrophrodisia) Salirophilia (salinus: salty, philia: attachment to) refers to people who are aroused by tasting salty body fluids such as perspiration. Perspiration at one time was thought to have magical qualities and was used in a potion to counteract love spells. The male wore out a pair of new shoes by walking and then drank wine from the right shoe which naturally mixed with sweat from his foot.

This reversed the spell and caused the man to feel hate toward the enchantress.

(See also COCKTAILS, KLISMAPHILIA, LACTAPHILIA, SHOWERS, UROPHILIA and VAMPIRISM)

SATAN WORSHIP Satan worship as we know it today did not exist until after Christianity adopted the philosophy of the separation of good and evil from Zoroastrianism (628-551 B.C.E.) and Manichaeanism (250-1200 C.E.). The latter was the former religion of one of the Catholic Church's founding fathers and proponent of this theory, St. Augustine. Satan worship became an escape by which persecuted Christians and others vented their hostility toward the Church.

The confusion created between Satan worship and witchcraft (Wicca) seems to have been in the blending of Christian and pagan rituals. The new Satanists used their own Christian rituals and belief of what Satan represented but in a manner that defiled and slandered the Church. Wicca had its own loose autonomous rituals, ones that existed thousands of years prior to organized third century religions.

The recognition of Satan is attributed to the Jews; however, the only mention of an angel named Satan representing evil is in the book of Job.  Incidently, Job was not a Jew, but his story was included in the N'veeim (Torah). The Lucifer of Genesis was a light giver, the morning star, and foremost the bearer of knowledge to humans. He opened their consciousness to good and evil and as punishment God cast him from heaven. This event is similar to that told of the Greek's heroic god, Prometheus whose name means forethought or before learning. This god stole fire from Zeus and gave it to mankind. Zeus as punishment cast him from heaven and chained him to a rock on earth where vultures daily ate at his liver. Zeus also in retribution created the first woman, Pandora, who opened a box to let evil out among man.

The most popular Satanic ritual was that of the "Black Mass." Many early Christians believed in the supernatural powers of ritual and the Christian Mass was conducted by a priest who supposedly became a personal mediator or liaison to God. The rationale of the congregants was that if God granted this priest's supplications for the church then they could hire the priest to use his power to petition God for personal favors. Good requests could become evil by simply inverting or changing part of the ritual. Early priests began conducting a Mass of the Dead in which they beseeched God to cause the death of certain enemies of paying parishioners, others ended rituals with sexual orgies and infant sacrifices. Priests that were discovered conducting these type of rituals were excommunicated by the Church. Black Masses became popular and these defrocked priests were hired to read the missal backward or substitute key words such as Satan or evil when appropriate, the altar was simply a naked virgin, the room was black as were the robes and candles. The Host was made of feces and the consecrated wine of urine or blood, or sometimes defiled by having a prostitute insert it into her vagina or urinate on it. There were several notable figures who used these rituals for their own gain. Gilles de Rais, who originally acted as a Marshal of France and escort of Joan of Arc, had rituals conducted to help him regain his lost wealth. In addition to Masses with black candles and other Satanic paraphernalia he began molesting and sacrificing young boys, eventually being reported to the authorities by his wife. The Marquise de Montespan, a mistress of King Louis XIV, used Masses to guarantee the King's continued sexual attraction to her. She was herself used as the altar and an infant sacrificed and its blood drained to make into a wafer that was given to the King. After 12 years he began to look for a younger mistress and the marquise turned vengeful and engaged in a series of Masses

of Death. These were unsuccessful but the King soon became aware of a plot against him and upon an investigation discovered 74 conspirators, many of whom were Catholic priests.

Black Masses again became popular during the 18th century in Hellfire Clubs. These were actually sex clubs where women dressed in nun's habits, naked females posed as altars, Masses were performed, the nuns used sex toys disguised as stick horses, and once everyone was sufficiently aroused the orgy began. These groups lost their popularity until the early 20th century when reports of Black Masses again surfaced. The Hermetic Order of the Golden Dawn spawned the father of today's cults, Aleister Crowley. Mr. Crowley broke away from the Golden Dawn and eventually joined another cult, the Ordo Templi Orientis of Germany and embellished it with sex acts, drugs, and animal sacrifice. Crowley died in 1947 but left behind several cult books on magick and a legacy of followers. One OTO member was Jack Parsons (1915-52), a prominent scientist in Pasadena, California, who was known for hosting ritual orgies including Hollywood stars. Parsons became involved with a scheme to incarnate the "Whore of Babalon" into the womb of a female. The spell failed. Parsons died in an explosion at the age of 37 while conducting a chemical experiment in his basement (*Satan Wants You*, by Arthur Lyons, pp. 44-83).

There are only two large organized Satanic Churches recognized by the government in existence in the United States today; The Church of Satan and the Temple of Set.

The Church of Satan was founded in 1966 by Anton LaVey. Mr. LaVey at one time worked in circuses and not only gained insight into the abnormal and people's fascination with it, but gained proficiency in promoting and choreographing the unusual. He was an avid reader of the occult and this combined with his earlier career contributed to the establishment of the Church of Satan and the direction it took. LaVey promoted his church by writing books on Satan worship and using advertising campaigns that included photos of a nude woman on an altar. This Church has nine creeds or Satanic Statements that describe its goals:

1. Satan represents indulgence instead of abstinence.

2. Satan represents vital existence instead of spiritual pipe dreams.

3. Satan represents undefiled wisdom instead of hypocritical self-deceit.

4. Satan represents kindness to those who deserve it instead of love wasted on ingrates.

5. Satan represents vengeance instead of turning the other cheek.

6. Satan represents responsibility to the responsible instead of concern for psychic vampires.

7. Satan represents man as just another animal—sometimes better, more often worse than those that walk on all-fours—who, because of his "divine spiritual and intellectual development," has become the most vicious animal of all.

8. Satan represents all of the so-called sins, as they all lead to physical, mental, or emotional gratification.

9. Satan has been the best friend the Church has ever had, as he has kept it in business all these years.

© Anton Szandor La Vey, 1966 c.e.

The Temple of Set was formed in 1975 by more conservative members from the Church of Satan. This group revived the worship of the Egyptian god Set. Set and Horus were originally brothers who were friendly to the dead. Horus the Elder represented the day and Set the night. The Egyptians later changed their philosophy and attributed all that was evil to Set and all that was good to Horus. Set was depicted as an animal with a head that is not possible to clearly identify. It has been guessed to be that of a camel, snake, or crocodile. Egyptologists call it the "Set beast." The exact image is unconfirmed because most of the statues were destroyed after this period. This religion emphasizes an intellectual self determinism and personal responsibility for life as opposed to the more common nature worshippers who maintained security by insisting on obedience to rituals and thought. Membership for the Temple of Set is restricted to those willing to dedicate much of their efforts to study.

Today there are many small cults throughout the United States and Europe that are autonomous, consisting of one leader and a few friends who use rituals seen in movies. The most notorious was one led by Charles Manson during the 1960's. Manson led his members in blood rituals, taught them "knife throwing, throat slitting and skull boiling." His "family" also participated in filming human sacrifices of young girls (*Rape and Ritual, A Psychological Study*, by Bradley A. Te Paske, p. 60).

Satanic cults are very rarely involved in human sacrifice and those that do engage in this are often small autonomous cults led by an individual.

(See also RITUAL SEX, SACRIFICES and SEX MAGICK)

SATYRIASIS (Coitolimia, Compulsive cruising, Gynecomania, Hyperphilia, Idiosyncrat, Pareunomania, Tragolimia) Satyrs are notorious half-goat and half-men Greek mythological characters who attended the god Bacchus and were known for their lechery and hedonism. Satyriasis is the male equivalent of female nymphomania.

There is no predetermined number of times that a person is expected to engage in sexual activity; therefore, a definition of satyriasis that specifies a numerical component is invalid. Cultures as well as individuals differ dramatically in sexual activity. Rather for a definition we might use similar criteria as for addictions: namely, if the activity is compulsive to the degree that it interferes with the person's ability to function in society and to support themselves it is a problem. A person who finds that their sexual needs far exceeds the ability of one partner to provide, sometimes sacrifices the affection and bonding possible with them for polite sex with a multitude of temporary partners.

A satyrist may have problems with being able to experience normal emotions so that when the temporary excitement of the chase and conquest wears off they, unlike others, are unaware of residual feelings of intimacy, and move on to the next person. A child who is not shown consistent love and nurturing may also be unable to trust or expect this from others as an adult. Bonding then does not occur with one person, instead nurturing and security is restricted to the act of sex itself. Other satyrists may simply enjoy the chase and conquest more than sex with a stable partner.

There may be a hormonal imbalance where the body produces an abnormal amount of testosterone, dopamine, or other chemical that would increase the person's desire for sex.

(See also NYMPHOMANIA and ORGASMS)

SCARFING See AUTOASPHYXIOPHILIA

SCARRING See CICATRIZATION

SCATOPHILIA See COPROPHILIA

SCOPOPHILIA (Mixoscopia, Scoptolagnia; Allopellia—having orgasm from watching others engage in sex) Scopophilia (skopein: looking a certain direction, and philia: attachment to) refers to sexual arousal gained from looking at people or events. This would include voyeurism, but is broader in that the people being watched may also consent, i.e. candaulism or group sex.

A leading television evangelist recently gained notoriety for engaging in scopophilia with prostitutes who would masturbate while he watched.

The scopophile may be aroused by watching an activity that involves a fetish or sex object. Men may watch women urinate, try on shoes, browse through erotic sections of a magazine rack, or ride Sybian (the mechanical dildo).

(See also VOYEURISM)

SCRATCHING (Dermographism; Amychesis—female who scratches partner

during height of passion) Scratching has been done during foreplay and sex throughout history. The *Kama-Sutra* recommended that people use this method to leave permanent love marks:

Generally speaking marks made with the nails should be imprinted on the armpits, the throat, the breasts, the lips, the jagdana or midriff, and the thighs. The nails can be used to make eight marks, by scratching or pressing: sounding, half-moon, the circle, the lines, the tiger's nail or claw mark, the peacock's foot, the hair's leap and the blue lotus leaf. The art of imprinting the marks of love is familiar to all. Nail marks may not be made on married women; however it is permitted to make special marks on the hidden parts of their bodies, as a fond memory and in order to heighten one's love. Even when they are old and have almost been effaced, nail marks remind a woman of previous moments of love and revive her passion, which might otherwise be simply lost. A young woman on whose breasts such marks are to be seen can impress even a stranger who sees her from a distance. A man who bears nail and teeth marks on this body is successful with women, even those who resist love.

People today are generally more cautious about leaving marks on their partner without their consent.

(See also BITING, CICATRIZATION, FLAGELLATION and PINCHING)

SCROTAL INFUSION (Ballooning, Scrotal inflation) Scrotal infusion is the process by which a solution is injected into the scrotal sack. It is also referred to as ballooning or scrotal inflation, although these terms might be taken to mean expansion by air or gas and for safety reasons that impression is best avoided by using the word infusion which denotes expansion by fluid.

The visual effect of the scrotal infusion resembles a water balloon. Men do not report any pain from this procedure and claim that one advantage is found the next morning when the solution filters into the penis causing it to swell to the size of a beer can. Men claim exclusive license to this type of sex play. There is no sealed part of the female anatomy that has a hollow sack which lends itself to expansion.

Paraphernalia used for this procedure were scissors, first aid tape, a 20 gauge angiocath or hypodermic needle, a one liter 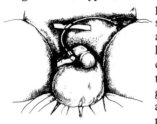 plastic bag of saline solution, an IV pole or hook on the ceiling, plastic tubing, latex gloves and packaged alcohol prep pads.

The saline solution was warmed to body temperature ahead of time. The bag was then held against the inside wrist to determine a comfortable temperature. Incidentally, the temperature is not for the comfort of the patient but rather to prevent the scrotal sack from shrinking as it normally does when exposed to cold water or ice. This shrinking would hamper the expansion process that is essential for infusion.

The bag was hung from a hook and spiked with the tubing which was then pinched closed not contaminating any of the ends. The scrotal area was swabbed with the alcohol prep pad, and the needle was inserted about one inch directly below the base of the penis in the middle of the scrotum. The partner waited for a moment to make certain that he had not pierced a vein (evident by blood backing up into the needle), the needle or angiocath was then taped flat and upright against the top of the scrotum. The tubing was then opened and adjusted so that it drained at a rate of about 60-90 cc's a minute.

The male stood because gravity helps to facilitate the expansion. However, fainting is a natural response and the person was monitored closely and had a bed or table behind him on which to lie if necessary.

Scrotal infusion is an activity that is difficult for most observers to understand. The men who experiment with this form of body modification have explained their various motives or desire to experience different feelings, to be unique, for the shock value, to prove that these are their genitals and they will do with them as they please, and to visually set their genitals apart from all others.

The saline in the scrotal sack absorbs into the body within about three days. Some people inject more saline than the scrotal sack can accommodate and this will immediately overflow through a small opening into the abdomen. CAUTION: This is a blood sport that requires proper sterilization procedures and is therefore not considered a safe sex practice. Improper placement of the needle may also damage local nerves.

("Scrotal Inflation and Other Genital Modifications," by J.B., QSM lecture, December 1, 1990)

(See also BONDAGE/LACING, PIERCING, SAFE SEX/SCROTAL INFUSION and SUTURING)

SENSORY COMPENSATION Sensory compensation is the body's natural mechanism by which we regulate the amount of outside stimulus to a manageable level. Our brain divides our attention between all the input available, and with this information interprets the environmental cues. We do not need all five senses for the brain to process or interpret external cues; we can do this with only one sensory aid. Of all our senses our strongest or most distracting is that of sight. Sound is the second most distracting sense and smell the third. Most people are aware of a similar compensation effect with the blind whereby they develop or become more focused on their remaining senses. This compensation does not require a long period of time, rather it can be artificially achieved in only a matter of minutes.

Sensory compensation is used in sex games by isolating the desired sense to be enhanced, for instance touch, and depriving the person of their ability to use the other four senses. The person is placed in a comfortable room that is void of odors or sound and not given anything to eat or hold in their mouth. They are then either blindfolded or the room is made dark, depending on whether the game entails activities that necessitate light. This deprivation of all senses but one results in the person becoming focused on tactile stimulation. A feather stroked across the body becomes more intense as does direct contact with their nipples or genitals. Their sensitivity to pain will also increase; therefore, care is taken to avoid strong stimulus.

Sensory compensation may be used to enhance any of the five senses, achieving various effects.

(See also SENSORY DEPRIVATION, SENSORY ENHANCEMENT and SENSORY OVERLOAD)

SENSORY DEPRIVATION

Sensory deprivation differs from sensory compensation in that one tries to eliminate all five senses. Deprivation may include activities such as sensory deprivation chambers, samadhi tanks, or suspension.

Tanks, wherein people defy gravity by floating or are suspended in water, can be very disorienting. Suspension is not as dramatic but has also produced results such as vertigo, hallucinations, and confusion. A safeword that acts to signal the partner to end the deprivation is essential for this activity.

Long term deprivation often produces hallucinations and altered states of consciousness. Hallucinations are a risk for almost anyone who becomes isolated; for instance, those in sensory deprivation chambers, sailors who reported hearing and seeing female sirens, and those who get lost in jungles. Tribesmen in South America have legends of men becoming victims of "Japujaneju," an evil female spirit, who often appears to them as their consort luring them deeper into the forest. People sent into space or just for a winter in Antarctica are often required to take psychological tests in advance.

A more pertinent and dramatic sexual effect of sensory deprivation is that often after only one-half hour a mere touch to the body or genitals can produce orgasm. Also, the first visual impression experienced after one is released from sensory deprivation can be very intense and long lasting. Many partners use this opportunity to express tenderness and love, or otherwise present themselves in a manner in which they would like to be remembered.

Sensory deprivation may be isolated to only part of the body such as the nipples or genitals. This is done with a numbing lotion or encasement. ("Sensory Deprivation and Bondage," by Adashi, Society of Janus lecture, May 24, 1990)

(See also SENSORY ENHANCEMENT, SENSORY OVERLOAD and SUSPENSION)

SENSORY ENHANCEMENT

Methods that enhance our senses are listed throughout this book and include techniques that range from the use of simple lubricants and massage to the more painful form of cock and ball torture.

The natural desire to increase the amount of stimuli for sex is found in some young children when they first learn to masturbate. One young girl would, during the summer, lay naked on burning patio bricks because it enhanced masturbation. In a similar fashion a young boy put pieces of cloth in a freezer and then removing one would lay it over his penis to facilitate masturbation. These methods probably intensified their sexual response because pain triggers the body's defense mechanisms by producing adrenalin. This may be of particular importance for youth who often do not have the sexual experience to build arousal by the use of sexual fantasies. Even those children who do use fantasy when masturbating don't use visions of what we consider regular or normal copulation. One very young girl described the thoughts she used while playing with herself. She visualized a monster, one seen in a movie, engaging in a bizarre form of urination from his mouth. One would guess that this girl used fear as a stimulant for arousal instead of pain as in the former cases. [Personal communications.]

Regardless of the method a person uses it is important to understand that people have different pain tolerances; therefore, what looks like it would cause pain to one person may in reality feel pleasurable to others. People who are under stress or who are "type A personalities" are thought to have a higher pain threshold than others.

(See also ABRASIONS, ACOUSTICOPHILIA, ACUPRESSURE, BATHS, BED OF NAILS, BEE

STINGS, BITING, CLAMPS, CUPPING, DEPILATION, INUNCTION, MASSAGE, MYSOPHILIA, PINCHING, SCRATCHING and SITOPHILIA)

SENSORY OVERLOAD

Sensory overload occurs when there is more information produced from an environment than a person can assimilate. This does not necessarily mean that more things are occurring simultaneously but rather that they are unfamiliar or confusing. Disorientation occurs because the brain can not readily process this type of information.

Deliberate sensory overload is used by cults to accomplish a similar effect on their converts. Steven Hassan, once a high ranking officer in the Moonie movement, and now an exit counselor and leading expert on destructive cults and their indoctrination techniques, spoke of the risks of sensory overload in his recent book:

Put a person in a sensory deprivation chamber, and within hours he will start to hallucinate and become incredibly suggestible. Likewise, put a person into a situation where his senses are overloaded with noncoherent information, and the mind will go "numb" as a protective mechanism. It gets confused and overwhelmed, and critical faculties no longer work properly. It is in this weakened state that people become very suggestible to others. The mind needs frames of reference in order to structure reality. (Combatting Cult Mind Control, p. 47.

An example of this in a sex scene is that of a person who is not experienced with S/M walking into a play party where various sorts of bondage, humiliation, and flagellation are being engaged in by people. This can create manifestations that are best described as having a fog over most of the room, tunnel vision, vertigo, and minimal focus. Advantages of sensory overload in sex play is that it makes the person become more submissive and reliant on their partner because it strips them of the ability to sort out ideas on their own. Confusion also creates this effect and is accomplished by giving a partner double-bind commands, those that contradict each other so that no matter what they do they can be criticized.

Awareness of the dynamics involved in all cases of controlled sensory overload by a second party is important. There are occasions when this type of bonding and influence from the partner is advantageous and also instances when it is inappropriate. An obvious case is that of spouse abuse where one partner constantly criticizes the other causing them to feel unsure of their own decisions, inferior, and unable to function without the abuser.

(See also BLINDFOLDING, BONDAGE, SENSORY ENHANCEMENT, SENSORY COMPENSATION, SUSPENSION and VERTIGO)

SERENADES

Serenades were popular in Europe during the 17th and 18th centuries.  Young men played their violins and sang on the streets beneath the windows of their lover. The English were quick to follow the romantic Italians' example but with different results. English men drank until midnight to get up their nerve, and then didn't quit singing until near dawn. Of course, this may well have been the quickest way to persuade a father to consent to his daughter's marriage simply to get her suitor to stop.

(See also COURTSHIP and EROTOGRAPHOMANIA)

SEX ALMANACS

There are several magazines and books that provide up to date information on international activities that are of interest to sexually active people. *The Safer Sex Maniac's Bible* is a comprehensive pocket sized guide that is published in London annually by Miss Tuppy Owens. Tim Woodward's magazine, *Skin II*, provides a current world listing of clubs, activities, publications, and shops, and San Francisco has several magazines with information about upcoming events: *Spectator, Drummer, Sandmutopia Guardian & Dungeon Journal,* and *Dungeon Master.* Sex clubs or organizations often keep up to date on local social functions.

(See also SEX CLUBS, SEX CONFERENCES, SEX HOTELS and SEX SHOWS)

SEX BOUTIQUES   There are several sex boutiques in the United States, most of which are owned by women. Inside, they resemble a fine lingerie store that carries sex toys, fur mitts, erotic videos, books, and body lotions. San Francisco's Romantasy Boutique, owned by Ann Grogan, also has drawings and work by local artists, bondage equipment for novices, night classes in stripping for your lover, beginning bondage, and many other topics. Special clients are treated to private lingerie shows several times a year with hors d' oeuvres and special entertainment at the end of the show. The Los Angeles area has two Love Boutiques that also sponsor home parties for women.

(See also SEX TOYS)

SEX CLUBS   Sex clubs that sponsor social activities for those with unusual sexual proclivities seem to have become more prevalent in modern times. Ancient worshippers of fertility religions engaged in their favorite 'perversions' openly without being criticized by others. Of course, most of these societies did not condone the same conduct between holidays, although there may have been secret organizations that did.

Clubs were formed in opposition to the Church's condemnation of pagan festivals in 16th century France. Two of these organizations, the Society Joyuse and the Society of Dijon, rescued the Feast of Fools, under the guise of its being a social activity. People were thus able to continue this observance for a while. The Feast of Fools itself was offensive to the Church because it included cross-dressing, complete mockery of Church rituals, flagellation, wearing masks, and the throwing of black pudding (some say feces) into the crowds.

In the 18th century an Englishman named Sir Francis Dashwood began a brotherhood of Medmenham. He purchased and remodeled an abbey in Medmenham for this purpose. In 1760 this group began holding their meetings there and the once stoic abbey now displayed sexual statues and paintings with lewd inscriptions throughout the interior and exterior. Their interest in sex was not restricted to the carnal enjoyment of art; they also had a library that contained a comprehensive collection of erotic literature. The members entered the abbey dressed as friars and their lady guests dressed as nuns. The Grand Master began club services at an altar with a cursory sacrament being offered to their baboon deity. This was followed by other simple rituals. The food was elaborate and libations abundant. Once members satisfied their initial hunger they selected a nun with whom to consummate the revelry. This brotherhood met twice a year and survived almost 20 years.

Today we have several hundred diverse clubs around the world. International advertising is fairly inexpensive and computerized printing of newsletters has made it simpler to form clubs. People with fetishes as obscure as large penises, big balls, hairy bodies, mud wrestlers, shaving, cigars, used condoms, genital modification, and throwing pies have been able to find others with similar interests willing to form clubs. Some of the larger clubs include New York's Eulenspiegel Society, the Chicago Hellfire Club, and Los Angeles' Threshold. The San Francisco area may have as many as a hundred clubs but the most prominent are the Back Drop, Outcasts, ETVC, Mother Goose Club, and the Society of Janus.

BACK DROP CLUB   The Back Drop is a fetish and fantasy club that was founded in 1966. It probably has the largest membership and sponsors the most events. Their private clubhouse is open to members from noon until 10:00pm, seven days a week. Classes include information on wrestling, photography, leather fabrication, slave training, cross dressing, spanking, and water sports. The club sponsors many interesting social events as well. There are Roman Holidays with gladiators, slaves, costumes, a Roman feast, parties for transvestites, a weekly slave auction, video nights, fashion shows, and a flea market once a month where members can exchange or sell their sex equipment.

ETVC The ETVC is a club for transvestites, transgenderists, transsexuals, their spouses, and therapists. The club has over 400 members to which it provides regular social functions, support groups, outreach programs, and a library. ETVC offers its members the opportunity to dress up for the evening and socialize with others. Their social events include an annual beauty pageant, outings, lingerie shows, poker games, casino nights, and more. They also offer classes on the finer arts of passing as female.

MOTHER GOOSE PRODUCTIONS The Jack and Jill Off masturbation parties are sponsored by the Mother Goose Club. Here people must follow simple rules pertaining to safe sex (penetration is not allowed) and the use of condoms, latex gloves, and dental dams. Social rules require that a person asks for permission before touching another and respond politely to anyone who says no. People must either dress in costume or wear nothing at all. The parties are open to people of any sexual preference. Unlike group sex houses, bi-sexuality is permitted and men are not required to bring a female in order to attend. The club provides hors d'oeuvres but some people bring whipped cream, chocolate syrup, or kama sutra oils to enhance their sex play. Some people engage in light bondage or S/M but most people are novices without prior group sex experience. There are usually about a hundred members at the parties and the age of the people is slightly younger than what is found at group sex houses. There also seem to be more wet spots on the linens by the end of the evening. The same Mother Goose Club sponsors Jack Off parties for men and Jill Off parties for females.

OUTCASTS The Outcasts is a female S/M organization that sponsors theme parties and a monthly lecture that may be anything from discussing the politics of being a black lesbian sadomasochist to piercing and lacing demonstrations. This group sponsors a booth at the SF Lesbian and Gay Freedom Day Parade and often catches the attention of spectators when they, the Dykes on Bikes, lead the parade or when they demonstrate whippings at their booth.

SOCIETY OF JANUS The Society of Janus was founded in 1974 by Cynthia Slater and has grown to have approximately 450 members. Similar to other S/M clubs they sponsor play parties that have themes such as Slave Auctions, Halloween Parties, Bondage and Beauty Pageants, Beat Your Valentine, and Costumes. One sees a variety of activities at these parties such as bindings, foreplay, bondage, mummifications, suspension, spankings, whippings, and use of sex toys. Rules and activities vary according to organization but they discourage genital penetration, fisting, urophilia, coprophilia, and other more specialized interests. A description of what one would see at Janus' Bondage and Beauty Pageant is as follows:

Upon entry through a locked door one pays their cover charge and receives a ballot. The social room is filled with figures clad with black leather, jeans, and a few business suits. Their faces show expressions ranging from sober, anxious, and preoccupied, to warm, friendly and festive. Voices and rustling can be heard through a doorway that opens to a large dungeon where people are busy placing their partners in bondage for the contest. People know one another and there seems to be a friendly exchange of humor, advice and assistance. A woman brushes by and you turn to see her leading a naked man by a leash attached only to his genitals. By this time many of the other participants are in different stages of dress. A beautiful young woman wearing a wedding dress is in one corner, her bodice is pulled down and on her nipples are rings that support small weights, and her feet are apart; being held in place with spreader bars. The front of her dress has been raised to expose her genitals from which another weight hangs from a chain and ball that has been inserted into her vagina. On the floor to their right is a man in black latex who has his arms and legs bound with belts, his genitals protrude, and have a paper plate surrounding them. Spaghetti is being sensually eaten off the plate by his consort. Two women are standing near the center, one encasing her naked partner in elaborate macrame. On stage are two people who have been bound in a standing position and their hoods attached to the ceiling with chains. A woman is standing near them with her hands cuffed behind her back. She is bare-chested and held in position by chains that are snapped to her nipple rings. Along the side wall is a woman who has been placed in a cage wearing only a slave collar. Near her is a naked man who has been cuffed onto a rape rack and his mistress is gently torturing his exposed scrotum with a riding crop. A crowd has now gathered around a woman who has been blindfolded and tied onto a chair, her arms are pulled back and her legs are spread to the sides. Her master displays a rather large butcher knife and reaching down slices two holes in the front of her sweater to expose her naked breasts. There are about twenty entries in all and one must vote for the best entry in each category. Ballots are handed in and about ten winners with a best of show are announced and brought onto the stage to receive their awards.

European sadomasochist groups include Club Doma in the Netherlands, Club Sunrise in Sweden, DSSM in England, Papillon in Canada, and SMil in Denmark and Norway. S/M support groups such as the New York group called the Lesbian Sex Mafia have formed as well.

Anti-censorship groups exist to protect people's ability to engage in safe and consensual sexual behavior. Some of these include Californians Against Censorship Together, Committee to Preserve Our Sexual & Civil Liberties, England's Campaign Against Public Morals, France's Centre du Christ Liberateur pour Sexual Minorities and, the Dutch Society for Sexual Reform. Other organizations exist that support all personal freedoms. These are the American Civil Liberties Union, National Coalition Against Censorship, and America's Libertarian political party.

(See also SEX ALMANACS, SEX CONFERENCES and STRIPPING)

SEX CONFERENCES There are several sex conferences, conventions, and symposiums held each year. These are sponsored by organizations such as the National Sexuality Symposium, the Society for the Scientific Study of Sex, the World

Association for Sexology, The Annual National Conference on Sexual Compulsivity/Addiction, National Organization of Circumcision, the International Conference on AIDS, Mensa Sexyg, and the International World Sex Conference. Most of these are designed for medical professionals or people with an academic interest in sexology. There is informal entertainment and some sponsor erotic costume balls or dances. Special interest groups such as bi-sexuals, infantilists, leathermen, extended families or polygamists, and swingers also sponsor annual conferences.

LIFESTYLES Lifestyles is an organization that hosts conferences for couples either contemplating or living in open marriages. It was founded in 1974 by Bob McGinley, Ph.D., a psychologist who felt it was important to organize a forum where people could exchange accurate knowledge about swinging and find emotional support in coping with other's resistance to their chosen lifestyle. This group has several conferences a year but its primary conference is often held during the summer in Las Vegas. Couples have the opportunity to attend outstanding lectures by prominent psychologists, hypnotists, writers, and workshop leaders. At night they are entertained by banquets, erotic costume balls, and lingerie discos. Private orgies and wife swapping are informal and arranged by some individuals. The vendor booths acquaint couples with the newest on-line computer programs for swinging, magazines, swinger vacation packages, toys, sex jewelry, personalized stationery, lingerie, and S/M paraphernalia. Many couples outside the swinging community attend these conferences because of their entertaining programs and the refreshing sex-positive attitude shared by conference attendees.

NATIONAL SEXUALITY SYMPOSIUM The National Sexuality Symposium was founded by Katheryn Roberts in 1990 and co-sponsored by Lifestyles, the Institute for Human Sexuality, and the San Francisco Sex Information Switchboard. In addition to the conference, Ms. Roberts publishes a quarterly magazine and sponsors a monthly lecture and dance in the San Francisco area. The agenda and entertainment are similar to those of the Lifestyles conferences but there are more counselors and singles who attend with much less emphasis being placed on private parties. Lectures in 1991 included topics such as "Alternate Personas" by William Henkin, Ph.D. and Sybil Holiday, "Communication is the Best Lubrication" by Isadora Alman, MFCC, "Sex and Drugs" by David Coleman, "Creating Successful Relationships" by Stan Dale, "Feminist Erotica" by Nina Hartley, "Sex and Censorship" by Bobby Lilly, "Sex Games for Couples" by Walter Shelburne, Ph.D., "Erotic Massage" by Kenneth Ray Stubbs, Ph.D., and "Erotic Film Making for Fun and Profit," by Janet Taylor.

THE SOCIETY FOR THE SCIENTIFIC STUDY OF SEX   This society was organized in 1957 for sexologists and professionals such as psychologists, professors, physicians, students, or people who have made a major contribution to the study of sex. Applications by new members are reviewed by the Board. In addition to conferences, SSSS publishes a quarterly journal of sex research and a newsletter. They have also created a Foundation to fund scientific research in this field. The organization was founded by Hugo Beigel, Harry Benjamin, Albert Ellis, Henry Guze, Hans Lehfeldt, and Robert Sherwin. Prominent past presidents include Wardell Pomeroy, Richard Green, and John Money.

The lectures are clinical but anyone with a sincere interest in human sexuality could easily become engrossed with the wealth of information provided. Past lectures have included "Is it limerance or is it lust" by James Weinrich, Ph.D., "Lesbian erotic archetypes" by JoAnn Loulan, M.A., "Gambling and sexual behaviors of older people" by Adele Zorn, Ph.D., and "Erotic Wars: What happened to the sexual revolution?" by Lillian Rubin, Ph.D.

WORLD CONGRESS FOR SEXOLOGY
The World Congress for Sexology is sponsored once every two years by the World Association for Sexology. These congresses are five-day international events. They began in 1974 and have been held in Paris, Montreal, Rome, Mexico City, Jerusalem, Washington, New Delhi, Heidelberg, Caracas, and in 1991 was held in Amsterdam. The 1993 congress is scheduled for Rio de Janeiro and the 1995 for Osaka. Professionals in sex therapy and education attend these conferences but others are also welcomed. The lectures are designed to provide attendees with a broad variety of information. Topics in 1991 included "Psychosexual development", "Plasticity of primate sexual and reproductive strategies", "Therapeutical approaches towards victims of sexual torture, "Sex and aging", "Therapy of erectile dysfunction", "Sexuality and chronic kidney disorders", and so forth.

(See also EROTIC BALLS, SEX CLUBS, SEX HOTELS, SEX MUSEUMS, SEX RESTAURANTS and SEX SHOWS)

SEX GAMES   A game is defined by Webster's as "any specific amusement or sport involving physical or mental competition under specific rules." Sex games include board games where people use dice, pawns, and a deck of cards; each giving explicit sex instructions. People can create their own sex games by making the prize a fantasy fulfillment for the winner of any ordinary game. Others formulate their own game as in the case of Adult April Fool's parties.

Adult April Fool's parties are organized so that each participant draws their assignment for the evening from a hat. Samples of these assignments include having to make an obscene phone call to someone at the party from another room, asking one's date if they mind you signing the waiting list for the midnight orgy, organizing a striptease show from volunteers at the party, offering a dollar to five different people to spend a minute alone with you in a dark bedroom, propositioning three people, pretending to be Dracula and having to nibble three people on the neck, kissing three strangers, announcing that you are recently engaged and then propositioning a guest, convincing someone other than your date to take a shower with you, and finally, talking someone of the opposite sex into letting you borrow their underwear for a few minutes. Alternatively, everyone has to write out either their most bizarre, their favorite, or their fantasy sex scene without signing the paper. All of these are placed in a hat and drawn out at midnight and read aloud. If people are willing they may also be called on individually at this time to read their original assignment to the group and relay their experience.

Many sex games are simply modifications of more common ones. The child's game of Spin the Bottle is modified this way so that instead of only receiving a kiss, the person who has the bottle point at them gets to request a sexual favor of anyone else in the circle. A circus game called the Ring Toss was also adapted into a sex game. This involves having men lie in a row and one by one the women throw a sponge ring onto the erect penis of the man they want. The owner of the penis and the winner then engage in sex. Strip Poker is probably the most common game. Teenagers often play it with the modification that everyone can stop when they get to underwear. Strip poker has also been modified for sex play by letting the winner of each hand select the person of their choice to engage in sex for five minutes; they then return to the table to play another hand.

There are numerous sex games on the market. Chippendale's has a two sided jigsaw puzzle of their young male strippers. There is a game called Dirty Words, where

players gain points by the number of sentences they can make with the 23 cubes containing words such as "ear, touch, bite, love, moist, lips, burn, moan, cream, crotch", and so forth. Forum Novelties makes a game, Private Parts,, that is similar to Pin-the-Tail-On-the-Donkey, except the lost appendage is a penis. There is a similar version for those who prefer to play with a female poster. Dirty Pictures, is a game that requires the players to draw a picture of words or phrases such as lust and the players who guess correctly get points. Sexual Lotto, is in the format of bingo except instead of numbers people match sexual instructions. Getting to Know You. . .Better, is designed to give one insight into their partners by the way they answer the questions on each card. A slightly more provocative game is Sexual Secrets, by TDC Games in which players draw a card and complete sentences such as "The first time I touched a naked woman I..., or "The thought of making love to two men at the same time really makes me..." An Enchanted Evening, is a board game that lists simple questions or acts for players to comply with in order to finish the game and have their secret fantasy fulfilled. The latter is written on paper by each player preceding the game. One of the games involving actual sex is called The Fantasy Role-Playing Card Game For Couples, by American Playtime. In this game the cards assign and describe roles to the players such as school teacher, nurse, prostitute, novice, and dominatrix. The instructions suggest that the players have the following props on hand before beginning the game: "blindfold, body powder, feather, honey or whipping cream, music for dancing, oil or lotion, soft ropes, sheet or cover." A slightly similar game is Dirty Dare, by Baron/Scott where the object is for a player to complete two dares in categories such as physical, messy, entertaining, and hot to the satisfaction of the other players in order to win. The props suggested for this game are: "ice cubes, whipped cream, eggs, oil, ketchup, mustard, peanut butter, bananas, pickles, powder, flour, and honey."

Computer board game programs such as Intersextion, are available through some of the adults only networks.

(See also AUCTIONS, COMPUTER SEX, DOMINANCE/SUBMISSION and FANTASY PLAY)

SEX HOTELS   Sex hotels permit swinging although most don't actively support it. Nudist resorts sometimes have private cabins and couples are permitted to discreetly approach others; however, some nudist resorts will ask people to leave if they are caught soliciting. Brochures with park rules often inform new members of their preference.

A west coast hotel that supports nudity and provides an atmosphere conducive to swinging is California's Edgewater West Adult Resort. Here are 80 rooms opening onto a private tropical setting with jacuzzis, swimming pools, fish ponds, and its own night club. The management also provides exciting entertainment for holidays. For example, the entertainment for July 4th, 1991 consisted of a Roman toga dinner party. Fruit was served by wenches (sometimes from on top of their breasts), followed by a banquet including breads in the form of penises and breasts. Entertainment included a belly dancer and a male stripper who removed everything but the baby oil rubbed onto his body by a mob of ravishing women. Dessert was served from a rolling cart upon which was a beautiful nude female covered with fruit and whipped cream for dipping. The hotel rules concerning swinging are that when couples are in their rooms they close their drapes for privacy, leave them open if they want others to watch from outside, and leave their sliding glass door and drapes open as an invitation for others to join them. Couples who enjoy nudity but who are not interested in swinging themselves stay at the hotel because they find the relaxed and friendly environment refreshing.

San Jose California once had a small motel swingers frequented. Here they would leave their doors slightly ajar and place a photo of themselves on the outside as a courtesy. This practice is sometimes seen at swinger conventions when the whole hotel is reserved for their use. Other sex hotels include Beck's Inn in Fayetteville, North Carolina, Eden Patio, and the Club Amour in France. Rio de Janeiro has several sex motels as does Japan. The Japanese cater to fantasy and one may select from one of a number of scenes.

People are encouraged to bring their own partner to sex hotels because a husband does not enjoy paying to share their wife with ten single men without having a female partner for himself.

There are several S/M hotels throughout Europe and Japan where the hotel has a dungeon available for use by its guests. Swinging may not be condoned by the managers. Some S/M hotels are private chalets that have equipped dungeons (usually designed for only one couple).

(See also SEX CONFERENCES and SEX CLUBS)

SEX HOTLINES   Sex hotlines are supported by charities, government, or private sponsorship. Hotlines provide answers to questions people have about sexuality and act as a referral service to therapists or special interest organizations. They are not there to entertain obscene phone callers. In fact, the operators (most are volunteer) are instructed to hang up or end any conversation where they suspect the caller is trying to masturbate or become verbally abusive.

One of the more general purpose sex hotlines is The San Francisco Sex Information switchboard. The types of questions volunteers are permitted to answer are more diverse because it is supported by private donations, fund raising parties, and training fees. Volunteers are not usually qualified therapists. Therefore they are required to complete 50 hours of training on subjects that range from homosexuality, diseases, S/M, zoophilia, incest, relationship counseling, surrogate work, and transsexuality before staffing the switchboard. Once on-line the volunteers cannot counsel individuals. They are restricted to listening, relaying information, and making referrals.

Callers typically ask questions about anal sex, S/M, cross dressing, fetishes, disease, birth control, incest, and relationship problems. The switchboard has a large catalog with hundreds of referrals for callers interested in special sex clubs or sex related entertainment. The hotline does not make referrals for dates, escorts, or prostitutes. The switchboard can only recommend that the person attend social functions or answer personal ads. A few of San Francisco's other hotlines are Men Overcoming Violence in

Their Relationships, Men Who are Violent to Women, and the AIDS Hotline. There are also hotlines for gays, bi-sexuals, rape victims, and diseases.

(See also DISEASES and PHONE SEX)

SEX MAGICK   Sex magick combines witchcraft rituals, visualization, breath control, and tantra for an ultimate sexual experience. Wiccans who practice sex magick are rare and it is difficult to gain entry into the coven.

Covens are often formed according to sexual preference; gay, bisexual, or heterosexual. Some members have sex with a partner and others masturbate. The rituals and chants differ from coven to coven; however, their basis in repetition tends to be a common thread. Rituals enhance emotions by conditioning. The mind anticipates the climax of the event and causes the body to automatically respond. Most of the rituals used in sex magick are based on Wicca and can be found in books such as *The Spiral Dance*, by Starhawk or many of the others on witchcraft or Western tantra.

Sex magick requires a proficiency in visualization skills. One must be able to visualize assorted colors, to create smells, tastes,  sounds, or moods and to change them at will. One popular exercise for novices is that of visualizing an apple with its colors, shapes, smells, and tastes; then eating it until only the core is left. Another important visualization technique, the tree of life, teaches the student how to create and channel energy. The person sits in a comfortable position and visualizes being connected to the floor. Next they grow roots that slowly sink into the earth, penetrating deeper and deeper until they pass the water table, the rock, and into the core of the earth. Here they feel the heat and pull this energy back into their body, the genitals, through the spine, past the heart, into the neck, and out the top of the head. When a person is able to visualize the apple and the energy flow they are then able to visualize their fantasy god and the divine powers which are used to enhance the sex act.

Two basic types of breathing are used during sex magick. Deep slow breathing has a calming effect on the body, it prolongs arousal by creating and storing energy rather than burning it up. Rapid and shallow breathing generates and burns energy. This type of breathing is done just prior to the sex act for a more intense orgasm. (Refer to OXYGEN REGULATION)

Ritual items used in sex magick include a chalice, an athame (two-edged knife), a red candle, a bell, a censer (an enclosed incense burner that swings by chains), and cauldron (incense pot).

The sex magick ritual begins with each person showering with warm water. This prepares a person physically by relaxing the muscles and helping one focus on the subtle pleasure sensations of their body.

The incense in the censer is lit and 3 tablespoons of rock salt is dissolved into the water filled chalice. The group sits together in a circle and does a series of deep breath meditations. The priestess brings the chalice to the center and each person places their fingers on the rim visualizing and perhaps verbalizing the casting of their personal list of pains and sorrows into the salty water. As this is accomplished the water symbolically turns dark and murky. The priestess then takes the chalice, stands, holds it above her head and calls on the goddess of the moon to change the water of their afflictions into pure crystal clear water. Everyone then joins in the chant:

> She changes all she touches and all she touches she changes, she changes all she touches and all she touches she changes...change is, touch is, touch us, change us, change is, touch is, touch us, change us...

The priestess proceeds by declaring that the water is pure as a bright white light. The goddess is asked to bless the water and is then offered the first libation (a drop is spilled). Each person takes a sip stating that they accept this change in their lives.

Some circles follow with a second cleansing meditation. A crystal, pentagram, or earth piece is held and used to ground what wasn't caught the first time. Each person lies on their back with their palms to the earth, holding on to the selected earthly medium, visualizing that they are floating down into the earth like mud when the rain hits it, down so deep into the earth that they reach the core, then bringing that warmth slowly back up into the body, re-energizing, and vitalizing it. Each person feels the power rise through the body, lighting it up like a neon sign.

The circle next banishes evil spirits that may be present in the room. The priestess enters the center of the circle with an athame and calls to the spirits of evil to be gone. All the members then respond with "We banish you, we banish you, we banish you, begone."

The priestess will then cast the circle by pointing to the sky with her athame and saying "Oh noon sky above, and earth below I salute you" while she draws a pentagram with the athame. She or an assistant then takes the salt water chalice, dipping their fingers in and flinging drops toward the East saying: "With salt and water I purify the East." The censer is swung back and forth before the East as the person recites: "With fire and air I invoke and charge the East. Oh guardians of the watchtower of the East, powers of air we invoke and call you, be here now, (a ritual bell is rung) awake, awake oh spirits of the East."

The priestess next takes her athame and joins the East to the South. The same ritual with salt water, censer, and the bell is performed for the powers of fire (afterward lighting the incense in the cauldron on the altar). The priestess continues in the same manner to the West for the powers of water and then the North for the powers of the earth. The priestess steps once again to the center of the circle and raises her athame as she chants "The circle is cast, we are between the worlds beyond the bounds of time where night and day, birth and death, joy and sorrow meet as one. Blessed be. Oh center above and center below we purify you. We invoke you with fire and air (swing

censer) and we call you. Awake, awake oh center (ring bell).

All now join in a chant of:

Isis, Astarte, Diana,
Hegate, Demeter, Kali,
Inana,

Repeat four times.

Osiris, Horis, Merlin,
Monanin, Helios, Shiva,
Horned One

Repeat four times.

Coven members now lie naked on the floor with each of their bodies in the shape of a pentagram for the god identity meditation. Here each person takes on the form of a sex divinity. In this position each point of the pentagram (head, left hand, left foot, right foot, and right hand) is identified as a part of life's cycles: sex, self, passion, pride, power. These words are repeated as each person visualizes each of these processes. A second meditation is done with love, wisdom, knowledge, law, and power. The last meditation consists of each person visualizing the life cycle: birth, initiation, consummation, repose, and death. Each person experiences the power and energy of being a god or goddess and each proceeds through the sex ritual in this new identity.

One person now lies down and their partner moves their hands over their body but without touching it. This pushes old energy out of the body and is done by running the hand from waist up past the head and from waist down the legs; the waist line is never crossed. The old energy is now replaced with positive new energy from the consort by slowly blowing onto the goddess along the same lines which the energy was released. The partner must be able to feel the breath move up and down their body because this is the initial stimulation that causes sexual arousal.

The couples exchange places and repeat the performance on their consort. Once accomplished, the energy is again exchanged, but this time with a vampire suck. The couple takes turns kissing and sucking at the neck while visualizing a flow of white energy entering into their body through their mouth. After each person is satisfied, the vampire sucking is done to each nipple and then to the genitals.

The two now join in the sacred sex act as they continue to visualize the life cycles of the earth and their connection with it as divine entities. The lovers remain joined until both return to a centered or relaxed state. There may be a tingling or throbbing sensation throughout the body caused by the excess generation of energy.

The circle is finally opened as people in the group hold hands and say "The circle is open, but unbroken, blessed be." A kiss is then passed around the circle in a clockwise direction. (Sex magick lessons from Karaqua, 1991, San Francisco)

Adding ritual to an act creates a mystique and heightens the intensity of arousal. This is true even for those without partners. An individual form of sex magick is practiced by an organization called the Temple of Psychic Youth (TOPY) which operates by mail. Its members perform individual sex rituals known as the 23 ritual. This ritual is done on the 23rd of each month at 11:23pm. The member lights a candle, focuses on a favorite sexual fantasy, has an orgasm, and then puts some of the ejaculate or vaginal secretions on a piece of paper. Spit is then added along with a drop of blood and a pubic hair. These are attached to the paper and then mailed back to the headquarters of the organization.

(See also RITUAL SEX, SATAN WORSHIP and VISUALIZATION)

SEX MUSEUMS There are several museums that have a collection of sexual artifacts or paraphernalia on display. The Venus Temple in Amsterdam has in its collection a mannequin of Marilyn Monroe in the famous pose from her movie *The Seven Year Itch*. It is rigged so that when one pushes a button a burst of air causes her skirt to blow upward exposing her legs and undergarments. They also have a collection of old photographs and two phone booths where one can listen to a recording of a typical fantasy hotline.

A Peruvian museum has an adults only section that displays ancient pottery portraying various sex acts. There are also numerous private collections that are occasionally exhibited to the public, such as the Robert Mapplethorpe photo exhibit and Frederick's of Hollywood's collection of lingerie worn by movie stars.

Although not a museum, the famous Konarak temple near the southeastern shore of India is a popular tourist attraction. It was built by King Narashima Deva around 1250 C.E. and carved on its walls are many sex scenes presumed to have been taken from the *Kama Sutra*. Sex was sacred to Indians as one of their Hindu scriptures suggests, "It is not so important to know thyself as to be thyself; self-abandonment to desire begets freedom from the same." Indians celebrate the festival of Shanipuja at this temple once a year. Women who survived illnesses during the previous year lie garlands of flowers on a stone penis which symbolizes generative power.

(See also SEX BOUTIQUES)

SEX POSITIONS People are beginning to experiment with various sex positions without the shame or guilt that has been imposed since the Catholic Church accepted the laws of the Stoics who in 100 B.C.E. declared that couples could only have sex in a supine position with the male on top. These patriarchal laws led to 2,000 years of inability to orgasm for many women and sexual repression in general. Today sexual positions are engaged in to facilitate deeper penetration, allow access to different parts of a partner's body, and to regulate pressure on the penis or clitoris.

A man who ejaculates quicker than he would like can use a missionary position with the woman on top or any other position that offers the least pressure and friction (in addition to using extra lubrication or a condom). Conversely, a person who takes longer to ejaculate may select positions that increase stimulation such as from behind, missionary with the woman's legs raised over his buttocks, a scissor position where the penis hits the side of the vagina or where the woman's legs are held together.

Positions that facilitate orgasm for women who prefer clitoral stimulation are those with the man lying (spoon position) or standing behind while simultaneously reaching around to stimulate her clitoris with his fingers. Clitoral stimulation can be accomplished in the missionary position as well. This is done by withdrawing the penis a couple of inches so that the tip remains in the vagina and the base rests against the clitoris. The penis is then rotated in circles or thrust up and down or back and forth, but always remaining in contact with the clitoris.

The use of chairs, pillows, swings, day beds, and counters can help one create new sex positions.

Gay sex positions often include the 69 position for oral sex, the spoon for anal entry with one reaching around with their hand for manual stimulation, and missionary where the bottom partner's legs are wrapped around the buttocks of the top male. Lesbians use the 69 position, sometimes with their legs wrapped around each other in a position that resembles a ball. Those who use strap on dildos are able to use many of the same positions engaged in by others.

Jessica Stewart compiled an excellent book on this subject entitled *The Complete Manual of Sexual Positions*. It has over 200 photographs and includes positions for group sex as well.

(See also AXILLISM, COITUS A CHEVAL, COITUS A MAMMILLA, COITUS INTERFERMORIS, GENUPHALLATION and HEAD STANDS)

SEX RESTAURANTS There are several types of sex restaurants. Some, such as the Hjarlter Dam, a Swiss restaurant, allow dominant women to anchor their slaves to a table or chair leg. Many American restaurants and bars during the 70's allowed other discreet forms of sex play such as fellatio under the table or toe jobs at the table.

The Japanese have coffee shops called the No Pan Kissa that are equipped with mirrored tiles on the floor to assist customers who may want to look up the dresses of their waitress. Incidently, the waitresses' uniforms do not include underwear.

London, the home of whipping enthusiasts, has School Dinners where patrons are caned by the waitresses if they don't finish their vegetables.

(See also SEX HOTELS, SEX SHOWS and SEX MUSEUMS)

SEX RINGS A sex ring refers to pedophilia involving several children and one or more adults. There are several types of sex rings. "A solo ring consists of one adult who is sexually involved with small groups of children. There is no transfer of the children or of photographs to other adults. A syndicated ring includes several adults who form a well-structured organization for the recruitment of children, the production of pornography, the delivery of direct sexual services, and the establishment of an extensive network of customers. In a transitional ring there may be more than one adult with several children, but the organizational aspect of the syndicated ring is missing. The transitional rings may be moving toward the organizational status of the syndicated ring; for example, the photographs may be sold" ("Response Patterns in Children and Adolescents Exploited Through Sex Rings and Pornography", by Ann Wolbert Burgess, R.N., D.N.Sc., Carol R. Hartman, R.N., D.N.Sc., Maureen P. McCausland, R.N., M.S. and Patricia Powers, R.N., M.S., *American Journal of Psychiatry*, 141:5, May 1984, pp. 656-662). The authors point out that boys were preferred most often, and in a study of 66 children 75% of the "victims demonstrated patterns of negative psychological and social adjustment after the rings were exposed." Activity in one ring included as many as 17 boys going to a coach's home after school where the boys sat "in a circle drinking beer and smoking marijuana", then the man dressed in a samurai outfit and signaled the boys to begin their sex ritual. After the orgy, which the coach photographed, "one boy would be designated to have sex with the man."

Children are less likely to report this type of sexual abuse because their friends and siblings are also involved; making it appear more normal. Financial rewards also serves to provide additional enticement. CAUTION: Any sexual activity between adults and children, including sex rings, is illegal.

The psychological injury sustained by these children and their parents is profound, and the punishment for the perpetrator is severe. The temporary excitement and financial gain is not worthwhile. Children should also be forewarned about such adult activities.

(See also INCEST, PEDOPHILIA, PORNOGRAPHY, PROSTITUTION and RAPE)

SEX SHOWS (Autagonistophilia—person performing) Sex shows vary according to the laws of the hosting country, expertise of the participants, creativity of the owners, and amount of money they are willing to spend for special effects.

Sex shows in Amsterdam consist mostly of erotic dancing where several solo females perform followed by the finale with a heterosexual couple thrusting in time with the music. While the sex act is sensual, one is left with the impression that they were

watching a dance routine. Other clubs have women from the audience come onto the stage to fellate the male performers. A sister city, Den Haag, features sex shows at Club DOMA, a posh private S/M club. An audience of attractive couples and a few older men sit in black leather booths watching a stage performance of light bondage and S/M. These are mostly women who bring each other to climax throughout the different segments of the show. Occasionally a volunteer from the audience is brought on stage to assist in the production.

Dallas, Texas has a private couples only club that has sex shows provided by an elected couple each week. These two partners then go through their routine for the entertainment of the others.

Paris has a restaurant called *Les Deux Boules* where couples lie in nets and engage in sex above the tables of customers who dine below. Germany's *Mon Cheri* club provides a bubble bath for customers to relax in with the female performers.

Bangkok probably has the most variety. One club has a woman pulling a 25 foot knotted cord out of her vagina. Others insert cigarettes, blow smoke rings, and pull out a string of double edged razor blades—one by one. This is accomplished by placing the group of blades together with paper around them as they are inserted. Their removal requires the skill of an older performer who slowly pulls on the string and makes sure that the pressure is on the side protected by the paper. Other women are trained to shoot baskets with boiled eggs or to insert a whole peeled banana and drop chunks into a cup. Some have learned to break balloons by inserting a dart gun into their vagina and shooting darts with their vaginal muscles. The bottle dance, where a woman squats and lowers herself onto the neck of a bottle, also has a long history among prostitutes.

The Philippines has sex shows near Clark Air Force Base where women pick up a stack of coins two to three inches high with their vagina and then release the coins one by one. Others shoot ping pong balls across the room from their vaginas, or act out fake stabbing scenes with realistic props. One show at the Thunder Dome has two naked women in a pool of water fighting as though one will drown the other.

The Gargoyle club in London once had an act where a man threw bowie knives at a naked woman who was bound to a wheel.

A Vietnamese club had a woman sitting on a swing that was attached to a pulley. This allowed a man to lie on the floor below the opening cut in the swing and raise and lower the female onto his penis.

San Francisco is the home of the internationally renowned O'Farrell Theatre. The females are college age and all resemble beauty contestants. Performances are restricted to females using dildos or performing cunnilingus on each other due to a city ordinance prohibiting sex with men on stage. The theatre has regularly scheduled performances throughout the day in each of its rooms. The main theatre has a stage where there are continual strip shows and lap dancers to entertain the audience. The Cine Stage has two female body builders that do Jazzercise and weight workouts to music and then end the show with a dildo routine. The stage, Behind the Green Door, has showers where females stand in front of the water and dance; soon all but two dancers leave the stage to lie on the customer's tables giving private shows to those who tip. The Kopenhagen Room has couches along the walls on which customers sit in the dark and watch a couple of strippers have sex in the center of the room. All are provided with flash lights to shine on parts of the body they find the most intriguing. The Ultra Room is rather

unique. Here two dancers perform sex in a room surrounded by private booths with windows and a small space through which to slide tips. Above the windows are metal handles that the women use to hold themselves up with while putting a foot on each side of the booth's window. A dildo with a suction cup is stuck to the glass and the woman then mounts it in such a way that the person in the booth sees her open vagina thrusting up and down on a large rubber penis. She may also fellate the dildo afterward or have the other dancer join her for a special fisting show. A different sex theater during the late 1970's had an additional feature. The dancers inside the room slipped silk cords through the small slot below the window (normally used for tips), the man tied one end around his penis, and the dancer tugged at the other end until the man ejaculated.

(See also EROTIC BALLS, SEX CLUBS, SEX CONFERENCES and SEX MUSEUMS)

SEX SURROGATES   Sex surrogates are trained to work with psychologists in helping clients overcome sexual problems. The surrogate normally pays $1,000 to attend a 12-week training program where they learn anatomy, human sexual response, communication, and other subjects pertinent to surrogate work. Masters and Johnson first reported results of treatment for sexual dysfunctions with sex surrogates. The study included 41 men and 13 different

surrogates over an 11 year period. Of these men 32 recovered from their problems (Masters WH, Johnson VE, 1970, *Human Sexual Inadequacy*, London: J and A Churchill, London).

The use of sex surrogates flourished during the 1970's but thereafter sharply declined. Benefits obtained from this type of personal therapy can be substantial. People suffering from psychological impotence, premature or retarded ejaculations, accidents, disfigurements, and those with penis implants are trained to deal with the complication, and they often improve when working with surrogates. Many problems are related to emotional bonding and the client is also taught to work through ordinary dating relationships with the surrogate. Unlike a dating relationship the person is not permitted to drop the surrogate when they feel uncomfortable or prefer someone new. The client's therapist encourages them to work through their conflicts so that they can survive in a normal relationship. Many clients never experience genital penetration with their surrogate. Those who do have intercourse with the surrogate do it toward the end of the treatment program. Once the client is able to have intercourse they are often considered cured and no longer in need of a surrogate.

Surrogates are average looking males and females who often work with either sex. Average looks discourage abuses such as those who might fabricate sexual problems to be able to work with attractive partners. Another reason therapists prefer average looking surrogates is that this is a more realistic aspect of life. Middle aged men are encouraged to give up their fantasies of only wanting to have sex with 20 year old gorgeous blonds. A surrogate teaches them to value a person for more meaningful attributes.

Surrogates come from a variety of backgrounds. Some are from sex related fields but for whatever reason, prostitutes do not seem attracted to this profession. Each surrogate is expected to have a personal relationship of their own. This is designed to help prevent the surrogate from unintentionally using the client for their own emotional support.

The normal duration of treatment is once a week for 7 to 14 weeks although some older clients take 20-40 weeks. A surrogate may see from one to 10 clients a week and will charge approximately $200 for a two-hour session. The surrogate rarely has sex with more than one or two of these clients a week. ("Sex Surrogates", by C. Cohen and J. Robinson, Mensa Sexyg Gathering Conference, February 17-18, 1990)

(See also IMPOTENCE and SEXOLOGISTS)

SEX TOYS See ABRASIONS, BONDAGE, CLAMPS, COCKRINGS, CUPPING, ELECTRIC SHOCK, FORNICATORY DOLLS, GENITAL/ANAL INSERTS, GROPING APPARATUS, ICE, JEWELRY, KLISMAPHILIA, KNIVES, KOKIGAMI, MEDICAL SCENES, OXYGEN REGULATION, PENETRATION TOYS, POWER TOOLS, SEX GAMES, STAPLING, SWINGS, and SYBIAN

SEXERCISE Sexercise is a name for exercises engaged in during intercourse and/or those that tone muscles used for sex.

Sexercise includes such exercises as 30 or 40 deep sucking movements up and down the penis during fellatio which is excellent for keeping facial muscles toned. Sexercise can also be in the form of push-ups or pelvic thrusts during coitus or keeping the buttock muscles squeezed together for as long as possible. Women can practice squeezing their pubococcygeus muscle around the penis. This is the same muscle that is used to stop the flow of urine. Once developed, a woman can massage the penis with these vaginal muscles. This is also referred to by some as the "snapping pussy" or kystapaza that has made some Asian prostitutes famous. Men are able to do something similar by raising and lowering the penis. Leg muscles can be exercised by one partner squatting over the face or genitals of the other.

Partners can be creative with sexercise, even using special music as an accompaniment. Penetration is not always necessary. A naked couple may merely decide to go through regular exercises together that require body contact.

(See also KABAZZAH and MASTURBATION)

SEXOLOGY There are many physicians and psychologists who are renowned for their understanding of and contributions to the science of sex. The following is only a sampling.

IWAN BLOCH Dr. Bloch (1872-1922), author of *Psychopathia Sexualis, Sexual Life of Our time,* and *Vita Sexualis,* made a major contribution to sexology. His early research on syphilis led him to conclude that sexual problems could not be understood based exclusively on theology, medicine, law, or anthropology. He felt that "the two fundamental pillars of sexual investigation—biologic observation and cultural research—demanded a restricted, independent rigorous science that would unite all the various methods of observation in one" (*Strange Sexual Practices* by Iwan Bloch, Introduction by Dr. Victor Robinson).

HAVELOCK ELLIS Ellis (1859-1939) was an English physician, son of a sea-captain who took him as a young boy aboard his ship to Australia and Peru. This early exposure to different cultures later instilled in Ellis a tolerant attitude regarding individual sexual choices. Adolescence again saw him in Australia and it was here that he studied medicine. His renowned seven volume book, *Studies in the Psychology of Sex,* gained world-wide attention. Sex was only one of the subjects that caught his interest. He wrote 17 books on politics and medical science within 44 years. Ellis led a quiet revolution to free people of their prejudice against those whose sex lives were different.

SIGMUND FREUD Freud (1856-1939) began as a neurologist in Vienna and became the father of psychoanalysis. His clinical work with patients who had experienced sexual trauma during childhood led him to develop theories regarding the effect sexual development has on behavior. Although not popular among his colleagues, Freud gained a following. His books were soon burned in Nazi Germany which banned them as representative of a "Jewish science." He died of cancer in England a year after the Nazi invasion of Austria. His contribution to sexology was his having the courage to take sex seriously during a period when others evaded serious research or discussion of the subject (*The Sex Atlas*, by Erwin J. Haeberle, pp. 488-489).

MAGNUS HIRSCHFELD Hirschfeld (1868-1935), like his father, was a physician, although his first studies were in philosophy. While traveling in Africa he saw civilizations that were tolerant and accepting of sexual deviances. This made him more tolerant and helped convince him that puritanical European society had inflicted unnecessary sexual mores on people. He later began a movement to petition the Reichstag to remove a law in the Criminal Codes against homosexuals. Soon he created the Institute for Sexual Science. At the Institute the clinic offered free medical advice, the university section had lectures that were open to the public; there was also a marriage counseling center, and a library that was available for anyone's use. Hirschfeld wrote books such as *Sappho and Socrates, Natural Laws of Love, Homosexuality*, and his 3,000 page *Sexual Pathology*. He was compassionate and fought in court as a medical expert to defend people charged with sexual offenses. He was also responsible for the initial discovery that hormones played a role in sexual behavior, and that "sexual anomalies are caused by irregularities in development." At the end of his life he found himself exiled, his Institute destroyed, his books publicly burned, and his colleagues imprisoned (*Sexual Anomalies and Perversions*, Publisher's Preface, pp. 17-25).

VIRGINIA E. JOHNSON Johnson (1925-) married William Masters and worked together with him to gather data from laboratory testing of couples engaging in sex. Volunteers were hooked up to instruments to monitor their physiological responses as they engaged in sex. Johnson and Masters also filmed many of these couples. The data collected was published in their book, *Human Sexual Response*. The information they gathered also provided the basis of a treatment program they offered to couples. (See also William H. Masters.)

ALFRED KINSEY Kinsey (1894-1956) was an entomologist who, appalled upon discovering how little scientific knowledge was available about human sexuality, decided to launch a systematic study. In 1948 he astounded the public with the release of his findings from 16,000 interviews in *Sexual Behavior in the Human Male*. His method of gathering information has been criticized by some. But considering the almost impossible challenge of gathering random samplings from people who are willing to be honest about their sex life, he accomplished an enormous feat.

RICHARD VON KRAFFT-EBING Krafft-Ebing (1840-1902) was a psychiatrist and neurologist. He became interested in sexual deviancy while staying with his grandfather in Heidelberg, Germany. This grandfather was an attorney who defended people charged with sex offenses in a Puritanical society. Krafft-Ebing studied and gained an expertise in "hypnosis, hysteria, criminal psychopathy, geriatrics, epilepsy, menstrual psychoses, migraine, and masochism." He is known primarily for his book *Psychopathia Sexualis* (which was the first comprehensive listing of sexual aberrations), for emphasizing "the importance of clitoral orgasm," and bringing the scientific discussion of homosexuality into the open (*Psychopathia Sexualis*, Introduction by Franklin S. Klaf).

WILLIAM H. MASTERS Masters (1915-) is a medical researcher who concentrated his studies on hormone replacement therapy for postmenopausal women during an era when major discoveries were being made in this field. He is better known, however, for his research in couple sex therapy. In 1971 he married his research partner Virginia Johnson. (See Virginia E. Johnson.)

JOHN MONEY Money (1921-) has written several popular books: *Straight, Gay and In-Between, Lovemaps, Love & Love Sickness, The Destroying Angel, Traumatic Abuse and Neglect of Children at Home*, and *Venuses Penuses*. He "is internationally known for his clinical and research work in the new and growing science of developmental sexology. In sexology he first formulated and defined the concept of gender role and identity. His clinical contributions include hormonal treatment for male sex offenders, sex reassignment in transsexualism, and the psychoendocrinology of birth defects of the sex organs" (*Lovemaps* jacket cover). Money has also coined many new words, giving us the tools to communicate more precisely regarding complex gender changes and paraphilias. (For reference purposes, a complete list of these terms follows:

Acrotomophilia, Adolescentilism (paraphilic), Androgynophilia, Andromimesis, Apotemnophilia, Asphyxiophilia, Autagonistophilia, Autassassinophilia, Autonepiophilia, Autophilia, Biastophilia, Catheterophilia, Chrematistophilia, Chronophilia, Displacement Paraphilia, Ephebophilia, Erotophonophilia, Exigency theory, Fetishistic/Talismanic Paraphilia, Formicophilia, G-I/R (gender-identity/role), Gender coding, Gender crosscoding, Gendermap, Gender Role, Gender transposition, Gerontalism—paraphilic, Gerontophilia, Gynemimesis, Gynemimetophilia, Hybristophilia, Hypophilia, Infantilism—paraphilic, Infantophilia, Inclusion Paraphilia, Juvenilism—paraphilic, Kleptophilia, Marauding/Predatory Paraphilia, Mercantile/Venal Paraphilia, Morphophilia, Munchausen's syndrome by proxy, Narratophilia, Nepiophilia, Normophilia, Olfactophilia, Paleodigms, Peodeiktophilia, Phylism, Pictophilia, Raptophilia, Sacrificial/Expiatory Paraphilia, Sex adjunctive, Sex adventitious, Sex derivative, Sex irreducible, Sexosophy, Skoptic Syndrome, Solicitational/Allurative Paraphilia, Somnophilia, Stigmatic/Eligiblic paraphilia, Stigmatophilia, Subrogation/understudy paraphilia, Symphorophilia, Telephonicophilia, Transvestophilia, and Vandalized lovemaps. For definitions of some of these terms see *Gay, Straight, and In-Between*, Oxford University Press, 1988)

WILHELM REICH Reich (1897-1957) was a psychoanalyst who studied under Freud. He brought about much of his later misfortune by mixing sex and politics. He compiled volumes of research on human sexuality and was the first to analyze orgasms and divided them into four phases. Several of his students went on to make great contributions as well. One developed Gestalt therapy and another founded Esalen. He was also a scientist who discovered, among other natural phenomena, the "bion and T bacilli, which are microscopic forms that originate from the disintegration of organic or inorganic materials, and which lie at the border between the living and non-living worlds." His works, in Nazi Germany, soon brought about his expulsion from the Communist Party and in the mid-

1930's he escaped under threat of death. Even in America he was subject to much harassment. His books were banned and burned, and his laboratory was vandalized. The Food and Drug Administration obtained an injunction to prevent Reich and his followers from using the word "orgone" and Reich was later arrested on "a technical violation of an injunction, and died in prison." Books such as *The Mass Psychology of Fascism, The Function of the Orgasm, The Sexual Revolution,* and *Listen, Little Man* survived. There are also institutes such as the Orgone Biophysical Research Lab, in El Cerrito, California that continue his research on orgone energy (*Natural Energy Works* catalog, p. 2). His theories on orgone are not generally accepted in the scientific community but his works on sexuality and the effects of a sexually repressive government on human health are once again receiving attention. (Personal communication with Robert Moore and Don Eckerstrom of the Healing Dynamic Center, in Arizona.)

There are many more physicians, psychiatrists, researchers, anthropologists, and writers who have made major contributions to our understanding of sexuality but whose individual contributions, for space considerations, cannot be mentioned. Today counselors and researchers can obtain a degree in sexology. One such doctorate program is offered at the Institute for the Advanced Study of Human Sexuality (1523 Franklin Street, San Francisco, California 94109). They may be contacted for referrals to qualified sexologists in one's local area.

(See also BIRTH CONTROL, CELIBACY and ST. AUGUSTINE)

SEXUAL HARASSMENT Section 703 of Title VII of the Civil Rights Act of 1964 reads "Unwelcome sexual advances, requests for sexual favors, and other verbal or physical conduct of a sexual nature constitute sexual harassment when (1) submission to such conduct is made either explicitly or implicitly a term or condition of an individual's employment, (2) submission to or rejection of such conduct by an individual is used as the basis for employment decisions affecting such individual, or (3) such conduct has the purpose or effect of unreasonably interfering with an individual's work performance or creating an intimidating, hostile, or offensive working environment....The victim as well as the harasser may be a woman or a man. The victim does not have to be of the opposite sex."

One difficulty in understanding sexual harassment is that similar sexual 'communication' made to 10 separate people elicits 10 different reactions ranging from anger and rejection to a favorable response. Deeper understanding requires that we look at why sexual harassment occurs and why harassees feel victimized. Almost all 'recognized' and reported sexual harassment is of women by men. However, females employed in upper management have become more aggressive and some intimidate their subordinate male workers similarly. Females lacking this power use more covert forms of harassment. (See RAPE)

Developing males typically learn to overcome fear. They face continual pressure, such as defeat by unscrupulous competitors. They must submit to the rage of superiors. They must often fight to get what they want or deserve. They learn by experience that the stronger male takes what he wants, then fights to keep it. Some men have difficulty changing from competing in their daily lives to vying for the attention of women.

There are various types of sexual harassment of women by men. Some men are merely egalitarian—they tell jokes and discuss sex with women just as they would with men. They do not expect to be physically intimate with the woman and may not want such intimacy. Other men need flattery or special attention; they seek the love and nurturance that sex implies and are more prone to developing relationships. When such a man is rejected, he often becomes angry and may seek revenge to assuage his pain. If he is unscrupulous, he may threaten the woman or try to harm her reputation or career. Other men are insecure about whether their friends like them and will only harass women in front of such

male friends. These men realize that they are being insulting but are exhibiting acts of 'bravery'. The same type of bravery is observed in primitive tribes where one hunter would run ahead of a group to attack a large animal or enemy.

Females are not usually taught to overcome or work through their fears. It is considered culturally acceptable in many societies for them to be victims, depending on a father figure to solve problems. Women often compete with peers using appearance, wardrobe, or seduction techniques that are also part of courtship rituals designed to attract male sexual attention.

Women grow up physically weaker than men. This creates an important psychological handicap. Females worry about possible rape or assault any time they walk down a dark street alone. Some women experience similar fear in their own homes. Few men can comprehend such concerns but it helps to understand because it can affect a woman's emotions when a man approaches her. She implicitly realizes that he could overpower her at any moment. And yet, the male is usually oblivious to her concern.

Sexual harassment involves a 'political' power game between men and women (power is defined here as the control of something someone else wants). So a woman has power, provided she says "no" to sexual advances, and a man can usurp that power only if he gets a favorable sexual response or takes what he wants by unscrupulous tactics such as threatening her with dismissal (his power ploy).

This subtle power struggle makes sexual harassment an important issue among feminists attempting to keep the scales balanced. Another concern about sexual harassment noted by the heterosexual majority is the inclusion of opinions regarding male sexuality from lesbian leaders of the feminist movement. While lesbians may be the first to notice female repression and job discrimination, the lesbian view of male sexuality is different from the attitude of heterosexual women. Sexual harassment between heterosexual men and women is dampened, because in any relationship a partner is judged on over-all performance, attributes weighed against faults. Heterosexual women involved in close, loving relationships with men can make this adjustment, but lesbians typically cannot. This is particularly true of lesbian feminists who have been raped by men. Heterosexual women are more willing to accept men's desires, for example 'raunchy' magazines, and their lust for women. Lesbians are much less likely to feel this compassion, or benefit from the power heterosexual men bestow on women they find attractive. In this context, similar separation of the sexes led single male clergy to support burning thousands of witches between the 13th and 17th centuries. Because they didn't have relationships with women, they were unable to regard them as human.

Women also differ from men in being less sexually attracted to men as a group. A female in love with one man often finds the touch of any other male offensive, whereas monogamous men do not seem to be as threatened by flirting, sexual conversation and casual touching.

In addition to the physical fear of rape, another major fear influencing women in their reactions to sexual harassment is social fear of engaging in so-called 'deviant' behavior.

Social disapproval and repression of sex is deep seated in many cultures. Society has imposed harsh judgments against those defying the narrow confines of 'normal' sex. This has endured for so many generations that people in most cultures are no longer aware of the basis of these beliefs nor of their origins.

Considering conditions in 17th through 19th century Europe we can see the origins of many of our negative attitudes about sex. During this time some of our ancestors were shackled to the front walls of churches and humiliated by people in their communities for minor sex offenses. Women who taught birth control or became pregnant out of wedlock were accused of heresy. As punishment their breasts were pinched off by a hot "Breast Ripper," or their vaginas ripped out by the "Oral, Rectal, and Vaginal Pear." The latter was used on the rectum of gays, who also faced the possibility of being sawn in half for their 'sin' while still alive.

Women who merely spoke up in church or against male authority were put into "Branks" or "Scold's Bridles" (metal masks) and staked in public squares where their fellow church members smeared them with feces or mutilated their breasts and genitals sadistically. People who refused to attend church on Sunday regularly despite warnings, would also be tortured for heresy.

Medical science panicked people by next reporting that loss of semen, for example in masturbation, caused insanity and created the same abnormalities as castration. Parents began having their children's genitals infibulated or blistered to prevent them from this fate.

It is against this backdrop that many people of today's generation respond to discussions of sex with fear and apprehension. This type of unfounded, superstitious fear promotes ignorance, sexual repression and harsh judgments against those trying to develop a more mature and rational opinion of sexual variance. This is the foundation of the second fear that affects many people's definition of sexual harassment—the social fear of engaging in so-called 'deviant' behavior.

In dealing constructively with sexual harassment, the harassee's discomfort or fear must be communicated explicitly to the harasser who must reply in a way showing that he or she understands the objection before the communication is ended.

Some women assume incorrectly that a disgusted facial expression conveys disapproval. They are enraged that a man continues in the face of such a warning. This is the thinking of a 'trained' victim afraid to communicate feelings to another person. On the other hand no harasser should be held responsible for such conduct unless the offended party clearly communicates disapproval. This disapproval should also be valid. People are not obliged to avoid sexual discussions any more than discussions on religion or politics, which will also inevitably offend some people.

People who find their working environment intolerable have a better case when they document occurrences of harassment, obtain witnesses, and show that they communicated their feelings to the offender and to management. Charges of sexual harassment are reported to field offices of the U.S. Equal Employment Opportunity Commission.

(See also RAPE)

SHAVING See DEPILATION

SHOWERS (Mysophilia—arousal from soiled clothing or foul decaying odors) Sexual showers refer to the expulsion of natural fluids onto a partner's body for arousal. A golden shower is comprised of urine, a milk shower of milk, a spit shower of saliva, a brown shower from feces, semen from semen, and Roman showers from vomit.

Semen showers are the most common and certainly the most accepted. These are done between the breasts, abdomen, buttocks, or on the face. Some are 'forced' to ejaculate on their own face as a form of humiliation in S/M games. American porn actors almost always ejaculate on the buttocks or abdomen of their partners. Some showers are staged with the assistance of a mechanical penis that ejects an egg white mixture.

Milk showers consist of a lactating woman squeezing her milk onto a partner, a non-lactating partner using commercial milk to rub over their own breasts, or someone pouring it onto the partner. (See also LACTAPHILIA)

Spitting is most often used as a lubricant but is also done in S/M games involving humiliation. (See SPITTING)

Golden showers are common during adolescence with the 'shooting' of insects, animals, and friends. Some write their names in the snow and others compete for who can shoot the longest distance. A large percentage of men questioned as to whether they had urinated on partners in the shower indicated that they had, some doing it without their partner's knowledge. Golden showers are sprayed on the face, body, genitals, or mouth of a partner. Some consider this to be a form of humiliation but others love the warm sensation, closeness, and trust it provides. (Refer to chapter on UROPHILIA.)

Brown showers refer to partners who defecate on one another. This may also be done using enemas, some of which may consist of diluted wine or food. (Refer to COPROPHILIA and COCKTAILS)

The Roman shower, or emetophilia, is rare. In such cases people typically drink wine or urine and then vomit these contents onto a partner or into a bowl. One form is called a chocolate mousse and consists of a combination of a  Roman and brown shower. The person swallows whipped cream and then their partner gives them an enema with chocolate pudding. Once prepared the person defecates the pudding onto the partner and then vomits the whipped cream on top. This creates a dessert for one or both.

Some may be tempted to make judgments about those who engage in this behavior. However, among practitioners are several Christian ecstatics who were later canonized. Alacoque and later Madame Guyon both spoke of irresistible desires to clean up the vomit of sick patients with only their tongue and St. John of the Cross found pleasure in sucking on the sores of lepers. CAUTION: The exchange of body fluids is not considered a safe sex practice.

SIDERODROMOPHILIA Siderodromophilia (siderodromo: trains; philia: attachment to) refers to those who are aroused by trains. Couples sometimes reserve a cabin and will have sex standing in front of the window as the train passes through a town or a station. Others squeeze into bathrooms or sneak quickies in corners. Trains provide more privacy and opportunity to socialize than airplanes or buses.

(See also COITUS A CHEVAL, DOGGING, HODOPHILIA and TUNNEL OF LOVE)

SIN See PECATTIPHILIA

SITOPHILIA (Botulinonia—sex with sausage) Sitophilia (sito: food; philia: attachment to) refers to those who use food for sexual purposes. Masturbation aids are found in the form of corn cobs, squash, cucumbers, bananas, sausages, warm melons, liver in a milk carton, or a jar of honey.

One gastronomic game is used in bondage scenes. The male partner is first immobilized, a paper plate is cut so that a  2" diameter hole is made off-center. The plate is held over the male genitals and these are pulled through so that the genitals now look as though they are being served on a platter. Luke warm spaghetti and meatballs are served onto the plate and, with fork in hand, a helpless male is told he is about to be fed his own balls. It doesn't matter who eats the meatballs but each strand of spaghetti is sensuously wrapped around the penis and sucked through the lips before being eaten.

Another use of food is that of taking a plum that is slightly slit, pitted, and pushed onto an erect glans penis. Once secure this can be inserted into a partner's vagina, adding volume and pressure for both partners. Banana carving contests are used as erotic teases at adult parties. A row of contestants are lined up, given a banana, and then told to compete with each other for who can carve the most realistic penis with only their teeth. Some strippers use a cucumber in a pseudo-castration scene where they have a man hold a cucumber between his upper thighs and then proceed to fellate the green erection. As the audience becomes enthralled the stripper bites off the tip of the cucumber. People sometimes suck on a lime before oral cunnilingus to make their taste buds swell, creating more texture when rubbed against sensitive genital tissue. There are special caterers that design cakes and pastries with a sexual theme.

People also stuff objects like grapes, small tomatoes, peeled and cooled hard boiled eggs, and small pieces of ice into the rectum for erotic pleasure. (Refer to section on ANAL SEX.)

Another use of food consists of combining it with body secretions. One couple devel-

oped a game where the wife, after dismissing herself during a formal dinner to go to the woman's restroom, upon returning would dip her finger in some food and put her finger to her husband's lips asking him to try it. People at the table, if they noticed at all, thought he was only tasting food, while in fact she had first dipped her finger in urine. The same is done with vaginal secretions.

People aroused by lactating breasts sometimes drop cream onto a partner's nipples and then lick it off. Sex surrogates use food to get some clients back in touch with their body. The surrogate gets the client excited and salivating by slowly rubbing their favorite food on their body. This reconditions their bodies to respond to touch. Food orgy parties are organized by individuals where friends bring either an erotic arrangement of food on a dish to share, or food that feels sensuous when rubbed onto a partner and licked off; afterward everyone soaks in a hot tub. There are all-male games such as "Shoot the Cookie" where males stand in a circle around a cookie and masturbate. The rule dictates that the last one who ejaculates on the cookie has to eat it.

Food can be used for a form of flagellation. A regular client of an Oregon bordello during the 1940's would pay to have two prostitutes watch him strip naked, put on high heels, get into a tub of bath water, and walk back and forth. His only request was that they throw oranges at his buttocks as he paced. He would then get out, pick up the oranges, replace them in his paper bag, dress, and leave. (Personal communication.)

(See also COCKTAILS, LACTAPHILIA, PIE THROWING and STUFFING)

SLAPPING See FLAGELLATION

SLAVES (Famulus) There is great variety in how people use sex slavery. The most famous sex slave was the Biblical Samson who was captured by the Philistines and, according to the Talmud, used to inseminate their wives in order to produce a race of superhumans. They blinded him so that this task would be easier.

Most do not live as slaves 24 hours a day but rather practice it for a few hours once a month or so. Slaves may serve one master exclusively or may be passed from one master to another. One master wrapped his sex slave in a sheet and drove her to a  friend's home to be used for his pleasure. Slaves may cook and serve guests at a special dinner or accompany their master to a party and care for their needs there. The slave may sleep in the bed with their master or on a rug next to the bed, in a box, or cage. 'Captive' slaves may have to be bound at night. Slaves usually prefer providing personal service such as bathing, brushing hair, polishing nails, shaving, massage, and holding a dildo or vibrator. ("Slave Fantasies", Society of Janus lecture, July 27, 1989)

Slaves need a reminder of the status that renders them different from others. Sex slaves identify themselves by wearing slave collars, an "o" finger ring, a brand, a special necklace, or chastity belt.

K. C. Rourke, a professional dominatrix and personal slave, describes the nuances of these relationships:

In order to understand the nature of Master/ slave relationships, it is important to realize that this slavery is imposed neither by law nor by social custom; even a slave who is defiant is a slave by personal choice. However, the nature of that choice and its implementation vary; sex slaves may be categorized according to why they chose their slavery, and how they see themselves and their masters.

In examining this question, it is helpful to look at three pairs of personality characteristics: passive/aggressive, dominant/submissive, sadistic/masochistic. Each pair forms a scale; every personality can be rated somewhere on each scale. The scales are independent of one another; a person can be, for instance, aggressive, submissive and masochistic.

The first pair relates to how a person sees (him)herself in relation to her environment: does she prefer to make things happen or let things happen? The second pair relates to how she sees herself in relation to other people: is she a leader or a follower? The third set relates to pain: does she seek to experience it, or inflict it? (In this instance, pain may be defined as physical and/or psychological, and many people are fairly neutral on this scale).

The first category of slave is the captive. She finds it exciting to have volition removed by another. If she has guilt feelings about sex, the loss of control may enable her to let go and enjoy 'forbidden' pleasures. She must be convinced, however, that her freedom has indeed been taken away, and will frequently test the control of the dominant. She might even require that she be physically captured and subdued, and only respond to the Master when she's sure he's in total command. In this kind of relationship, restriction and ritual play an important part, and contracts may be negotiated in advance.

The second category is the passive slave. This is a person who doesn't want to take responsibility for his/her actions, and seeks someone to take that responsibility away. This kind of slave will seek out a full-time dominant, rather than occasional or contractual play. S/he is frequently a passive-aggressive person who forces others to make decisions so that s/he is free to blame them when things don't turn out to his/her liking. ("I don't know exactly what I want, but I know this isn't it and it's your fault!") This can be very draining to a dominant, because the so-called slave is actually running the show and putting a great deal of pressure on him.

The third category is sometimes called a SAM (Smart-Ass Masochist). This person has learned early in life that the only way to get attention is to do something bad and get punished. The alternative, in their minds, is to be ignored completely. In many cases they were even told by their parents that they were being punished "because I care about you..." and have come to confuse punishment with parental and other love. Their only goal in a Master-slave relationship is to misbehave and earn punishment. They, too, can be exhausting for a Master unless he is a committed sadist with a strong need to hurt or humiliate others.

The fourth category of slave can be referred to as the seeker or apprentice. This is a person who feels a strong need for guidance or direc-

tion. S/he will seek out a Master or Mistress s/he respects and admires, giving up authority in exchange for the guidance (training) s/he desires. S/he will go to great lengths to win the approval of the Master, and show him what s/he can do. If the Master disciplines such a slave, it is a loving affirmation of his authority and his acceptance of their service. If he wishes to punish them, he need only express disappointment with them. In many cases this type of slave is an aggressive and energetic person who lacks confidence and self-esteem, and needs encouragement, instruction and/or permission from a respected person. Many are highly intelligent and imaginative, and are more needful of validation than of actual training; others, through the training they receive, develop the confidence they need to function better independently. This kind of slave gradually becomes a great asset to a Master or Mistress.

The general guidelines for full time slave training include things like getting a written contract in which the slave agrees to give up (store) all personal possessions and live with the master, serving him or her completely for a specified period of time. The slave's contact with the outside world is often restricted or forbidden during this time. A slave needs to be made to feel that they are isolated with no one to rescue them, making them totally dependent on their new master regardless of their character. Slaves are not allowed to make any decisions for themselves. The master provides clothes (some go nude), food and water, and controls the times at which the slave may use the bathroom. These necessities are often used as rewards when getting the slave to submit to something in which they wouldn't ordinarily engage. Slaves generally pass through emotional phases of consensual role playing to irritation, defiance, anger, and submission, before they finally revere and bond to their master. This process is similar to spousal abuse or the Stockholm syndrome where prisoners, such as Patty Hearst, bond to their captors. Ritual, a form of psychological bondage, causes a slave to lose their own identity and become a willing receptor of someone else's desires. Special forms of address are used for the top such as Lord, Goddess, Mistress, and Master. Bottoms are called worm, Fido, slave, whore, or baby.

Slaves are sometimes taught to perform in the same manner as trained dogs. Hand signals are used to command a slave to stand, sit, speak, kneel, fetch, or kiss their master's feet. (*A Tangled Web: The Art of Slavery*, by Lady Tanith)

Lady Tanith, a professional dominatrix, also has a clientele of slaves that correspond by mail. A sample of one of the letters written to her by a slave is as follows:

You are Queen Satanja, Queen of all the land. I have been captured by your female warriors who have selected me to be your pleasure for the evening. My name is Tarus, General of the forces you have just defeated. My other warriors who have lived have been sent to the House of Pleasure where they will sexually please your best warriors...you will relate this to me. As I am brought in, you will be on your throne. You have no men in your empire...only the most beautiful women but those men you have captured in battle are your servants...you have a harem of men, that are at your beck and call for all sorts of sordid sexual orgies....

In this session you will teach me how to please you and your favored warriors....you will take every liberty with me that you want....you will:
-constantly curse at me...calling me all sorts of evil names
-seduce me as you tease and tantalize me and make me the captured animal of your royal court
-spit upon me
-continually tell me how I will be pleasing all of your female slave sluts at the orgies as you sit on the throne and watch
-make me worship your royal and beautiful body..within your royal limits...I will worship any part you wish including feet
-blindfold me for a portion of the session as you bring in your other female slave sluts to please you while I can only hear the moans of pleasure and lust....call them by name and tell them what to do to you.
-Eventually your seductive powers overcome me.

Bottom's disease refers to a slave whose self-esteem is so low that they consent to servitude because they prefer not to assert themselves. Most slaves, however, find a temporary period of service to be cathartic, similar to that of returning to childhood without the pressures of the business world. At the end of a couple of months or a year they are ready to face life's challenges again. Others feel it is a method by which to express their unconditional love and devotion to a partner and to have a partner return that love to them as individuals rather than because of their job status or what they own. ("Slave Training", by Lady Tanith, Back Drop lecture, January 26, 1991)

(See also DOMINANCE/SUBMISSION, FANTASY PLAY, HUMILIATION, PARAPHILIAS and RITUAL SEX)

SNUFF FILMS Actors in these films kill young victims during sex scenes. Snuff films are illegal and only sold underground; therefore, information on this subject is difficult to obtain.

One snuff film was briefly mentioned in the January 1986 issue of *Penthouse* in an article about Satanism by Dr. Joel Norris and Jerry Allen Potter in which they tell of a woman who uncovered a snuff film of a child being torn apart by its abductors. Today, most are filmed in Hong Kong and these also feature dismemberment.

An account of an American snuff film was given by a man working for an X-rated video company in England. In a personal interview he spoke of several snuff films seen in Germany during the early 70's. Most depicted strangulation and for that reason he could not guarantee that what he saw was authentic. However, one movie did have a scene that would have been difficult to stage. This movie was filmed in the Southern United States and was of a group of men driving along highways picking up female hitchhikers. They then bound their victims and took them to a small motel. Here the men would blindfold, gang bang, and perform sadistic acts such as ramming a broom handle up their vaginas before finally strangling them. The last female was treated much the same. They placed different items in her mouth to fellate; the final one being a hand gun with a silencer on the end, and as she sucked on this, the man pulled the trigger. Her naked body slammed against the wall behind and her bloody head caved in with the impact. (Special effects artists in the movie industry consulted by law enforcement agencies have confirmed that any mutilations can be duplicated with special effects techniques.)

People who purchase these movies probably do so out of curiosity or because this has long been a fantasy. For some it seems to bolster their own sense of power. Those who actually murder most often take their own photos or video of the event. (Interview with Detective James Rodriquez.) CAUTION: The greatest harm buyers of these films do is to provide incentive for producers to continue having innocent victims murdered.

(See also LUST MURDER, MUTILATION, PEDOPHILIA and SEX RINGS)

SOMNOPHILIA (Sleeping princess syndrome) Somnophilia (somnus: to sleep; philia: attachment to) refers to those who are sexually stimulated by fondling or having sex with a sleeping partner.

Many case studies of somnophiles show childhood histories of having covert sex with a sibling that was either asleep or pretending. They condition themselves to become aroused by a sleeping partner and when the circumstance changes they become impotent or ineffective. Professional therapy is often effective in helping a couple overcome this barrier to intimacy. CAUTION: This activity becomes unethical when done on minors sleeping in the same bed or with a partner who would not ordinarily consent.

(See also AMAUROPHILIA, FROTTAGE and NECROPHILIA)

SOUNDING (Urethral self-instrumentation) Sounding (subondare: to submerge) is the medical term for a metal rod used to find and dilate strictures in the urethra or other body cavities. Gonorrhea often left scar tissue that had to be removed in this manner. The sound instrument is slowly inserted down the urethra stretching open any scar tissue that is in its path. These instruments are purchased from medical supply houses.

People use sounding in S/M play for both increased sensation and to transfer power to the hands of the dominant. Other people use things such as rubber fishing worms, cotton swabs, or ice. The rubber fishing worms have a smooth surface, are flexible, and can be sterilized in a pressure cooker. Those who use ice freeze sterile water in paper straws and, once removed from the freezer for a few minutes, slide it out of the container. Ice is much more dangerous because of the risk of accidental breakage inside the urethra before it melts.

Physicians have found objects such as hairpins, plastic tubes, and even a small snake in people's bladders.

The most common type of sound used is the Van Buren which is curved at one end and ranges from .20 to .28" in diameter (the equivalent of the French sound sizes of 16 to 22). This is popular because once placed into position the end presses in the vicinity of the prostate gland which can then be gently stimulated.

A different variety of sounding consists of using 1/4" diameter stainless steel balls. These are counted, pushed into the urethra, and left there as the man masturbates. Upon ejaculation the seminal fluids push the balls out in a way that resembles a machine gun. The steel balls are again counted to verify that none remain in the urethra.

A pseudo type of sounding involves the practice of a partner pushing small amounts of warm water, champagne, or chips of ice into the very tip of the penis during fellatio. CAUTION: Sounding can cause serious injury. Signs of damage to the urethra are a change in the frequency one urinates, orange or brown urine, or pus. A doctor should be consulted if any of these symptoms occur. Even if treated, however, urinary tract infections can lead to kidney infections, kidney failure, and sometimes death.

(See also CATHETERS, MEATOTOMY and SAFE SEX/SOUNDING)

SPANKING See FLAGELLATION

SPECTROPHILIA (Incubus, Succubus)
Spectrophilia (spectral: phantom or ghost; philia: attachment to) refers to sexual arousal by intercourse with spirits, ghosts, angels, or gods.

At one time many believed that nocturnal emissions were caused by spirits. The medieval Europeans named the male spirit Incubus. He was believed to cause nightmares and to lie on top of women, seducing or raping them. This was a delusion that was common among females without sex partners, particularly in convents. Conversely, the Succubus was thought to be a female demon that would lie underneath and seduced men, draining them of semen at night. The Babylonian Lilith was even more cruel, demanding sacrifices of the male organ and sometimes a man's life.

Most accounts of spectrophilia were documented during the witch trials from the forced confessions of innocent victims. Nocturnal emissions, impotency, and every other sort of sexual problem was blamed on intercourse with evil spirits.

Sexual hysteria also became common during the Inquisition and men accused women of casting a glamour or spell on them causing them to lose their penis. The men suffering from hysteria could not see their own organs. Two Dominicans, Kramer and Sprenger, wrote of one of these cases warning people that "such members are [not] really torn right away from the body but that they are hidden by the devil...so that they can be neither seen nor felt":

A certain young man had had an intrigue with a girl. Wishing to leave her, he lost his member: that is to say, some glamour [spell] was cast over it so that he could see or touch nothing but his smooth body. In his worry over this he went to a tavern to drink wine; and after he had sat there for a while he got into conversation with another woman who was there, and told her the cause of his sadness, explaining everything and demonstrating in his body that it was so. The woman was shrewd and asked if he suspected anybody.

The man did and the woman suggested that he ask the girl to remove the spell. He left the tavern and upon finding the girl made his demands. She refused saying she was innocent but when he began strangling her she wisely agreed to remove the spell saying, "Now you have what you desire." He then touched his penis and found it to be restored.

This fear was experienced by Thai men during the Vietnam war. It was referred to as the "Thai Shrinking Penis Syndrome." These men felt that their penises were getting smaller and would tie a string around them to prevent their penises from disappearing inside their abdomens. A Thai physician logged the penis sizes of Thai men and later wrote a paper on the subject.

This hysteria recently surfaced in 1991 among people in Nigeria who believed people were casting spells on them and a simple handshake could cost their genitals or breasts. An article in the *London Observer* explained:

One of the first incidents took place in the lobby of the Central Bank, when a visiting man declared that his testicles had been snatched. Although he stripped naked, there are conflicting reports as to whether he was able to prove his loss. What is certain is that bystanders fled. Police have arrested more than 150 people for spreading rumors of stolen testicles, and at least three lynchings are reported to have occurred when hysterical crowds have taken alleged culprits to task....Testicles are reported to fetch a high price in the fetish market—up to $1,000—and are in high demand at present.

The most famous instances of spectrophilia, however, are those of the Virgin Mary and God. G. L. Simons wrote of this in his book:

Some writers, finding it difficult to believe that even God could impregnate the Virgin Mary without her losing her virginity, developed the idea that she was impregnated through the ear by the archangel Gabriel, or by God himself...In some early paintings the Holy Ghost is seen descending as a dove with the divine sperm in its bill; in other pictures the seminal words are seen passing through a lily, on their way from Gabriel's mouth to Mary's ear...In one early carving the sperm come direct

from God's mouth through a tube which led under her skirts (Sex and Superstition, p. 103, reproduced with permission of Blackie & Son Ltd.).

The number of reported Incubi and Succubi and other forms of neurosis increased during the 12th century after the Church imposed harsh restrictions against sexual activity.

(See also CHOREOPHILIA, FANTASY, FERTILITY RITES, HIEROPHILIA, ORGASMS, SEX MAGICK and SEX RITUALS)

SPERM BANKS   Sperm banks are facilities where sperm is deposited for future use in fertilization of a woman. The first infant was born using this technology in 1953. In 1989 there were about 40 sperm banks or human semen cryobanks affiliated with the American Association of Tissue Banks.

Men who are considering a vasectomy or those who must undergo chemotherapy or radiation therapy have a need for this service. A donor's semen is first checked for fitness and then frozen in liquid nitrogen tanks. The cost for freezing sperm is around $250.00 and a five year storage fee in 1989 was $650.00.

Cryobanks also provide services such as infertility profiles, sex selection, sperm washing, cervical mucus penetration assays, and anti-sperm antibody testing.

Some sperm banks provide sperm to be used by women for impregnation. Male donors qualify by filling out a survey form and, once approved, provide sperm for use by anonymous recipients. This screening is important not only for genetic consideration but because many sexually transmitted diseases can be transferred in this manner: "Neisseria, gonorrhea, mycoplasma hominis, Ureaplasma urealyticum, chlamydia trachomatous, trichomonas vaginalis, HIV, and hepatitis B virus" ("Micro-organisms Present in Donor Semen, Screening and Detection," by DJL Palmer, J. Cuthbert, J. Mukoyogo, MS Obhrai, and JR Newton, *British Journal of Sexual Medicine*, April 1990, p. 114). Religions vary on their interpretation of whether this procedure is morally acceptable.

Not all women use sperm banks to secure semen. Some spouses agree to having a friend or acquaintance inseminate their wife while others, including some lesbians, have the male ejaculate in a jar and use a turkey baster for insertion. Women who are unable to carry an infant to term sometimes use a surrogate mother who is impregnated by the husband. There are many more emotional and legal complications involved with this method and courts most often uphold the birth mother's wish to keep her child regardless of previous financial arrangements or contracts.

A listing of banks can be obtained from the American Association of Tissue Banks, 1350 Beverly Road, Suite 220A, McLean, VA 22101.

(See also EUGENICS)

SPITTING   Spitting is used during sex games both as a form of humiliation and as a fetish. Spit itself once had magical qualities. Kirghis tribes living on the border of China and the USSR once believed they could heal the diseased by whipping them until they bled and then spitting in their face.

Spit is often used during sex as a convenient lubricant for kissing, fellatio, and vaginal or anal penetration.

A spit fetishist is sexually aroused by having their partner dribble spit into their mouth or on their body. There have also been women who were specifically attracted to certain men because of the masculine manner in which they could spit.

(See also FETISHES, HYGROPHILIA, HUMILIATION and SHOWERS)

STAG PARTIES   Stag or bachelor parties are given by males in honor of a friend's marriage and they vary according to the morals of those involved. The tradition of the stag party may be a holdover of the ancient puberty rituals that preceded mass weddings.

Typical entertainment includes a stripper or sex video and a few will relocate their party to a bordello. Others have hired professional dominatrixes to teach the guest of

honor what to expect in his new role as a husband.

This is also the occasion for pranks and a few grooms have found themselves dropped off alone in a desolate area with only a few hours left before the wedding. One man actually awoke from a drunken stupor to find that his friends had put him on a cargo ship that had embarked for Alaska during the night.

Females have begun having their own stag parties, to which male strippers sometimes provide entertainment. Gay partners both attend bachelor parties and they also occasionally engage same sex strippers.

(See also SEX SHOWS and STRIPPERS)

STAPLING   Stapling is done in S/M scenes as a form of control over a partner's genitals. Surgical skin staplers with an auto-release are preferred but a few people have used the standard office type (this is not advised due to the staples not being sterile. They are also longer and  more painful). The prongs of the surgical staples are about 1/8" long and curved inward so that they stay in place until removed. A special surgical remover is required for this procedure.

During S/M play people may staple the edges of the scrotal skin to the thighs, the outer skin of the penis to the abdomen, the outer labia together, the buttocks together (painful unless there is a lot of loose skin), and a few have stapled the lips of the mouth. All of the genital staplings are considered a form of site specific bondage (i.e. the mouth stapling would take the place of a gag) or a chastity device. The stapler is operated at a quick snap which reduces some of the pain as the staple enters the skin ("Surgical Suturing and Stapling," by A. Kraus, QSM lecture, August 4, 1990). CAUTION: Staple play is considered a blood sport and therefore unsafe sex.

(See also BONDAGE/LACING, INFIBULATION, SAFE SEX and SUTURING)

STATIONERY Custom stationery is available for people of any sexual preference interested in erotic expression. Illustrations range from romantic scenes of two clothed people in an embrace to group orgies. People use this stationery to send to lovers, as announcements of an address change, invitations to sex parties, thank you cards, or calling cards. Personalized cards may be ordered by sending photographs of oneself. Those desiring an improvement in physique, such as adding a few inches to the size of the penis or breasts, may request those changes.

STIGMATOPHILIA Stigmatophilia, a term coined by John Money, (stigma: mark, philia: attachment to) refers to those who are aroused if their partner has a tattoo, pierced jewelry, body modification, or scarring on their bodies or genitals. (See also CICATRIZATION, JEWELRY, PENIS MODIFICATION, RINGING and TATTOOS)

STRANGLING See OXYGEN REGULATION

STRETCHING (Catatasis—penis, Kolpeuryntomania—vagina) Stretchings may be permanent or temporary. Both types of stretching are done to modify the appearance of the genitals or nipples and may cause some discomfort.

Testicles tend to rise when one nears orgasm and forcing them to stay toward the

bottom of the sac delays ejaculation. Orgasm itself is prolonged and intensified when it does occur. Weights or other special devices are used to accomplish temporary stretching. Metal rings or leather bands fit around the top of the scrotal sac to squeeze the testicles downward. CAUTION: Excessive pressure can cause small blood vessels to break and too much pressure on the testicles themselves is dangerous.

Some people have chosen to permanently stretch their foreskin, nipples, penis (causes

impotence), or labia. This process takes several years to accomplish. The skin is not stretched enough to create pain because this causes lacerations that fill in with scar tissue. Skin that is gently stretched develops microscopic tears that fill in with normal tissue; eventually extending the length of the desired body part. Those using an insert such as a bar or ring gradually pull on it to lengthen the appendage. Those interested in increasing the size of a hole increase the size of the insert over time until the hole gets to the desired diameter. This is similar to people in African tribes who stretched their ear lobes or lips.

The African Baganda, Bagishu, and Suaheli tribes once stretched their inner labia so that they would hang at least two inches below the vagina. This was called the Hottentot apron or mfuli and supposedly

had its origin from girls who masturbated so often that the labia became extended. It is said that men, preferring wives with high sex drives, selected these women first. Soon other women had to compete by stretching their labia. Men discovered that they also enjoyed the extra sensation of having the labia engulf the penis during penetration. These preferences resulted in men refusing to marry women who had not had this labia modification. Young Hottentot girls used two different methods for elongation. Some took a weed and used that to rub and pull on the labia until it had stretched to the desired length. Others tied the labia together with a string and hung a rock on the end. The effect of this was evidently less aesthetic than the former and was described by some as resembling the crop of a turkey.

There are also men who have a compulsion to stretch a female's vagina during penetration. They may also use sheaths for this purpose. The stretching needs to induce discomfort or pain before the man with such a compulsion is satisfied.

(Refer also to WEIGHT TRAINING)

STRIP POKER There are many versions of strip poker, the card game based on the rules of regular poker. Some players write out the sexual activities they are willing to perform and for what price before playing poker. Fake or play money is divided equally and used during the game. Clothes may be bartered if one runs out of money. Once the game is over people add up their winnings and buy the sexual activity they can afford from the other players.

The most common form of strip poker is simply playing for articles of clothing instead of money and more adventurous players will play for specific types of sex acts. If there are more than two players the winners may be given their choice of sex partners for five minutes after each round of poker.

Cheating makes the game more intriguing but one must be willing to face the consequences if caught by their partner. Erotic decks of cards may be used but for those not tempted to show others their hands.

(See also COMPUTER SEX and SEX GAMES)

STRIP SEARCH Strip searches are used in S/M scenes involving police arrests, prison riots, customs searches, prisoners of war, or alien abductions.

The general procedure requires the captive to face a wall with their hands in the air. Their partner then pats them down with their hands on the outside of their clothes. Next the prisoner is asked to empty the contents of their purse or pockets onto a table for inspection, followed by all their clothing. Everything is closely inspected for drugs, microfilm, bugging devices, weapons, or sex toys. The prisoner stands naked with their hands behind their head during this time.

The body is searched and procedure requires that every body opening is checked (bacteria collected from an anus should not be transferred to a vagina). Once the prisoner is found to be completely clean he or she is released, seduced, or relocated to a prison cell.

(See also HUMILIATION and INTERROGATION)

STRIPPING (Ecdyosis—arousal from removing clothes in front of others, Gynonudomania—compulsion to rip clothes off others) Stripping refers to people who voluntarily take off their clothes for an audience. Strippers are male, female, heterosexual, and gay. Private strippers advertise in local magazines in Las Vegas and will come to hotel rooms to perform. Most professional strippers work in clubs with a few becoming celebrities who travel across the country to appear at private clubs. Male strippers, such as the Chippendales of southern California, perform in clubs, others work for stripping telegram companies, private parties, or for gay theaters.

There are certain general rules that strippers use when undressing. These begin with selecting music conducive to dance and wearing easy-to-remove clothes; ones in which they feel attractive and sexy. The toes are kept pointed throughout the routine and any part of the body that is being unveiled is protruded toward the audience; with the exception of some teasing movements. The removal of pants, skirts, or underwear requires that the stripper bends over and slowly pulls the article of clothing down across the buttocks, letting it drop to the floor. Hands are run along the contours of the body to accentuate and tease. There are many other guidelines used by successful strippers. An excellent educational video was done by Gio, titled *How to Strip for Your Man*.

(See also CHOREOPHILIA and SEX SHOWS)

STUFFING Stuffing refers to the insertion of objects into the vagina or anus. This usually involves food or beverages when done in consensual sex play. People use cherry tomatoes, boiled eggs that have been peeled, strawberries, bananas, cucumbers, whipped cream, or whatever other food is favored by the partner.

A famous court case of a 1920's comedian known as Fatty Arbuckle involved testimony that he had stuffed ice and then a champagne bottle up a starlet's vagina. She later died of complications from the lacerations, but he was acquitted after the third trial.

Killers and rapists sometimes stuff the vagina of their murder victim with items lying around the room. One man shoved a victim's false teeth into her vagina without her knowledge. They were discovered a month later when she requested a standard sexually transmitted disease test. The awareness of his actions was complicated by the fact that when he assaulted her he broke her jaw ("Unusual Vaginal Foreign Body," by Peter Watson, *British Journal of Sexual Medicine*, September 1988, p. 294).

Not all stuffing is done by a partner. One woman inserted a rubber ball into her vagina at a party where she had been drinking. It was not discovered until 20 years later ("Vaginal Foreign Body of Very Long Duration," by Benjamin Piura, *British Journal of Sexual Medicine*, Nov. 1986, p. 308). CAUTION: The vaginal cavity is sensitive to foreign chemicals.

(See also BONDAGE/SPECULUM and SITOPHILIA)

SUBLIMINAL TAPES Subliminal refers to the part of the mind that is just beneath the conscious mind, and which is susceptible to repetitive stimuli. Many listen to tapes designed to help them overcome smoking, overeating, low self-esteem, stress, fear, and for slave training in the S/M community.

While scientists seem to agree that a person may perceive subliminal messages, there is little evidence that commercial tapes of this sort effect change in a person's behavior. Dr. Anthony Greenwald of the University of Washington did studies where he mixed the labels on tapes given to volunteers and discovered that the subject on the label had more impact than what was actu-

ally on the tapes. Yet a different study indicated that some people feel a higher level of security or self-esteem after receiving subliminal messages. Nothing, however, reveals that a person would ever kill or commit suicide because of a subliminal message as was suggested in the trial of Judas Priest, a rock band, concerning a subliminal message in their album that said "Do it."

An S/M audio tape, therefore, would only help a slave adjust to the idea of servitude or might help a shy or anxious slave overcome their initial apprehension. S/M tapes are made by the slave's master or by a hypnotist. The tape itself gives messages about being submissive and receiving rewards for this type of behavior.

Sex therapy tapes are also available that are supposed to help people relax and improve their sex life.

(See also HYPNOSIS and VISUALIZATION)

SUBMISSION See DOMINANCE/SUBMISSION

SUBPERSONALITY Subpersonalities are similar to multiple personality disorders except that the personality change is only temporary and awareness is never lost. The regular personality seems to be suppressed enough for it to be difficult to respond appropriately. Multiple personality disorders seem to be caused by repetitive or ritualized abuse that is in contrast with the rest of the child's life; such as molestation by a parent. Subpersonalities are based on either a single instance, or constant trauma and stress. Subpersonalities seem to surface when a person recalls this period of time. This often occurs during therapy or for others during sex.

Therapists sometimes deliberately use childhood subpersonalities when working with a patient's problem. It seems that when a person remembers the pain or trauma, their consciousness shifts and the therapist is able to communicate directly with the child. While they are in this state the therapist gives them the comfort, nurturing, or explanations not received as a child.

This consciousness does not have to be the child personality, it can also be an angry adult. This was true for one woman who sometimes experienced subpersonalities during sex. She was traumatized by serious physical abuse beginning in infancy. Sex partners who brought up subjects that reminded her of the abuse or her father caused her to shift into one of two characters. The first was a young child who became sexually frigid, wanted to be held, and was unable to say anything except "no" without great effort. The other character was an angry adult male rapist who pinned down the partners and sexually assaulted them. (Personal communication.)

A partner that regresses into a child will show signs of going physically limp, weak, withdrawing, and not being able to verbalize the cause for this sudden response. If this occurs during sex their partner helps by simply holding and nurturing them as they would a child. Questions that are complex or that require more than a simple answer cause frustration in the partner suffering from this regression. This is a temporary condition which passes as soon as the old memories fade. If this occurs often and affects a couple's normal sex life a professional therapist may be of assistance.

(See also FETISHES and PARAPHILIAS)

SUPPORT GROUPS Support groups have recently become popular. These seem to have taken the place of close extended families as Americans have relocated for college and better job opportunities. Support groups differ from professional therapy in that no one person offers guidance. Everyone is there because they identify with the same problem.

Most groups spawned off a successful Alcoholics Anonymous program started in 1935 by Bill Wilson and Dr. Robert Smith. These men proved that association and support from a fellow sufferer was more therapeutic and successful than the vast range of existing methods. Al-Anon, the next large support group, was started by Lois Wilson in 1951 for partners of alcoholics.

Today there are support groups for overeaters, transvestites, drug addicts, sex addicts, gays, bi-sexuals, shoppers, workaholics, parents of sex offenders, bereavement, parents of children who died

violently, incest survivors, gamblers, child molesters, celibates, sexual enthusiasts, women who love too much, prostitutes, polygamists, spouses who are abused, abusing spouses, a lesbian's pagan group, and many more.

Twelve-step programs begin their meetings with an introduction, and a short presentation, next opening the floor to anyone who would like to share their thoughts with the group. Large groups sometimes impose a time limitation so that as many people as possible will have the opportunity to share. The typical opening comment is: "Hi, I'm Bill and I am a sex addict" (or whatever is appropriate). Others reply with "Hi, Bill" and Bill then continues to tell about events or feelings that came up since his last visit. People are not allowed to offer advice, ask questions, or criticize anyone else in the group. Anonymity is respected and all take an oath not to repeat anything said in the meeting to others.

Women's pagan support groups differ slightly from other twelve-step programs in that the women sit in a circle, open the meeting with a grounding ritual to mentally detach themselves from the outside world and to focus on the meeting. People speak only when they feel ready to share their problems and are restricted to a few minutes. The forum is much more flexible than other groups because their bond is a religious one rather than a specific addiction. Once everyone has had an opportunity to speak, they join hands and sing chants before breaking the circle. The added ritual creates more of a cathartic effect than the typical twelve-step closing remarks of "It works, keep coming back."

Therapists often encourage patients to attend one or two support group meetings between visits. This sometimes speeds recovery and reduces the cost of therapy.

(See also SEX CLUBS)

SUSPENSION Suspension refers to hanging someone in the air from an overhead support which allows for some movement. Semi-suspension is when only a portion of the person's weight is off the ground.

The most cruel form of suspension was recorded during the Inquisition where people were tortured by hanging them by their genitals. Today's S/M community uses suspension for pleasure.

One man is said to have masturbated by hanging upside down and banging his penis against a door. Some use boot cover devices that fit around a person's own boots and hang from a hoist by an eye bolt mounted in the bottom of the boot cover. The person's arms are left free until after they are in a hanging position. This allows them to help manipulate their body as it is being raised off the floor. Likewise, the arms are freed before lowering the person back onto the floor.

Another method of suspension involves placing padded leather cuffs on a person's wrists and ankles and a leather belt around their waist. These are attached to chains hanging from a hoist or other object. A parachute harness is often used in this type of suspension instead of the leather belt. CAUTION: Safety requires all suspension equipment and chains to be checked before hanging a person on them. Welded chain is the safest and metal pulleys make the lifting easier. Panic snaps are also used on the lines in case the person needs to be released immediately. A person is not left in an upside-down position for more than a few minutes. Additional caution is also exercised with people who are near sighted because there is a potential risk of retinal detachment due to the oblong shape of their eyeball and the extra pressure caused by the accumulation of blood. Anyone seeing light flashes should immediately see an ophthalmologist.

A person bound or suspended with their arms above their head may faint. This is common. They are laid down and will revive without assistance within a few minutes. Those who become nauseous or develop headaches are released at once. Mummification used with suspension has a calming effect but can also cause disorientation. ("Suspension," by T. DeBlase, QSM lecture, March 23, 1990)

(See also BONDAGE and SENSORY DEPRIVATION)

SUTTEE   Suttee (virtuous woman) is the East Indian practice of burning a widow with her husband. This is thought to have begun over 3,000 years ago among northern Aryan tribes. One could escape this socially imposed suicide if a man took hold of the widow's hand as she lay on her dead husband's funeral pyre. This gave her status as the second man's wife and she could live. Suttee was first justified in poor villages where if a family lost its bread winner it could not survive. Thus, it was considered merciful to have the wife, who often could not remarry anyway, commit suicide. This freed her children for adoption by other families. The practice continued even once these tribes became more stable. Suttee came to be encouraged in the upper levels of society by the Brahmans who often received the couple's wealth after the wife's death. It was these priests that objected the most when in 1829 Lord William Bentinck forbade the practice of suttee. Some widows still felt compelled to join their husbands in death and to prevent this they were sometimes tied to a stake at a distance during the burial.

Today Indian husbands who wish to marry someone else or to be free of their wives arrange an accidental fire in the kitchen. The wife is sometimes bound or held by in-laws to accomplish this feat. Others, trying to capitalize on dowries, will first request more money from their father-in-law. If he doesn't pay, his daughter gets burned alive in the kitchen, leaving the husband free to marry someone else and collect her dowry.

(See also MARRIAGE)

SUTURING   Suturing (sutura: to sew) is done in S/M play as a form of pseudocastration, bondage, or infibulation of the genitals. Sterile techniques are always used for this procedure (see SAFE SEX).

The couple decides the type of suturing scene in which they wish to engage and then gathers the items needed for the procedure. The preferred type of suture is non-absorbable silk because it is the easiest to tie. The needles used are cutting needles in either size 00 or 000. People without access to medical supply houses use sterilized stainless steel needles and prepackaged white polyester thread. A sterilized thimble is also used due to the toughness of the skin and the force needed to push the needle.

A button is sometimes used to keep the suture threads from pulling through the skin or just for decoration, particularly on the end of the penis.

A purse string stitch is used around the front of a breast or the scrotum. It is the same as a straight stitch but it forms a circle which is then pulled tight with the protruding ends of the suture and tied. This holds the flesh in a puckered position until the suture is cut.

A Parker-Kerr stitch is used to hold an object such as a penis or dildo underneath 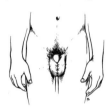 the sutures. These stitches are done by anchoring the first stitch and then lying the object (dildos are covered with a condom) on the area. The suture is pulled over the object and the next stitch is put into the skin on that side. Next the suture is pulled over to the other side of the object and anchored into the skin. The distance between the stitches on each side is determined by the length and weight of the object.

Most stitches use square knots. Continuous stitches are used in suturing two breasts together down the front inseam or sewing the labia together. Single knots are used in pseudo castration where the penis is tucked down and the 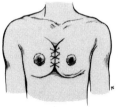 scrotum skin is pulled up around the penis. Sutures are then placed along the top to close the seam. This type of castration is only possible with men who have loose or large scrotal sacs. The outer skin on the penis is sometimes pinched up and sutured, but it is dangerous to go very deep because the delicate tissue beneath can be damaged. CAUTION: Please be aware that there are vital structures, such as nerves, arteries, veins, tendons, bones, and joint spaces *immediately* beneath the skin in some areas.

Permanent disability can result from accidently suturing one of these structures. ("Surgical Suturing and Stapling," by A.K., QSM lecture, August 4, 1990)

(See also BONDAGE/LACING, INFIBULATION, PIERCING and RINGING)

SWINGING   See GROUP SEX and WIFE SWAPPING

SWINGS   (Slings) Swings are made of fabric, leather, or wood and provide support for those suspended from the ceiling. Sex swings appear to be an ancient Eastern invention designed for ultimate sensual pleasure.

A partner lies back in a semi-reclining position with their legs spread and raised in the air. This position offers direct access to the genitals and the swing is at a height that allows easy penetration. This arrangement offers a feeling of control for one partner and a feeling of nurturance and surrender to the one in the swing. Swings are also popular for massage because all parts of the body are accessible.

(See also SEX POSITIONS, SEX SHOWS, SYBIAN and TANTRA)

SWITCHES   The term switch is used by those in the S/M community for those people who alternate the role of a bottom/submissive and top/dominant. This is usually done out of necessity because there are many more bottoms than tops, others simply enjoy the role change. It is also often the case that people refuse to submit to a top who has not learned the empathy and S/M techniques gained from first being a bottom.

(See also BOTTOM, DOMINANCE/SUBMISSION, HUMILIATION and TOPS)

SYBIAN   Sybian is the name given to a $1,395.00 mechanical dildo device that is in a class of its own. The device is housed in a half cylinder shaped saddle that a person rides to orgasm, after orgasm, after orgasm. The Sybian differs from other dildoes in that it not only vibrates at different speeds and intensity but it rotates as well. These are controlled by two regulator dials on a control box. The Sybian was test marketed at swinger conventions and modified for best results before it was released to the public. Riders were given buttons that read "Sybian Test Pilot."

Some seem to become addicted to operating the control box for women. Females

orgasm at different frequencies. Men quickly learn which ones are most intense for the woman they are with and gain immense pleasure in controlling how many orgasms she experiences and when. Men have found the device just as stimulating when they replace the dildo attachment with a butt plug. Some bars have replaced their mechanical bronco rides with the Sybian.

(See also GENITAL/ANAL INSERTS and SEX TOYS)

SYMPHOROPHILIA Symphorophilia (symthoma: casualty; phoron: producer; philia: attachment), coined by John Money, refers to one who experiences sexual arousal from creating casualties by, for example, burning down apartments, hospitals, or orphanages. This is done for the pleasure of causing death and catastrophe rather than just watching the flames.

One famous case between 1899 and 1930 was of Peter Kurten, also known as the Dusseldorf Murderer. He was unlike most other sociopaths in that he varied his attacks, weapons, and victims. It did not matter whether they were female, male, child or animal. The following poem written by Kurten will show this clearly:

In the case of Ohliger, I also sucked blood from the wound on her temple, and from Scheer from the stab in the neck. From the girl Schulte I only licked the blood from her hands. It was the same with the swan in the Hofgarten. I used to stroll at night through the Hofgarten very often, and in the spring of 1930 I noticed a swan sleeping at the edge of the lake. I cut its throat. The blood spurted up and I drank from the stump and ejaculated.

Kurten admitted to 79 crimes of his own as well as finding intense pleasure in witnessing catastrophes or accidents. He finally confessed to his unsuspecting wife, having her turn him in to the police for the reward offered on the Dusseldorf Murderer. His confession was prompted by fear of his fantasies to burn down an orphanage.

It may be impossible to know but one wonders if politicians like Hitler, who began wars or exterminations of groups, found sexual pleasure in doing so. Hitler did have the exterminations in concentration camps filmed.

(See also HYBRISTOPHILIA and LUST MURDER)

T

TANTRA Tantra refers to the Vedic Hindu doctrine that is designed to extend sexual unity and bonding. Couples find this brings more ecstatic pleasure than a quick orgasm. Hindus at one time only used this technique under the guidance of a guru or other couple to ensure that the correct procedures were followed. There were sex techniques similar to tantra among the American Cherokee Indians, Chinese, some African tribes, and sex magick, although the ritual and goals are often different.

Tantric students fine tune their senses so that each becomes one with the universe and with their partner. Meditation and breathing techniques are used to control and extend the arousal period so that the penis stays functional for nearly an hour. The couple has many positions with which they can regulate the flow of energy between them. Eye contact and matching breaths is an integral part of the exercises as well. Proficiency takes time and discipline; therefore, this is not a technique that lends itself to casual sex between strangers.

There are many books and several organizations that teach tantra to couples. Peak Skill Publishing offers books such as *Sexual*

Energy Ecstasy by David Alan Ramsdale, MA and Ellen Jo Ramsdale and *Intimacy & Sexual Ecstasy* by Jonathan Robinson, MA as well as videos and other tantric products (See Bibliography). ("A Taste of Tantra," by Coleman and McCusker, Lifestyle Conference, August 17-18, 1990)

(See also KABAZZAH, KAREZZA, SEX MAGICK and SEX MUSEUMS)

TAPHEPHILIA   Taphephilia (taphe: burial; philia: attachment to) refers to those who are aroused by being buried alive. Geoffrey Mains, in his book *Urban Aboriginals,* mentions one Los Angeles man who had his friends mummify him in rubber or leather and temporarily bury him (p. 90).

(See also BONDAGE and OXYGEN REGULATION)

TATTOOING   Tattooing involves puncturing the skin with needles and injecting indelible dyes to permanently color the skin. The two oldest verified color tattoos were found on a 4,000 year old Bronze Age man who was discovered preserved in an Austrian glacier and on a 4,200 year old Egyptian priestess of the goddess Hathor. It has been practiced by light skinned Egyptians, Greeks, Native American Indians, South Pacific tribes, and Japanese, among others. Our early ancestors  stuck needles dipped in pigment into the skin, or else soaked thread in carbon and pulled it through the skin. They also applied soot or pigments directly to the skin and punctured the area with needles.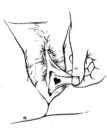

The designs of early tattoos consisted of patterns of dots and simple lines. The Indonesians began using bolder geometric designs and the Japanese, after using it as punishment on criminals between the 7th and 16th centuries, changed it to the colorful, elaborate, and artistic work that is seen today.

Tattooing was brought back to Europe by sailors who had become fascinated with this art form. People paid to hear sailors tell of their travels and see their tattoos.

Tattooing sometimes had sexual significance. There were tribal chieftains who had vulvas tattooed on their chests. The Haitians, Berads, and Basivis women wore penis tattoos and others tattooed their faces as a charm against sterility.

People also tattoo their genitals. Helen Fisher, in her book *The Sex Contract,* tells of "Ulithian women of the western Pacific [who] tattoo the inner lips of their vulvas to enhance their beauty." Men have also been tattooed on their genitals and at least one inside the urethra that had been opened with a subincision.

Havelock Ellis wrote of a man who had a tattoo fetish. The man relates his experience as "when I got a tattooist to place the figure of a butterfly on the upper side of my penis, I experienced a few minutes after leaving the shop, the phenomena of erection and ejaculation accompanied by a feeling of physical exaltation so great that it almost prostrated me afterwards" (*Studies in the Psychology of Sex,* by Havelock Ellis).

Tattoo machines operate on a 12 volt battery with one to three needles being used in the sleeve of a hand gun. These needles, like those of a small sewing machine, move up and down at a very fast speed depositing ink as they pierce the skin to a depth of less than one millimeter. The tattooed area is rubbed with an anti-bacterial or antibiotic ointment and covered with a sterile bandage. This is removed one or two hours later when the area is washed with lukewarm water. The client is told to prevent the ink from dissipating by avoiding heat on the area (i.e. hot tubs, baths, saunas, sun bathing, and swimming) for the next couple of weeks. Tattoos on the shaft of the penis are not difficult or particularly painful but those on the glans are harder to get the ink to stick in place because of frequent bleeding and are more painful. The labia is not very painful but, because it is a mucous membrane, lines tend to lose their sharpness and blur; therefore, simple line drawings are preferred.

Tattooing is also used to color in the areola on the breasts of women who have had mastectomies and nipple reconstruction.

Because of AIDS, tattoo artists have begun using fresh needles for each customer.

(See also PENIS MODIFICATIONS and RINGING)

TEASING (Tantalolagnia—arousal from teasing) Teasing is done to sexually excite a person but without the intent of fulfilling their desires once aroused. It is an overt form of flirting. This may be done with words, sounds, promises, provocative attire, gestures, or caresses. Creating a desire for something begins a process in the brain that creates tension until it is either obtained or substituted by something else.

Teasing may be used to increase passion during sex by refusing to be penetrated or by threatening to withdraw if the partner doesn't orgasm within the time it takes to count down from ten. A gentle push against the groin as the count approaches two or three can intensify their response. CAUTION: Teasing strangers or people with whom one has no intention of engaging in sex is inhumane, if not dangerous.

(See also COURTSHIP and SEXUAL HARASSMENT)

TELEGONY Telegony was the belief that the first man to inseminate a woman would automatically be the father of any child she bore afterward. This was an advantage as far as adultery was concerned because husbands did not worry about bastard children. However, telegony created a tremendous problem for widows and divorcees. Men refused to marry these women because they felt the children born would not be theirs but that of her first husband.

(See also ADULTERY, CUCKOLDRY and MARRIAGE)

TESTICLES (Gemellus, Gonads) Testicles are the male organs that hang in the scrotal sac and produce spermatozoa. They are the equivalent to the female ovaries and begin life in the abdominal cavity before dropping to the scrotal sac. Testicles are part of the visceral or intestinal cavity and this is why abnormal pressure or trauma induces such extreme nauseating pain. One is usually larger than the other and they both rise when exposed to cold or when nearing orgasm.

The testicles were once so sacred that oaths were given while someone held the testicles of the man swearing in their hand, thus the terms testimony and testify. Women once assisted their husbands in quarrels by grabbing the opponent by his testicles and squeezing. Legislation soon passed that penalized women by cutting off the offending hand.

Testicles are often used in S/M games. They are squeezed in cock and ball torture, have weights hung on them, are separated with straps, and held in the mouth and gently rotated. Rarely, they are pierced.

An organization called the Ball Club was founded for those who have a special interest in testicles. A quarterly newsletter allows members to run personal ads or submit articles, erotic stories, photos, and artwork. Not all the ads are from men. The following is extraordinary even for this newsletter.

Sadistic butch bi-female and lover/ slave into severe ball torture and the tears and suffering it can cause. Long, hard sessions of ball crushing, beating, burning, needles and knives...

(See also TORTURE and WEIGHTS)

THALPOTENTIGINY Thalpotentiginy refers to those people who find heat or warm weather sexually arousing.

(See also PSYCHROCISM)

TICKLING (Knismolagnia and Titillagnia—arousal from tickling) Tickling involves light touching of the vulnerable areas of our body's defense system causing us to want to retreat. Tickling used during foreplay will cause increased stimulation in a partner; however, this has to be transferred to sexual arousal before it is of benefit. Women of the Baganda tribe became adept at seducing their husbands by tickling their armpits. Tickling was also used in religious worship. Goldberg, in *The Sacred Fire*, wrote of a Russian sect called the Ticklers whose religious service consisted of the men tickling the women until they passed out.

Tickling is often used with bondage in S/M games. The stimulus may at first seem pleasurable but over a long period of time can become unbearable. The person may also become desensitized to tickling after repeated stimulation. Instruments used for tickling are fingers, rabbit fur, ostrich feathers, and soft bristled brushes.

People advertise in personal ads for partners willing to engage in this form of sex play. Videos are available by mail, such as "Tormentor's Delight" which has a nude woman tied with her hands above her head and tickled by a hooded monk, and "Tickling Senorita" that shows a coed tied to a bed and tormented with a feather by a classmate. CAUTION: Passing beyond some people's limits can result in choking, vomiting, or incontinence.

(See also BONDAGE and SENSORY ENHANCEMENT)

TIMOPHILIA   Timophilia (time: worth; philia: attachment to) refers to those who are sexually aroused by wealth or status. The Roman emperor Caligula, known for his carnal lusts, entertained himself by wallowing in piles of gold.

Some people take treasured objects to bed with them. Jimi Hendrix was said to have slept with his guitar and some women will take a new fur coat, dress, diamond ring, or other prize to bed with them and touch it throughout the night. It is said to produce a similar feeling of comfort and possession that a lover would give.

It is often difficult to discern where the desire for the power that money brings ends, and the erotic excitement begins. Wealthy men quickly learn the aphrodisiac qualities money has for seducing the woman of their choice. This desire is not restricted to one sex because there have also been many personal ads appearing throughout the last hundred years from men wanting to marry wealthy women.

(See also FETISHES, MASTURBATION and PARAPHILIAS)

TOILET TRAINING   Toilet training is the term used for submissives learning the art of coprophagy or urophilia. The toilet slave may be made to lick a toilet clean, lie on their back as their partner squats above their face, or to lick their genitals clean after they relieve themselves. Some use the portable commodes or shower chairs available for rent at medical rental stores. One partner sits in the chair and the other lies beneath  and carries out whatever orders they are given. Some people use these chairs for cunnilingus because of the way the edges of the commode spread and expose the genitals.

A person who has a strong desire to be a toilet slave, but who is not yet accustomed to consuming human wastes, is often started with a substitute such as warm beer or chili. These are inserted into the vagina or anus and the person learns to consume these substitutes before graduating to real secretions.

A few professional dominatrixes will train toilet slaves. The following quote is from a letter written to a dominatrix by a slave after their first session:

Toilet Slave John smiled back at his Lady as he quickly removed his clothes and fell to his knees before her. He was momentarily overwhelmed with feelings of gratitude that he had found her. He had not served a Mistress for a long time, but the other two Mistresses whose Total Toilet he had become some years before, and with whom he had developed almost loving Mistress-Slave relationships, had taught him that for a Toilet Slave to be completely successful in his duties, there must be an intangible "X" factor present which enabled him to not only worship, love, and adore his Mistress, but to worship, love and adore her shit. He must glory in, and make love to, her shit. He must desire her shit above all else, knowing that because in a very real sense eating her shit was the ultimate act of degradation, it therefore became the ultimate act of love, giving his Mistress ultimate feelings of pleasure and power.

As he looked up at her, Toilet Slave John felt that "X" factor with the Lady to a degree he had not felt in years. For a minute they just smiled at each other, and there was that feeling of beginning a long journey together, and then she said, crisply, "Okay, now, little Toilet Slave, let's get it going!" She began working a number of globs of tissue-burning ointment and other substances on cotton swabs as far as she could —in and out, in and out, in and out— into Toilet Slave John's miserable toilet-flusher worm of a cock. She called it "cock-fucking." Then after a quick round with her whip, she inserted two irritant-soaked cotton swabs into his toilet flusher, leaving them there as she tied a leash around the base of his miserable worm and balls and led him crawling through the house for the amusement of her Mistress associates before dragging him into the bathroom

Toilet training is not for everyone but for some it brings intense pleasure and satisfaction. CAUTION: Eating feces can spread many serious diseases, including hepatitis, shigella, amoebic dysentery, cholera, and various parasitic worms. It may be the most dangerous kind of unsafe sex.

(See also COPROPHAGY, COPROPHILIA and SHOWERS)

TOPS The term top is used by those in the S/M community for those who choreograph or direct sex play with a partner. They are the authority figure. This is a much broader term than sadist which implies arousal from seeing a partner injured or in pain. A top may simply require that their partner attend a dinner function without underwear.

More specific titles may be used during a fantasy game such as teacher, reverend father, mistress, and goddess.

(See also BOTTOM, MASOCHIST, SADISM and SWITCH)

TORTURE Torture refers to inflicting pain to extract information from a noncooperative person. The definition has recently broadened to include the infliction of pain without the explicit intent to gather information or a confession.

Governments have employed torture for their purposes for thousands of years. Those cultures not using torture relied on divine intervention. Here a suspect that was accused of a wrongdoing had to endure a trial by ordeal; passing the test proved his

innocence. Neither torture nor trial by ordeal was totally successful for getting at the truth. The concept that a person who is tortured will divulge all the information the enemy desires with accuracy is erroneous. The captors sometimes are able to scrutinize information better when they capture several prisoners and compare their stories or interrogate prisoners on several occasions and watch for discrepancies in their statements. The Europeans became so calloused to torture during the witch burnings and the Inquisition that it was used for punishment for those sentenced to death. King Charles I himself was one of these victims. Judges pronounced the following death sentence on him:

You shall go from hence to the place from whence you came, and from that place shall be drawn upon a hurdle to the place of execution, and there shall hang by the neck till you are half dead, and shall be cut down alive, and your privy members cut off before your face and thrown into the fire, your belly ripped up and your bowels burnt, your head to be severed from your body, your body shall be divided into four quarters, and disposed as His Majesty shall think fit.

Other cultures used things such as the American Indian torture of slowly masturbating a man to death, the French torture of inserting a glass tube in a prisoner's urethra and breaking it with a hammer, or the Afridi women's torture of prying a man's mouth open with wood and urinating in it until he drowned. The use of torture to obtain information is now against national policy and a group called Amnesty International works to obliterate it in the rest of the world.

Many of the torture games used among S/M enthusiasts include techniques used by different governments. A fantasy torture scene can be based on Romans, Inquisitors, Japanese, American Indian, Military, German SS, female Amazon warriors, and so forth.

Genital torture techniques are the most popular. People put testicles in small vise grips, do ball crushing (twisting the sac 90, and squeezing the testicles together with the hand until the person submits), whipping the genitals, using an irritant on the mucous membranes, rubbing the area with Dragon Skin paper (similar to a plastic sandpaper), attaching clamps or clothespins, using alternate heat and cold, impaling the genitals with needles or a small nail, using electrical cock rings or an elastrator clamp to put a rubber band on scrotum (used for castration of animals by veterinarians—it is not left on for more than 5 minutes for a human). The difference between S/M torture and the political type is that the victim can end the game at any time and serious damage is avoided at all costs. CAUTION: Chemicals can burn skin, and torture devices can cause damage. ("Male Tit and Genitorture I and II," by Tony DeBlase, QSM lectures, June 1 and 8, 1990; "Private Pleasures, Intimate Pain; An Exploration of the Subtle Art of Cunt Torture," by V.A., QSM lecture, June 1990)

(See also ALGOPHILIA, CICATRIZATION, MASOCHISM, SADISM, TESTICLES and WEIGHT TRAINING)

TOUCH (Toucheurism—arousal from touch; Sarmassophilia—arousal from kneading flesh) Touching a person creates a sensation from pressure placed on the skin. (Sensual arousal from tactile stimulus may include pain for some people. This is discussed under the heading ALGOPHILIA).

Touch allows us to simultaneously receive and transmit feelings. It is the only sense that can be shared between two people. The skin has, beneath its surface, various receptors or nerve endings that react to specific types of touch. For instance, the Merkel's Disk and Meissner's Corpuscle detect light touch, the end bulbs of Krause nerves sense cold, Ruffini Endings detect heat, free nerve endings feel pain, and the Pacinian Corpuscle senses deep pressure, and seems to override all other sensations. These receptors are more dense in certain areas than others and because of this these locations provide more pleasure when stimulated. There is a simple "two-point discrimination" test that one does with a hairpin and ruler to determine the most erogenous zones on our bodies. The tips of the hairpin are spread with the points

varying from two millimeters to seven centimeters in distance and run along the surface of the skin. The objective is to determine at which point one can feel the sensation of two pin tips instead of one. The closer the two points can be recognized together the more sensitive the area is to touch. The following chart is an example of the variances:

BODY SECTION	# OF MILLIMETERS
Tip of tongue	1-2 mm
Clitoris	3-4 mm
Glans Penis:	
pretumescent	5-9 mm
tumescence	9-15 mm
posttumescent	3-4 mm
Anus	4-5 mm
Nipples	8-10 mm
Lips	4-5 mm
Neck	50-60mm

The sense receptors seem to be abundant in the areas that center on body functions necessary for survival. Our bodies are designed to trigger a production of endorphins which in turn create a pleasure response in our brain each time we engage in one of these activities (i.e. eating, nursing, coitus, and defecation). The brain assumes we are eating each time there is pressure applied to the lips or tongue, that we are nursing when it is applied to the nipples, and so forth. It is because of this natural mechanism that we are able to enhance the sex act by applying touch and pressure to areas of our bodies other than the genitals.

The desire to touch is a primal need and is genetically transmitted. One social function of touch was to keep people in group formations. The desire for this was termed centripetal movement. Clans served many functions in enabling humans to survive. They decreased the number of times people would encounter a predator, increased the power of the clan through intimidation of numbers, and took advantage of the expertise of those best knowledgeable at hunting or gathering food. Groups also increased the chances of fertility and survival of the young. The discovery of agriculture and breeding animals alleviated this need and made it more advantageous for man to spread out into much smaller units (*Sociobiology*, by Henry O. Wilson, pp. 26-27). Touch is crucial for infants and remains important throughout our lives. Jillyn Smith speaks of this in her book, *Senses & Sensibilities:*

Without touch, children die. As late as the second decade of this century, the death rate in U.S. foundling institutions for infants under one year old was nearly 100 percent. Dr. Fritz Talbot of Boston brought the idea of tender loving care back with him from Germany in the 1940s....Introduction of "mothering" regimens in institutions dramatically reduced the mortality rates of children. Recent studies have shown that premature infants who were massaged for 15 minutes three times a day gained weight 45 percent faster than others who were left alone in their incubators. The massaged infants did not eat more than the others. Their weight gain seemed to be related to effects of touch on their metabolism (p. 199).

Children as they become older seek to replace the nurturing once received from parents with security objects, fetishes, pets, and peer contact. Males often develop a socialized misconception that touch should only precede coitus. Men will often either not engage in touching unless they feel they can follow through with sex or will instigate sex more often than their partner would like when hugging or caressing would suffice.

There are people who are able to orgasm solely by being touched in areas other than the genitals. A recent issue of *Sex Over Forty* cited the personal experience of a psychologist who unexpectedly had an orgasm when her lover caressed her hand while she was reading a magazine. The article goes on to state that "Medical research on touch has shown that it improves many situations by: lessening anxiety, calming fears, decreasing pain, lowering blood pressure, reducing stress, soothing the sick and alleviating loneliness" ("How touch affects intimacy," by E.D. Whitehead and S. Zussman, September, 1990 issue of *Sex Over Forty*).

People involved in sadomasochism use mild to intense tactile stimulation to accomplish the same type of orgasm others have with penis/vagina sex. In fact, group S/M club play parties often have a rule that genitals may not be handled and yet many achieve orgasms.

(See also ACUPRESSURE, AXILLISM, BINDING, BITING, CORSETS, CUPPING, PINCHING, SCRATCHING, SENSORY ENHANCEMENT and TICKLING)

TOURNIQUETS   Tourniquets are used to stop the flow of blood from an artery. There are six main arterial pressure points but only the brachial and femoral are used in sex play. People who play with tourniquets do it primarily because they enjoy the tingling sensations produced once the tourniquet is removed.

Tourniquets are applied by first elevating the arm or leg, placing a padding directly over one of these major arteries, wrapping 2" width fabric around the arm or leg, tying the ends, inserting a pencil or stick into the knot and twisting it like a clock hand with 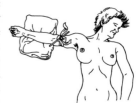 just enough pressure to stop the pulse. The exact time is written down so that the tourniquet can be loosened within 5 minutes. CAUTION: Tourniquets may cause permanent nerve damage or arterial embolization of an atheromatous plaque (which can cause loss of a limb). It can be extremely dangerous.

(See also BINDING, BONDAGE, CLAMPS and CORSETS)

TRANSSEXUALS   (Gender crosscoding, Gender dysphoria—person whose behavior matches the opposite sex, Gender transposition—the changing of behavior between sexes) A transsexual is defined as a person who has had an overwhelming desire to be the opposite sex. As children they are often confused about their true sexual identity. It is not until at about the age of five or six they are faced with the physical evidence of being different. For many this means growing up depressed over the fact that their genitals do not match the mental picture of themselves. Once a transsexual goes through a sex change they are then referred to only as male or female.

The vocabulary used to differentiate among this group is not adequate. A transgenderist is said to refer to those who begin the process of a sex change, usually breast implants and sometimes ingestion of hormones, but who has no desire to complete the castration portion of the surgery. They prefer to be able to pass as either male or female without making a commitment to either.

In 1952 Christine Jorgensen had the first successful sex change surgery in Denmark and since that time about 6,000 Americans have followed suit.

In order for a transsexual to qualify for surgery they have to have spent three months under the supervision of a therapist who recommends the procedure, begin a year's hormone treatment, and during this time the person must live as their new sex 24 hours a day. The hormones change the bone mass slightly, cause the growth of new hair and in some female-to-males their hairlines may begin to recede. Men may find that they become less tense and females more aggressive. Electrolysis is used to get rid of unwanted hair. For some this can be the most expensive portion of the sex change. If a person takes the hormone treatment for a year and then changes their mind about the sex change before surgery the effects of hormones will not completely reverse themselves.

The surgery from male to female costs anywhere from $5,000-15,000 not including therapy, voice lessons, hormones, and electrolysis. Some surgeons have become experts in this procedure and most untrained eyes cannot detect a difference in their patient's genitalia from that of a natural female. During a typical surgical procedure the scrotal sac is cut open and the testicles thrown away. The penis is sliced open and its contents are discarded as well. The surgeon then inserts his fingers into the vaginal area and opens a cavity in which the penile shell is turned inside out and pushed inside to create a vagina. In time the dry penile tissue will become mucosal and resemble an ordinary vagina in texture. The scrotum is then used to form the labia and a piece of the penis and erectile tissue used to form the clitoris.

The surgery for female to male costs from $10,000-20,000 and has not advanced to the point where a constructed penis is fully functional. The scrotum is formed from the labia and synthetic testes inserted to resemble the male organs. Many prefer to live with the elongated clitoris which is as sexually functional as before. Others opt for a phalloplasty that has a prosthetic device enabling him to insert his new penis into a vagina and orgasm himself because the other end of the device puts pressure on the clitoris. The third option is for a phalloplasty which uses skin grafts to form a flaccid penis that can be used for urination but often a patient finds they have a problem with urinary infections and urine leaking out of the wrong area. Ejaculation is impossible despite the alternative selected.

A support network is available for transsexuals and others called E.T.V.C. CAUTION: The sex change does not solve all of a person's problems; it often creates additional ones. Families and friends may ostracize the person and they may even lose their job. Ex-men find they lose social status and that new jobs as a female often pay less.

(See also CASTRATION, DRAG QUEENS, HERMAPHRODITE and TRANSVESTITES)

TRANSVESTITES (Acault—Burmese, Berdaches—male who performs role of wife in some tribes, Eonism, Gynephonia—effeminate voice, Transvestophilia—arousal from transvestism, Virimimism—adoption of masculinity)

Transvestites are people who find erotic pleasure in crossdressing. This does not include women in history who have passed as men simply to obtain better paying jobs or a higher social status. Nor does it include drag queens, female impersonators, or those involved in petticoat or victorian lace discipline. In other words, crossdressers who are not sexually aroused by crossdressing are not transvestites.

Crossdressing was practiced in many societies. Balboa was appalled by it among "Chiefs at Quarequa in Panama. Here he said, was 'the most abhominal and unnatural lechery,' practiced by 'the Kynges brother and many other younger men in women apparell, smoth and effeminately decked, which by the report of such as dwelte abowte hym, he abused with preposterous venus.' Balboa delt summarily with the offenders, throwing forty of them to his dogs" (*Sex in History*, by Reay Tannahill, p. 293, citing Anglerius' *Opera . . . Oceani decas*, pp. 89-90).

Crossdressing sometimes had religious significance. An American Indian tribe believed that if a man dreamed of the moon goddess he must dress like a woman, perform those duties, and have sex with men. In other tribes the medicine men had to crossdress as a condition of this office.

One of the more notorious transvestites was a Roman named Heliogabalus who would dress as a woman and evict prostitutes from their bordellos, taking over their clientele. He eventually fell in love with a slave and at the wedding dressed in a gown, afterward going through a defloration scene. Heliogabalus was assassinated by his soldiers upon discovering his plot to abdicate and make his husband the emperor, declaring himself empress of Rome. Others included the harem of the 17th century Queen Zingua of Angola Africa who kept her husbands dressed in female attire. Catalina de Erauso was a 17th century Spanish nun who left the convent dressed as a man, became a soldier, and fought in South America before being discovered. A century later two female crossdressers fought on a pirate ship until they were captured by the Jamaican government and sentenced to death in 1720 (*The Mysteries of Sex, Women Who Posed as Men and Men Who Impersonated Women*, by C.J.S. Thompson).

European men dressed in elaborate costumes, bright colors, and wore wigs and makeup until the end of the 18th century, when they adopted dull colors and simple styles. Crossdressing allows men to at least temporarily break with this tradition and experience some pleasure in their appearance. This is referred to by some as fashion envy.

Transvestites primarily wear opposite-sex clothes for the purposes of sexual arousal. For this reason they tend to choose items they associate with sexy women, such as lingerie, stilleto high heels, and bikinis.

Male crossdressers often have the attitude that women are pampered. When these men crossdress they are able to forget the stresses from the office and to relax. Their rigid male persona does not normally allow for this type of pampering. Transvestites frequently exaggerate sex-role stereotypes by assuming very masculine roles (truck drivers or construction workers) in their careers. One transvestite was not able to be sexually submissive to a female partner in his male persona but insisted on being submissive in his female role. He chose to go without sex rather than submit to a whipping in his male character; a whipping that he asked for in his female role.

A transvestite seems like the perfect date for a bi-sexual female. However, several who have attempted dating transvestites have stated that while their date looked and acted like a female they still had strong male energy. Therefore, instead of becoming aroused by being with a female (or male) the sexual response became confusing and dissipated because one felt more like they were with a man who was dressed like a woman. There are many wives of transvestites who adjust to the crossdressing in their sex lives; however, similar to fetishes a partner can often feel they do not rank in first place.

The transvestite's selection of female attire can become strange at times as in the following case cited by Robert Tralins:

One evening I became very blue and I decided that perhaps it would've been the time of the month for me, so I went down to the pharmacy and purchased a box of sanitary napkins and a sanitary belt. I even stained the napkin with a dot of blood from my penis and then I went out again....I wondered how it would feel if I also bought a tampon and inserted it in my rectum (*The Sexual Fetish, Case Histories of Bizarre Erotic Hangups*, p. 148).

Magazines, videos, newspapers with personal ads, and businesses cater to this preference. (ETVC Anniversary Party and Lingerie Show, May 25, 1989) CAUTION: Transvestism is illegal in America if one is found loitering or soliciting. There are support groups for transvestites such as ETVC in San Francisco that provide social opportunities for those desiring to crossdress away from home. Most of the S/M bars and bondage clubs also welcome crossdressers.

(See also ADOLESCENTILISM, ANDROIDISM, ANDROMIMETOPHILIA, COSTUMES, DRAG QUEENS, FEMALE IMPERSONATORS, PETTICOAT DISCIPLINE, TRANSSEXUALS and VICTORIAN LACE)

TRICHOPHILIA (Hirsutophilia—arousal from armpit hair, Gynelophilous and Pubephilia—pubic hair fetish, Tripsolagnia—arousal from having hair manipulated or shampooed)

Trichophilia (tricho: hair; philia: attachment to) refers to hair fetishes. Children often fixate on hair at an early age, some developing a strong preference or fetish for a certain style, length, or color.

Female pubic hair can vary greatly from woman to woman. *The Illustrated Book of Sexual Records* cites an example of a woman whose pubic hair hung to her knees and another whose hair was so prolific that locks of it rose in the front to near the navel and behind up several inches on the buttocks. Other women are endowed with very little.

Females seem to notice chest hair, some developing an intense attraction to it. There have been women who could only orgasm if their partner had a hairy chest; and those who could only orgasm if he didn't.

Men with hair fetishes sometime resort to stealing hair. Many cases exist of men who have been arrested for snipping off a stranger's hair for their collection. Hirschfeld wrote of one man who had labelled each of the 31 pigtails in his collection with the hour and date he had taken them. The man was repulsed by the idea of having sex with a woman and needed to separate the hair from the individual. Men will also hire prostitutes to let them fondle and masturbate into their hair. Krafft-Ebbing told of a man who had been married to a famous bearded lady and upon her death searched until he found another. Lust murderers sometimes scalp the pubic area (gynelophism) of their victim to keep as a trophy. Gays also have hair fetishes. Hirschfeld cited one in a collection of his work called *Sexual Anomalies and Perversions*:

When the patient (a highly placed civil servant now aged 50) was seven years old, it happened one night that when he was already in bed the maid-servant, who was leaving, came up to him and embraced him. The patient still remembers quite clearly how he pushed his fingers through her hair. At the age of puberty he begun to experience sexual excitement whenever he saw or touched nicely dressed hair. But from then on, excitement was only induced by the hair of men; the hair of women exercised no effect whatever on him, and even in men he was only interested in sleek, dark brown hair, which had to be brushed right back...He derives particular pleasure and sexual excitement from dressing other people's hair. He executes this operation in the following manner: He stands behind the other man, applies hair oil, which, together with combs, he always carries with him, then he combs the hair back. As the comb reaches the top of the head, ejaculation takes place...the patient, whose behavior has frequently attracted attention, is known by the nickname of "The Hairdresser" (pp. 548-9).

A recent article in *TIME* magazine referred to a judge who was arrested by state troopers. It appears that the judge offered a "defendant leniency if he let the judge shampoo his hair. Further, suggested His Honor, the young man could get even more leniency if he brought in friends for a wash and rinse as well. . .Last week the magistrate apologized and pleaded guilty to official oppression, or misusing his office. He then resigned." ("Miscellany, Hair Justice," *TIME*, May 18, 1992, p. 26)

A small world-wide group of long hair enthusiasts exists whose members exchange photos, videos, and letters.

(See also DEPILATION, FETISHES, PUBIC DRESSING and PUBIC HAIR SCULPTURING)

TROILISM   Troilism (trois: three) refers to three people having sex. This may be two men and one woman, three men, two women and one man, or three women.

(See also CANDAULISM, GANG BANGS, GROUP SEX, ORGIES and MENAGE À TROIS)

TROUBADOURS   Troubadours lived during the 11th to 13th centuries at which time many were killed for heresy by the Church. These men taught birth control, that sex should be enjoyed, and that love should be considered in selecting a marriage partner. Troubadours turned the hearts of many away from stoic tradition with their romantic ballads. Singing minstrels were not novel, these men had long roamed through villages singing poems to impress wealthy men. In return they received food or lodging. The Inquisition brought an important change because now the land owners left on campaigns and minstrels soon discovered that their previous songs were of little interest to the lord's wife, who now controlled the funds. During the adaptation, songs began to take on the flavor of romance, unrequited, and immortal love. These were now dedicated to the wife of the feudal lord, who perhaps for the first time had a man bestow this type of attention upon her, and she rewarded him well. It is doubtful that too many troubadours ever consummated a liaison. However, their philosophy of romance and courtship filtered into the upper classes who had the free time to indulge in contemplations of titillating or torrid affairs.

(See also COURTSHIP and SERENADES)

TUNNEL OF LOVE   Amusement parks up until the 1960's often had three to four minute boat rides that passed through a dark tunnel. Couples often took this opportunity to sneak kisses. These tunnels of love lost their popularity when contraceptive pills became available and premarital sex became socially acceptable.

(See also CHAPERONS, COITUS A CHEVAL and COURTSHIP)

U

URINE   See UROPHILIA

UROPHILIA   (Golden showers, Water sports, Undinism, Urolagnia, Ondinisme, Renifleurism) Urophilia (uro: urine; philia:  attachment to) refers to those who derive sexual pleasure from acts involving urine. For some their gratification stems from engaging in an activity their mother condemned. Boys who were not allowed to fondle their penis were usually granted permission to hold it while urinating. Boys also discovered that urination could be a powerful weapon, one that could cause almost any target to retreat. This combination of rebellion, power, and sensuality became a potent aphrodisiac difficult for some to resist.

A few women also found erotic pleasure in urine. A sexologist named Merzbach recorded a case in the late 19th century of a young lady who not only masturbated by holding a bottle of men's urine under her nose but hung around men's rooms so she could smell the urine and masturbate openly as she watched men leave. Men secrete androsterone, a sex hormone, in their urine, and there is a possibility that this could have caused her attraction. It at least works for the male guinea pig who sometimes seduces uncooperative lovers by urinating on them.

Urine at one time was thought by many to have magical powers. Captain Edward Moor in 1810 referred to an odd superstition in his book, *Hindu Pantheon*:

The greatest, or, at any rate the most convenient of all purifiers is the urine of a cow. Images are sprinkled with it. No man of any pretensions to piety or cleanliness would pass a cow in the act of staling without receiving the holy stream in his hand and sipping a few drops...If the animal be retentive, a pious expectant will impatiently apply his finger, and by judicious tickling excite the grateful flow.

The American Zunis danced over a bowl of urine and would occasionally ingest it as a remedy for stomach problems. The African Nandis washed their hands in urine and then rinsed with water. They believe that if only water were used it would kill their husbands. Germans too believed in the magic properties of this liquid. Sometimes young brides would add a little to their husband's coffee to cast a love spell on him. Others used human urine to cure jaundice, anorexia, gout, toothache, colic, fevers, and insomnia. An American woman in Texas during the 1950's used this home remedy on her husband to cure the sore eye. The account indicated that he wasn't as convinced as his wife because she had to hold him down while urinating in his face. Ghandhi drank his own urine to reabsorb nutrients back into his body.

Urophiles engage in such activities as urinating on a partner's body, genitals, face, or in their mouth. It may be used for humiliation, punishment, or reward, depending on how the bottom feels about urine. Urine is not safe if the person has AIDS or hepatitis, therefore some partners substitute warm apple juice.

Bladder control is often used as a form of torture. Emperor Tiberius devised a method whereby he served his victims their fill of wine and then before they could urinate he had a cord tied around their penis to close off the urethra.

Sex games may also include mixing the liquid with food as portrayed in the movie called "Yellow Jello" where the actress mixes her urine with jello, stirs it, eats, and then rubs it on her body.

Finally there is a "golden enema" which is accomplished by inserting the penis into the vagina, waiting for it to become flaccid, and then, urinating. Only a very few have mastered this technique. CAUTION: Urine may contain bacteria and viruses and is not considered safe sex. ("Water Sports," Society of Janus lecture, June 8, 1989)

(See also CATHETERS, COCKTAILS, KLISMAPHILIA, SHOWERS and SITOPHILIA)

URTICATION   Urtication (urtica: nettle) refers to those who use stinging nettles to stimulate the skin. This was done to the limbs of the paralyzed to bring sensation to the person.

People have modified this practice for sex games. Nettles are favored because of several natural qualities. The active ingredients do not spread to other areas but are restricted to the site at which the plant comes into contact. Nettles have tiny hair-like projections rather than thorns which can break and stick in the skin. The skin also becomes  sensitized without the injury that certain types of flagellation can produce.

Skin exposed to nettles will redden and in a short time produce small bumps. The person will feel a sharp hot sting that fades to a warm tingling glow which may last several hours.

Nettles may be applied in various ways. Some lie the stems down and press the hairs into the skin, others hold them in a cluster and tap it against the chosen area, or put them into a bottom's underwear. Men who wear condoms have found that briefly applying nettles to the penis before putting on the condom can compensate for the sensation lost by the latex barrier. CAUTION: People using nettles should check new partners for allergic reactions and if flagellating the person with a cluster avoid the neck and face area.

(See also BEE STINGS and PYROPHILIA)

V

VAMPIRISM (Blood sports—sex play involving blood, Hemotigolagnia—fetish for sanitary pads, Menophilist—fetish for menstruating women)

Vampirism refers to drinking blood. Folklore is filled with odd tales of the living dead that drain others of their blood. Blood, similar to urine, is thought to have magical qualities and has been used in many religious ceremonies. Faustina, the wife of emperor Marcus Antoninus, drank the blood of dying gladiators to ensure fertility and epileptics believed that drinking the blood from a decapitated criminal would cure them.

There may be a health benefit to self-vampirism. Animals respond to wounds by licking them. They have a hormone in their saliva that promotes the regeneration of destroyed cells. Humans also have an enzyme that destroys some viruses and the urge some have to lick bloody wounds may be natural.

Vampirism varies and may include cunnilingus during a woman's menstrual cycle, biting that draws blood, making a small cut in one's skin, or using a hypodermic to collect blood from a vein. A recent case involved an Argentinean who was captured after attacking fifteen women in their beds and sucking blood from their necks in the period of only one week. Many vampires, lacking a cooperative partner draw their own blood, some doing this once, adding an anti-coagulant, and storing it in the refrigerator for the next few times they want to masturbate. Some even date partners with large veins because looking at these is arousing.

Drug addicts sometimes develop a sexual response to drawing blood back into the hypodermic syringe, some having described the experience as similar to orgasm. It is possible that the past generations found legends of vampires particularly exciting because of their exposure to phlebotomy, or bloodletting. A culture that thought nothing of having a barber surgeon drain their blood into a bowl would have less aversion to using a modified version of this in their sex play. The caning that was popular in England may have been indirectly connected to this desire as well. Even today there are those that get more of a pleasure from a caning if blood is drawn. The same is true for piercing or other blood sports.

Today's sex vampires sometimes seduce drunk men in bars and talk them into letting them make a cut on their skin during sex. It is more difficult for a male vampire to find women willing to be cut than it is for females to find willing males. The magazine *EXPOSED* featured an interview by Bill Reynolds with a member of a New York vampire society. This group makes small cuts on each other before indulging in orgies. One scene was described as starting with two sisters being cut, and then performing cunnilingus in front of the group as blood covered their bodies. This scene was followed by a group orgy. Another official vampire group is headquartered in Stockton, California, and there are several individual practitioners in San Francisco.

Some people have become sexually intrigued with this practice and formed clubs, dating services, computer bulletin boards, and commercial 900 telephone party lines. CAUTION: Vampirism is a blood sport and, as such, is considered unsafe sex.

(See also BLOOD SPORTS and PHLEBOTOMY)

VERTIGO Vertigo refers to dizziness or disorientation. Children often twirl in circles to be able to experience this unusual sensation. Humans as well as animals take advantage of this peculiar effect in their sex games. The African clawed frog often grabs a female during coitus, spins her around until she becomes dizzy, and as she weakens he again mounts her and copulates. Humans use similar tactics but add a blindfold to speed the process. They also use swings or suspension devices. The latter creates a more complete disorientation. CAUTION: Vertigo can cause nausea in some people.

(See also OXYGEN REGULATION and SENSORY OVERLOAD)

VICARIOUS AROUSAL (Vicarphilia—arousal from exposure to behavior of others) Vicarious arousal (vicis: substitute) refers to one who acts in the place of another, or in this case one who receives vicarious arousal from the actions of another.

Some men derive sexual satisfaction from insisting that their lover dress in provocative and revealing clothes when they go out into public. Others are often attracted to influential people, celebrities, those who engage in dangerous sports, or anyone who leads an exciting life. Criminals who have to serve prison sentences often find they have a waiting list of women who want to write to and sometimes marry them. Adrenalin is produced by our bodies when we become excited or frightened. This in turn causes the release of sex hormones in both males and females. Some people confuse the meaning of this type of response toward a person's activities as sexual attraction. This reaction can occur with each episode and after a while a person may think they are in love with the partner. CAUTION: Mistakes can be avoided in love affairs if an effort is made to learn more about their partner and to ask themselves whether they would still be infatuated if this person lacked the thing that one found exciting.

(See also EROTOMANIA and HYBRISTOPHILIA)

VICTORIAN LACE Victorian lace is feminine lingerie that is often made of silk and lace. Some males find this style of lingerie is erotic and would prefer to have their sex partner wear this rather than pantyhose.

Women who have top management jobs often wear lace undergarments to compensate for the otherwise sterile exterior. The idea that they are wearing something sexy makes them feel more attractive and self-confident. This preference is not exclusive to women; male transvestites also wear this type of clothing.

Victorian lace is used in S/M games to evoke a strong negative reaction from some males and lesbians. These people feel humiliated and submissive when forced to wear sexy lace and frills. Feminine lace in this society takes away the power one may ordinarily enjoy by dressing in leather or business suits. Therefore a person who wears this symbol of subservience not only submits to a partner but to the prejudices of a society. For some it can be more demeaning than wearing a dog collar and drinking out of a doggy bowl.

(See also CORSETS, DRAG QUEENS, INFANTILISM and PETTICOAT DISCIPLINE)

VICTORIANISM Victorianism is the term used to describe the sexual repression and prudery that sprang up during the last half of the 19th century. It was named such because Queen Victoria (1837-1901) reigned during this period. Unlike Puritans, the Victorians lacked a religious foundation for their fear of sex. Many became unduly concerned about their children masturbating because of medical reasons. Physicians such as Dr. Boerhaave had begun writing about the physical maladies attributed to masturbation as early as 1708. He said that "the rash expenditure of semen brings on a lassitude, a feebleness, a weakening of motion, fits, wasting, dryness, fevers, aching of the cerebral membranes, obscuring of the sense and above all the eyes, a decay of the spinal chord, a fatuity." Other physicians concurred with this opinion but it was not a topic that concerned the majority until when in 1835 Dr. John Todd made a monumental impact on readers when referring to interviews with superintendents of two insane asylums, writing that they supported his personal views on masturbation. They "will say, not only that this is the cause of bringing many of their patients there but an almost insuperable obstacle in the way of their recovery." Parents panicked and began engaging in all sorts of horrendous preventative tactics. These included infibulation, burning the genitals of the child, circumcision, castration, chastity belts, and cages for the penis.

Soon any type of sex came to be blamed for behavior that fell outside their conservative social mores. Clitoridectomies were done to young children as well as women whose husbands decided that they were oversexed. In the middle 1800's an American doctor named Marion Sims, known for developing gynecological surgical tools, performed many of these. He needed females to develop and test these inventions and because he did not use anesthesia he found very few volunteers. He began experimenting on slave women and for those whose owners were skeptical, he simply purchased the woman to use in surgery. Once he had perfected his tools he moved from his home in Alabama where he had built his own private "hospital," and performed surgery, to open the first Women's Hospital in New York (*The Horrors of the Half-Known Life*, by G.J. Barker-Benfield, p. 101).

Sex continued but it was not discussed in public. People became ashamed of not being able to control a natural function. Those who did manage to suppress their desires often became intolerant and judgmental of those not suppressing their lusts.

(See also ILLEGAL SEX)

VIRGINS (Aphallata, Parthenity; Hymenoclasis—surgical defloration, Hymenorrhexis—defloration of hymen, Stupprator—man who prefers virgins) The word virgin refers to those people who have not engaged 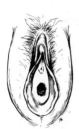 in penetration. In females the presence of a hymen is the determining factor. Females who engaged in only fellatio or anal sex technically retained their virginity. The hymen covers the vaginal opening but almost always has some sort of small hole in it large enough to insert a finger. This membrane is torn with the penetration of a penis and will remain this diameter until she stretches it by childbirth.

Some ancient traditions required that virgin brides give themselves first to stone gods (phallus), kings, slave owners, father-in-laws, or feudal lords. This was called the right of the first night, *jus primae noctis*, and is still forced onto the Untouchables in parts of India. There were other cultures where the bride was deflowered by someone other than her husband because of the superstitious belief that evil would befall him. Allen Edwardes and R.E.L. Masters described a typical defloration scene following a Northern African Arab wedding:

In the evening of the betrothal or actual wedding, the little girl (ranging in age from three to nine) is led by her father-in-law into an empty bedroom, where he strips her naked...most seigneurs are gentle and careful. Seating her on their knees, they will kiss the child and fondle her body—especially her little vulva, until "it starts to tickle." The man will say to the girl: "Let me feel the little turtle you have inside your legs." The 'alemah is reassured and does not resist; only haste and cruelty cause the child to cry and struggle to get away. Freeing his erect organ from his clothes, the considerate seigneur will then straddle the girl over his thighs, which he opens so that her own legs are forced or stretched as wide apart as possible. So doing, he slowly lowers her upon his glans penis, which he works between the labia and round and round the little orifice by holding the child by the waist and swaying her to and fro and from side to side...(The Cradle of Erotica, p. 132).

Virginity became important when men began paying dowries, some demanding that their merchandise be undamaged. There may have been a legitimate reason for this other than morality. Marriages arranged between a father and bridegroom might have encountered problems if the young woman had a lover before the marriage. These lovers could assist her in escaping, become antagonistic, or continue the affair after the wedding. An unconsummated love would be less of a threat.

Sex with a virgin is avoided by some people while others find it novel, feel honored, enjoy the feeling of power in defiling a virgin, are relieved that they cannot be compared with anyone else, or have a religious ethic that would create prejudice against a partner who was not virgin.

Women remain virgins due to reasons such as warnings of parents, the absence of a serious lover, fear of pregnancy and sexually transmitted diseases, or the lack of interest in sex. Religion too had a strong influence. During the Middle Ages young virgins under the influence of Church propaganda committed suicide rather than marry and lose their sacred virginity.

Bordellos often catered to men who paid extra for virgins. Bordello owners discovered that they could soak alum in a piece of cloth and insert it into a girl's vagina for a few hours and be able to pass her off as virgin several times. Some sex shops carry a formula called "China Shrink Cream" which is supposed to work within five minutes. One early surgical procedure was the suturing of torn hymens of prostitutes in bordellos, so they could be "re-virginized."

(See also BORDELLOS, GEISHAS, PEDOPHILIA and SEX RINGS)

VISUALIZATION   Visualization is the ability to see an event, object, or person in one's mind and is used in almost any type of sex.

Sex magicians use visualization to see energy flow, thoughts, divinities of air, fire, water, earth, and heaven as well as personal sex divinities. A person is able to increase the intensity of a trance (or divine identity) by visualization skills. The objective of sex magick is to visualize oneself and one's partner as gods that have come down to join in a fertility ritual. Well developed visualization skills allow one to identify with the god of choice so that the sex experience becomes a sacred and much more powerful experience.

Tantra utilizes visualization to see and direct the energy flow, breath, and to see themselves and partners as sacred.

Visualization is used in S/M play by placing a person in a blindfold or dark room and then making strange noises or threats which cause the person to visualize scenes that frighten or arouse them. Fantasies become more vivid and more intense under these circumstances.

People sometimes visualize having sex with a different person than the one in their arms. This is often done in the case of fetish objects because without this substitute some are unable to keep an erection.

(See also FANTASY, FANTASY PLAY, RITUAL SEX and SEX MAGICK)

VOMIT   See EMETOPHILIA and SHOWERS

VOYEURISM   (Allopellia, Cryptoscopophilia, Inspectionism, Mixoscopia, Parascopism, Peeping Tom) Voyeurism involves the act of watching other people for the purpose of sexual arousal. Often the voyeur stations himself outside a person's home and watches through a window. Teenagers sometimes engage in this activity out of frustration before they become sexually active themselves. Watching people having sex while being afraid of being caught is more arousing than looking at photos in magazines. This becomes a problem for men when it becomes their primary sexual outlet or when they are arrested.

This activity is not limited to males. One woman would slip into her backyard every night so that she could watch through the windows of a male neighbor. This man had the habit of wearing a t-shirt without underwear as he prepared dinner and relaxed for the evening.

Voyeurism seems to surface in many people when it involves a celebrity and a photographer who catches them in revealing attire. This was particularly true with Jacqueline Onassis who was stalked by photographers waiting for a bikini shot when she thought she was sunbathing in privacy. The same is true today of Princess Diana of England. Recently a photographer who managed to get a photograph of the princess in a bathing suit on a private yacht sold it for $135,000. This amount indicates that there are thousands of pseudo-voyeurs who find pleasure in getting a glimpse of the forbidden or the innocent. The embarrassment or outrage of the victim makes it all the more appealing.

(See also EXHIBITIONISM, ILLEGAL SEX and SCOPOPHILIA)

WEDDINGS Weddings, as we know them, have evolved in the last few hundred years. Marriage between two parties was generally carried out with a simple vow. The eventual involvement of a priest seems to have arisen from the practice of the couple going to church to say a Bride Mass after their vows. The couple often waited in front of the church for their friends, said their vows, and then entered the church. G. Rattray Taylor explained that "[i]t was only in the tenth century that the priest took to supervising the marriage at the door, and not until the sixteenth that it became obligatory to conduct the whole of the ceremony inside the church" (*Sex in History*, p. 28 as quoted from *A History of Matrimonial Institutions* by G.E. Howard). Marriage without the participation of a priest was later condemned as illegal by the Church. Taylor described a sample European wedding:

The bridal procession would set out from the house of the bride's father: first, the bride, accompanied perhaps by two pages, . . . Next would come the musicians, fiddling and blowing, then a group of maidens. These would all be dressed in the same way as the bride, in order to confuse any demons . . . some of the bridesmaids would be carrying . . . wheat sheaves on their heads—symbols of fertility and memories of Ceres . . . At nightfall there would be a banquet and dancing at the house of the bride's father . . . The married couple retire with their friends . . . Next comes the ceremony of throwing the stocking. . . Now appears the priest, and the benediction posset . . . blesses the bed, sprinkling holy water on the couple and censing the room, to dispel the demons who will undoubtedly be attracted by the performance of the sexual act (Sex in History by G. Rattray Taylor, pp. 29-30).

Other cultures dictated that the bride had sex with someone else prior to the husband. (See section on Virgins) The Nasamonian custom even required that all the wedding guests take their turn deflowering the bride (*The Mothers*, by R. Briffault, MacMillan Publishing).

According to Reader's Digest's *Stories Behind Everyday Things* the wearing of white wedding gowns originally signified joy, not chastity, and for brides among other cultures colors such as red, green, or black are common. The wedding rings were a symbol of purchase for some cultures. The designation of the third finger "probably comes from the ancient Greeks. Their first, faulty dissections of the human body led them to believe that a particular vein, the vena amoris, ran from that finger straight to the heart" (pp. 216-217).

Most of our other customs such as carrying a bride over the threshold, the honeymoon period, throwing things at the bride and groom, are remnants of bride capture, which existed in some parts of Europe until the early 20th century.

Many people today have arranged weddings that were more intriguing than normal church weddings, incorporating their favorite sport or activity into the ceremony. Couples take their vows while skydiving or in helicopters. Those in the S/M community have weddings where the partner who is to be submissive displays this by enduring a whipping or performing some other servile act. They may both have genital piercings done to signify their bond to each other. One male couple threw an S/M play party during which they gathered the group around and took their vows. They were both dressed in American Indian fantasy wear, and as a symbol of their bond the dominant cut the ponytail off his partner to keep as a memento in his medicine bag.

A different couple of which one was a female bi-sexual and the other a post-surgical male transsexual decided to have two ceremonies. In the first one the groom dressed according to custom and the bride wore a gown. The second ceremony was conducted with both of them dressed in wedding gowns.

(See also MARRIAGE)

WEIGHT TRAINING   Weight training refers to sex games where weights are hung from the nipples, genitals, or a piercing.

An eighteenth century writer, Andre Andrea de Nerciat, in his book *Aphrodite*, wrote of a male character being tested by having a 150 pound weight hung upon his tumescent organ "which he easily carried for three minutes." This seems an unlikely feat and if Nerciat based this on reality it was probably from torture techniques conducted in prisons or during the Inquisition which did include hanging people by their genitals from the ceiling.

Small weights hung on the glans are used today by some Eastern mystics to negate the function of their penis. Some have been stretched to hang between the knees and are worn rolled up against the body.

Clamps are often attached to each nipple and small weights are gradually added to increase the sensation. This will be more painful than merely using the clamps alone. Those who engage in this activity put the clamps and weights on themselves before using them on others.

Labia, penis, or scrotal weights are used in the same manner as those on nipples.

Weights are used to pull the testicles down as a method to delay orgasm. Others use them as a test of endurance. The Chicago Hell Fire Club had a national contest to see who could hold the most weight hung on the testicles. Five pound weights were added at intervals as the men bent their knees to have them applied. Three men tied for first place with 85 pounds each; none were willing to become sole champion by allowing the last five pounds to be added.

Weights are also hung from piercings. This is done both from permanent piercings that have jewelry inserted and from temporary piercings where the weight is attached to a suture, a fish hook, or the needle itself. This type of weight play would include lacing, bell dancing, or Sun dancing (an American Indian ritual where a man is pierced through the muscles of the upper chest with a stick and hung by strings from a tree limb until the stick breaks). CAUTION: Sterilization techniques are used any time the skin is broken in weight training. Too much weight on the testicles can do serious damage.

(See also BINDING, BONDAGE, STRETCHING and TORTURE)

WHITE SLAVERY   White slavery refers to the enticement or abduction of white women to work as prostitutes in foreign countries. Today the term is also used for women of any race that are transported to other countries (including the United States) under false pretenses and used for prostitution. These usually go through a training or breaking period where they are taught fellatio, anal sex or other sexual variations which will earn a higher fee. Those who refused to cooperate were sometimes starved to death. Foreign women were preferred by procurers because these were easier to exploit since the girls rarely spoke the language of the country and had no friends or money with which to escape.

A late 19th century racket run by a madame from China involved hiring young female actresses and singers, particularly those who had discreetly supplemented their income with part-time prostitution. Several women would be offered the chance to tour other countries with a musical company and even went through rehearsals and a couple of engagements in other countries before being left stranded without money in China. The madame, who was originally from America, would accidently happen upon them in their hotel and befriend them. Eventually, as a favor she would offer them a temporary job in her establishment to earn money with which to buy a return ticket. Most were stricken with syphilis before they could make it home and died in China.

Women were easier to get into other countries by deceit because if they knew their fate it was difficult to keep them quiet while aboard ships or through customs. A girl who thought she was to have a better life was much more willing to cooperate by lying to government agents or sneaking through barriers. Women, even after realizing their fate, did not all submit. Some where tortured to death because of this. One of the more recent cases of brutality occurred in 1964 in Mexico, where three sisters were convicted of running a sex slave service. "Girls were abducted—and then branded on the thigh or the breast with a red-hot iron; then they were locked up for months in tiny cells to break their spirits. When the girls were thought ready— through starvation, beating, and gross sexual exploitation—to satisfy any brothel frequenter, they were sold to establishments in Mexico or elsewhere. Some girls were beaten to death; one was burned alive; some were buried or tied to a bed by means of barbed wire" (*The Illustrated Book of Sexual Records*, by G. L. Simons, p. 102).

The other type of white slavery took place during the 19th century in America. African slaves had been so interbred with white blood that many had red or blond hair and blue eyes. An instance of two of these was cited by J. A. Rogers:

Tower describes the sale of a slave who was "whiter than many, nay, than most of the Anglo-Saxon ladies, of medium size, well-developed, beautiful black hair, black and sparkling eyes. The auctioneer cries, 'Why gentlemen, she is fair enough to become the sweetheart of a governor,' then rudely drawing the covering from her neck and shoulders, he exhibited a bust as plump and purely white as the snow-tinged image of Venus". . .Rev. Calvin Fairbank describes the sale of a slave-girl in Montgomery County, Kentucky, thus: "He turned his victim's profile to that excited crowd and lifting her skirts laid bare the beautiful symmetrical body from her feet to her waist and with his brutal sacrilegious hand smote the white flesh, exclaiming, 'Ah, gentlemen, who is going to be the winner of this prize?' The girl was one-sixty-fourth Negro" (Slavery Unmasked by P. Tower, p. 307(1856) and How the Way was Prepared by C. Fairbank, p. 30(1890); cited in Sex and Race, pp. 205-206).

Many of these women were sold to bordellos to work as prostitutes in the South.

The United States as well as other countries are still hosts for sex slaves. Procurers get these women into different countries by promising them husbands or jobs and leave them at a secured bordello without hope of rescue. CAUTION: If one can't succeed at modeling, performing arts, or finding a husband in one's own country it is not reasonable to think that there is a better chance in a country where one doesn't speak the language, doesn't have business contacts, friends, or the money to support oneself. Of course, many job offers are legitimate but without a backup plan there is always the possibility of being victimized.

(See also AUCTIONS, PROSTITUTION and SLAVES)

WIFE SWAPPING (Swinging) Wife swapping is an ancient custom in several cultures. Eskimo men left their wives with a neighbor when they ventured on hunting trips and during this time she performed wifely duties for the neighbor. This was an essential custom in a country where a woman and children might not survive weeks of harsh cold alone. The Chinese, not too long ago, had a custom of renting out their wives when the husband had to be away for several months. If she got pregnant and delivered a child while being rented it belonged to the man who was renting her. The Chukchee of North Asia practiced a wife swapping arrangement where if one of the men in a group had to travel or had some other reason for visiting, the husband would fix him a bed and offer him his wife. These favors were of course later reciprocated and single men were rarely permitted this hospitality. Other cultures engaging in formalized wife-swapping included certain African tribes, natives of Hawaii, and Tibet. Many ancient cultures had religious holidays where wife swapping or promiscuity were one of the featured attractions for the devoted worshippers.

American soldiers in World War II just after the siege on Germany are reported to have played a game of musical beds with local women who exchanged sex for food. Each soldier started with a woman and then upon cue the women would change beds in the dark and after a while the lights would come back on so that couples could see with whom they were having sex.

Today wife swappers have several options available to make the experience more enjoyable. Swingers have sail boats and yachts that are chartered for private parties. Groups reserve blocks of rooms on regular cruise ships. Of course, here, clothing and discretion is no longer optional. Couples lacking their own friends with whom to swap are able to attend conventions such as Lifestyles that provide opportunities for couples to travel to vacation resorts and meet others with the same interest.

(See also CANDAULISM and GROUP SEX)

WORKSHOPS There are many sex, intimacy, or relationship workshops available. Esalen Fields in Big Sur teaches people to accept themselves and others without judgments as do the Stan Dale's Human Awareness Institute workshops in the San Francisco area. The Human Awareness Institute workshops also help people work on sexual intimacy and sexual biases. People attend several levels and have to be prepared to become more and more intimate as they continue the training.

Karen Mendelsohn, the founder of San Francisco's QSM, sponsors workshops on various S/M practices. These workshops include training for bondage, whipping, piercing, and such forms of psychological play as humiliation and interrogation. QSM offers a multi-part "Introduction to S/M" series to give novices an overview of all forms of S/M play.

There are many other workshops such as tantra, sex magick, group sex, and so forth.

(See also SEX CLUBS, SEX CONFERENCES and SUPPORT GROUPS)

WORSHIP Sex or body worship is more profound than a slave master relationship. The devotee must perform ritualized acts of worship to their god or goddess. This may be as simple as kneeling and describing the partner's beauty, complimenting them on their selection of clothes, or idolizing their body, their breasts, and genitals. Worship can become more complicated when mixed with ancient rituals. In these scenes an altar is prepared that has a goblet, knife, string, incense, and red candle. The idolater is to kiss the goddess and drink of her urine from the goblet. She may also smear blood or feces on a wafer and offer it for him to eat. Those interested in safe sex substitute apple juice and peanut butter for body fluids. CAUTION: The use of body fluids is not considered a safe sex practice.

(See also DOMINANCE/SUBMISSION, HUMILIATION and MASOCHISM)

WRESTLING (Cratolagnia—arousal from strength, Sthenolagnia—arousal from displaying strength or muscles)

Wrestling is arousing for both those who prefer to engage in it themselves and those who watch other people perform.

Personal wrestling is similar to other physical exercising in that it produces adrenalin and creates a more intense level of pleasure. Hirschfeld cited the case study of a 40 year old Hungarian art dealer whose sole method of inducing orgasm was to exercise:

I had my first pollution on a train journey at the age of 12 or 13, and I was puzzled and anxious. Soon after I developed the horizontal bar mania, and I made exercises on it until violent orgasm and ejaculation were induced...between the twentieth and thirtieth exercise, without manual contact...I did this on average every three days...I attribute my powerful biceps and chest muscles to this peculiar method of masturbation (Sexual Anomalies and Perversions, by Magnus Hirschfeld, p. 131).

Most gays and some heterosexuals are able to wrestle with their partners. Those who can't sometimes hire a prostitute or a professional dominatrix.

Videos such as *Amazon Dancers, Amazon Women* and Deadly Amazons feature female body builders and are available for those who want to watch women in different arrays of dress wrestle men. Male wrestlers can be found on television or at public matches. Bars sometimes have female mud wrestlers that became popular during the 1970s throughout portions of the world.

(See also BONDAGE and CAT FIGHTING)

X Y Z

XENOPHILIA (Xenolimia, Xeno-dynamic—only potent with strangers) Xenophilia (xeno: stranger; philia: attachment to) refers to someone who is sexually aroused by strangers. Xenophiles may feel increased passion when meeting new acquaintances and if they are able to seduce this person they quickly lose interest, i.e. a one-night stand. Others may frequent bordellos always asking for a different woman or wanting to try women of various nationalities. Some, otherwise heterosexual men, will take the opportunity that anonymity offers when they travel to experiment with men or children. J.A. Rogers, a writer who lived for a while in the West Indies said, "so fond were the English sailors of black boys that whenever the fleet came on its annual visit, the local pharmacists had to lie [sic] in an extra supply of unguents [lubricants] (*Sex and Race*, p. 129).

The use of costumes or wigs in sex play provides excitement for many people; however, not everyone is comfortable having sex incognito and partners should never be coerced into participating.

(See also PARAPHILIAS and PHOBOPHILIA)

YONI WORSHIP The female yoni (genitals) preceded the phallus in being revered because of its power to give life. Stone carvings of vaginas were discovered to be as ancient as 35,000 B.C.E. The yoni had magical qualities and a woman could heal the sick or scare away storms and devils by simply exposing her genitals.

The yoni was usually carved in a round stone with three line indentations. Later it took also the form of a horseshoe that was thought to bring good luck when nailed upside down above one's doorway.

(See also CHARMS and PHALLOPHILIA)

ZELOPHILIA Zelophilia (zelosus: zeal or jealousy; philia: attachment to) refers to one who becomes aroused by jealousy. This arousal may be triggered by either partner becoming jealous. Zelophiles who become aroused from their own jealousy are reacting to the fear of loss and the adrenalin it produces. Some of these people take their lovers to a group sex house or otherwise put them in situations that will solicit attention from rivals thereby deriving intense sexual arousal from watching their lover approached or succumb to coitus.

(See also HEDONISM, JEALOUSY, LOVE and PECATTIPHILIA)

ZOOPHILIA Zoophilia involves sex between humans and animals and generally takes many more forms than does sex between humans. Some of our ancestors felt that sex with animals held a magic power and their gods were able to create offspring by these sacred unions. Herodotus mentions an ancient Egyptian temple at Mendes where goats were trained to have sex with both sexes as part of their fertility rituals. Ancient Egyptians also used coitus with female crocodiles to increase male virility. Certain folk-lore taught that zoophilia was a cure for venereal diseases and it was engaged in for this reason by some.

It was assumed throughout most of history that offspring could be produced by these unions and many cultures prohibited the act for this reason. Several males defended themselves after having been caught during the 19th century by announcing that they practiced coitus interruptus to prevent impregnating the beast. The incidence of zoophilia between young boys, cows, and sheep became so prevalent during the 17th century that the Catholic Church tried to ban the employment of male herdsmen. Zoophilia often carried with it the penalty of death for both participants; however, one exception to this rule was cited by Inge and Sten Hegeler in their book *An ABZ of Love.* "In 1750, Jacques Ferron was hanged for having had intercourse with a female donkey. Several respectable citizens (including the abbot of the local monastery) appeared as witnesses and declared that they had known the donkey for many years and that it had always behaved itself virtuously and as a good donkey should. The court then acquitted the donkey, declaring that it obviously must have been raped" (p. 23).

Literature and art include portrayals of zoophilia. Michelangelo painted a scene of Leda and the Swan (Zeus), and Agostino Carracchi did an engraving titled *Satyr and Nymph* in 1590 of a half man/goat having explicit intercourse with a woman. In literature, *A Night in a Moorish Harem* by Lord George Herbert includes a poetic account of a girl's sexual encounter with a stallion:

Mohammed was my favorite stallion. He was more fleet than the wind, and so gentle that he obeyed my slightest word. He was of a bright wine color and his shape was perfect. His head was small and gracefully set on his arching back. His brown eyes had almost human intelligence. His limbs were slender, and he walked so proud that he seemed to spurn the ground.

He came up to me, and after I had fed him from my hand, I spent some time braiding his mane. Then, for want of something else to do, I thought I would take a bath. A pool where the water gathered from a spring which fed the oasis made a fine bath. it was shaded by palm trees from the sultry heat which glowed on the surrounding sands. After bathing I threw myself at length on the short grass and stretched myself lazily on my back at full length.

Mohammed came and stood over me as if for company in our loneliness. I amused myself by making him stand with his forefeet on either side of my chest. Nothing could have induced him to step on me, not even if a gun had been suddenly fired. But there was nothing to startle him. We were entirely alone.

Pretty soon—as stallions will when standing in perfect repose—his shaft hung dangling out. In a spirit of mischief I put up both my feet and took it between them and began rubbing it gently. It gradually stiffened, and its crest hung down between my thighs and pressed against the lips there. He put his head down and touched my bosoms with his velvety nostrils. I still continued to rub up and down his shaft. It suddenly shot out, and, stretching my sheath to its greatest tension, penetrated me to my loins.

I was ravished with the fierce thrill and the stallion's gushing sperm. It found no room in my distended orifice and spurted out of it again like a fountain descending over my belly and thighs. Luckily for me, the distance between his loins and mine was sufficient to prevent anything but the end of his shaft from entering. Otherwise I know not but that it would have been driven through the length of my body and come out my mouth.

As it was I scrambled out from under him with my lust completely quenched. From my waist to my knees I was dripping with the stallion's thick milky sperm. I hastened to wash it off and to bathe and cool my smarting sheath in the pool. For a long time I had to keep Mohammed away from me with a switch, but I did not strike him hard. I could not bear to hurt him for the consequences of my own folly.

Regardless of the relationship of religious or civil laws some people have a preference for animal sex partners. Kinsey reported that as many as 17% of boys raised on farms have had at least one sexual encounter with an animal. The percentage for zoophilia in the general population was reported as 8% for males and 3% for females.

One San Francisco prostitute who publicly performed coitus with a Newfoundland dog on stage stated that any woman who had experienced sex with a dog would never again be satisfied with a man. (The sexual preference for a dog is called cynophilia.)

A sheepherder in South Africa evidently became so proficient that he devised a technique whereby he cut two holes at the bottom of his jacket in which to insert the hind legs of sheep to anchor them in place for coitus. He quite willingly offered this advice to anyone at the local town tavern. The other popular sex position with sheep was to place each of the sheep's hind feet into the man's boot. True animal lovers will tell you that pigs are preferred over sheep because they are much more willing partners.

Mexican border towns were once famous for their donkey shows. A prostitute would allow a donkey to penetrate her vagina while on stage and a red ribbon was then placed on the penis marking the length she was able to take in. Other prostitutes would then take their turn to see if they could break the record.

The act of zoophilia usually involves a person manually masturbating the animal, having mouth to genital (zoofellatio), penis 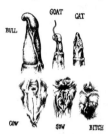 to anus, or penis to vagina contact. The animals used are generally dogs, horses, donkeys, cows, deer, sheep, pigs, gerbils, snakes, turkeys, chickens, and geese. Snails or insects are used for sensory enhancement in either masturbation or bondage games. The genital anatomy of some of these animals are depicted in the following drawings:

The various types of zoophilia have been divided into the following categories:

ANDROZOONS Androzoons are male animals that are trained for sex with humans. Animals trained for men are gynezoons. Many are only trained for oral sex (zoolinction) and this is done by putting their favorite food on a person's genitals. There are also professionals who train androzoons for other individuals.

Two thousand years ago androzoons were used in the Constantinople Amphitheater to rape and sometimes kill victims for the amusement of the crowds. The most common were apes, bulls, cheetahs, dogs, giraffes, wild boars, and zebras. Theodora, the daughter of one of these trainers, married the Roman Emperor Justinian. She evidently trained some of her own animals as she was notorious for a stage performance in which she laid on her back with her legs raised and her genitals facing the audience. Theodora's assistants would then drop kernels or grain into her open vagina. Her trained geese were then allowed to come onto the stage and pick the kernels out with their beaks (*Perverse Crimes in History*, p. 49).

Sex with animals is not always consensual. One Englishman was convicted of sodomy and indecent assault because he repeatedly forced his wife into coitus with his dog. There are also rumors of men wrapping gerbils with duct tape and penetrating them anally. CAUTION: Animals used for this purpose tend to be embarrassing as they lack discretion as to who or when they mount.

AVISODOMY Avisodomy (Avis: bird, sodomy: anal sex) is the ancient practice of having sex with a bird. As the man is about to orgasm he breaks the neck of the bird causing the bird's cloaca sphincter to constrict and spasm, thus creating pleasurable sensations for the man. The ancient Chinese used geese for this purpose and the Parisian brothels provided turkeys for their clients. Chickens are used on farms by a few young men today in the United States for this purpose. A portion of the stimuli for a few may be due to the feeling of power derived when killing the bird.

BESTIALSADISM Bestialsadism includes people who derive sexual pleasure from torturing or mutilating animals. For example, one San Francisco man shot a wild pig while hunting, chased away the dogs, and had sex with the dead animal. He then returned to his campsite with the animal and repeated the performance for two of the women in the group while they took photos. (Personal communication.) Many lust murderers and anthrophagists, some at a young age, begin torturing animals before moving on to human victims. The animal is hurt or mutilated while the person masturbates or has intercourse with it. Others do not harm animals themselves but orgasm when they witness fowls being killed by cooks or by coachmen lashing their horses. There were also men who once hired prostitutes to torture and kill animals while they watched. Professional counseling by a therapist is important if this occurs during childhood. Young children can transfer the anger they feel to animals, just as their fear of parents can manifest itself as a phobia of insects, heights, animals, etc. The common mishandling of animals by inexperienced children should not be confused with deliberate infliction of pain, injury, or death. Nor is avisodomy to be included as bestialsadism, the reason being that the killing of the bird was not out of anger, but rather for sexual pleasure.

Sexual arousal is caused by the release of specific chemicals in the brain. These are already heightened due to the anger that triggers the act, and intensified even more from revenge, fear of being caught, and vicarious anxiety from seeing pain, blood, or death. This combination creates sexual arousal for many people. Refer to the sections titled Masochism, Sadism, and Paraphilias for a more complete discussion of this phenomenon.

EROTICA Bestial erotica is used by those who become sexually aroused by the sight of mating animals. The person may actually be repulsed by the sight but later will become aroused to the point of masturbation. One such case was a nun who became so aroused by the sight of two flies in sexual union that each time she felt compelled to masturbate. She estimated this as having happened over 400 times (*Studies in the Psychology of Sex*, by Havelock Ellis, 1900, Vol. I, p. 73).

Some children or people become fascinated at the sight of a male animal ejaculating and will sometimes take an active role by masturbating the animal themselves. These people generally have no intention of having coitus with the animal themselves.

Bestial erotica and fantasies that include animals are common and have no apparent harmful effects.

FELLCHING Fellching (fellah: to plow or fell: fierce, cruel, causing death, animal's hide) is the act of inserting a live animal into the anus or vagina for the purpose of receiving sexual pleasure from their body movements. Fellching is done with gerbils, rodents, or fish.

Some of the Ponape men of the Croline Islands insert a fish into a woman's vagina and then slowly lick it out as a form of foreplay. (*Patterns of Sexual Behavior*, by C. Ford and F. Beach, p. 51)

Remains of small rodents have been found in the lower intestines and rectums of cadavers during autopsies. (Personal communication with student at the University of California at Davis.) These animals are said to have been placed into a plastic bag or condom and inserted into the anus after it has been stretched. The bagged gerbil is put into a lubricated toilet paper roll which is pushed into the rectum and at the right moment the empty roll is yanked out leaving the gerbil and bag inside. (Personal communication.) CAUTION: This form of fellching is extremely dangerous. The rectal wall is very thin and can tear easily. It may lead to peritonitis and death.

FORMICOPHILIA (Entomocism—insects) Formicophilia (formica: ant; philia: attachment to) refers to the use of insects for sexual purposes. Ants, flies, or insects are used to crawl over the genitals or other portion of the body.

People use insects to tickle, to induce fear, inflict pain, or to create a sensuous feeling. Bugs are either attracted to a specific area by the use of honey or are placed in a jar and held over a certain part of the body.

Cleopatra is said to have had a small box that could be filled with bees and placed against her genitals for a stimulation similar to that of vibrators. A few young men have been known to remove the wings of a fly, submerge themselves in bath water, and then allowing their penis to stick out of the water, put the fly on it to crawl around. (Personal communication).

People who use fear select the type of insect that frightens or disgusts their partner. This insect is allowed merely to crawl over the victim's body which causes a rush of adrenalin that is later transferred to sexual passion for their partner.

Others are only interested in the stinging or pain that can be inflicted by insects. American Indians, Asians, and others used insects in torturing captives. Today some governments still advocate interrogation that includes insect torture. One such method is the stripping of a prisoner and staking him to the ground where hundreds of ants will bite him. Another is to put ants, mosquitos, biting flies, wasps, or bees in a jar and hold the open end against his nipples, armpits, and genitals (*Physical*

Interrogation Techniques by Richard W. Krousher, p. 88). A slightly different torture technique is called the "Bath of Flies" and requires the prisoner to be blindfolded and bound with their wrists above their head and their feet together. They are next rubbed with honey or other sweet smelling liquid with special attention being given the mouth, armpits, ears, genitals, and anus. This attracts flying insects and will supposedly cause insanity if done for over a couple of hours. A few use stinging insects for sex play. One man would lie on the grass in his back yard during the summer and have ants crawl over his body becoming sexually aroused as they began to bite. Another captures bees in a glass jar, puts each on his penis just below the glans, and holds them there until they sting. (See BEE STINGS)

NECROBESTIALISM Necrobestialism (Necro: death, bestial: animals, act of) refers to those people who are sexually aroused by having sex with dead animals. This may include the bestialsadist who kills the animal before or during the torture, as well as those who choose to have sex with animals they already find dead. The Suaheli and Arabian fisherman along the coast of Africa until a hundred years ago believed that unless they had anal sex with the seacows that they netted or that had washed up dead they would be dragged out to sea the next day and drowned by the seacow's dead sister. Many locals would therefore make these fishermen swear by the Koran that they did not have sex with the seacow they were selling at the local market.

OPHIDICISM Ophidicism (ophidi: serpent; ism: act) refers to those who use snakes for sexual pleasure. Snakes were used by women throughout history as sexual companions and vaginal inserts. (See separate section on OPHIDICISM.)

PSEUDOZOOPHILIA Pseudozoophilia (Pseudo: pretended, zoo: animal, philia: attachment to) refers to sexual fantasy games where a partner plays the role of an animal.

The Roman emperor Nero would play a game where he dressed in skins of wild ani-

mals and then attacked the genitals of people who had been bound to stakes. Tiberius had young boys trained to swim after him and come up underwater to suck and nibble at his genitals. He called them his "minnows." He also had an island where he kept young men and women who roamed the woods and pretended to be nymphs and satyrs. An Egyptian, Ali Goher, played a game where his friends would squat, cackle, and lay eggs by sleight of hand. He would then yell, "Hello hens, here's your cock" as he began his orgy of anal sex (*Perverse Crimes in History*, p. 196).

Coitus à cheval is played by having one partner pretend to be a horse, dress up and have the other ride them. (See COITUS À CHEVAL) Sex slaves sometimes take the role of a pet dog and are made to wear a leash, eat and drink out of dog dishes, fetch newspapers, lick genitals, be toilet trained (house broken), etc.

Some people make animal noises during sex, and others wear a mask or sometimes use a partner they find unattractive and pretend they are an animal. Stuffed animals, masks, and puppets are likewise used for fellatio or masturbation in sex games. One of San Francisco's leather bars has an event called the S/M Circus where people dress as different exotic animals and are taught to perform the same as their animal counterparts. One lion tamer was brave enough to put his head in the mouth of his large cats. The audience didn't get to see the actual event because he turned his back to them and spread his cape around the two squatting beasts. CAUTION: There are infections or diseases that one must consider including rabies (rare), certain types of blood poisoning, parasites, bites, and fleas. Some androzoons scratch their partner's back which could lead to infection. Another risk worth considering for men is that a female dog's vagina will constrict and lock the penis in position during coitus. One man was reported as having gone to an emergency room, with dog intact, to have the staff inject the dog with a muscle relaxant so that he could withdraw his penis. One boy in Nebraska, while having a dog engage in rectal entry, was injured enough during withdrawal to need stitches (*Omaha Clinic*, March 1893). A donkey caused the death of his female partner in Chicago by falling on her, and other women have received vaginal lacerations from being unable to free themselves of the dog's swollen penis. One woman died from hemorrhaging after someone walked into the room and startled the dog, causing it to tear the vaginal vault trying to free himself. Sex with a partner that has little intelligence, superior strength, and who panics easily is risky (*Studies in the Psychology of Sex,* by Havelock Ellis).

(See also BEE STINGS, FORMICOPHILIA and OPHIDICISM)

GLOSSARY OF TERMS

Abduction: to kidnap or carry a person away by force, also used in sex play

Abrasions: scratching or rubbing off skin

Abstinence: celibacy

Acmegenesis: orgasm

Acomoclitic: preference for hairless genitals

Acousticophilia: arousal from sounds

Acrophilia: arousal from heights or high altitudes

Acrotomophilia: sexual preference for amputees

Actirasty: arousal from exposure to sun's rays

Acucullophallia: circumcision

Acupressure: pressure points on body that induce certain responses, some sexual

Adolescentilism: cross-dressing or playing the role of an adolescent

Adultery: having sex outside a marriage

Agalmatophilia: arousal from statues or manikins; also called pygmalionism

Agenobiosis: married couple who consent to live together without sex

Agonophilia: person who is aroused by partner pretending to struggle

Agoraphilia: arousal from open spaces or having sex in public

Agrexophilia: arousal from others knowing you are having sex

Albutophilia: arousal from water

Algophilia: arousal from experiencing pain

Aliphineur: person using lotion to arouse partner

Alloerasty: use of nudity of another person to arouse partner

Allopellia: having orgasm from watching others engaging in sex

Allorgasmia: arousal from fantasizing about someone other than one's partner

Allotriorasty: arousal from partners of other nations or races

Alphamegamia: arousal from partner of different age group

Altocalciphilia: high heel fetish

Alvinolagnia: stomach fetish

Amatripsis: masturbation by rubbing labia together

Amaurophilia: preference for a blind or blindfolded sex partner

Amomaxia: sex in a parked car

Ambisexual: bi-sexual

Amelotasis: attraction to absence of limb

Amelotation: loss of a limb

Amokoscisia: arousal or sexual frenzy with desire to slash or mutilate women

Amphisexual: bi-sexual

Amychesis: act of scratching partner during sexual passion

Anaclitism: arousal from items used as infant

Analinctus: licking anus

Analingus: rimming or penetration of anus with tongue

Anasteemaphilia: attraction to taller or shorter partners

Androgyny: having both male & female characteristics

Androgynophilia: bi-sexual

Androidism: arousal from robots with human features

Andromania: nymphomania

Androminetophilia: arousal from female partner who dresses like male

Androsodomy: anal sex with a male partner

Anililagnia: arousal from older female sex partner

Anisonogamist: attraction to either older or younger partner

Anocratism: anal sex

Amomaxia: sex in parked car

Anomeatia: anal sex with a female partner

Anophelorastia: arousal from defiling or ravaging a partner

Anophilemia: kissing anus

Anoraptus: rapist who only attacks elderly women

Antholagnia: arousal from smelling flowers

Anthropomorphism: attributing human characteristics to half-human half-animal characters

Anthropophagolagnia: rape with cannibalism

Anthropophagy: cannibalism

Apellous: circumcision

Aphallatia: celibacy

Aphrodisiacs: drugs stimulating a sexual response

Apistia: adultery

Apotemnophilia: person who has sexual fantasies about loosing a limb

Arachnephilia: arousal from spiders

Arrhenothigmophilous: nymphomania

Arsometry: anal sex

Artificial insemination: deposit of sperm into the vagina by methods other than male penetration of the vagina

Asceticism: religious self-denial often including celibacy

Asphyxiaphilia: arousal from lack of oxygen

Asthenolagnia: arousal from weakness or being humiliated

Astyphia: impotence

Asynodia: celibacy particularly due to impotence

Auctions: public sale with item or sex slave going to highest bidder

Autagonistophilia: exhibitionism, arousal from exposing naked body or genitals to strangers while on stage or while being photographed

Autassassinophilia: arousal from orchestrating one's own death by the hands of another

Autoerotic Asphyxia: arousal from oxygen deprivation and sometimes risk of dying

Autogynephilia: arousal from crossdressing

Automasochism: arousal from inflicting intense sensations or pain on one's own body

Autoerotica: self induced arousal (i.e. fantasies or other aids)

Automysophilia: arousal from being dirty or defiled

Autonepiophilia: infantilism; arousal from dressing or being treated like infant

Autopederasty: person inserting their own penis into their anus

Autophagy: self-cannibalism or eating own flesh

Autosadism: infliction of pain or injury on oneself

Avisodomy: breaking neck of bird while penetrating it for sex

Axillism: penis penetrating an arm pit

Ball dancing: bell dancing; self flagellation by hanging fruit from hooks in skin

Bardajes: young gay male lover

Barosmia: arousal from smell

Basoexia: arousal from kissing

Bath house: commercial baths, some of which allow sex on premises

Bed of Nails: lying on a bed of nails for sensory enhancement

Bee stings: the use of bees, such as to sting genitals

Bell dancing: self-flagellation with bells or other ornaments hanging the skin

Belonephilia: arousal from use of needles

Bestiality: zoophilia; sex with animals

Bestialsadism: cruelty or mutilation of animals

Bi-Sexuality: people with sexual attraction for both sexes

Biastophilia: those preferring to violently rape their victims

Bigynist: sex between one male and two females

Bihari surgery: cutting ligament above penis to make it appear longer

Bindings: wrapping feet or genitals with string or lace

Bivirist: sex between one female and two males

Blastolagnia: person aroused by young females

Blindfolding: covering the eyes

Blood Sports: sex games which involve blood

Borderline self-mutilator: automasochism

Body Painting: temporary designs drawn on body

Body Worship: sex game where partner is made to adore another's body

Bondage: physical or mental restriction of partner

Bordellos: houses of prostitution

Bottom: passive partner who experiences stimuli during sex games, masochist, slave, submissive

Botulinonia: using a sausage as a dildo

Bouginonia: female masturbation from the use of objects such as dildos that stretch open the vagina

Brachioprotic eroticism: a deep form of fisting where the arm enters the anus

Bradycubia: slow movement during penetration

Branding: burning patterns or initials into flesh

Buggery: anal sex

Bundling: partners sleeping together clothed and without sex

Bushie Mall: agoraphilia; sex in an open area

Butt plugs: anal inserts used for masturbation

Candaulism: spouse who watches partner having sex with someone else

Caning: whipping that uses a switch or cane to discipline partner

Capnolagnia: arousal from watching others smoke

Castration: removal of the scrotum, testicles, ovaries, or penis

Cat Fighting: women fighting without rules and often tearing off each other's clothing

Catamites: young gay male lovers

Cataphilist: male submitting to female

Catatasis: stretching of the penis

Catheters: insertion of plastic tube into urethra

Catheterophilia: arousal from use of catheters

Celibacy: abstinence from sex

Chaperon: person who escorts a young couple to ensure they don't engage in sex

Charms: objects used to bring good luck and ward off evil

Chastity: sexual abstinence

Chastity Belts: leather or metal belts used to prevent genital penetration

Chemise Cagoule: long heavy night shirt with hole for penis

Chezolagnia: masturbating while defecating

Chipil: Couvade syndrome

Choreophilia: dancing to orgasmic release

Chrematistophilia: person aroused by having to pay for sex or having sex partner steal from them (see also harpaxophilia)

Chronophilia: arousal from passage of time; arousal from older partner

Chubby Chasers: people who are aroused by obesity in partner

Cicatrization: scarring

Circumcision: the removal of foreskin on genitals

Clamps: metal, plastic, or wood fasteners used on nipples or genitals

Claustrophilia: arousal from being confined in small space

Clitoridectomy: surgical removal of the clitoris

Clitorilingus: licking a clitoris

Clitoromania: nymphomania

Cock Rings: rings placed around the base of the male genitals to maintain erections

Cocktails: drinking of body secretions from a glass

Coitobalnism: sex in a bathtub

Coitolimia: tremendous sexual drive

Coitophobia: fear of sexual intercourse

Coitus: sexual penetration with orgasm

Coitus analis: anal sex

Coitus à Cheval: couple having sex on the back of an animal or one acting out role of horse

Coitus à Mammilla: penetration of penis between breasts

Coitus à Unda: sex or sex games in water

Coitus Intrafermoris: penetration between legs

Coitus reservatus: birth control method where male withdraws penis before ejaculation

Colobosis: mutilation or castration of penis

Condoms: latex or animal intestine used as shield to guard against skin-to-skin contact with partner's genitals

Constrictions: bondage using rows of strings

Compulsive cruising: compulsive search for sex partners

Computer sex: the use of computers for sex games, communication, and erotic photography

Commasculation: homosexuality

Concubinage: use of female slaves as sex partners; living with sex partner without being married

Confessions: admitting a sin; in some cases to arouse potential partner

Coprography: writing obscene words or phrases, usually in public toilets

Coprolagnia: arousal from feces

Coprolalia: arousal from using obscene language or writing

Coprophagy: the consumption of feces

Coprophilia: arousal from playing with feces, also called scat

Coproscopist: arousal from watching a person defecate

Corephallism: anal sex with young girl

Corsetting: body modification or oxygen restriction from using corsets

Corvus: fellatio

Costumes: the use of costumes in sexual fantasy play

Courtesans: the mistress of a king or nobleman

Courtship: the period before marriage where a person tries to entice the other into a commitment

Couvade: custom where male mimics child birth or is confined at time of wife's delivery

Couvade syndrome: a male who experiences symptoms of pregnancy in sympathy for wife

Cratolagnia: arousal from strength of partner

Cross dressing: a person who wears the apparel of the opposite sex

Crurofact: leg fetish

Cryptoscopophilia: desire to see behavior of others in privacy of their home, not necessarily sexual

Cuckoldry: a man whose wife has sex or becomes impregnated by a man other than himself

Cunnilalia: to talk about female genitals

Cunnilingus: oral sex on a woman

Cupping: drawing blood to the surface of skin by placing heated glass jars onto the skin

Cutting: cicatrization, or scarring of skin for sexual purposes

Cyesolagnia: pregnant woman fetish

Cymbalism: lesbianism

Cynophilia: arousal from sex with dogs

Cyprieunia: sex with a prostitute

D'Eon, Chevalier: French cross-dresser from whom the term "Eonism" is derived

Dacnolagnomania: lust murder

Dacrylagnia: arousal from seeing tears in the eyes of a partner

Dacryphilia: person who is aroused by seeing their partner cry

Dame de voyage: dolls designed for genital penetration, often used by sailors

Danse du ventre: erotic or fertility dancing; belly dance

Dating services: agencies arranging for strangers to meet each other, usually for a fee

Day belts: chastity device used for short day excursions

De Clerambault's syndrome: erotomania

Defecolagnia: arousal from defecation

Defilement: arousal from partner or self becoming dirty or wet

Deliberate self-harm syndrome: automasochism

Dendrophilia: arousal from tree or fertility worship of them

Depilation: shaving, waxing, or other type of hair removal

Dermagraphism: marks left on the skin of a partner by biting, scratching or sucking

Dermaphilia: doraphilia; sexual stimulus from skin

Deviance: paraphilia; practice that deviates from the majority of society

Dildos and Plugs: instruments used for genital penetration

Dippoldism: sexual arousal from abusing children

Discipline: punishment and control of a partner in sex play

Diseases (STD or VD): sexually transmitted diseases, also called venereal diseases

Divertissement: paraphilia

Docking: slipping one partner's foreskin over the glans penis of another

Dogging: couples who engage in sex in their car while others watch from outside

Doleros: algophilia; arousal from pain

Dominance/Submission: power exchange between partners

Doraphilia: arousal from animal fur, leather, or skin

Douches: rinsing out the anus or vagina with liquids

Dowry: sum of money or goods paid to parents of future husband or wife

Drag queens: gay men who dress in female attire

Dungeons: rooms that are decorated for SM play

Dysfunctions: physical disorders relating to sex

Dysmorphophilia: arousal from deformed or physically impaired partners

Ecdemolagnia: arousal from traveling or being away from home

Ecdyosis: arousal from removing clothes in front of others

Ecorchement: flagellation

Ecouteurism: listening to others having sex without consent

Ederacinism: to tear out sex organs by the roots as in a frenzy or to punish oneself for sexual cravings

Ejaculatio praecox: premature ejaculation

Electric Shock: using electric shock for sensory enhancement

Electrophilia: arousal from electrical stimulus

Electrolysis: an electrical method of removing hair

Elopement: hasty and clandestine marriage without consent of family members

Emetophilia: Roman shower; arousal from vomit

Endytolagnia: arousal only from partners who are clothed

Endytophilia: arousal only from partners who are clothed

Enema: the insertion and expulsion of fluids into the anus

Enema cocktail: drinking purged contents of enema

Entomocism: the use of insects

Entomophilia: arousal from insects or using them in sex play

Eonism: crossdressing

Eopareunia: engaging in sex while young

Ephebophilia: attraction to adolescent sex partner

Episioclisia: suturing of the labia majora; infibulation

Eproctolagniac: person aroused by flatulence

Eproctophilia: arousal from flatulence

Erotica: sexual literature and photos

Erotographomania: arousal from writing love poems or letters

Erotomania: people who develop an unreasonable love of a stranger or person not interested in them

Erotophobia: fear of sexual love

Erotophonophilia: lust murder

Essayeurs: men who were hired by bordellos to become sexual with women so that timid clients would follow their lead

Eugenics: belief that only the fittest should impregnate women

Eunuchs: castrated men

Executions: a legal death sentence, some people become aroused by watching executions

Exhibitionism: exposing body to inappropriate and nonconsenting people for arousal

Exmuliebrate: castration

Exophilia: neophilia; fetish for the unusual or bizarre

Fainting: passing out or losing consciousness

Famulus: slaves, family

Fantasy: mental image or illusion, sometimes sexual

Fantasy Play: acting out sexual fantasies

Fellatio: oral sex on a male

Fellching: sucking semen out of vagina or anus; or inserting animals into anus or vagina

Female impersonators: men who dress in women's clothing, often for pay

Fetishes: an object that replaces people as primary object of love

Fibula: bar that runs through foreskin of male and attaches to semi-circle device, used by Romans to prevent intercourse

Ficaro: bordello

Fisting: inserting a fist or hand into the vagina or anus

Flagellation: striking a person with an object

Flatulence: passing gas from bowels

Flatuphilia: arousal from having partner pass gas

Flirting: pretending to have affection for another person

Floating hog ranches: boats used to transport prostitutes to the Western U.S. and from which they conducted business in route

Florentine girdle: chastity belt

Flower boats: Chinese boats used for prostitution

Foot binding: the wrapping of feet, done by Chinese and others

Foot fetish: podophilia

Formicophilia: zoophilia; sex play with ants (see also Entomophilia)

Fornicatory Dolls: plastic blow up, rubber, or mechanical dolls used for penetration

Fratrilagnia: arousal from having sex with one's brother

Frottage: rubbing body against partner or object for arousal

Furor uterinus: nymphomania

Furtling: the use of fingers underneath cut-outs in genital areas of photos for arousal

Galateism: agalmatophilia; sexual attraction to statues

Gamahucheur: cunnilingus

Gamophobia: fear of marriage

Gang Bangs: sex with a series of waiting partners

Gay: person who prefers same sex lover

Geishas: Japanese women used as social companions

Gemellus: testicles

Gendermap: "A developmental representation or template synchronously in the mind and brain depicting the details of one's G-I/R. It includes the lovemap but is larger, insofar as it incorporates whatever is gender coded vocationally, educationally, recreationally, sartorially, and legally as well as in matters of etiquette, grooming, body language, and vocal intonation." (John Money)

Genitals: sex organs of either male or female (penis, testicles, scrotum, clitoris, vagina, G-spot, cervix, etc.)

Gendoloma: the use of sexual fantasies to hasten orgasm

Genofact: genital fetish

Genuphallation: insertion of penis between the knees of a partner

Gerontophilia: attraction to a partner whose age is that of different generation

Girdle of Venus: chastity belt

Glory holes: a hole in a partition that allows a person on the other side to engage in sexual activity

Goddess Worship: a toilet scene using Witchcraft rituals

Godemiche: dildo in the shape of a penis with scrotum used for masturbation

Golden enemas and Douches: urine deposited into anus or vagina

Golden showers: urinating onto a partner's body

Gomphipothic: arousal by the sight of teeth

Gonads: testicles

Graophilia: arousal from older female partner

Graffiti: drawing or inscription on public walls, sometimes sexual; coprography

Graphelagnia: arousal from photographs of nudity or sex

Green bower: motels or establishments that catered to short-term rentals of rooms by couples to be used for sex

Gregomulcia: arousal from being fondled in a crowd

Groping: feeling of unknown or unidentified person in boxes, suits, etc.

Group Sex: sex with more than one partner or in close proximity of others

Groupies: erotomania; people who are devoted to or who follow celebrities

Gymnocryptosis: females talking about sex life of husbands

Gymnophilia: arousal from nudity

Gynandromorphous: hermaphrodite

Gynecaeum: area where Greeks kept wives at home and separated from other men

Gynecomania: compulsive desire for female sex partners

Gynecozygous: lesbians

Gynelophilous: arousal from pubic hair

Gynelophism: scalping hair on pubic area, usually done by lust murders

Gynemimesis: male-to-female cross dressing

Gynemimetophilia: person aroused by a male impersonating a female

Gynephonia: effeminate voice

Gynonudomanic: compulsion to rip clothes off others

-gyny: female or having female organs

Handkerchief Codes: color codes to identify sexual preferences

Haptosis: non-consensual sexual touching

Harem: area where Arabs kept wives at home and separated from others

Harem effect: lesbianism

Harlotry: prostitution

Harmatophobia: fear of sexual incompetence or making a mistake

Harmatophilia: arousal from sexual incompetence or mistakes, usually in female partner

Harnesses: body harnesses used in suspension or penis restriction

Harpaxophilia: arousal from being robbed or burglarized

Hebephilia: men aroused by teenage boys

Hedonism: act of indulging in pleasure

Hedonophilia: sexual arousal from engaging in pleasurable activity

Hedralingus: licking anus

Hemerotism: daydreaming or fantasizing about sex or nudity

Hemotigolagnia: arousal from bloody sanitary pads

Hermaphrodite: person who has both part female and male genitalia

Hetaerae: the highest class Greek prostitute or female companion

Heterophilia: arousal from members of the opposite sex

Heterosexualism: arousal from members of the opposite sex

Hierophilia: arousal from sacred objects

Hirsutophilia: arousal from armpit hair

Hodophilia: arousal from traveling

Homilophilia: sexual arousal from hearing or giving sermons

Homoeroticism: sexual arousal from person of same sex

Homophilia: sexual arousal from person of same sex

Homophobia: fear of same gender sex partner

Homosexuality: arousal by partners of the same sex

Hot Wax: sex game where hot wax is melted onto partner

Humiliation: degrading partner to establish sexual power

Hybristophilia: love of someone who has committed an outrage

Hygrophilia: arousal from body fluids or moisture

Hymenoclasis: surgical defloration of virgin

Hymenorrhaphy: suturing of the hymen; infibulation

Hymenorrhexis: defloration of hymen

Hyperphilia: compulsive desire for sex

Hyphephilia: arousal from touching skin, hair, leather, fur or fabric

Hypnosis: act that induces a level of sleep

Iantronudia: arousal from exposing oneself to a physician, usually by faking an ailment

-iasis: pathological condition

Iconolagny: arousal from pictures or statues of nude people

Idiosyncrat: compulsive desire for sex

Idrophrodisia: arousal from the odor of perspiration, especially from the genitals

Impotence: the inability to achieve enough tumescence to penetrate a partner with one's penis

Incest: sex with close family member

Incubus: a spirit who was thought to lie on top of women and have sex while they slept

Infanticide: the practice of killing a newborn child

Infantilism: cross-dressing as a young child for sex play

Infibulation: closing penis/vagina with suture or ring

Inflatable dolls: plastic dolls that are designed for genital penetration

Inspectionism: voyeurism

Insufflation: blowing air into a body cavity

Intergenerational: sex between partners with 20+ years age difference

Interrogation: to ask questions, sometimes under duress

Inunction: anointing or rubbing person with oil or lather

Invert: arousal from person of same sex

Invirility: impotence

Ipserotic: Narcissism

Irrumation: fellatio

Ischolagny: avoidance of women to prevent arousal

-ism: act or abnormal condition classified by prefix (i.e., transvestism)

-ist: person expert in field or adherent of prefix (i.e., sadist)

Iterandria: arousal from person of same sex

Jack gagger: a husband that procures men to pay for sex with his wife

Jactitation: a false boast that causes harm to others, sometimes sexual

Juvenilism: dressing or acting out role of a juvenile, sometimes sexual

Kabbazah Sex: tantra sex, male passive, female active

Karezza Sex: coitus reservatus

Kegel exercises: exercise of the pelvic muscles that control orgasm

Kleptolagnia: arousal from stealing

Kleptomania: compulsion to steal

Kleptophilia: arousal from stealing

Klismaphilia: arousal from enemas

Knismolagnia: arousal from tickling

Kokigami: the wrapping of the penis in a paper costume

Kolpeuryntomania: stretching of the vagina

Labiorrhaphy: suturing of the labia

Lacing: suturing body parts to another object for bondage

Lactaphilia: arousal from lactating breasts

-lagnia: lust, arousal

Lagnocolysis: celibacy

Lagnolalia: discussion of sexual subjects

Lagnonector: person who kills in order to have sex with corpse

Lagnoperissia: nymphomania

Lap dancing: squatting above a sitting person and rubbing against them to create arousal without touching genitals

Latex: rubber or plastic suits worn by people with this fetish

Lectamia: bundling

Lena: female panderer or procurer for prostitute

Leno: male panderer or pimp for prostitute

Leptosadism: mild form of sadism

Lesbian: woman who prefers female lover

Levirate marriage: marriage of widow without a son to deceased husband's brother

-lingus: suffix meaning with the tongue

Love: attachment, fondness, and devotion

Love addiction: irresistible compulsion to fantasize about or to be with a partner

Love map: "A developmental representation or template in the mind and in the brain depicting the idealized lover and the idealized program of sexuo-erotic activity projected in imagery or actually engaged in with that lover." (John Money)

Love potions: potions that are thought to increase a person's sexual desire

Lubricants: a substance that reduces friction, often used to facilitate penetration

Lung-yang: arousal from person of same sex

Lust Murder: murdering a person one feels a sexual attraction toward

Lygerastia: tendency to only be aroused in darkness

Macrogenitalism: arousal from large genitals

Maieusiophilia: arousal from pregnant women

Mammagymnophilia: arousal from female breasts

-mania: suffix indicating an abnormal preoccupation, compulsion, or craving for an act or object

Manuxorate: male using his hand to masturbate

Maritate: female masturbating alone

Martymachlia: group sex

Maschalophilous: arousal from armpits

Masochism: ability to transfer emotions caused by pain to erotic feelings or as median in which to analyze weaknesses and strengths

Massage: rubbing of the body to increase circulation

Massage Parlors: a business establishment that specializes in massage

Mastigothymia: flagellation

Mastix: female sadist

Mastofact: breast fetish

Masturbation: orgasm not involving penetration of partner

Matrincest: sex with one's mother

Matronolagnia: arousal from older female partner

Maturation: the process of aging including sexual changes

Mazoperosis: mutilation of breasts

Mazophallate: rubbing penis between breasts

Meatotomy: dilating urethra with a medical dilating device, the urethra is stretched to eventually facilitate a finger or a penis

Medical scenes: sex play that involves using medical instruments or settings as props

Medocure: the clipping or perfuming of the penis

Medolalia: talking about the penis

Melolagnia: arousal from music

Ménage à trois: a husband and wife having sex with a third party

Menophilist: arousal from menstruating women

Menstrual taboo: separation of spouses during female's menstrual cycle

Merinthophilia: arousal from being bound

Merlin: an artificial vagina used for penetration

Miscegenation: sex between races

Misogynist: a man who hates women

Misogyny: hatred of women by either sex

Mixoscopia: orgasm dependent on watching others having sex

Moriaphilia: arousal from telling sexual jokes

Morphophilia: arousal from person with a different physique

Mortality: inevitable death

Mucophagy: consuming mucous secretions as in nasolingus

Mummification: wrapping the full body in a manner that prevents movement

Munchausen's syndrome: arousal from reopening a wound

Mutilation: tearing the skin or otherwise deforming a person's body

Mysophilia: arousal from soiled clothing or foul decaying odors

Nanophilia: sexual attraction to a short partner

Naphephilia: arousal from touching or being touched

Narcissism: self love

Narratophilia: person who is aroused by discussing sex with others

Nasolingus: arousal from sucking nose of partner

Nasophilia: nose fetish

Natural family planning: birth control by rhythm method

Necrochlesis: sex with a female corpse

Necrocoitus: penetration of corpses

Necrophagia: cannibalism of corpses

Necrophilia: sex with corpses

Necrosadism: sadism or mutilation of corpses

Negotiation: arranging transactions for conduct with sex partner

Neophilia: arousal from novelty or change

Nepiolagnia: arousal by infants of opposite sex

Nepiophilia: arousal by infants of opposite sex

Nepiphtherosis: attempted sex with an infant

Nepirasty: arousal from handling infant often experienced by childless females

Niddah: abstaining from sex 1/3 of the time to create arousal during rest of month

Nomavalent: arousal from traveling or new places, usually impotent at home

Nonmonogamy: multiple sex partners

Normophilia: those only aroused by acts considered normal by their religion or society

Nosolagnia: arousal from knowing parnter has terminal illness

Nosophilia: arousal from knowing partner has terminal illness

Nudity (Recreational): nudity in group settings, beaches, nudist camps, etc.

Nudomania: arousal from nudity

Nymph: young woman or nature goddesses

Nympholepsy: trance state induced by erotic fantasies

Nymphomania: uncontrollable desire of woman for sex

Nymphophilia: adult males who are attracted to young females

Nymphotomy: removal of the inner labia

Obscene Phone Callers: people who become aroused by making phone calls, using vulgar language, or trying to elicit a reaction from the other party

Ochlophilia: arousal from being in a crowd

Oculolinctus: licking partner's eyeball

Oculophilia: eye fetish

Odaxelagnia: arousal from biting

Odontophilia: arousal from tooth extractions or tooth fetish

Oedipus complex: repressed desire to have sex with parent of opposite sex

Old maid's insanity: erotomania

Olisbos: dildos

Olfaction: the sense of smell

Olfactophilia: arousal from odors

Omolagnia: arousal from nudity

Onanism: masturbation or withdrawing penis from vagina before ejaculation

Ondinisme: arousal from urine

Oneiropornism: dreaming about prostitutes or sex

Open marriage: adultery

Ophidicism: use of snakes, sometimes for sexual purposes

Ophidiophilia: arousal from snakes

Oral sex: contact between the mouth and genitals; use of the mouth in sex play

Ordune: arousal from photographs of nudes or sex

Orgasms: climax of sexual excitement, often accompanying ejaculation

Organofact: fetish for some part of the body

Orgies: group sex

Osculocentric: arousal from kissing

Osmolagnia: arousal from odors

Osmophilia: arousal from odors

Osphresiolagnia: arousal from odors

Othello's syndrome: jealousy

Oxygen regulation: regulating intake of oxygen for sexual enhancement

Ozolagnia: arousal from odors

Pageism: male submitting to female

Panderer: a procurer or go-between for prostitutes and clients

Paraphallus: dildos

Paraphilia: sexual arousal to unusual or socially unacceptable object or act

Parascopism: voyeurism, especially through bedroom windows

Pareunasthenia: impotence

Pareunomania: compulsive desire for sex

Parthenity: virgin

Parthenophagy: cannibalism of young girls

Parthenophilia: sexual desire for virgins

Parthenos: virgin

Passivism: submission

Pathicus: passive recipient in gay anal sex; catamite

Pathicant: a minor who engages in anal sex with an adult

Pathophobia: phobia of contracting a sexually transmitted disease

Patrolagnia: sex with one's own father

Pecattiphilia: arousal from sinning or possibly guilt

Pederasty: anal sex

Pediophilia: arousal from dolls

Pedophilia: sex with minors

Peeping Tom: voyeur

Penetration toys: devices used for penis insertion during masturbation

Penis ligation: the tying of the foreskin of a penis

Penis modification: physical alteration of penis

Penosugia: fellatio

Peodeiktophilia: exhibitionism

Peritomy: circumcision

Perogynia: mutilation of females

Personal ads: advertisements designed to attract sex partners

Perversion: sexual acts that differ from the majority; paraphilia

Petticoat discipline: the use of cross dressing adolescent boys by their mothers as a form of control

-phagy: practice of eating object specified by prefix

Phallolalia: talking about penises

Phallophilia: large penis fetish or preference

Pheromones: natural chemicals or hormones that induce sexual response

Philemanmania: compulsion to kiss

-philia: suffix that indicates an abnormal sexual attachment to what is specified by acronym

Phlebotomy: arousal from bloodletting

Phobias: an irrational fear of an object or situation

Phobophilia: arousal from fear or hate

Phone Sex: verbal sex between partners on a phone

Phygephilia: sexual arousal from being a fugitive

Pictophilia: arousal from pictures, video or movies with a sexual subject

Pie throwing: arousal from being hit with a pie

Piercing: inserting needles into skin for arousal

Pimps: procurer for sexual partners that pay

Play: the consensual acting out of a role or game, sometimes sexual

Play room: room equipped with sex paraphernalia and used primarily for sex play

Podophilia: arousal from feet

Polyandry: one wife with multiple husbands

Polygamy: one person with multiple marriage partners

Polygyny: one person with multiple wives

Polyiterophilia: arousal only after having sex with a series of partners

Polymorphous: having several forms of arousal techniques

Pompoir: vaginal muscle control that masturbates penis when inserted

Pornography: depictions of sex that are considered unacceptable by one's society

Posthetomy: circumcision

Power tools: electric or battery operated tools that can be used in sex play, although this was not their original function

Preblysis: premature ejaculation

Prisha: religious separation of males and females

Proctophallism: anal sex

Proctotitillia: tickling anus

Procurer: a person who solicits or provides prostitutes for clients

Professional dominatrix: woman hired to function as a top or sadist

Prostitution: sex performed for financial gain

Pseudo: pretended act

Psycholagny: orgasm induced from psychic or mental stimulation

Psychopathic: person who indulges in own pleasure without regard for hurting others

Psychose passionelle: erotomania

Psychrophilia: arousal from being cold or watching others freeze

Psychrotentiginous: arousal from cold weather

Pubephilia: arousal from pubic hair

Pubic dressing: coloring or adding ornaments to pubic hair

Pubic Hair sculpturing: removing pubic hair so that the remainder forms a pattern (i.e. a heart)

Pudendacure: pubic dressing for female

Purdah: veil used on women to hide their face

Puritans: a protestant group that became excessively strict regarding morals

Pygmalionism: agalmatophilia; statue fetishism where person rubs their body against statue

Pygophilemania: arousal from kissing buttocks

Pygophilia: arousal from contact with buttocks

Pygotripsis: arousal from rubbing buttocks

Pyrophilia: arousal from fire or of its use in sex play

Quadoshka: American Indian form of tantric sex

Queening: sitting on the side of a person's face as a form of bondage

Rape: nonconsensual sex involving coercion, empowerment or anger

Rape rack: bondage device which leaves victim's genitals exposed for sex or rape

Raptophilia: arousal only from raping a victim

Red light district: area with bordellos and perhaps street prostitutes

Relics: an object that has historical or special interest

Renifleur: person aroused the smell of urine or by sniffing underwear

Retifism: shoe fetish

Rhabdophilia: arousal from being flagellated

Rimming: penetration of anus with tongue

Ringing: insertion of permanent jewelry into a body piercing

Ritual Sex: sex performed with specific rules of conduct (i.e., Wicca, weddings, slave training)

Robotism: attraction to or the use of robots in sex play

Roman Showers: vomiting on partner, usually after drinking urine or wine

Sacofricosis: cutting a hole in pant pocket to facilitate masturbation in public

Sadism: empowerment and arousal derived from injuring others

Sadomasochism by proxy: arousal from watching others disciplined; Dippoldism

Salirophilia: person ingesting human sweat or saliva (fluids with a salt content)

Sapphosadism: lesbian sadism

Sarmassophilia: arousal from kneading flesh

Satan worship: religious rituals performed to Satan as a god

Satyriasis: men who have an uncontrollable desire for sex

Scarfing: the use of a scarf in strangulation for sexual arousal

Scat: arousal from using feces in sex play

Scopophilia: arousal from being stared at oneself

Scoptolagnia: arousal from seeing the genitals of the opposite sex

Scoptophilia: arousal from looking at sexually stimulating scenes

Scortum: prostitution

Scrotal infusion: infusion of saline into the scrotal sack so that it enlarges

Selgolalia: telling stories that include sex

Sensory compensation: our body's regulation of incoming stimulus to a tolerable level

Sensory deprivation: using lack of sensations to create desire

Sensory enhancement: increasing arousal by increased body sensations

Sensory overload: inability of our body to absorb and comprehend incoming stimulus

Seraglio: the Chinese practice of keeping wives secluded at home from other men

Serenades: musical performance during courtship given outdoors at night

Sergeism: infliction of injury to suppress arousal, automasochism, based on story of Sergius by Tolstoy

Sex addiction: compulsion to have sex

Sex Magick: the use of witchcraft rituals for sexual purposes

Sex rings: organized groups of children being sexually exploited by one or more adults

Sex surrogates: people who are trained to help people overcome sexual dysfunctions

Sex toys: mechanical objects used to assist in masturbation or sex play

Sexautism: tendency to be preoccupied with sexual thoughts

Sexercise: exercises designed to improve muscles used for sex

Sexologists: people who study the science of sex

Sexoschizia: bi-sexual

Sexual aberration: paraphilia

Sexual anomalies: paraphilias

Sexual inversion: arousal from person of same sex

Sexual sadist killer: lust murderer

Shaving: removing the hair with a razor of a partner or oneself for arousal

Showers: depositing body fluids onto a partner's body

Shunammitism: bundling

Siderodromophilia: arousal from trains

Siphnianize: anal masturbation

Sitophilia: arousal from food

Slapping: slapping partner for arousal

Slaves: person who contracts to be sex slave

Sleeping princess syndrome: those aroused by partner who appears to be asleep

Slings: swings or other forms of support for suspension from which a person may engage in sex

Smegma: secretions from gland under foreskin of penis or clitoris

Snapping pussy: constrictions of muscles used for orgasm; sexercise

Snuff films: films that portray the actual murder and mutilation of one of the actors

Sodomy: oral or anal intercourse involving penetration with male, female, or animal

Somnophilia: fondling stranger in their sleep

Sororate marriage: right of spouse to engage in sex with sisters-in-law or sometimes brothers-in-law

Sororilagnia: sex with one's own sister

Sotadism: anal sex

Sounding: insertion of an object into the urethra

Spanking: using hand to slap partner's buttocks for sensory enhancement and arousal

Spay: castration

Spectrophilia: either coitus with spirits or arousal from image in mirrors

Speculum: dilating device used by physicians when doing pelvic exams and in SM medical scenes

Spermatophobia: fear of semen loss

Sphagia: a sacrifice used to placate the gods, the whole offering was completely burned

Sphincter: anal or urethral muscle that closes to prevent passage of urine or feces

Splitting: splitting the penis from the glans toward the base

Stabbing: insertion of a sharp object into flesh

Stag parties: private parties where only men and possibly a female stripper or entertainer are permitted

Stapling: inserting a U-shaped wire into skin during sex play

Statuophilia: agalmatophilia; sexual attraction to statues

Sthenolagnia: arousal from demonstration of strength or muscles

Stigmatophilia: arousal from partner who is stigmatized (i.e., tattoos, piercings, scars)

Strabismus: arousal from eyes of partner

Strangulation: controlling oxygen by restricting windpipe or blood vessels in neck

Stretching: stretching body or genitals for arousal

String bondage: constrictions; wrapping string around body at certain intervals for arousal

Strip poker: card game where the losers remove articles of clothing

Strip search: interrogation process where sex partner is stripped and searched

Stripping: removal of clothes, sometimes performed on stage in an erotic manner

Stuffing: insertion of objects into vagina or anus

Stupprator: man who is aroused by virgins

Subincision: cutting part of the glans penis from the tip toward the base

Subliminal tapes: audiotapes that give messages intended to alter habits

Submission: surrender to and trust of a partner

Subpersonality: a temporary personality or character change but one where the person does not lose all consciousness with their current surroundings, they are often from childhood

Succubus: a female spirit who was thought to lie underneath men and have sex with them while they slept

Support groups: groups of people that find solace in discussing a common problem

Suspension: suspending body for sensory deprivation and bondage

Suttee: religious practice of killing wife upon husband's death and burial

Suturing: stitching flesh together

Swinging: group sex or wife swapping

Swing: an object that allows a person to be suspended and move back and forth

Switch: people who play either the top or bottom role (sadist or masochist)

Sybian: a vibrating dildo that sits on top of an object that resembles a saddle

Symphorophilia: arousal from arranging a disaster, crash, or explosion

Syntribate: rubbing thighs together to masturbate

Tachorgasmia: premature ejaculation

Talisman: charm, sometimes used in love spells

Tantalolagnia: arousal from teasing

Tantra: yoga type sexual discipline

Taphephilia: arousal from being buried alive

Tattooing: tattooing for arousal and marking

Tea Room: slang term for restrooms used for hustling and fellatio

Teasing: to excite sexually but without fulfilling implied message

Teledildonics: arousal from computer sex games

Telegony: belief that first man impregnating woman will be the father of any subsequent children

Telephone scatophilia: arousal from obscene phone calls

Telephonicophilia: arousal from using phone calls for sexual conversations

Teratophallic: large penises

Terror play: sex play using terror or fear for arousal

Thalpotentiginy: arousal from heat

Thelectize: clitoridectomy

Thesauromania: compulsion to collect objects or clothing belonging to females

Thlipsosis: arousal from pinching others

Three-legged bloomers: bondage underwear garment that has sleeve for head that opens to genitals of partner

Thusiai: a sacrifice of food cooked on an altar and eaten later by priests or worshippers

Thygatria: sex between father and daughter

Tickling: light touch that sometimes causes a laughter response

Timophilia: when a person's primary arousal comes from gold or wealth

-tion: suffix indicating a state of being

Titillagnia: arousal from tickling

Tithiolagnia: having an orgasm while nursing

Toilet Training: urinating or defecating on a partner as a form of slave training

Top: term used for partner who controls stimuli during sex games

Torture: inflicting pain to get information or for revenge, also used in sex play

Tourniquets: a device that compresses blood vessels to control bleeding, sometimes sexual

Toucheurism: touching a stranger for arousal

Tragolimia: compulsive desire for sex regardless of attraction of partner

Transsexual: person who are in the process of physically changing sexes

Transvestite: person who is aroused by crossdressing

Transvestophilia: arousal from crossdressing

Traumaphilia: arousal from wounds or trauma; automasochism

Trial marriage: couple who lives together for a period to determine compatibility for marriage

Tribadism: lesbianism; sex by rubbing

Triborgasmia: wife who masturbates husband

Trichophilia: hair fetish

Tripsolagnia: arousal from having hair shampooed

Tripsolagnophilia: arousal from massage

Tripsophilia: arousal from massage

Troilism: arousal by being third party in sex scene

Troubadours: 11th-13th century musician poets that popularized love and chivalry

Tunnel of love: carnival boat ride that passed through a dark tunnel allowing couples a moment of privacy

Tyrannism: cruelty; sadism

Undinism: arousal from water

Uranism: arousal from person of same sex

Urethral self-instrumentation: sounding; inserting object into urethra for arousal

Urolagnia: arousal from urine

Urophilia: arousal from urine

Urtication: the use of nettles to create extra sensation

Vampirism: consuming blood of partner for arousal

Vertigo: dizziness, sometimes used to enhance sex acts

Vertugadin: large hooped skirts that also acted as chastity devices

Vibrators: tools that are inserted and which vibrate

Vicarphilia: arousal from other people's exciting experiences

Victorian lace: sexual discipline using crossdressing as punishment

Victorianism: a 19th century English society that was notorious for bigotry and restrictive about morals

Vincilagnia: arousal from bondage

Virgin: person not having experienced penetrative sex with another person

Virimimism: adoption of masculinity

Visualization: an image formed by the mind, sometimes used in sex rituals and often in sexual fantasy

Voyeurism: arousal by watching others without their consent

Water sports: the use of urine for arousal; urophilia

Waxing: removal of body hair by a sticky substance applied to a strip laid against hair and pulled off

Weddings: marriage ceremonies

Weight training: the use of hanging weights on genitals or hooks for arousal

Whipping: striking or flagellating a partner for sensory enhancement

White slavery: the sale of one race to another for purposes of prostitution

Whore house: bordello

Wife swapping: exchanging spouses with another couple for sexual purposes

Worship: reverence of an object or person

Wrestling: a physical struggle between two or more people, used as sexual arousal by some

Xenodynamic: person who is only potent with strangers

Xenolimia: arousal from strangers

Xenophilia: arousal from strangers

Yoni worship: worship of the female genitals

Yoshiwara: Japanese prostitutes

Zelophilia: arousal from jealousy

Zooerasty: arousal from animals

Zoophilia: arousal from animals

Zwischenstufe: arousal from person of same sex

APPENDIX OF SUPPLIERS

The following businesses and clubs have assisted in providing me with valuable information. Many have been previously referenced in this encyclopedia but without an address.

ART:

Fine Art Depictions of SM
by Michael Rosen
Shaynew Press
P.O. Box 11719
San Francisco,
CA 94101

Phoebe Gloeckner
Illustrator
PO Box 31682
San Francisco,
CA 94131

Kokigami
(Japanese paper
costumes for the penis)
Ten Speed Press
P.O. Box 7123
Berkeley, CA 94707

No! No! Greetings
(personal erotic draw-
ings and stationery)
PO Box 221
Norco, CA 91760

O Card Corporation
(Erotic greeting
cards by
Olivia De Berardinis)
P.O. Box 111
Roslyn, NY 11576

FANTASY MAGAZINES:

KATHARSIS
(Gladiators, torture, evil
women, aliens, cruci-
fixion)
P.O. Box 2266
Daytona Beach, FL
32015-2266

FETISH FILMS AND MAGAZINES:

Cocoa 'n Creme, Your
National Guide to
Interracial Swinging
PO Box 811218
Chicago, IL
60681-1218

FETISH TIMES
(newspaper)
B&D Company
P.O. Box 7109
Van Nuys, CA 91409

GIO ("How to Strip for
Your Man" video tape)
PO Box Box 349
Orchard Hill, GA
30266

MILKY
(Lactating women)
Parliament News, Inc.
P.O. Box 3959
North Hollywood, CA
91609

OVER 40
(40 to 60 year old
nudes) magazine
Leisure Plus
Publications, Inc.
4th Floor
New York, New York
10013

PLATINUM (Films)
4501 Van Nuys Blvd.
Suite 215
Sherman Oaks, CA
91403

Skin II
23 Grand Union Centre
Kensal Road
London W10 5AX
ENGLAND
Ph: 081-968-9692

HOTLINES, CLUBS OR REFERRAL SERVICES:

Back Drop Club
(Fetish & fantasy)
P.O. Box 1369
El Cerrito, CA
94530-1369

Ball Club
(large testicles)
PO Box 1501
Pomona, CA 91769

The Big Board (Obese
partner referrals)
567 Blackhawk Club
Drive
Danville, CA 94526

BUFF
(Foreskin restoration)
6471 Silverheel Circle
Huntington Beach, CA
92647-6541

Californians Against
Censorship Together
1800 Market Street
Suite 1000
San Francisco, CA
94102
Ph: 415/548-3695

Club Mud
Box 277
Rio Nido, CA 95471

ETVC (Transvestites &
transsexuals)
P.O. Box 6486
San Francisco, CA
94101

Hung Jury
(dating service)
PO Box 417
Los Angeles, CA 90078

KARAQUA
(sex magick lessons)
821 Leavenworth, #12
San Francisco, CA
94109
Ph: 415/441-2571

Lifestyles Organization
2641 W. La Palma
Suite A
Anaheim, CA 92801

Mother Goose
Productions
(Jack & Jill Off parties)
P.O. Box 3212
Berkeley, CA 94703

NOSE (National Org.
of Sexual Enthusiasts)
PO Box 8733
Atlanta, GA 30306

National Sexuality
Symposium
PO Box 620123
Woodside, CA 94062
Ph: 415/851-4751

New Friends
Dating Service
(for people with herpes)
P.O. Box 1235
Capitola, CA 95010

QSM (S/M lectures
and classes)
PO Box 882242
S.F., CA 94188-2242
Ph: 415/550-7776

San Francisco Sex Info.
P.O. Box 640054
S.F., CA 94164-0054
Ph: 415/621-7300

SMALL, ETC.
PO Box 294
Bayside, NY 11361

Society of Janus (S/M)
P.O. Box 6794
San Francisco, CA
94101
Ph: 415/985-7117

Transvestite
transformations
Sybil Holiday
Ph: 415/558-9531

JEWELRY:

Clit Clamps
c/o Judy Kirk
13428 Maxella Avenue
Suite 314C
Marina Del Rey, CA
90292

Sweater Bumpers
PO Box 1854
Los Lunas, NM 87031

**LEATHER
RELATED BOOKS
AND
MAGAZINES:**

Desmodus, Inc.
(Drummer,
DungeonMaster or
Sandmutopia)
P.O. Box 11314
San Francisco, CA
94101

Lady Tanith (letters)
PO Box 7925
Berkeley, CA
94707-0925
Ph: 415/7887

Piercing Fans Int.
Quarterly
The Gauntlet
2377 Market Street
San Francisco, CA
94111

Religion of the
Month Club
(articles on feces)
PO Box 2430
Santa Clara, CA
95055-2430

**PIERCING
STUDIOS:**

Fakir Musafar
(also branding,
cupping, and seminars)
Insight Institute
PO Box 421668
San Francisco CA
94142-1668
Ph: 415/324-0543

Raelyn Gallina
PO Box 20034
Oakland, CA 94620
Ph: 510/655-2855

The Gauntlet
2377 Market Street
San Francisco, CA
94111
Ph: 415/431-3133

**SEX BOUTIQUE/
STORES:**

DESMODUS
24 Shotwell
San Francisco, CA
Ph: 415/252-1195

Mr. S Leather
1779 Folsom Street
San Francisco, CA
Ph: 415/863-7764

Romantasy
(also catalog orders
and corsets)
199 Moulton St.
San Francisco, CA
94123
Ph: 415-673-3137

SEX HOTELS:

Edgewater West
10 Hegenberger Road
Oakland, CA
Ph: 510/632-6262

SEX TOYS:

Wayne Cooper
LifeStyle Products
PO Box 4022
Hopkins, MN 55343
612/443-2689

**TANTRA
WORKSHOPS:**

S. Wadel or David
Coleman
1470 DeHaro Street
San Francisco, CA
94107

TATTOO ARTISTS:

Mad Dog Tattoo
43A Juniper Street
San Francisco, CA
Ph: 415/552-1297

UNIVERSITIES:

Institute for the
Advanced Study of
Human Sexuality
1523 Franklin Street
San Francisco, CA
94109
Ph: 415/928-1133

BIBLIOGRAPHY

Aldridge A., Gregory E. 1990. "COMPUTER EROTICA." San Francisco: Lecture at Mensa Sexyg Gathering Conference.

Alexander P. 1987. "Prostitution: A difficult issue for feminists" SEX WORK, WRITING BY WOMEN IN THE SEX INDUSTRY. Delacoste F., Alexander P., eds. San Francisco: Cleis Press.

Almodovar N.J. 1990. "SEXUAL LIFESTYLES AND THE CRIMINAL" Las Vegas: Lifestyle conference.

American Social Health Association. 1989. "A female condom?" THE HELPER. North Carolina.

Antelman S.M., Knopf S., Kocan D., Edwards D.J. 1989. "Persistent sensitization of clonidine-induced-hypokinesia following one exposure to a stressor; possible relevance to panic disorder and its treatment." PSYCHOPHARMACOLOGY (Vol 98, 1989) Spring-Verlag.

Arentewicz G., Schmidt G., eds. 1983. THE TREATMENT OF SEXUAL DISORDERS, CONCEPTS AND TECHNIQUES OF COUPLE THERAPY. New York: Basic Books, Inc.

Arnold C. 1986. PAIN, WHAT IS IT? HOW DO WE DEAL WITH IT? New York: William Morrow and Co., Inc.

Arulch K.S. 1961. Ganzfried, S., ed. CODE OF JEWISH LAW. New York: Hebrew Publishing Co.

A.V. 1990. "PRIVATE PLEASURE, INTIMATE PAIN; AN EXPLORATION OF THE SUBTLE ART OF CUNT TORTURE." San Francisco: QSM lecture.

1990. BAREFOOT DIGEST ANNUAL ad in Fetish Times. B&D Co., PO Box 7109, Van Nuys, CA 91409.

Barker-Benfield G.J. 1976. THE HORRORS OF THE HALF-KNOWN LIFE, MALE ATTITUDES TOWARD WOMEN AND SEXUALITY IN NINETEENTH CENTURY AMERICA. New York: Harper & Row Publishers.

Bean J. W., 1990. "CLOTHESPINS: THE SCENE FROM THE CORNER STORE." San Francisco: QSM lecture.

Blackwood B. 1935. BOTH SIDES OF BUKA PASSAGE. Oxford: The Clarendon Press.

Blanchard R., Hucker S.J. 1991. "Age, transvestism, bondage, and concurrent paraphilic activities in 117 fatal cases of autoerotic asphyxia", THE BRITISH JOURNAL OF PSYCHIATRY (Vol 159 p371-377).

Blank J. 1982. GOOD VIBRATIONS, THE COMPLETE GUIDE TO VIBRATORS. Good Vibrations, 3492 22nd Street, San Francisco, CA 94110.

Blinder M. 1989. CHOOSING LOVERS. Malcomb Illinois: Glenbridge Publishing Ltd.

Bloch I. 1931. MARQUIS DE SADE, HIS LIFE AND WORKS. The Brittany Press.

Bloch I. 1933. STRANGE SEXUAL PRACTICES. New York: Falstaff Press, Inc.

Bogren L.Y. 1986. "The Couvade Syndrome." INTERNATIONAL JOURNAL OF FAMILY PSYCHIATRY (Vol 7 No 2 pp123-135).

Bohannan P. 1988. Rubin A., ed. "Beauty and Scarification Amongst the Tiv." MARKS OF CIVILIZATION. Los Angeles: Museum of Cultural History, University of California at Los Angeles.

Bourke J. 1891. SCATOLOGIC RITES OF ALL NATIONS. Washington D.C.: W. H. Lowdermilk and Co.

BR Creations. 1989. "CORSETS." San Francisco: Outcast lecture.

Brannon J.M., Larson B., Doggett M. 1989. "The extent and origins of sexual molestation and abuse among incarcerated adolescent males." INTERNATIONAL JOURNAL OF OFFENDER THERAPY AND COMPARATIVE CRIMINOLOGY (Vol 33:2 pp161-171).

Brauer A., Brauer D. 1983. EXTENDED SEXUAL ORGASM—ESO. New York: Warner Books, Inc.

Briffault R. 1931. THE MOTHERS. New York, London: MacMillan Publishers.

Brown D.E., Edwards J.W., Moore R.P. 1988. THE PENIS INSERTS OF SOUTHEAST ASIA. Berkeley California: Center for South and Southeast Asia Studies, University of California at Berkeley.

B. J. 1990. "ELECTRICAL APPLICATIONS." San Francisco: QSM lecture.

B. J. 1990. "SCROTAL INFLATION AND OTHER GENITAL MODIFICATIONS." San Francisco: QSM lecture.

Bryk F. 1935. Sexton M.F., trans. VOODOO EROS (English 1964). New York: United Book Guild.

Bunker Stockham A. 1894. TOKOLOGY. Chicago.

Burg B.R. 1982. "The sick and the dead: The development of psychological theory on necrophilia from Krafft-Ebing to the present." JOURNAL OF THE HISTORY OF THE BEHAVIORAL SCIENCES (Vol 18 pp242-254).

Burgess A.W., Hartman C.R., McCausland M.P., Powers P. 1991. "Response patterns in children and adolescents exploited through sex rings and pornography." AMERICAN JOURNAL OF PSYCHIATRY (Vol 141:5 pp656-662).

Burkan T., Burkan P.D. 1983. GUIDING YOURSELF INTO A SPIRITUAL REALITY (FIREWALKING). Twain Harte California: Reunion Press.

Busch H., Silver B. 1990. KOKIGAMI, THE INTIMATE ART OF THE LITTLE PAPER COSTUME. Berkeley: Ten Speed Press.

Bylinsky G. 1966. MOOD CONTROL. New York: Scribners Press.

Califia P. 1988. THE LESBIAN S/M SAFETY MANUAL. Lace Publications, POB 10037, Denver, CO 80210-0037.

Califia P. 1988. SAPPHISTRY, THE BOOK OF LESBIAN SEXUALITY. The Raiad Press, Inc.

Campbell J. 1988. HISTORICAL ATLAS OF WORLD MYTHOLOGY: THE SACRIFICE. New York: Harper & Row.

Campbell J. 1988. THE WAY OF ANIMAL POWERS. New York: Harper & Row.

Camphausen R.C. 1991. THE ENCYCLOPEDIA OF EROTIC WISDOM. Rochester, Vermont: Inner Traditions International, Ltd.

Carroll C. 1989. PIERCING FANS INTERNATIONAL QUARTERLY (PFIQ, NO. 15). The Gauntlet, 519 Castro Street, Box 73, San Francisco, CA 94114.

Carter S., Sokol J. 1987. MEN WHO CAN'T LOVE. New York: M. Evans and Co., Inc.

Catton C., Gray J. 1985. SEX IN NATURE. London: The Oregon Press Ltd.

Cauthery P., Stanway A., Cooper F. 1985. THE COMPLETE GUIDE TO SEXUAL FULFILLMENT. Buffalo New York: Prometheus Books.

Celeste. 1990. "PLAY PIERCING AS ART AND SENSATION." San Francisco: QSM lecture.

Celeste. 1990. "PLAYING WITH FIRE." San Francisco: QSM lecture.

Chesser E. 1971. STRANGE LOVES, THE HUMAN ASPECTS OF SEXUAL DEVIATION. New York: Popular Library, William Morrow & Company, Inc.

Church G., Carnes C. 1972. THE PIT. New York: Outerbridge & Lazard, Inc.

Church, P. 1989. "Impotence." HARVARD MEDICAL SCHOOL HEALTH LETTER (Sept & Oct). Boston: Harvard University.

Cohen N. 1992. "Controversy over court ruling on sado-masochism." LONDON INDEPENDENT.

Coleman D. McCusker N. 1990. "A TASTE OF TANTRA" Las Vegas: Lifestyle Conference.

C. J.C. 1990. "TERROR." San Francisco: QSM lecture.

Cone R. 1989. "Prisoners of love." PACIFIC NORTHWEST (May).

Conway C. 1992. "Angst." Stanford Medicine, (Spring 1992). Stanford, California: Stanford University.

Cooper W.M. 1890. A HISTORY OF THE ROD. London: William Reeves.

Cunningham S. 1983. EARTH POWER, TECHNIQUES OF NATURAL MAGIC. St. Paul, Minnesota: Llewellyn Publishers.

d'Arno Q. 1985. INQUISITION, TORTURE INSTRUMENTS FROM THE MIDDLE AGES TO THE INDUSTRIAL ERA. Florence: Qua d' Arno Bilingual Publishing.

D'Emilio J., Freedman E. 1988. INTIMATE MATTERS, A HISTORY OF SEXUALITY IN AMERICA. New York: Harper & Row Publishers.

Daily D., ed. 1988. THE SEXUALLY UNUSUAL GUIDE TO UNDERSTANDING & HELPING. New York, London: The Harrington Park Press.

Dalby L. 1983. GEISHA. Berkeley: University of California Press.

Davis D.J. 1873. HISTORY OF THE CITY OF MEMPHIS.

de Rosa P. 1988. VICARS OF CHRIST, THE DARK SIDE OF THE PAPACY. New York: Crown Publishers, Inc.

DeBlase T. 1989. "MALE TIT AND GENITORTURE I AND II." San Francisco: QSM lectures.

Decker M. 1992. "BREATH CONTROL AND CAROTID ARTERY PLAY." San Francisco: QSM lecture.

de Leeuw H. 1943. CITIES OF SIN. New York: Willey Book Co.

Dingwall E.J. n.d. VERY PECULIAR PEOPLE. Rider.

Dorman A., Kane J.J. 1989. TIME MAGAZINE (Oct 30) "And now emotional aftershocks." New York, Atlanta.

Dunlop J.L. 1989. "De Clerambault's Syndrome." BRITISH JOURNAL OF SEXUAL MEDICINE (pp306-307).

Durkheim E. 1963. INCEST, THE NATURE AND ORIGIN OF THE TABOO. New York: Lyle Stuart.

Eckert W.G., Katchis S., Donovan W. 1991. "The Pathology and medicolegal aspects of sexual activity." THE AMERICAN JOURNAL OF FORENSIC MEDICINE AND PATHOLOGY (Vol 12:1).

Edwardes A., Masters R.E.L., 1963. THE CRADLE OF EROTICA. New York: The Julian Press.

Ellis A. 1963. INCEST, THE ORIGINS AND THE DEVELOPMENT OF THE INCEST TABOO. New York: Lyle Stuart.

Ellis H. 1906. STUDIES IN THE PSYCHOLOGY OF SEX. Philadelphia: F.A. Davis Company.

Ellis H. 1936. STUDIES IN THE PSYCHOLOGY OF SEX. New York: Random House.

Ellis P., Mellsop G. 1985. "De Clerambault's syndrome—A nosological entity?" BRITISH JOURNAL OF PSYCHIATRY (Vol 146:90, pp90-93).

Fareck N., ed. 1980. THE MANY FACES OF SUICIDE. New York: McGraw Hill.

Farrar S. 1983. WHAT WITCHES DO. Custer Washington: Phoenix Publishers, Inc.

Fast J., Bernstein M. 1983. SEXUAL CHEMISTRY, WHAT IT IS—HOW TO USE IT. New York: Pocket Books, Simon & Schuster, Inc.

Fehlinger H. 1945. Herbert S., trans. SEXUAL LIFE OF PRIMITIVE PEOPLE. New York: United Book Guild.

FETISH TIMES (No. 191), B&D Co., PO Box 7109, Van Nuys, CA 91409.

Fielding W.J. 1942. STRANGE CUSTOMS OF COURTSHIP AND MARRIAGE. New York: Blue Ribbon Books, The New Home Library.

Fisher H.E. 1983. THE SEX CONTRACT. New York: Quill, William Morrow and Company, Inc.

Fiske P. 1990. "DISCIPLINE." San Francisco: QSM lecture.

Fledermaus, ed. 1989. "Personal ad." DRUMMER (No. 133). San Francisco: Desmodus, Inc.

Fledermaus, ed. 1981. "The shocking art of electrical torment." DUNGEON MASTER (Vol 8). San Francisco: Desmodus Publishers.

Fledermaus, ed. 1981. "When in Rome." DUNGEON MASTER (Vol 11). San Francisco: Desmodus Publishers.

Ford C.S., Beach, F.A. 1951. PATTERNS OF SEXUAL BEHAVIOR. New York: Harper & Brothers.

Forward S., Torres J. 1986. MEN WHO HATE WOMEN & THE WOMEN WHO LOVE THEM. New York: Bantam Books.

Frazer J.G. 1910. TOTEMISM AND EXOGAMY (Vol 4). London: MacMillan.

Freedman H. 1977. SEX LINK-WHAT THE ANIMALS DO ABOUT IT. New York: M. Evans & Company, Inc.

Gadon E.W. 1989. THE ONCE AND FUTURE GODDESS. New York: Harper & Row Publishers, Inc.

Gallina R. 1990. "CUTTING." San Francisco: QSM lecture.

Gallina R. 1989. "PIERCING." San Francisco: Outcast lecture.

Gartrell N. 1986. "Increased libido in women receiving trazodone." AMERICAN JOURNAL OF PSYCHIATRY (Vol 143:6, pp781).

Gerich W. 1990. "Just Deserts." BUF (Vol. 22 No. 1). River Edge, New Jersey: BUF Publications.

Gilder R. 1931. ENTER THE ACTRESS, THE FIRST WOMEN IN THE THEATRE. New York: The Houghton Miffline Co.

Ginzburg R., ed. 1962. EROS (Spring). New York: Eros Magazine/Ralph Ginzburg.

Gio. 1990. HOW TO STRIP FOR YOUR MAN video. Gio, PO Box 349, Orchard Hill, GA, USA 30266.

Goldberg B.Z. 1958. THE SACRED FIRE, THE STORY OF SEX IN RELIGION. New York: University Books.

Goldman M.J. 1991. "Kleptomania: Making sense of the nonsensical." AMERICAN JOURNAL OF PSYCHIATRY (Vol 148:8 pp986-996).

Goodland R. 1931. A BIBLIOGRAPHY OF SEX RITES AND CUSTOMS. London: George Routledge & Sons, Ltd.

Goodman G.S. 1984. "Children's testimony in historical perspective" JOURNAL OF SOCIAL ISSUES (Vol 40).

Gordon F. 1990. "ASK THE DOCTOR." San Francisco: lecture.

Gottlieb A. 1974. SEX DRUGS AND APHRODISIACS. Manhattan Beach, California: Twentieth Century Alchemist.

Gove, P.B., ed. 1986. WEBSTER'S THIRD NEW INTERNATIONAL DICTIONARY. Springfield, Massachusetts: Merriam-Webster, Inc.

Graff, N. 1991. "A RITUAL OF JOINING." JOURNEYING, c/o B. Love, 101 First St, Suite 155, Los Altos, California 94022.

Graff, N. 1992. "SLEEPING BEAUTY." JOURNEYING. Los Altos, California.

Graham H.D., Gurr T.R. 1969. VIOLENCE IN AMERICA. New York: Signet Books.

Gregor T. 1985. ANXIOUS PLEASURES, THE SEXUAL LIVES OF AN AMAZONIAN PEOPLE. Chicago: The University of Chicago Press.

Greyson B. 1985. "A typology of near-death experiences." AMERICAN JOURNAL OF PSYCHIATRY (Vol 142:8 pp967-969).

Grogan, A. 1992. ROMANTASY BOUTIQUE CATALOG, 1999 Moultan, San Francisco, CA 94123.

Grubman-Black S. 1992. BROKEN BOYS/MENDING MEN. New York: Ivy Books.

Guralnik, D.B., ed. 1972. WEBSTER'S NEW WORLD DICTIONARY OF THE ENGLISH LANGUAGE. New York, Cleveland: The World Publishing Co.

Haeberle E.J. 1981. THE SEX ATLAS. New York: The Continuum Publishing Co.

Hal. 1990. "ROPE HARNESS AND OTHER SIMPLE BONDAGE TECHNIQUES." San Francisco: QSM lecture.

Hall S. 1972. GENTLEMAN OF LEISURE-A YEAR IN THE LIFE OF A PIMP. New York: A Prairie House Book, Rapoport Printing Corp.

Harlow H. 1971. LEARNING TO LOVE, A LANDMARK SUMMARY OF RESEARCH FINDINGS. New York: Albion Publishing Co., Ballantine Books, Inc.

Hassan S. 1988. COMBATTING CULT MIND CONTROL. Rochester New York: Park Street Press.

Hegeler I., Hegeler S. 1963. AN ABZ OF LOVE. Copenhagen Denmark: Chr. Erichsen's Forlag.

Hemingway E. 1932. DEATH IN THE AFTERNOON. New York: Scribner.

Herbert G. 1902. A NIGHT IN A MOORISH HAREM. New York, London: Erotica Biblion Society.

Herrman B. 1991. "FISTING." San Francisco: QSM lecture.

Herrman B. 1991. TRUST/THE HAND BOOK: A guide to the sensual and spiritual art of handballing. Alamo Square Press, PO Box 14543, San Francisco, California 94114.

Hirschfeld M. SEXUAL ANOMALIES AND PERVERSIONS. London: Torch Publishing Co., Ltd., Stanley Sidders, with acknowledgments from Encyclopaedic Press Ltd.

Hite S. 1981. THE HITE REPORT ON MALE SEXUALITY. New York: Alfred A. Knopf.

Holiday S., Henkin W. 1989. "ALTERNATE PER-SONAS." San Francisco: Society of Janus lecture.

Holmberg A.R. 1946. THE SIRIONOS. Unpublished Ph.D. dissertation. Yale University.

Howard G.E. 1904. A HISTORY OF MATRIMO-NIAL INSTITUTIONS. Chicago: University of Chicago Press.

Irwin J., Livnat S., Ader R. 1990?. "Stressor associ-ated cues influence immune function." NEURAL CONTROL OF IMMUNE SYSTEM III. Queen's Univ. Kingston, Canada K72 3N6, and Univ. of Rochester, NY 14642.

Jacobus X. 1898. UNTRODDEN FIELDS OF ANTHROPOLOGY. Paris.

John and Honeybear 1990. "ABC'S OF SWINGING." Palm Springs, CA: Lifestyle Conference lecture.

Jones I. 1982. "Self-injury: Toward a Biological Basis." PERSPECTIVE BIOLOGICAL MEDICINE (Vol 26 pp37-150).

Jordon W. 1968. WHITE OVER BLACK. Chapel Hill, North Carolina: University of North Carolina Press.

Jung C..G. 1953. THE COLLECTED WORKS OF C.G.Jung (Bollinger Series XX, Vol 5). New York: Pantheon Books.

Kahaner L. 1988. CULTS THAT KILL, PROBING THE UNDERWORLD OF OCCULT CRIME. New York: Warner Books.

Kale A., Kale S. 1975. TANTRA, THE SECRET POWER OF SEX. Bombay: Jaico Publishing House.

Katchadourian H., Lunde D. 1972. FUNDAMEN-TALS OF HUMAN SEXUALITY. New York: Holt, Rinehart and Winston, Inc.

Kennedy C., ed. Aug. 1989. "Sexual abuse of chil-dren." MAYO CLINIC HEALTH LETTER. Rochester, Minnesota.

Kennedy C., ed. Dec. 1989. "Impotence/penile implants??" MAYO CLINIC HEALTH LETTER. Rochester, Minnesota.

Kiefer O. 1934. SEXUAL LIFE IN ANCIENT ROME. London: Abbey Library.

Kim A. 1985. NINJA MIND CONTROL. New York: Citadel Press Book, Carol Communications.

Kinsey A.C., Pomeroy W.B., Martin C.E., Gebhard P.H. 1953. SEXUAL BEHAVIOR IN THE HUMAN FEMALE. New York: Pocket Book, Simon & Schuster.

Kinsey A.C., Pomeroy W.B., Martin C.E. 1948. SEXUAL BEHAVIOR IN THE HUMAN MALE. Philadelphia: W.B. Saunders Co.

Klein M. 1990. "Censorship and the fear of sexu-ality." Amherst, New York: THE HUMANIST.

Krafft-Ebing R. 1965. PSYCHOPATHIA SEXU-ALIS. Originally published by Stein and Day Publishers. Reprinted with the permission of Scarborough House. Lanham, Maryland.

Krafft-Ebing R., Freud S., Ellis H. 1963. Kirch A., ed. THE SEXUAL REVOLUTION. New York: Dell Publishers Co., Inc.

K. A. 1990. "SURGICAL SUTURING AND STAPLING." San Francisco: QSM lecture.

Krousher R.W. 1985. PHYSICAL INTERROGA-TION TECHNIQUES. Port Townsend, Washington: Loompanics Unlimited.

Kurtz P. 1991. THE TRANSCENDENTAL TEMPTATION-A CRITIQUE OF RELIGION & THE PARANORMAL. Used with permission of Prometheus Books. Buffalo, New York: Prometheus Books.

LaFarge. 1988. "You're going to put a what up my what?? Catheters & sounds: The basics of urethral insertion." DUNGEON MASTER (No. 34). San Francisco: Desmodus Publishers.

LaVey A. 1989. THE SATANIC WITCH. Los Angeles: Feral House.

Leacock E. 1980. Etgienne M., Leacock E., eds., "Montagnais women and the Jesuit program for col-onization." WOMEN AND COLONIZATION: ANTHROPOLOGICAL PERSPECTIVES. New York.

Leibenluft E., Gardner D.L., Cowdry R.W. 1987. "The inner experience of the borderline self-muti-lator." JOURNAL OF PERSONALITY DISOR-DERS. (pp1317-1324).

Levene P. 1985. APHRODISIACS FACT & FIC-TION. Dorset England: Javelin Books.

Levine S. 1980. "Crime or Affliction? Rape in an African Community." CULTURE, MEDICINE AND PSYCHIATRY (Vol 4. pp151-165). Boston and Dordrecht, Holland: D. Reidel Publishing Co.

Levy H.S. 1972. CHINESE FOOT BINDING. New York: Bell Publishing Co.

Lewinshohn R. 1958. HISTORY OF SEXUAL CUSTOMS. New York: Harper & Row.

Lindsay P. n.d. THE MAINSPRING OF MURDER.

Llinas R. 1988. BIOLOGY OF THE BRAIN, FROM NEURONS TO NETWORKS. New York: W.H. Freeman & Co.

LONDON OBSERVER. 1991. "Handshakes draw squeals of fear." London.

Lowen A. 1965. LOVE AND ORGASM. New York: The Macmillan Co., Signet Books.

Ludwig E. 1937. Lindsay M.H., trans. THE NILE, THE LIFE-STORY OF A RIVER. New York: The Viking Press.

Lue T. 1990. "IMPOTENCE." Lecture: Palo Alto, CA.

Lyons A. 1988. SATAN WANTS YOU. New York: Warner Books, Inc.

MacDonald J.H. 1973. "False Accusations of Rape." MEDICAL ASPECTS OF HUMAN SEXUALITY. (Vol 7:5 pp170-194).

Mains G. 1984. URBAN ABORIGINALS, A CELEBRATION OF LEATHERSEXUALITY. San Francisco: Gay Sunshine Press.

Malin M.H. 1987. "A preliminary report of a case of necrophilia." Paper presented at the Eighth World Congress for Sexology, Heidelberg, West Germany, June 14-20.11

Mannix D. 1976. FREAKS, WE WHO ARE NOT AS OTHERS. San Francisco: Re/Search Publications.

Mannix D. 1958. THOSE ABOUT TO DIE. New York: Ballantine Books, Inc.

Mantegazza P. 1935. SEXUAL RELATIONS OF MANKIND. New York: Falstaff Press.

Marmor J. 1976. McCary J.L., Copeland D.R., eds. "Normal and deviant sexual behavior." MODERN VIEWS OF HUMAN SEXUAL BEHAVIOR. Chicago: Science Research Associates, Inc.

Masters R.E.L., Lea E. 1963. PERVERSE CRIMES IN HISTORY. New York: The Julian Press.

Masters W., Johnson V. 1970. HUMAN SEXUAL INADEQUACY Boston: Little, Brown, J and A Churchill, London.

McCary J.L. 1976. McCary J.L., Copeland D.R., eds. "Sexual myths and fallacies." MODERN VIEWS OF HUMAN SEXUAL BEHAVIOR. Chicago: Science Research Associates, Inc.

McCord W., McCord J. 1964. THE PSYCHOPATH, AN ESSAY ON THE CRIMINAL MIND. New York: D. Van Nostrand Co., Inc.

McGrath M. 1990. "Injections that cause erections." MEN'S HEALTH (Vol 6).

Mead M. 1928. COMING OF AGE IN SAMOA. New York: William Morrow & Co.

Miczek, Thompson, Shuster. 1990. "Analgesia following defeat in an aggressive encounter: Development of tolerance and changes in opiate receptors." ANNALS OF THE NEW YORK ACADEMY OF SCIENCES, STRESS-INDUCED ANALGESIA (Vol 467).

Miller T.W., Veltkamp L.J. 1988. "Child sexual abuse: The abusing family in rural America." INTERNATIONAL JOURNAL OF FAMILY PSYCHIATRY (Vol 9 No 3 pp259-275).

Money J. 1991. BREATHLESS ORGASM. Buffalo, New York: Prometheus Books.

Money J. 1988. GAY, STRAIGHT AND IN-BETWEEN. New York: Oxford University Press.

Money J. 1980. LOVE AND LOVE SICKNESS, THE SCIENCE OF SEX, GENDER DIFFERENCE, AND PAIRBONDING. Reprinted by permission of the publisher. Baltimore Maryland/London: The John Hopkins University Press.

Money J. 1986. LOVEMAPS, CLINICAL CONCEPTS OF SEXUAL/EROTIC HEALTH AND PATHOLOGY, PARAPHILIA, AND GENDER TRANSPOSITION IN CHILDHOOD, ADOLESCENCE AND MATURITY. New York: Irvington Publishers, Inc., and Prometheus Books.

Money J. 1986. VENUSES PENUSES. New York: Prometheus Books.

Moor E. 1810. HINDU PANTHEON.

Mountfield D. 1984. ILLUSTRATED MARQUIS DE SADE. New York: Crescent Books.

Musafar F. 1989. "BRANDING AND BURNING." San Francisco: QSM lecture.

Musafar F. 1991. "BRANDING AND CUPPING." San Francisco: Society of Janus lecture.

Musafar F. 1989. "RITUALS." San Francisco: Society of Janus lecture.

Nan. "FINE ART OF CANING."

Nerciate A.A. 1950(approx.) APHRODITE. Paris.

Niemoeller A.F., 1935. AMERICAN ENCYCLOPEDIA OF SEX. New York: The Panurge Press.

Norris N., Potter J.A. 1986. "The devil made me do it." PENTHOUSE (Jan).

O'Relly E. 1967. SEXERCISES. New York: Pocket Books, Simon & Schuster, Inc.

Oltmanns T.F., Neale J.M., Davison G.C. 1991. CASE STUDIES IN ABNORMAL PSYCHOLOGY. New York: John Wiley & Sons, Inc.

OMAHA CLINIC. 1893. (article on bestiality). Omaha Nebraska.

Otto H. 1990. "Living up to your orgasmic potential" Chapel Hill, North Carolina: SEX OVER 40.

Owens T. 1991. THE SAFER SEX MANIAC'S BIBLE, Pub: Tuppy Owens, PO Box 4ZB, London W1A 4ZB, England.

Palca J. 1989. "News and comment." SCIENCE (Vol. 245) Washington D.C.: American Association for the Advancement of Science.

Palmer D.J.L., Cuthbert J., Mukoyogo J., Obhrai M.S., Newton J.R. 1990. "Micro-organisms present in donor semen, screening and detection." BRITISH JOURNAL OF SEXUAL MEDICINE.

Panati C. 1989. PANATI'S EXTRAORDINARY ENDINGS OF PRACTICALLY EVERYTHING AND EVERYBODY. New York: Harper & Row Publishers.

Pareek S.S. 1989. "Unusual penile swelling—bulleetus." BRITISH JOURNAL OF SEXUAL MEDICINE.

Partridge B. 1960. A HISTORY OF ORGIES. New York: Crown Publishers, Inc.

Peters E. 1985. TORTURE. New York: Basil Blackwell, Inc.

Petrie F. n.d. EGYPTIAN TALES.

Phillips R. 1991. UNTYING THE KNOT. Cambridge: Cambridge Press

Piura B. 1986. "Vaginal foreign body of very long duration." BRITISH JOURNAL OF SEXUAL MEDICINE (pp308-309).

Polley J., ed. 1980. STORIES BEHIND EVERYDAY THINGS. Pleasantville, New York: Reader's Digest Association, Inc.

Procopius. 500C.E.—1927, trans. SECRET HISTORY. New York: Covici-Friede, Publishers.

Quartermaster. 1989. "Fundamentals of flagellation." SANDMUTOPIA GUARDIAN (No. 5, April). San Francisco: Desmodus, Inc.

Rama S., Ballentine R., Hymes A. 1979. THE SCIENCE OF BREATH. Honesdale, Pennsylvania: The Himalayan International Institute.

Ramsdale D.A., Ramsdale E.J. 1985. SEXUAL ENERGY ECSTASY: A PRACTICAL GUIDE TO LOVEMAKING SECRETS OF THE EAST AND WEST; "The Tantric Joy of Sex" 2nd Edition. ISBN 0-917879-03-1, Peak Skill Publishing, PO Box 5489, Playa Del Rey, CA 90296

Rappaport R.G. 1988. "The serial and mass murderer: Patterns, differentiation, pathology." AMERICAN JOURNAL OF FORENSIC PSYCHIATRY (Vol 9:1 pp39-48).

Reese P. TRELLIS SINGLES 2540 California #112, Mountain View, CA 94040, USA

Reeves Sanday, P. 1979. THE SOCIO-CULTURAL CONTEXT OF RAPE.

Reynolds B. 1991. "Sex for blood; New York's elite vampire club part 1." EXPOSED (Vol 1, No. 1). Anton Enterprises, Inc., PO Box 34013, Los Angeles, CA 90034.

Richards B. 1977. THE PENIS. London: Valentine Products, Inc.

Riddle, G. 1989. AMPUTEES & DEVOTEES. Halcyon Books, PO Box 2092, Sunnyvale, CA 94087.

Ringrose C.A.D. 1989. "Case report quad 'P' therapy for rapid relief from sexual aberration." BRITISH JOURNAL OF SEXUAL MEDICINE.

Robinson F., Lehrman N. eds. 1971. FROM PLAYBOY: SEX AMERICAN STYLE. Chicago: Playboy Press.

Robinson J. 1991. INTIMACY & SEXUAL ECSTASY. Video. Peak Skill Publishing, PO Box 5489, Playa Del Rey, CA 90296.

Robinson V., ed. 1936. ENCYCLOPAEDIA SEX-UALIS. New York: Dingwall-Rock, Ltd.

Roe C.G. 1910. PANDERS AND THEIR WHITE SLAVES. New York: Fleming H. Revell Co.

Rogers J.A. 1967. SEX AND RACE (Vol. I, II, III). New York: Helga M. Rogers.

Rose C., Sweet E. 1991. "DANCING WITH THE SPIRITUAL FLAMES." San Francisco: QSM lecture.

Rosen M.A. 1986. SEXUAL MAGIC, THE S/M PHOTOGRAPHS. Shaynew Press, PO Box 11719, San Francisco, CA 94101.

Rosen M.A. 1990. SEXUAL PORTRAITS, PHO-TOGRAPHS OF RADICAL SEXUALITY. San Francisco: Shaynew Press.

Rosenthal S.H., ed. 1982. "Sexual changes in men over forty." Chapel Hill, North Carolina: SEX OVER FORTY.

Rossi W.A. 1976. THE SEX LIFE OF THE FOOT & SHOE. New York: Ballantine Books.

Roth L.H., ed. 1987. CLINICAL TREATMENT OF THE VIOLENT PERSON. New York: The Guilford Press.

Rule B. 1986. EVERYDAY LIFE IN THE HAREM. London: W.H. Allen & Co.

SAMOIS. 1987. COMING TO POWER. Boston: Alyson Publishing, Inc.

SAN FRANCISCO CHRONICLE (June 21, 1991).

SAN FRANCISCO EXAMINER. (March 19, 1992). "Toe sucker charged with sexual abuse."

Saunders E.B., Awad G.A. 1991. "Adolescent Female Firesetters." CANADIAN JOURNAL OF PSYCHIATRY (Vol 36:6, pp401-403).

Schain W.S., Wellisch D.K., Pasnau R.O., Landsverk J. 1985. "The sooner the better: A study of psychological factors in women undergoing immediate versus delayed breast reconstruction."

AMERICAN JOURNAL OF PSYCHIATRY (Vol 142:1 p40).

Schiff A.F. 1975. "An Unusual Case of Pseudo Rape." JOURNAL OF FORENSIC SCIENCES (Vol 20:4 pp637-641).

Schmidt J.E. 1967. CYCLOPEDIA LEXICON OF SEX. New York: Brussel & Brussel, Inc.

Schneidman M. 1992. STANFORD MEDICINE. Spring 1992. Stanford, California: Stanford University.

Schurig D. 1905. JOURNAL DE MEDECINE. Paris.

Schwartz B. 1988. THE ONE HOUR ORGASM. Houston: Breakthru Publishing.

Schwartz J.R. 1990. THE OFFICIAL GUIDE TO THE BEST CAT HOUSES IN NEVADA. Straight Arrow Publishers, Box 1068, Coronado, CA 92118.

Schwartz M.F., Masters W.H. 1984. "The Masters and Johnson treatment program for dissatisfied homosexual men." AMERICAN JOURNAL OF PSYCHIATRY (Vol 141:2 p173).

Scott G.G. 1983. EROTIC POWER, AN EXPLO-RATION OF DOMINANCE AND SUBMIS-SION. New York: Citadel Press, Carol Publishing.

Scully D. 1990. UNDERSTANDING SEXUAL VIOLENCE, A STUDY OF CONVICTED RAPISTS. Boston: Unwin Hyman, Inc.

Segal J.H. 1989. "Erotomania revisited: F r o m Kraepelin to DSM-III-R." AMERICAN JOURNAL OF PSYCHIATRY (Vol 146:10, pp1264).

Sez S. 1990. "ARE YOU A SWINGING VIRGIN." Las Vegas: Lifestyle Conference lecture.

Sifakis C. 1982. THE ENCYCLOPEDIA OF AMERICAN CRIME. New York: Facts on File, Inc.

Silber S. 1980. HOW TO GET PREGNANT. New York: Warner Books, Inc.

Silver B. Bennett J. 1989. THE NAUGHTY VIC-TORIAN HAND BOOK, FURTLING. New York: Workman Publishers Co., Inc.

Simons G.L. 1982. THE ILLUSTRATED BOOK OF SEXUAL RECORDS. New York: Delilah Communications Ltd.

Simons G.L. 1973. SEX AND SUPERSTITION. New York: Harper & Row. Reproduced with permission of Blackie & Son Ltd., Glasgow, Scotland.

Smith J. 1989. SENSES & SENSIBILITIES. New York: John Wiley & Sons, Inc.

Society of Janus. Anon. 1989. "BONDAGE WITH ROPES." San Francisco: Society of Janus lecture.

Society of Janus. Anon. 1989. "SLAVE FANTASIES." San Francisco: Society of Janus lecture.

Society of Janus. Anon. 1989. "WATER SPORTS." San Francisco: Society of Janus lecture.

Stanway A. 1988. A WOMAN'S GUIDE TO MEN AND SEX. New York: Carroll & Graf Publishers, Inc.

Starhawk. 1989. THE SPIRAL DANCE. New York: Harper & Row.

Stekel W. 1929. SADISM AND MASOCHISM. (Vol I & II). London: John Lane the Bodley Head.

Stekel W. 1964. SEXUAL ABERRATIONS. New York: Grove Press, Inc.

Stewart J. 1990. THE COMPLETE MANUAL OF SEXUAL POSITIONS. Media Press, 9135 Alabama Ave, Suite B, Chatsworth, CA 91311.

Stone M. 1976. WHEN GOD WAS A WOMAN. San Diego, New York, London: Harcourt Brace Jovanovich.

Sullivan L. 1985. INFORMATION FOR THE FEMALE-TO-MALE CROSSDRESSER AND TRANSSEXUAL. L. Sullivan, 1827 Haight St, #164, San Francisco, CA 94117.

Sun L.H. 1992. "One very popular surgeon." SAN FRANCISCO CHRONICLE (Jan 12).

Swingers' Digest. 1989. "Personal ad." The Directory, PO Box 18144, San Jose, CA 95158.

Tanith L. 1991. FANTASCENES; GAMES LOVERS CAN PLAY, Lady Tanith, PO Box 7925, Berkeley, CA 94707-0925.

Tanith L. 1991. "SLAVE TRAINING." Richmond CA: Backdrop lecture.

Tanith L. 1991. A TANGLED WEB: THE ART OF SLAVERY, A TRAINING MANUAL FOR MISTRESSES, MASTERS AND SLAVES VERSION 1.1. PO Box 7925, Berkeley, CA 94707-0925.

Tannahill R. 1980. SEX IN HISTORY. Briarcliff Manor, New York: Stein and Day.

Taylor G. 1954. SEX IN HISTORY. New York: The Vanguard Press.

Te Paske B. 1982. RAPE AND RITUAL, A PSYCHOLOGICAL STUDY. Toronto: Inner City Books.

Thomas H., Thomas D. 1942. LIVING BIOGRAPHIES OF RELIGIOUS LEADERS. New York: Garden City Publishing Company, Inc.

Thomas P., ed. 1989. COCOA 'N CREME, YOUR NATIONAL GUIDE TO INTERRACIAL SWINGING. Connection Magazines, PO Box 03549, Cleveland, Ohio 44103.

Thompson C.J.S. 1974. THE MYSTERIES OF SEX, WOMEN WHO POSED AS MEN AND MEN WHO IMPERSONATED WOMEN. New York: Causeway Books.

Townsend L. 1989. THE LEATHERMAN'S HANDBOOK II. New York: Carlyle Communications.

Tralins R. 1969. THE SEXUAL FETISH. New York: Paperback Library, Coronet Communications, Inc.

Tripp C.A. 1975. THE HOMOSEXUAL MATRIX. New York: McGraw-Hill.

Turner E.S. 1954. A HISTORY OF COURTING. London: Michael Joseph Ltd.

Underhill E. 1972. MYSTICISM. New York: World/Meridian.

Vale V., Juno A., eds. 1989. MODERN PRIMITIVES. San Francisco: Re/Search Pub

Valensin G. 1969. A COMPLETE GUIDE TO THE WORLD OF SEX, SEX FROM A TO Z. New York: Berkley Publishing Corp.

Vatsyayana. 250C.E.—1980. de Smedt M., ed. THE KAMA-SUTRA. New York: Crown Publishers.

Vergara A. 1974. THE NEW ART OF BELLY DANCING. Millbrae, California: Celestial Arts.

von Krafft-Ebing R. 1965. Klaf F.S., trans. PSYCHOPATHIA SEXUALIS. New York: Bell Publishing Company, Inc.

von Schrader D. 1978. ELEMENTARY FIELD INTERROGATION. Delta Ltd.

W. Karen. 1989. "CLOTHING AND COSTUME." San Francisco: Society of Janus lecture.

Wahl C.W., ed. 1967. SEXUAL PROBLEMS-DIAGNOSIS AND TREATMENT IN MEDICAL PRACTICE. New York: The Free Press.

Ward J. 1989. "MALE PIERCING." San Francisco: QSM lecture.

Ward J. 1989. "NIPPLE PIERCING." San Francisco: QSM lecture.

Waring M. 1988. FORESKIN RESTORATION. Metairie, Louisiana: Opportunity Press, Inc.

Watson P. 1988. "Unusual Vaginal Foreign Body." BRITISH JOURNAL OF SEXUAL MEDICINE (p294).

Weinrich J.D. 1987. SEXUAL LANDSCAPES, WHY WE ARE WHAT WE ARE, WHY WE LOVE WHOM WE LOVE. New York: Charles Scribner's Sons.

Whitehead E.D., Zussman S., eds. 1990. "How touch affects intimacy." Vol IX.4) Chapel Hill, North Carolina: SEX OVER FORTY.

Williams B. 1990. ECSTATIC RITUAL, PRACTICAL SEX MAGIC. Dorset England: Prism Press.

Williamson C. 1990. "Ganienkeh." THE MAGAZINE (Issue 38) by Katharsis, PO Drawer 2266, Daytona Beach, FL 32115-2266.

Wilson E.O. 1975. SOCIOBIOLOGY. Cambridge, Massachusetts: The Belknap Press of Harvard University Press.

Wilson E., Wilson A. 1972. THE SERENA TECHNIQUE OF BELLY DANCING. New York: Drake Publishers.

Winchel R.M., Stanley M. 1991. "Self-injurious behavior: A review of the behavior and biology of self-mutilation." AMERICAN JOURNAL OF PSYCHIATRY (Vol 148:3 pp306-316).

Wiseman J. 1989. PERSONAL AD-VENTURES. Gentle Persuasion Press, 2966 Diamond St, Room 212, San Francisco, CA 94131.

Woodward T. SKIN II. Pub: 23 Grand Union Centre Kensal Road, London W10 5AX, England

Wyly J. 1989. THE PHALLIC QUEST, PRIAPUS & MASCULINE INFLATION. Toronto: Inner City Books.

Yates A. 1987. "Should young children testify in cases of sexual abuse?" AMERICAN JOURNAL OF PSYCHIATRY (Vol 144:4 pp476-480)

INDEX